	EDUCATION				PLACE OF BIRTH	CITIZEN-SHIP	RESIDENCE, APRIL 1, 1935							
11	12	13	14	B	15	C	16	17	18	19	20	D	21	22
33	M	No	8		Massachusetts			Same House			No		Yes	
27	M	No	8		New York			Same House			No		No	No
6	S	Yes	1		New York			Same House			No		No	No
52	M	No	8		New York			Same House			No		Yes	
48	M	Wo	5		New York			Same House			No			
24	S	No	8		New York			Same House			No		No	No
52	M	No	0		Lithuania		AL	Same Place			No	Yes	No	No
50	M	No	0		Lithuania		AL	Same Place			No	Yes	No	No
20	S	No	8		New York			Same Place			No	Yes	Yes	
17	S	No	8		New York			Same Place			No	Yes	Yes	
55	M	No	0		Lithuania		AL	Same Place			No	Yes	No	No
49	M	No	0		Lithuania		AL	Same Place			No	Yes	Yes	
24	S	No	H4		New York			Same Place			No			
22	S	No	H3		New York			Same Place						
21	S	No	H3		New York			Same Place						
20	S	No	H3		New York			Same Place					No	No
60	M	No	0		Lithuania		AL	Same			No		No	No
65	M	No	0		Lithuania		AL	Same			No			
25	S	No	H4		New York			Same House			No		Yes	
36	M	No	8		New York			Same House			No		No	No
37	M	No	H2		New Jersey			R	Bergen	New Jersey	No		Yes	
48	M	No	0		Lithuania		AL	Same House			No		Yes	
50	M	No	0		Lithuania		AL	Same House			No		Yes	
23	S	No	H4		New York			Same House			No		Yes	
20	S	No	H2		New York			Same House			No		No	No
63	Wd	No	7		Lithuania		AL	Same House			No		No	No
18	S	No	8		New York			Same House			No		No	No
15	S	Yes	H1		New York			Same House			No		No	No
12	S	Yes	6		New York			Same House			No	Yes	No	No
53	M	No	3		Poland		PA	Same Place			No	Yes	Yes	
53	M	No	0		Poland		AL	Same Place			No	Yes	Yes	
18	S	No	H2		New York			Same Place			No		No	No
15	S	Yes	H1		New York			Same Place			No		No	No
57	M	No	4		Poland		AL	Same Place			No		No	No
56	M	No	6		Poland		AL	Same Place			No		No	No
22	S	No	H2		New York			Same Place			No		No	No
40	Wd	No	5		Poland		AL	Same Place			No		Yes	
21	S	No	H2		New York			Same Place			No		Yes	
17	S	Yes	H3		New York			Same Place			No		No	No
46	M	No	1		Pennsylvania			R	Lackawanna Pennsylvania		No		No	No

This Is Who We Were In The 1960s

FOR PERSONS 14 YEARS OLD AND OVER

ALL AGES									
MOTHER TONGUE (OR NATIVE LANGUAGE)		VETERANS				SOCIAL SECURITY		USUAL OCCUPATION, INDUSTRY, AND CLASS OF WORKER	
Language spoken in home in earliest childhood								USUAL OCCUPATION	USUAL INDUSTRY
38	II	39	40	41	I	42	43	44	45	46	47
English						Yes	Yes	all		

This Is Who We Were: In The 1960s

Based on material from Grey House Publishing's
Working Americans Series by Scott Derks

Grey **H**ouse
Publishing

PUBLISHER: Leslie Mackenzie
EDITORIAL DIRECTOR: Laura Mars
ASSOCIATE EDITORS: Diana Delgado; Sandy Towers
PRODUCTION MANAGER: Kristen Thatcher
MARKETING DIRECTOR: Jessica Moody
COMPOSITION: David Garoogian

Grey House Publishing, Inc.
4919 Route 22
Amenia, NY 12501
518.789.8700
FAX 845.373.6390
www.greyhouse.com
e-mail: books @greyhouse.com

Publisher's Cataloging-In-Publication Data
(Prepared by The Donohue Group, Inc.)

This is who we were : in the 1960s / Grey House Publishing.— [1st ed.]

607 p. : ill. ; cm.

"Based on material from Grey House Publishing's Working American Series by Scott Derks."
Includes bibliographical references and index.
ISBN: 978-1-61925-248-6

1. United States—Economic conditions—1961-1971. 2. United States—Social conditions—1960-1980.
3. United States—Civilization—1945- 4. United States—History—1961-1969. 5. Nineteen sixties.
I. Derks, Scott. Working Americans— II. Grey House Publishing, Inc.

HC106.6 .T45 2013
330.973

TABLE OF CONTENTS

Section One: Profiles
This section contains 30 profiles of individuals and families living and working in the 1960s. It examines their lives at home, at work, and in their neighborhoods. Based upon historic materials, personal interviews, and diaries, the profiles give a sense of what it was like to live in the years 1960 to 1969.

Section Two: Historical Snapshots
This section includes lists of important "firsts" for America, from technical advances and political events to new products and top selling books. Combining serious American history with fun facts, these snapshots present, in chronological categories, an easy-to-read overview of what happened in the 1960s.

Section Three: Economy of the Times

This section looks at a wide range of economic data, including food, clothing, transportation, housing and other selected prices, with reprints of actual advertisements for products and services of the time. It includes figures for the following categories, plus a valuable year-by-year listing of the value of a dollar.

Section Four: All Around Us—What We Saw, Wrote, Read & Listened To

This section includes reprints of newspaper and magazine articles, speeches, and other items designed to help readers focus on what was on the minds of Americans in the 1960s. These printed pieces show how popular opinion was formed, and how American life was affected.

Section Five: Census Data

This section includes state-by-state comparative tables and demographic trends for metropolitan areas from 1960 to 1970.

ESSAY ON THE 1960s

America: The Rebellious Child

Following the placid era of the 1950s, the seventh decade of the twentieth century made quite a reputation for itself through rebellion and protest. No aspect of American society escaped this social upheaval entirely unscathed. The 1960s contained tragic assassinations, momentous social legislation for African Americans, remarkable space achievements, the awakening of the Native American rights movement, and some of the nation's largest antiwar protests in its history. Music, hairstyles, and the willingness of people to speak out would all be transformed, and anti-establishment sentiments rang out loud and clear by the hippie crowd, a crowd that advocated the loosening of sexual mores, alternative lifestyles, and increased drug use. It was the beginning of the Beatles and the tragic end of the non-violent phase of the Civil Rights Movement. While the nation's "silent majority" slapped "Love It or Leave It" bumper sticker on their cars ("It" being America) thousands of highly vocal, well-educated middle class citizens carried signs in the streets to protest American's involvement in Vietnam. It was truly a time of wrenching conflict in search of social change.

This Is Who We Were: In The 1960s profiles Americans who were at the center of a number of social issues. Here is where the country stood on these issues nearly 50 years ago.

Immigration: Amid the turbulence swirling around many issues, America remained a safe haven for the politically and economically repressed refugees around the world. As an aftermath of the Cuban revolution, for example, 1,800 Cuban refugees a week were arriving in Miami in 1962. This evolved into the formalized Cuban airlift of 3,500 refugees a month in 1965. That same year, President Lyndon Johnson signed into law the Immigration and Nationality Act of 1965 and pledged "that those who seek refuge here in American will find it."

Sports: Transformative events occurred in a number of sports. The burgeoning success of NASCAR was slowed by the death of driver Fireball Roberts, and the question of whether or not the sport had become too dangerous. The appearance of performance-enhancing drugs in football and horseracing captured headlines, while professional athlete salaries continued to rise and television sports coverage exploded. The NBA expanded from eight to 17 teams, and player Wilt Chamberlain defined the game with his grace and power.

Music: Branching into several directions, music of the 1960s witnessed the founding of the Motown record label, and the British invasion led by the Beatles and the Rolling Stones. As the same time, American folk music grew into a major movement, pioneered by the likes of Woody Guthrie, Pete Seeger, Joan Baez, and the Mamas & the Papas. Psychedelic rock, represented by the Doors, the Grateful Dead, and Jefferson Airplane, also gained a huge following.

Education: In addition to its stated objective of educating the nation's youth, America's local public schools were placed at the center of the nationwide war on poverty. More and more studies had linked years in school to lifetime earning potential, and strengthened the connection between dropping out of school and going to prison. All the while, educators were coping with student threats to protest the Vietnam War, parental threats to protest sex education classes, meeting the mandate for school integration, and declining school tax revenues impacted by inflation.

Achievements: Extraordinary space achievements marked the 1960s. Ten years after President Kennedy announced that he would place a man on the moon, 600 million people around the world watched as Neil Armstrong gingerly lowered his left foot into the soft dust of the moon's surface. The landing was one of America's greatest triumphs and an exhilarating demonstration of American genius. Other life altering achievements included release of Enovid 10, the first oral contraceptive, and the participation of the Gay Liberation Front in the Hiroshima Day March, the first homosexual participation as a separate constituency in a peace march.

At War: The Cold War became hotter during conflicts over Cuba and Berlin in the early 1960s. Fears over the international spread of communism led to America's intervention in a foreign conflict that would become a defining event of the decade: Vietnam. By 1968, Vietnam had become a national obsession, leading to President Lyndon Johnson's decision not to run for another term, and fueling not only debate over the country's role in Vietnam, but also more inflation and national division. Antiwar marches grew in size until millions of marchers filled the streets of New York, San Francisco, and Washington, DC at the end of the decade.

Economy: From 1960 to 1964, the economy expanded; unemployment was low and disposable income for music, art, vacations, and other leisure activities grew rapidly. American consumers bought 73 percent fewer potatoes and 25 percent more fish, poultry, and meat, and 50 percent more citrus products and tomatoes, than in 1940. Factory workers earned more than $100 a week—their highest wages in history. In 1960, approximately 40 percent of American adult women had paying jobs, and the struggle to bring economic equality to blacks during the period produced massive spending for school integration. Between 1950 and 1965, inflation soared from an annual average of less than 2 percent to a budget-popping average of 9.5 percent. Upper class investors, once content with the consistency and stability of banks, sought better returns in the stock market and in real estate.

INTRODUCTION

This Is Who We Were: In The 1960s is an offspring of our 13-volume *Working Americans* series, which was devoted, volume by volume, to Americans by class, occupation, or social cause. This new edition is devoted to one decade—the 1960s, and is the third in a single-decade series that includes the 1940s and the 1950s. It represents all classes, dozens of occupations, and all regions of the country. This comprehensive look at the decade in America when demonstrations were commonplace and traditional values were questioned, presents American history through the eyes and ears of everyday Americans, not the words of historians or politicians.

This Is Who We Were: In The 1960s presents 30 profiles of individuals and families—their life at home, on the job, and in their neighborhood—with lots of photos and historical images of the time. These stories are told through typical Americans, some struggling and some successful, but all authentic.

Together, the profiles, with the other sections outlined below, present a complete picture of what it was like to live in America in the 1960s, from the African American in Washington D.C. who taught himself how to win a gold medal for weight lifting in the 1960s Olympics, to the Nashville country music record producer who signed Loretta Lynn, Patsy Cline, and Chet Atkins.

Section One: Profiles

Each of 30 profiles in Section One begins with a brief introduction that anchors the text to the decade. Then, each profile is arranged in three categories: Life at Home; Life at Work; Life in the Community. The detailed Table of Contents that precedes this Introduction gives specifics about jobs and geographic region.

Section Two: Historical Snapshots

Section Two is made up of three long, bulleted lists—and what significant lists they are! In chronological order—Early 1960s, Mid 1960s and Late 1960s—these include an amazing range of firsts and turning points in American history, from the signing of the Civil Rights Act into law to the famous "bed-in for peace" by John Lennon and Yoko Ono, during which they recorded "Give Peace a Chance."

Section Three: Economy of the Times

One of the most interesting things about researching an earlier time is learning how much things cost and what people earned. This section offers this information in spades. Each of three categories—Consumer Expenditures, Annual Income of Standard Jobs, and Selected Prices—offers actual figures from three years—1961, 1966, and 1960—for easy comparison and study.

At the end of Section Three is a Value of a Dollar Index that compares the burying power of $1.00 in 2012 to the buying power of $1.00 in every year prior, back to 1860, helping to put the economic data in *This Is Who We Were: In The 1960s* into context.

Section Four: All Around Us

There is no better way to put your finger on the pulse of a country than to read its magazines and newspapers. This section offers 48 original pieces—articles, book excerpts and speeches—that influenced American thought in the 1960s, From articles declaring "Negro Singer to Wed White

Actress," "JFK IS ASSASINATED," and "In the Round, Viet Talks Resume," this section is the eyes and ears of America in the 1960s.

Section Five: Census Data

This section includes two elements, both invaluable in helping to define the times in which those profiled in this book lived. First, 16 State-by-State comparative tables that rank data from the 1960, 1970, and 2010 census. Topics include Population, Education, Housing, Home Value, and Rent. Second, General Demographic Trends for Metropolitan Areas, 1960 to 1970, is a study by the U.S. Census of Population and Housing Trends. This section includes, for each state, a map, tables, and narrative.

This Is Who We Were: In The 1960s ends with a comprehensive Bibliography, arranged by topic, and a detailed Index.

Olympic Weightlifter in 1960

Jim Bradford was a self-trained weightlifter. As a teenager, he developed his own technique for success while training at his local YMCA basketball court in Washington, D.C. His first national event was the Junior Nationals in 1946. In 1960, at 32-years-old and competing in his last Olympics, he wanted gold.

Life at Home

- Jim Bradford weighed 247 pounds on his fourteenth birthday.
- Until he discovered a copy of the weightlifting magazine *Strength and Health*, he was just an overweight black teen walking the streets of the nation's capital.
- Inspired by the pictures and the personal stories of weightlifters, Jim began working out at home.
- But after a dumbbell mishap in the second-floor bedroom of his home sent plaster crashing upon his family downstairs, Jim was dispatched to the 12th Street YMCA.
- There he began working out, largely training himself, relying heavily on strength, not technique.
- As a result he taught himself to lift with virtually no split of his legs on the way up, only bending his back as he lifted the bar over his head.
- This technique was developed, he later confessed, from fear of dropping the weights on the YMCA basketball court and getting barred from the court for having scarred the floor.
- After four years of training and competing on a local level, a very muscular Jim entered his first national event, the 1946 Junior Nationals.
- There he learned some of the lifting techniques of veteran weightlifters and made slow progress.
- Four years later, at age 22, he won the Junior Nationals and placed third in the Senior National Championship.
- In 1951 he placed second in the Senior Nationals and earned a spot on the 1951 World Championship team.
- Here Jim battled aging teammate John Henry Davis, the reigning "World's Strongest Man" and world champion since 1938.
- But John Davis was hurt, and Jim Bradford was young and hungry. At the conclusion of the snatch lift, John Davis was in terrific pain, his undefeated reign truly endangered.
- As the clean and jerk competition began, the arena was charged with energy. Everyone knew that history was about to be made.

Jim Bradford was a self-trained Olympic weightlifter.

- Jim made his first clean and jerk smoothly, and Davis did the same, through the pain.
- Jim answered with an easy second attempt, which was also matched by Davis, who was barely able to leave the stage after the lift.
- Jim knew that if he made his last lift at a still-higher weight, Davis would be forced to match him, risking permanent injury.
- A gold medal and the glory of winning the World Championship were in Jim's grasp-a lifetime dream come true.
- But winning meant defeating an injured legend and stripping a teammate of his undefeated status.
- Jim declined this last lift in the spirit of sportsmanship.
- John Davis retained his title as World's Strongest Man, and newspapers heralded Jim's decision as one of the greatest acts of sportsmanship in the history of athletics.
- Jim won a silver medal at the 1952 Olympics in Helsinki.
- He joined the Army, serving in the Korean War, and his weightlifting career was interrupted.
- In 1954 he was called upon to replace an injured member of the World Championship team.
- Jim jumped on an airplane without hesitation and placed second, winning valuable points for the United States.
- By the time the 1960 Olympics in Rome rolled around, he was ready for one more opportunity on the world stage.
- This time he wanted the gold.
- He was 32 years old; married, with three children; and earned $56 a week as a documents clerk in the Library of Congress.
- His monthly mortgage was $105—half his income.
- Since paid leave would have jeopardized his amateur status under Olympic rules, Jim took an unpaid leave from his clerk position, which he could barely afford.

Life at Work

- One of the oldest sports of the modern Games, weightlifting was one of the final events at the 18-day-long 1960 Olympics in Rome.
- At the opening parade of nations, African American Rafer Johnson marched at the head of the US delegation, causing a stir as the first black athlete to carry the American flag in the highly visible ceremony.
- The 305 US men looked sharp in the US Olympic team dress uniform: McGregor-Doniger olive-green sports coat, Haggar slacks and Van Heusen beige knit shirt.

The USA running team at the Olympics in Rome.

- After weeks of anticipation and the thrill of marching in the opening ceremony, Jim Bradford was brimming with energy.
- The US men's contingent was housed in large buildings in the middle of the Olympic Village, sharing 50 suites, each of which held 3 to 8 athletes.
- Americans had their own dining facility, open 22 hours a day, from 5 a.m. to 3 a.m.
- The dining room was operated by an Italian chef with 76 employees, who cooked mostly beef, to suit the tastes of the Americans.
- Jim loved to travel.
- While at a competition in Warsaw, Poland, the year before, he had made a point of meeting locals, attempting their language and eating indigenous foods.

- To the media, the weightlifting competition, comprising seven weight classes, was the perfect metaphor for the clash of the two superpowers—the United States and the Soviet Union—in a time of "Cold War."
- Americans had collected more gold medals during the two previous Olympics, in Helsinki and Melbourne, but current momentum favored the Soviet strongmen.
- Jim's American coaches believed that winning the weight contest in Rome "would be our best propaganda weapon" in the Cold War.
- The political tension that invaded the 1960 Olympics had begun two years earlier when a delegation of US track and field athletes became the first team to visit the USSR since the start of the Cold War.
- Russians, cheered on by the home crowd, scored a 172-170 victory, which was interpreted in the wider world as a victory for the Communist way of life.
- A lot more than a gold medal was on the line.
- When it was Jim's turn to compete, the Soviets had won four matches and the team title.
- Jim prepared by spending hours meditating in the Olympic Village, visualizing the handling of immense weights.
- In weightlifting the mental preparation was as critical as the physical.
- In the first round, Jim easily pressed 374.5 pounds.
- He made his 396.5-pound press with apparent ease.

The Cold War brought contention into the Olympic games.

The 1960 Olympics opening ceremony.

- The Soviet opponent, Yuri Vlasov, made his lift, but the judges ruled Vlasov's lift was illegal, and the lead went to Jim.
- In the next round, the snatch, Vlasov was the clear winner, by 11 pounds.
- Jim's lead was precariously thin, and he was concerned.
- It appeared the gold medal would be decided by the clean and jerk.
- That's when the officials announced the initial ruling against Vlasov had been overturned on appeal.
- Jim protested vehemently, but Vlasov was given a comfortable lead going into the last event.
- Eventually, the Soviets claimed the gold.
- Rumors of drug use by the Soviet team didn't bother Jim.
- He came from the old school: excuses didn't count.
- But to lose because of the judges' ruling was too outrageous for words.
- Officials asked that he not create an international incident.
- Silence in the face of injustice was a terrible burden for Jim to carry.

Life in the Community: The Olympic Village, Rome

- The Olympic ideal of pure athletic competition staged once every four years was designed to rise above the competing ideologies and international disputes raging around the world.
- In 1960 the increasingly hot rhetoric of the Cold War was only one of many intrusions of strife into the Games.
- One week before the opening ceremony, the American pilot Francis Gary Powers was convicted of espionage charges in a Moscow court after his U-2 reconnaissance plane was shot down over Russia.
- Just days before the closing ceremony, Soviet premier Nikita Khrushchev staged a dramatic appearance at the UN General Assembly in New York, railing against the United States and the West and pounding his delegate desk with his fists and then, allegedly, with one of his shoes.
- Questions were raised concerning which flag East Germany and West Germany would use in the competition; the unified German team marched under a neutral flag in the opening ceremony. A major uproar erupted when the athletes from Taiwan attempted to march as the delegation of China.

Olympic Stadium in Rome, 1960.

- At the same time, new nations—particularly in Africa—were lobbying for more participants in a wider variety of events, women wanted to run longer distances and civil rights activists in South Africa wanted the International Olympic Committee to live up to its Olympic Creed and expel the apartheid delegation from South Africa.
- Simultaneously conflict was raging over the definition of an "amateur athlete."
- Increasingly the rigid rules on "amateur" status were being challenged by athletes, who saw everyone but themselves making money from their efforts.
- Seventy-two-year-old Avery Brundage, president of the International Olympic Committee, was the personification of the Olympic movement—and the object of considerable ridicule.
- Endorsements, sponsorships and subsidized work programs were all strictly forbidden—although some athletes had begun quietly taking money to wear certain shoes.
- Rafer Johnson, a competitor in the decathlon, was told he would be ineligible for the Olympics if he appeared in *Spartacus*, an upcoming film about a slave revolt in ancient Rome.

The USA delegation included 305 athletes.

- The Olympic Committee ruled that Johnson had been hired not for his acting ability but because he was a famous athlete.
- Johnson declined the role.
- Champion hurdler Lee Calhoun lost his eligibility for a year because he and his wife got married on the *Bride and Groom* TV game show and accepted gifts and a honeymoon.
- All these issues were played out before a worldwide television audience.

- In the United States, CBS News paid $600,000 for the exclusive rights to broadcast the summer Olympics (and additional footage) for the first time.
- Under its contract, CBS could broadcast approximately 1 hour and 15 minutes per day, up to 20 hours of programming, from August 25 to September 11.
- The Italian broadcasting network RAI decided, largely without consultation, which events would be covered and provided the necessary camera work, which then required that CBS transcribe the Italian picture, cast at 625 lines per second, into the standard US picture of 525 lines per second.
- Ponderous TV cameras, each weighing more than 60 pounds, lumbered through the broadcast sites, tethered to cables the circumference of boa constrictors.
- Tapes of each event were flown by commercial aircraft to the United States, a 9.5-hour trip.
- Jim McKay, a former *Baltimore Sun* police reporter, would then edit the film, write the copy and provide the voiceover, all from a studio in New York City's Grand Central Station.
- *Encyclopedia Britannica* was a major source of background information for the broadcasts.

Olympic athletes ignored the international strife that was brewing outside the games.

"1,500 Will Cover Olympics,"
Pacific Stars and Stripes, July 31, 1960

About 1,500 newsmen, photographers, and radio and television commentators will cover the Olympic Games in Rome from August 25 through September 11.

The Italian organizing committee issued 1,200 passes to newsmen from all over the world, and 300 photographers and radio and television men…

Rome's telephone company also has put 2,500 telephones and 500 phone booths at the disposal of the press. The telephones are scattered in various sports arenas and in the main press center…

The organizing committee made several separate accords with various television companies in Europe, the United States and Japan to telecast the games.

Seventy foreign radio organizations have asked the Italian Radio Company (RAI) for technical equipment for their services in connection with radio information in the games.

To meet such a great demand RAI set up a radio center at the Rome Music College near the Foro Italico, which will be the site of many Olympic events…

Technical installations at the radio center include 58 special studios which will be placed at the disposal of various foreign countries for production of their radio programs.

RAI installed more than 800 circuits to ensure links between the radio center and the competition arenas, and to the international center of the Italian State Telephone Company. . .

More than 250 operators and technicians, from various RAI stations throughout Italy, will be brought to Rome for the games and will be used exclusively for this radio service.

To handle the flood of news copy expected to amount to hundreds of thousands of words a day, special telegraph, cable and radio circuits are being opened between Rome and major cities on every continent.

Our sportsmen represent the new socialistic order where mental health and moral purity are harmonically tied with physical development. Sports and physical development are the habit of the nation. They are the source of the good spirit, happiness, hard work, and long lives of the Soviet people.

—*Pravda,* August 22, 1960

Olympic Weightlifting Terms

Press: The barbell is lifted from floor to chest and then chest to overhead in two smooth movements with a slight bend but no shifting of the feet.

Snatch: The weight is lifted floor to overhead in one explosive movement; the lifter is allowed to shift his feet.

Clean and jerk: The weight is taken from floor to shoulder height, held there briefly, then lifted overhead with a squat and spring of the legs.

Television Programmer in 1961

Steve Brewster, at 28, worked for ABC, broadening the appeal of the upstart's programming. Losing Olympic coverage, he promoted the creation of Wide World of Sports, *but thought ABC's decision to cover the presidential debates was a mistake. He was surprised by the positive reaction the debates received.*

Life at Home

- Steve and Gretchen were rarely home together, often seeing each other only on weekends.
- Their apartment was completely furnished and kept ready to entertain on short notice, but they rarely had time.
- The walls were white, and most of the furniture was modern; they avoided putting pictures and other objects on tables to avoid a cluttered look.
- Steve worked a 12-hour day, often 6 days a week, while Gretchen often traveled for movie shoots to remote locations, mostly for minor roles.
- Gretchen cut several TV commercials, which brought her financial rewards, but she feared she would not be cast in movies if she appeared in too many commercials.
- For the right person, Los Angeles was the land of opportunity, but competition was intense.
- Gretchen really wanted a baby but was afraid of what childbirth would do to her figure and career; Steve kept saying that they would have children once he "made it."

Life at Work

- Wages on a television or movie set were strictly controlled and regulated by contracts.
- For a TV western, an extra earned a minimum of $25.47 for eight hours, during which he or she might spend two or three hours just waiting for something to happen.
- Actors earned $5.00 more if they did not mind getting wet and $8.07 more if they rode a horse; driving a team of four horses added an extra $20.50 to the paycheck.
- For seven years after merging with United Paramount Theaters, the ABC television network had been battling for ratings respectability with the other two networks.
- This was accomplished in 1960–61 with a lineup heavily composed of shows in the action-adventure format; news, public affairs, sports and daytime programming were virtually nonexistent.
- Steve focused on broadening the appeal of the ABC network, since too much of its lineup was based on the

Steve Brewster was a television programmer for ABC.

type of action-adventure show that can lose favor overnight.

- The network's *77 Sunset Strip* and *The Untouchables* were doing well, but many of the new action-adventure clones were getting poor ratings; *Klondike*, featuring Ralph Taeger and James Coburn, was already slated for cancelation.
- Some other shows were showing weakness, and Steve was asked to develop new strategies for ABC.
- One of his peers, Steve's competitor for advancement at the network, launched the first adult cartoon show, *The Flintstones*.
- Positioned in the 8:30 p.m. time slot, when children were in bed, and sponsored by Winston cigarettes, *The Flintstones* was getting a mixed reception.
- Nearly everything else was bombing, including the reappearance of comedian Jackie Gleason in a quiz show format so insipid that the program was pulled after one week.
- ABC's only apparent hit of the season was *My Three Sons*; CBS appeared to be striking gold with *The Andy Griffith Show*—the appeal of which was completely lost on Steve.
- Steve was betting on sports. Although ABC had already stubbed its toe on sports, he thought that spending heavily for sporting events would give the network revenues and respectability—and allow him to be promoted.
- In 1959, to deepen its reach and gain leverage for the summer Olympic Games, ABC paid $167,000 for the exclusive television rights to the 1960 Winter Olympics in Squaw Valley, California.
- When ABC failed to get the rights to the summer Games as well, the network canceled plans for covering the winter Games entirely; CBS picked up the rights for both.
- Unfortunately for ABC, the ratings for the winter Games were high, boosting excitement for the summer Games. CBS extensively employed videotape to provide same-day coverage of the summer Games from Rome, dramatically increasing the immediacy—and ratings—of the Olympics.
- CBS emerged a winner, with ABC the clear loser.
- Many at ABC, including Steve, were infuriated that the network had not been willing to show the Winter Olympics, even if commercial sponsorships were scarce, to establish itself as a solid network player.
- ABC's only major, long-running sporting event was boxing, which was considered a joke; both NBC and CBS had long ago abandoned coverage of weekly boxing matches, a staple of the early 1950s.
- Steve was now promoting ABC's involvement with the brand-new American Football League; linking ABC and the upstart AFL would help both, he believed.
- Plans were under way for the creation of a Saturday afternoon program called *Wide World of Sports*, hosted by former CBS sportscaster Jim McKay.

ABC aired the Kennedy/Nixon presidential debate, with favorable ratings.

- Based on the idea that many different sports could be featured during a single show, *Wide World of Sports* was getting heavy promotion.
- The format was modeled on the Olympic coverage pioneered by CBS—live or pretaped segments bringing together action highlights from various venues.
- No one was sure it would work, but Steve was excited that ABC would be trying something new.
- Gaining respectability through sports had an immediate appeal, since upgrading ABC's news and public-affairs programming, everyone believed, would take more time.
- Because of the intense pressure to challenge CBS and NBC, Steve did not think that ABC would have patience with any programming that developed slowly; ABC needed hits.
- ABC's history of supporting news broadcasts was weak; the network was the last of the three to create a nightly news show, settling in the early 1950s for a weekly commentary program by former radio analysts Paul Harvey and Walter Winchell.
- Even when news was added in 1953, featuring CBS refugee John Daly, most of the ABC affiliates refused to carry the 15-minute news program.
- To strengthen its news position and control distribution, ABC moved its news programming into prime time, which it controlled, in 1958–59, using the 10:30–10:45 p.m. time slot.
- News at ABC was still considered a lost cause. Steve believed daytime soap operas and sports were the tickets to ratings respectability.
- ABC's first attempt at producing documentaries, under the title of *Bell & Howell Close-Up!*, was heavily panned, and Steve's fellow programmer was fired.
- The revamped *Bell & Howell "Close-Up!"* series, broadcast by Time-Life stations, was gaining respectable reviews for its interview with Fidel Castro on the verge of announcing he was a communist, and for "Walk in My Shoes," an episode concerning the lives and experiences of American blacks involved in the civil rights movement.

- In the fall of 1960, during the presidential campaign, Steve had been unsure of the wisdom of his network producing two of the four presidential debates.
- Privately he had wondered how many "eggheads," who could have been watching a sitcom, would be willing to tune in to see John Kennedy and Richard Nixon discuss the issues.
- He was surprised and delighted when the presidential debates produced a windfall of good publicity for television and praise for its ability to allow millions of people across the entire country to share simultaneously in an important and historic event.
- He was less pleased by the comments of FCC commissioner Newton Minow, who called television a "vast wasteland."

Life in the Community: Los Angeles, California

- In the 1940s Los Angeles was the film center of the world. Ninety percent of all motion pictures made in the United States were made there.
- During that time Hollywood studios were producing up to four hundred movies a year for the American audience.
- Los Angeles's cherished position as entertainment capital of America was challenged in the 1950s by a dramatic decline in movie attendance from its wartime peak and by live television productions from New York.
- With the advent of taped programming, Hollywood talent and studios were both in vogue for television production, and many shows were produced in the facilities once used for movies.
- While movies had the glamour, Los Angeles's aerospace industry—housed south of the LA International Airport—had become the main intellectual center of missile design and fabrication in the non-Communist world.
- California Institute of Technology, located in suburban Pasadena and referred to reverently as "a young MIT," played a key role in the scientific development of aviation and rocketry.
- In Greater LA, the RAND Corporation, a nonprofit strategic think tank created and largely funded by the US Air Force, attracted to the area physicists, chemists, mathematicians, astronomers, social scientists and other scholars interested in doing research.

Speech: Newly appointed FCC Chairman Newton Minow, March 9, 1961, at the National Association of Broadcasters

"I invite you to sit in front of your television set when your station (or network) goes on the air and stay there without a book, magazine, newspaper, profit-and-loss sheet, or ratings book to distract you—and keep your eyes glued to that set until the station signs off. I can assure you that you will observe a vast wasteland. You will see a procession of game shows, violence, audience participation shows, formula comedies about totally unbelievable families, blood and thunder, mayhem, violence, sadism, murder, Western bad men, Western good men, private eyes, gangsters, more violence, cartoons, and—endlessly—commercials, many screaming, cajoling, and offending, and most of all, boredom. True, you will see a few things you enjoy, but they will be very, very, few, and if you think I exaggerate, try it. Is there one person in this room who claims that broadcasting can't do better? Is there one network president in this room who claims he can't do better? Why is so much of television bad? We need imagination in programming, not sterility; creativity, not imitation; experimentation, not conformity; excellence, not mediocrity."

Television in 1961

January: *The Avengers.* Britain's ABC network presented the spy duo of Dr. David Keel (Ian Hendry) and a mysterious character referred to simply as Steed (Patrick MacNee).

March: Newton Minow was sworn in as chairman of the Federal Communications Commission.

April: Death of *Omnibus.* Age: Nine years. In its final season, the show was relegated to a Sunday afternoon slot once a month on NBC.

April: *ABC Final Report* (ABC). The first network attempt at late-night news each weeknight. At first, the program was only carried by ABC's owned and operated stations, but in October it expanded to the entire network.

June: Worthington Miner's syndicated theater presentation, *Play of the Week,* was canceled.

June: *PM East/PM West.* Westinghouse entered late-night television, syndicating 90 minutes of talk and variety five nights a week. One half of the program came from New York (with Mike Wallace), while the other half originated from San Francisco (with Terry O'Flaherty). In February 1962, the West portion was dumped.

July: John Chancellor took over NBC's *Today* from Dave Garroway.

September: *DuPont Show of the Week* (NBC), after four years as a series of floating dramatic specials for CBS, switched to NBC, changing formats as well. The weekly series now included drama, documentary, and variety presentations ranging from "The Wonderful World of Christmas" (with Carol Burnett and Harpo Marx) to "Hemingway" (narrated by Chet Huntley).

September: Walt Disney's *Wonderful World of Color* (NBC). Robert Kinter, who had signed Disney to television when he was with ABC, brought the popular family program with him to NBC. For the first time, the show aired in color (which ABC had always shied away from), beginning with the premier episode, "Mathmagic Land," featuring Donald Duck and a new animated character, Professor Ludwig Von Drake.

September: *Gunsmoke* expanded to 60 minutes, while the cream of six years of the half-hour shows was rerun on Tuesday nights under the title *Marshal Dillon*.

October: *Calendar* (CBS). Harry Reasoner hosted a 30-minute morning show combining hard news and soft features. Reasoner's wry essays, co-written with Andrew Rooney, were a high point of the program.

December: *The Mike Douglas Show.* The former band singer started a 90-minute afternoon talk show on Westinghouse's KYW in Cleveland. By October 1963, the show was syndicated nationally.

FALL 1961 SCHEDULE

MONDAY

Network	7:00	7:30	8:00	8:30	9:00	9:30	10:00	10:30
ABC	Expedition	Cheyenne		The Rifleman	Surfside Six		BEN CASEY	
CBS	local	To Tell The Truth	Pete And Gladys	WINDOW ON MAIN STREET	Danny Thomas Show	Andy Griffith Show	Hennessey	I've Got A Secret
NBC	local		National Velvet	The Price Is Right	87TH PRECINCT		Thriller	

TUESDAY

Network	7:00	7:30	8:00	8:30	9:00	9:30	10:00	10:30
ABC	local	Bugs Bunny Show	Bachelor Father	CALVIN AND THE COLONEL	THE NEW BREED		ALCOA PREMIERE	Bell And Howell Close-Up
CBS	local	Marshal Dillon	DICK VAN DYKE SHOW	The Many Loves Of Dobie Gillis	Red Skelton Show	ICHABOD AND ME	Garry Moore Show	
NBC	local	Laramie		Alfred Hitchcock Presents	DICK POWELL SHOW		CAIN'S HUNDRED	

WEDNESDAY

Network	7:00	7:30	8:00	8:30	9:00	9:30	10:00	10:30
ABC	local	STEVE ALLEN SHOW		TOP CAT	Hawaiian Eye		Naked City	
CBS	local	THE ALVIN SHOW	Father Knows Best	Checkmate		MRS. G GOES TO COLLEGE	U.S. Steel Hour / Armstrong Circle Theater	
NBC	local	Wagon Train		JOEY BISHOP SHOW	Perry Como's Kraft Music Hall		BOB NEWHART SHOW	DAVID BRINKLEY'S JOURNAL

THURSDAY

Network	7:00	7:30	8:00	8:30	9:00	9:30	10:00	10:30
ABC	local	The Adventures Of Ozzie And Harriet	Donna Reed Show	The Real McCoys	My Three Sons	MARGIE	The Untouchables	
CBS	local	FRONTIER CIRCUS		NEW BOB CUMMINGS SHOW	THE INVESTIGATORS		CBS Reports	
NBC	local	The Outlaws		DR. KILDARE		HAZEL	Sing Along With Mitch	

FRIDAY

Network	7:00	7:30	8:00	8:30	9:00	9:30	10:00	10:30
ABC	local	STRAIGHTAWAY	THE HATHAWAYS	The Flintstones	77 Sunset Strip		TARGET: THE CORRUPTORS	
CBS	local	Rawhide		Route 66		FATHER OF THE BRIDE	The Twilight Zone	Eyewitness
NBC	local	INTERNATIONAL SHOWTIME		Robert Taylor's Detectives		Bell Telephone Hour / Dinah Shore Show		FRANK McGEE'S HERE AND NOW

SATURDAY

Network	7:00	7:30	8:00	8:30	9:00	9:30	10:00	10:30
ABC	Matty's Funday Funnies	The Roaring Twenties		Leave It To Beaver	Lawrence Welk Show		Fight Of The Week	Make That Spare
CBS	local	Perry Mason		THE DEFENDERS		Have Gun, Will Travel	Gunsmoke	
NBC	local	Tales Of Wells Fargo		The Tall Man	NBC SATURDAY NIGHT AT THE MOVIES			

SUNDAY

Network	7:00	7:30	8:00	8:30	9:00	9:30	10:00	10:30
ABC	Maverick [from 6:30]	FOLLOW THE SUN		Lawman	BUS STOP			
CBS	Lassie	Dennis The Menace	Ed Sullivan Show		General Electric Theater	Jack Benny Program	Candid Camera	What's My Line
NBC	The Bullwinkle Show	Walt Disney's Wonderful World of Color		CAR 54, WHERE ARE YOU?	Bonanza		DuPont Show Of The Week	

Automobile Salesman in 1961

Wes Cameron built his company into the world's largest Ford dealership through the hard sell and the power of television. He appeared in his own commercials to promote his dealership, becoming a TV personality. In a local poll, he was more popular than national entertainers Ed Sullivan and Steve Allen.

Life at Home

- Wes Cameron pushed, prodded and sold his way to his dream, creating the largest car dealership in the nation.
- Irish on one side of his family and Italian and German on the other, he was endowed with a natural enjoyment of people and a gift for conversation that together made him a natural salesman.
- Wes was a member of many charitable, civic and religious groups. A Roman Catholic layman, he appeared on TV talkathons for charity. He also coached a Little League team that won a district championship.
- He supported several religious causes in the area and even provided clergymen with cars at cost.
- His dealership sponsored an annual Lake Michigan endurance swim as part of his $1 million annual advertising budget.
- He and Violet lived in a sprawling, nine-room ranch house in Lincolnwood, a Chicago suburb, with their son and two daughters.
- Wes also owned three motorboats, a summer home in the country and a winter home in Florida.
- His property in Lincolnwood included a 30' x 60' swimming pool, which he shared with neighborhood children, even hiring a lifeguard to watch over them. Although he built the pool for exercise, he also swam 44 laps every afternoon at the Illinois Athletic Club.
- He began his selling career at age 8, when he sold soda pop in his neighborhood; at age 12, after his father died, he took a paper route and an after-school job at a service station to help his mother and sister pay the bills.
- Wes never went to college. Instead, he first parlayed his fascination with cars into the job at the service station and later became the owner of his own gas station.
- After serving time in the Army during World War II, Wes took advantage of the car shortage in 1943, setting up a used-car lot.

Wes Cameron was a car salesman who believed in the hard sell.

Violet Cameron and her family enjoyed a large home in Chicago, a house in the country, and another in Florida.

- In 1945 he bought a failing Ford dealership, but Ford gave the lucrative franchise to someone else, after which Wes opened a Hudson automobile dealership.
- While appearing on TV with other Hudson dealers to promote a wrestling match, he found his calling; his appearance was such a big hit that he took over the wrestling sponsorship and became one of the on-air personalities.
- After that came a TV variety show of his own, a barn dance and late movies, with Wes making his pitches at intermission.
- Before long, Wes was Hudson's number-one U.S. dealer, selling more than 10 percent of the factory's products, but his eagerness brought both success and problems.
- When he began offering a "lifetime guarantee" against defective parts in his cars, customers complained that he met their objections by insisting that the parts were worn by age, not by defect.
- His aggressive salesmen were accused of illegal practices, including "bushing"—persuading the customer to sign a blank contract, then filling in numbers different from those agreed upon—and his file at the Chicago Better Business Bureau grew thick.
- When Wes saw that Hudson was not keeping up with the times, sticking to its backward styling, he switched to Ford.

Life at Work

- Wes learned to take full advantage of the power of television, appearing in his own commercials to promote his dealership and, in the process, becoming a TV personality.
- A handsome man with curly blond hair and steely blue eyes, he possessed a voice that captured attention, whether he was speaking in person or on television.
- Standing 6'1", he ended his commercials by looking into the viewer's eyes and intoning the words, "God bless you."
- In one Chicago poll, he was more popular than national entertainers Ed Sullivan and Steve Allen.
- Rival dealers complained that their own mothers sang the praises of "that honest Mr. Cameron."
- Sales consistently rose at the dealership after he took over the franchise, except during the recession of 1958.
- By 1961 sales were at a record $41 million a year, although the company's net earnings were just $117,000—down 55 percent from the previous year, reflecting the narrow profit margin a car dealer had in a highly competitive market.

- In 1960 dealers nationwide averaged a $22 profit on each new car sold; as a result dealer failures were up 43 percent.
- Wes's profit margin was higher. He believed that dealers had to be flexible; "If they can't sell a car for a $300 to $400 profit," he said, "they won't sell it. If we can only sell a car for a $50 profit this month, we have to sell it for a $50 profit. Maybe next month we'll take $40. Maybe the month after that, it will be $100. We have to take what the market will bring."

Ford was one of the most popular cars in the 60s.

- He was disdainful of efforts to create a factory-fixed fair-price agreement, saying, "A lot of dealers are sitting around waiting to be legislated into making a living."
- The customers, he believed, were sharper, shrewder and better informed than in the past, with many realizing that dealers were overstocked and anxious to deal; as a result, haggling was in its heyday.
- Everyone wanted a bargain; dealers were especially frustrated by buyers who shopped around from dealer to dealer, using one salesman's figures to bring down another's.
- Wes had a staff of 94 salesmen to cover the six-block-long dealership complex on Chicago's West Side.
- Personally selling more than a thousand cars a year, he had an amazing memory for names and could make complete strangers comfortable in minutes.
- When selling, he played shamelessly on nationalities: if the customer was Irish, he put on a brogue; if the customer was Jewish or Italian, he had a few phrases to match.
- In 1960 his Ford dealership sold 21,000 cars—9,000 new and 12,000 used, more than any Ford dealership in the world. His secret was to make every customer believe he was getting the same deal the salesman would offer his very own brother.

- To maintain the quality of his empire, Wes paid close attention to the details. During his daily tour, he looked in on the new-car showroom to make sure it was clean and that sales were moving at a steady clip; in the service department, he leafed through service orders to detect any patterns that might indicate a problem. He also dropped in on the repair waiting room to talk with customers so their stay would be more pleasant.
- "If you're in the automobile business today," he would say, "and your only profit is from selling new cars, you aren't going to make money. You have to be in insurance, financing, repair—the whole ball of wax."
- If Wes had had his way, dealers would have been consulted more often when automakers were planning new models. He remarked, "If I have $4 million invested in my company, then I should be invited to see what I'm going to have to sell."
- Between 1951 and 1961, the number of U.S. new-car dealerships shrank from 47,000 to 32,000, with another 25,000 selling only used cars.

- New-car dealers offered a choice of 17 standard-sized car models and 89 compacts, most offering a variety of models, motors, options and accessories; it was possible to buy a Chevrolet in more than a hundred thousand different combinations.
- Once American dealers introduced compact cars, the sales of foreign automobiles dropped dramatically—helping to drive the American economy, which was still showing signs of post-recession weakness.
- National inventories hovered at one million cars; some dealers still had unsold 1960 models on their lots.
- To help spur sales, Ford announced the new Falcon Futura, which featured large hubcaps, an opulent interior, bucket seats, deep pile carpets and all-vinyl upholstery.
- To compete, General Motors planned several new compact convertibles for the next model year, and Pontiac decided to introduce the sporty, two-door Tempest coupe.
- Detroit researchers believed that the economic mood of the nation was ripe for "the economic-luxury market."

Life in the Community: Chicago, Illinois

- In 1961 the television program *The Untouchables*, depicting the crime sprees of Chicago mobster Al Capone, was in its third

Chicago enjoyed a steady tourist trade.

year, continuing to stir controversy; letters to newspapers raged against the image it was creating for Chicago, and charges of defamation emerged from the estate of Al Capone.
- In 1960 Yiddish-theater star Dina Halpern had founded the Chicago Yiddish Theater Association, adding a new dimension to a growing theater scene in once-staid Chicago.
- The city was still celebrating its role in electing John F. Kennedy, the first Roman Catholic president of the United States, although accusations abounded that voter fraud, engineered by Chicago mayor Richard Daley, was the only reason John Kennedy had carried Illinois—and subsequently the nation—in a close vote.
- Chicagoan Ray Kroc bought out Dick and Mac McDonald for $2.7 million as part of his plans to further expand the McDonald's fast-food chain.

"The Arabian Bazaar," *Time,* **March 24, 1961**

"Aggressive salesmen use so many tricks and traps to sell to the customer-ranging from legitimate gamesmanship to downright shabby conduct-that customers enter a showroom on guard. A sample of unscrupulous tactics:

The highball: The salesman offers an unrealistically high price for the customer's trade-in, then jacks up the price of the new car (often with accessories) to cover the too-high trade-in, or backs off altogether.

The lowball: The salesman quotes a rock-bottom price for the new car to win the customer, then later hikes up the price, declaring that a mistake has been made or that the quoted price was for another model.

The double dip: Two salesmen work on a customer, pretending to be in competition with each other. When the first salesman is turned down, another moves in with a better deal. Later, the two split the commission.

The bush: The salesman persuades the customer to sign a blank contract after he has agreed to certain terms, then fills in figures different from those agreed on, or adds additional costs for such fictitious items as delivery charges, handling costs and excise tax (which is already included in the price). The bush is illegal in some states.

A variation on the bush is to fill out the contract at the agreed-upon figures, sending the customer away satisfied. Then the salesman calls later and informs the customer that a mistake has been made and the car will cost more money-figuring that he will pay the difference rather than go through the whole haggle again. Some salesmen try to close a deal by insisting, 'I can only get it for you at this price today'—though they will be glad to quote the same price tomorrow. Another salesman rushes off into the back room to check the new, low, low price with his boss, but often simply goes for a drink of water. He comes back breathless, bearing the news that his boss has lost his mind and agreed.

Downtown Chicago, Illinois.

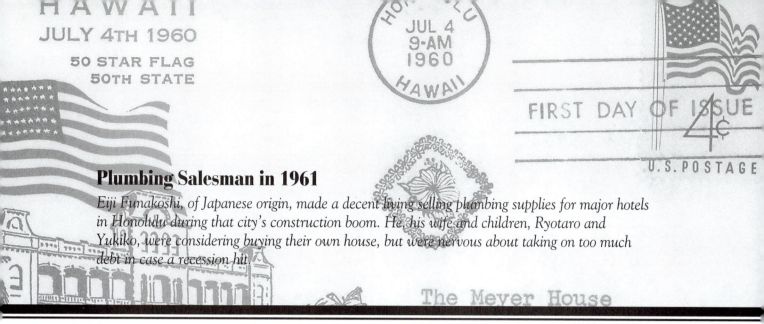

HAWAII

JULY 4TH 1960

50 STAR FLAG
50TH STATE

JUL 4
9·AM
1960
HAWAII

FIRST DAY OF ISSUE

4¢

U.S. POSTAGE

Plumbing Salesman in 1961

Eiji Funakoshi, of Japanese origin, made a decent living selling plumbing supplies for major hotels in Honolulu during that city's construction boom. He, his wife and children, Ryotaro and Yukiko, were considering buying their own house, but were nervous about taking on too much debt in case a recession hit.

The Meyer House

Life at Home

- The construction boom in Honolulu raised the family income.
- Both Ryotaro and Yukiko began to talk about college. In the past they had not considered leaving the Islands for school because of the expense, but their recent prosperity had made it possible for them to consider stateside schools.
- The Funakoshi family was also thinking about buying a house; subdivisions with wide, winding streets were being constructed at a torrid pace.
- At the same time, the family knew that if a recession hit Hawaii or the building trade, Eiji's income would rapidly diminish. They were afraid of taking on too much debt.
- Early in the year, the Funakoshis attended a New Year's Day wedding ceremony for a Japanese couple; weddings were a popular part of the traditional New Year's excursions from Japan to Hawaii.
- This family annually made contributions to charities, including the United Fund, of $458.
- To protect his family, Eiji spent $545 a year on life insurance, and he also put a little of his income aside toward a retirement fund.
- Food and beverages accounted for 28 percent of this family's budget; shelter required 16 percent.
- Even though the costs of eggs, dairy products and fresh produce were very high in Hawaii, costs for heating fuel and heavy clothing for the winter were minimal.
- Like most Islanders, this family used a Hawaiian word, *keiki,* to refer to a child; likewise they expected to see the words *kane* and *wahine* on bathroom doors to signify "men" and "women."
- The Funakoshis were very supportive of Hawaiian statehood.
- Statehood, especially for the large population of Japanese ancestry living in the Islands, was a symbol of social acceptance, the chance to be first-class citizens.

Eiji Funakoshi made a good living selling plumbing supplies to high-end hotels.

WASHINGTON TO WAIKIKI BY JET advertisement

TRAVEL SERVICES DEPT.—AAA
1712 G Street, N.W.—MEtropolitan 8-4000, ext. 243
Washington 6, D. C.

Please send me information on the AAA "Washington to Waikiki Tour" which departs on November 4, 1963.

Name: _____

Address: _____

_____

Office Phone _____ Home Phone _____

Membership Number _____

WASHINGTON TO WAIKIKI BY JET

14-day tour for only $640 including hotel accommodations

The dream of a lifetime, at a rock-bottom price . . . Hawaii, with its spectacular scenery from mountaintop to the crystal depths offshore, awaits you at the other end of the Northwest Orient jet flight from Dulles International Airport. Deadline for reservations is September 2; departure is set for November 4, 1963. Make your reservation early! Go AAA to Hawaii. AAA offers more than 80 other tours by air, rail or ship to all points in the free world . . . places like Europe, South America, Alaska and Canada, the Orient, the Near East. When you think of travel, anywhere, any time, think of AAA!

Hawaii's tourist industry was booming.

Life at Work

- Already an experienced salesman, Eiji found selling plumbing supplies for major hotels and developments under construction exciting. The money was good, but, more important, he felt he was part of Honolulu's progress.
- Financially Eiji was having the most successful year of his life; Honolulu in particular had bought into the idea that "progress is better, more progress is best."
- Following statehood Hawaii's economy boomed, particularly construction.
- The popular joke was that Hawaii's new state bird was the Dillingham crane, referring to the long steel tower used for erecting tall buildings.
- Recent high school graduates fulfilled the need for unskilled labor in the construction industry, but skilled workers were needed to keep pace with the current demand.
- In 1961 there was more private construction in Hawaii than during the 16-year period between 1925 and 1941.
- Nine-tenths of the construction was on the island of Oahu; in rates of growth and dollar volume, construction exceeded even the tourist industry.
- One of Eiji's major clients was Roy Kelley, the "wizard of Waikiki," who was the largest hotel developer in the state, with approximately 2,200 rooms under his control.
- Kelley's moderately priced rooms made Waikiki an affordable place for the middle-income visitor.
- A typical single hotel room built by Kelley cost $8.50 to $12.00 a night.

Life in the Community: Honolulu, Hawaii

- The Republic of Hawaii was annexed as a U.S. territory in 1900. It retained its earlier motto, "Ua Mau Ke Ea O Ka Aina I Ka Pono," or, "The Life of the Land Is Preserved by Righteousness."
- The 390-mile chain of the new island territory was located 2,100 miles west-southwest of San Francisco.
- At statehood in 1959, 85 percent of the population resided on Oahu, home of the state's capital city, Honolulu.
- After World War II, Hawaii was confronted by a shortage of housing, particularly between 1954 and 1958.
- In 1960 nearly everyone was talking about a "new Hawaii" that would be the financial, commercial, cultural and educational hub of the Pacific. The resident population was 642,000, but rapid immigration began to strain the resources of the fragile islands.
- Hawaii turned the economic disadvantage of being in the middle of the Pacific into an

Major hotels were being constructed to keep up with demand.

Honolulu, Hawaii.

advantage; the Islands became a world travel center, the operational center for the nation's defense in the Pacific and a major center for shipping.

- Hawaii's mild temperature and fertile soil were excellent for growing tropical fruits and vegetables; approximately 75 percent of the world's canned pineapple was produced on the Islands.
- Sugar and pineapples were the leading economic drivers in Hawaii; defense spending on military bases was third and tourism, growing rapidly, was fourth.
- Hawaiian sugar producers led those of all other states in wages and yields per acre.
- Hawaii had always been a paradise, but only for the well-to-do; following statehood, thanks to tourism, more workers were feeling the spread of prosperity.
- Statehood also changed Hawaii's image in the tourist market by broadening its appeal; to the Islands' natural beauty and "exotic" Polynesian ambiance were added staples of American culture, such as hamburgers and typical hotel amenities.
- The development of the tourism industry depended on a major technological breakthrough: regular passenger jet service from the American mainland.
- In the 1960s the economy fare from the mainland to Honolulu was $110.00 for prearranged groups and conventions.
- When Pan American began Boeing 707 service to Hawaii in September 1959, the trip from California was reduced from a tedious 15 hours to just 5 hours.
- A super-speed deluxe airliner from Hawaii to California cost $79.10 and included free hot meals; fly now, pay later arrangements; and sleeper seats. Trips to Wake Island cost $154.40; Guam, $176.00; Okinawa, $200.00 and Tokyo, $284.00.
- Tourism soon rivaled both sugar and pineapple production as the Islands's major industry.
- The number of visitors in 1960 rose 44 percent over the total for 1959; tourism was expected to double in the next five years.
- Unlike in the past, tourists came to Hawaii all year around; the tourist "peaks" disappeared.

- Surveys showed that 35 percent of visitors were returnees—people who had enjoyed the Islands on an earlier visit.
- Waikiki Beach, where 100 hotels were located, was a major tourist destination.
- By 1960 one out of every three marriages in Hawaii was racially mixed. The population of the Islands had become one-third Asian, primarily Japanese; one-third partly Hawaiian, Filipino or Puerto Rican; and about one-third *haole*, or white.
- Families of which the head of the household was of Chinese or Japanese ancestry earned the largest annual median incomes.
- A survey of median income by race showed that Caucasians averaged $5,986 annually; Chinese, $6,730; Filipino, $4,355; Hawaiian, $5,200 and Japanese, $6,842. The average for all groups was $6,055.
- The average wage per hour of field workers in Hawaii in 1960 was $1.63 plus fringe benefits of $0.48. By contrast Louisiana paid $0.71 per hour, Florida, $1.01 and Puerto Rico, $0.51.
- The average weekly wage for all Hawaiian industries in 1960 was $73.19; mining paid $113.62 a week, and the wholesale and retail trade paid $63.32.
- During the preceding year, the cost of living in Hawaii had risen 3 percent; domestic gas rates, shoes, automobile fuel, hospital-room rates and recreation led the increases.
- During World War II and the Korean War, hundreds of thousands of military personnel trained in or traveled through Honolulu, creating a natural thirst to return.
- In 1961 Elvis Presley starred in *Blue Hawaii,* the first of three movies he made on location in Hawaii in the 1960s, tying his considerable appeal to the Islands.

Diamond Head is a volcanic cone on the Hawaiian island of O'ahu.

Civil Rights Pioneer in 1961

Septima Clark taught school in South Carolina for 40 years before being fired for refusing to resign her membership in the NAACP. The action occurred after the South Carolina legislature banned state employees from any association with civil right organizations. Clark had been Vice President of the organization's Charleston chapter since 1956.

Life at Home

- Septima Poinsette was born on May 3, 1898, in Charleston, South Carolina.
- Her mother, Victoria Warren Anderson, was raised in Haiti and excelled in its challenging educational environment, which was modeled on that of Europe.
- As a young woman, Victoria came to live in the United States, where she met and married Septima's father, Peter Porcher Poinsette.
- Peter, a Muskhogean from the Sea Islands of Georgia, was born a slave on a coastal plantation.
- Freed at the end of the Civil War, he found work on a steamship that traveled between Charleston and New York.
- Once married, Victoria and Peter took up residence in Charleston.
- Septima was the second of their eight children.
- Septima's mother, having been reared outside of the American South, had never been a slave and did not allow the prevailing prejudice to inhibit her from demanding opportunities for her children.
- In the first grade, Septima went to a public school called the ABC Gallery, under less-than-perfect conditions.
- There were approximately a hundred other students in her class. The facility had outdoor bathrooms and bleachers for seating, and beatings were administered daily for disciplinary infractions.
- So Septima's mother sent her instead to a private school in the home of a woman and her niece.
- It was common at the time for black women to run small schools in their homes.
- The woman who ran this private school reserved admission for the children of "free issues"—African Americans who had never been slaves—since they were considered to be of higher social standing.
- The head teacher was very strict, because she believed that the children of free issues should be held to a higher standard of behavior.
- The school's rules extended beyond the classroom and the school day; children could be whipped for infractions in their spare time away from school.

Septima Poinsette Clark taught school in the South Carolina school system for 40 years.

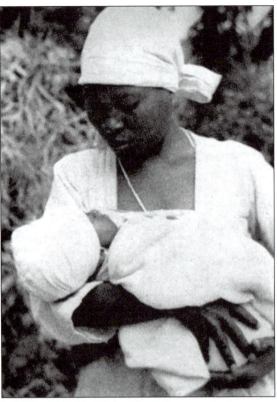

Infant Septima and her mother, Victoria.

- For instance, if the teacher saw a student outside a store eating candy from a paper bag, it was considered unacceptable behavior and grounds for a beating.
- When she was about eight years old, Septima returned to public school, attending Mary Street School for two years, followed by two years at Burke Industrial School, where she completed the seventh grade.
- Septima recalled, "I shall never forget those years. They were the most important for me, and I shall to the end of my days be grateful to my parents for them. They were hard years, years of struggle for both my father and my mother. There were eight children to feed and clothe, and always there was little money with which to provide even the bare necessities. But love made the household a home, and though constant toil from sunup until the late hours of the night was the year-round routine, it was a happy home. Despite the hardships, the children were able to trudge off each day to school after a hot breakfast and with a lunch, and there were hot meals when they returned from school. Some days there was even a penny with which to buy a piece of candy, for in our childhood days a penny would indeed buy a little treat."
- On completion of the seventh grade, Septima had earned a teaching certificate. The Charleston public schools, however, still were not hiring black teachers.
- Two circumstances—Septima's high scores on an exam, which would exempt her from having to complete the eighth grade, and her mother's insistence that she continue her schooling—led her to matriculate at Avery Normal Institute in the ninth grade.
- Avery was a coeducational school for African American students.
- The school was developed at the turn of the twentieth century by the American Missionary Association, and it was sponsored by the Congregational Church.
- Avery was staffed primarily by white teachers from the North, predominantly from New England.
- In order to pay her tuition at Avery, Septima worked for a couple who lived across the street from her parents, serving as a companion, housekeeper and babysitter for the woman while her husband was away on business.
- Septima and the woman were close in age and became good friends.
- The woman would make lovely dresses for Septima, and the two would go on outings together.
- At Avery Septima loved the library and astronomy.
- She loved the teachers for their dedication. They taught her how to cook and sew.
- When Septima was a junior at Avery, Benjamin F. Cox, a black man, became president of the institute.
- Cox brought many positive changes to Avery, improving the facilities and expanding the curriculum.
- With Cox came the appointment of black teachers to the faculty.
- Black teachers and white teachers living together in the faculty dormitories was unacceptable to the white establishment in Charleston, and the city outlawed this arrangement.

Septima worked on developing a curriculum for adult students.

- Thus Avery Normal Institute had to dismiss its white teachers.
- In her senior year at Avery, Septima passed another teaching exam, earning her a first-grade teaching certificate.
- Her teachers encouraged her to seek enrollment at Fisk College in Nashville, Tennessee, but at $18 per month, Fisk cost more than Septima's family could afford, and she began looking for work as a teacher.
- Charleston's public schools did not employ black teachers at the time, so in 1916 Septima found work at Promised Land School on Johns Island, off the coast of South Carolina.
- Septima met her future husband, Nerie Clark, in January 1919.
- He was a sailor aboard the USS *Umpqua*, which docked in Charleston Harbor.
- During a three-day leave in May 1919, Nerie returned to visit Septima.
- The two were married a year later.
- Septima's family did not approve of or consent to the relationship, because they did not think the two had had sufficient time to become acquainted.
- Septima and Nerie had a daughter, named Victoria after Septima's mother, but the baby died soon after birth.
- Nerie never met his daughter, because he was away at sea when she was born.
- Soon after Nerie's return, he and Septima moved to North Carolina to live with his family.
- There Septima became pregnant again.
- Nerie left the Navy, and the couple moved to Dayton, Ohio.
- Septima's second child, a son, was born in a Dayton hospital.
- The child was named Nerie, after his father.
- While Septima was still in the hospital following her son's birth, she found out that her husband had an ex-wife, of whom she had been unaware.
- Septima also learned of another woman in Dayton with whom her husband had practically been living.
- At this time Nerie Clark asked his wife to take their newborn child and move away from Dayton as soon as possible.
- Septima moved back to Hickory, North Carolina, to live with her in-laws.
- Ten months later, Nerie was dead from kidney failure.
- Septima transported Nerie's body back to his family home in the mountains of North Carolina, and she stayed there to teach for a year.
- Then she moved with her son back to Johns Island and resumed teaching at Promised Land School.
- But the island winters proved to be too harsh for her child, and the rigors of her schedule were too great for her to provide him with adequate care.
- Though it would bring her anguish, Septima entrusted her son to the care of his paternal grandparents.

Life at Work

- On Johns Island there were 14 schools for black students, staffed by one or two teachers each.
- For white students, there were three schools, each staffed with one teacher.

Racism was part of life for Septima.

- Septima was rated a principal, earning $30 per month from the State of South Carolina, with an additional $5 per month as a supplement from Charleston County.
- She shared the responsibility of teaching 132 students with one other teacher, a fellow graduate of Avery Normal Institute.
- The white teachers on Johns Island were responsible for as few as 3 and not more than 18 students; those with teaching certifications comparable to Septima's were paid $85 per month.
- The school itself was a log cabin-like building with an open fireplace for which the students had to collect their own firewood.
- The only materials provided for the school were an ax, a water bucket and dipper, a table and chair and some makeshift benches and chalkboards.
- Teachers had to provide their own chalk and erasers.
- Of greater concern was the wide range of children's skills and ages; individual instruction was a daily task.
- Moreover, those students old enough to work were contractually obligated to labor on the plantations on behalf of their families; attendance at school was erratic.
- In 1918 Septima accepted a job teaching sixth grade at Avery Normal Institute, and she moved back to Charleston.
- She was paid $30 per week.
- "The experience of teaching at Avery was one of the most important and formative experiences of my life. It was then that I first became actively concerned in an organized effort to improve the lot of my fellow Negroes. Sometimes I have the almost certain feeling that I was providentially sent to Avery that year."
- During the next decade, Septima held a series of teaching positions and began attending interracial meetings in Columbia, South Carolina.
- In the summer of 1930, Septima went to Columbia University in New York, studying math, curriculum building and astronomy.
- At Columbia she learned to incorporate the vernacular of her students into the reading lessons in order to improve their comprehension and teach them new words.
- She studied astronomy so she could include information about, and words pertaining to, the natural world in the lessons she taught.
- In the summer of 1937, Septima went to Georgia to study at Atlanta University; specifically, she wanted to learn more about working with rural populations.
- One of her professors was W. E. B. Du Bois, the intellectual leader of the National Association for the Advancement of Colored People (NAACP).
- Many of Septima's fellow students in Atlanta were from rural areas where work on plantations and on contract farms were common.

> **"JOIN THE FIGHT FOR FREEDOM"**
> **CAMPAIGN of N.A.A.C.P.**
>
> ....196.......
>
> Received from...
>   *(Name)*
>
> ....
>   *(Address)*
>
> Paid $.............
>
> Signed ....
>   *Solicitor*
>
> Address ....
>
> If you receive no acknowledgement from National Office, write Lucille Black, Membership Secretary, 20 West 40th Street, New York 18, N. Y.

Septima was fired for her association with the NAACP.

Anti-black protesters took their concerns to Washington D.C.

- Often these students found her attention to the racial inequalities and injustices of the day threatening and controversial.
- "But nevertheless, I went on, and I got to the place where I had to give my concerns regardless of where I was. The problem, I realized, was not only whites against blacks. It was men against women; it was old against young. You had all those things to fight all the time regardless, and it's still a constant fight."
- Working her way through college while teaching, Septima earned a Bachelor of Arts degree in 1942 from Benedict College in Columbia, South Carolina.
- Once she had completed her B.A., she wanted to pursue a Master's degree.
- In 1944 she began classes at Hampton Institute in Virginia.
- Over the course of three summers, she worked toward and earned her Master's.
- During the 18 years that Septima lived in Columbia, her teaching salary increased from $780 to $4,000 per year.
- In addition to earning two degrees during that time, she also helped to fight for and win equal pay for black teachers.
- Black teachers in Columbia had earned only around half of what white teachers with equivalent education and experience made.
- The NAACP took up the cause, sending Thurgood Marshall, then its chief legal counsel, to represent Septima and her colleagues.
- In 1945 Judge Julius Waties Waring ruled in federal court that teachers with comparable credentials must be compensated equally, regardless of race.
- School officials drafted the National Teacher's Exam for the purpose of evaluating teachers.
- Septima was one of 42 teachers to take the exam the first time it was administered.
- She scored an A, and with it, she earned a raise from $62.50 to $117 per month.
- In 1947 she moved back to Charleston to take care of her mother, who had suffered a stroke.
- She became involved with the Young Women's Christian Association (YWCA), serving as the chairperson of administration for the black YWCA.
- Through her work with the YWCA, she became close personal friends with Judge Waring and his wife Elizabeth.
- It was a friendship anchored by a shared belief in the justice of an integrated society and their mutual efforts toward building one.
- Judge Waring's court rulings and friendships caused controversy. Friends ceased to associate with him and his wife, they were refused service at local businesses, and they had to be accompanied by guards in public.
- Ultimately the Warings were forced to leave Charleston.
- Septima was criticized by her colleagues and her principal for her friendship with the Warings; her neighbors worried that she would bring trouble to the entire neighborhood.

Black students had a difficult road to walk in the 60s.

A propaganda postcard, claiming the Highlander Falls School was a breeding ground for communism.

- She was the target of obscene and threatening phone calls, and she had to live daily with the reality that her work and her associations made her a target for all those who would resort to violence in an effort to maintain a culture of white supremacy.
- In 1954 Septima went to the Highlander Folk School for the first time.
- The school, set on 200 acres on the Cumberland Plateau, in Monteagle, Tennessee, was the only place in the South at that time where interracial education and organization were taking place.
- At Highlander every aspect of life was communal and integrated; for many it was their first experience in this kind of environment.
- After her initial visit to Highlander, Septima became very active in the work of the school, transporting groups there from South Carolina, leading workshops, and drafting pamphlets.
- In 1954 she collaborated on two pamphlets: "A Guide to Action for Public School Desegregation" and "What Is a Workshop?"
- "At Highlander I found out that black people weren't the only ones discriminated against. I found out that whites were against whites. The low-income whites were considered dirt under the feet of the wealthy whites, just like blacks were. I had to go to Highlander to find out that there was so much prejudice in the minds of whites against whites. I didn't dream—I thought that everything white was right. But I found out differently. I found out that they had a lot of prejudice against each other."
- Septima continued to teach elementary school in Charleston and work with local civic organizations as the civil rights movement developed throughout the United States, particularly in the South.
- She also kept up her involvement at Highlander, returning in the summer of 1955, when she worked with and got to know Rosa Parks.
- Throughout the South the white establishment—including, in most cases, local government entities such as legislatures and law enforcement—was reacting to the changes being achieved through the coordinated efforts of civil rights organizations.
- Following the 1954 *Brown v. Board of Education* decision, in which the Supreme Court deemed segregated schools to be unconstitutional, the white power structure of the South sought to disable the NAACP, the driving force behind much of the legal action and resulting change.
- To this end the heads of state legislatures in the South called special sessions ruling that the NAACP must make public its membership lists.
- The NAACP refused to do so.
- The individual states reacted in different ways, some obtaining injunctions to stop the operation of the NAACP.
- In 1956 the South Carolina legislature passed a law banning all persons employed by either the city or the state from any membership in, or association with, civil rights organizations.
- Having been a long-time member of the NAACP, Septima became the vice president of the Charleston chapter in 1956.
- She refused to sever her ties with the organization despite the state's ruling.

- As a result she was fired from the teaching position she had held for 40 years and lost the pension she had earned along with it.
- She attempted to organize the teachers of South Carolina to fight the injustice of the new law, but there was little response to her letters and entreaties.
- The culture of intimidation was working, she saw; teachers feared for their lives and livelihoods and would not fight the new law.
- It was at this moment that Septima came to the realization that what she was asking of the people she was trying to mobilize was more than they were prepared to take on.
- She remembered thinking, "I'm going to have to get the people trained. We're going to have to show them the dangers or the pitfalls that they are in, before they will accept. And it took many years."
- Septima was offered a job at the Highlander Folk School as director of workshops, and she moved to Monteagle in June 1956.
- In her new role, she traveled widely, and she continued to be active in her Charleston community as well.
- While at Highlander Septima developed the "citizenship school" model, which she then implemented throughout the South.
- The objective of the citizenship schools was to teach black adults to read and write and also to teach them the information necessary to become registered voters.
- The first citizenship school was started on Johns Island, South Carolina.
- It was a collective effort by Septima, Highlander head Myles Horton and a man from Johns Island named Esau Jenkins.
- Jenkins wanted to run for election to the school board, but he couldn't get elected unless his supporters were allowed to cast ballots.
- Voters told him that if he could help them learn the requisite information to pass the voter registration tests, then they would vote for him.
- Jenkins had attended Highlander, and he worked with Horton and Septima to develop a curriculum for these adult students.
- When it came time to open the school on Johns Island, no church, school or civic organization was willing to assume the risk associated with such an undertaking.
- With financial support from Highlander, the Progressive Club, a voter education group started by Jenkins, bought a building in which to hold citizenship school classes, at a cost of $1,500.
- The site housed a cooperative store, which operated out of the front of the building, while the citizenship school classes took place in a windowless room in the back.

Septima and her colleagues created a positive environment for black and white students alike.

- This nonviolent, direct action—educating black voters so that they could claim their political voice—had to be concealed to prevent violence.
- The first citizenship school teacher was Septima's cousin Bernice Robinson.
- The method of teaching involved students telling stories about their daily activities.
- They would then record the stories and read them back to the class.
- Any challenging words would be used in the spelling lessons.
- Classes were organized with attention to civic participation and empowerment.
- Following the success of the Johns Island Citizenship School model, Highlander developed a program to train teachers to lead citizenship schools all over the South.

- Septima recalled, "Working through those states, I found I could say nothing to those people, and no teacher as a rule could speak with them. We had to let them talk to us and say to us whatever they wanted to say. When we got through listening to them, we let them know that they were right according to the kind of thing that they had in their mind, but according to living in this world, there were other things they needed to know. We wanted to know if they were willing then to listen to us, and they decided that they wanted to listen to us."

- Because of its integrated environment and its work in training and educating blacks and the rural poor to empower themselves, Highlander Folk School was accused of advocating communist ideals and activities, and it fell under the scrutiny of the FBI.

- "Anyone who was against segregation was considered a communist," Septima recalled.

- "White Southerners couldn't believe that a Southerner could have the idea of racial equality; they thought it had to come from somewhere else."

- In 1959, during Highlander's twenty-fifth anniversary celebration, the Rev. Dr. Martin Luther King Jr. was photographed sitting near a reporter for *The Daily Worker*, a communist newspaper.

- The reporter had not made her affiliation with the communist paper known when seeking admission to the celebration.

- Throughout the South, the photograph was used as propaganda to "prove" that Highlander was a communist training center.

- This prompted the authorities of the State of Tennessee to investigate the "subversive activities" taking place at the school.

- The state legislature met and solicited the district attorney to bring any suit against Highlander so that the school's charter might be revoked.

- Though it was integration on the Highlander campus that Tennessee authorities wanted to end, they couldn't bring that charge against the school with a reasonable expectation of winning because the Supreme Court had already ruled that segregated schools were unconstitutional.

- Ultimately the state felt most confident that it could successfully charge Highlander with the possession of alcohol and intent to sell it.

- On July 31, 1959, nearly 20 Tennessee police raided the Highlander Folk School.

- They detained Septima, and "finding" moonshine at the residence of Myles Horton, they arrested her and some of the students.

- In court Septima testified that the liquor found the night of the raid had at no time been in her possession.

- Despite incongruities in the statements of the prosecution's witnesses, the court upheld the possession charge.

- The initial consequence was an order that the administration building be temporarily padlocked.

- Subsequently, the Grundy County Circuit Court revoked the school's charter.

- "I wasn't going to let them scare me to death. I just wouldn't let them. But it wasn't an easy thing, because when you'd go home, you would keep thinking what they could do and what they might do, because they were very, very harassing and very mean, very much so."

- By early 1961, 82 teachers who had received training at Highlander were conducting citizenship classes in several Southern states.

- In the summer of 1961, the legal status of Highlander was so tenuous that the citizenship school program was relocated to the Dorchester Co-operative Community Center in McIntosh, Georgia.

- The project of the citizenship schools was taken up by the Southern Christian Leadership Conference (SCLC).

- Septima, for a time, was both employed by Highlander and working on behalf of the SCLC.

- She traveled widely in the South and throughout the country recruiting and fundraising for the citizenship school program.

Life in the Community: Charleston, South Carolina

- Charleston had a long colonial history and was the original capital of the Carolina Colony.
- It was established to serve as a major port city, an expectation it fulfilled.
- As such it was the primary location for the unloading and selling of humans captured in Africa and transported to be sold as slaves in the colonies (later, the United States).
- As a result of its role as a trade center, Charleston became the wealthiest city south of Philadelphia and the fourth-largest in the colonies by the mid-1700s.
- More than half of Charleston's population was made up of slaves.
- In the nineteenth century, black slaves and domestic servants continued to make up the majority of the city's population.
- South Carolina grew increasingly adamant that states' rights superseded the power of the federal government.
- In 1832 the state passed an ordinance whereby it could nullify the mandates of the federal government.
- Federal troops were, therefore, dispatched to Charleston's forts to collect tariffs. The state's history of conflict with and resistance to the federal government had begun.

The Civil War wreaked havoc on the city of Charleston.

- On December 20, 1860, following the election of Abraham Lincoln as president, South Carolina's General Assembly voted to secede from the Union.
- Thus began the Civil War.
- Charleston incurred heavy bombardment and severe damage during the war.
- In 1865 Union troops moved into Charleston and took control of much of the city.
- Following the Civil War, federal troops were dispatched to South Carolina to oversee Reconstruction.
- The war had devastated both Charleston's economy and its infrastructure.

Charleston was an important seaport.

- Freed slaves faced poverty, discrimination, intimidation and various abuses and other forms of disenfranchisement.
- Many former slave owners refused to free their slaves.
- South Carolina languished economically for the remainder of the nineteenth century.
- Once one of the nation's wealthiest states, South Carolina by 1890 was near the bottom in per capita income.
- Illiteracy impacted 45 percent of the population; public health was so poor that 44 percent of the state's military volunteers for the Spanish-American War were rejected.
- Cities began aggressively developing textile manufacturing as a sign of progress; the standard work week was 66 hours before a 1907 law reduced it to 60 hours.

- Charleston's public school system was one of the best in the state, but statewide, private education continued to play a major role. In 1916 one in eight high-school students was enrolled in a private school.
- The outbreak of World War I brought a handful of federal military training centers to the state and dramatically increased the activity in the Charleston Naval Yard.
- But agriculture, particularly the growing of cotton, continued to dominate the economy.
- In 1939 approximately 80 percent of the state's male high school and college graduates moved elsewhere in search of better opportunities.
- A survey in 1945 showed that 40 percent of those desiring a college education indicated they planned to go to school out of state.
- Following the World War II, industrial recruitment accelerated; within nine months, Charleston had attracted 19 new companies employing 812 people.
- There followed major investments of federal dollars as a large military presence in the region helped to shore up the city's economy.

Early Charleston, South Carolina.

"30 More Virginia Schools to Integrate This Week,"
The Martinsville Bulletin (Virginia), September 3, 1961

Seventy-three Virginia schools will admit Negro pupils—30 of the schools for the first time—at opening sessions this week.

Negro enrollment in the commonly white schools is estimated at 537, more than double the Negro enrollment in the 1960-61 term.

Last year, 211 Negroes attended 43 white schools in 11 localities, while for the 1961-62 session, that figure has jumped to 73 schools in 19 localities.

Enrollment of Negro pupils in the predominately all-white classrooms is expected to proceed without incident and no special precautions are being taken anywhere in the state.

Heaviest concentration of integration in the state is in the Northern Virginia area across the Potomac River from Washington. These for localities—Alexandria, Falls Church, Arlington County and Fairfax County—account for more than half of the Negroes admitted.

The other localities are scattered from Virginia's Tidewater to the Blue Ridge Mountains.

Most of the Negro students were assigned to the schools by the state Pupil Placement Board, which only last week assigned seven more Negroes to white schools in five localities. Others were ordered admitted by federal judges.

Reverend Dr. Martin Luther King, Jr.'s
Address to the AFL-CIO Convention [excerpt], 1961

"How can labor rise to the heights of its potential statesmanship and cement its bonds with Negroes to their mutual advantage?

First: Labor should accept the logic of its special position with respect to Negroes and the struggle for equality. Although organized labor has taken actions to eliminate discrimination in its ranks, the standard for the general community, your conduct should and can set an example for others, as you have done in other crusades for social justice. You should root out vigorously every manifestation of discrimination so that some international, central labor bodies or locals may not besmirch the positive accomplishments of labor. I am aware this is not easy or popular-but the eight-hour day was not popular nor easy to achieve. Nor was outlawing anti-labor injunctions. But you accomplished all of these with a massive will and determination. Out of such struggle for democratic rights you won both economic gains and the respect of the country, and you will win both again if you make Negro rights a great crusade.

Second: The political strength you are going to need to prevent automation from becoming a Moloch, consuming jobs and contract gains, can be multiplied if you tap the vast reservoir of Negro political power. Negroes given the vote will vote liberal and labor because they need the same liberal legislation labor needs…

If you would do these things now in this convention-resolve to deal effectively with discrimination and provide financial aid for our struggle in the South—this convention will have a glorious moral deed to add to an illustrious history."

"Desegregation Developments, Education," *The Americana Annual 1962, An Encyclopedia of the Events of 1961*

As the eighth school year after the U.S. Supreme Court's desegregation decision began, only three states—Alabama, Mississippi, and South Carolina—continue to have complete segregation at all levels of the public education system.

The number of Negroes attending classes with white children was still small. As of November 1961, according to the *Southern School News,* 7.3 percent of the 3,210,724 Negro children enrolled in schools of the 18 previously segregated states were attending biracial schools. However, of the 233,509 Negroes in mixed classes, 88,881 were in Washington, DC, 47,588 in Maryland, 20,636 in Kentucky, an estimated 35,000 in Missouri and 15,500 in West Virginia, 10,555 in Oklahoma and 8,448 in Delaware. In the rest of the previously segregated states, fewer than 7,000 Negroes were in mixed schools.

The increase of 31 in the number of the segregated school districts in the fall of 1961 was extremely small, and led to the enrollment of only 392 additional Negroes in previously all white schools. Nevertheless, the segregation steps taken were significant. Three of the largest cities in the south—Atlanta, Dallas, and Memphis—were desegregated, and all fall school openings were without violence…

Outside the South, efforts were being made in 1961 to eliminate what is called de facto segregation. Such moves were underway in Chicago, New York, Pasadena, Montclair, New Jersey, and New Rochelle, N.Y.

Baseball Barker in 1961

Charles Plautard's dream of wearing a St. Louis Cardinal jersey took shape as a boy, working at his father's newsstand near Busch Stadium. Realizing that he was not big league material, he did the next best thing, and took a job hawking "red hots here" at Busch Stadium, where he could root for his beloved Cardinals every game.

Life at Home

- Charles Plautard was born in the central Broadway section of St. Louis, Missouri, the only son of Pierre and Anne-Marie Plautard.
- The Plautard name was first introduced to the area by French fur traders, who built a post on the site of the city in 1764.
- Charlie's father was the owner and operator of a small newsstand on Broadway near Busch Stadium, home of the St. Louis Cardinals baseball team.
- Charlie loved the Cardinals, and most of all he loved to follow the exploits of Stan "the Man" Musial.
- Like thousands of young boys growing up in the Gateway City, Charlie dreamed of one day wearing a Cardinals red jersey and being interviewed by *St. Louis Globe-Democrat* sportswriter Bob Burnes.
- Playing highly competitive high-school baseball made Charlie realize that although he was a decent player, he was no threat to take Stan the Man's job in the Cardinals outfield.
- In 1959, at age 17 and in need of a job, Charlie sought employment at Busch Stadium, relishing the opportunity to simultaneously earn money and root for his beloved Cardinals.
- It was a slow process, with dozens of disappointing trips to the ballpark as he waited his turn for a job.
- His persistence finally paid off when he became a vendor at Busch Stadium.
- He was first assigned to sell the heaviest, least popular drinks, but he was a baseball barker nonetheless.
- Within two years he was earning enough money working at the ballpark and at his father's newsstand to rent his own apartment.
- The *St. Louis Post-Dispatch* classifieds advertised a "clean bachelor apartment, completely furnished, $57.50 per month."
- One of his first purchases for his new apartment was an Avril playmate hi-fi with long-distance radio so he could listen to his team's away games on the Liberty Mutual Broadcasting network.

Charles Plautard was a die-hard Cardinals fan and a vendor at Busch Stadium.

- To save money on records, he signed up for a record club that offered him any five of his favorite records, mailed to him for $1.97.
- Working as a stadium vendor was physically demanding, so to stay in shape, he bought a set of 110-pound, vinyl-jacketed weights with two dumbbells from Sears Roebuck, for $20.
- Charlie became known for his parties, with the music of José Feliciano, a 19-inch GE TV and lots of Budweiser beer—with the new tabbed aluminum cans.
- Food and beverages had been a feature of baseball parks since 1859.

Life at Work

- Charlie Plautard was so excited about applying for work as a vendor at Busch Stadium that he arrived two hours before game time, only to be greeted by a throng of other boys and men with a similar goal.
- Unfazed, he joined the rest of the crowd awaiting the arrival of the food concessions manager, who picked from the crowd those who would have the opportunity to sell drinks and snacks during the game.

Famous Cardinal player Stan Musial was a hero to Charles.

- The manager would scan the crowd and then point, one at a time, until his daily quota of workers was filled.
- Work as a concessionaire was for one day only, so the selection process was repeated on every new game day.
- The manager possessed a keen memory for faces and for the work ethic of those he had hired previously.
- He didn't need a fancy evaluation sheet to know who was watching the game when they should have been selling, or who attracted so little attention to themselves that they never made any sales.
- Charlie returned day after day for weeks before he was given an opportunity for the first time.
- On the day he was chosen, he was lined up along the wall with the other prospective workers after the usual veterans had already been hired.
- The boss gave him a look and then pointed in the direction of the other hires.
- Charlie was given a crate of 7-Up and his instructions.
- He learned to wave and holler to draw attention to himself.
- It was June 21, 1959, and on that day Stan Musial doubled twice—the 652nd and 653rd hits of his career—to break Honus Wagner's National League record during the doubleheader against the Pirates.
- Working two games in a row was exhausting but exhilarating. After that Charlie was consistently picked on game day.
- During the earliest decades of professional baseball, an array of food was available: peanuts, soft drinks, Cracker Jack popcorn, ice cream, cherry pie, cheese, chocolate, hard-boiled eggs, sandwiches, coconut-custard pies, planked onions and even tripe.
- Vendors also hawked beer, soda water and chewing gum.
- In fact, a controversy surrounding the selling of beer led to the formation of a new league.
- The National League, sensitive to the image of ballparks as the scene of too much drinking and gambling, and generally unsuited for women, tried to eliminate all ballpark alcohol.
- Yet Cincinnati Stadium had a long tradition of beer and whiskey sales, averaging $3,000 a season and supporting several of the city's largest industries.
- Rather than face the financial damage of a no-beer ballpark, Cincinnati quit the National League and formed what would later become the American Association, inextricably linking beer and baseball.
- The products given to each vendor to sell were determined by seniority.
- For those at the top, that meant hot dogs.

- They were lighter in weight and far more profitable than soda.
- The hot dog, or red hot, was created, so the story goes, by the pioneer concessionaire Harry Stevens on a cold day at the Polo Grounds in New York City, when ice cream wasn't selling.
- Stevens allegedly sent an assistant out for frankfurters, which were sausages sold by the local German groceries.
- He boiled the sausages in water and put them in long buns so the fans could hold and eat them.
- But it was the vendors yelling "Get them while they're hot, get your red hots here" that attracted the attention of sports cartoonist Thomas Aloysius Dorgan (TAD).

Baseball players endorsed weightlifting equipment.

- When Dorgan published a sketch of the concession workers serving the frankfurters and coined the term "hot dogs," the name stuck.
- As success continued for the Cardinals, so, too, for Charlie.
- During his first season as a vendor, he moved up far enough to sell ice cream, and the Red Birds kept winning.
- Baseball's popularity was soaring. Innovator/owner Bill Veeck added the players' names to their uniforms, and ballparks nationwide were averaging 14,000 fans per game.
- In 1962, after three years of selling, Charlie finally made the big time and was named a hot dog man at Busch Stadium.
- Some vendors developed special tosses or behind-the-back passes to impress the crowd, but Charlie was known for one thing—good service.
- He loved hawking his wares to the crowd using the traditional "red hots here" yell, like the vendors of old.
- With his booming voice and winning personality, he was popular among the fans and became one of the top earners at the stadium.

- The average fan spent between $0.70 to $0.90 per game on drinks and snacks, making the concessions worth $12 million a year.
- The 1962 season began with an 11–4 Cardinal victory over the New York Mets, a team making their baseball debut.
- Stan Musial was on a tear, and with each game, it seemed, he shattered another record.
- On June 22, while Charlie watched from the stands, Musial became major league's all-time leader in total bases, with 15,864.
- In all, Musial broke four all-time records at Busch Stadium. He was the best but not the only part of a memorable baseball year for Charlie.
- On September 23, the Dodgers's Maury Wills singled and stole second and third to tie Ty Cobb's record of 96 stolen bases in a season, and in the seventh inning, Wills added one more steal to set a new record.
- Best of all, the Cardinals won the game, 11–2.

Life in the Community: St. Louis, Missouri

- During the first half of the 1800s, St. Louis was the "Gateway to the West," attracting entrepreneurs such as Adolphus Busch, who immigrated to America in 1857 and established a brewing business with his father-in-law, Eberhard Anheuser, in 1866.
- In 1873 Adolphus Busch discovered a process of pasteurizing beer that allowed the beer to withstand temperature fluctuations.
- This permitted the firm to distribute its beer on a wider basis.
- In conjunction with Carl Conrad, a St. Louis restaurateur, Busch developed a light beer called Budweiser, believing that consumers would prefer it to the darker brews that dominated the market.
- In 1953 Augustus "Gussie" Busch bought the St. Louis Cardinals team, and Anheuser-Busch purchased the old Sportsman Park, renaming it Busch Stadium.
- St. Louis quickly developed a reputation as a baseball town.
- Fans rarely booed, always knew the pitch-count, could anticipate a hit-and-run and appreciated good defensive play—from both teams.
- In keeping with Busch Stadium's unique tradition, hometown fans did not sing "Take Me Out to the Ballgame" for the seventh-inning stretch but instead clapped along to the Budweiser musical theme.
- "Take Me Out to the Ballgame" was played at Busch Stadium in the eighth inning.

St. Louis, Missouri.

"Musial Signs for Last Time, Office Job Awaits St. Louis Star," *San Mateo Times,* January 5, 1962

Stan Musial signed his 1962 contract with the St. Louis Cardinals today saying, "This looks like my last year in baseball."

"I'll try to make this a real good one," Musial said in a morning news conference.

The contract amount was not disclosed. Musial, who said he will be 42 this winter, added, "I don't want to be the oldest player to ever play."

The guess last year was that Musial signed for about $75,000. It was announced that there had been "an adjustment downward."

"That's because of the taxes, and the adjustments amount to very little," Musial said.

Golf Caddie in 1962

Raymond Walker was eight-years-old when his father killed his mother, then himself. Six years later, the young African American left his aunt's Baltimore's public housing apartment, moved in with a friend, and began work as a caddy at the city's fancy country club, despite never having been on a golf course.

Life at Home

- Raymond Walker grew up in the Cherry Hill public housing project, which included a sprinkling of federally subsidized apartments and low-cost, privately owned homes.
- When Raymond was eight years old, his father killed Raymond's mother and then himself, leaving behind a suicide note that said he was worried about money and ashamed he would be unable to purchase any Christmas gifts for his children.
- Only two items were found with the note: a $25 money order made out to Raymond's grandmother for the care of the children and Raymond's newly printed package of school pictures, which he had proudly given to his mother before he went out to play.
- His parents died at 4:30 in the morning in his father's powder-blue 1950 Plymouth station wagon, which they had parked near the construction site of the new colored high school.
- *The Afro-American*, Baltimore's biweekly black newspaper, put the murder-suicide on its front page for two consecutive issues.
- Raymond's parents were buried separately, three days apart; Raymond refused to attend either funeral, even though he always believed he was his father's favorite child.
- The children's grandmother, already suffering from cancer, died a month later, so three aunts agreed to raise the children, each taking one child.
- Raymond moved to a public housing unit with his Aunt Etta, her husband and their six children.
- Nine people shared an apartment with only four rooms: a kitchen, a living room and two bedrooms, all with concrete floors.
- The apartment also had a single bathroom with a tub, but no shower, while the kitchen had two sinks: a shallow one for washing dishes and a deeper one for laundry, which was done using a washboard.
- Raymond's aunt and uncle slept in one of the two bedrooms, which they shared with their youngest daughter, who still slept in a crib. The two next-youngest children bedded down on the sleeper couch in the living room, while the four oldest boys shared the other bedroom, two in each twin bed.

Raymond Walker's parents died when he was young, and he lived with his aunt and cousins.

Raymond's aunt believed in education, and wouldn't let him think of quitting school.

- Meals often included fried salt pork, syrup and bread.
- On Fridays dinner was usually fried fish; Saturday's dinner was baked beans and hot dogs from the A&P. On Sundays the family ate fried chicken.
- When money ran low, supper consisted of a pot of navy beans or pancakes. Spam and potted ham were also staples.
- To make ends meet, Raymond's aunt often sent one of the children to shop at a grocery store where everything could be bought in individual units—one egg for the family that could not afford a dozen, or a few loose cigarettes instead of a pack.
- When Raymond got in trouble, his aunt would holler, "I'm going to give you some medicine you don't want to take!"
- The house was a football field away from the edge of the city dump, and some in the community made ends meet by picking through the mounds of garbage for something to eat— "shopping at the dump," the kids on the street called it.
- Because of its closeness to Baltimore's harbor, the trash dump got most of the fruits and vegetables that failed to clear customs, giving neighbors another reason to "go shopping."
- Sometimes, Raymond and his friends would go to the dump simply for sport—to kill rats by beating them with sticks as they ran for cover.
- When one of Raymond's friends got a BB gun, they formed hunting teams; one group of boys would beat the trash pile to make the rats run, while the others would take turns shooting the gun at the fleeing rodents.
- When times were good, Saturdays were spent at the lone neighborhood movie theater; Raymond's aunt would give him a quarter and say, "Don't come home until dark."
- It cost $0.14 for children under the age of 15 to get into the theater, leaving $0.11 for a snack.
- Raymond usually invested a nickel in a box of Jujyfruits, even though he didn't like the black or green ones.

Life at School and Work

- Raymond's aunt believed in education and would not discuss his dropping out of school; the children's father had forced the girls to leave school in the seventh grade, saying, "All they gonna do anyway is git married and have a bunch of babies."
- All three aunts wanted more for the children.
- Raymond's elementary school provided milk and graham crackers during the morning break, and he often was chosen to go to the pick-up area and get a half-pint carton of milk and graham crackers for each student in the class.
- For a class of 32 students, the school provided 16 half-pint cartons of regular milk and 16 of chocolate milk.
- Raymond would return and hand out the milk and crackers; the duty gave him real power, since he decided who got the chocolate milk.

Raymond had a "Quo Vadis" hair cut, made popular by the MGM movie.

- Anyone who wanted chocolate milk worked hard to stay on Raymond's good side—an important shield provided by a teacher aware that children could be cruel to a classmate whose parents had died tragically.
- The school, like Raymond's home, constantly smelled of burning trash; the glow from the burning trucked-in garbage was a local landmark.
- In Junior High Raymond enjoyed a reputation as the class clown; he and his buddy were as much competitors as they were a team.
- Once Raymond's partner in comedy got in trouble for taping a mirror to his shoe so he could look up a classmate's dress.
- For many students, lunch at school was often last night's leftovers, ranging from fried fish heads to potted ham- or egg-salad sandwiches, which often smelled on a hot day.
- The school had books for the students to read while in class but not enough for each student to take one home for homework. Therefore the books were read aloud in class, with each student taking a turn.
- Raymond was aware of his poverty. He wore Converse sneakers to school every day, even during snowstorms.
- When a hole wore through the bottom of a sneaker, he stuffed it with cardboard to keep his feet dry.
- In the eighth grade, Raymond wore brogans with steel taps on the first day of school; this later became a school fad.
- In 1962 Raymond completed the ninth grade at an integrated school, having never attended school with whites before.
- At the beginning of the year, his aunt gave him $20 to buy clothes and supplies; he got two pairs of khaki pants and a couple of shirts from a surplus store, found shoes at a pawn shop, and still had enough money left to buy a loose-leaf notebook.
- But money issues remained.
- Following the Christmas break, the teacher asked each child to stand and talk about what they got for Christmas.
- He couldn't tell everyone that he got socks and underwear, so he created a fantasy Christmas for himself, complete with basketballs and his own record player.
- Once during the year, he stayed out of school for a week, embarrassed that he could not afford a haircut; when his teacher discovered the reason for his absence, she came to his house, gave him a dollar and took him to a barber.
- As they left the barbershop, she simply said, "I will see you at school tomorrow."
- Based on his test scores, but not his grades, Raymond was selected to attend Baltimore City College, the city's most prestigious public school for boys, the following fall.
- As the school year came to a close, though, he and his aunt fought over who had the right to the money sent by the Welfare Department, and Raymond finally moved out of the apartment.
- Then he had to carry his own weight.
- Raymond moved in with two friends in Cherry Hill and began work at the white country club across town.

- The first time he walked up the long road to the country club, the members of which were predominantly wealthy Jewish professionals, his stomach did flip-flops.
- Even though he was eager to be a caddie, Raymond had never been on a golf course before, let alone a course at a fancy country club.
- The club had opened in the summer of 1927 as a retreat for the wealthiest of the Eastern European Jews who had come to the United States around the turn of the century.
- Many of the newly arrived came to Baltimore, known as the American Jerusalem. Often, however, they did not see eye to eye with the German Jews who had emigrated a generation earlier. So the Eastern European Jews set up their own social clubs and eventually established their own country club, starting with 92 members and a nine-hole golf course.
- The club was an important center for the city's Jewish life; every Saturday night, parties for members were held at the club.
- On his first day, Raymond arrived a little after 7 a.m., with the morning dew soaking through his Converse sneakers and making his socks cling to his feet.
- The parking lot was filled with Cadillacs, Lincolns, and even a Jaguar and a Rolls-Royce.
- Three black men in their early twenties were taking turns chauffeuring cars to the parking lot.
- The senior caddie, who was past 60 years old, knew the rules of the club—including the unwritten rules, which were passed from caddie to caddie. These included keeping one's mouth shut, staying out of the golfer's way—and totally avoiding the pro shop.
- On Saturdays the urgency to "get a bag" was always apparent, even though it meant carrying a bag of clubs over nearly four miles of rolling terrain in the heat of summer.
- Most caddies carried two bags of clubs, one on each shoulder, and were paid $4 per bag for a full 18 holes of golf, which normally took four hours.
- A golf bag, with its many pockets, was filled not only with clubs but also with balls, tees, rain clothes, an umbrella, shoes, sweaters and hats—all combining to push the average weight of a bag to 50 pounds.
- If a caddie did not get any work during an entire day, he was given "caddie welfare"—$2 to cover lunch and the bus ride home.

- The club also provided a caddie class on Sunday mornings, from 6:30 a.m. until 8:30 a.m., so young men from "the Hill" could learn the rules of golf.
- At the class Raymond learned golf protocol, such as who goes first on the second shot, how to replace a divot, when to walk, when to talk and how to keep score.
- He was one of several kids from the Hill who had found their way to the country club that summer.
- Until then Raymond, like many from his community, had encountered white men mostly as policemen, mailmen and milkmen.
- Even though at the beginning he did not know his fellow black caddies very well, Raymond felt a brotherhood with them and with anyone else who came from the same public housing project.
- In the caddie shack, where Raymond waited for work, the floor was rough and uneven, making the daily crap game a contest of nerves as well as of chance.

Baltimore passed an equal employment ordinance, opening up more jobs to blacks.

The Greyhound bus took Mommy and Daddy and me on a vacation. We saw lots of things. I like the animals and the mountains and the big trees the best. I met lots of new people. New people are nice. The bus driver was nice. He let me wear his cap. I had a good time. So did Mommy and Daddy. They like the Greyhound bus too. They said maybe next year we could go again. I hope they don't forget.

Raymond had a reputation as the class clown, and was keenly aware that he stood apart from other children.

- Monday was Ladies' Day at the club; on other days there were restrictions on when women could play, but on Mondays the club belonged solely to them.
- When he caddied on Mondays, Raymond was even more careful about being polite.
- The murder of 14-year-old Emmett Till—in 1955, in Mississippi, after Till allegedly whistled at a white woman-and the pictures in *Jet* magazine of Till laid out in an open casket still haunted Raymond.
- Raymond learned that on most rounds, he had to be invisible; golfers—men and women—discussed extramarital affairs and generally behaved as if he were not there, without apology or acknowledgment.
- After work the caddies often went to a restaurant called Luigi's, where Raymond invariably ordered a plate of fried chicken, collard greens and potato salad.
- From there he regularly caught the number 37 bus back to Cherry Hill.
- Most evenings he hung out with two friends at the nearby shopping center, often in their favorite spot between the liquor store and the pool hall.
- Too young to go into either place of business, they occasionally convinced someone of legal age to buy them a bottle of Thunderbird, Purple Cow or Richards Wild Irish Rose. But Raymond only watched, because he did not like to drink.
- Not far away was the beauty parlor, where women went to get their hair "fried, dyed and laid on the side."
- Friday night was a busy night at the barbershop, where men and boys in need of a clipping sat waiting for their chance in the chair, well past the 9 p.m. closing.
- Raymond, like many boys his age, had a "Quo Vadis"—a hairstyle made popular after the 1951 MGM movie found its way into black theaters; after the hair was cut closely with clippers, a razor was used to produce a rounded look resembling the hairstyles in the movie.
- The barbershop became particularly crowded on the nights that heavyweight fights took place; everyone gathered to listen to the fights on the radio.
- When Sonny Liston became the world heavyweight boxing champion in September 1962, knocking out Floyd Patterson in the first round of their championship bout, men could be heard shouting up and down the street.

Life in the Community: Baltimore, Maryland

- The closeness of the apartments in the public housing project where Raymond lived promoted a strong sense of community.
- The mothers often talked to on another other over the backyard clotheslines or across the metal rails that divided the front porches.
- The men, few of whom owned a car, often walked together to and from the bus stop or sat side-by-side in the shade of the trees that dotted the small hill behind the row houses.
- A husband and wife, plus their children, occupied almost every apartment in his building; there were few single parents.
- Growing up, Raymond spent most afternoons on the tiny strip of land in back of the row houses, where he and the other boys shot marbles and played catch using a ball with no hide, held together only with tape.

- The girls spent their time jumping rope and playing jacks.
- Sometimes the street in front of the apartments would fill up with kids on skates-which would lead to forming a line, created when a kid skated down the middle of the street as fast as he could with a hand extended out behind him; quickly, other skaters grabbed hold and offered a hand to someone else.
- The last person was often a daredevil or naïve, because once the lead skater screeched to a stop, the line created a human slingshot that fired the last person down the street like a rocket.
- Raymond's first experience resulted in a bruised behind and a reputation for toughness that kept a lot of guys off his back.
- The neighborhood blended African American and Jewish culture; some people joked that Baltimore's Pennsylvania Avenue was the longest road in the world because it connected Africa to Israel.
- Raymond's mother had worked in a clothing store catering to working-class black women.
- The store was located near Pennsylvania Avenue and was owned by the son of a Jewish immigrant who had fled czarist Russia at the turn of the twentieth century.
- The owner let Raymond fold the boxes used to package the clothes, paying him a nickel, which Raymond immediately converted into a bag of candy corn or jellybeans.
- Baltimore's 1910 land-use ordinances mapped out black neighborhoods and white neighborhoods, designating undeveloped areas to be reserved for blacks or whites and in some cases converting black neighborhoods to white.
- These residential segregation ordinances, similar to laws passed in other Southern cities, prompted the founding of the National Association for the Advancement of Colored People (NAACP).
- By the 1930s segregation was well organized in the city, with blacks segregated by law into separate schools, hospitals, jobs, parks, restaurants and railroad cars.
- In 1952, after seven years of NAACP picketing, Ford's Theater agreed to admit African Americans.
- That same year downtown department stores agreed to sell to black customers, although they were not permitted to try on the clothing.
- The next year the municipal parks were desegregated and the first city department began hiring black employees.
- In 1956 the city passed an equal-employment ordinance, and the state ended the practice of listing separate job openings under "white" and "colored."
- By 1958 most movie theaters and first-class hotels accommodated African Americans.

"Colored admission" was still part of the landscape in the early 60s.

Record Producer in 1964

Estelle Stewart Axton was white, and grew up on a Tennessee farm. At age 40, despite her husband's protests, Estelle joined her brother's record company, and quickly became the South's premier record producer for black artists. Her Stax Records became home to Otis Redding, Rufus Thomas, Booker T. and the MGs, and Isaac Hayes.

Life at Home

- Estelle Stewart was born on September 11, 1918, in Middleton, Tennessee, and grew up on a farm.
- She moved to Memphis as a schoolteacher and married Everett Axton.
- Estelle was working as a bookkeeper at Union Planters Bank in Memphis when, in 1958, her brother Jim Stewart asked her for help in developing an independent record label he planned to call Satellite Records.
- He wanted to issue recordings of local country and rockabilly artists.
- All he needed was $2,500 to buy a one-track Ampex recording machine. In exchange he would make Estelle his partner.
- When Estelle talked to her husband about it, his first response was, "No way!"
- But the more Estelle thought about the concept, the more she liked it.
- Eventually, she convinced her husband that they should remortgage their house to obtain the needed sum, and, in 1959 she joined Satellite as an equal partner.
- Estelle Stewart Axton was white, was 40 years of age and had two children.
- Initially, the brother and sister set up shop in an abandoned, rent-free grocery store in a small community 30 miles from Memphis.
- At the time the newspapers were full of headlines concerning *Sputnik*, the new Russian satellite that had become first human-made object in space.
- It appeared to represent the future, so they named their company Satellite Productions. But this attracted a trademark lawsuit and resulted in a name-change to Stax Records, comprising the first two letters of their last names, Stewart and Axton.
- The following year Estelle and Jim discovered the unused Capitol Theatre in a black Memphis neighborhood and turned it into a recording studio and record shop; the cost was $150 a month.

Estelle Stewart Axton became the South's premier record producer for black artists.

Jim Stewart and singer Carla Thomas.

- Once the studio was set up, they opened a record shop next door in a space that formerly housed the theater's candy counter; Estelle kept her day job at the bank.
- To get inventory for the store, Estelle took orders for records from her co-workers at the bank and then went to Poplar Tunes, the largest record store in town, bought the records for $0.65 and resold them for $1.00.
- Initially the record store kept Stax Records studio afloat.

Life at Work

- None of Estelle's and Jim's early records were successful until a popular black disc jockey, Rufus Thomas, and his 16-year-old daughter, Carla, came to the studio to pitch some ideas.
- Rufus Thomas's most successful recording had been an "answer" song entitled "Bear Cat," created in response to Big Mama Thornton's "Hound Dog" and released in 1953. ("Hound Dog" would later be successfully covered by a white singer named Elvis Presley.)
- That day Rufus Thomas and Carla Thomas previewed "'Cause I Love," written by Rufus, and convinced Estelle and Jim to record and distribute it.
- About 15,000 copies later, Atlantic Records head Jerry Wexler offered $1,000 for the right to distribute "'Cause I Love" nationally—giving the studio some exposure and some cash and demonstrating for Stax's white owners the potential of black music.
- Their recording studio itself had acoustical drapes handmade by Estelle, a control room built on the movie theater stage, insulation on the one outside plaster wall to reduce echo, and baffles made with burlap hung from the ceiling.
- The end result was a very live recording environment issuing a reverberation effect similar to that of the concert hall; this would become an important component of what was later known as the Stax Sound.
- Stax Records's big break came when Rufus and Carla Thomas returned to the station with another idea, another song.
- "As soon as Jim and I heard that song, we knew it was a hit. It's funny, when you hear a song, you know if it's got something in it that will sell," Estelle later said.
- With the $1,000 they had received from Atlantic Records, Stax Records recorded "Gee Whiz, (Look at His Eyes)" and established itself as a hitmaker.
- Carla Thomas, who commandeered the title of Queen of Memphis Soul, grew up in the projects, in close proximity to Palace Theater on world-famous Beale Street.
- In 1952, at the age of 10, she became a member of the high school-oriented Teen Town Singers.
- Thomas stayed in school, attending classes and completing her schoolwork, while rehearsing on

The Mar-Keys touring band was all white, but it was a racially integrated group that recorded.

Booker T. and the MG's was just one of Stax Records' famous artists.

Wednesdays and Fridays after school and performing at the radio station on Saturdays.

- Somehow she found the time to write "Gee Whiz" when only 16, using a 32-bar, AABA pop-song structure.

- Sales of "Gee Whiz" began slowly in 1960, but in January 1961, when Thomas was midway into her first year at Tennessee A&I University in Nashville, the success of the single propelled her into the spotlight as she performed on television on *American Bandstand*.

- The song provided a launching pad to Thomas's first album, and it gave Stax Records national exposure and label recognition. Atlantic Records again signed on to handle distribution.

- Estelle's next hit arrived courtesy of a neighborhood group, the Mar-Keys, playing "Last Night," an instrumental. The Mar-Keys was a racially integrated R&B group that included Estelle's son. But when the band toured, its members were all white.

- The song was played on WLOK radio before it became a record, generating enormous interest in the Memphis area. At the time, however, Jim Stewart was reluctant to cut a record.

- Estelle, known as Lady A, finally got it onto the marketplace by pleading, cussing and finally betting $100 it would be a hit; she knew that the kids could "twist" to the record.

- Memphis radio station WHBQ introduced the record to white audiences and played it over and over before it went national. Estelle collected her $100.

- The neighborhood surrounding Stax Records would embrace the sobriquet Soulsville, in honor of performers such as Aretha Franklin, Johnny Ace, and James Alexander of the Mar-Keys.

- The Stax sound was different from that of its rival, Motown Records in Detroit, which was known for more polished urban, smooth sounds.

- "Once you crossed the Mason-Dixon Line and got down to Memphis," Rufus Thomas said, "it was altogether different."

- In 1959, a young black songwriter named Berry Gordy Jr. formed Motown for the express purpose of aggressively marketing black rock 'n' roll to a white audience.

- Motown turned out hit records in assembly-line fashion—each one technically perfect, efficiently marketed, and designed to have a broad crossover appeal.

- Gordy carefully supervised the repertoire of Motown's performers and required them to take classes in diction, stage presence, and choreography.

- As a result Gordy developed headliner acts such as Diana Ross and the Supremes, the Temptations, and Michael Jackson of the Jackson Five.

Berry Gordy was a young songwriter who formed Motown Records.

- Estelle's and Jim's system was less formalized and more prone to an occasional misfire.
- Stax became one of the most successfully integrated companies in the country—from top management and administration down to its artists.
- "We didn't see color," Estelle said. "We saw talent."
- By 1963 Stax was releasing two or three records per month and four or five albums per year.
- All the while, from her perch at the record store, Estelle led impromptu songwriting workshops on new releases by competitors.
- Every word of a song was parsed by the music crowd as thoroughly as if it were from an ancient manuscript.

Artists recording at the Stax Records' studio.

- The elements of a song's appeal were identified and then analyzed to determine why they worked.
- At the same time, jazz great Phineas Newborn Jr. might drop by and play the piano for hours, while David Porter, who worked across the street bagging groceries, was learning the craft of songwriting.
- Saturdays were set aside for musicians, amateur and professional alike, to audition—establishing yet another link to the community.
- Singer Otis Redding got his start at Stax with "These Arms of Mine," recorded at the end of another band's recording session. Rufus Thomas continued his string of hits with "Walking the Dog," which he wrote while watching an attractive woman dance one night.
- In 1963 three albums were issued by Stax: Gus Cannon's "Walk Right In" (also covered by the Rooftop Singers), an anthology entitled "Treasured Hits from the South," and Rufus Thomas's "Walking the Dog."
- The bottom-line profits of Stax in 1964 were steady but unspectacular, with a majority of its records being sold to black customers through inner-city, mom-and-pop record stores.
- Meanwhile, Motown Records was in its ascendancy, with the Supremes, Mary Wells, the Miracles, the Temptations, and Stevie Wonder all topping the pop charts.
- In Detroit, Motown based its image around "Hitsville, U.S.A.," while Stax's identity was based on being "Soulsville, U.S.A."
- One of Stax's assets was its ability to grow talent.
- When impoverished musician Isaac Hayes began coming in, Stax's system made room for the talented youngster with the miraculous ear and special knowledge of arrangement.
- And when Hayes combined his talents with Otis Redding's, they became ambassadors of the Memphis Sound.

Life in the Community: Memphis, Tennessee
- Majestically perched on a bluff on the eastern bank of the Mississippi River, Memphis had long been a place apart.
- While Tennessee consisted of rolling hills that nurtured country music, Memphis was as flat as the Delta and historically a breeding ground for classic blues, black gospel, and rockabilly.
- The city had long served as a stopping-off point for large numbers of travelers—black and white—mesmerized by the opportunities promised by the Great Migration to St. Louis or Chicago.
- Urban by definition, Memphis was still rural in mindset as the 1960s unfolded.
- The city was musically known as the nurturing ground for both the pentecostal music of the Church of God in Christ and the sophisticated Big Band blues embodied by B.B. King.

- Out of this polyglot mix grew Memphis Soul, defined as stylish, funky, uptown soul music, a sultry style produced at Stax and at Hi Records, using melodic unison horn lines, organ, bass, and a driving beat on the drums.
- When Jim Stewart and Estelle Axton converted the old movie theater at the corner of McLemore Avenue and College Street into a recording studio, they gave witness to the level of homegrown talent in the area.
- Their record store became one of the hipper local hangouts, attracting musicians, songwriters, and vocalists, all eager to hear the latest sounds.
- "I think there would have been no Stax Records without the Satellite Record Shop," Booker T. Jones, of Booker T. and the MGs. "Every Saturday I was at the Satellite Record Shop—that's where I went after school; I got to go in there and listen to everything."
- The shop also served as a testing ground for new recordings; Estelle often played recently recorded demo tapes for the record-shop patrons.
- Their reactions often determined whether the new record would be changed, dumped or promoted heavily.
- Hi Records was started by three Sun Studio musicians—Ray Harris, Bill Cantrell and Quentin Claunch—as well as Joe Cuoghi, one of the owners of Poplar ("Pop") Tunes.
- Hi Records's early releases were primarily rockabilly.
- Just as the Mar-Keys's "Last Night" helped Stax, the success of Bill Black's Combo changed Hi from a rockabilly label to an instrumental powerhouse during the early 1960s.

Memphis, Tennessee.

"The Stax Story Part Six, Porter and Hayes Producers,"
Hit Parader, February 1968

Isaac Hayes and Dave Porter have written about 150 songs together for Stax artists and also produced most of them. So far their most successful collaboration has been with Sam and Dave on songs like "Hold On, I'm Coming" and "Soul Man"; in addition, Isaac plays piano on his own sessions in many of the other Stax sessions.

Isaac was born in 1942 on a farm in Covington, Tennessee, and raised by his grandparents who worked as sharecroppers. His mother died when he was an infant and he never saw his father. When Isaac was seven, the family moved to Memphis. He won several music scholarships, but he couldn't afford to buy an instrument, so he took the vocal training. He had to drop out of school to help support the family, and took singing jobs in local nightclubs where he also taught himself to play piano. Gradually, he worked into full-time gigs and met Dave.

Dave was born in Memphis in 1942, one of nine children. He grew up never knowing what his father looked like. "It was just my mother and a bunch of kids. I ran around barefoot and we were so poor it hurt." He sang in church regularly and wrote a class poem in the sixth grade. He formed a singing group in high school and wrote original songs—"which were really horrible." Then he got a job in a grocery store across from Stax and watched the musicians coming and going. In his spare time he sang in nightclubs and hung out around the Stax studio. "Then I met Isaac. We worked as a duet and wrote 30 straight flops, but we learned a lot."

HP: Who writes the lyrics and who writes the melodies?

Dave: Normally I write the lyrics and Hayes comes up with the melodies.

HP: Do you ever work with Steve Cropper?

Dave: Yes, we do. Steve's a tremendous writer himself. We get together with Steve on arrangements. Isaac: Sometimes the three of us work together or we work with Steve individually.

HP: Who are the main singers you produce?

Dave: Sam and Dave, Carla Thomas, Johnny Taylor, some of Otis Redding, Mabel John, Rufus Thomas, Jean and the Darlings, a new group we have. We've also been working with some new songwriters, Homer Banks and Alan Jones, and a girl named Betty Crutcher. They're very good.

HP: Do you write songs with particular artists in mind?

Dave: Normally we tailor-make songs for a particular person. We block out all other things so that we can find a trait that the artist can protect the best.

Isaac: If we write something for another Stax artist, we present it to the producer in charge. Maybe we'll give something to Booker T., who produces William Bell.

HP: What's the difference in writing material for Johnny Taylor and Sam and Dave?

Isaac: With Sam and Dave, we have to create excitement in the material. With Johnny, the material has to be more subtle.

Dave: Johnny is selling 100 percent message. He's capable of getting any message over. So we concentrate on that. With Sam and Dave, we concentrate on sound, gimmicks as well as message.

HP: Sam and Dave must do a lot of improvising on your material.

Dave: Not necessarily. When we write a song, we include ad-libs. This keeps the message together. This gives the audience a chance to grasp everything.

Isaac: We'll throw in little phrases they can use on the side. Once they get the song down, they naturally use their own interpretation when they're delivering the tune.

HP: Isaac, you play piano on a lot of things, don't you?

Isaac: Yes. I play piano on all the records Dave and I produce. I'm on quite a few others, too. Wilson Pickett cut "99 1/2" and "634-5789" down here, and I played on those. I'm on Albert King's records. I also play piano and organ with the Monkeys. Booker T. usually plays organ on all the records, but sometimes we switch. Booker's playing is slower and smoother than mine.

HP: Were both of you born in Memphis?

Isaac: I've been in Memphis since I was seven, but I was born a few counties away. I came to Stax three or four times with bands and vocal groups trying to sell records. I played saxophone at the time. I finally got on as a session man. Porter came to me and we worked together in nightclubs as a team. I used to work in a meatpacking plant but I got laid off. I joined a band and decided to stick with it until I made it.

Dave: I was born in Memphis and I've been here all 25 years. I lived in the neighborhood of Stax since its inception. Stax started about five years ago, and I was one of the first artists on the label, with a record that didn't do anything. I sang on a corny R&B thing called "Old Gray Mare." It was one of the first records cut here. Hayes came in on a few sessions, and when we talked, we found many similarities in our thoughts. We decided to try it as a team. Before I came to Stax, I was working across the street in a grocery store pushing carts, and at night I sang in nightclubs.

HP: Describe how your work is different from Holland Dozier at Motown?

Isaac: I really don't know how they work or what the formula is, but it seems to me they do have a formula. We try to make our tunes more natural.

Dave: The truth is, we work with a formula, too. We have a plan. We know what to look for on any tune we write. Before we okay an idea, it must possess the things we're looking for. We count on the rhythm and the naturalness of it, whereas Holland and Dozier, which we admire to the fullest, seem to go more for sound. They have strong lyrics, but they're going for a specific sound. We hope our things sound good, too, but we concentrate on the natural feelings. There might be a mistake here and there, but if it feels good, we leave it in.

Isaac: We regard a mistake as being natural. We put ourselves into the stories we're writing. I also make my music complement the words.

HP: What's your favorite song that you've produced as a team?

Dave: "Hold On, I'm Coming" by Sam and Dave.

Isaac: That's my favorite, too.

"Music: Folk Music Revival," Robert Shelton, folk music critic, *Encyclopedia Yearbook,* 1964

In 1963, folk music entrenched itself as an established part of the popular music industry of the United States. Attendance at folk concerts reached record proportions; nearly one out of every three pop music discs had some folk flavor, and the term "hootenanny" became a household word.

The current revival of interest in folk music stems from 1957, when the Kingston Trio burst on the scene. There had been earlier waves of popularity in the cities and among collegians in folk music, which is actually the oldest form of music in the world.

The largest previous revival had been during World War II, when such names as Leadbelly, Burl Ives, Josh White, Richard Dyer-Bennet, Woody Guthrie, and Susan Reed dominated the scene. Another spurt occurred in 1950 with the popularity of Pete Seeger and the Weavers in the North and Hank Williams in the South.

But by 1963, the picture had changed considerably. The chief impetus probably came from the American Broadcasting Company's *Hootenanny* television show. The program, which started as a half-hour musical visit to various college campuses during the spring of 1963, received favorable notice from the critics and grew to an hour by autumn.

With as many as 11 million people watching the *Hootenanny* show on Saturday night, the impact of the mass audience was irrefutable. It immediately reflected itself in the establishment of a "hootenanny craze"-touring companies of that name, dozens of records. Besides the rather low-level "folk music" the show-and its offshoots-offered, the craze had its good side effects. It obviously affected the record turnout for Newport Folk Festival of July.

The television show and the Newport Folk Festival represent the two polarities of American folk music. *Hootenanny* has come to represent the most commercial, least probing and most superficial approach to the folk song. The Newport Festival dealt in folk music of integrity, performances that spoke as musical expression as well as social document of a high order. The festival, which has its counterparts in programs at the University of Southern California, Chicago, Cornell and elsewhere, stressed traditional, little-known, authentic singers in performance, workshops and panels. The television show is primarily run for profit, has become embattled with either an outright boycott or indifference by major performers in the field, chiefly because of its overt blacklisting of Pete Seeger as well for its low esthetic concept...

Between these two poles lies American folk song, a commercial product and artistic product. It can be heard in the bright and urbane stylings of Peter, Paul and Mary, the only pop music group ever to have had three discs among the nation's top five simultaneously. It can be heard in the purling, sensuous voice of Joan Baez, singing the ancient ballad of the Anglo-Scots-American tradition. It can be echoed in the angry, passionate poetry of the newest major star of the folk cosmos, Bob Dylan, the songwriter who reflects a growing tension of social protest in his music. It is in the contemporary folk songs of the many followers of Dylan. It is the songs of the Negro integration battler, chanting "We Shall Overcome" in the South.

Investor and Art Collector in 1965

David Creswell's trained eye and playful imagination led him in two directions: preserving Baltimore's architectural heritage and collecting African art. Between deflecting his city's pursuit of urban renewal and traveling to Aftica and France in search of treasures, Creswell managed to build his worth to more than $50 million.

Life at Home

- Raised in a privileged environment, David came from a family whose fortune was made in banking and oil, and he grew up surrounded by impressionist paintings in his home.
- He went to prep school before attending Rhode Island School of Design.
- When David was a sophomore in college, his parents both were killed in a private airline crash; the courts ruled that the accident was the result of faulty airplane maintenance.
- David inherited millions from his parents' estate, and he was awarded $28 million in compensatory damages from the accident.
- Settling in Baltimore, he worked briefly for an architectural firm before establishing his own company, which became the platform for many of his crusades against the destruction of the city in the name of the "New Baltimore."
- David also published a wide variety of books and essays on the architecture of the inner city, many of which were focused on saving the concept of inner-city neighborhoods, not simply preserving quality architecture.
- Even before his parents' deaths, he traveled extensively, living in a world dominated by ideas, images and visions—a unique blend of reality and fantasy that others might not immediately see.
- David did not hesitate to rent gardens or even entire buildings as party settings for his friends; when his imagination was aflight, money was no object.
- His friends looked forward to the charming, hand-drawn, whimsical Christmas cards he created and mailed each holiday season.
- One year the motif consisted of an intricate landscape with looming castles and futuristic but highly detailed trees. To give a festive look to the more than 1,500 cards he created, David hired an artist to apply gold leaf to specific details of the drawing.
- David was delighted when rural French furniture style captured headlines in the United States; the Mediterranean influence of heavily distressed

David Creswell came from family money, and spent his time studying architecture and collecting African art.

finishes on pecan, pine and cherry would, he thought, be a "vast improvement for most Americans."
- He also liked the textured and colored walls being displayed in many of the more sophisticated magazines.
- David's three-story brownstone apartment in Baltimore was burglarized and badly damaged on New Year's Eve.
- Although the apartment contained millions of dollars' worth of African art treasures, meticulously gathered over 20 years, the thief took only David's television set, silver and watches—but then spray—painted the walls and smashed many of the African masks.
- After years of being the guardian of architectural standards in Baltimore and of the inner city's fabric, David was shocked and disheartened to have been recompensed in this way. He spent much of the year in Paris, attempting to recover.
- In Paris David could enjoy the "culture of the world" without taking a plane anywhere, although he planned a side trip to East Asia to satisfy his taste for authentic Asian food.
- To ensure that he would have appropriate accommodations in Paris, he kept his rented apartment available despite his extended absences.
- David had his home in Baltimore completely redone to wipe away the "sting of invasion" left by the burglary.

Life at Work

- For more than a decade, David had consistently been a voice for neighborhood preservation as Baltimore wrestled with blight and corruption and, arguably, an inferiority complex.
- He was a regular visitor—and often a loud voice—at zoning meetings, at which developers petitioned for wholesale changes, often involving the leveling of entire neighborhoods.
- One of his books on neighborhood preservation was considered a model "call to arms" for neighborhood organizations nationwide, especially those in urban areas.
- His ideas and writings often clashed with the desire of the city's commercial establishment to create a "New Baltimore"—often, David thought, at the expense of the old.
- David was ambivalent about the passage in 1965 of the Housing and Urban Development Act, which expanded urban renewal and public housing while authorizing rent supplements for lower-income families. Although the intent of the new law appeared beneficial, experience had taught him that large, federally financed programs too often resulted in the bulldozing of entire neighborhoods in the name of progress.

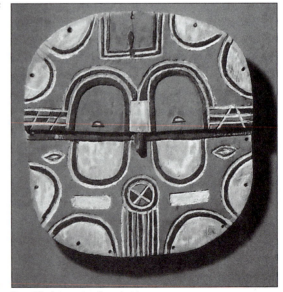

- When not raising his voice at public meetings in defense of inner-city Baltimore, David wrote about preservation and toured the world collecting high-quality African art.
- His passion for art led him to spend days at the Musée de l'Homme in Paris, studying books and visiting galleries that displayed "primitive" art.
- He was particularly fascinated by the concept of "total art," which called attention to the beauty of ordinary household utensils as well as of ritual or religious articles; he did not hesitate to buy everyday objects such as arm and ankle bracelets, stools and headrests, in addition to very rare Dogon, Kota, Fang and Baule sculptures.

David had a passion for primitive art.

- African sculpture was made by animists who conferred a soul onto inanimate objects, even tools and spoons.
- David organized an all-Africa art show in Paris, funding much of it himself, to demonstrate to the world the value and quality of primitive African art.
- He arranged for the display of 100 objects from as many different tribes, spending thousands of dollars of his own money arranging and promoting the show, which included a massive gala featuring African musicians and dance groups he flew in for the occasion.
- The show was well-attended but poorly reviewed; many critics, especially those in the United States, thought that the rustic art of Africa had little to say to the modern world, denying that the work was art or fretting that it was not signed or dated.
- The concepts of the sculptors' anonymity and the unimportance of a work's age seemed to baffle many Western critics.
- One of David's chief criteria for art was its intended use; to interest him, an object had to have been made not for tourists but with a ritualistic significance.
- He also looked for African art that showed use and wear, rarely buying objects in pristine condition.
- David purchased his first piece of African sculpture when he was 26-two years to the day after his parents died in the airplane crash—and he owned more than 600 objects, including masks, jewelry, reliquaries, statues, beadwork and textiles. Some was displayed in his home, and the rest was in storage.

- Many of the works came from French and Swiss collectors, but David often acquired art in Europe from immigrants who had left African colonies that had achieved nationhood.
- David donated two of his finest pieces to the Louvre.
- One of David's favorite purchases, from Ivory Coast, was a female Baule Kpan mask. Its arresting, 18-inch-tall curved face crowned by a high headdress of carved braids and chignons, had closed eyes; a long, straight nose and a small, oval mouth with teeth showing; David found its simplicity arresting.
- The mask was once used as part of a masquerade, a daylong performance in which an entire village marked the death of a notable person or celebrated an important event.
- Another piece bought during the same collecting trip, from Gabon, was a Bakwele dance mask, the beauty of which came from the omission of all irrelevant detail.
- Much of Africa's finest art had left the continent or been destroyed years before; in countries where Islam was embraced, the destruction was particularly devastating.

Life in the Community: Baltimore, Maryland

- In the 1960s Baltimoreans felt their city was changing in positive ways, explaining, "We used to say, 'We hope you like our city, sir. But if you don't, you can go to the Devil.' We don't feel that way anymore."
- After seeing their city fade in the lengthening shadows of Philadelphia and Washington, and watching centuries-old companies merge with New York-based corporations, Baltimore was ready to change.
- Local newspapers campaigned against Baltimore's "branch-plant" status as the city's firms merged with companies such as General Electric, W.R. Grace and Olin Mathieson Chemical Company.
- Meanwhile other Chesapeake ports began challenging the role of the Baltimore port, long geared to the fortunes of the railroads that linked it to the Midwest.
- Therefore large sums of money was poured into improvements, including trade missions to London and Brussels to drum up new international commerce for Baltimore's piers.

Early Baltimore, Maryland.

- Commercial leaders loved to talk about the "New Baltimore," symbolized by the $125-million Charles Center complex of commercial buildings.
- At the same time, two major office buildings with a total of 600,000 square feet of office space were built; the buildings swiftly enjoyed an 80-percent occupancy rate.
- Most of the new building also meant tearing down—often, bulldozing once—elegant neighborhoods with barely remembered histories.
- David continued to use history and his own knowledge and mischievous personality to force developmental compromises; "Not all change is bad, but neither is all change good," he often reminded the zoning boards.
- Instead of vainly attempting to stop major developments, he often looked for ways to redirect the destruction away from irreplaceable homes and buildings.
- Not all in Baltimore was changing, however; The Maryland Club, a sanctuary for the city's leaders, had yet to admit its first woman.

Developmental Psychologist in 1965

Susan Walton Gray belonged to the generation of psychologists who challenged the belief that a child's genes were his or her destiny. Her work, and that of like-minded colleagues, provided the inspiration for Head Start, a federal program that groomed preschool children from poor families to succeed in school.

Life at Home

- Susan Walton Gray was born on December 5, 1913, to a wealthy family in the small town of Rockdale in Maury County, Tennessee, about 70 miles southwest of Nashville.
- She was the second of three children born to Dan R. Gray Sr. and Elizabeth Wolfenden Gray.
- The family was originally from New England, where it had been involved in iron manufacturing since the 1700s.
- Susan's uncle, J. J. Gray Jr., owned the Rockdale Iron Company, a pig iron furnace that owned a patented process.
- Susan lived around much poverty, especially among African Americans; in later years she would describe the world of her childhood as a "feudal society" revolving around her uncle's blast furnace.
- Her father practiced falconry and raised basset hounds; he was highly individualistic, and she did not feel pressure to assume traditional female roles: "I got the notion as a little child I was just as good as anybody."
- The Grays sold their furnace in 1926 as part of a $30 million merger, and Susan's parents moved into a house in Mount Pleasant, about eight miles northeast of Rockdale.
- She enrolled in Randolph-Macon Woman's College in Lynchburg, Virginia, in the early 1930s, in the midst of the Great Depression.
- She recalled feeling very guilty when an economics professor said, "The trouble with you young ladies is that you don't think an intelligent thought can ever be achieved by someone with dirty fingernails."
- From then on she became concerned about social injustice.
- Susan majored in the classics—Latin and Greek—but she also liked math and biology, and she took some psychology courses.
- She was intrigued by the work of Mary Margaret Shirley, a psychologist who was writing *The First Two Years*, an important work in developmental psychology.
- She graduated from Randolph-Macon with her bachelor's degree in 1936 and taught fourth grade in public schools, but she soon realized that this was not what she wanted to do for the rest of her career.
- She decided to pursue a higher degree, and she was encouraged by some friends and mentors to study psychology.

Susan Walton Gray's belief, that environment played a big part in a child's development, laid the groundwork for the Head Start Program.

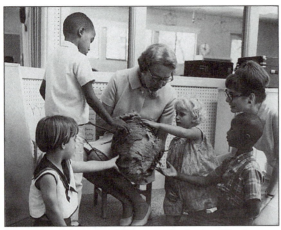

Susan believed that many children were disadvantaged by poverty.

- Susan went to George Peabody College for Teachers in Nashville, where she earned her Master's degree in 1939 and a doctoral degree in developmental psychology in 1941.
- During World War II, she taught for four years at Florida State College for Women in Tallahassee and published research on the vocational aspirations of young black children.
- After the war the president of Peabody recruited her to return to the school and build its psychology department.
- When she joined the faculty in 1945, Susan was the only psychologist at the school—male or female. A second woman psychologist arrived in 1958.

- Susan's most famous professional achievement was the Early Training Project, born of her need to have a program in which graduate students from Peabody could perform research, her belief that psychologists should perform socially useful work and the concern of the superintendent of the Murfreesboro, Tennessee, schools over a decline in achievement scores of black children.
- Susan never married or had children of her own—not uncommon in her day, when a woman's choice was between a career and a family.
- "I don't know whether I feel good about it or not," she said in later years.
- Susan was elected president of the Southeastern Psychological Association in 1963; she was the first woman to hold this post.
- She had a strong will and great intellectual curiosity, and she always asked probing questions.
- Susan took an interest in photography, and she shot thousands of photos of subjects ranging from children living in poverty in Appalachia to close-ups of flowers.
- An Episcopalian and very much a Southern lady, she served tea and cookies in the afternoons.
- With her knowledge of Latin and Greek, she would play games with her colleagues, using obscure words.
- Despite her proper manner, she drove a sporty Ford Thunderbird in the early 1960s; one of her graduate students recalled that Susan received speeding tickets more than once on her frequent drives between the campus in Nashville and Murfreesboro, 33 miles away.

Life at Work

- Susan said her career path was more a matter of serendipity than planning.
- Peabody professors Julius Seeman, Raymond Norris, and Susan Walton Gray started Peabody's doctoral program in school psychology in 1957, and they won a federal grant to support this emerging branch of education training.
- In 1959 Susan started an experimental preschool program called the Early Training Project.
- Many educators at the time believed that a child's intelligence was innate and could not be changed by training.
- But Susan believed that many children in her kindergarten classes were disadvantaged by poverty and social disabilities; she also believed a child's "educability" could be enhanced by early education of the child and training for parents.
- According to colleague Penny Brooks, "The timing of her work was perfect. The crack in the door was the need for a program for the War on Poverty. And it was the '60s—a time when there was growing emphasis on the social environment as the cause of all ailments. …The Civil Rights Movement was raising awareness of people who were disadvantaged, and these factors aligned to make it a time of hope—race and income are not necessarily destiny.…Enter the Early Training

Project. It showed that early training and intervention could make important differences in the future of children."

- A nationwide survey of October 1964 enrollments found that nursery schools were predominantly private and generally beyond the reach of low-income families.
- Most kindergartens were public, but they were absent in many areas.
- The US Health, Education and Welfare Department (now the US Department of Health and Human Services) released its report in August 1965. "Large numbers of American youngsters who are most in need of a hand up in the early stages of the educational processes are not getting it," said Wilbur J. Cohen, who was then the department's acting secretary.

Susan's Early Training Project proved that early intervention made important differences in children's futures.

- Among five-year-olds nationwide, the percentage enrolled in kindergarten or other grades hovered around 20 percent from the 1920 through the 1940 Census.
- But enrollments of five-year-olds rose to 35 percent in 1950, and 45 percent in 1960.
- The South as a whole had a 23 percent enrollment rate for five-year-olds in 1960, while the rate for other regions ranged from 53 percent to 58 percent.
- In Tennessee the rate was 20 percent in 1960.
- Susan thought that despite the opinion prevailing among many at the time, children from poor families weren't destined to fail and could reach their full potential with careful help.
- Her Early Training Project was designed to provide this help.
- Four- and five-year-olds from poor, mostly black neighborhoods in Murfreesboro attended a summer school.
- Others involved with the project made regular visits to the children's homes and worked with mothers, sharing their skills in preschool education.
- In Columbia, Tennessee, a town near where Susan grew up, researchers created a control group. They identified a similar group of preschoolers and charted how well the preschoolers performed over the years with no intervention.
- Susan carefully measured the progress of these students as they started school, and she also charted changes within families.
- Her research showed that children from poor families had a better chance of success when they started the first grade if they had participated in a well-designed preschool.

Working with mothers, the Early Training Project shared professional skills in preschool education.

- She also found that those around the child—mothers and siblings—also benefited as the project's methods diffused among families and neighbors.
- "We have been struck by great strengths in most of the homes we have visited," Susan wrote.
- "One is the deep, underlying concern of the parents for their children. Not only do they have the same goals and aspirations as more affluent parents, they also have a deep reservoir of potential for improving their lives.... This deep concern for the welfare of their children and

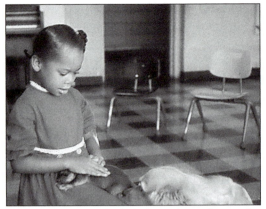

Children from poor families had a better chance of success if they participated in a well-designed preschool.

latent ability to cope with life's demands provide the opportunities for an intervention program working with mothers, a program designed to enable them to become more effective as teachers of their young children."

- "Home visiting is not a panacea for the problems of low-income families in present-day society," she continued. "Still, if we can enable parents to become more effective educational change agents, we thereby make a lasting contribution toward improved lifestyles and general welfare in such low-income homes, and toward a more satisfying future life for their children."

- Research similar to that conducted by the Early Training Project was being done by several other researchers across the country.

- Twelve such teams formed a consortium in the early 1960s in order to pool their data to test their findings more rigorously.

- President Lyndon B. Johnson had launched a series of federal programs called the War on Poverty. In 1964 Sargent Shriver, who was in charge of the new agency overseeing the programs, joined his wife, Eunice Kennedy Shriver, on a visit to Tennessee to present a grant at Peabody for another program and to visit the Early Training Project.

- Only a year before, Eunice's brother, President John F. Kennedy, had been assassinated in Dallas.

- Susan drove the Shrivers to Murfreesboro in her Ford Thunderbird, along with another Peabody psychologist, Carl Haywood, who recalled that they visited facilities and homes where the preschool experiment had been taking place.

- The Shrivers thought they had seen children who were "mentally retarded," but Haywood said the children were picked only for their poverty status—social impediments, not physical ones.

- On the flight back, Sargent Shriver turned to his wife and remarked on the success of the Early Training Project.

- "I could do this with regular children all across America," he said.

- The Shrivers credited that visit as a crystallizing moment for the inception of Head Start; the program was approved by Congress that year, and the first summer program began in 1965.

- Head Start's first program lasted for eight weeks in July and August of 1965, involving 561,000 children, ages four and five, at 13,344 centers across the country.

- The program's first year cost $95 million: 90 percent came from federal grants and 10 percent from local matches.

- The centers employed more than 40,000 teachers and other professionals.

- Assistance also came from 45,000 neighborhood residents, most of whom were paid the federal minimum wage of $1.25

Program head Sargent Shriver, center left, and Lady Bird Johnson, to Shriver's left, officially launching Head Start.

an hour, and approximately 250,000 volunteers.

- Head Start was one of numerous antipoverty programs launched as part of Johnson's Great Society program. Head Start's underlying philosophy was that discrimination and poverty were preventing schools from properly developing human talent.
- Later Susan wrote: "A start has been made for these young people and others like them, but there is still far to go before such young people as a group can realize the potential that is within them."

Life in the Community: Nashville, Tennessee

- To tackle the issue of poverty in America, Congress passed the Economic Opportunity Act of 1964 and the Elementary Education Act of 1965.
- Contained in the Economic Opportunity Act were both the Job Corps and Head Start.
- Head Start was viewed as preparing children of the poor to enter the social-sorting process of school on more equal terms with children of the middle class.
- Head Start was founded as America passed through the most turbulent years of the civil rights movement.
- One of the program's motives was to give disadvantaged children, many of them belonging to minorities, a better chance to succeed in school as the schools were desegregated.
- Job Corps focused on unemployment and delinquent youth, disadvantaged students for whom education did not provide equality of opportunity, and ways to break the cycle of poverty.
- In many parts of the United States, race and poverty were intertwined.
- The civil rights movement in Tennessee was more peaceful than in many Southern states, but the road was long and difficult.
- Nashville was one of the crossroads of the movement.
- Tennessee had been a slave state before the Civil War.
- In 1866, one year after the war's end and the abolition of slavery, the state enacted a law requiring separate school systems for white children and black children.
- Laws expanding and stiffening segregation were passed into the 1930s.
- In many counties, it was difficult for blacks to register to vote, and families faced reprisals if they tried.
- Highlander Folk School, founded in Monteagle, Tennessee, in 1932, worked mostly with labor unions for its first 20 years, fostering education among adults to increase their power in their communities.

- By 1951 Highlander began shifting to establishing "citizenship schools" to teach blacks to read and write so they could register to vote.
- Many people who would become prominent in the early civil rights movement attended sessions at Highlander.
- Among them was Rosa Parks, who went to Highlander just a few months before her arrest in Montgomery, Alabama, for refusing to yield her bus seat to a white passenger sparked the 13-month-long Montgomery bus boycott of 1955–1956.

Highlander Folk School, Monteagle Tennessee.

"Head Start Project May Bring Changes to America's Education,"
Delta-Democrat-Times, Greenville, Mississippi, November 4, 1965

NASHVILLE, Tenn.—The impact of the federal government's hastily conceived Project Head Start may already have caused a permanent alteration in the entire structure of American education, an article in the new magazine *Southern Education Report* said today.

This suggestion by some educational observers was noted by writer Erwin Knoll in a survey of the vast program's activities during the past summer. The SER article is titled "Hasty 'Landmark.'"

The preschool training program, Knoll wrote, "has already established itself, in the view of many observers, as the most formidable weapon in the arsenal of the federal War on Poverty." But its proponents, he said, believe it will reach far beyond the lives of the nation's poor.

Head Start "has encountered its share of administrative problems and political controversy," the article said, including racial conflict in the South, religious friction in the Middle West, salary disputes in New York and enrollment difficulties in Alaska. "Nonetheless," Knoll [wrote], "the program has enjoyed broader support than most other aspects" of the government's antipoverty campaign.

Knoll's report appeared in the second issue of *Southern Education Report,* published bimonthly in Nashville under a grant from the Ford Foundation to the Southern Education Reporting Service. The objective, fact-finding enterprise is directed by a board of Southern educators and editors.

Head Start's summer program enrolled 561,000 children in communities around the country. As the session drew to a close at the end of August, President Johnson called it "a landmark, not just in education, but in the maturity of our own democracy," and announced the program would be extended on a year-round basis.

Dr. Julius B. Richmond, dean of the medical faculty at the State University Upstate Medical Center in Syracuse, New York, and director of Project Head Start, said:

"Even at this early date, we can say that gains of the children in widely varying programs have exceeded the expectations of our planning committee. Since the child development centers are comprehensive in nature, we have seen improvement in nutrition and health, and vocabularies have shown striking improvements. The children have gained confidence in their relations with people, and they are much richer in their understanding of the world around them.

Many long-term observers of the development of young children have been somewhat surprised at the apparent effectiveness of our programs, particularly in view of their brevity. They tend to attribute much of this success to the small groups (a pupil-teacher ratio of 15-to-1) and to the teacher assistants and aides who helped to provide individual attention."

Delegates to the White House Conference on Education in July said Project Head Start presaged a nationwide commitment to universal public preschool education. Reporting on the discussion in a panel session on early childhood education, James E. Allen Jr., New York State commissioner of education said:

"The continuation of Head Start and other such preschool programs was deemed essential. The incorporation of such programs into regular school programs was considered to be highly desirable, with the provision that the co-operation and involvement of the entire community and its whole resources be continued. And paramount in the deliberations on the subject of preschool education was an all-pervading feeling that the momentum of Head Start should not be lost."

Entrepreneur and Restructurer in 1965

Norton Simon was an entrepreneur who lived by the three Ps - power, paranoia and publicity. He used all three to build a multi-million-dollar empire by taking over mismanaged companies and increasing their profitability. His first success was Hunt Foods, which began life as an insolvent orange-juice bottling company.

Life at Home

- Norton Simon was born into a moderately successful Jewish family in Portland, Oregon; his father ran a family-owned department store and dabbled in real estate and a steel products company.
- When Norton was 14, his mother died, and Norton's father moved the family, including Norton's two younger sisters, to San Francisco to live with relatives.
- Norton was an indifferent pupil who rejected rote learning and arrogantly read novels during class.
- Both father and son possessed a photographic memory and the ability to rapidly add or multiply several figures at once in their heads.
- Norton joined a group of boys who called themselves "The Nocturnes," whose primary expertise was playing craps.
- Already an entrepreneur, Norton bought bags, towels and tissues from paper manufacturers after school and sold them to San Francisco stores.
- Then, at 16, he leased a vaudeville theater and was on the road to profitability when his father persuaded him to pull out of show business.
- His money then went into the stock market, where he developed an effective system of hedging; later, he would emerge from the 1929 stock market crash with $35,000 when others lost everything.
- At his father's insistence, he enrolled in the University of California at Berkeley, but he withdrew from his prelaw studies within the first six weeks to run a sheet-metal distribution company.
- "The university," Norton said years later, "was involved with requirements, and I was interested in learning only what I wanted to learn."
- In 1927 he invested $7,000 in an insolvent orange-juice bottling plant in Fullerton, California; he renamed it Val Vita Food Products Company.
- Using a business formula he would continue to refine throughout his life, Norton cut costs, switched from bottles to cheaper cans, undersold competitors and eventually switched the plant from orange juice to tomatoes.

Norton Simon believed hat life was controlled by the three Ps — power, paranoia, and publicity.

- During the next decade, Val Vita sales rose from $43,000 to $9 million; then, abruptly, Norton sold the business to Hunt Brothers Packing, a moderate-sized canner in the San Francisco area.
- For some time he had been buying Hunt stock; with the money he made from the sale of Val Vita—almost $4 million—he bought even more and made a play for control.
- After a considerable struggle, he won control of Hunt Brothers in 1943 and changed the name to Hunt Foods.
- Its most dominant products were prepared tomato sauce and ketchup.

Norton had a passion for classic art.

Life at Work

- At Hunt Foods Norton Simon immediately displayed a combination of toughness and imagination that would foster controversy.
- To cut costs he bought his own can-making company and installed it next to the factory; to promote his brand name, he spent 7 percent of revenue on advertising—almost triple the industry average—including 52 full-page ads in *Life* magazine in one year.
- To make his package more attractive, he insisted on printing the labels directly onto the cans; to move his goods more efficiently, he bought his own trucks.
- Then, in a move that would unsettle the industry, he broke one of the hallowed rules, announcing that after decades of catering to grocery store chains by canning "private-label" products to be sold under the store brand name, Hunt was eliminating the marginally profitable private packaging operation and the competition it created on the store shelf.
- This antagonized the big distributors.
- Unshaken, Norton simply bought up several small canneries that had done private-label packaging and converted them to handling Hunt products.
- The entire conflict came to a head after the World War II, when the demand for consumer food goods was great and distributors' need for products high.
- Many distributors vowed to boycott Hunt products once their contracts had run out, but Norton's heavy advertising campaign was so successful that most stores were compelled to stock Hunt's ketchup whether they wanted to or not.
- With Hunt tomato products as his base, Norton expanded.
- First came the Ohio Match Company, which was churning out millions of matchbooks with Hunt recipes on the covers.
- Norton began buying in, and by 1946, he held a controlling interest.

Norton bought several small private-label canneries, and converted them to handle Hunt products.

With Hunts as a base, Norton bought controlling interests in a number of large companies.

- Using the profits of Ohio Match, Norton purchased a huge interest in Northern Pacific Railroad; when skyrocketing stock prices preventing him from gaining a controlling interest, he sold out at a $2.8 million profit and started buying into cottonseed oil.
- Then he acquired New Orleans-based Wesson Oil for $76 million; he quickly doubled its size and strengthened its marketing.
- Next, he noticed that publishing stocks were undervalued because of the potential competition posed by television; in this adventure he won *McCall's* magazine, but he lost most of the staff when they walked out in protest.
- Norton's new team then produced a magazine that increased the company's circulation by 60 percent and the company's profitability by 550 percent.
- Norton also made aggressive overtures to companies as diverse as Wheeling Steel, Canada Dry and Knox Glass, earning him the reputation of being a corporate raider.
- It was a charge he rejected on the grounds that he typically kept and improved the companies he bought.
- Norton generally looked for companies with stock that was undervalued in the market, a wide pool of investors, and—most important—profits restrained by unimaginative management.
- Typically he would begin by buying stock either personally or through one of his companies, but always on the sly.
- Once he held a sizable chunk, Norton would come charging into a stockholders' meeting, firing questions at directors, demanding to know why performance was not better and waving charts and graphics with statistics to back up his points.
- Norton was never conventional—but he was always interesting.
- *Fortune* magazine called him the least popular businessman in California.
- Even his most loyal employees said he was not easy work for: "He demands your best all the time," said one.
- But he did have the ability to listen to everyone, and he acquired a reputation for hiring and promoting talented women.
- "I was always breaking up the cartel-like combinations in the business world," he said. "I was always coming in and cutting the price to the point where it busted up their combination most, while still making my profit."
- Norton's other passion was art—exquisite paintings by the world's finest artists: Picasso, Monet, van Gogh, Cézanne, Gauguin and Rembrandt.
- The leap from ketchup to culture, and the money spent, attracted considerable attention to the secretive and cautious Los Angeles-based businessman.

Norton demanded 100% from his employees every day.

- And despite his $100 million wealth, Norton made a point of studying the quality and pedigree of every art purchase as intensely as he had the balance sheet of any company he had ever acquired.
- After Norton Simon purchased Rembrandt's portrait of his son Titus for $2.2 million in 1965, they both appeared on the cover of *Time* magazine.
- Even *Time* was unable to discern whether Norton was an art connoisseur who engaged in business or a businessman who collected art.
- Franklin Murphy, chancellor of the University of California at Los Angeles and Norton's closest friend, said, "Most businessmen tend to be rather traditional and representational in their approach to business. But I think of Norton as a Cézanne or Picasso—unconventional, constantly probing and testing, constantly dissatisfied."

HUNT'S

Hunt Foods factory.

Life in the Community: Los Angeles, California

- Los Angeles was founded on September 4, 1781, by Spanish governor Felipe de Neve as El Pueblo de Nuestra Señora la Reina de los Angeles del Río de Porciúncula ("Village of Our Lady, the Queen of the Angels of the River of Porziuncola").
- It became a part of Mexico in 1821, when Mexico won independence from Spain.
- In 1848, at the end of the Mexican-American War, Los Angeles and the rest of California were purchased by the United States as part of the Treaty of Guadalupe Hidalgo.
- Los Angeles was incorporated as a municipality on April 4, 1850, five months before California achieved statehood.
- Often known by its initials, *LA*, and nicknamed the City of Angels, Los Angeles constituted one of the nation's most substantial economic engines, excelling in agricultural processing, manufacturing and entertainment.
- One portion of Los Angeles—Hollywood—was known as the "Entertainment Capital of the World," leading the world in the creation of motion pictures, television productions and recorded music.
- Railroads arrived when the Southern Pacific completed its line to Los Angeles in 1876.
- Oil was discovered in 1892, and by 1923, Los Angeles was producing one quarter of the world's petroleum.
- By 1900 the population had grown to more than 102,000.
- In the 1920s, the motion picture and aviation industries kept the area's economy growing, ensuring that the city suffered less than other areas during the Great Depression.
- In 1932, with the population surpassing one million, the city hosted the Summer Olympics.
- The postwar years saw an even greater boom, as urban sprawl expanded the city into the San Fernando Valley, known for its agriculture.
- California had a long history in the fruit- and vegetable-packing business, with many companies dating from the 1860s.
- Demand was so high that, starting in the 1880s, women of Mexican descent were recruited as workers.
- Fruit- and vegetable-canning tended to be highly seasonal work, with most of the peaks in the summer and the lows in the winter.

- Previously dominated by mom-and-pop canners, who suffered most from the Depression, fruit-canning became the domain of the big-money corporations.
- During the period from 1939 to 1950, California produced more canned fruits and vegetables than any other state.
- Canneries processed apricots, peaches, blackberries, pears, tomatoes, eggs, apples, cherries and salad fruit.
- In 1946 the state's share of the U.S. fruit-packing market was approximately 50 percent.

Early Los Angeles, California.

The History of Hunt Foods

- Hunt Foods was founded by Joseph and William Hunt in 1888 in Sebastopol, California, as the Hunt Brothers Fruit Packing Company

- The brothers relocated to nearby Santa Rosa in 1890, and then to Hayward in 1895.

- Their canning operation grew rapidly, focused on canning the products of California's booming fruit and vegetable industries.

- In 1943, Hunt was taken over by Norton Simon's Val Vita Food Products, founded in the early 1930s.

- The merged firm kept the Hunt name and was incorporated as Hunt Foods, Inc.

- The new management decided to focus the company on canned tomato products, particularly prepared tomato sauce.

- Besides canned tomato sauce, the Hunt brand appeared on tomato paste; diced, whole, stewed, and crushed tomatoes; spaghetti sauce; ketchup; barbecue sauce; and canned potatoes.

Longshoreman in 1966

Arthur Caplan was 40-years-old and had worked as a longshoreman on the Portland, Oregon docks for 20 years. Despite an uneven work schedule, Arthur's annual income was very good. He often opted to work weekends, when pay was higher, and stay home on a weekday as needed to spend time with his children or work on house projects.

Life at Home

- Because of the uncertainty of work schedules and weekly paychecks, the Caplans had an uneven cash flow.
- Despite the uneven hours and pay, Arthur's yearly income was very good.
- Each day Arthur decided whether to appear in the hiring hall to obtain a job for the day or to stay home; this provided an added measure of independence and self-discipline to the job.
- This independence also allowed Arthur to work a very flexible schedule—always realizing that no work (or pay) might be available in the coming weeks.
- Paula, who did not work outside her home, was never sure when her husband would be at home or at work.
- To help bridge the sometimes-long periods of inactivity, this family used its savings and the longshoremen's credit union when money was tight.
- Until the creation of the credit unions in the 1950s, loan sharks had charged the workers very high interest rates during financially difficult times.
- Like many longshoreman families, the Caplans maintained a large garden—a source of great pride as well as vegetables for the family table; they lived outside Portland to accommodate the garden.
- Nearly all of their male friends were longshoremen, and nearly all were married; a single man was regarded as a "kid" until he "grew up," took a wife and began the highly regarded task of raising children.
- It was not uncommon for Arthur's and Paula's brothers and sisters to drop by the house unannounced; entertaining informally—often in the kitchen—was one of the reasons they bought an old farmhouse with a large kitchen.
- Women were expected to care for the home and children, and rarely would Arthur prepare his own breakfast if Paula were home.

Arthur Caplan loved his job as a longshoreman.

- Arthur's irregular hours allowed him to spend considerable time with his children.
- He took time out to help train his sons in sports, including boxing and fistfighting—both family traditions.
- Arthur had gained fighting experience in the Marines during the Korean conflict.
- A flexible work arrangement helped Arthur to handle his own remodeling, including installing a new vanity in their home.
- Having a lot of property allowed the Caplans to pursue their family hobby as "rockhounds," searching for semiprecious stones and fossils and displaying their large collection of "finds."
- They rarely planned major trips or activities for the weekends because pay on Saturday and Sunday was one-and-a-half times the normal pay scale, making it a preferable time to work.
- Fossil-hunting expeditions or visits to Paula's mother's home were more often enjoyed during the week.

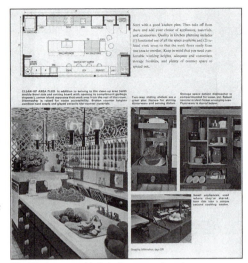

Flexible hours enabled Arthur to work on home renovation projects.

Life at Work

- Approximately 1,200 longshoremen worked in the Portland, Oregon, area; along with their families, they represented a close-knit community of about 5,000 people.
- All were members of the International Longshore and Warehouse Union (ILWU); the West Coast-dominated ILWU was not affiliated with the International Longshoremen's Association, which was the largest longshoremen's union on the East Coast.
- Longshoremen worked for themselves, not for a company; most gained a sense of community through their union and their self-image as longshoremen.
- Compensation for Portland longshoremen included complete coverage for medical care at the Bess Kaiser Hospital and dental care for children.
- Longshoremen were predominantly native-born Americans of northern European ancestry, especially English, Scandinavian, and German; many of their ancestors first settled in Wisconsin, Minnesota, the Dakotas or Pennsylvania.
- Longshoremen liked to project an image of themselves as rough-and-ready individualists who were part of a very tight-knit community.
- The strike of 1934 was so important in the history of the union that it was commemorated with the Bloody Thursday Parade, employing the Industrial Workers of the World motto "An injury to one is an injury to all."
- Work schedules were driven by when ships arrived in port and the cargo they carried; the work—and therefore the pay—could be erratic.
- Some days the docks were overloaded with boats; on other days no work can be found for the longshoremen. In addition, weather is always a factor.
- Ships only made money when they are moving goods; they did not earn profits when sitting idle or being loaded in port.
- Thus most owners wanted loading, unloading, and servicing of ships to take place quickly, placing pressure on the longshoremen to work rapidly and on unpredictable time schedules.

Maritime themes were common in businesses in and around Portland.

- Weather in the Pacific or in the mouth of the Columbia River dictated how many ships would reach port and how much work could be done.
- Like his fellow longshoremen, Arthur often worked seven days straight for several weeks in a row but then had no work for three or four days in a row.
- The work itself was physically demanding and could be extremely hazardous; most longshoremen sustained injuries on the job, and some were crippled or killed.
- Longshoreman had to have confidence in their personal ability to handle demanding situations and emergencies, and they expected these same skills among their fellow longshoremen.
- During the course of 1966, Arthur worked 1,777 hours, or about 34 hours a week on average.
- Yielding to pressure from the ILWU, in 1961 Portland Local 8 allowed blacks to work as casual men—the first step in the traditional recruitment procedure—then as union members; the younger men by then dominating the docks were more open to black workers than were their elders.
- The hiring hall also served as a social center for the men; card games and gossip were staples of the hall.
- Attempts to change the hiring hall system of dispatching longshoremen to their jobs, established in 1934, were resisted in 1948 and again, to Arthur's satisfaction, in 1966.
- The Portland hiring hall was located in a converted church; hiring took place twice a day, at 7 a.m. and again at 5 p.m., for the night shift.
- Gangs were dispatched on strict yearly earnings basis; the gang with the lowest earnings was dispatched first and to the longest job, while the gang with the highest earnings was dispatched last and to the shortest job.
- Board men, who worked independently, bid for jobs based on a daily lottery system that determined the order in which each man bid for a job.
- Many longshoremen believed that a "nine-to-five" routine was too restrictive and insufficiently remunerative.
- Men who were noted fistfighters had prestige among the longshoremen, so long as they adhered to the group's standards of fair play and were not bullies.

Life in the Community: Portland, Oregon

Willamette River, Portland, Oregon.

- Portland, Oregon, is located at the confluence of the Willamette and Columbia Rivers and owes much of its history and prosperity to its prominence as a seaport.
- Portland was the second-largest port on the Pacific Coast in total waterborne commerce; its "city proper" population was 365,000. Including the surrounding five-county metro area, the population was 774,205.
- The state of Oregon had a population of less than two million; nearly a third lived in or near the Portland metropolitan area.
- Portland was the largest city in Oregon; no other city exceeded 100,000 residents.
- Ethnically the city was settled by Germans, Scandinavians, and immigrants from New England and the old South; no ethnic group ever dominated or directed the development of the state.
- Ethnic neighborhoods, common in other large cities, were largely unknown in Portland or in Oregon.

- Portland began its history as a seaport, with the lumber schooner trade plying the Pacific Coast between the Pacific Northwest and the more heavily populated areas of southern California and San Francisco.
- In the early days, Portland was a timber worker's town, and many loggers and sawmill workers easily transitioned to waterfront work; loggers were also familiar with the rigging and gear required on the docks.
- With the lumbermen came their ideas about unions, particularly the egalitarian—often called radical—ideas of the Industrial Workers of the World.

Sea lions sunning themselves on the Oregon coast.

- Historically, most of Oregon's timber was shipped to the East Coast, Europe, and the East Asia.
- After the downfall of the Nationalist regime of Chiang Kai-shek, Portland shipped little to China.
- Bulk wheat brought from the inland wheat-growing areas came to dominate trade through the port; the timber industry was in decline.
- Other than tourism, two significant industries dominated Oregon: agriculture to the east of the Cascade Mountains and timber to the mountains' west.
- One researcher concluded that the "predominantly old-line Americans and Scandinavians agree wholeheartedly on the principle of social egalitarianism, and thus reject the concept of social mobility as intrinsically worthless."
- Although a tightly integrated social group, the longshoremen of Portland were scattered throughout the city; no clustering took place near the docks.
- The docks were stretched out along the Willamette River over a distance of some 10 miles, making it impractical for longshoremen to live near their work, since they did not know from day to day on which dock they would be working.

The Portland Longshoremen

An old-time longshoreman explains why he began working around the docks even though he told his mother in 1927 he was saving his money to buy a ranch: "I told my mother, this is a stopgap, I want to get enough money to buy a ranch. But it seemed as though-oh, we banked our money in the Hibernia Bank on Third and Washington, and we got quite a little bit together. I don't know, twelve or thirteen hundred dollars. And that bank went broke. And it seemed as though one thing after another happened all through the years. And then I will admit the waterfront began to get to me. And I would think to myself, now I've just barely got an eighth grade education. Now where can I work now where can make $45.00 a week? Because of this crowd I was running with there were kids working in banks, a couple of tailors, this and that, and I had more money than any of them. And I got to thinking-everything was all adding up. There was the freedom. There was the quick pay. You didn't have to wait a month for your pay. When you went up the gangplank, the mate would pay you off in gold. Every job was different. Every ship was different. Every man you worked with, you worked with a different man every day. You meet all kinds, types, every kind of man in the world. You got to see the whole world passing right there in front of your eyes. I guess I fell in love with the waterfront."

Disillusioned Beatle Fan in 1966

Diana-Jane Richburg became enamoured with the Beatles when she was 15, and had Beatle-watching parties with her friends when the musical group appeared on television. After John Lennon's comment that the Beatles were more popular that Jesus, however, she organized anit-Beatle protests and the destruction of Beatle records and memorabilia.

Life at Home

- Diana-Jane Richburg was named after her mother's two singing sisters.
- Diana-Jane grew up loving all kinds of music: Christmas, country, gospel and rock.
- When she turned 15, her father, owner of the second-largest car dealership in Birmingham, Alabama, took her on a father-daughter trip to New York City.
- She experienced her first plane trip, her first Broadway play, her first subway ride and her first exposure to a new musical group from England known as the Beatles.
- Diana-Jane returned to Birmingham with tales of tall buildings, rude cab drivers and the music of John, Paul, George and Ringo.
- The already popular Diana-Jane drew an instant crowd in January 1964 when she showed off a recording of "Please Please Me" that she had gotten in New York.
- Even the school's biggest skeptics took notice when the Beatles appeared on *The Ed Sullivan Show* on February 9 and sang five songs, including "All My Loving," "She Loves You" and "I Saw Her Standing There."
- In all, 11 girls gathered in the Richburgs' living room that Sunday night to see the Beatles perform on television, while across the nation, approximately 71 million Americans witnessed the launch of Beatlemania.
- No major crimes were reported in New York City during the hour the show was broadcast.
- Mrs. Richburg had trouble seeing what all the fuss was about and why everyone kept screaming so loudly they couldn't hear the music.
- Yet it was hard to miss in all that screaming the physical and sexual energy the music unleashed.
- Mr. Richburg was greatly amused that his little trip to New York City had yielded such big dividends: a deliriously happy teenager.
- When the Beatles returned for a second *Ed Sullivan* appearance one week later, two dozen girls crowded the Richburg home.

Diana-Jane Richburg's love affair with the Beatles had its ups and downs.

- Then, for the Beatles's third *Ed Sullivan* appearance on February 23, Diana-Jane's father installed three television sets in the showroom of his automobile dealership and told his daughter to invite the whole school.
- Hundreds came, most with special permission from their parents, since they would be out after nine o'clock on a school night.
- Diana-Jane was in seventh heaven; *her band* was sweeping the nation!
- She loved them all, especially Paul McCartney.

Diana-Jane organized her friends to help in her protest of the Beatles.

Life at School

- Diana-Jane Richburg was at the lake swimming with her friends when she first heard the news in the summer of 1966.
- John Lennon had said publicly that the Beatles were more popular than Jesus.
- At first Diana-Jane laughed and told her friends, "They probably are."
- Then, slowly, the significance of what Lennon had said sank in.
- No one should say they were more popular than Jesus, she thought.
- She even discussed Lennon's comment with her mother.
- When disc jockeys Tommy Charles and Doug Layton suggested on WAQY—known locally as WHACKY radio—that Birmingham boycott the Beatles, Diana-Jane was a convert.
- The controversy had been initiated months earlier, on March 4, 1966, when the *Evening Standard* in England published an interview between Maureen Cleave and John Lennon entitled "How Does a Beatle Live?"

The Beatles popularity boasts landed them in hot water with some of their fans.

- In the article Lennon was quoted as saying: "Christianity will go. It will vanish and shrink. I needn't argue about that. I'm right, and I will be proved right.
- "We're more popular than Jesus now. I don't know which will go first—rock 'n' roll or Christianity. Jesus was all right but his disciples were thick and ordinary. It's them twisting it that ruins it for me."
- The British public took little notice of the comment.
- Four months later an American teen magazine called *Datebook* published Lennon's statement without reprinting the original article, and featured it as part of a cover story called "The Ten Adults You Dig/Hate the Most."
- The American reaction was instantaneous.
- Radio stations across the country, especially in the South and the Midwest, stopped playing Beatles records.
- Death threats poured in, directed against John and the other Beatles as well.
- Bonfires appeared, with Beatles pictures and albums providing the fuel.
- Beatles spokesmen repeatedly attempted to explain that "John was certainly not comparing the Beatles

Many fans loved the Beatles unconditionally.

with Christ. He was simply observing that so weak was the state of Christianity that the Beatles were, to many people, better known. He was deploring, rather than approving, this."

- Explanations did no good, however.
- In Cleveland the Reverend Thurman H. Babbs threatened to excommunicate any member of his congregation who listened to the Beatles.
- In the South the Ku Klux Klan burned the Beatles in effigy and nailed Beatles albums to burning crosses.
- In Birmingham Diana-Jane took a leading role in organizing the protest.
- The initial plan to burn a pile of Beatles records was shelved when the city refused to issue a fire permit.
- But that did not stop several grocery stores from setting up collection points for Beatles records and memorabilia so that they could be crushed.
- Diana-Jane gathered her entire Beatles collection—except for the 45 she got of "Please Please Me" that glorious weekend in New York City.
- She then organized the junior class to publicize the drop-off locations advertised by WAQY.
- Fourteen drop-off locations around the city were established; Birmingham would show the world the Beatles couldn't get away with this.
- When Diana-Jane Richburg arrived at the first Ban the Beatles drop-off location, she immediately became nervous; only a handful of albums were there.
- A driver since she was 14 years old, Diana-Jane had borrowed one of her father's model cars for an inspection tour of the drop-off locations and talked two of her friends into coming along.
- At the second location, there were even fewer records, but at the third site a crowd was gathered.
- From a distance she counted a dozen people in the parking lot unloading albums.
- Diana-Jane was just on the edge of a cheer when she realized most of the fellow protesters were young—junior-high young—without a popular one in the bunch.
- Diana-Jane's friends were equally taken aback and immediately began to discuss who really listened to WAQY anyway.
- Besides, with school not starting for another month, organizing the student leaders was going to be hard.

Life in the Community: Birmingham, Alabama

- Birmingham, founded in 1871, was Alabama's largest city, with a population of 275,000.
- Birmingham was located in an area of central Alabama that was rich in mineral resources, including iron ore, coal and limestone deposits.
- Consequently Birmingham's economy was dominated by iron and steel manufacturing; the heavily industrialized city was long known as the "Pittsburgh of the South."

Birmingham, Alabama had a large black population.

Anit-black protests were not uncommon in Birmingham.

- Once the city's transportation links with the rest of the state took shape, the city grew rapidly and became the foremost transportation center of the mid-South.
- U.S. Steel was Birmingham's primary industrial powerhouse; when it closed its mills in the city during the Great Depression, the economic effects were catastrophic.
- Birmingham's economy did not recover until the advent of World War II brought the steel mills back to life.
- By the 1880s more than half of the city's industrial workers were black.
- Rigidly segregated Birmingham became a focus of civil rights protests in the early 1960s.
- Local civil rights leaders led by Reverend Fred Shuttlesworth invited Reverend Martin Luther King Jr. to help lead a campaign of demonstrations intended to pressure merchants and local business leaders into backing repeal of the municipal segregation ordinances.
- In May 1963 the campaign succeeded; although some grew impatient with the pace of implementation, Birmingham's public accommodations were legally desegregated, and the public schools were integrated that September.
- In that same month, however, the 16th Street Baptist Church, a target of earlier violence, was bombed, killing four young girls attending the Sunday church service. A perpetrator associated with a Ku Klux Klan group was identified by a witness but was charged only with possession of dynamite without a permit; he received only a hundred-dollar fine and a six-month jail sentence.
- The bombing galvanized support across the nation for the civil rights movement.

"Beatle Squabble Called Publicity Stunt,"
Martinsville (Virginia) Bulletin, August 9, 1966:

Editor, The Bulletin:

Ban the Beatles, Yea! Yea! Yea! Kick the mopheads out in the name of Christianity! That's the cry of a segment of the broadcasting industry who would like you to believe they are banning the Beatles to preserve the purity of the airwaves. Not so, gentle friends. Why do the very people who promoted the Beatles and other off-key singers now seek to destroy the giant they created? Ostensibly, because of a magazine article quoting Beatle John Lennon as saying his group is more popular than Jesus. But quite obviously this Ban-The-Beatles movement is simply the latest gimmick devised by publicity hungry broadcasters to gain a larger share of the shallow thinking audience.

If, indeed, there was a real interest in the good quality and high moral standards of the material presented on these stations, there would be no reason for banning the world's Number One singing foursome. Without these stations' exposure, they would never have gained their status as national heroes. And without the broadcasters' help, many other screamers who call themselves entertainers would be missing from the so-called top-40 and top-100 music charts.

Our new breed of public-spirited announcers thinks nothing of following a Ban-The-Beatles announcement with the wails of a narcotics addict or the mumbling of one whose mind is so numb from alcohol that he can't utter an intelligible word.

I say if radio stations are going to set themselves up as judges of an artist's morals, they should also sit in judgment of his talent. If this ever happens, we can expect scores of recording stars who claim to be entertainers to be taken off the air.

Some stations use the democratic approach in their Ban-The-Beatles publicity stunt. After quoting John Lennon as saying the Beatles are more popular than Jesus, they invite their teenage audience to call the station and vote to ban or not to ban. While the calls come in, the turntables are spinning, and the screams and moans of the Beatles' contemporaries fill the airwaves! It's ironic that while the Beatles are being voted out, other record stars whose morals are probably no better and whose talent certainly is no better, are being rewarded.

A disc jockey who is truly interested in providing wholesome, high-quality entertainment should use a little discretion in selecting all the records he plays. After all, as just about any radio personality will tell you, without him, the Beatles could not have made it to the top. John Lennon of the Beatles may think they're more popular than Jesus. It seems to me those who continue to promote the Beatles or their brand of entertainment think themselves more popular than God.

A Disgusted Reader

If I had said that television is more popular than Jesus, I might have got away with it. It's a fact, in reference to England, we meant more to kids than Jesus did, or religion at that time. I wasn't knocking it or putting it down. I was just saying it, as a fact and it's true, more for England than here. I'm not saying we're better or greater or comparing us with Jesus Christ as a person or God as a thing, or whatever it is, you know, I just said what I said and it was wrong, or was taken wrong, and now it's all this!

—John Lennon

1966 Beatles Timeline

January 21: George Harrison married Patricia Anne Boyd.

February 21: The single "Nowhere Man" was released by Capitol Records.

March 4: Journalist Maureen Cleave of the *Evening Standard* interviewed John Lennon and asked a question concerning Church and God.

April 6: The Beatles began recording *Revolver* at Abbey Road studios.

May 27: The single "Paperback Writer" was released.

June 6: The Beatles appeared on *The Ed Sullivan Show.*

June 14: The "butcher cover" for the *Yesterday…and Today* album, which depicted the Beatles dressed up in white smocks amidst decapitated baby dolls, was pulled.

June 15: *Yesterday…and Today* was released.

July 4: After the Beatles performed before 50,000 fans at Manila's National Football Stadium, reports were circulated that the president of Manila was insulted by the Beatles' failure to show up at his children's party; as a result, the Beatles were kicked and punched as they left Manila.

July 29: Lennon's "We're more popular than Jesus" comment appeared in Datebook.

August 2: A ban on playing Beatles records began in Birmingham, Alabama; by August 6, 30 radio stations had removed all Beatles records from airplay.

August 6: Beatles manager Brian Epstein held a press conference in New York for damage control over John Lennon's "anti-Christ" remarks.

August 8: The *Revolver* album was released; The singles "Yellow Submarine" and "Eleanor Rigby" were released.

August 11: John Lennon met with the American press to explain what he had meant by his "We're more popular than Jesus" remark.

August 12: The North American Beatles tour began in Chicago.

August 29: The Beatles held their final U.S. performance in San Francisco's Candlestick Park.

September 19: John Lennon flew to Spain to star in the movie *How I Won the War,* in which he played the part of Private Gripweed.

September 20: George Harrison went to India to study the sitar with Ravi Shankar.

October 17: The *Amazing Beatles* was released.

November 6: John Lennon visited the Indica Gallery in London where he met Yoko Ono displaying her art.

November 24: The Beatles began recording *Sgt. Pepper's Lonely Hearts Club Band.*

December 16: The Beatles Fourth Christmas Record, *PANTOMIME: EVERYWHERE IT'S CHRISTMAS,* was issued to fan club members.

"Fan Rallies to Defense of Beatles," *Martinsville (Virginia)*
Bulletin, August 26, 1966

Editor, The Bulletin:

I hope this letter will help many people to realize the truth about the Beatles. They didn't really make that statement to be bragging. They were actually complaining. Many disc jockeys have led us to believe that the Beatles said they were better than Jesus, but they said they were more popular than Jesus.

This is true. The Beatles are more popular than Jesus and so are the Supremes, Rolling Stones, rock 'n' roll music, money, parties, liquor and almost anything else you can think of. If you don't believe me, let me give you some examples: (1). If most people were given a choice of going to church or to a party, game, the movies, etc., I'm sure they would pick the latter. (2). A person would spend $500 to better his social image but it is hardly likely that he'd give $500 to the church. (3). Many people would sit down and read paperback books for hours but would they read a Bible for that long? (4). You could ask a person plenty of questions about Vietnam, rock 'n' roll music, etc., and he could answer every one of them, but how many questions could he answer about the Bible? Very few, if any.

John Lennon was really disgusted because the state of Christianity is so weak that nobody worships God as they are supposed to. Let's face it. Most people only go to church because they feel it's their duty. Even when a parent gives his child a quarter to put in Sunday School, he'll only put in a dime and spend the rest for candy.

This sudden banning of the Beatles is just a mass misunderstanding led mostly by disc jockeys who were too dense and thick-headed to analyze the statement. Even when the person that got the statement from the Beatles contradicted the disc jockeys' interpretation and the Beatles' manager himself appeared to the nation on CBS news and gave John's true intentions in making the statement they (the disc jockeys and others who banned them) were still too obstinate to recognize the truth in the Beatles' statement.

I don't think banning was right because the Beatles are the best thing that's happened to the rock 'n' roll industry. They've opened up new trends as well as built up the economy of both the U.S. and Britain. They've written many beautiful songs which have been performed by stars like Frank Sinatra, Andy Williams and the Hollywood Strings. They are a model which all American teenagers would do well to copy. The Beatles started in the cellars of Liverpool and rose to the top—even to play at the London Palladium and a command performance for the Queen of England, who gave them medals of honor.

By copying the Beatles many would-be juvenile delinquents of England have now formed groups of their own. The Beatles are four nice, mannerable, clean-cut lads who were brought up by strict parents who taught them to love and respect God.

Many people who banned the Beatles really didn't like them at first and thought this was a good way to get rid of them. And many others took the statement at face value without a second thought to what Mr. Lennon meant. Therefore, some people are violating one of the cornerstones of the American Democracy by condemning a person without hearing both sides of the issue. These record stores that banned the Beatles couldn't care a fig about what the Beatles said; they're just hoping to cash in on the publicity.

Some adults want to get rid of the Beatles because they hate rock 'n' roll music. They're always knocking rock 'n' roll and expect teenagers to regress to the musical styles they enjoyed as teens, such as Benny Goodman and Lawrence Welk.

There are many rock 'n' roll groups far worse than the Beatles. So why pick on the Beatles? They always look neat and clean on stage and many other groups look sloppy with hair falling to the shoulders and stupid looking clothes on.

If these would-be savers of the U.S. and Christianity would spend more time with problems which really affect teens such as the sale of dope, sex out of wedlock and the dropout rate, they would then be really helping to raise the standards of America and what we Americans really stand for.

Signed,

Beatle Fan Forever

We'd done about 1,400 live shows and I certainly felt this was it. It was nice to be popular, but when you saw the size of it, it was ridiculous, and it felt dangerous because everybody was out of hand. Even the cops were out of line…It was a very strange feeling. For a year or so I'd been saying, "Let's not do this anymore." And then it played itself out, so that by 1966 everybody was feeling, "We've got to stop this." I don't know exactly where in 1966, but obviously after the Philippines we thought, "Hey, we've got to pack this in."

—George Harrison after the Beatles' last American concert in Candlestick Park

---

African American Baseball Player in 1966

Luther Henderson was a 22-year-old African American baseball player. A natural athlete, he was offered college scholarships to play basketball and football, but decided on a professional baseball career because a baseball contract would bring immediate cash to his family. He played first base for the Washington Senators and was hailed as the next Ted Williams, baseball Hall of Famer.

Life at Home

- Luther lived outside Washington, DC, in an apartment the Senators helped him locate; he wanted a house, but his teammates had told him to go slow with his spending because "rookie money" could disappear.
- During the season, he traveled with the team three to four days a week; he was excited about being in the majors but found Washington, DC, intimidating.
- Because he was afraid to drive in the city, he took cabs to work.
- He learned that city women were more aggressive than women he had known back home; when he was in the minor leagues, he had found it difficult to meet women, but as a Washington Senator, he was approached by women for dates.
- At age nine he had begun picking cotton 12 hours a day in Mississippi, alongside his mother; to forget the bleeding sores on his hands, he fantasized about becoming a major league baseball player.
- From an early age, it was his dream to help his mother escape poverty and picking cotton, which paid $2.50 for every hundred pounds.
- At age 14 he and his family left sharecropping and moved into the city of Greenville, on the Mississippi River.
- His mother did housework for others, making approximately $20 a week.
- To help support his mother, he dropped out of high school during his sophomore year, but the principal worked out a special arrangement that allowed Luther to work in a dry-cleaning plant and still attend classes on a rearranged schedule.
- Eventually he was able to play baseball, basketball and football in high school. Southern California offered him a football scholarship, while Oklahoma wanted him to play basketball; he selected professional baseball in part because he knew a contract would bring immediate cash to his family.
- Luther signed at the earliest possible moment: midnight of the day he graduated from high school.
- When he got the signing bonus of $10,000, he went home, asked his mother to sit at the kitchen table, and

Luther Henderson played first base for the Washington Senators.

At nine-years-old, Luther worked in the fields.

put a pile of money in front of her, telling her she would never have to work again.
- Now that he was in the majors, he planned to build his mother a home.
- His only real interest was baseball, which he loved to talk about morning, noon and night—on trains and buses and in hotel lobbies.
- His tastes ran to brightly colored clothes; when he had money for the first time, he enjoyed spending it.
- While on a road trip, he bought himself a Sunbeam electric toothbrush for $14.99, and in the same store he found for his mother an electric knife with twin reciprocating blades for $16.99.

Life at Work
- A rookie baseball player with the Washington Senators, Luther was called up from the minor leagues after the season began.
- At 6'2" and 220 pounds, he was considered a big professional athlete, although he moved with the grace of a smaller man.
- Luther signed a professional contract at age 18, immediately following his high school graduation night in Greenville, Mississippi.
- Considering the potential he had shown, his signing bonus of $10,000 was low, probably owing to his lack of exposure in Mississippi.
- The scout who found Luther was the first African American scout ever employed by the team.
- Traditionally, when a scout found a promising prospect, he would write a letter to the director of the minor league system, but when the scout saw Luther play in high school, he raced to a telephone.

- Luther played in the minor-league system for four years, hoping for a shot at the major leagues.
- To gain additional experience, he played winter baseball in Nicaragua, increasing his confidence in his ability to play at the highest level of his sport.
- In high school and in the minor leagues he had played third base, but with the Senators he played first base.
- Over his first season in the majors, he improved his batting average by taking the advice of veteran players, who told him to use a heavier bat; he began to swing a 36-inch bat, which resulted in better control and fewer strikeouts.
- His teammates enjoyed telling stories about his power, including his game-winning home runs off the scoreboard in center field.
- His biggest weakness was chasing bad pitches just outside the strike zone, although he learned to be more patient at the plate.
- Competing managers predicted he would hit .340 to .350 once he learned the strike zone and understood how to read major-league pitchers.
- In his first season with the Senators, Luther batted sixth in the lineup and had a .289 average; but the Senators were given little chance of winning the pennant.
- The Senators never enjoyed the popularity in Washington of the National Football League's Washington Redskins, for whose games tickets were often as hard to get as a White House invitation.

Life in the Community: Washington, DC

- Washington was a city of amazing diversity and contrasts, ranging from the posh Georgetown section to the poverty of the inner city.
- Washington had two major products: government and tourism.
- Approximately 35,000 civil servants drove into the city every day from the Virginia and Maryland suburbs; the Washington metropolitan area comprised approximately 3 million people.
- Approximately 20 million people enjoyed the city's tourist attractions each year.
- Demonstrators, whose causes and concerns were numerous, were also attracted to the city in large numbers.
- In 1966 civil rights activists known as the Free DC Movement picketed and boycotted Washington retail businesses that were not supporting a move toward home rule for the city.
- Only 61 square miles in area, the federal city had a population of approximately 700,000, of whom 70 percent were black.
- The city's "bedroom" counties—Fairfax in Virginia and Montgomery in Maryland—had the highest median income level of any counties in the nation.

Luther was an excellent ball player.

- Lawyers made up the largest single group of professionals in the city; there were close to 20,000 attorneys in Washington, half of whom worked for the government.
- Until Brasília became the capital of Brazil in 1960, Washington was the only capital city in the world that was planned before it was built.
- In 1966 the area's 3,500 carpenters went on strike, affecting many heavy construction projects in the DC area.
- That year Congress approved $2.9 billion over three years to help build college classrooms.
- Howard University announced a plan to train 45 poor high-school dropouts as teacher's aides in Washington's elementary schools.
- Three African Americans ran for two council seats in the nearby town of Seat "Seat Pleasant" is the correct name.
- Pleasant, the first time a black had been on the ballot in the town of 6,800 across the District of Columbia line in Prince George's County; one black candidate won.

Mexican Immigrant in 1966

Miguel López was 22-years-old when his brother returned home to Mexico from six months in the U.S. with more money than Miguel could make in a year. That was when Miguel decided to travel north of the border. He became a farm worker in California, sent money home to Mexico, and joined the National Farm Workers Association.

Life at Home

- Born in Monclova, a city in the state of Coahuila in northeastern Mexico, Miguel López grew up working alongside his parents and five younger siblings in the fields, harvesting wheat and sugarcane.
- Work was inconsistent—sometimes there would be work every day, while at other times there would be no work for weeks.
- A friend had a brother who had worked in the United States for six months and returned to Mexico with more money than Miguel could make in a year.
- Miguel had always prided himself on being a hard worker; he was physically strong and eager for the chance to prove himself in the United States.
- He dreamed of earning money to bring back to his family in Monclova.
- On July 3, 1963, he traveled by train with a group of 15 other young men from Coahuila to Ciudad Juárez, in the neighboring state of Chihuahua at the northern border of Mexico.
- Miguel carried with him only a small satchel of clothing and a pack of cigarettes.
- The first step to employment north of the border was approval by a U.S. official after a brief face-to-face interview.
- Prospective workers were asked about their work experience and had to show the calluses on their palms to prove they did farm labor.
- Then they were searched for weapons or drugs and sprayed with DDT, a powerful insecticide.
- Of the 16 young men from Coahuila, Miguel was among the 10 who were selected to work in the U.S.
- The rest were sent back home.
- He was given papers to sign, but, with no knowledge of English, he did not know what was written on them.
- These papers were his work contract documents, outlining the terms and conditions of the Bracero

Miguel Lopez traveled from Mexico to the US to earn more money for his family.

Program, allowing him to work in the United States.
- After completing the paperwork and having his picture taken for his work permit, Miguel waited in Ciudad Juárez for several days with very little food.
- Distracted by both his excitement about beginning work in the United States and his anxiety about not knowing what he would find there, he barely noticed the hunger.
- He thought about how proud his father and mother would be on receiving the money that he would send them from the United States.
- Finally the Mexican workers were instructed to board a crowded train to cross the border into El Paso, Texas.
- It would be several years before he crossed the border again.

Miguel's first job in the U.S. was picking cotton in El Paso, Texas.

Life at Work

- Miguel López's labor contract with the Bracero Program was for three months.
- The Bracero Program began in 1942; its goal was to support U.S. agriculture during World War II.
- The program was controversial, because it increased competition and lowered wages for Mexican Americans already working in the agricultural industry in the United States.
- Bracero contracts for skilled agricultural workers ranged from four weeks to six months and included adequate, sanitary, free housing; low-cost meals; occupational insurance; and transportation back to Mexico.
- These terms were often not upheld by U.S. farms that employed braceros.
- Miguel was selected by a farmer in El Paso to pick cotton.
- He earned $2.20 per 100 pounds of cotton picked and was able to gather 300 pounds a day.
- Miguel was paid $35 to $45 per week; most weeks, he was the top earner at the farm.
- The national minimum wage was $1.25 per hour; in Texas, migrant farm workers averaged $0.81 per hour.
- Miguel worked seven days a week from 6 a.m. to 5 p.m.
- The work was hard, but Miguel was extremely satisfied to have steady work and to be receiving good pay.
- Every Saturday after work, his boss took the workers into the town to buy food and cigarettes.
- The farmer was young and inexperienced; he had inherited the farm from his father, who had died in a tractor accident.
- Dealing with the Mexican workers was intimidating for the youthful white boss, so he avoided interacting with them when possible.
- Miguel spent his money carefully, and once a month he sent money home to his family.

- With his cotton-crop earnings, he sent home a total of $300 and saved $20 to buy clothes for his family when he returned to Mexico.
- By late September, when Miguel's contract was almost over, he learned from other workers about opportunities for picking grapes in California, where the pay was even better.
- Before he left Texas, he mailed a letter home with a check for $46 and a promise to return to Mexico as soon as he could with more money.
- Miguel then boarded a train to Delano, California, and didn't look back.
- The journey of nearly 950 miles took eight days.
- While he missed his family, Miguel was excited at the prospect of continuing to work and earn more money before he returned home.
- On their arrival in Delano, the workers were transported to a grape vineyard.
- Most of the workers at the vineyard lived in the area year-round.
- Unlike most other crops, grapes require attention for ten months out of the year.
- Miguel's primary role was girdling, or cutting into the bark of the grapevine, disrupting the natural flow of water, thus forcing the fruit to swell.
- At the grape vineyard, workers were segregated by nationality—Puerto Ricans, Filipinos, Mexicans, African Americans or Anglos.
- Miguel shared a room with three other Mexicans; he had his own cot and shelves.
- Fifty-six men shared a common bathroom with four toilets, three shower stalls, and six sinks.
- The cost of room and board was $2.10 per day.
- Three meals a day were provided in the common area, usually tortillas or sandwiches with iced tea.
- The food wasn't bad, but often there was not enough.

Miguel sent home a total of $300 during his cotton-picking days.

- Once or twice a week Miguel would miss a meal because he was at the end of the food line.
- When not in the fields, Miguel played basketball or card games with other Mexican workers.
- Though the work was tedious, it required a great deal of concentration to make cuts in the correct place.
- Miguel earned $1.10 per hour—more than he had earned in the cotton fields, but still less than the minimum wage.
- After several years of working in America's fields, Miguel López considered himself to be Mexican American, even though he was still an undocumented worker.
- If he had returned to Mexico after his three-month work permit expired in 1963, he could have applied for a permanent visa and returned to the United States legally.
- Yet with his success in California, Miguel did not want to go home, and he never completed the necessary paperwork.
- No longer a bracero, Miguel joined the National Farm Workers Association (NFWA) in 1965, based on promises

of higher wages, better living conditions and contract protection.

- On September 16, 1965, Mexico's Independence Day, Miguel joined the 1,200 members of the NFWA and voted to join in the Delano Grape Strike.
- The more than 200 workers at Miguel's vineyard participated in the strike.
- While he did not work for four months, Miguel was deeply moved by the passion of César Chávez and the struggle for social justice.

- In early 1966 Miguel found work again in Delano, with a vineyard that had signed a contract with the United Farm Workers (UFW).
- As a result of his union membership, he now earned $1.70 per hour.

Life in the Community: Delano, California

- The first convention of the National Farm Workers Association (NFWA), founded by César Chávez, was held in Fresno, California, on September 30, 1962, more than a year before Miguel arrived in Delano.
- After that the NFWA worked to organize farm workers in dozens of agricultural towns in California, concentrating on offering farm workers modest benefits and meaningful services.
- The NFWA was against the Bracero Program because the braceros, as temporary laborers, worked for less money in worse conditions than union workers.

Picking grapes in California paid better than picking cotton.

- The Delano Grape Strike began in September 1965 when the mostly Filipino American members of the Agricultural Workers Organizing Committee (AWOC) walked out against Delano-area grape growers.
- The NFWA and the AWOC merged to form the United Farm Workers Organizing Committee on August 22, 1966. On being accepted into the AFL-CIO in 1972, the organization changed its name to the United Farmworkers Union.
- Using nonviolent tactics, including inspiring a consumer boycott, the United Farmworkers achieved the goals of the strike, and it ended in 1970.

Mexican Immigration Timeline

1848 The Mexican-American War (1846-1848) ended with the Treaty of Guadalupe Hidalgo, in which Mexico lost 55 percent of its territory (present-day Arizona, California, New Mexico, and parts of Colorado, Nevada and Utah).

The U.S. paid Mexico $15 million for war-related damages and to ensure that existing property rights would be protected for Mexicans now living in the boundaries of the U.S.

1853-1880 Fifty-five thousand Mexican workers immigrated to the United States as agricultural laborers.

1904 The Border Patrol was established by the U.S. to stop Asian workers from entering the U.S. through Mexico.

1910 Thousands of Mexicans fled across the border when the Mexican Revolution began.

1910-1930 The total number of Mexican immigrants recorded by the U.S. Census tripled from 200,000 to 600,000.

1911 The Dillingham Commission identified Mexican laborers as the best solution to the Southwest labor shortage; Mexicans were exempted from immigrant "head taxes" set in 1903 and 1907.

1917 Prospective immigrants to the U.S. were charged an entry tax of $8 and given a literacy test as a result of the U.S. Immigration Act of 1917.

Between 1917 and 1923 more than 72,000 Mexicans entered the U.S.

1921 The U.S. Immigration Act of 1921 restricted the immigration of Southern and Eastern Europeans.

Mexican workers were formally admitted at Border Patrol stations and charged a tax upon entering.

1924 Mexican immigration reached 89,000.

Congress created a 450-man Border Patrol, shared by the Mexican and Canadian borders.

1930s Five hundred thousand Mexicans living in the U.S. were deported back to Mexico.

Around 60 percent of those deported were children born in the U.S. or legal citizens of Mexican descent.

1931 Mexican American parents won their case against the Lemon Grove, California School Board to prevent their children from segregation from white children.

1941 The League of United Latin American Citizens held protests against discrimination by the Southern Pacific Railroad, which refused to give skilled apprenticeships to Mexican Americans.

1942 Mexican nationals were allowed to work in the U.S. on a temporary basis, mostly in the agricultural industry, through the Bracero Program. In the first three years of the program, over 200,000 temporary workers from Mexico, the Bahamas, Canada, Barbados, and Jamaica entered the U.S.

1952 Immigration and Nationality Act, also known as the McCarran-Walter Act, gave priority to skilled workers and family members of U.S. citizens while stating that all races were eligible for naturalization.

1954 The U.S. Immigration and Naturalization Service deported over one million Mexicans during Operation Wetback in an effort to reduce illegal immigration in the southwest.

1964 The Bracero Program ended due to a surplus of agricultural workers and increased mechanization such as the mechanical corn harvester. The program had permitted temporary employment for nearly 4.5 million Mexican nationals.

Labor leaders began working toward unionizing farm workers.

1965 The Immigration and Naturalization Act of 1965 eliminated the national origin quotas of the 1920s and set annual limits of 170,000 Eastern Hemisphere European immigrants and 120,000 Western Hemisphere immigrants. For Western Hemisphere immigrants, visas were available on a first-come, first-served basis. Spouses, children and parents of U.S. citizens were exempt from the numerical limits.

Getting the Nation to Pay Attention to Farm Workers, http://www.ufw.org

Roberto Bustos was an original 1965 striker and captain of the 400-mile march from Delano to Sacramento in 1966. "I'll always remember Cesar coming into the office one day and saying, 'We are going to go to Sacramento.'

I was very enthusiastic about the idea and was already loading up my car with all my things, and then he gave me the harsh news that we would be marching from Delano to Sacramento! At that moment I thought the man had lost his mind. I looked at the map and saw that the journey was 245 miles.

I didn't think I could walk that distance, and I was right. Ultimately it came close to 400 miles since we made several stops in different towns and never went on a straight path. We stopped at Ducor, Terra Bella, Visalia and Fresno, among others.

But the day the march started, March 17, 1966, I had no idea of the impact this journey would have. We were expecting support but never to be joined by 10,000 supporters as we arrived at the Capitol in Sacramento. It was overwhelming seeing so many people join us and support us in our struggle. When we had started on our way up we only had 70 farm workers with us. The march took a total of 25 days and finally finished on April 10, 1966.

We walked over 15 miles a day, every day. At times I thought we wouldn't make it. In fact, had we not been given new boots by a company in Porterville, we probably wouldn't have.

The march was very significant, and not just because it was a chance for the governor to see what we were going through. It also allowed the rest of the nation to pay attention to what was happening in Delano. Before the march we had no press coverage whatsoever. It was as if 5,000 workers were not on strike.

Today I leave with the honor of not just being captain of the march but with the legacy and history of what the march signified: the recognition the American public gave to the farm workers' struggles."

Daughter of Oil Executive in 1966

Theresa Blasi was eight-years-old and a world traveler. She spent eight months of the year attending school in New Jersey, and four months in Sardinia, Italy with her oil-executive father, mother, and four-year-old brother. When in Italy, Theresa missed baloney sandwiches, but was happy to have brought along her Barbie doll collection.

Life at Home

- In Sardinia Theresa and her little brother spent their days running up and down nearly deserted beaches where seawater was pumped into flats and dried; the resulting raw salt was refined into table salt.
- During her first days on the island, she was disturbed when she periodically heard the explosions used to dislodge the raw salt, but soon she understood and grew accustomed to the noise.
- The family lived in a NATO compound, even though her father was an Esso oil company executive overseeing the design and construction of an oil refinery in the area.
- Theresa's mother kept her out of school during the trip because Theresa was so far ahead of the other students; a previous assignment in Malaysia had included a period of intensive education at a British army base school that put Theresa well beyond her grade level in academic achievement.
- Theresa was told that the Sardinian school had no openings, so that instead of attending "regular" school, she would have a tutor.
- The tutor was a sincere young man who had little success in controlling a rambunctious eight-year-old intent on constantly showing off.
- Once, to demonstrate her coloring skills to him, she used green chalk to fill in all the white portions of her mother's new oriental rug—to the dismay of all the adults concerned.
- When not with the tutor or playing on the beach, Theresa attempted to find friends among the NATO kids.
- On some days she would stand for hours near the entrance to the military post exchange—the commissary where groceries were sold—in the hope that someone would see her and ask if she wanted a green Popsicle.
- Since her family was not military, Theresa didn't think she was allowed to go into the PX, even though her parents had said it would be okay.
- With no ability to speak Italian, she spent much of her time with Americans and Canadians assigned to the NATO facility.
- Even this was not always safe ground; one day the mother of one of her Canadian friends asked her if she wanted to sit on the

Theresa Blasi, at eight-years-old, spent four months of the year in Italy, while her father worked as an oil executive in a Sardinian refinery.

Theresa traveled the Italian countryside with her mother.

Chesterfield, referring to the couch; she froze, petrified of saying or doing the wrong thing.

- The trip opened her eyes to the wider world and introduced her to foods and customs she had never encountered at home.
- While at the market, she and her mother visited a butcher shop where dead rabbits were hanging on display.
- She also learned to appreciate eating fish, a staple of the Sardinian diet, even when it was served with head and tail still attached. Still, she missed the baloney sandwiches she so enjoyed at home in the States.
- She had brought her collection of Barbie dolls with her, and she spent hours playing with, talking to and dressing the dolls. One had blond, swirling hair that made her look elegant, while the other was more conservative, with reddish hair pulled back into a bun.
- Theresa's assortment of Barbie clothes and accessories included a bright pink skirt, fishnet stockings and even a makeup kit.
- If she had not been able to bring her Barbies to Sardinia, Theresa would not have wanted to go at all.
- In addition to her Barbie dolls, she also enjoyed dressing several Liddle Kiddles dolls, which had come with their own pink cribs and tiny sandboxes.
- During the family's stay in Sardinia, Theresa's mother decided to take both of the children on a train trip to Venice and Florence.
- The train was crowded with soldiers, many of whom sat on their suitcases because seats were not available.
- During the trip Theresa bought a salami sandwich from a vendor at one of the train stations; she didn't think to get a drink or ask if the sandwich included any hot peppercorns—which it did, in abundance.
- During the two-week tour, they rode on many trains, and Theresa took hundreds of black-and-white pictures with her Kodak 126 camera.
- They visited a Murano glassworks factory on an island in the Venice lagoon.
- Theresa thought her brother was annoying the entire time, although she was glad to have company.
- The best part of the trip was choosing the change purse her mother bought for her, made of royal blue Italian leather with ornate gold trim.
- Theresa was born in New Hampshire while her father was completing his ROTC requirement there but by age eight she had already traveled extensively; at four, she was in Germany and at six, in Malaysia; in between, she was at her home in New Jersey.

Life at School

- When Theresa returned from Sardinia and started the second grade in New Jersey, she found that her classmates were ahead of her in some subjects but behind her in others; her education in Malaysia and tutoring in Sardinia had left her out of sync with the other students.
- Although she did well in Miss Post's class and was delighted to be with her friends again, she found the transition hard at times.
- Everyone sat in neat rows and did their work as they were told.
- Theresa did not like to go into the hallways without her friends; when she walked down the hall by herself, her steps produced an echo, so she always tried to leave class with a group.

- She enjoyed the Little Golden Books, especially *Dumbo*, the story about the elephant with the biggest, floppiest ears ever.
- Next she was captivated by the movie *Born Free* and the idea of raising lions.
- Shot in Kenya, the movie won two Oscars—and Theresa's heart; she begged and begged to be allowed to see it a second time.
- Although Theresa's mother was careful to limit Theresa's television viewing, she did approve of *The Andy Griffith Show*.
- Theresa's mother liked Andy and Opie, but she thought Aunt Bea was like a member of her own family.
- Another favorite was *Batman*, which aired twice a week; at least once a week, the family would gather around the black-and-white television set and watch the show together.
- Every house in the neighborhood had its specialty: one house was the "strawberry milk" house; in another, there were always blue lollipops; the neighborhood twins had a classroom in their basement; the Bennett boys had a fort.

Theresa loved The Andy Griffith Show.

- Theresa's family's specialty was Kool-Aid; everyone knew that her mom always kept Kool-Aid for the kids, no matter how many arrived or when.
- One father loved to load his tiny Triumph Spitfire convertible with as many children as possible for the short trip to the gas station; recently, Theresa had been one of the lucky ones to get a ride.
- At the end of the street in their housing development, the neighborhood kids discovered a huge vineyard, where there were thick old grapevines perfect for swinging.
- With vines so long, a role in the next Tarzan movie could not be far away, although over the years several would-be Tarzans broke an arm practicing.

Another favorite of Theresa's was Batman.

- Some afternoons were spent playing army; the boys all had toy "guns" and shot each other, while Theresa and her friend served as the nurses.
- At night, especially on weekends, Theresa and her friends sometimes went to a nearby pasture from which they could secretly watch movies playing at the local drive-in theater.
- Sometimes Theresa's entire family went to the drive-in; the two children were dressed in their pajamas before they left the house in case they fell asleep during the movie.
- Theresa loved being able to play there on the jungle gym in her pajamas.
- For school Theresa always dressed well, as dictated by her mother.
- Many of the shirts her mother bought were ribbed or had stripes.

- Theresa loved wearing the flowered corduroy outfit her mother found.
- After telling her mother that she liked the color chartreuse, because it was fun to say the word, Theresa was given a pair of electric green polyester pants for her birthday. The pants practically glowed in the dark.
- She wore her birthday present to school only once, and she was teased about it for an entire day; when she got home, Theresa buried the pants in the farthest, darkest corner of her dresser drawer.
- She also hated the red coat her mother made her wear; she was sure she was the only child in the entire school who had a coat with fake fur—or any fur at all.
- Besides, the fake fur on the collar always shed and went up her nose.
- She did like the red-plaid school lunchbox her mother bought for her, which went with many of her outfits.
- When she discovered one Saturday that her mother had failed to wash her favorite jeans and only dresses were available to wear, Theresa immediately vowed to run away.
- But when her mother offered to help her pack, Theresa burst into tears and decided not to leave home.
- When she was tempted to misbehave, Theresa knew what supposedly would happen; a spanking paddle painted with the words "For the Cute Little Deer with the Bear Behind" hung prominently in the kitchen.

Theresa always dressed well, in smart clothes mostly chosen by her mother.

Life in the Community: New Jersey and Sardinia

- New Jersey was known for its factories and industrial output, and it ranked first in the United States in chemical products, thanks to its large number of pharmaceutical, basic chemical and paint industries.
- The state also was known for food processing, as well as for the manufacture of apparel, electrical machinery and stone, clay and glass products.
- One of New Jersey's signature special events was the annual Miss America Pageant, which took place in Atlantic City.
- The environment in Atlantic City was entirely different from what Theresa had experienced in Sardinia, an ancient island with a deeply embedded culture that it had absorbed from many lands, including nearby Italy.
- The first invaders were the Phoenicians, followed by the Carthaginians, Romans, Arabs, Pisans, Genoese and Spaniards.
- In Rome's Etruscan Museum and the museums of Cagliari and Sassari could be found hundreds of tiny, exquisite Sardinian bronzes from the eighth century BCE.
- Throughout the island there remained 3,000 little fortresses dating from prehistoric times to about the third century BCE.
- In 1966 more than a billion dollars was being invested in Sardinia for dams, public works, communications, subsidies for agriculture and construction of luxury hotels and tourist facilities.
- Sardinia already supported two universities graduating doctors, engineers, architects, lawyers and academics.

- Scattered throughout the island were hundreds of fierce shepherds who spoke a dialect resembling Latin, continuing to tend their flocks.
- It was said that the shepherds always had to be tough and vigilant; sheep rustling had a long tradition in Sardinia.
- Also still important in Sardinia were traditional handicrafts, including the creation of hand-woven carpets, tapestries, coverlets, unusual baskets, and carved wood chests.

Oil refinery in Sardinia, Italy.

"Pleasures and Places: Sardinia," by Philip Dallas, *Atlantic Monthly,* March 1966

The foreigners who are now moving into Sardinia are Milanese, Parisians, Swiss, Germans, English and Romans. They are setting up highly automated factories and luxurious hotels; but they are moving in by proxy and behind a smoke screen of lawyers, engineers and architects, who fly in and out continually on brief visits, meeting their Sardinian opposite number who are overseeing the practicalities of the various enterprises. Simultaneously, hundreds of Sardinians are moving out, bringing their already small number to less than a million and a half on an island the size of West Virginia…

Each of Sardinia's two principal cities-Cagliari in the south and Sassari in the north-has its sphere of influence and a youthful sense of rivalry. If Cagliari puts up a high-rise building, Sassari must have one too, no matter how little it needs one. However, Cagliari is a historic, if not a prehistoric, city, while Sassari is only eighteenth century, though not without a considerable provincial charm.

Artist in 1966

Reid Miles was an artist who worked with typefaces, moody photography, and a minimalist color palette to help Blue Note Records establish itself as one of the hippest of all jazz labels. Working for Esquire magazine before being hired to design album covers, Miles designed 500 jazz album covers with a Blue Note look that matched the Blue Note sound.

Life at Home

- Born in Chicago on July 4, 1927, Reid moved to Long Beach, California, with his mother following the stock market crash and the separation of his parents in 1929.
- After high school, Reid joined the Navy and, following his discharge, moved to Los Angeles to enroll at Chouinard Art Institute.
- By that time, the record industry, once a fledgling in the business world, had grown up dramatically; jazz was America's number-two export, behind only Hollywood movies.
- It was also the Golden Age of jazz, when this distinctly American sound dominated pop music.
- Duke Ellington, Billie Holiday, Benny Goodman, Tommy Dorsey, Ella Fitzgerald, and Count Basie were known worldwide as jazz icons and stylistic leaders.
- To take advantage of the rapidly rising popularity of the music, the major record labels emphasized quantity over innovation, required their stars to record numerous albums each year.
- In 1937 RCA booked Tommy Dorsey and His Orchestra for 22 recording sessions to maximize their earning potential while the band was still popular.
- Smaller bands were ignored, and young musicians were expected to conform.
- Into this niche slipped Blue Note Records.
- The tiny record label was founded in 1939 by Alfred Lion, who became interested in jazz while living in Germany.
- Lion became a lifelong devotee of jazz on December 23, 1938, when he attended a sold-out performance at Carnegie Hall featuring "talented Negro artists from all over the country who have been denied entry to the white world of popular music."
- Many of Lion's earliest recording sessions started at 4:00 a.m., when musicians got off work from a night gig.
- Lion ignored most of the commercial rules concerning recording—such as the "appropriate" length of a tune—delighting the jazz musicians and attracting additional talent.

Ried Miles was a photographer whose work was called "moody" and used a monochrome palette.

- Lion's partner, Francis ("Frank") Wolff, was equally committed to the evolving world of jazz; he was also a talented photographer.
- Wolff's warm, intimate photographs of musicians emphasized the informal, fluid nature of the genre.
- His portraits dominated the cover designs of Blue Note Records.
- At the same time, the phonograph record itself was evolving.
- Around 1910, 78-rpm records had replaced the phonograph cylinder as the medium for recorded sound.

Alfred Lion and Frank Wolf were committed to the evolving world of jazz.

- The 78-rpm records were issued in both 10" and 12" diameter sizes and were usually sold separately, in brown paper or cardboard sleeves that carried little more than the name of the retail store.
- Beginning in the 1920s, bound collections of empty sleeves made of plain paperboard were sold as "record albums" in which customers could store their records.
- Starting in the 1930s, record companies began issuing collections of 78-rpm records by one performer on specially assembled albums.
- In 1938 Columbia Records's Alex Steinweiss invented the concept of album covers and cover art.
- Other record companies followed his lead, and by the late 1940s, record albums routinely featured individual, colorful paper covers.
- Reid Miles worked for *Esquire* magazine in the early 1950s before he was hired by Frank Wolff to design album covers for Blue Note Records.
- Although Blue Note had employed talented artists to design its covers, the jazz label still lacked a look.
- Reid changed that—almost immediately.
- Almost single-handedly, he defined the look of cool jazz: a harmonious blend of modernism with a distinct personality.

Life at Work

- Reid Miles's five hundred jazz album covers for Blue Note Records defined "cool" in the era of Thelonious Monk.
- One of his first covers featured Thelonious Monk with the word *Thelonious* split across two lines with a hyphen between the *o* and *n* set in dark type; the word *Monk* was in white against a background of ocher-yellow.
- Then, with the type dominating the design, Reid placed a small Frank Wolff photograph at the corner of the frame to complete the Blue Note look.
- The unexpected, stylized, nonconformist look on the album sleeves coolly echoed the innovation of the music inside; Reid gave Blue Note a look that matched the "Blue Note Sound."
- This unconventional, eclectic design was embraced by Albert Lion, who sought out the "different" and liked

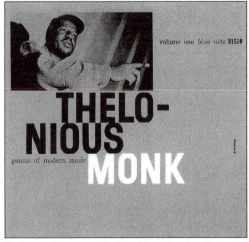

Reid gave album covers for Blue Note Records a distinctive look.

Miles Davis, right, with Frank Wolf, in the Blue Note studio.

Reid's ability to creatively incorporate Woolf's moody, mostly black-and-white photographs with innovative cropping, unconventional typefaces and off-balance designs.

- But Reid was restless, constantly changing, frequently reinventing his look to keep it fresh.
- He specialized in the unexpected—manipulating type and employing unconventional fonts and severe cropping of photographs.
- Few of the covers were full-color; Reid preferred using black and white with only one other color.
- "Typography in the early 1950s was in a renaissance, anyway. It happened especially on album covers because they were not so restrictive as advertising," Reid said.
- Reid enjoyed unrestricted access to Frank Wolff's atmospheric photography and broad discretion concerning the album's final look and feel.
- Fans raved that a Reid Miles sleeve was as recognizable and distinctive as "the trumpet timbre of Miles Davis or the plaintive phrasing of Billie Holiday."
- Personally Reid wasn't particularly interested in jazz and often traded away the albums that Blue Note gave him.
- He professed to have much more of an interest in classical music, but he didn't hesitate to mirror the atmosphere of a jam session in his artwork.
- "Frank tried to get the artist's real expression ... the way he stood. Reid was more avant-garde and more chic, but the two together worked beautifully," according to Albert Lion.
- "Frank always hated it when I cropped one of his photographs of his artist through the forehead," Reid said.
- For a decade, his look wowed and inspired. Hired in 1956, Reid exited ten years later when Blue Note was sold, having grown up and risen to maturity with jazz.

Life in the Community: New York City

- By mid-century jazz bands around the world took their stylistic cues from the American orchestras based in New York City, where innovation and creativity were in no short supply.
- There jazz lovers could hang out at Gabler's Commodore Music Shop and debate the merits of "hot" jazz or the perfect size of a jazz band.
- New Orleans, Chicago, Kansas City and others all staked a special claim to the development of jazz, but New York City was where big events took place.
- It was at Carnegie Hall in 1914 that James Reese Europe and His Clef Club Orchestra performed his "popular music," syncopated transition from ragtime to jazz.
- By 1923, the Club Alabam "Club Alabam" in New York was home to Fletch Henderson's influential orchestra, which deviated from New Orleans style by adding three saxophones and dropping a clarinet.
- This created a true reed section, one of the fundamentals of Big Band jazz.

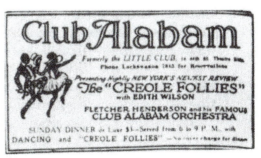

- By 1934 the Benny Goodman Orchestra broadcasts out of New York were a national sensation, using a formula that emphasized Big Band orchestration while leaving room for instrumentation.
- At the start of World War II, jazz had attained enough momentum and maturity to stage a revolution within itself with the emergence of bebop.
- By the end of the war, eager patrons lined up at New York's Royal Roost on Broadway to hear fully integrated orchestras, whose very existence served as a catalyst for innovation.
- New York City was also in the center of the musical action in the 1950s as Thelonious Monk developed his pioneering modulations known as "Zombie Music."

The History of Blue Note Records

1925   Sixteen-year-old Alfred Lion, the future founder of Blue Note Records, was profoundly influenced by a live performance he attended in his native Germany of Sam Woodyard and His Chocolate Dandies.

1930   During his first trip to United States, Lion purchased more than 300 records unavailable in Germany.

1938   To escape the rising tide of Nazism, Lion emigrated to the United States, where he feasted on the variety of music ranging from spirituals to swing to boogie-woogie pianists Albert Ammons and Meade Lux Lewis.

1939   After Lion recorded Ammons and Lewis, 50 discs were produced and soon sold.

1941   Photographer Francis Wolff left Germany and joined Lion.

1942   Blue Note suspended record production in deference to the war effort; Lion was drafted into the Army.

1948   Blue Note started recording emerging talent such as Thelonious Monk, Bud Powell and Fats Navaro.

1951   Blue Note moved from 78 rpms to the 10-inch platform and began using album cover art designed by Paul Bacon, Gil Melle and John Hermansader.

1953   Recording engineer Rudy Van Gelder's attention to audio detail, such as the audibility of the high hat cymbal, began to mold the distinctive Blue Note sound.

1956   Reid Miles began working with Lion and Wolff as Blue Note's graphic designer.

1958   Rising star Andy Warhol designed a Blue Note album cover featuring Kenny Burrell.

1964   Blue Note registered hits with "Song For My Father" by Horace Silver and "The Sidewinder" by Lee Morgan.

1965   Recording giant Liberty purchased Blue Note Records from Alfred Lion and Francis Wolff.

Super Glue Inventor in 1967

Dr. Harry Coover invented Super Glue by accident, while working on a clear plastic that could be used for precision gun sights for soldiers. Not only that, but a spray-on version of the sticky stuff was just the thing to stop the bleeding of wounded soldiers in the Vietnam War—a fact for which soldier Ted Grant was eternally grateful.

Life at Home

- Ted Grant always sang the praises of the man he credited with saving his life: Dr. Harry Coover, known to Ted only as "Dr. Super Glue."
- The two men, born 30 years apart, never met; indeed, Dr. Coover never heard Ted's name.
- Their paths crossed because of glue; Dr. Coover was an accidental glue guru, and Ted was a man in need of his invention.
- Born in Newark, Delaware, on March 6, 1919, Dr. Coover received his BS from Hobart College and continued his studies at Cornell University, where he earned an MS degree in chemistry in 1942 and a PhD in 1944.
- Shortly thereafter he began working for Eastman Kodak's chemical division in Rochester, New York.
- Ted was born in Lancaster, South Carolina, where both his parents worked third shift at the Springs Textile Mill.
- His parents assumed that Ted would join them when he turned 16 and no longer had to attend school.
- Ted, however, had other ideas; he loved how he looked in a football uniform and especially cherished the attention lavished on an aggressive linebacker eager to make the tackle on every play.
- Coaches whispered that college football might be in his future.
- And 1965, Ted's junior year in high school, was the perfect time to showcase his athletic skills, they said, particularly in a town where football was a religion.
- The year 1965 was also the year an incredibly stable adhesive known as Super Glue—invented previously by Dr. Coover—was to be used for medical treatment on the bloody battlefields of Vietnam—a place Ted could not then have located on a world map.

Dr. Harry Coover invented Super Glue while researching a material for gun sights during the Vietnam War.

- For most of human history, research into adhesive glues had focused on joining together two pieces of wood or other cellulose products using another natural substance.
- The role of natural adhesives, such as hides, starch, dextrin and gum, remained important because of their tendency to cost less than synthetics.
- The most critical advance of the early twentieth century came with the patenting of Bakelite, the first synthetic polymer resin.

Ted Grant, whose life was saved by Cooper's invention, was drafted into the Vietnam War.

- This invention by Leo Baekeland led to polymer science, which also stimulated research into new adhesives.
- During World War II, Dr. Coover was part of a team conducting research with chemicals known as cyanoacrylates in an effort to make a clear plastic that could be used for precision gun sights for soldiers.
- While working with the chemicals, the researchers discovered that they were extremely sticky, a property that made them very difficult to work with.
- Moisture caused the chemicals to polymerize, and since nearly all objects have a thin layer of moisture on them, bonding would occur in virtually every testing instance.
- The research team rejected cyanoacrylates and moved on; a war was under way, and there was no time for distractions.
- "Serendipity had knocked, but I didn't hear it," Coover commented years later.

Life at Work

- Linebacker Ted Grant had been waiting the whole game for the fleet tailback from Rock Hill High to run a naked reverse in a close game between traditional rivals.
- Ted was sure he could hit the tailback hard enough to take him out of the game; a helmet to the hip was the perfect plan.

Ted's passion was football until he broke his leg in two places.

- The only thing Ted did not calculate on was the fumble caused by his sensational wallop.
- In the resulting scramble for the loose ball, Ted's teammates drove viciously to recover the fumble, breaking Ted's leg in two places.
- Ted clearly remembered the standing ovation he received when he was carried off the field; the trip to the hospital and the next two days were less clear.
- What he realized after two months in a cast was that his football career was over.
- Ted's father wasted no time securing him a job at the mill.
- Ted was just going to work on the second shift the day his draft notice arrived.
- After 18 months in the mill, Ted was ready for a change; he was more familiar with the location of Vietnam now that 540,000 US troops were committed to the fight and the American death toll had reached 33,000 soldiers.
- In 1951 Dr. Coover was transferred to Kodak's chemical plant in Kingsport, Tennessee, where he rediscovered the cyanoacrylates and recognized in them a new potential.

- He had been overseeing the work of a group of Kodak chemists who were researching heat-resistant polymers for jet-airplane canopies.
- When a researcher applied one of the compounds between the lenses to test its effect on light, the lenses would not come apart.
- The researcher became upset at the loss of expensive equipment, but Dr. Coover saw things differently.
- They did further tests on the cyanoacrylate monomers, and this time Dr. Coover recognized that these sticky adhesives had unique properties: they required no heat or pressure to bond.
- He and his team tried the substance on various items in the lab, and each time, the items became permanently bonded together.
- Dr. Coover—and his employer—knew they were on to something; Coover received patent number 2,768,109 for his "Alcohol-Catalyzed Cyanoacrylate Adhesive Compositions/Superglue" and began refining the product for commercialization.
- His company packaged the all-purpose adhesive as "Eastman 910" and began marketing it in 1958; it was named Eastman 910, as Dr. Coover explained, because "You could count 1, 2, 3, 4, 5, 6, 7, 8, 9, 10 and it was bonded."
- During the 1960s Eastman Kodak sold cyanoacrylate to Loctite, which repackaged and distributed it under a different brand name, Loctite Quick Set 404.
- By the mid-1960s, Dr. Coover became something of a celebrity; appearing on the television game show *I've Got a Secret*, he lifted the host, Garry Moore, off the ground using a single drop of Super Glue.
- During the Vietnam War, Dr. Coover developed a cyanoacrylate spray based on the same compound, which was sprayed onto soldiers' serious wounds to quickly halt bleeding so that the injured could be transported to medical facilities instead of morgues.

Ted was wounded during an ambush in the Vietnam jungle.

- Cyanoacrylates were then used for sealing dental repairs, lesions, and bleeding ulcers, and for suture-free surgery.
- Meanwhile, US Army Private Ted Grant had discovered that the steaming jungle of Vietnam was unpredictable and dangerous.
- While walking point on a routine patrol, he realized that an ambush lay ahead.
- Acting on finely tuned survival instincts, he signaled the squad to halt and was silently moving his fellow soldiers back when the shooting began.
- Three Americans were killed immediately, while Ted was wounded in three places: his shoulder, leg and hand.
- He was bleeding profusely.
- When the medic arrived, he bandaged some of Ted's wounds and then glued several other wounds shut with a spray-on Super Glue not yet authorized for medical use.
- The crude system worked temporarily and gave medics time to move the critically wounded soldiers to the safety of a hospital; the glue saved Ted's life and became his badge of honor.
- Back home, drinking beer at the Dixie Tavern in Lancaster, South Carolina, Ted always drank a toast to the man who saved his life: Dr. Super Glue.

Life in the Community: Kingsport, Tennessee

- Tennessee Eastman Company in Kingsport, Tennessee, got its start thanks to World War I and the scarcities it caused.

Eastman Kodak founder George Eastman.

- Raw materials such as photographic paper, optical glass, gelatin and many chemicals, including methanol, acetic acid and acetone, were unavailable to the powerful Eastman Kodak Company.
- At the close of the war, Eastman Kodak founder George Eastman decided to ensure that he always had an independent supply of chemicals for his photographic processes.
- In his search for suitable quantities of methanol and acetone, Eastman turned his attention to the southern United States and its forests, as well as to Kingsport, Tennessee.
- In 1920 Tennessee Eastman was founded, with two major platforms—organic chemicals and acetyls.
- From the primary feedstock of pyroligneous acid, many of Eastman's basic chemical building blocks were manufactured, studied and perfected.
- Products such as calcium acetate, sodium acetate, acetic acid and acetic anhydride became the bases for other major company platforms.
- During World War II, a powerful explosive called RDX was manufactured for the U.S. government at Holston Ordnance Works at Tennessee Eastman sites.
- At the peak of production, the ordnance plant was producing a million and a half pounds of explosives each day.
- Eastman's portfolio of products continued to expand, and by the 1960s, Tennessee Eastman Company was manufacturing products that became familiar features of everyday life: polyester fibers for apparel and home furnishings, plastics for the automobile industry and a growing number of industrial chemicals.
- Kingsport, Tennessee, itself was first chartered in 1822, and over time it became an important shipping port on the Holston River.
- Goods originating in the surrounding region were loaded onto barges for the journey downriver to the Tennessee River at Knoxville.
- The town lost its charter after a downturn in its fortunes precipitated by the Civil War.
- Rechartered in 1917, Kingsport was an early example of a "garden city," designed by city planner and landscape architect John Nolen of Cambridge, Massachusetts.
- It carries the nickname "The Model City" from his plan, which organized the town into areas for churches, housing, commerce and industry.
- The plan included some of the earlier uses of traffic circles, or roundabouts, in the United States.
- Kingsport was among the first municipalities with a city-manager form of government, and its school system was organized on a model developed at Columbia University.
- Most of the land along the river was devoted to industry.
- Indeed, most of Long Island, in the Holston River and within the Kingsport city limits, as well as an equally large area on the river's east bank were occupied by Tennessee Eastman Chemical Company.
- Lancaster, South Carolina, was established in the mid-1700s by Scots-Irish and English settlers from Lancaster, Pennsylvania, itself named for their homelands in England.
- During the Civil War, troops under General William Tecumseh Sherman occupied the town in early 1865, during Sherman's Carolinas Campaign.
- Following the war, Colonel Leroy Springs founded Springs Cotton Mill in 1895; this industrial enterprise became one of the largest textile plants in the world.
- For most the twentieth century, Springs Industries shaped the fortunes of Lancaster and its citizens.

Immigrant Medical Student in 1967

Peng Liu was born in China, and started life in privileged surroundings, with servants, cooks and a private school education. As the Communist regime took hold, he was separated from his mother and brothers and life became increasingly difficult. He was granted a student visa in 1966, and arrived in San Francisco as a medical student.

Life at Home

- Peng Liu was born in 1939, ten years before his native city of Shanghai fell under Communist control and the People's Republic of China was established.
- From the late 1800s, his family owned many successful textile factories in Shanghai; they exported silk and other fabrics to the United States and Europe.
- Peng was aware at a very young age of the differences between rich and poor.
- He grew up with servants, cooks, gardeners and chauffeurs, and, with his two younger brothers, he attended the best private schools in Shanghai.
- As in many wealthy Chinese homes, Peng was surrounded by Western influences, ranging from tennis courts to crystal chandeliers to Frank Sinatra's music.
- He enjoyed going to school, especially when Western movies and cartoons were shown in his English classes.
- After the success of the Communist Revolution in China in 1949, English classes were no longer included in the curriculum at Peng's school.
- Instead he was required to study the language and history of Russia.
- As a teenager Peng was aware of the Communist regime, but he did not recognize the implications of Communist control until later; he was more interested in listening to records, going out with his friends and talking to girls.
- Western influences were tolerated in the early years of Communist China, but when Peng was a teenager, he was told to hand over his record albums to be destroyed by the authorities.
- When his family lost control of their factories to the Communists in 1950, Peng's father applied for a visa to travel to Hong Kong, which was under non-Communist British rule.
- Eventually, in 1952, he was granted a one-month travel visa after lying to the authorities about his plans, saying he was visiting relatives in Hong Kong in order to persuade them to return to China with him.

Peng Liu escaped the Communist regime in China, to become a medical student at the University of California.

- In truth Peng's father wanted to relocate his family to Hong Kong to escape the tight grip of Communist rule in Shanghai, and possibly to open another textile factory there.
- Surmising his father's intentions, the government kept a close watch on Peng's family, who remained in Shanghai.
- As the news of his father going to Hong Kong spread, Peng and his brothers were harassed in school and accused of being the sons of a Hong Kong spy.
- Thirteen-year-old Peng became isolated from his friends and classmates, whose parents feared that association with Peng might link their own families to political dissent.

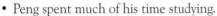

Peng's father went to Hong Kong, planning to relocate his family there.

- Peng spent much of his time studying.
- As was required for all children, Peng and his brothers were part of the Pioneer Movement—an organization to teach children the principles of communism.
- His mother cried silently as she tied the red scarves on their necks each morning before school.
- She expressed disdain for the idea that children and adults alike had to pretend they believed in something they didn't in order to avoid political persecution at the hands of the Communist leaders.
- Peng's school, now run by the government, was saturated with anti-American propaganda.
- At the age of 14, Peng became part of a youth group in preparation for Party membership.
- His mother began working as a teacher, and she became increasingly frustrated with the restrictions of the Communist regime, which forced previously wealthy Chinese to work for the government.
- She communicated with his father secretly, through letters written in code.
- In 1958 letters were discovered in a "routine" search of their home.
- Peng and his brothers were taken from their mother, who was arrested for disloyalty to the Communist Party.
- Peng never saw his mother again.
- The three boys were taken to separate communes in the countryside, where they were assigned duties such as working in the fields and scrubbing floors.
- Three years later, in 1961, Peng's father finally located his sons and applied for a visa for 17-year-old Peng to join him in Hong Kong.
- On arriving in Hong Kong, Peng learned that both of his younger brothers had died, most likely of starvation or of a disease such as tuberculosis.
- Even though Peng's formal schooling had been interrupted in 1958, he had excelled in academics, especially math and science, so his father immediately helped him apply to schools.
- Peng was admitted to the University of Hong Kong in 1962 after passing rigorous entrance examinations.
- His father encouraged him to study medicine, and Peng maintained the highest grades in most of his courses.
- In Hong Kong Peng's father had established another small but very successful silk factory; fearing future Communist takeover, however, he decided to leave Asia in search of more secure freedom in the United States.

Peng and his brothers were taken from their mother, who was arrested for disloyalty to the Communist Party.

Peng's early childhood was spent comfortably in a roomy house.

- Through his silk-export business, Peng's father had become familiar with US business practices, and he knew a few Chinese and American businessmen in San Francisco.
- For more than 60 years, the Chinese Exclusion Act had banned Chinese nationals from immigrating to the United States.
- After fighting alongside China as allies in World War II, the United States passed a series of laws, including the Immigration Act of 1965, that permitted the immigration of Chinese.
- Following his graduation from the University of Hong Kong, Peng applied for a student visa to continue his studies in the United States.
- After earning a passing score on the Test of English as a Foreign Language (TOEFL) and submitting the appropriate documentation, he was admitted to the University of California in San Francisco.
- Peng arrived in San Francisco as a medical student in 1966, full of hope.

Life at School

- Peng Liu enjoyed the environment of San Francisco during his first full year in the United States.
- There were a lot of trees and parks, and it was very clean compared with Shanghai or Hong Kong.
- Peng enjoyed the atmosphere of the American university, but he struggled with using English in both academic and social situations.
- He was most comfortable in the classes that included chemistry and math, especially when working with numeric formulas and graphs.
- The informal nature of Peng's classes surprised him.
- In China students did not converse with teachers or ask questions in the middle of class.
- One day his chemistry professor actually admitted that he had made a mistake when writing a formula on the board.

San Francisco, California.

- Even more surprising to Peng was that a student had pointed out the error.
- Peng could not remember any of his Chinese teachers ever admitting to an error.
- He was also surprised that students were allowed to eat and drink in class, and that some teachers walked around the classroom or sat on desks as they lectured.
- Peng often wrote down questions for his professors because they had difficulty understanding his English.
- He frequently became "lost" during the English-language lectures, and he re-read all of his notes and lecture materials many times after class.
- With the exception of a rare few, he thought, his American professors gave him high grades for less work compared with his teachers in China.
- He liked his apartment, which was provided by the university as part of his research assistantship through the medical school, but he was very lonely.
- Peng did not make friends easily and spent most of his time on his studies.
- He had difficulty interacting with the American students and was amazed at the confidence that they displayed.

San Francisco had a thriving Chinatown.

- He felt as though he did not fit in with the other students; most seemed loud, arrogant and disrespectful.
- One afternoon, after his biology class, Peng was reviewing his notes while waiting to catch the bus back to his apartment.
- It was raining, and Peng was grateful that there was a covered seating area at the bus stop.
- Suddenly he heard the screeching of car tires and looked up to see a red Chevrolet fast approaching the bus stop, just before feeling a wet splash of cool mud cover the entire front side of his body.
- As the car quickly sped away, Peng heard roaring laughter as one of the students in the car mimicked his Chinese language in a singsong voice.
- His heart sank as he wiped mud from his glasses and tried to salvage his notes, written in a combination of English and Chinese.
- The few other Chinese medical students at his university who had started the program before him seemed to have taken on the attitudes of the American students.
- Moreover, they were from different cities in China and spoke dialects of Chinese that were nearly incomprehensible to Peng.
- Although he preferred to stay within the familiar atmosphere of his small apartment and the university, Peng traveled to Chinatown each Saturday morning with David Li, a 58-year-old professor of biology who was originally from Hong Kong.
- Established in the 1850s, San Francisco's Chinatown was the largest and oldest Chinatown in the United States.
- There Peng came into contact with many other people from Hong Kong, and also some from Shanghai.
- While he was appreciative of the opportunity to get fresh fish and vegetables, he often found the experience of Chinatown depressing.
- In contrast to the university campus, the streets of Chinatown were dirty, with rats scurrying underfoot and children running in the street.
- It reminded Peng of the industrial district of Shanghai he had seen as a very young child, with dilapidated buildings and street beggars.
- The Chinese here were struggling, working for very little money in laundries or restaurants, often living in cramped quarters with several other families.
- But at least, Peng thought, it was better for them here than back in China, where the oppressive Cultural Revolution was taking place.
- After graduating from medical school, Peng hoped to work as a dermatologist in the United States.
- While doctors were respected in China, he would earn a better salary in the United States.

Life in the Community: Chinatown, San Francisco, California

- The first Chinese immigrants to the United States, two men and one woman, arrived in San Francisco on the American brig *Eagle* in 1848.

- Once the "Chinese School" was created in 1859, Chinese American children were not permitted into any other public schools in San Francisco.
- Anti-Chinese ordinances were passed in San Francisco in 1870 to limit their housing and employment opportunities.
- In 1880 the United States and China signed a treaty giving the United States the right to limit but "not absolutely prohibit" Chinese immigration.
- The 1882 Chinese Exclusion Act banned immigration of Chinese laborers to the United States and prohibited Chinese from becoming naturalized citizens.
- The estimated 15,000 Chinese living in San Francisco's Chinatown lost nearly everything in the earthquake and fire of April 1906.
- Following the disaster, most Chinese left for Oakland; the city attempted to remove the 400 Chinese remaining in the city in order to appropriate the commercially valuable Chinatown district, but the plan failed after the consequences in lost tax revenues became clear.
- In 1910 the Angel Island Immigration Station

San Francisco's Chinatown played a vital role in preserving the identity of ethnic Chinese in the U.S.

opened; it operated as a detention and processing center for Chinese immigration.
- Thousands of Chinese immigrants spent weeks or months at Angel Island, undergoing interrogations by U.S. immigration officials.
- Angel Island was closed after a disastrous fire in 1940; by that time some 250,000 Chinese immigrants had been processed there.
- On December 17, 1943, halfway through World War II, President Roosevelt signed the repeal of the Chinese Exclusion Act, ending more than sixty years of legalized racism and discrimination.
- The McCarran-Walter Act of 1952 made all races eligible for naturalization; restrictions on Asian immigration, however, remained unchanged.
- In the 1960s Chinese immigrants from Hong Kong began arriving in San Francisco in large numbers; because of their lack of proficiency in English, many had to accept unskilled employment in Chinatown despite their professional status in Hong Kong.
- The Immigration and Naturalization Act of 1965 abolished the national origins quota system that had been the basis of American immigration policy since the 1920s, replacing it with a preference system focusing on immigrants' skills and family relationships with citizens or U.S. residents.
- The arrival of Cantonese-speaking immigrants from Hong Kong and mainland China led to replacement of the Hoisanese/Taishanese dialect that had prevailed earlier with standard Cantonese.
- As the oldest Chinatown in North America and the largest Chinese community outside Asia, San Francisco's Chinatown continues to serve a vital role in preserving the history and identity of ethnic Chinese in the United States.

Chinese Immigration Timeline

1848 Chinese immigration began in California with the beginning of the gold rush.

1850 The Chinese American population in the U.S. was about 4,000, out of a population of 23.2 million.

The U.S. Census reported only two Chinese, working as house servants in Los Angeles.

1854 Chinese was included on a list of racial groups not allowed to testify against whites in the California Supreme Court.

1860 The Chinese American population in the U.S. was 34,933 out of a total population of 31.4 million.

1864-1865 Central Pacific Railroad Company recruited thousands of Chinese workers to build the first transcontinental railroad.

1870 The Naturalization Act limited American citizenship to "white persons and persons of African decent," preventing Asians from gaining U.S. citizenship.

1871 Anti-Chinese violence erupted in Los Angeles and other cities across the U.S.

About 75 percent of the U.S. Chinese population was in California.

1882 Congress passed the Chinese Exclusion Act, banning further entry of Chinese nationals to the U.S.

Since 1850, approximately 250,000 Chinese had entered the U.S.

1890 The Chinese American population was recorded as 107,488 out of a total of 62.9 million.

1891 The first public telephone pay station was started in San Francisco's Chinatown, called the Chinese American Telephone Exchange.

1892 The Geary Act was introduced, extending the Chinese Exclusion Act. Chinese resident laborers were required to obtain a certificate of residence or face deportation or imprisonment.

1898 The Supreme Court ruled that anyone born in the U.S. was a citizen.

1906 A massive earthquake and fire destroyed all records in San Francisco, including immigration records.

1910 The Chinese American population in the U.S. was 94,414 out of a total population of 92.2 million.

The Angel Island Immigration Station in California opened to process Chinese immigrants who were restricted by the Chinese Exclusion Act.

Prospective immigrants endured intense, specific questioning to weed out "paper sons," or those who had false documentation that claimed relation to a Chinese U.S. citizen.

1924 The Immigration Act of 1924 placed further restrictions on immigration using a national origins quota.

1930 The Chinese American population in the U.S. was recorded as 60,000 out of a total population of 123.2 million.

Chinese wives married to American men prior to May 1924 were allowed to enter the U.S.

1940 The Angel Island Immigration Station closed due to a fire in the administration building.

1941 The United States entered World War II after the Japanese attacked Pearl Harbor. China was an ally of the United States.

1943 Congress passed the Magnuson Act, which repealed the Chinese Exclusion Act; an annual Chinese immigration quota of 105 was established and Chinese were also granted the right to become naturalized citizens.

The Yale Institute of Far Eastern Languages was founded to teach Chinese language and culture.

1945 World War II ended when the U.S. dropped an atomic bomb on Hiroshima and Nagasaki, Japan, and Japan surrendered to the U.S. and its allies.

The War Brides Act enabled 118,000 wives and children of U.S. military men to immigrate to the U.S., including Chinese.

1949 The Chinese Civil War ended with the Communist conquest of Mainland China. The Communist Party of China established the People's Republic of China.

1950 The Chinese American population in the U.S. was 150,005 out of a total population of 151,325,798.

1952 The Immigration and Nationality Act, also known as the McCarran-Walter Act, ended exclusion of immigrants based on race, but included a racial quota system.

1953 The Refugee Relief Act authorized 214,000 non-quota immigrant visas for refugees.

1955 The Chinese Chamber of Commerce was established in Los Angeles to promote and encourage the development of the Chinese American business community.

1958 A movement in Communist China referred to as "The Great Leap Forward" began, designed to turn China into a leading industrial power and resulting in widespread famine.

1959 The U.S. Immigration and Naturalization Service began the "Confession Program" (1959-1966), which enabled Chinese immigrants who had entered the country illegally to confess their status and become eligible to be naturalized citizens.

1962 The Kennedy Emergency Immigration Act permitted 15,000 Chinese immigrants to enter the United States between 1962 and 1965 as a result of "The Great Leap Forward" and Communist oppression in the People's Republic of China.

1965 National origin quotas were eliminated as part of the Immigration Reform Act of 1965.

A quota of 170,000 immigrants, with a maximum of 20,000 per country, was established with categories of preference set for each.

"Chinaman's Chance," *Time*, September 8, 1967

To sightseers tramping its cluttered avenues, San Francisco's Chinatown has always displayed a pungent blend of yang and yin. Those intertwined opposites-good and evil, sweet and sour, light and dark-describe not only Chinese philosophy but also the inner contradictions of a district whose neon signs and tourist bustle mask a swarming, sweatshop world of long hours, low pay, hard work and fear. For all its outward ambiance, the largest Chinese enclave outside Asia is one of America's most wretched slums.

Over 40,000 Chinese are jammed into the 42 blocks of Chinatown proper between Bush Street and Broadway, Kearny and Powell. About 30,000 have spilled north and west into adjacent residential districts; 10,000 more live throughout the Bay Area.

They first came by the thousands to California—Gum San, land of the Golden Mountains—when the gold fields and railroads beckoned, and in smaller streams when the U.S. set up immigration quotas and California passed its racial exclusion laws in 1892. Despite the restrictions, so many Chinese have entered the U.S. in the past seven decades that perhaps as many as half the people of Chinatown are there in violation of the immigration laws.

Since Mao Tse-tung took over the Chinese mainland, immigration via Hong Kong has swelled incrementally: more than 4,000 Chinese a year now settle in the Bay Area, creating a job shortage so severe that exploitation is the order of the day—and night. The traditional Chinese family fabric has visibly frayed. With mothers working, delinquency climbs. Tenement squalor sustains a tuberculosis rate double that of San Francisco as a whole.

Working conditions are no better. The major sources of jobs are restaurants, curio stores and the sewing shops, comprising 151 small, family-oriented contract clothing factories employing about 20 seamstresses apiece. Paid on a piecework basis, the women often labor from 8:30 a.m. until after midnight, seven days a week, fingers darting frenetically to make ends meet. Asked why she would work at least 12 hours a day for a net income of $26 a week, one mother of five said succinctly: "You have to in Chinatown."

Ever since one Chum Ming sailed east from his native Kwangtung in 1847 to grow up with the country, California's Chinese have been victimized by their language problems (even today, no more than 40 percent speak fluent English), their fear of deportation, and traditional kowtowing to fate and station. San Francisco's youngest, brightest Chinese Americans leave for the suburbs at a rate of up to 15,000 a year, and Chinatown has become a way station for immigrants and a ghetto of the old and unemployed poor.

Only recently has Chinese pride permitted a lowering of the all but impenetrable veil that shrouded their condition from the outside world. California's Labor Commission and the San Francisco Central Labor Council have heard depressing testimony from Chinatown residents about working conditions in the district. Last week, led by the International Ladies' Garment Workers Union, labor opened a campaign of pickets, sanctions and the threat of boycott against eight Chinatown sewing shops and a contracting firm. Although the goal is not immediate unionization, the 25,000-member culinary workers union is waiting in the wings, and a labor spokesman called the drive "the opening gun in a campaign we hope will eventually end substandard wages and conditions in Chinatown shops, stores, factories and bars."

Band Member in 1968

Marshall Borowitz began playing the guitar at nine-years-old. After five years of music lessons, he started a cover band, which played together for one year. Marshall left the band and, at 16, started another band called One Night Stand. When the band was offered a one-month gig in South Carolina, Marshall and One Night Stand had one incredible summer.

Life at Home

- When he named his band "One Night Stand," Marshall Borowitz felt delightfully wicked and provocative.
- Later, when the bar closed down at 3:00 a.m. every night and the equipment still had to be packed and hauled to the VW bus, the mildly naughty name sounded like the monthly schedule set by his booking agent.
- Getting frisky at the end of an evening with the local groupies was pretty difficult when there was a three-hour drive still ahead.
- Band life on the road was, in a word, frustrating.
- Marshall was born on July 1, 1947, in Stamford, Connecticut, a product of the postwar years and part of what would come to be ubiquitously called the Baby Boomer generation.
- He grew up as the middle child in the family, the son of an IBM executive and a mother who loved to play bridge and drink whiskey sours after five o'clock.
- It was simply assumed that Marshall would attend college—he was never asked—and follow the pattern set by his do-gooder older sister, who knew how to get along.
- Marshall did not always know how to get along.
- During his teenaged years, he had thoroughly absorbed the raucous comedy albums of Lenny Bruce and spent many late-night hours listening to Bob Fass on WBAL, where he first heard Arlo Guthrie singing his 15-minute-long antiwar song "Alice's Restaurant."
- The entire universe was exploding with exciting music.
- Bob Dylan's *Blonde on Blonde*, the Jimi Hendrix Experience's *Are You Experienced?*, Cream's *Disraeli Gears*, and the Beatles' *Sgt. Pepper's Lonely Hearts Club Band* had all been released in 1967.
- What was the use of attending college to read seventeenth-century literature when a revolution was under way in the twentieth century?
- The Beatles were the modern Shakespeare; music had become the most comprehensive form of communication thus far invented by humankind.

Marshall Borowitz started his first band when he was 14-years-old.

One Night Stand was offered a one month job at the beach in South Carolina.

- The evidence was everywhere: Muddy Waters, Jefferson Airplane, Janis Joplin, Steppenwolf, Country Joe and the Fish, the Who, Otis Redding, the Rolling Stones.
- Two rock music-inspired magazines chronicled this explosion of creativity: Paul Williams's *Crawdaddy!*, created in 1966, and Jann Wenner's *Rolling Stone,* which followed in 1967.
- *Rolling Stone* signaled its expansive view of the cultural change under way when it informed its readers that it would be dedicated "not just to the music, but everything it represents."
- Music companies such as Elektra Records recognized the uniqueness of the moment; for example, Elektra assigned one employee (with the job title "company freak") to work with super talents such as Jim Morrison.
- Marshall became giddy at the sound of Janis Joplin singing "Me and Bobby McGee," and acquired enormous guilty pleasure from listening to the Rascals performing "Good Lovin'," "I've Been Lonely Too Long," and "People Got to Be Free."
- It was his older sister—the one he didn't want to be like—who convinced him that he had a good enough singing voice to accompany his masterful guitar work.
- One Night Stand, his band, was a kind of present to himself—his liberation vehicle after his junior year in high school.
- Several musicians in the area were looking for something to do; earning money as a band appealed to all.
- Before settling on the band's moniker, they tried out "Slippery When Wet," "Nighttime Itch Cream" and "Better with Beer." Each was rejected for a different reason.
- The next stage involved determining what kind of band they wanted to be: rock, blues rock, folk rock, or straight R&B?
- The cornucopia of emerging musical trends during his growing-up years made it difficult for Marshall to isolate a style.
- When he was ten years old, Marshall saw Buddy Holly and the Crickets play "It's So Easy" on *American Bandstand*; he was enthralled by the energy radiating from the band.
- The next year he wanted to be Bobby Darin singing "Mack the Knife," or a member of the R&B Drifters belting out "There Goes My Baby."
- And, like everyone else, he took a shot at Bob Dylan's singer/songwriter approach and discovered how high that hill had become.
- His first band, enthusiastically named the Seagram 7 (even though it only had five members), could predictably begin a dancing frenzy with Lesley Gore's "It's My Party" and any song by Little Richard—especially "Tutti Frutti.'"

Life at Work

- When Marshall Borowitz and his band One Night Stand were invited to take a one-month summer slot in North Myrtle Beach, South Carolina, in July 1968, Marshall couldn't believe his luck.
- The parental pressure factory was already heating up concerning his unwillingness to commit to college in the fall.
- Not only could he escape Connecticut for the sun and surf of South Carolina for part of the summer, but this fortuitous change of events would allow him to escape the "stink eye" his mother gave him every morning.
- Besides, being a part of the emerging cultural scene was special work.
- Rock music was on the verge of taking over the world, Marshall believed.

- The musical *Hair* was awakening society to the issues of the day, *Rolling Stone* magazine had become his Bible, and the entire nation, it seemed, had paused to mourn the death—in an airplane crash near Madison, Wisconsin—of Otis Redding, whose greatest hit, "Sittin' on the Dock of the Bay," was recorded three days before his death.
- But Marshall's first struggle was to convince the band.
- The drummer had a girlfriend he couldn't possibly leave for the summer, while the lead singer had agreed to work for his father, an optometrist, grinding glasses and helping to run his office.
- The bass guitarist had been planning to drive out West—but going south to the wide beaches of South Carolina sounded good enough for him.
- Eventually they all came around.
- The next challenge was the music. Although Marshall enjoyed the crosscurrents of cultural sound, he was unsure that the band's repertoire was sufficient for a teenage hangout magnet where the current dance craze was "The Shag."
- Marshall had seen the six-count, partnered dance featuring defined steps at the Myrtle Beach Pavilion the summer before, but he had failed to master the fancy footwork required.
- The dancers would be listening to songs by the Tams, the Temptations, the Drifters. To please this crowd of well-dressed dancers, the band would need to expand its play list.
- Problem number three was money-immediate cash.
- Once they arrived in Myrtle Beach, the gig included room and board and $79 each per week—more than enough incentive to leave Connecticut for South Carolina's annual bikini invasion.
- Recently gasoline had gone up to $0.37 a gallon, with rumors of it topping $0.40 per gallon by summer's end. And they still needed to buy replacement speakers and coordinate their clothes so they would look right.
- Marshall wanted the band to wear color-coordinated, shiny shirts during the first and second set and then change into a laid-back Hawaiian motif for the third and fourth sets.

The Myrtle Beach Pavilion–the band's job site—was surrounded by girls in bikinis.

- Problem number three, however, was promptly solved: Marshall's father okayed the entire scheme and agreed to front the necessary money—provided it was paid back.
- After two weeks of frantic rehearsing, at least six shouting matches over music selections and two boyfriend-girlfriend breakups, the band was ready.
- Or at least that's what they thought.
- Traditionally, every textile factory in North Carolina, South Carolina and Virginia closed down the week of July 4, providing its employees with a vacation and allowing time to bring in workers to completely clean and repaint the mill.
- In the Carolinas going on vacation meant one thing: Myrtle Beach.
- Marshall and his bandmates had never seen so many cars on so few roads; 60 miles outside their destination, cars came to a stop and barely moved.
- The VW bus they drove, which was originally bought in the cooler climate of Connecticut, didn't recognize the words *air conditioning.*

Traffic was always an issue in Myrtle Beach.

- When they finally arrived at Ocean Drive, they were hot and exhausted, but they were scheduled to play that night.
- Two members of the band took a nap on the beach and came back so sunburned they could barely walk; Marshall got everything set up and crossed his fingers.
- By the time they opened their first song, two hundred rampaging vacationers, eager for excitement, were milling around the dance floor.
- They didn't respond to the first three songs—two by the Rascals.
- That's when Marshall hauled out "Tutti-Frutti" and the room began to rock; he followed it with some James Brown.
- The second night was better; the third night was the best.
- That's when he met Penny, whose Southern accent was wider than her bikini bottom.
- It was also the night the drummer climbed off the stage and helped get the dancing going.
- By the end of the week, word was out: One Night Stand was the band to see.
- Their Tams imitations were terrible and their Beach Boys sound was off-key, but the mood was just right when they played.

- Marshall became hypersensitive to news in the music world: the opening of the Kaleidoscope Club, featuring Canned Heat and the Jefferson Airplane; Country Joe and the Fish's attempts to answer the question, "What does a piano sound like when dropped from a great height?," and the breakup of Buffalo Springfield.
- After two weeks they had their routine down: play till 2:00 a.m., party till 4, sleep till noon, eat cereal, spend time on the beach, spend time with new girlfriends, scrounge up something to eat at an all-you-can-eat restaurant and be on stage at 8:00 p.m.

- Marshall didn't want the summer to end, even though Penny had returned to Salisbury, North Carolina, and had not yet been replaced.
- He wanted music to be his life, and his mantra was taken straight out of *Rolling Stone* magazine.
- Writer Ralph Gleason wrote in the June 22, 1968, *Rolling Stone*: "At no time in American history has youth possessed the strength it possesses now. Trained by music, linked by music, it has the power for good change the world. That power for good carries the reverse, the power of evil."

Life in the Community: Myrtle Beach, South Carolina

- The Spanish explored the Myrtle Beach area as early as 1514, and in the 1700s Blackbeard's pirates inhabited its bays and inlets.
- Indigo plantations were established in the area, but transportation difficulties left most of the beach uninhabited until 1902, when the first railroad was created by the Burroughs and Chapin families.
- The arrival of the railroad began the transformation of Myrtle Beach from an isolated agricultural community into a summer beach resort.
- Still a sleepy community when the Great Depression arrived, Myrtle Beach, with its long stretch of white sand beaches, offered wealthy industrialist John T. Woodside the opportunity to purchase some 65,000 acres.

Myrtle Beach, South Carolina.

- His construction of a golf course and the magnificent Ocean Forest Hotel inaugurated Myrtle Beach's resort culture.
- Horry County officials made full use of New Deal programs to develop infrastructure and service institutions supporting the region.
- World War II further enhanced the development of Myrtle Beach; the region's population swelled with the creation of Myrtle Beach Army Air Force Base.
- Beginning in 1951 Myrtle Beach annually hosted Canadian-American Days during Ontario's spring break in March; tens of thousands of tourists flocked to the area for a week's worth of special events.
- These events and the construction of dozens of golf courses expanded the holiday season from four months to seven.
- The area was incorporated as a town in 1938 and became a city in 1957; the building of beach motels accelerated.
- The city's name refers to the wax myrtle shrub, which grows abundantly throughout the area.
- In May 1968, largely for marketing ease, the communities of Ocean Drive Beach, Cherry Grove, Crescent Beach and Windy Hill were combined into North Myrtle Beach.

Billboard's Top Songs: 1968

1. "Hey Jude," The Beatles

2. "Love Is Blue," Paul Mauriat

3. "Honey," Bobby Goldsboro

4. "(Sittin' on) The Dock of the Bay," Otis Redding

5. "People Got to Be Free," Rascals

6. "Sunshine of Your Love," Cream

7. "This Guy's in Love With You," Herb Alpert

8. "The Good, the Bad and the Ugly," Hugo Montenegro

9. "Mrs. Robinson," Simon and Garfunkel

10. "Tighten Up," Archie Bell and The Drells

11. "Harper Valley P.T.A.," Jeannie C. Riley

12. "Little Green Apples," O.C. Smith

13. "Mony, Mony," Tommy James and The Shondells

14. "Hello, I Love You," The Doors

15. "Young Girl," Gary Puckett and The Union Gap

16. "Cry Like a Baby," Box Tops

17. "Stoned Soul Picnic," Fifth Dimension

18. "Grazin' in the Grass," Hugh Masekela

19. "Midnight Confessions," The Grass Roots

20. "Dance to the Music," Sly and the Family Stone

21. "The Horse," Cliff Nobles and Co.

22. "I Wish It Would Rain," Temptations

23. "La-La Means I Love You," Delfonics

24. "Turn Around , Look At Me," Vogues

25. "Judy In Disguise (With Glasses)," John Fred and His Playboy Band

26. "Spooky," Classics IV

27. "Love Child," Diana Ross and The Supremes

28. "Angel of the Morning," Merrilee Rush

29. "Ballad of Bonnie and Clyde," Georgie Fame

30. "Those Were the Days," Mary Hopkin

31. "Born to Be Wild," Steppenwolf

32. "Cowboys to Girls," Intruders

33. "Simon Says," 1910 Fruitgum Company

34. "Lady Willpower," Gary Puckett and The Union Gap

35. "A Beautiful Morning," Young Rascals

Woman Golf Pro in 1968

Sally O'Neill played with her father's golf clubs when she was three, broke 100 at 9, and shot 73 when she was 14. After ten years of playing amateur golf, Sally turned professional when women's golf was enjoying unprecedented popularity—and her first day on the job was a dream come true.

Life at Home

- Sally was only three years old when she first picked up her father's golf club and pretended to take a swing.
- At nine she broke 100, and at 14 she shot 73 on a public course near her house.
- Her father's friends loved to carp about the frustration that golf engendered, to reassure themselves that golf was a "real" sport even though no one wore helmets.
- Sally understood the absolute joy of a smooth swing, a soft loft and a perfect landing.
- Sally also knew how it felt to make those periodic bad swings, but she always recalled her father's advice—hold on to the good moments.
- Sally's mother had fallen in love first with golf, then her husband, then her daughter and then alcohol.
- By the time Sally was six, her mother mostly loved alcohol.
- By second grade, Sally had learned not to invite friends over to the house.
- Her mother spent most afternoons passed out on the living room couch and didn't like the sound of giggly girls.
- Sally found refuge with her great-uncle at the pro shop, where he checked in players, sold equipment and kept the golf merchandise straight.
- Together they would prepare the evening meal and try to coax Sally's mother into eating something.
- Afterward they would play board games that emphasized patience, flexibility, planning ahead and keeping your cool.
- In later years, after Sally had left home, she always played board games before a major match, because it calmed her nerves.
- On late afternoons, when it was too late to start a round, Sally and her great-uncle would walk the course and swing at a few golf balls.
- First she developed her short game and practiced incessantly, punching the ball onto the green from 30 yards out.
- Only when she had her grip right and her confidence secure was she allowed to pick up a driver.

Sally O'Neill turned pro when women's golf was enjoying unprecedented popularity.

New golf courses were popping up everywhere.

- Some days her father would arrive at the golf course in time to walk a few holes before they went home.
- The 1960s was a time of great expansion for women's golf.
- By the time Sally was consistently winning tournaments in the early 1960s, every major men's tournament was either on television or preparing to be televised.
- New golf courses were popping up everywhere, and earth-moving equipment was allowing golf course designers to create imaginative new contours in the land.
- Riding mowers were making course maintenance less expensive, while encouraging larger and more complex greens and tees.
- Expanded air travel was allowing many to play on faraway courses, especially in the South, where the development of warm-weather grasses was creating new opportunities.
- It was also the age of television.
- Golf's premiere moment had come in 1953 on the final round of the Men's World Championship of Golf, for which a single camera had been positioned atop the grandstand.
- In that setting golfer Lew Worsham needed a birdie three to reach a playoff with Chandler Harper for the $25,000 first prize.
- After a perfect tee shot, Worsham faced a wedge approach for roughly 120 yards.
- From there he drove a low shot that continued to roll for 60 feet, straight into the hole for an eagle, to an outright victory.
- That historic moment, witnessed by thousands, ushered in television coverage of the 1954 Open and the Masters Golf Tournament in 1955.

Life at Work

- Sally O'Neill's first day at work was a dream come true.
- After a decade of playing amateur golf, Sally O'Neill had turned pro.
- Just standing next to Ladies Professional Golf Association star Kathy Whitworth was a thrill, but learning that she was paired to play a practice round with her hero was both intimidating and exhilarating.
- Unlike many of the wunderkinds who dominated the Ladies Professional Golf Association, Sally O'Neill was in her mid-twenties before she turned pro.
- But she fully understood what Kathy Whitworth meant when she said, "Golf just grabbed me by the throat. I used to think everyone knew what they wanted to do when they were 15 years old."
- Kathy's parents owned a hardware store in Texas, where she grew up as the youngest of three daughters, and she learned golf using her grandfather's clubs on the nine-hole course built for employees of El Paso Natural Gas.
- Two years after taking up the game at age 15, Whitworth won the 1957 New Mexico Women's Amateur golf tournament, a success she repeated the next year.

Sally's first day on the job was a dream come true.

- Although unpolished, Whitworth had all the shots—from a stellar bunker game to creative recoveries she honed as a teen.
- When she was 20, her father and a couple of local businessmen agreed to subsidize Whitworth's career at $5,000 a year for three years.
- She made $1,217 the first year and came within a hair's breadth of quitting.
- She stayed on the tour after her parents advised, "You have three years. If you don't make it, just come home and we'll do something else."
- It was a story well known to Sally, who didn't have even one year's worth of cushion.
- At 26 she had one shot at making the pro circuit.
- A failed marriage was behind her, and she only saw gold ahead.
- On the first tee, Sally positioned herself like a pro, drove like a pro and acted like a pro.
- That lasted through three holes.
- Even though it was only a practice round, Sally was immensely aware that Kathy Whitworth was already ahead, having birdied the first and third holes.
- Sally started to panic—how could she possibly compete at this level every day and make a living?
- On the par-four fourth hole, Sally sliced her tee shot, fired a second shot in the bunker, put the third shot into the back corner of the green, chipped the fourth shot 30 feet beyond the hole, missed the cup on her fifth shot and then dropped in a two-footer for a double bogey six.
- She was so embarrassed, she couldn't even look at Kathy.
- Number five was better, but shaky.
- Number six was a disaster. Number seven was even worse.
- On number eight, a par-five dogleg littered with water traps, Kathy teed off first, then stepped beside Sally and said, "Looks like you're trying to copy some of my early rounds when I was just getting started."
- Sally understood.
- She parred the eighth and ninth holes and then fired a 34 on the back nine.
- When Kathy and Sally parted at the end of the day, Kathy said quietly, "I'll be watching you tomorrow."

Life in the Community: The Ladies Professional Golf Association (LPGA)

- The early years of the twentieth century were dominated by British women golfers; few American women won major trophies.
- Sisters Harriot and Margaret Curtis—holders of the U.S. Women's Amateur title in 1906 and 1907, respectively; Margaret repeated in 1911 and 1912—played in the British Ladies Amateur Golf Championship but never dominated.

Early years of women's golf.

- Glenna Collett Vare, who captured six U.S. Women's Amateurs between 1922 and 1935, was known for her rhythmic, smooth swing, which produced long, straight shots—but she never won the British Ladies Amateur.
- It was not until 1947 that the British Ladies Amateur title went to an American: Babe Didrikson Zaharias, a superb athlete who had previously won gold medals at the 1932 Olympics for the javelin and the 80-meter hurdles.
- In 1950 the Ladies Professional Golf Association was formed, with 11 women as its charter members; the effort was underwritten by Wilson Sporting Goods.

- In addition to Didrikson Zaharias, freckled-faced Patty Berg emerged as a star of the LPGA, and she served as its first president.
- By 1952 the LPGA boasted a schedule of 21 events—nearly three times the number of tournaments held just two years before.
- Prize money for the LPGA Tour reached $200,000 in 1959.
- The LPGA received its first television coverage in 1963, during the final round of the U.S. Women's Open Championship.
- By the end of the 1960s, prize money had grown to $600,000 and the schedule offered 34 events.
- "Kathy Whitworth Leads in Tourney," Robert Grimm,

Mansfield News Journal (Ohio), August 25, 1968

SPRINGFIELD—Kathy Whitworth, playing her best with big money on the line, fired a three under par 69 Saturday to take a one-stroke lead over Carol Mann after the first round for $35,000 in the Ladies World Series of Golf.

Miss Whitworth, the defending champion in the third annual event, recovered from a bogey on the first hole of the six-woman tournament and played nearly flawlessly the rest of the way.

Her competition faltered in the steamy 90-degree temperature over the 6,194 yard Snyder Park course here.

Miss Mann, recovering on the back nine from an almost disastrous start, was one stroke behind with a 38-32-70 score, followed by Sandra Haynie at even par 72. Susie Maxwell Berning and Sandra Post were at 73 and Mickey Wright was trailing with a six over par 78.

Miss Whitworth played steady golf at one time and at one time on the front nine held a four-stroke lead over Miss Mann. But the six-foot three Miss Mann, leading money winner on the LPGA tour this year, wound up her round in a sensational way, with consecutive birdies on the 16th and 17th holes and an eaglethree on the par five 140-yard 18th hole.

Ski Lodge Operators in 1968

Woody and Eva Duker operated a ski lodge in Winter Park, Colorado at a time when the ski industry in Colorado was experiencing phenomenal growth. They made all their income from December to April and, if it was a good season, they traveled in May and June. To improve business, the Dukers lobbied for a recent innovation—artificial snowmaking.

Life at Home

- The Dukers maintained a double room in the back of the lodge as their home, constantly commingling life at home with life at work.
- Their lodge was one of the oldest in the area; although their facilities were aging, their customers were loyal.
- Yet they worried that if they did not install saunas, improve lighting and upgrade the lodge, people would stop coming.
- On the other hand, if they were to make all the improvements, they were unsure they would attract enough customers to stay in business.
- The skiing season extended from December through April; during the season the Dukers made all of their income for the year.
- In May and June they liked to travel—if the ski season had been lucrative enough.
- The previous year, their ski lodge, and Winter Park in general, had experienced a 12 percent drop in business from the prior year.
- They hoped that the 1968–69 season would be better.
- To try to ensure more business, this couple joined a group lobbying for artificial snowmaking, a recent innovation in some ski areas.
- They thought it would help them create a longer season and that by laying a snow base earlier, they could attract more skiers who knew that an adequate base would always be available.
- Snowmaking was not only expensive but required tremendous quantities of water; some large Eastern ski areas spent $50,000 or more to produce snow during a season.
- Snowmaking was feasible only in locations where the nightly temperature range was from 20 to 25 degrees; Winter Park certainly qualified.

The Duker's operated a ski lodge, attached to their home, in Winter Park, Colorado.

- In 1963 Ski Broadmoor and Geneva Basin in Colorado had both installed snowmaking equipment; by 1968 snowmaking facilities were available on the lower practice slopes at seven ski areas.

- Communities such as Aspen and Vail were developing year-round recreation centers to attract visitors; Woody and Eva were eager to be less dependent on just five months' activity to support them the entire year.
- A recent decision by the federal government to group holidays on Mondays, creating three-day weekends, looked like it might increase their business, but this was still uncertain.
- Winter Park had a long history as a ski resort; many in Denver considered Winter Park the place for "locals" to ski.
- A recent survey of skiers had revealed that Vail, Winter Park, Aspen, Stowe, and Mammoth were their favorite weekend ski areas.
- The survey also showed that the skiers' favorite resorts were Vail, Aspen, Winter Park, Europe, Sun Valley, Alta, Jackson Hole, Squaw Valley, Steamboat, Stowe, and Breckenridge.
- The Dukers feared that the real action was now at Aspen's Buttermilk Mountain or at Meadow Mountain, near Vail.

Life at Work

- The ski industry in Colorado, including in Winter Park, was experiencing phenomenal growth.
- The number of skiers visiting Colorado during the 1966–67 season had increased 14-fold since the 1955–56 season.
- Nonresident skiers spent an estimated $41.3 million during the 1966–67 season, compared with $3 million in 1955-56.

- Overall lift-ticket sales throughout Colorado increased 15.2 percent from 1965–66 to 1966–67—but competition was cutting into income.
- Statewide the ski-lift ticket sales increased to $1,221,300.
- Yet in Winter Park the number of skiers using the lifts dropped from 203,000 during the 1965–66 season to 179,200 in 1966–67, a decrease of 11.8 percent.
- The Winter Park community was concerned; Arapahoe Basis, Buttermilk Mountain, Crested Butte, Monarch, and Snowmass had all had a 20 percent or more increase in ski-lift usage.
- Some areas were experimenting with night skiing to improve revenues and increase usage; most of these areas, such as Arapahoe Basis, Durango, Meadow Mountain and Snowmass, were on the lower slopes.
- As the number of ski areas increased, attracting more skiers, the number of lodges also swelled.
- Going into the 1968–69 season, there were 20 lodges operating in Winter Park.
- Most tended to be geared to family skiers, offering a warm, friendly atmosphere but little emphasis on nightlife.
- Rates ran from a low of $3.50 for a single to a high of $28 for a double.

- The Dukers' lodge charged $10 a night for a single and $18 for a double, breakfast and dinner included.
- Winter Park was the last ski area in the United States to be served by a genuine snow train, operated by the Rio Grande Railroad on Saturdays and Sundays during the season.
- Locals believed that one of the most awe-inspiring sights in skiing was seeing the train disgorge its load of a thousand or more Denver skiers.
- Yet such weekend activity was not optimal for the ski lodge, which needed week-long visitors to maximize its profits; weekend guests only rented for one or two days, while staff was working all seven.
- Winter Park was known for grooming its slopes to withstand the onslaught of visitors, using the Bradley Packer-Grader, which chopped off moguls.
- Topography was Colorado's—and Winter Park's—greatest asset; its light-powder snow was extremely good and offered a great variety of experiences to the vacation skier. It was also high-altitude skiing, which, for some, took a little getting used to.

Winter Park was known for well-groomed slopes and well-maintained equipment.

- Winter Park attracted skiers who considered skiing a leisure activity; it also attracted big names in racing, both for training and for actual races.
- On weekends Winter Park was packed with Denver skiers who made the one-hour drive up the mountain—often on a whim.
- Many skiers, including tourists who arrived in Denver by air, made their skiing destination decision based on which area had the "best powder" for maximum skiing conditions.
- Many thought that Rocky Mountain powder was easier to ski than any other snow in the world.

Life in the Community: Winter Park, Colorado

- Skiing had an impact on every part of Colorado's, and Winter Park's, economy.
- Businesses tied to the success of the season included airlines, auto-rental agencies, service stations, real-estate developments, restaurants, lodging places and ski clothing and equipment manufacturers and retailers.
- On average a skier spent more than $300 on skiwear and equipment before hitting the slopes.
- The cost of skis was about $170; boots cost $80 and bindings, $30; ski poles ran $35 a pair; and gloves cost $30 a pair.

Ski lessons were popular.

- The state boasted 38 ski areas in operation; 22 were open daily and 16 operated on weekends only.
- Most were located below the timberline, at 7,000 to 11,000 feet in altitude; the altitude protected the slopes and made them less susceptible to sudden thaws and freezes, giving Colorado a natural advantage over other ski regions.
- During the 1967–68 season, more than $41 million was spent in Colorado by nonresident skiers; Colorado accounted for more than 27 percent of all skiing expenditures in the 12 Western states.

The Winter Park Ski Industry

- Up until the turn of the century, skiing was largely a means of survival, not recreation.
- Ski clubs formed in the 1920s, but in the days before rope tows or T-Bars, skiers walked up the trail for the privilege of a short ride down the mountain.
- The dream of creating a mountain ski area was assisted by the completion of a railway line in the 1930s.
- George E. Cranmer was the father of the Winter Park ski area; he dreamed of a mountain city park that could become a winter sports center.

Many Denver residents often drove to Winter Park for a ski weekend.

- He envisioned this city park—60 miles from the city—as a recreational "gift to the children of Denver"
- He was supported by a group of prominent Denver businessmen who formed themselves into the Arlberg Club.
- A clubhouse was built on the Mary Jane Placer claim in 1933; the U.S. Forest Service cut trails by 1937.
- In 1938, the U.S. Forest Service granted the City of Denver a special-use permit for some 6,400 acres of land for winter sports and recreational development.
- That same year, the Denver City Council accepted a grant from the Federal Emergency Administration of Public Works to construct park improvements to include ski tows and ski-ways.
- In 1939, the city of Denver acquired 100 acres of land at the mouth of Jim Creek, adjacent to West Portal.
- To assist in the promotion of this new ski area, the name West Portal was changed to the more family-oriented "Winter Park."
- A crowd of 10,000 turned out for the first annual three-day "Winter Sports Festival."
- By 1942, a snow train carrying 500 Denver children began the tradition of weekend skiing Cranmer dreamed about.
- By 1946, with the war ending, skier volume broke all records; Winter Park was firmly established as a ski destination.
- Skiers could stay overnight in a bunkhouse for $0.50.
- By 1949, ski trains carrying up to 1,500 people were arriving in Winter Park for a weekend of fun.
- The *Chicago Tribune* praised the access to the area by train; skiing in the Denver area increased by 75 percent, with more than 26,500 skiing during the 1949-50 season.
- New lifts increased capacity in the 1950s; at the same time, Winter Park began grooming its slopes-an innovative feature.
- The popularity of Winter Park spread during the 1960s Olympics at Squaw Valley, where many of the area's ski patrols participated in the international event.
- By 1967, the Winter Park Ski School had grown to 28 instructors because of demand.

"Why Ski Colorado?" *Colorado Skiing, 1968*

"Colorado's light, silky powder snow is unique in the American West. It has to be skied to be believed. Powder snow is abundant in Colorado because of the dependable west winds that bring bounteous moisture from the Pacific. Colorado snow is dry and powdery because the wind's long journey over the desert has evaporated the excess moisture out of the clouds before the sharp cold of the Rockies makes it fall. Colorado powder remains sparkling and white because the dry, smog-free air keeps the snow crisp and white long after it falls.

Colorado ski lodges are new—built within the last five to 10 years, for the most part. This means up-to-date facilities: baths, saunas, comfortable beds, adequate heating, and heated swimming pools. It also means modern means of management, assuring prompt replies to your inquiries, and a minimum of confusion and reservations, even at peak seasons.

As a state, Colorado is less than 100 years old, scarcely two generations from frontier times. As a result, Colorado people still have much of the old-time frontier openness and friendliness to the stranger that is lost in many overcrowded parts of America. Sprinkled in with native Coloradans are many newcomers: Swiss, Austrian, German, Italian, and French skiers, as well as Eastern Americans who have 'gone West' to ski, and never returned."

Survey of Vail (Colorado) Skiers: Conclusions, 1968

"He is younger than we had previously believed—29.2 years, as compared with our hypothetical 35-year-old average skier. Even accounting for holiday and weekend incursions of students, this average age indicates a departure from the classic long-stay resort guest pattern. Apparently, higher incomes among young college graduates, greater mobility, and increased vacation time have allowed a younger crowd to enjoy the type of winter resort experience once reserved for the affluent middle-aged.

There is a curious inconsistency in the length of stay as compared to the type of (lift) tickets sold. The average stay is 5.2 days (6.4 days for the in-week guest). Yet only 22 percent of those surveyed bought five- or seven-day tickets and seven percent bought packages, while 46 percent bought single day tickets! It is obvious that many customers prefer to keep their options open, skiing when they wish, rather than locking themselves into a week of daily skiing. In this respect, the Vail skier is more like the European skier, whose activity pattern is relaxed and varied, than the traditional western resort customer, who skis determinedly, every day, during his vacation.

As might be expected, the Vail skier, like most other sportsmen, somewhat over-evaluates his abilities. Note that he has listed as his favorite slopes at Vail the three most difficult areas: The Bowls, Prima, and Riva Ridge. Yet 49 percent of all surveyed are beginning or intermediate skiers, who have no business skiing such slopes. Dreams of glory intrude even into the dry pages of a customer survey…

As brought into sharp focus by this survey, the Vail customer is nearly ideal from a ski resort marketing point of view. He is young, affluent, highly mobile, well-educated, largely white-collar in profession.

Even more significant, in view of the product Vail offers, is his dedication to skiing. A skier for nearly seven years, he intends to devote a month of each year to the sport. His family skis, too, and nearly everyone owns his ski equipment (88 percent).

He is largely undemanding, in terms of the more sophisticated frills of resort life, so long as the skiing is good. If lifts run smoothly, and slopes and snow are right, he is a happy, satisfied customer. Only a few small clouds darken his horizon. Because many others like him have discovered Vail, there are lift lines at peak holiday times, and prices for Vail-type facilities seem too high."

Electronics Worker in 1968

Marian Whitley worked at a leading electronics manufacturing plant—one of the first corporations in Memphis to hire black workers. Her husband, Richard, farmed the family land and hired himself out to neighboring farms. Marian, Richard, and their young daughter, lived in a mobile home on the property Marian inherited from her father.

Life at Home

- In addition to farming the family land, Richard hired himself out to neighbors, many of them white, in the spring and fall; he also sold fertilizer to earn extra income.
- In addition to growing vegetables for sale and use at home, he prided himself on his hunting skills; deer, squirrel and turtle were part of the family diet.
- Marian was one of the 40,000 people who drove into Memphis to work each morning.
- Developers were buying nearby farms for the expanding suburbs of rapidly growing Memphis; land speculation was rampant. The family had not decided whether or not to sell the family farm if asked.
- They were uncertain where they would move to if they agreed to sell the farm; most African Americans in Memphis—even those with money—lived in the often-substandard homes in the older section of town, because Memphis had few integrated neighborhoods.
- The approach of the suburbs also brought libraries; Memphis had nearly 20 library branches. Janet considered herself a good reader, and the library was important to her.
- Both parents believed that their third-grade daughter would have a better life with more opportunities than they had had, especially if she did well in school.

Marian Whitley worked at one of the first corporations in Memphis to hire black workers.

Life at Work

- Marian's employer, a nationally known electronics company, began manufacturing operations in Memphis in 1947, with 100 employees producing electronic components such as headphones and condensers.
- By 1968 the plant employed 1,200 workers, spread evenly over three shifts.

- Most of the workforce comprised middle-aged white women, who worked at machines producing small, delicate components.
- The first black employee had been hired in 1961, during a period of expansion.
- African American workers were added at the Memphis facility because of corporate pressure and a gradual change in the racial climate in Memphis as cafeterias, drinking fountains, public restrooms and similar facilities were desegregated.
- At the plant racial relationships were considered good by both black and white workers; in the cafeteria black workers normally sat together, apart from the white workers, out of tradition and choice.
- Black leaders thought that the changes in hiring practices took place not because of marches or demonstrations but because of the nondiscriminatory workplace requirements placed on government contracts.
- Most African Americans hired by the company had a high school diploma, and one-third had college experience; approximately one-fourth of the white workers did not have a high school diploma, and only seven percent had attended college.
- By 1968 half of all new hires were black women; only 16 black men were employed among the 1,200 workers.
- Typically the jobs required little training.
- The plant experienced little unionization.
- The electronics manufacturing industry, dominated by companies such as Westinghouse and General Electric, was growing rapidly.
- From 1923 to 1958, total employment in the electronics manufacturing industry grew threefold; electric-power consumption, measured in kilowatt hours, grew 16-fold.
- In 1968 sales of appliances and electronic products increased 9.0 percent, and profits, 18.2 percent, over the prior year.

Life in the Community: Memphis, Tennessee

- Memphis, at the extreme southwestern corner of Tennessee, sat high on a bluff overlooking the Mississippi River; it was the county seat of Shelby County.
- Memphis's economy had always been tied to the river; the city grew as a center where cotton bales were sold, loaded onto riverboats and shipped down the waterway.
- Firestone, RCA, International Harvester, General Electric and other well-known companies settled in the city, once known best for the blues, gambling and catfish.
- Over time, following a national pattern, neighborhoods near downtown Memphis became more African American, while new all-white suburbs sprang up around the city.
- With a population of nearly 550,000, Memphis was the largest city not only in Tennessee but in the region, including the bordering states of Mississippi and Arkansas.
- About 200,000 of Memphis's residents, or 40 percent of the city's population, were black.
- Many migrants from the cotton and soybean farms of the Mississippi delta settled in the

Memphis, Tennessee, showing Mississippi River and Riverside Drive by Moonlight

Memphis, Tennessee.

city; just 56 percent of Memphis's population had been born in Tennessee, and more than 25 percent had lived in Memphis for fewer than five years.

- Approximately 57 percent of the African American families had incomes below the poverty level of $3,000 a year, while only 13.8 percent of white families lived below the poverty line.
- At the 1960 census, the median educational level of Memphis's African American residents over 25 years old was 6.7 years; the median educational level for whites over 25 was 11.1 years.
- Achievement tests showed black eighth-graders testing two grades behind white eighth-graders.
- The Shelby County school system was not desegregated until 1963; in 1968 the vast majority of the public schools were still de facto segregated.
- In 1968 only 3 of 13 city councilmen were black; just 5 percent of all school board members were African American.
- Early in 1968 civil rights activists encouraged black sanitation workers to strike, supported by the American Federation of State, County, and Municipal Employees' Union (AFSCME) and black ministers in the area; Reverend Martin Luther King Jr. took a leadership role.
- Pay for garbage workers was $70.00 a week; all of the supervisors were white, while workers typically were African Americans recruited from farms.
- The mayor considered the strike to be unwarranted, declaring "I don't make deals." King was branded an irresponsible rabble-rouser.
- From their pulpits Memphis's black ministers compared the strikers with Old Testament prophets who crusaded against injustice; they took up special collections for the workers and asked their congregations to join them in daily marches to downtown Memphis.
- In less than a week, $15,000 was raised to support the strikers; sales in downtown businesses dropped by 35 percent.
- On March 14, 1968, NAACP executive secretary Roy Wilkins spoke to a rally of 9,000; four days later, Reverend Martin Luther King Jr., spoke to an audience estimated at 25,000 and called for a one-day general strike of all workers.
- Riots broke out during a downtown march on March 28; a 16-year-old was killed, 60 people were injured and 300 demonstrators were arrested; the mayor called for martial law and brought in 4,000 National Guard troops.
- The president of the local Chamber of Commerce blamed the violence on activist preachers, saying, "If the Negro ministers would tend to their ministering instead of trying to stir things up, we wouldn't have had this trouble."
- King returned to Memphis from Atlanta on 3 April. Speaking to the sanitation workers and supporters, King told them, "I've seen the Promised Land. I may not get there with you. But I want you to know tonight that we, as a people, will get to the Promised Land."
- Reverend Martin Luther King Jr. was shot and killed on April 4, 1968, at the Lorraine Motel in Memphis. Memphis, along with cities across the nation, experienced rioting that night.
- The city eventually agreed to pay the garbage workers an extra $0.10 per hour and to permit union dues to be handled through a credit union and then paid to the AFSCME.

Civil Rights in Memphis

- On December 1, 1955, 42-year-old Rosa Parks helped launch a movement by refusing to surrender her bus seat to a White passenger; the federal courts ruled segregation of the Montgomery, Alabama, buses unconstitutional in 1956.

- In response Memphis post office employee O.Z. Evers filed a suit against the Memphis bus company in 1956 to desegregate that city's buses.
- Black banker and NAACP board member Jessie Turner filed a desegregation suit against the Memphis Public Library in 1958.
- John F. Kennedy promised during his 1960 presidential campaign to exercise "moral and persuasive leadership" to enforce the 1954 Supreme Court decision calling for desegregated schools.
- By 1960 a generation of high school Black students had grown up knowing that the Supreme Court had ruled the educational apartheid they were experiencing was against the law of the land.
- Resentment and frustration burst to the surface in the 1960s across the nation.
- Challenges to the official barriers to Blacks seeking public accommodations included sit-in demonstrations at drug stores, freedom rides on public buses across the South, and marches in hundreds of cities across the nation, although principally in the South.
- Student sit-ins began nationwide in 1960; 41 Memphis College students were arrested for entering two segregated libraries.
- The racially mixed Memphis Committee on Community Relations urged voluntary desegregation; the buses were desegregated in the fall of 1960, libraries in October, and the Overton Park Zoo in December of that year.
- To avoid a Black boycott, the Memphis downtown merchants agreed to volunteer desegregation in January 1962—provided that no changes were required during the 1961 Christmas season.
- Thirteen Black students integrated four Memphis schools in the fall of 1961 without incident; officials were so fearful of riots that even the teachers were not informed of the planned integration of their classrooms until the night before.

Signs of segregation were throughout the city.

- In 1962 the movie theaters of the city were integrated secretly. With the cooperation of the theater managers, a Black couple was selected to integrate the Malco Theatre. When nothing happened to the couple, the following week two Black couples were sent to integrate another theater; by April, 1963, 14 theaters had been integrated in this way.
- When publicity about the progressive work of the Memphis Committee on Community Relations appeared in the Memphis newspaper, the White chairman, a respected former Memphis banker, received anonymous letters addressed to the "nigger lover" and stating, "race mixing is communism."

- As part of an agreement to voluntarily integrate the 20 largest restaurants in the city, and thus avoid picketing, the restaurant owners insisted that the *Memphis Appeal* not report that integration of the eating establishments was taking place.
- Until 1965 the Tennessee Department of Employment Security maintained segregated offices; employers who wanted White workers called one office, for Black workers, another separate facility.

Student Body President in 1968

Carl Cochrane, at 17-years-old, was the president of his school's student body, a member of the National Honor Society, excelled in both school plays and mathematics. And, like any other high school student in 1968, Carl wrestled with the impact of the Vietnam War, the murder of Martin Luther King, and the right time to try for his first kiss.

Life at Home

- Carl Cochrane was not only president of the student body at his high school but head of the National Honor Society, the beta club and the drama club; he got invited to all the best parties, even though he often didn't go.
- His SAT scores totaled 1180, split fairly evenly between math and verbal; with these scores and an all-A average, he was assured of acceptance into almost any college he chose.
- He wanted to attend the College of William and Mary in Virginia and enter the prelaw program, although he was unsure of exactly what that entailed.
- He loved the challenge of math, the memorization of history, and his biology teacher.
- His father was a college theater professor, and his mother was a drama teacher at his high school; there was always a play, a rehearsal or some other drama-related activity going on. Up and out in the morning, free in the afternoon and back to the theater for rehearsals at night was a schedule Carl had experienced his entire life.
- Meals, prepared by his father, often were hurried, and it was not unusual for dishes to be stacked up in the sink after dinner until the next morning, when breakfast was prepared.
- If it were not for Daisy Douglas, the black maid who came each morning, the household might not run at all.
- Daisy was paid $35 a week.
- A typical dinner might include fried chicken and well-cooked vegetables, rice, gravy and a salad.
- The only seasonings allowed in the house were salt, pepper and barbecue sauce; his father claimed that his stomach had been ruined in graduate school and in the military, and he could only tolerate bland foods.
- Carl was the only child at home; his brilliant, flamboyant and dominating brother Greg had left for Yale, while his younger sister was at Whitten Village, a home for retarded children.

Carl Cochrane was president of his high school's student body.

- It was liberating to be out from under the shadow of his big brother, but Carl was lonely, also; when Greg was around, something was always happening—good, bad or wild.
- Although college was expensive, the Cochranes believed in education; learning was good—money would take care of itself.
- Carl spent most afternoons working as a clerk in a small law office, two to three hours each day, for $1.25 an hour; he used his paycheck to support his music habit, particularly to upgrade his drum kit.
- His band, the Claystone Blues, practiced often and loudly; paying gigs were rare, most often consisting

Carl loved math and history.

of junior-high parties and small dances in the neighboring towns of Fort Mill or Chester.
- Carl loved the role of entertainer—especially as a drummer, but he was learning to enjoy stepping up to be lead singer as well.
- His songs often tracked from the greatest-hits list of the Tams, the Drifters, Billy Stewart, the Swinging Medallions and Otis Redding.
- The group rarely did Motown, preferring Southern soul to the overproduced, as they thought, sounds of Detroit.
- The music world was still buzzing about the Beatles's groundbreaking 1967 album *Sgt. Pepper's Lonely Hearts Club Band*, featuring experimental sounds, nontraditional instruments, enigmatic songs and a psychedelic ambience that seemed to express a new direction in art and music; it also was the first album ever to include printed lyrics on its cover.
- Whenever Carl stepped into the theater world of his parents, he immediately moved backstage; he had developed considerable expertise in the technical aspects of running a play.
- He loved being known as the "lighting guy," because so few could compete for the role.
- Both his mother and father took great pride in their heritage; they collected antique furniture.
- Their collection included an Elizabethan chest with *1670* carved on its lid, a three-legged carved Jacobean chair, two-hundred-year-old Chippendale chairs, original paintings by some of America's most renowned artists and, in the dining room, 12 sets of china.
- Even though the family had collected all the china from their ancestral lines, Carl's father still brought home dinner plates given away at the grocery store as premiums.
- In Carl's open, high-ceilinged bedroom were an oak rolltop desk found in North Carolina, the bed in which his father and ten uncles and aunts had been born, and a collection of statues, including a figure of David and a World War I Uncle Sam with only one arm.

The Cochrane home was large and welcoming.

- The house was chilly, owing to its high ceilings, poor insulation and retrofitted heating system.
- The two-story, colonial-style house, purchased when Carl was in the fourth grade, cost $8,000.
- His parents had borrowed $10,000 from the bank, investing the extra $2,000 in a heating system that was never quite up to the task of warming the rambling, 6,000-square-foot home.
- But hot or cold, people were always welcome; the door was always open to students, former students, actors, friends, great-aunts, friends of great-aunts and the lonely.

- Carl's mother loved to entertain with grand gestures, as though she were performing a role never quite relinquished.
- As a result everyone felt welcome at almost any time of the day or night.
- This was especially true at Christmas, when the entire family erected an all-white Christmas tree in the front hall.
- Following a longstanding family tradition, the boys cut a 10-foot sweet gum tree growing near the railroad tracks that had lost all of its leaves.
- Then they carefully wrapped each and every limb in cotton ticking to create the image of a multilimbed tree just after a snowstorm.
- To enhance the effect, each limb was trimmed with silver tinsel, with the tinsel icicles placed one at a time on the tree, each at a precise distance from the last.

Carl's parents both taught in theater-related disciplines.

- The display, when seen through the front door, was impressive enough to stop traffic on the street, once even attracting a photographer from *Southern Living* magazine.
- The house also attracted stray animals; cats, dogs and mice all found a place there.
- But keeping the house running took work; after returning home from his job, Carl often assisted his father in physical work around the house—hauling furniture, digging roots out of the sewer lines or cutting down trees; they also constructed theater sets.
- Because the family had only one car, Carl often cut his Friday-night dates short so he could be back to take Aunt Katie home before it got too late.
- He led a split life; nine months in his hometown and the three summer months in Manteo, North Carolina, at the Lost Colony, an outdoor theater production company.
- There, night after night, the story of the arrival of English settlers in the New World and the birth of young Virginia Dare was performed for tourists, who were invariably mesmerized both by the drama itself and by the energy that accompanied outdoor theater.
- When Carl was small, his mother played the glamorous role of Queen Elizabeth II, directed by his father; in his earliest days, Carl was the newborn baby featured in the play.
- In the mid-1950s, their pictures appeared prominently in *National Geographic* in a feature on the outer banks of North Carolina; his mother was shown in costume, while Carl and his father were featured eating watermelon.
- Growing up at the theater, he enjoyed the rhythms of the work, the controlled chaos and the teamwork.
- Better yet, he spent hours rehearsing with the college girls who annually arrived to learn acting or dancing.
- During the school year, his constant love was Jill Clarke, an energetic, beautiful pixie; they spent hours talking and thinking and dreaming about the future.
- Jill's governing rule was: during dates both of her feet stayed on the ground at all times.

Jill Clarke was the love of Carl's life.

- They had been dating for two years, ever since their first cotillion dance, held annually at the town's Moose Lodge.
- During his summers away, Carl had found that some of the young women attracted by the summertime bliss of professional acting had less strict governing rules.
- But a lifetime of going to Manteo year after year had had its penalties.
- Traditionally, when school ended, nearly every high school student in the state journeyed to Myrtle Beach for a week, to party.
- By the end of each summer, when Carl returned to town, the revelry that supposedly took place during First Week had been magnified in retellings to epic proportions, making Carl envious.
- His time away working at the Lost Colony also meant he could not participate in the late-summer football practices that were a ritual of high school life; as a result he never went out for the team.

Carl enjoyed participating in school productions.

- He and several of his buddies worked on repairing a 1957 Triumph TR3 given to Carl by his friend Leon; over nearly a year, they replaced the rusted metal floor with plywood, found a hood, tinkered with the engine and installed seats by nailing the seat belts to the floor.
- When the moment of victory arrived, the engine roared to life, and Carl took his first exhilarating ride—until the police arrived.
- Because they could not afford a muffler, Carl and his friends had used a straight pipe to vent the exhaust, producing a highly pleasing roaring sound that attracted both the neighbors and the local police.
- Carl got a stern warning, but there were no other repercussions.

Life at School

- As student body president, Carl started every day by making the school announcements over the intercom.
- Trips by the 4-H Club, victories by the school's sports teams and requests that no one walk on the gym floor until the finish dried all got top billing.
- Good school spirit was important to Carl; it signaled that all was well.

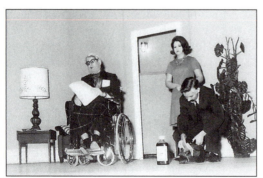
Carl's drama classroom was always alive with activity and sound.

- Although he was not involved in sports, he loved the excitement of the football games and holding his girlfriend close when the team did well.
- Everyone knew him, both because of his active student role and because his mother was one of the school's most popular teachers.
- Her drama classroom was always alive with motion and sound, including exaggerated physical action and loud, dramatic speeches—activities not permitted elsewhere.
- The previous fall the school's production of *The Man Who Came to Dinner* had attracted 150 student actors and technicians; the show had run three

consecutive nights in the 1,200-seat school auditorium, and each performance had sold out.

- For a second year, students from the nearby black high school had been allowed to attend Carl's all-white school through the "freedom of choice" plan.
- The ninth, tenth, eleventh and twelfth grades achieved a racial mix of approximately 5 percent black and 95 percent white.
- Many of the African Americans who chose to attend the white school were the children of black teachers and other professionals.
- Carl believed the freedom of choice plan gave everyone an equal opportunity, although he was concerned that many of the black students had been placed in the less-challenging tracks, along with the kids from the textile mills.
- Few of the freedom-of-choice kids were in his college preparatory classes, although several were doing well on the football and basketball teams.
- To cope with the new sensitivity expressed by the black students, the marching band had learned to play the song "Dixie" more slowly and somberly so it would be less offensive.
- When Carl's mother had invited the entire high school drama club—including the three black members—to the Cochrane home for a celebration party, there had been whispers that this integrated social gathering could attract members of the Ku Klux Klan; to everyone's relief, none had appeared.

Carl was a popular president of his high school class.

- When Carl gave everyone a tour of the house, he had included a visit to his room, where there hung a framed Confederate flag that had been carried by a relative during the Civil War; at least one of the black students was shocked.
- It was during a spring-semester school trip to Washington and Lee College in Lexington, Virginia, that Carl had learned of the murder in Memphis of Reverend Martin Luther King Jr.
- Carl was traveling with a group of eight from the high-school newspaper; the leaders decided to stick with the prearranged schedule, including a trip to the Natural Bridge and then a tour of the college.
- Silently Carl had spent considerable time trying to sort out what the shooting would mean, while looking for an appropriate gift to take home for his girlfriend.

Carl thought carefully about his stand on the Vietnam War.

- That night several members of the group had been positive they could see Washington, DC, burning when the riots broke out, but Carl had been unsure of where his sight ended and his imagination began.
- When Carl returned home, the school principal had called the student leaders together to discuss the situation and to set policies for controlling potential violence at the school.
- Carl was also trying hard to understand the Vietnam War, the protests against it and what his own position should be.
- After the riots at the Democratic Convention in Chicago, he had bought a bumper sticker reading, "America: Love It or Leave It," but he did not immediately put it on the family car, because he was no longer sure that this slogan truly reflected his opinion.

137

- Although many young men from the local textile mill village, particularly those who dropped out of school to work, had been drafted into the army, Carl knew no one who had actually died in the conflict.
- He was also aware that under current law, his entry into college the following year would provide an exemption from the draft—but for how long?
- No one truly believed the war would push on for very much longer; even if the United States was in the wrong, North Vietnam was a tiny country with too few people and resources to resist the power of American weaponry.

Life in the Community: Rock Hill, South Carolina

- Compared with neighboring Fort Mill, the town of Rock Hill, South Carolina, seemed big and cosmopolitan, thanks to the presence of Winthrop College in the town center.
- Historically the town had been dominated by a handful of textile companies; around the mills there had grown up villages comprising hundreds of small homes.
- Since 1923, Winthrop College, a women's college, had been a fully accredited member of the Southern Association of Colleges and Secondary Schools.
- In 1968 the college had 115 faculty members, six large dormitories, five classroom buildings and a library with more than 150,000 volumes.
- The six-acre Glencairn Garden had been opened to the public by its owner and then donated to the city; everyone could enjoy the hundreds of azaleas, camellias and other Southern favorites planted there.
- For entertainment, though, high-schoolers consistently traveled to the South Park section of Charlotte, North Carolina, to listen to popular musical acts such as the Temptations or Dionne Warwick.

Native American Activist in 1969

Harry Smallboy was frustrated that America could be so obsessed with civil rights for African Americans while, at the same time, ignore legitimate injustices that played out against Native Americans every day. After years of prejudice and inequality, Harry decided to join his fellow Native Americans fighting for fishing rights in Washington state.

Life at Home

- Harry Smallboy was sick to death of being called chief, red, injun and Tonto.
- He was particularly bored with the propensity of little boys with toy cowboy pistols to "shoot" at him while shouting, "Bang, bang, you're dead. Fall down."
- Long ago he had ceased to think any of this was funny.
- The abuse was particularly bad when Hollywood was displaying its latest version of America's Western past.
- Twenty-nine years old and a native of Los Angeles, California, Harry was convinced that it was time for Indians on the West Coast to fight for their rightful place in the economy.
- He was inspired by the occupation of Alcatraz Island in San Francisco Bay by Indians claiming that an 1868 treaty entitled them to the site, since the abandoned prison on Alcatraz was surplus federal property.
- For the first time, he realized that the actions of a handful of courageous individuals could speak for thousands of people unable to voice their frustrations.
- Approximately 800,000 American Indians lived in the United States; of this number about 450,000 resided in or were connected to reservations.
- The vast majority lived west of the Mississippi River; the Navajo Reservation in parts of Arizona, New Mexico and Utah was the nation's largest, with 120,000 people living in an area the size of West Virginia.
- The majority of reservation Indians claimed incomes below the poverty level of $4,000, with the average reservation income being $2,600.
- Seventy-five percent of all reservation homes were substandard; 50 percent were dilapidated beyond repair.
- Only half of all reservation homes had indoor sanitation facilities.

Harry Smallboy fought for the rights of Native Americans.

- Urban-based Indians such as Harry earned an average of $4,500, thanks to better opportunities and, often, more education.
- The incomes of urban Indians and black males were nearly the same.
- Harry earned a public-high-school diploma and had experienced one bewildering year of college.
- That level of education had earned him a job in a warehouse stacking boxes and lots of red-man-sneaky-Indian-HOW jokes from his coworkers.
- Most of the time, Harry said little, only correcting others when they referred to him as being part Indian; he preferred to think of himself as an Indian who was part white.
- His mother's grandmother was enormously proud that her father had been white and said so frequently.
- Harry believed that pervasive racism had convinced her that her "white" side was superior to her "red" side.
- Despite having been raised in the urban environment of Los Angeles, Harry identified strongly with his Indian heritage, and he felt that the heritage of his people was being swept away in the name of "progress."

Harry's grandmother was proud that her father was white.

- Fewer than 10 percent of Native Americans earned their living from agriculture; fewer than 5 percent were employed in crafts.
- Vocational agriculture had been removed from the curricula of federal Indian schools in the 1950s.
- In Washington state, where Harry's people originated, the Indians were losing the right to fish for salmon, all because whites had overused, polluted and dammed the rivers.
- Purely on impulse he quit work and drove to Washington to join a "fish-in" protest, even though he had never seen a salmon in the wild and didn't really like to fish.

Fishing was central to the survival of Native Americans in Washington state.

Life at Work

- The fishing-rights dispute in the State of Washington had dragged on for 15 years without resolution, yet to Harry Smallboy, the issues were clear.
- Prior to the arrival of the whites, his people—the original inhabitants of Washington state's coastal waters—had been among the wealthiest Native Americans, thanks to salmon fishing.
- Fishing was central to their survival and was specifically protected in the various treaties signed by his ancestors—treaties that were written to last for as long as "the grass grows and the sun comes up in the east and sets in the west."
- But for nearly a hundred years, the rights of his ancestors had been under assault.

- The Puyallup now owned only 33 acres of land; the Nisqually claimed 2 acres and the Snohomish, 16 acres. The three-hundred-member Muckleshoot tribe—to which Harry belonged—shared a reservation of just a quarter of an acre.
- Deprived of their land, tribal members were forced to fish off the reservation.
- The various treaties declared this to be within their rights, although fish and game officials said otherwise.
- For most of the 1960s, state officials had been dragging Indians into court, challenging their right to fish for salmon and steelhead trout.

The fishing-rights dispute had been around for 15 years.

- One year earlier another round of litigation had started when the state confiscated the boats and gear of two dozen people.
- Going to court proudly dressed as Muckleshoot Indians had become a way of life for his people.
- The Washington Indians were generally the losers—until they produced pictures of an incident in which the fish and game officials had used billy clubs to pummel protesters and then kicked and punched the women and children.
- But injustices continued, especially when the treaty right of the Indians conflicted with the desires of wealthy sport fishermen determined to land steelhead trout.
- The state even launched a nationwide advertising campaign using the slogan, "Come to Washington, a sportsman's wonderland," as if the state had decreed the steelhead trout a "white man's fish."
- Once in Washington, Harry heard jokes about the steelhead swimming to America with the *Mayflower.*
- Mostly he heard resentment from fishermen disgusted with the concept that they needed the white man's permission to fish, hunt or gather nuts.
- At one meeting a man shouted in anger, "The white man didn't plant the trees, bring the deer or raise the fish, but he wants to give me—a Puyallup-permission to use the land, the air, the water."
- Another man who had volunteered to join the next "fish-in/arrest" was a Vietnam War veteran, back from his third tour of duty; he had already been arrested twice for illegal fishing and was prepared to be arrested again.

Native Americans were routinely arrested for illegal fishing.

- They then talked of demonstrations, road blockades and land takeovers as ways to express Indian outrage over injustice, poverty and white dominance.
- The legacy of being born Indian in America was dismal: an average life span of 40, due to disease, alcoholism and malnutrition; an infant mortality rate more than twice the national average; an unemployment rate ten times the national average; the highest teen suicide rate among the groups distinguished by the U.S. Census and liver disease from alcoholism at a rate five times higher than that of the white population.
- They laughed about the white reaction to Native American protests that mocked the Thanksgiving

and Columbus Day holidays—but lowered their voices in case the police had them under surveillance.

- Voices grew tense when it became time to stage another fish-in and risk arrest.
- Harry hung close to the Vietnam vet as he gathered up nets and fishing tackle.
- The time had arrived for Harry Smallboy—Muckleshoot Indian—to make his stand for his people.

Life in the Community: Puget Sound, Washington

- In the 1700s the indigenous inhabitants of Puget Sound spoke numerous languages; they did not have one name either for themselves or for people outside the region.
- Gradually they began to lump all traders into two categories: "King George men" or "Bostons."
- After the Americans established control of the area, "Bostons" served to identify all immigrants.
- In a similar fashion, "Indians" was used to designate a native Washington state population as diverse and changeable as the "Bostons."
- At the time the first fishing rights treaties were signed in the early 1850s, white settlers had had little interest in salmon fishing.
- The protection of fishing rights was explicitly demanded by native leadership, because salmon fishing was central to their way of life.
- Non-Indian commercial fishing began to grow after the first salmon cannery appeared on the Columbia River in the 1870s.
- By the turn of the century, tribal fishing was being squeezed out by white commercial fishing at the mouth of the river.
- As commercial mechanization increased, Indian salmon harvests fell.

Early Puget Sound, Washington state.

- But salmon fishing and its related activities continued to be at the heart of the Puget Sound Indian culture, even after the building of large-scale hydropower plants reduced salmon runs in the 1930s and 1940s.
- Then, in the 1950s, as dams and pollution further decreased the salmon runs, Washington state game authorities began to require tribal fishers to observe state conservation laws, not ancient treaties.
- The Muckleshoot, Puyallup and Nisqually asserted their treaty fishing rights and continued to fish.
- Then, in January 1961, James Starr and Louis Starr Jr., both from the Muckleshoot tribe, and Leonard Wayne, a Puyallup, were arrested for fishing on the Green River; the court found they were fishing legally according to fishing treaty rights.
- The State of Washington then started a sustained drive to end Indian treaty fishing rights in any way possible, including abolishing the tribes.
- This was especially true after the Washington Supreme Court decided in December 1963 that the state did not have the power to regulate Indian fishing for conservation purposes.
- The first fish-in as an act of political protest occurred January 1, 1964.
- This was followed by a fish-in featuring actor Marlon Brando, who was arrested, attracting huge media attention.
- Native fishermen, too, were arrested and received jail terms—and then went back to the river to fish and be arrested again.

- In 1964 the courts ruled that the Muckleshoot Indians were not a tribe, because no delegates of a tribe known by that name had signed the Treaty of Point Elliott (1855); the Muckleshoot, however, were descended from Duwamish and Upper Puyallup peoples who inhabited Central Puget Sound and were signatories to the treaty.
- In 1965 a county judge ruled the Puyallup Indians were no longer a tribe because they had lost their land.
- The protests and fish-in events continued.
- In 1966 black activist Dick Gregory and his wife were arrested at a fish-in, and Gregory was sentenced to 40 days in jail; Gregory commented: "If more people went to jail for rights, fewer would go for wrongs."
- Battles between the tribal members and state fish and game officers became media events; the Native Americans would assert their right to fish and state officials would confiscate Indian fishing boats and gear—all in front of television cameras.
- The Native American movement was galvanized.

Timeline of American Indian Activism

1961 The National Indian Youth Council was organized to encourage greater self-sufficiency and autonomy.

1964 The Survival of American Indians formed to stage "fish-ins" to preserve off-reservation-fishing rights in Washington State.

The Sioux made their first landing at the vacated Alcatraz prison, during which five Sioux Indians claimed the island under the Fort Laramie 1868 Sioux Treaty enabling Sioux Indians to take possession of surplus federal land.

1966 Senator George McGovern introduced a resolution highlighting the increased desire of Indian people to participate in decisions concerning their people and property.

1968 United Native Americans was founded in the San Francisco Bay Area to promote self-determination through Indian control of Indian affairs at every level.

The American Indian Movement was founded in Minneapolis to protect the city's Native American community from police abuse and to create job training and housing and education programs.

Mohawk Indians formed a blockade at the Cornwall International Bridge between the U.S. and Canada to protest U.S. restrictions on Native peoples' free movement between the two countries.

Congress passed the Indian Civil Rights Act, which required states to obtain tribal consent prior to extending any legal jurisdiction over an Indian reservation.

1969 The American Indian Center in San Francisco burned down; the loss of the center focused Indian attention on taking over Alcatraz for use as a new facility.

The 19-month occupation of Alcatraz began when a diverse group of about 90 Indians took over the abandoned island property.

Members of the American Indian Movement arrived at Alcatraz and gathered ideas about confrontational activism and land seizure as tools to confront the federal government's Indian policies.

The right of taking fish, at all usual and accustomed grounds and stations, is further secured to said Indians, in common with all citizens of the Territory and of erecting temporary houses for the purpose of curing, together with the privilege of hunting and gathering roots and berries on open and unclaimed lands. Provided, however that they shall not take shell-fish from any beds staked or cultivated by citizens.

—Fishing-rights treaty between Territorial Governor
Isaac Stevens and Western Washington tribes, 1854

And when the last Red Man shall have perished, and the memory of my tribe shall have become a myth among the White Men, these shores will swarm with the invisible dead of my tribe, and when your children think themselves alone in the field, the store, the shop, upon the highway, or in the silence of the pathless woods, they will not be alone…At night when the streets of your cities and villages are silent and you think them deserted, they will throng with the returning hosts that once filled and still love this beautiful land. The White Man will never be alone.

—Chief Sealth at the Medicine Creek Treaty ceremony, 1854

Invading Alcatraz, by Adam Fortunate Eagle, from Native American testimony by Peter Nabokov

We set out from San Leando, my family and I, with our tribal outfits packed, and with $24 in beads and colored cloth arranged in a wooden bowl for the symbolic purchase of Alcatraz Island from the government. With a feel of optimism we were soon on the Nimitz Freeway driving for Fisherman's Wharf in San Francisco, and Pier 39.

The weather on Sunday morning, November 9, 1969, was beautiful and calm. This was a pretty strange thing we were doing. Indian people, twentieth-century urban Indians, gathering in tribal councils, student organizations, clubs, and families, and joined by concerned individuals from all over the Bay Area, with the intention of launching an attack on a bastion of the United States government. Instead of horses and bows and arrows of another era, we were riding in Fords and Chevys, armed only with our Proclamation but determined to bring about a change in federal policy affecting our people…

At Fisherman's Wharf, we parked and joined a growing group of Indian students. When I learned that our scheduled boat was nowhere around I suggested that we stall while I looked for another. Richard Oakes went to the end of the pier to read our Proclamation, with Indians and television crews in tow, while I looked around. Then I noticed this beautiful three-masted barque that looked like it had come right out of the pages of maritime history. Its name was the Monte Cristo, and its owner, who, with tight pants and ruffled shirt looked like Errol Flynn, was Ronald Craig.

When I approached, he said, "Hey, I'm curious—what's going on over there with all those Indians?" I explained the fix we were in, pointing out the media contingent that had come to cover the landing. "I'll take you," he said, "on condition we get permission from the Coast Guard and that we carry no more than 50 people. The boat rides deep because of the keel. And I can't land on the Alcatraz dock. We'll circle a couple of times, a sort of sight-seeing tour to get your message across, OK?"

After he counted to make sure we were only 50, he fired off the little cannon on the bow. Here were Indians sailing on an old vessel to seek a new way of life for their people. I thought of the *Mayflower* and its crew of Pilgrims who landed on our shores. The history books say they were seeking new freedoms for themselves and their children which were denied in their homeland. Never mind that Plymouth Rock already belonged to someone else. What concerned them was their own fate, their own hopes. Now, 350 years later, its original citizens, to focus national attention on their struggle to regain those same basic rights, were making landfall on another rock.

Sex Education Advocate in 1969

Dr. Mary Calderone, at age 60, co-founded the Sex Information and Education Council of the United States, designed to help teachers, therapists and other professionals teach sex education with a "positive approach and moral neutrality." Mary's efforts were condemned not only by some parents and church groups, but by conservative political groups.

Life at Home

- As an outspoken advocate for sex education in the public schools, Dr. Mary Steichen Calderone promoted the concept that human sexuality was a multifaceted and vital part of a healthy life that should not be hidden under a shroud of secrecy or limited to smutty magazines.
- Born in Paris on July 1, 1904, Mary never lacked for intellectual stimulation.
- Her bohemian childhood was experienced at the feet of her father, photographer Edward Steichen; her uncle, poet Carl Sandburg; and many of the leading artists of the day.
- When Mary was six, she berated a family friend, the sculptor Constantin Brâncui, for his horizontal-headed bird pieces; the head position, she said, would undoubtedly hinder the bird from singing.
- Brâncui listened respectfully to the tike and afterward only sculpted birds with more upturned heads.
- Dancer Isadora Duncan asked Mary's father to let the girl join her dance troupe.
- Mary attended the Brearley School in New York City for her secondary education before entering Vassar College, from which she graduated in 1925 with a degree in chemistry.
- After her graduation, Mary decided to go into theater, and she studied for three years at the American Laboratory Theater.
- She married actor W. Lon Martin and had two daughters, Nell and Linda.
- Mary abandoned acting and divorced in 1933.
- During this period she underwent two years of Freudian analysis.
- In 1934 she took courses at Columbia University Medical School, placing her daughters Nell, eight, and Linda, six, in boarding school in Massachusetts.
- Nell died the next year of pneumonia, plunging Mary into the deepest and most bitter emotional crisis of her life.
- She spent that summer recovering at her father's place in Connecticut.

Dr. Mary Calderone advocated sex education in the public schools.

Mary earned a master's degree in public health.

- "I don't really know what I did except hate the world for taking my child," she said. "Then I felt suddenly that if I reached my hand backward and forward in time, hundreds of thousands of other mothers who had lost children would touch me. I was just one of many."
- "Nell was very much like me," Mary said. "She looked like me and had a powerful personality. I had to come back the week after she died and take my exams. A week later I had a hysterectomy scheduled. That was some three-week period."
- In 1939 she received a diploma from the University of Rochester Medical School, and three years later she earned a Master's degree in public health at Columbia University.
- There she met her second husband, Dr. Frank Calderone, who later served as chief administrative officer of the World Health Organization.
- They married in 1941 and had two daughters, Francesca and Maria.
- Mary worked as a physician in the Great Neck, New York, public school system.
- In 1953 she joined the staff of the controversial Planned Parenthood Federation of America as its medical director.
- In 1964 Planned Parenthood succeeded in overturning the American Medical Association's policy against physicians disseminating information on birth control, transforming contraception into part of mainstream medical practice.
- Meanwhile letters kept arriving at Planned Parenthood asking questions not just about sex but about sexuality in general.
- Mary came to realize that sex education was sorely lacking in American society.
- She believed that her work should not be limited to preventive measures against pregnancy but should integrate human sexuality into the field of health.
- That would require a new organization and a renewed commitment.

Life at Work

- In 1964, at age 60, Dr. Mary Steichen Calderone cofounded the controversial Sex Information and Education Council of the United States (SIECUS; later called the Sexuality Information and Education Council of the United States), which served teachers, therapists and other professionals.

Mary's insistence that sex education should begin as early as kindergarten offended conservative religious groups such as MOMS (Mothers Organized for Moral Stability) and MOTOREDE (Movement to Restore Decency). Nevertheless, her crusade for sex education with a "positive approach and moral neutrality" was launched.

Mary insisted that sex education should begin as early as kindergarten.

- Nationwide one school district after another was embroiled in angry arguments over sex education classes being promoted by SIECUS.
- Even though the National Education Association (NEA) had passed a resolution strongly affirming its support of the courses, communities in 35 states were debating the role of the public school in sex education.

- The arguments were not new to Mary; she had championed the cause for more than a decade, dating from to a time when sex was simply not discussed in public.
- The current controversy revolved around how specific the information should be, to what ages it should be taught and who should be teaching children about health and human development, including human sexuality.
- Although adamant about sexual freedom, Mary believed that the sex act ultimately should be reserved for marriage and that sexuality found its peak expression through the "permanent man-woman bond."
- Her extensive work popularizing sex education was compared to Margaret Sanger's campaign for birth control and Rachel Carson's support of the environment.
- The human child is sexual even before birth, Mary said during lectures across the nation.
- "We know now that the penis erects in the uterus. And when the infant is born, the parents immediately begin to communicate to the child that it is a boy or a girl. For example, fathers are more gentle handling baby girls. Gender identity is fixed by the age of two.

Mary was picketed by parents and church groups.

- "Finally, there is the disapproving attitude of the parents toward the child's discovery that his body is pleasurable. Parents reflect our sexophobic society."
- Controversy over sex education in U.S. schools intensified in the 1960s, but as early as 1912 the NEA had called for teacher-training programs in sexuality education.
- In 1940 the U.S. Public Health Service strongly advocated sex education in the schools, labeling it an "urgent need."
- In 1953 the American School Health Association launched a nationwide program in family-life education.
- Two years later the American Medical Association, in conjunction with the NEA, published five pamphlets that were commonly referred to as the "sex education series" for schools.
- By 1968 Mary had been condemned by the John Birch Society as "an aging sexual libertine"; it called the effort to teach about sexuality a "filthy Communist plot."
- Mary was picketed in Oklahoma: "Tulsa's Shame! Calderone Came!" read one placard.
- Fears about what sex education might do to schoolchildren spread to some parents and church groups.
- "I expected someone to take a potshot at me," she says of those early days.
- A best-selling 1968 pamphlet called *Is the School House the Proper Place to Teach Raw Sex?* targeted SIECUS, calling Mary the "SIECUS Sexpot" and claiming that she wanted to undermine Christian morality and corrupt children.
- Support for sex education among public health officials and educators did not sway its opponents; battles raged between conservatives and health advocates over the merits and format of sex education in public schools.
- They contended that Mary's promotion of sex education in schools was encouraging a premature and unhealthy participation in sex and usurping the role of parents in guiding their children's lives.
- Her reply was that if parents were doing their job properly, there would be no need for school-based sex education.
- Phyllis Schlafly, leader of the far-right Eagle Forum, argued that sex education resulted in an increase in sexual activity among teens.

- By the 1960s the United States was experiencing a powerful and widely publicized sexual revolution following the introduction of the birth control pill.
- Sex education programs in public schools proliferated, in large part due to newly emerging evidence that such programs did not promote sex but, in fact, helped delay sexual activity and reduce teen pregnancy rates.
- The classes took two approaches: abstinence education and safe-sex education.
- Abstinence education supporters insisted that the best way to address teen sexuality problems was to teach young people not to have sex at all; if girls did not have sex, they couldn't become pregnant and were dramatically less likely to contract a sexually transmitted disease (STD).
- Supporters of abstinence claimed that abstinence not only would prevent harmful psychological presumptions but would build skills designed for improving a relationship.
- Those advocating safe-sex education, including Mary, insisted that since many kids would still decide to have sex, it was more effective to teach them ways to protect themselves while doing so.
- At the same time, Mary had an expansive view of intimacy.
- During a lecture at Syracuse University's Institute for Family Research and Education, Mary said, "You must remember that, for most people, until very recently, sex was something you did in bed, preferably in the dark in one position … and fully clothed."
- The students laughed appreciatively.
- Then she said, "You know there is a word ending in -k which means 'intercourse.' Do you know what it is?" Several in the class gave the obvious answer.
- She then asked, "How about *talk*? That is sexual intercourse. We never talk to each other as nonsexual people. I am not talking to you as a nonsexual person. I am well aware of my sexuality and very happy with it."
- Mary stated that parents should not punish their children for doing the things that are part of being human.
- Even though masturbation was considered unhealthy and dangerous when Mary was growing up, most doctors came to view it as not only acceptable but desirable.
- "What you do is socialize. You teach that these are private things for the child alone. Then when he's older, sex will be with someone else whom he'll choose. Later, parents can teach children how to give and receive love because that is the real role of the family—not just providing shelter, food, education and recreation."
- Her theatrical and medical training, coupled with her dignity, poise and authoritative voice, helped Mary to get her message across: that children are born sexual beings and remain so until they die, and that people of all ages need and deserve a proper sexual education.
- Sex education in the schools should start in kindergarten, she said.
- Modern children, she insisted, were in desperate need of sex education because they were sexually vulnerable, "devoid of chaperones, supervision, rules and close family relations and subject to onslaughts of commercial sexual exploitation."

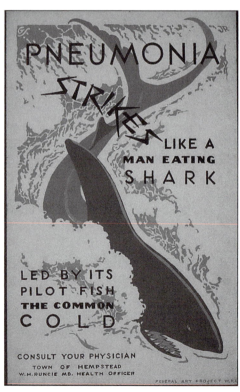

Life in the Community: The State of US Education

- As the 1960s came to a close, the country's schools struggled with society-based burdens from endemic segregation, illegal drugs and entrenched poverty.
- Teachers and administrators, often without adequate training, increasingly inherited the problems that swirled in the community outside the schoolhouse door.
- Americans came to question the ideology of public education; issues of income inequality, teen pregnancy and drug use were laid at the feet of US schools and their teachers.
- In the 1960s schools were seen as one of the primary battlefields in the War on Poverty, both by politicians and by inner-city families struggling for a larger piece of the American pie.
- Critics questioned whether "equality" in education was enough to ensure equality of opportunity for all.
- Teacher unionization, collective bargaining, judicial decrees, student rights and community control all competed as school administration priorities.
- Liberals and conservatives argued for alternative structures: vouchers, performance contracting, radical decentralization, free schools, alternative schools, home schools.
- Teachers deserted the profession in large numbers because of low pay and the downward spiraling of morale.
- Classes were overcrowded; more and more communities were embracing double sessions.
- As the nation's poor increasingly moved to urban areas to seek opportunity, the nation's white middle class—along with their children—fled the cities; Cleveland experienced a 26.5 percent decline in white population during the decade; Chicago, 18.6 percent; St. Louis, 31.6 percent.
- Affluent parents were losing confidence in the public schools, fueling a dramatic enrollment increase in private schools.
- Meanwhile educators focused public attention on the need for well-educated American talent as a weapon in the Cold War with the Soviet Union.
- In its 1954 ruling in *Brown v. Board of Education*, the US Supreme Court had reiterated its belief in the "importance of education to our democratic society," as "the very foundation of good citizenship."
- The court said that schooling "is a principal instrument in awakening the child to cultural values, in preparing him for later professional training, and in helping him to adjust normally to his environment. In these days, it is doubtful that any child may reasonably be expected to succeed in life if he is denied the opportunity of an education."

"Sex Education Opponents Blast Back," Marilyn Baker, *Montclair Tribune* (California), November 13, 1969

In this final installment of the sex education series, the spotlight is focused on those who adamantly oppose sex education, and why they feel it is wrong and what they base such opinions on, when voicing them.

Perhaps the most outspoken local critic of sex education is the Stanhope family, Clayton and Cleo Stanhope, and their 10-year-old daughter Susan.

All three have written letters, branding sex education in the least attractive terms, with Stanhope himself declaring that such education does little but cause the problems it allegedly corrects.

Mrs. Stanhope felt that past installments of the series were "a smooth cover-up job for sex education" primarily because the medical terminology for the sex organs was not spelled out in newspaper articles.

She added that such medical terms are apparently "A-OK for the toddlers" in the opinion of this reporter, hence, felt that such terms should be published in the newspaper "for those old fogey adults who never had the opportunity to delve into sex at such a tender age."

Stanhope himself based his blast on sex education on the fact that some 10-year-old children preferred baseball to sex education philosophy or other older pursuits.

His comment was, "Would these sex-crazed, meddling adults allow that to present 10-yearolds the same opportunities that young boys had without indoctrinating them with a mess of sex facts that can do nothing but wreck their young lives."

Ten-year-old Susan Stanhope took exception to a statement made via a letter to the editor which claimed "sex is NOT a communist plot and neither is sex education." The youngster demands that "the burden of proof is on the writer's shoulders…his proof should be forthcoming."

The statement from 10-year-old Susan Stanhope was her belief that the series was "just spouting the liberal clichés which one reads in the daily or weekly one-sided newspapers."

Another opponent of sex education is Dr. Richard Parlour and his wife Liz.

Dr. Parlour has prepared a six-page statement, which he titled "The Case Against Family Life Education," issued September 27 of this year.

In his statement, Parlour claims the title "family life education" was "cleverly chosen" to delude the American public about the actual subject matter.

Parlour brands as "fallacious and proven unsound" what he terms is the basic philosophy of family life education, that philosophy being "children should not be taught what to think; instead they should be given all this information so they can think for themselves."

"[This] is the philosophy that has created a generation of unhappy, confused, rebellious youth who have achieved their mark with record rioting, suicide, addiction, sexual promiscuity, epidemic venereal disease and rejection of everything established, even the good things," according to Parlour's statement.

Parlour believes that the classroom family life series undermines the "indoctrination process that parents should have established at home."

In another tack, Parlour also challenges the actual need for sex education, asking "How much is the life of an ordinary person enriched by reading The Kinsey Report?"

He adds, "Only rudimentary sexology is really necessary for adult mental health. The importance of sex in healthy living is an American obsession."

The doctor adds that "knowledge about sound family life is sorely needed," but does not feel this family life study should include the manner in which a couple beget a family.

Rather, Parlour supports "the time-honored and proven curriculum for children of reading, writing, and arithmetic, taught to the tune of the hickory stick."

One of the great issues of this era is the question of how to reframe our moral values in terms relevant to the needs and conditions of a world that grows more complex and demanding every day. Many of the moral dilemmas relate in one way or another to sexual behavior within, as well as outside, marriage.

—Dr. Mary Calderone, 1968

Civilian Antiwar Advocates in 1969

Greg and Ellen Watson, encouraged by their daughter's activism against the Vietnam War, participated in their town's Vietnam Moratorium. The ceremony included reading of the names of the war dead, and Ellen volunteered to read the E through J names, a group that included the name of their neighbor's son.

Life at Home

- Ellen Watson was never considered a radical in any sense.
- She rarely attended public meetings, except for the PTA and the Women's Club at her church, and she never, ever spoke up, unless it was to volunteer for the food committee.
- Ellen's husband, Greg, was even less flamboyant.
- Greg always preached to Ellen and their three daughters that he was performing his civic duty when he got up every day and worked hard to support those who didn't.
- So the sight of the Watsons at an antiwar rally was a strange sight indeed.
- After all, Greg had served in World War II, and Ellen's father had been decorated for his service in France during World War I.
- Ellen would claim that their daughter Carol had led them to this decision, but Greg insisted that the momentum had been building for a while.
- A sophomore at Marshall College in Huntington, West Virginia, Carol had been talking about the nationwide moratorium to protest the war that was planned for October 15.
- The youngest of the three girls, Carol was polite, adventurous and challenging.
- Moratorium participants were asked to stay home from school or work, and businesses were encouraged to close on October 15 to send a message to President Richard Nixon that the war should end now.
- After first broaching the subject of cutting classes in protest, Carol asked her parents how they would feel if she attended a rally—and, possibly, was arrested.
- Clearly this was not the type of thing children from Charleston, West Virginia, had been raised to do.
- Greg had been willing to support the war during the presidency of Lyndon B. Johnson, believing the president knew things he couldn't reveal; when the death toll continued to mount, however, Greg grew silent.
- He recalled that President Dwight D. Eisenhower had misled Americans about the U2 spy plane;

The Watsons voiced their opposition of the Vietnam War with some negative consequences.

151

President John F. Kennedy, about the Bay of Pigs; and President Johnson, about the Gulf of Tonkin incident. Now President Nixon was talking peace but continuing the war.

- It did not help that the United States was spending $2 billion a month to help a South Vietnamese government that appeared authoritarian and corrupt; at this pace, inflation would definitely be right around the corner.
- Besides, during the 1968 election campaign, candidate Nixon had announced he had a plan to end the war.
- Greg was a man who took politicians at their word, and he wanted to see the plan.
- For the first time, the Watsons talked about the war and the nearly 1,000 soldiers who had died in combat during the past two months.
- They began reading the *Washington Post* to see what the big-city papers had to say about it; none of what they read was good.
- The peace talks were in disarray, drug use among soldiers was rising, the politicians and generals were fighting each other and Negro civil rights leaders were saying that too many young black men were dying in Southeast Asia.
- The Hiltons, their neighbors down the road, still were unable to believe that they had lost their oldest son to the war, the son who was supposed to take over their hardware store when Bob Hilton retired; Big Bob had trained Little Bob in everything, from fertilizer to plumbing supplies.
- Everyone in town, it seemed, was at the funeral.
- Since the Hiltons were just simple folks who worked hard and minded their own business, they didn't know how to protest.
- Once Ellen decided that Carol was leading them in the right direction, she finally found the courage to tell Mary Sue Hilton that she was planning to attend the moratorium and read out the name of Robert Edward Hilton, among others.
- Ellen held her breath waiting for a reaction.
- Mary Sue simply said that that would be fine.
- Greg was experiencing similar struggles: how do you tell your coworkers at the car dealership that you think America should tuck tail and run from a fight?
- As parts manager, he was well respected for his work, knowledge and cooperative spirit, but he was hardly an opinion leader.
- What would people say when he didn't show up for work on the day of the moratorium?
- Should he just take the day off? Or should he be really bold and tell the boss to shut down that day?
- Greg was afraid they would think he'd turned hippie.
- Carol was pleased with her parents' decision, but her oldest sister, Helen, was furious.
- Helen vented over the phone to her father: This type of thing could harm her husband's law practice; the Watson name would be mud; her children—their grandchildren—would be shunned; could her parents even be trusted to keep the kids anymore?
- Greg finally told Helen to grow up; he hung up the phone on his daughter's ranting.
- Neither Ellen nor Greg expected Helen, her husband and the kids to appear for the customary Sunday supper after church.

Life at Work

- The night before the moratorium, Ellen created black crepe-paper armbands as a sign of solidarity, and although Greg said the armbands were silly, the next day he wore one anyway.
- Shortly after Ellen and Greg Watson arrived at the gathering site, near the town's war memorial, several people tried to start an antiwar chant, "Out Now, Out Now"; it quickly died out.
- A few moments later, efforts to sing "Blowin' in the Wind" fared little better.
- Ellen knew she needed all her energy just to read the alphabetized *E* through *J* names of the war dead.

- When the moratorium organizers learned that Ellen was willing to participate, they offered to let her go first, with the *A* through *D* names, but she thought that would be too hard for her.
- Being second would suit her just fine, if she could get through the *H*s without tearing up at the name Robert Edward Hilton.
- Most of the attendees had never publicly opposed anything before, and certainly not anything as significant as the US president's policy in Vietnam.
- For about ten minutes, they simply stood awkwardly; then, as the first candle was lit, Greg knew there was no turning back.
- For a moment he wished he could have mustered the courage to read the names himself, but then he looked at Ellen and realized how nervous she was.

- Unsure of what was proper etiquette at an antiwar rally, the organizers had decided in advance that church candles would be lit first and then an Episcopal priest would lead the Lord's Prayer, followed by the reading of names.
- The first name read was one Ellen did not know, but the second, Alfred Allen Anderson, was the son of a high school classmate.
- She hadn't even known of her friend's loss, but she realized she had no time to mourn now.
- The first reader was nearly through the *D* names: Edmund Perry Dallas…David Templeton Dukes…
- For Ellen these moments were terrifying and exhilarating; she felt like she was going to be sick but couldn't possibly go back on her commitment now.
- When she started reading the names out, she was startled by the flash of a photographer's camera; she realized that tomorrow all of Charleston would know what she had done.
- "Ellen from the church committee and the quiet Greg are now a hippie couple…What do you think of that?"
- Well, let them talk, she thought; Greg and Ellen Watson want the war to end.
- Then Ellen saw Mary Sue Hilton, still wearing black and carrying the American flag that had been draped on Little Bob's casket.
- Big Bob wasn't there, and Mary Sue seemed unsteady.
- She had come to hear the name of her son read out in public as one of America's war dead, while she clutched the flag.
- Mrs. Rice, dressed in her Sunday best, stood defiantly with a sign taped to her pocketbook reading, "God Bless Our President."
- Two teenagers drove by, yelling, "Dirty commies!" but they did not stop.
- The next morning the *Washington Post* reported that "uncounted and uncountable thousands of Americans demonstrated their opposition to the Vietnam War yesterday in one fashion or another all across the nation."
- According to the story, crowds ranged from 100,000 on the Boston Common to a rain-drenched 1,500 in San Francisco to 30,000 on the New Haven Green to 10,000 at Rutgers University to 5,000 in the center of Minneapolis to 50,000 on the grounds of the Washington Monument.
- The reporters said: "3,500 braved a six-inch snowfall in front of the state Capitol in Denver to hear speeches and the reading of names of the state's 567 war dead."

- Despite snow and 15-degree temperatures, 20 people had stood through the night in front of a war memorial on the Wyoming University campus at Laramie.
- Sixty-five people in small, conservative Charleston, West Virginia, felt about right, Greg told Carol, as she related her own protest activities.
- Carol had helped ring an old church bell for three days, striking the bell once every four seconds in memory of each U.S. soldier killed in Vietnam.
- There were only minor incidents of violence nationwide, and few arrests.
- In Phoenix, Texas, the mother of a sailor killed in the war demanded that his name be excluded from a list being read at a moratorium rally.

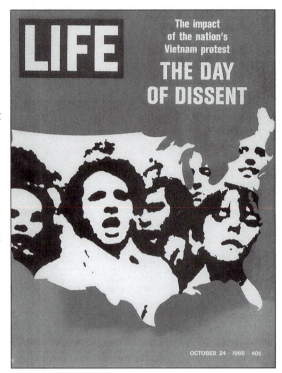

- The crowds were overwhelmingly white—generally, but not always predominantly, young and including a number of middle-class, "respectable" adults who had come to believe that direct action was necessary to end the war.
- After the rally at the Washington Monument grounds in Washington, DC, 30,000 people carrying candles marched past the White House.
- According to his aides, President Nixon kept a business-as-usual schedule, having stated that he did not propose to be the first American president to lose a war.
- He had begun a unilateral withdrawal of the bulk of American forces in Vietnam, and some military commanders had been reined in so tightly that a unilateral ceasefire prevailed.
- *Life* magazine called the one-day moratorium a "display without historical parallel, the largest expression of public dissent ever seen in the country."

Life in the Community: The October 15, 1969, Vietnam Moratorium

- The moratorium began as a campus-based program, with college-town canvassing, leaflet distribution, class-cutting, seminars, candlelight processions and readings of the names of the war dead at colleges and universities.
- The aim of the activities was to pressure President Nixon into altering his course and bringing the troops home faster than he intended.
- The nationwide protest was initiated by three activists: Sam Brown, David Hawk and David Mixner.
- They raised $75,000 and obtained pledges of support from more than a hundred student-body presidents.
- Brown, age 25, was the main fundraiser; he first became an activist with the National Student Association's "Dump President Johnson" movement, which led to Senator Eugene McCarthy's presidential challenge.
- Brown won a reputation as a first-rate choreographer of mass movements.
- Twenty-four-year-old Hawk, whose primary focus was opposition to the draft, had a background in civil rights work in Georgia, and he was a staff worker for Allard Lowenstein; Lowenstein had been a president of the National Student Association in the 1950s and by the 1960s was a well known civil rights and antiwar activist and liberal Democratic politician.

- At the time of the moratorium, Hawk faced imprisonment as a draft-resister; in spring 1969 he had directed a we-won't-go letter campaign in which 250 student presidents and editors wrote directly to President Nixon.
- Mixner, also 24 years old, was a union organizer who worked particularly with farm laborers—his father being one.
- Mixner was also a member of the McGovern Commission for Reform of the Democratic Party.
- The moratorium gained support from nationally recognized individuals, such as pediatrician and child-rearing expert Doctor Benjamin Spock and Coretta Scott King, wife of the slain civil rights leader Martin Luther King Jr.
- In Washington, DC, thousands gathered to participate in a candlelight parade led by Mrs. King.
- In her remarks, King said, "Forty thousand Americans have been given as sacrificial lambs to a godless cause. When will it cease? While we spend billions of dollars in Vietnam, we have ignored our problems at home."
- Sam Brown was planning another massive demonstration for November 14 and 15 if President Nixon failed to accelerate troop withdrawal from Vietnam.

"In Duluth, a Mother of Five Joins the Campaign against War," Nan Robertson, *The New York Times*, October 16, 1969

Mary Carolyn Lennon Fleege shivered in the frigid wind off Lake Superior at her first peace rally today, whispered a few "Hail Marys" to herself and tied a bit of white rag to her sleeve in public mourning for the men who died in Vietnam.

She sang antiwar songs and "America the Beautiful" in a light soprano in front of the county courthouse and confessed that never in her life had she done anything nearly so daring. Mrs. Fleege is a 34-year-old housewife with a broad, open Irish face, the mother of five small children and the wife of an engineer for the Minnesota Highway Department. She describes herself as a "ghetto Catholic" who has just begun to move out into a world of new and sometimes painful ideas.

Today, she took her children out of classes for 90 minutes to go to a memorial service at the Duluth campus of the University of Minnesota and later joined several thousand persons, mostly high school and college students, at the downtown demonstration. Her actions climaxed a year of private worry about the war.

For 30 minutes, Mrs. Fleege and the others sat mutely on the cold ground before the courthouse. When the rally dispersed, after the Mayor of Duluth had complimented those present on their good behavior, Mrs. Fleege went home to tend her children, put another load of washing through the machine and bake the supper casserole.

Vietnam War Timeline

1954 Forty thousand Vietminh surrounded Dien Bien Phu in North Vietnam, resulting in the French Army ordering a ceasefire on May 7 after 55 days of battle.

Eight nations signed the U.S.-sponsored SEATO treaty.

1955 President Eisenhower's administration sent the first U.S. advisers to South Vietnam to train the South Vietnamese Army.

1957 The Vietcong assassinated over 400 South Vietnamese officials.

1959 A specialized North Vietnamese Army unit was formed to create a supply route from North Vietnam to Vietcong forces in South Vietnam which became known as the Ho Chi Minh Trail.

1961 President John F. Kennedy ordered 100 "special forces" troops to South Vietnam.

1962 In Operation Chopper, U.S. helicopters carried 1,000 South Vietnamese soldiers near Saigon in the first U.S. combat mission against the Vietcong.

Operation Ranch, designed to clear vegetation alongside highways, set the stage for vast tracts of forest to be sprayed with "Agent Orange."

1963 United States servicemen in Vietnam numbered 16,500.

1964 The U.S. Congress passed the Tonkin Gulf Resolution, authorizing President Johnson to take "all necessary measures" to "prevent further aggression" in Vietnam.

China, North Vietnam's neighbor and ally, successfully tested an atomic bomb.

1965 The U.S. Congress provided $2.4 billion for the Vietnam War effort.

Operation Rolling Thunder began, a continuous bombing campaign of North Vietnam that would last for three years.

1967 Secretary of Defense Robert McNamara announced that U.S. bomb raids had been ineffective.

U.S. troops in Vietnam totaled 500,000.

1968 The North Vietnamese caught the U.S. by surprise with the Tet Offensive attacks on almost all the capitals of South Vietnam's 44 provinces.

The My Lai Massacre of over 200 unarmed civilians captured national attention.

1954 President Johnson announced he would not seek re-election, and ordered bombing to stop over 75 percent of North Vietnam.

President Nixon was elected president, and during a policy address on Vietnam in 1969, proposed an "8-Point Peace Plan" that would include mutual withdrawal of all non-Vietnamese forces.

1969 The first U.S. troop withdrawal occurred when 800 men were sent home.

President Nixon introduced his "Vietnamization" program to prepare the South Vietnamese to take over the U.S. combat role.

Congress gave the president the authority to institute the "draft lottery" system aimed at drafting 19-year-olds before older men.

"Vietnam Debate, Will it Help or Hinder Peace?,"
U.S. News & World Report, October 20, 1969

Fighting dropped off in Vietnam—but there was no breathing spell in Washington. Pressures, protests and discussion swirled around the White House. Critics—of all stripes—demanded the president "do something to end the war." There was argument, too, whether the protesters were doing more harm than good in the hazardous search for peace.

Almost before many realized what was happening, Richard Nixon found himself in the vortex of a Vietnam "Great Debate" not unlike the one that dogged Lyndon Johnson's last year in the White House.

President Nixon wanted a "60-day moratorium" on national discussion of Vietnam in hope that he could use the time to break the deadlock with the communists.

What Mr. Nixon got, instead, was a torrent of public reaction from prominent men in both of the major political parties, from the military, from campuses and elsewhere.

The president was confronted with a variety of demands.

Some insisted the war be stopped immediately, at whatever cost. Others wanted the president to set a rigid deadline for troop withdrawal—or risk having Congress set one for him.

At the other extreme, there were demands that the president reverse course, step up the war and strike a decisive blow against North Vietnam.

Through the swelling debate and argument ran only one common thread: "Do something."

Accompanying all this was a parallel and important issue: Will the mounting debate over Vietnam help or hinder the search for peace?

On October 7, the view of the Nixon administration was presented by Defense Secretary Melvin R. Laird, who charged that antiwar forces were trying to pressure the White House "into capitulation on Hanoi's terms."

Said the defense chief in a speech to the AFLCIO in Atlantic City:

"Hanoi's strategy is clear: Expect to achieve victory by waiting for us to abandon the conflict as a result of the antiwar protest in this country."

Other administration sources, speaking privately, were deeply embittered by the outburst of dissent in Congress and on the campuses. One official emphasized: "There is no doubt that each and every speech, and each and every demonstration helps the communist cause."

The president's critics gave no sign of letting up. A massive nationwide "Vietnam Moratorium" on October 15 won the open support of a group of senators and congressmen who urged that the demonstrations continue until all troops are brought home.

On October 8, Senator Frank Church (Dem.), of Idaho, and Senator Mark Hatfield (Rep.) of Oregon, teamed up to introduce in the Senate a resolution demanding complete disengagement from Vietnam.

The Church-Hatfield move, one of several of a similar nature, was regarded as a key proposal because of its bipartisan basis. At the heart of the resolution was a complaint that President Nixon was moving too slowly in bringing home the troops-a total of 60,000 during all of 1969.

"At the present rate of withdrawal," the resolution said, "American troops will be engaged in Vietnam for the next eight to 10 years."

The essential argument of "doves" is this: It has been decided to get out of the war, so let's get out right now.

"Antiwar for Everyman," *The New Republic,* **September 6, 1969**

On the nation's campuses, when young men still face the draft, the antiwar clock has begun to tick again. Beginning October 15 with a one-day "moratorium" (to sidestep the more inflammatory word "strike"), the Vietnam Moratorium Committee plans to retool the dormant campus antiwar machine and launch it on a campaign to pressure the Nixon administration to do either of two things: Negotiate a Vietnam settlement or get out fast. The emphasis in both cases is speed.

Moving from the teach-in of 1967-68 to the teach-out, college students this year will be asked to forsake the homogeneous campus and go out into the community, where the door-to-door canvassing techniques that worked so well for Sen. Eugene McCarthy in New Hampshire will be used. The committee hopes to involve labor, business, professional and academic groups in a revived antiwar effort which would escalate to a two-day moratorium in November, a three-day affair in December and so on. The goal is a national moratorium to protest the war-a day when normal activity ceases and everyone's business is some sort of antiwar activity.

The purpose of the October 15 Moratorium is that of "putting an end to the most tragic mistake in our national history—the cruel and futile war in Vietnam. We meet today to call our government away from folly into the paths that lead to peace."

Inventor of Sweet 'N Low in 1969

Ben Eisenstadt was convinced that the government's ban on cyclamates would bankrupt his company, which manufactured artificial sweetener that included the banned ingredient. Instead, a loyal customer base encouraged him to quickly reformulate Sweet 'N Low, without cyclamate, and sales of the product tripled.

Life at Home

- Ben Eisenstadt was born in New York City, on the Lower East Side of Manhattan, on December 7, 1906.
- His parents, Rose and Morris Eisenstadt, were Jewish immigrants to the United States from Poland; Morris worked on the waterfront, unloading ships.
- When Ben was seven years old, his father tripped on a scaffold and fell several stories before being saved by a hook that caught his pants.
- A year later Morris Eisenstadt was rushed to the hospital after suffering a massive heart attack.
- When eight-year-old Ben arrived at the hospital, he was told "Your father is with Jesus," signaling the start of a tumultuous late childhood and adolescence.
- Because his mother couldn't afford to raise three children, Ben was sent to live with his uncles, moving from apartment to apartment, often sleeping on floors and couches in the industrial wasteland of northern New Jersey.

- Ben lost contact with his mother and siblings when they fled to California following a gang fight that had resulted in death threats against his brother Robert.
- Ben attended school and worked in his uncle's teabag factory until 1927, when he began an apprenticeship with a Manhattan lawyer.
- Soon afterward, he enrolled in St. John's University School of Law; Ben graduated in 1929 as class valedictorian.
- After graduation Ben rented an office on Broadway, but because of the Great Depression, there were no clients.
- Ben took a job at a cafeteria his father-in-law operated in Brooklyn. Later he ran a couple of cafeterias of his own, eventually finding a measure of success with a cafeteria he opened in 1940 on Cumberland Street, in the Fort Greene section of Brooklyn, just across from the Navy Yard.

Benjamin Eisenstadt invented a cyclamate-free Sweet 'N Low.

- Brooklyn became a boomtown during World War II; in 1944, there were 900,000 military personnel in New York City.
- The end of the war turned the Navy Yard into a ghost town, leaving Ben bereft of customers.
- Recalled his uncle's teabag factory, he removed the lunch counter and stools and turned the Cumberland Cafeteria into the Cumberland Packing Company, which packaged tea.
- Ben's wife, Betty, had often complained about the messy and unsanitary sugar dispensers that filled nearly every restaurant.

Being across from the Brooklyn Navy Yard was good for Ben's cafeteria business.

- As his teabag venture limped toward oblivion in 1947, Ben—or Betty—had the brainstorm that changed the way Americans dispensed sugar: the same equipment that injected tea into teabags, they realized, could be used to put sugar into little paper packets.
- Why not make serving sugar clean and personal—to a single person, one packet at a time?
- At a time when restaurants used only open sugar bowls or heavy glass dispensers, the idea of individual, sanitary sugar packets was revolutionary.
- But Ben was so naïve that when he proudly showed his sugar operations to executives of a giant sugar company, the company simply set up its own sugar-packet operations.
- Ben's proposal to Domino Sugar representatives resulted in them calling back to say that they had duplicated his machine and would not need his services.

Sweet 'N Low, named after a poem by Alfred Lord Tennyson, quickly gained popularity.

- At the time Ben and Betty's son Marvin came to work with Ben, a contract with the small Jack Frost Sugar Company was keeping Cumberland alive, but without a branded line of its own, the company was a marginal operation.
- Cumberland Packing also produced packaged duck sauce for Chinese restaurants, perfume and tokens; the company grossed approximately $100,000 a year, most of which went back into the company in the form of investments in new machines and workers.
- Ben bestowed half of the factory on his son, teaching him the accountability of ownership.

Life at Work

- The father-son partnership of Ben and Marvin Eisenstadt got its first real test in 1956, when the two men were approached by executives of a pharmaceutical company seeking a sugar substitute that could be individually packaged.
- The executives wanted a medical product that could be sold to diabetics; in return, the Eisenstadts would control the packaging.
- To meet the challenge, Ben and Marvin hired Doctor Paul Kracauer, a chemist, to help them develop a mixture that would imitate the look and feel of sugar.
- Seeing a new opportunity, they mixed saccharin, a derivative of coal tar, with cyclamate, searching for the proper tastes—especially for a coffee sweetener.
- Saccharin had been around since the nineteenth century; it had suffered scandal connected to its inventor, had been used by President Theodore Roosevelt and was then banned for a short period by

President William Howard Taft—only to be redeemed when World War I dramatically reduced the worldwide supply of sugar.

- Considered a medicine for diabetics, saccharin was generally available only as a liquid or in pill form, and its use was restricted to diabetics and the obese, despite a growing demand for diet foods.
- Saccharin's bitter aftertaste was of particular concern.
- Initially, the various combinations Ben and Marvin tried failed to eliminate the bitterness of the saccharin or to create enough bulk for the mixture to fill an entire packet.
- Marvin found the answer in an old cookbook.
- With the addition of lactose, which bulked up food and leached out taste, they perfected the formula that would become Sweet'N Low.
- When they returned to the pharmaceutical company with their solution, the executives no longer had an interest in an individually packaged sugar substitute, believing that the market was too small.
- Taking care to patent the first granulated low-calorie sugar substitute, Ben named the product Sweet'N Low, after a song with words from a poem by Alfred Lord Tennyson; Ben distinguished the packaging from that of white sugar by giving Sweet'N Low a pink packet printed with a treble-clef musical logo.
- Now his timing was perfect: the man who had made spooning sugar passé with his first idea had created a sugar substitute just as the American health craze was in its infancy.
- With a claim of fewer than three calories per serving, Cumberland launched Sweet'N Low in 1957 as a product for anyone—and everyone—watching his or her weight.

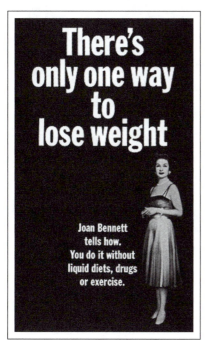

- A&P, one of the nation's leading grocery chains, contacted Cumberland and asked if it could distribute Sweet'N Low nationally.
- Very quickly, Cumberland's sugar substitute became the most popular brand of its type on the market.
- Sweet'N Low was a hit—a successful new product that swept to the top of a booming niche in the 1960s.
- The sugar-substitute market picked up further with the debut of diet sodas in 1962.
- Demand for Sweet'N Low rose accordingly; competing products quickly appeared, cutting into Cumberland's market share.
- Then, however, the federal government decided that the chemicals in Sweet'N Low had not been thoroughly studied.
- Some testing had indicated that cyclamates might cause cancer or birth defects in chickens and rats, and in 1969, the Food and Drug Administration decided to run more definitive tests on the chemical.
- After just three weeks of testing, the government abruptly declared a ban on cyclamate sweeteners.
- Preliminary results had shown the growth of cancerous tumors in rats; consequently, cyclamates were deemed unsafe for humans.

- The ban was announced in late October; all cyclamates were to be off the shelves by February 1.
- This might well have been the end of Cumberland Packing and Sweet'N Low.
- But Ben and Marvin were prepared, having anticipated a possible ban.
- Marvin was able to use his chemical expertise to devise a new formula for Sweet'N Low, made with saccharin but without the addition of cyclamates.
- As the ban loomed, the Eisenstadts went to their bank and borrowed $1 million; meanwhile, loyal dieters bought Sweet'N Low by the case, concerned that the product would disappear.
- While their competitors strategized in committee meetings, Ben and Marvin publicly removed all of their old inventory from grocery shelves across the country and buried it in landfills—in the glare of national television news cameras.
- Then Cumberland supplied its distributors with its reformulated product, judged safe to use.
- The dining public cherished its right to pour Sweet'N Low from pink packets into their drinks and—governmental ban or not—they were going to have a sugar substitute.
- As a result of adversity and excellent timing, Ben Eisenstadt's artificial sweetener once again dominated the U.S. market.
- Their competitors had failed to react so quickly, and several disappeared.
- Sales of Sweet'N Low tripled.

Life in the Community: New York City

- By the mid-nineteenth century, the German Jews of New York City were well established, and they had largely assimilated into New York society; thereafter a flood of the uneducated poor, many Jewish, poured into the city from Poland and Russia.
- In 1836 just 10,000 Jews lived in New York City; 75 years later, half a million lived on the Lower East Side alone.
- Entire towns dropped off the map of Eastern Europe, only to reappear on the streets of New York City.
- There was a great deal of tension and a yawning class difference between the relatively well off assimilated German Jews and the newcomers.
- For the first time, the 1920 Census showed Brooklyn overtaking Manhattan as the most populous borough of New York City.
- By 1924 two million Jews had arrived from Eastern Europe.

Early New York City.

- Growing anti-immigration sentiment in the United States at this time resulted in the National Origins Quota of 1924, which severely restricted immigration from Eastern Europe.
- As a whole the Jewish community took the lead in opposing immigration restrictions, which nevertheless remained in effect until 1965.
- In this period New York City was a major destination of African Americans swept up in the Great Migration; the influx of blacks from the South resulted in a flowering of African American culture during the Harlem Renaissance.

- For most of his term, New York City mayor Jimmy Walker, a Democrat supported by the notorious Tammany Hall political machine, oversaw a period of prosperity in New York; during Prohibition, which Walker had always opposed, "speakeasies" flourished in the city.
- Over toward Broadway was "Tin Pan Alley," the center of the city's music industry; the first modern musical, Jerome Kern's *Show Boat*, opened in 1927 as the theater district moved north of 42nd Street.
- The Great Depression, which soon spread to the rest of the United States and then the world, began in New York City with the stock market crash of 1929.
- The Depression was a time of unemployment and poverty, and it resulted in a period of increased government involvement in the economy.
- In 1931 the recently completed Empire State Building derisively became known as the "Empty State Building"; for many years, in the bleak business climate, it could not attract a sufficient number of tenants.
- In 1933 Republican reformer Fiorello La Guardia was elected mayor of New York City.
- An exuberant populist with a multiethnic sensibility, La Guardia was of both Italian and Jewish descent.
- La Guardia's term saw the continued ascent of Robert Moses, New York's powerful "master builder" of bridges, parks and parkways and a great proponent of automobile-centered modernism; over his long career, which began in the 1920s under Governor Alfred E. Smith, Moses completed massive construction projects that were and remained controversial.
- A large expansion of the subway system in the 1930s and, from the 1940s, municipal ownership of subway companies that previously had been privately owned gave New York City's subway system its lasting shape.
- Beginning in the late 1930s, New York saw a concentrated influx of intellectual, musical and artistic Europeans, refugees from the political turmoil in Europe, enhancing the international character of the city's culture.
- The 1939 New York World's Fair was a high point of technological optimism, meant to mark the end of the Depression; the fair also celebrated the 150th anniversary of George Washington's inauguration, at Federal Hall in Manhattan, as the first president of the United States.
- After the start of World War II, the fair's theme was changed from "Building the World of Tomorrow" to "For Peace and Freedom."
- The city was significantly affected by the war.
- For the duration of World War II, the Port of New York handled 25 percent of the nation's trade; much of this passed through the Brooklyn Army Terminal and the Brooklyn Navy Yard.
- By the war's end, the Navy Yard was the world's largest shipyard, with 75,000 workers.

"Crackdown on Food Additives Challenges Good Cooks,"
Harriet Van Horne, *Tucson Daily Citizen*, November 24, 1969

Unexpected blessings—some of them delicious—may soon be gracing our bill of fare.

It was high time the government cracked down on cyclamates, monosodium glutamate, and all those dubious additives described in squinty little letters on the label. Now good cooks have been challenged.

To the average housewife, HEW's subtracting of an additive leaves her with the uneasy feeling that she ought to go find a substitute additive.

If synthetic sweeteners produce cancer of the bladder of laboratory rats, why not be daring and try some other sweetener? Sugar is non-toxic but boring. Why not honey?

Honey in hot tea is delicious. Honey stirred into warm milk at bedtime makes a lovely posset. John the Baptist found wild honey dandy with a locust.

The Elizabethans put honey on everything, including their toothpaste, which explains why everybody from Queen Bess down had terrible teeth. But no rats have ever expired from a surfeit of honey. (A surfeit of locusts, well, maybe.)

The innocuous white powder called MSG gives convulsions to rats and migraine headaches to people who overeat in Chinese restaurants. (It was, in fact, this "Chinese restaurant syndrome" which led to further research on MSG.) As all cooks know, MSG is not so much a seasoning as a stimulant. It opens the taste buds and makes them say "Mmmm…"

Deprived of MSG, a housewife may have to revise her table of flavorings. Honest, black powder straight from the pepper mill should enjoy a new vogue. It has always worked more efficiently than MSG.

A whiff of curry powder may enliven the blended sauces nobody likes. Who knows? Fresh herbs may reassert their good green tang in roast meat and casseroles.

While food packagers suffer the agonizing reappraisal that always follows government bans, I wish some chemist with a decent respect for good food would invent an MSG that works in reverse. That is, an inexpensive white powder to close the taste buds. Close them firmly and politely when the food on the plate is inedible.

What embarrassment, what digestive distress we'd all be spared on those nights of horror when we must dine where the cuisine is not the glory of the house. Please, can I have a little GSM in my pillbox?

The government's new firm stand on pesticides should sweeten our lives, too.

Now, at last, we can eat an apple, skin and all, and not worry about when the twitching may start. (The classic pattern of DDT poisoning is random excitement, twitching, convulsions, death. Now you know.)

A ban on DDT, when it comes, may mean that raw carrots no longer taste of gasoline. And baked potatoes will be served in preference to the noodles in the add-water-and-mix sauce which, naturally will be chock-a-block with MSG, cyclamates, and if I may voice my own dark suspicions, sawdust and bone dust.

We spend enormous amounts of money on food in this country, but too many people have forgotten how to eat. And too many women, beguiled by jiffy mixes and frozen prefixed feasts, have never learned to cook.

We've come a long way, perhaps too far, from our seventeenth-century ancestors who knew how to pot a swan, preserve flowers in syrup and make "kissing comfits" to sweeten the breath.

"What's That Funny Taste? The Never-Ending Quest for Fake Sugar,"
Benjamin Siegel, *American Heritage,* June, 2006

Just as diet soda's multibillion-dollar industry stems from the unassuming Russian Jewish émigré Hyman Kirsch, so the history of artificial sweeteners is an immigrant story, one that begins in a Johns Hopkins University laboratory in 1879. Constantine Fahlberg, a "well-built, handsome, German-American," according to an article Scientific American published years later, was working there examining the properties of coal tar. Quite by accident, he stumbled upon a chemical that would forever sweeten the course of history.

"One evening I was so interested in my laboratory," Fahlberg told *Scientific American,* "that I forgot about supper until quite late, and then rushed off for a meal without stopping to wash my hands. I sat down, broke a piece of bread, and put it to my lips. It tasted unspeakably sweet. I did not ask why it was so, probably because I thought it was some cake or sweetmeat. I rinsed my mouth with water, and dried my mustache with my napkin, when, to my surprise, the napkin tasted sweeter than the bread. Then I was puzzled."

Fahlberg quickly realized what he had stumbled upon, a byproduct of coal tar that, strangely enough, "out-sugared sugar." After running back to the lab, he proceeded to violate several principles of scientific safety, tasting each and every chemical in order to figure out which one had accidentally found its way into his food. Stumbling upon saccharin, Fahlberg began secretly to study the compound, and in time went back to Germany to set up his own manufacturing company. Soon he was selling his product worldwide.

Diet soda was certainly the furthest thing from Fahlberg's mind; medicine was where saccharin would prove most useful, he thought, and suggested that the chemical be used in "fine wafers and other foods for invalids," hoping it would prove "invaluable in disguising and destroying all the bitter and sour tastes in medicine without changing the character or action of the drugs."

Fahlberg wasn't concerned with side effects. Saccharin "has no injurious effect on the human system," he said; "what effect has been noticed is rather beneficial than otherwise." And soon he was looking beyond medical applications: "In the future, the new sugar will be used by druggists, physicians, bakers, confectioners, candy makers, preserve and pickle makers, liquor distillers, wine makers, and dealers in bottlers' supplies."

However, saccharin was always viewed a bit suspiciously; from the earliest days of its marketing and even during the First World War's intense sugar rationing, some Americans saw the substance as a poor substitute for energy-rich sugar and perhaps even as something hazardous.

In 1937, Michael Sveda, the son of Czech immigrants and an amateur violinist

and woodworker, stepped out for a cigarette after a long day of working toward his chemistry Ph.D. at the University of Illinois. Like Constantine Fahlberg before him, Sveda realized that what he was putting in his mouth was unusually sweet. He walked back in the lab for another groundbreaking chemical taste test. He had stumbled upon cyclamate.

Cyclamates were everything that saccharin was not: They lacked the metallic aftertaste that plagued saccharin, and there were no initial concerns about safety. Hyman Kirsch used them to sweeten No-Cal, Royal Crown to sweeten Diet Rite Cola. For close to two decades, cyclamates went into everything from toothpaste to canned fruit.

Then came 1969 and the alarm about cyclamates causing cancer in rats. In the years that followed, aspartame would have its day, though that chemical, too, has been plagued by reports linking it with cancer.

While most technologies have changed dramatically in the last hundred years, artificial sweeteners aren't much more advanced than they were in Constantine Fahlberg's time, and the regular association of them with cancer may help explain why the diet-soda industry changes formulas every 20 years or so. Splenda, the brand name for sucralose, is the latest in the line of new artificial sweeteners. Like its predecessors, it was born when a researcher happened to taste a chemical he had merely been asked to "test."

Dieting in America

One of the earliest dieting programs was developed in the early nineteenth century by Presbyterian minister Sylvester Graham. Graham's diet involved ingesting fruits, vegetables, and other high-fiber foods while abstaining from spices and meats. The staple of Graham's diet was his own recipe called "Graham Bread," later known as the graham cracker.

Yet, rather than simply weight loss, Graham's diet was originally intended to curb gluttony and to prevent impure thoughts. Another early dieting fad of the late nineteenth century involved rules on chewing.

Dubbed "The Great Masticator," Horace Fletcher was the most famous proponent of such chewing diets.

Fletcher's maxim was that food ought to be chewed 32 times before being swallowed, claiming "Nature will castigate those who don't masticate."

These fads were followed by "diet pills" in the early twentieth century that claimed to contain tapeworms or tapeworm eggs.

One advertisement poster depicted a woman pensively standing before a mountain of food. The text reads, "Fat. The enemy that is shortening your life banished! How? With sanitized tapeworms. Jar packed. 'Friends for a fair form.' Easy to swallow." There are even reassuring phrases in this ad that note that sanitized tapeworms are "guaranteed harmless" and have "no ill effects."

During the 1950s, doctors prescribed diet pills to patients that contained amphetamines, which were used extensively during World War II to help soldiers overcome fatigue.

One of the side effects of amphetamine use was appetite suppression, but the use of amphetamines also led to substance abuse problems.

Doctors eventually stopped prescribing amphetamines for weight loss in the 1960s.

Vietnam War Bride in 1969

Bian Le, one of nine children, was sold, along with her six sisters, to other families so her parents could afford to send her brothers to school. She met US Air Force pilot Jim Scott at the teahouse where she worked. They married, and she traveled alone and pregnant to America, where Jim was recovering from a land mine injury.

Life at Home

- Bian Le was born in 1951 in Bien Hoa, a small village outside of Saigon.
- Her biological parents were very poor and unable to care for their nine children.
- Bian and her six sisters were given away or sold to other families so that her parents could afford to send their two sons to school.
- As was common among farming families in rural South Vietnam, Bian's foster parents adopted her as cheap labor to help farm their small property.
- On their farm, about 10 acres running along the Long Tau River, her foster family grew oranges, coconuts and bananas.
- As a child Bian worked 14-hour days in the fields under the hot sun.
- She often became so dehydrated that she would faint, only to be beaten by her foster father for wasting time.
- Bian's foster family had one biological son, Minh, and four other adopted daughters.
- In the spring of 1965, when Bian was 15 years old, she ran away from the farm with a friend; they went to Saigon with plans to sell vegetables and earn $40 a month.
- On arriving in Saigon, Bian became separated from her friend.
- With no money and nowhere else to turn, she took a job as a prostitute.
- She earned $100 a month working at a busy teahouse that was frequented by U.S. military personnel serving in the Vietnam War.
- She sent money home to her foster family every month for a year, until she learned that their neighborhood had been destroyed by the fighting.
- As a teenager struggling to survive, Bian did not identify with the Vietnam War; she only wanted the violence to end.
- Working as a prostitute, Bian became pregnant three times.
- Her first pregnancy resulted in a miscarriage, and she gave two infants up for adoption when they were only days old.

Bian "Betty" Scott came to America as a Vietnam War bride.

- She met Jim Scott, a US Air Force pilot, in the spring of 1968, at the teahouse where she worked.
- He was stationed at the Bien Hoa Air Force Base near Saigon.
- Fascinated by Bian's dark eyes and exotic beauty, Jim became a frequent customer at the teahouse.
- Despite the respect and kindness Jim showed her, including gifts of scarves and perfume, Bian did not view him differently from any other customer.

Jim Scott was an Air Force pilot.

- She had learned to guard herself against American soldiers.
- Jim was persistent in his affection toward Bian, and when she became pregnant in the fall of 1968, he begged her to return to the United States with him to raise their child.
- She was reluctant to leave the familiarity of Vietnam, but she finally agreed in order to escape the ongoing violence.
- Before they left, Jim sent for first- and second-grade American readers, and he sat with her almost every day to help her learn as much English as she could.
- Illiterate in her own language, she did not see much use for the books.
- When Jim suddenly stopped coming to see her, Bian assumed that he had either been killed or returned to the United States.
- She began making arrangements to give their unborn child up for adoption.
- One night Bian was awakened by US military officials who told her that Jim had been injured in a land-mine explosion and was recovering in America.
- He had told the officials that she was his wife and that they had plans for her to join him in the United States.
- Then Bian made a decision that required every ounce of her strength and courage: she left the teahouse for an unknown future in the United States.
- Bian arrived alone in the United States on April 20, 1969.
- Jim met her at the airport in Boston, where she endured passing through customs and filling out the necessary paperwork for her to legally stay in America.

Bian stayed home with the baby and had a difficult time adjusting to western culture.

- Many of the legal ceremonies, including her marriage, involved repeating English words after a U.S. official in a small, dark office with no windows, on the fourth floor of a large government building.
- Jim brought Bian home to his small house in Westover, Massachusetts. She gave birth to their son, Adam, three months later.
- After Jim recovered from his injuries, he returned to work at the Westover Air Reserve Base.
- Every Sunday Bian endured dinner with Jim's parents, who would stare at her and whisper behind her back.
- She knew that they wished she would go back to Vietnam so Jim could find a nice American wife.
- During dinner Bian kept her eyes lowered and remembered to use her fork instead of her hands, as Jim had told her, but she always ate quickly.
- Jim's brother's wife, Diane, grew up in a privileged family in Boston, Massachusetts, and worked as a schoolteacher.

- Diane suggested that Bian take on a "more American name, like Betty," which would be easier for everyone to pronounce.
- Humiliated, Bian, now Betty, nodded.
- In Vietnamese, the meaning of the word Bian is "secret," and in this strange new place, Bian felt her former life slipping away, like a secret that no one in the United States would ever know or understand.
- Once, while cleaning up in the kitchen after dinner, she overheard the family arguing that her marriage was a disgrace to the family.
- Her mother-in-law said that she and Jim had nothing in common and that she was just interested in his money.
- Bian would never become used to the American way of making hurtful comments.

Life at Work

- Jim's Air Force salary of $585 a month was more than enough to support his family.
- He encouraged Bian to stay home with the baby all day.
- Jim worked long hours, often not returning home until 7 or 8 p.m.
- Accustomed to working around the clock from the time she was a child, Bian quickly became lonely and restless at home.
- Learning about divorce for the first time in America, Bian also became afraid that her husband, whom she barely saw, would leave her with nothing.
- Driven by this fear and wanting something more than to care for her son, she took up a neighbor's offer to give her a job scrubbing floors.
- Knowing that Jim would never approve, she always left their house after he went to work, taking Adam with her, and arrived home before him in the evenings.
- She hid the money that she earned under a loose floorboard in the baby's nursery.
- The work was easy; Bian/Betty was paid $0.75 an hour.
- In the first six weeks, she earned $100.
- The minimum wage was $1.30, with the average salary $6,887.
- At work Bian/Betty spoke to no one.
- Her tall American boss shouted and gestured to tell Bian her duties each day.
- Bian had a difficult time adjusting to living in a wealthy, foreign culture.
- After growing accustomed to the city noises of Saigon, Bian thought Westover was too quiet; the only familiar sound was the airplanes overhead.
- In the first few weeks at Jim's house, she checked the kitchen constantly, making sure that there was food for the baby.
- Bian was overcome with loneliness.
- Before she began secretly scrubbing floors, she had interacted with only Jim and Adam for days at a time.
- She did not see another Asian person; immigration from Vietnam was rare.
- With a war still under way, Jim prohibited her from communicating with her friends in Vietnam, claiming it would risk his career in the Air Force.
- In Massachusetts Bian felt isolated from everything and everyone.
- She struggled with post-traumatic stress; she often awoke from nightmares of dead bodies in the streets or floating down the river.
- She tried to cope with depression and cried every day to return home to Vietnam.

Record Producer in 1969

Owen Bradley found music as he was recovering from an eye injury as a child. He opened his own record studio with his brother in 1952 and, when he focused more on "easy listening country" than traditional country, he found himself at the center of a controversy between honky tonk artists and those who saw a softer sound as their ticket to fame.

Life at Home

- Born in Sumner County, Tennessee, in 1915, Owen began his life within 100 miles of Nashville, the home of country music.
- While Owen was recovering from an eye injury as a child, his father gave him a crystal radio, which opened his ears to the musical worlds of both country and jazz.
- By the time he was 15, he was so obsessed with playing the piano that he quit school to perform with a local orchestra.
- In 1935, when he was 20 years old, Owen married Mary Katherine Franklin; the couple first met when both were in the eighth grade.
- That same year Owen won a position as an intermission player on radio station WSM in Nashville, making $5 per segment; the station and its music format were at the epicenter of country music at that time.
- In 1940 he graduated to regular house musician, playing piano, organ, and trombone.
- Serving in the military from 1943–1945, Owen wrote songs in his free time, including "Night Train to Memphis," which became a hit for Roy Acuff; he also played in a band led by Ted Weems, and when Weems departed, Owen became the bandleader.
- During the 1940s Owen learned the craft of country music and did music-recording sessions at the radio station while also leading his own Owen Bradley Orchestra, a popular dance band.
- His first recording in the WSM studio was "Blue Mexico Skies," sung by Zeke Clements.
- By 1947 Owen was music director for WSM and had come to the attention of Paul Cohen, head of Decca Records; Owen soon worked for Decca as a pianist and arranger.
- Decca's talent roster included Ernest Tubb, Kitty Wells, Patsy Cline, Loretta Lynn and Conway Twitty.

Owen Bradley was a record producer based in Nashville, Tennessee.

- Within a decade Owen became a record producer for Decca; in 1958 he left WSM and opened a Nashville branch for Decca, serving as its vice president. In some years he managed personally to create 30 or more albums.
- With his brother Harold, a guitarist who became a legendary studio recording musician, Owen opened his own studio in 1952, recording Kitty Wells, among other country stars.
- Owen produced Wells's "It Wasn't God Who Created Honky Tonk Angels," an "answer song" to Hank Thompson's "The Wild Side of Life"; Wells's song proved to be a breakthrough not only for Wells but for female country vocalists generally.
- In 1954 Owen and Harold built the "Quonset Hut" on 16th Avenue in Nashville and moved their studio there; they opened the new space in 1955, thus launching what came to be called Music Row.

As music director for WSM, Owen hired on-air talent.

- In 1961 Owen was named *Billboard's* country music Man of the Year.
- Already famous as a country music record producer, Owen converted an old barn near his home in Mount Juliet, outside Nashville, Tennessee, into a recording studio; it became a magnet for musicians seeking stardom.
- His original plan was simply to open up a space for his oldest son, Jerry, to cut demo tapes and possibly throw a party or two.
- After that the entire operation blossomed; in 1969 a thousand recording sessions would take place in the studio.
- Many country records stayed on the market for several years, especially those of superstars like Loretta Lynn, Patsy Cline and Kitty Wells—all of whom were Owen's clients.

Loretta Lynn was one of Owen's artists.

- After years of producing and performing, Owen had the confidence and the wealth to not worry about impressing anyone but himself.
- He had a fabulous ear for talent and loved to attract singers to his place.
- Building the studio provided the perfect balance of professionalism and fun.
- The building had many conveniences, especially its location close to his house, but the resonant tin roof rattled during Tennessee thunderstorms, forcing recording sessions to stop until the rain abated.
- Loretta Lynn's hit song "Don't Come Home A-Drinking (with Lovin' on Your Mind)" was recorded at Owen's studio.
- In just three hours at Owen's studio, Kitty Wells, the Queen of Country Music, once taped five songs for an album.
- Owen was proud that his son was in the music business.

Life at Work

- The music business was tough: Owen liked to tell singers that having a big hit is like having to go to a bank with no money in it; "You wonder where the next one is coming from."
- Once he converted the barn into a recording studio, Owen had more control over the sounds he produced.
- A consummate professional, he loved to describe his production style as being a referee for a bunch of musicians getting together and doing what came naturally.
- Owen had a hands-on approach, both managing the label and producing in the studio; he sometimes was accused of micromanaging, but he believed quality begot quality.
- He was known for choosing the right songs and coaxing the best possible vocal performances from his artists.
- His son and his brother both worked for the company, often playing backup on the records Owen created.

Elvis Presley was often backed by the Jordanaires, who recorded in Owen's studio.

- Frequently Owen had to balance the demands of Nashville artists with Decca's marketing ideas, yet he had a good relationship with the New York executives.
- When Decca insisted that Patsy Cline's record "I Fall to Pieces" needed to have more of a "pop" sound, Owen added a string section; the record went on to sell millions, climbing both the country and the pop charts.
- He "de-twanged" other songs he produced so that they would reach a wider audience.
- For most recording sessions, Owen incorporated a team of musicians hired for a particular album instead of using an artist's touring band.
- The studio musicians sometimes worked with five or six different singers during the week, adapting their style of playing each time.
- Critics claimed that Owen's studio-musician formula sucked the life out of country music, but Owen believed he had pumped the money back in, and that country had to keep developing to stay fresh.
- For years the name of the artist, not the song, had dominated the industry, but that changed; Owen thought that the song itself should be the star, not the artist or the recording—even though he represented some of the biggest names in the business.

Kitty Wells was one of Owen's artists.

- At the same time, groups like the Jordanaires, who backed Elvis Presley on many of his recordings, came to work almost exclusively for record studios, staying off the road; at $85 per session, each singer could earn $65,000 a year singing in the studio by day and eating home cooking at night.
- The records Owen produced reflected his musical skills, honed through years of playing; when the record was complete, the listener heard every instrument.
- What he liked best about the business was that everyone knew everyone else; over his career he had worked with Kitty Wells, Brenda Lee, Patsy Cline, Loretta Lynn,

Grandpa Jones, Burl Ives and Charlie Walker—all of whom contributed to Owen's wealth and fame.

- Many people considered Owen's greatest talents to be discovering extraordinary voices and then letting them shine.
- With Chet Atkins—an outstanding solo guitarist and session player,and, as a record producer and company vice president, Owen's counterpart at RCA Records—Owen was at the forefront of a movement that gave country music a softer sound by downplaying the steel guitar and country fiddles.
- This move toward "country pop" or "easy-listening country" caused tension between the artists committed to the traditional honky-tonk- or

Owen was moving away from the country fiddle sound of country music.

mountain-music sound of country and those who saw the softer sound as their ticket to fame and fortune.
- Owen denied that he was abandoning country music, insisting he was only updating the sound for modern radio audiences.
- Those in the business claimed that a record producer had to combine technology and art, managing both the creative and practical sides of a recording.
- Owen loved doing it all; in Nashville it was not unusual for one person to have the authority to sign an artist to a major record label, authorize the budget and then produce the artist's record in a studio at least partially owned by that same individual.
- It was not unusual for the producer to hold, through various means, at least part of the publishing rights to the songs.
- "Producer" was the most powerful individual job title in country music.
- Often entire records were cut in two or three days, with no overdubbing; the vocals, instrumental solos and background harmonies generally were done at the same time the basic tracks were cut.

Life in the Community: Nashville, Tennessee

- Encircled by the Appalachian Mountains, Nashville was the capital of country music for most of the twentieth century, gaining that title after its radio station WSM began broadcasting its "Barn Dance" program, on November 28, 1925.
- The radio show, sponsored by an insurance company, featured performers such as Uncle Jimmy Thompson and Sam and Kirk McGee.
- The station acquired the Grand Ole Opry tag in 1927, when announcer George D. Hay, whose
- country program followed an hour of classical music, made a pun on the theme of grand opera.
- The Opry staged its first outdoor tent show in 1932, attracting eight thousand people at $0.10 each.
- From 1941, when WSM (which stood for "We Save Millions," the insurance company's slogan) joined the NBC radio network, the Opry—and Nashville—obtained a wider audience.
- Featuring music with which rural America could identify, the Opry came to be heard across the nation and in Canada.
- The first major artist to record in Nashville was Eddy Arnold, in 1944.
- In 1950 Capitol Records became the first big label to launch a Nashville operation; within ten years all of the major record labels had Nashville offices and studios.
- "Music Row" became famous throughout the world, drawing millions of tourists to the city annually.
- Guidebooks comforted the uninitiated: "You don't have to be a connoisseur of country music to get a kick out of Nashville's country music boom. It's interesting to observe simply as a phenomenon, like the Grand Canyon and Niagara Falls."

- A mandatory stop for country music fans was the Grand Ole Opry House, built originally as the Union Gospel Tabernacle and still equipped with the very hard original pews.
- Reserved seats at the Opry were $3; general admission was $2.
- On Saturdays WSM Music City Bus Tours took visitors to the wooded clump where Gentleman Jim Reeves died in a plane crash, and to the homes of Webb Pierce, Tex Ritter, Skeeter Davis, Faron Young, Jim Ed Brown, Eddy Arnold and, of course, Audrey Williams, widow of the legendary Hank.
- At the Country Music Hall of Fame and Museum, for the $1 admission, country's faithful could view a ten-minute color film on the history of country music, see how a record was made, peer into a recording studio and then look at the memorabilia of the stars.
- Sights in the Hall of Fame included Eddy Arnold's first guitar, the hat Minnie Pearl wore at her Opry debut, Earl Scruggs's banjo, and Gabby Hayes's boots.
- An entire display case was devoted to the relics salvaged from the 1963 plane crash that took the life of Patsy Cline; the case contained her favorite wig, mascara wand, hair brush and a battered, Confederate-flagged cigarette lighter that still played "Dixie."

The Grand Ole Opry House was a favorite among visitors to Nashville.

- But Nashville was more than country music, as many of its long-time residents were quick to say; the city prided itself on being a regional financial, wholesale and retail center, drawing customers from middle Tennessee, southern Kentucky, northern Alabama and northeastern Mississippi.
- It did not wish to lose those other distinctions and become too heavily dependent on a single industry, even country music.
- In 1962 the municipal government of Nashville merged with the government of Davidson County to form a metropolitan government serving half a million people.
- The move was made because the inner city was deteriorating and city services were lagging: downtown land values and rentals were dropping, while few new buildings were being built.
- The metro government concept sparked a boom in Nashville; one very visible consequence was the Capitol Hill project, including construction of a new, domed auditorium.
- The National Life and Accident Insurance Company—the South's largest, with $1.5 billion in assets—constructed a 31-story, $15-million building near the Capitol Hill complex.
- In 1969 a $100-million downtown renewal program was announced, encompassing 14 city blocks.
- Banks such as Commerce Union and First American National were contemplating whole blocks as investment projects.
- The first attempt at creating a metro government, in 1958, had failed, opposed by center-city Democratic jobholders who feared the country crowd; black leaders, who thought it would dilute their voting power downtown; suburban businessmen, who feared higher taxes; and hard-core conservatives, who considered governmental centralization as a Moscow plot.
- By 1962, however, attitudes had changed, and the move passed with a comfortable majority.
- Forced to pay taxes for downtown problems, suburbanites suddenly became interested in finding solutions—according to city officials, who nevertheless stressed that Nashville's approach brought together all of the human resources of the suburbs and the inner city.

"First Angry Man of Country Music," by Tom Dearmore, *New York Times Magazine*, September 21, 1969

"Why, on the threshold of the 1970s, is the United States reverting to its rurigenous music of the 1930s? To some observers it is almost a comic anomaly that country-western music, the backwoods balm of the Great Depression, should in this time of affluence, technological domination and blasé youth suddenly gain millions of converts among those who once were repelled by it.

Indeed, the country seems to have gone 'country' crazy: 'The Beverly Hillbillies' goes on and on, 'Hee-Haw' is a Sunday prime-time prize of CBS's and 'country' singers have now 'made the network' with their own shows and are recording with the Boston Pops.

Country-western string music was the cultural adrenaline of the thirties and forties in all the little Dullsvilles of the South, suffocating in the humid heat of Saturday nights when the bawling jukebox voices drifted out of slot-in-the-wall honky-tonks. It told of the slovenly, busted boozer, the flawless sweetheart, the fast trains that held some mystic promise, the hobo's death, the cowboy's loneliness. Twangy gospel pieces mapping the road to salvation (a railroad to the pearly gates in more than one instance) were on the same Wurlitzers with lowdown music-to-swill-beer-by and the tearjerkers about home and mother. The form appeared in the twenties among the hillbillies and cotton pickers of the poor South—an amalgam of ancient folk balladry, Negro spirituals, fundamentalist gospel pop music and Prohibition jazz. It flowered in the early thirties when the farmers got their battery radios and heard songs both mournful and rousing from WSM in Nashville, wept as Jimmie Rodgers, 'The Singing Brakeman,' related how Hobo Bill died alone but smiling in a frigid freight car.

Many Americans despised it as the banal evocation of a tawdriness of life unworthy of notice, as a nasal cacophony, as ignorance put to music. But it now is not only rising in popularity at home, it is, as John Greenway points out in *The American West* (the magazine of the Western History Association), making headway abroad-it has devotees all over western Europe; there is a 'Tokyo Grand Ole Opry' on the air, featuring bands like Jimmy Tokita and His Mountain Playboys. American country singers have packed the London Palladium and drawn cheers in Hobart, Tasmania, equal to those in Nashville, Tennessee, the capital of country music."

"We were so poor and everyone around us was so poor that it was the forties before any of us knew there had been a Depression."

—Record producer Chet Atkins, on growing up on his father's 50-acre farm in the Clinch Mountains near Luttrell, Tennessee

SECTION TWO: HISTORICAL SNAPSHOT

The 1960s in America were revolutionary. The counterculture that developed in this decade crept into all aspects of everyday life. Large segments of society challenged mainstream values surrounding clothing, music, drugs, dress codes, and education, and new behavior in these, and other aspects of life and lifestyles, began to take hold. The decade is often called the Swinging Sixties, referring to the loosening of social taboos, especially in regard to racism and sexuality. Major social movements, specifically those targeted against the Vietnam War, and demonstrations for and against civil rights, continue to define the decade. These Historical Snapshots highlight significant firsts and milestones of the 60s, as oral contraception are approved and The Beatles become household words.

Early 1960s

- The National Association of Broadcasters reacted to a payola scandal by threatening fines for any disc jockeys who accepted money for playing particular records
- Four students from North Carolina Agricultural and Technical State University in Greensboro, North Carolina, began a sit-in at a segregated Woolworth's lunch counter, which triggered similar nonviolent protests throughout the Southern United States
- Joanne Woodward received the first star on the Hollywood Walk of Fame
- Adolph Coors III, chairman of the board of the Coors Brewing Company, was kidnapped for $500,000 and later found dead
- The United States announced that 3,500 American soldiers would be sent to Vietnam
- Arthur Leonard Schawlow and Charles Hard Townes received the first patent for a laser
- The United States launched the first weather satellite, TIROS-1
- *Ben Hur* won the Oscar for Best Picture
- A Soviet missile shot down an American Lockheed U-2 spy plane; the pilot, Francis Gary Powers, was captured, tried, and released 21 months later in a spy swap with the U.S.
- President Dwight D. Eisenhower signed the Civil Rights Act of 1960 into law
- The U.S. Food and Drug Administration announced that it would approve birth control as an additional indication for Searle's Enovid, making it the world's first approved oral contraceptive pill

- The nuclear submarine *USS Triton* completed the first underwater circumnavigation of Earth
- The Soviet Union beat Yugoslavia 2-1 to win the first European Football Championship
- The two leading U.S. presidential candidates, Richard M. Nixon and John F. Kennedy, participated in the first televised presidential debate

- Nikita Khrushchev pounded his shoe on a table at a United Nations General Assembly meeting to protest the discussion of Soviet Union policy toward Eastern Europe
- Entertainer Sammy Davis, Jr. married Swedish actress May Britt
- Basketball player Wilt Chamberlain grabbed 55 rebounds and scored 100 points in single games
- Production of the DeSoto automobile brand ceased
- President Eisenhower authorized the use of $1 million toward the resettlement of Cuban refugees, who were arriving in Florida at the rate of 1,000 a week
- Ham the Chimp was rocketed into space aboard *Mercury-Redstone 2* in a test of the Project Mercury capsule, designed to carry U.S. astronauts into space
- U.S. astronaut Alan Shepard became the first American in space aboard *Mercury-Redstone 3;* a suborbital flight that lasted for 15 minutes
- The U.S. Supreme Court declared in *Boynton v. Virginia* that segregation on public transit was illegal
- The U.S. Census listed all people from Latin America as white, including blacks from the Dominican Republic, European whites from Argentina, and Mexicans who resembled Native Americans
- The world population was 3,021,475,000
- The Congress of Racial Equality (CORE) organized Freedom Rides to integrate buses, trains and terminals throughout the South
- The minimum wage rose from $1.00 to $1.25 per hour
- Congress passed legislation making airplane hijacking punishable by death
- John Steinbeck's *The Winter of Our Discontent*, Irving Stone's *The Agony and the Ecstasy*, Joseph Heller's *Catch 22*, and Harper Lee's *To Kill a Mockingbird* were all bestsellers
- Readers voted *Peanuts*, *Li'l Abner* and *Pogo* the best comic strips of the year
- The IBM Selectric typewriter, self-wringing mops, electric toothbrush, Country corn flakes and Coffee-mate all made their first appearance
- The twist craze, led by Chubby Checker, began
- President Kennedy launched an exercise campaign urging all Americans to be more fit
- The Interstate Commerce Commission banned segregation on all interstate facilities

- The Civil War Centennial celebration began
- FCC Chairman Newton Minow called television "a vast wasteland" during a speech at the National Association of Broadcasters
- President Kennedy appointed a committee to study the status of women
- The DNA genetic code was broken
- A university poll reported that 72 percent of elementary and high school teachers approved of corporal punishment as a disciplinary measure
- Clark Gable died at the conclusion of filming *The Misfits*
- Robert Zimmerman, known as Bob Dylan, began singing in Greenwich Village nightclubs; his first recording opportunity was as a backup harmonica player
- Ray Kroc borrowed $2.7 million to buy out the McDonald Brothers and began the McDonald's empire
- Four thousand servicemen were sent to Vietnam as advisors to the South Vietnamese army
- The words Peace Corps, high rise, New Frontier, soul, zonked, and new wave all entered the language
- Cigarette makers spent $115 million on television advertising
- Canned pet food was among the three top-selling categories in grocery stores
- President Kennedy established the Peace Corps two months after his inauguration
- New York's First National Bank offered fixed-term certificates of deposit
- The right wing activities of the John Birch Society stirred concerns in Congress
- R.J. Reynolds acquired Pacific Hawaiian Products Company in an attempt to diversify away from tobacco products
- Sprite was introduced by Coca-Cola Company
- A Gallup poll recorded that 74 percent of teens interviewed believed in God; 58 percent planned to go to college. Of the 16- to 21-year-old girls interviewed, almost all expected to be married by age 22 and most wanted four children
- Electronic Data Systems was founded by H. Ross Perot
- 90 percent of American households had at least one television set
- The American Broadcasting Company (ABC) began color telecasts for 3.5 hours per week
- *Silent Spring* by U.S. biologist Rachel Carson was published which stated that more than 500 new chemicals were entering our bodies because of widespread insecticide use
- Diet-Rite Cola was introduced as the first sugar-free soft drink
- Tab-opening aluminum drink cans were introduced
- On May 28, 1962, the stock market plunged 34.95 points, the sharpest drop since the 1929 crash
- At the National Reactor Testing Station near Idaho Falls, Idaho, atomic reactor SL-1 exploded, killing three military technicians
- In his farewell address, President Eisenhower warned Americans of the increasing power of a "military-industrial complex"
- The U.S. launched its first test of the Minuteman I intercontinental ballistic missile

- The Beatles performed for the first time at the Cavern Club
- Max Conrad circumnavigated the earth in eight days, 18 hours and 49 minutes, setting a new world record
- The first U.S. Polaris submarines arrived at Holy Loch
- The Twenty-third Amendment to the Constitution was ratified, allowing residents of Washington, DC, to vote in presidential elections
- Soviet cosmonaut Yuri Gagarin became the first human in space aboard *Vostok 1*
- The Bay of Pigs Invasion of Cuba failed to overthrow Fidel Castro
- A bus full of Civil Rights Freedom Riders was fire-bombed near Anniston, Alabama, and the Civil Rights protestors were beaten by an angry mob
- *Venera 1* became the first manmade object to fly by another planet—Venus—but failed to send back any data
- President Kennedy announced before a special joint session of Congress his goal to put a man on the moon before the end of the decade
- Peter Benenson's article "The Forgotten Prisoners" was published in several internationally read newspapers, leading to the founding of the human rights organization Amnesty International
- Russian ballet dancer Rudolf Nureyev requested asylum in France while in Paris with the Kirov Ballet
- President Kennedy delivered a widely watched TV speech on the Berlin crisis, and urged Americans to build fallout shelters
- Civil Defense officials distributed 22 million copies of the pamphlet *Family Fallout Shelter*
- The Walt Disney anthology television series, renamed *Walt Disney's Wonderful World of Color,* began telecasting its programs in color
- Baseball player Roger Maris of the New York Yankees hit his sixty-first home run in the last game of the season to break the 34-year-old record held by Babe Ruth
- The Soviet Union detonated a 58-megaton-yield hydrogen bomb, the largest ever manmade explosion
- The *Fantastic Four #1* comic debuted, launching the Marvel Universe
- President Kennedy sent 18,000 military advisors to South Vietnam
- Nazi Adolf Eichmann was pronounced guilty of crimes against humanity by a panel of three Israeli judges and sentenced to death for his role in the holocaust
- "Barbie" got a boyfriend when the "Ken" doll was introduced
- The late-night television show, *The Tonight Show,* with Johnny Carson, began
- Demonstrations against school segregation occurred throughout the South
- President John F. Kennedy contributed his salary to charity
- The Dow Jones Industrial Average reached a high of 767
- Movie premieres included *To Kill a Mockingbird, Long Day's Journey into Night, The Manchurian Candidate, The Longest Day* and *Lawrence of Arabia*

- The Students' Nonviolent Coordinating Committee (SNCC) organized the freedom ballot in the South, aggressively registering blacks to vote in Mississippi, Alabama and Georgia
- Popular songs included "Go Away, Little Girl," "What Kind of Fool Am I?", "I Left My Heart in San Francisco" and "The Sweetest Sounds"
- At nine New York daily newspapers, unions staged a strike that lasted five months
- Walter Cronkite replaced Douglas Edwards on the *CBS Evening News*
- Jackie Robinson was the first African-American inducted into the Baseball Hall of Fame
- *One Flew Over the Cuckoo's Nest* by Ken Kesey, *Happiness Is a Warm Puppy* by Charles M. Schulz, *Sex and the Single Girl* by Helen Gurley Brown, and *Pigeon Feathers* by John Updike were all published
- *Mariner II* became the first successful interplanetary probe, confirming that the high temperatures of Venus were inhospitable to life
- *Who's Afraid of Virginia Woolf?* opened on Broadway
- Inflation was at 0.4 percent, unemployment at 5.5 percent
- Eighty percent of households had a telephone
- The world came to the brink of war when America and the Soviet Union faced off over the installation of Soviet missiles in Cuba
- New York City introduced a subway train that operated without a crew on board
- The Beatles' first record, "My Bonnie" with Tony Sheridan, was released by Polydor
- Leonardo da Vinci's *Mona Lisa* was exhibited in the United States for the first time, at the National Gallery of Art in Washington, DC
- Six members of the Committee of 100 of the Campaign for Nuclear Disarmament were found guilty of a breach of the Official Secrets Act
- First Lady Jacqueline Kennedy took television viewers on a tour of the White House
- John Glenn became the first American to orbit Earth, three times in four hours, 55 minutes, as a member of Project Mercury

- The U.S. Supreme Court ruled that federal courts could order state legislatures to reapportion seats
- The Century 21 Exposition World's Fair opened in Seattle, Washington
- The Hulk debuted with *The Incredible Hulk #1* by cartoonists Stan Lee and Jack Kirby
- Dayton Hudson Corporation opened the first of its Target discount stores in Roseville, Minnesota
- The U.S. Supreme Court ruled that mandatory prayers in public schools were unconstitutional
- The Supreme Court ruled that photographs of nude men were not obscene, decriminalizing nude male pornographic magazines
- The first Wal-Mart store opened for business in Rogers, Arkansas
- *Amazing Fantasy #15* featured the superhero character of Spider-Man, created by cartoonists Stan Lee and Steve Ditko

- President John F. Kennedy was shot and killed in Dallas, Texas
- Betty Friedan published *The Feminine Mystique*, challenging the image of the happy housewife
- Television premieres included *The Fugitive, The Patty Duke Show, My Favorite Martian, Petticoat Junction* and *Let's Make A Deal*
- Katherine Graham became president of The Washington Post Company, and the only female head of a Fortune 500 company
- The Beatles crashed the American music scene with their first big hit, "I Want to Hold Your Hand"
- U.S. factory workers earned more than $100 a week, a new record
- The March on Washington for Jobs and Freedom attracted thousands to hear Martin Luther King deliver his "I Have a Dream" speech
- Julia Child prepared boeuf bourguignon on television to launch her popular French cooking program
- Fifty women each week applied to *Playboy* to become "Playmate of the Month"
- American poet and novelist Sylvia Plath published her autobiographical novel *The Bell Jar*
- Sidney Poitier won the Academy Award for best actor in *Lilies of the Field*, while *Tom Jones* won best picture
- Broadway openings included *Barefoot in the Park, Enter Laughing, One Flew Over the Cuckoo's Nest* and the musical *Oliver!*
- Fourteen thousand people were arrested in 75 southern cities during civil rights demonstrations
- Mary Petermann discovered Petermann's particles, or ribosomes, the sites of protein synthesis
- Hit songs included "Wipeout," "Call Me Irresponsible," "If I Had a Hammer," "Puff (the Magic Dragon)," "Da Doo Ron Ron" and "The Times They Are a-Changin'"
- The Kodak Instamatic camera, the New York Hilton, Weight Watchers, the Trimline phone and Spiderman all made their first appearance
- Births among unwed teenage mothers were up 150 percent over 1940
- California passed New York as the most populous state
- Police Chief Bull Connors of Birmingham, Alabama, used police dogs, fire hoses and cattle prods on civil rights marchers to break up a demonstration
- New Hampshire authorized government-sponsored lotteries designed to raise money for education
- Congress approved legislation guaranteeing equal pay for equal work

Mid 1960s

- In the first meeting between leaders of the Roman Catholic and Orthodox churches since the fifteenth century, Pope Paul VI and Patriarch Athenagoras I met in Jerusalem
- In his first State of the Union Address, President Lyndon Johnson declared a "War on Poverty"
- Thirteen years after its proposal and nearly two years after its passage by the Senate, the Twenty-fourth Amendment to the Constitution, prohibiting the use of poll taxes in national elections, was ratified
- General Motors introduced the Oldsmobile Vista Cruiser and the Buick Sport Wagon
- The Beatles, having vaulted to the Number 1 spot on the U.S. singles charts for the first time with "I Want to Hold Your Hand," appeared on *The Ed Sullivan Show*, and were seen by an estimated 73 million viewers, launching the mid-1960s "British Invasion" of American popular music
- The Supreme Court ruled that congressional districts must be approximately equal in population
- Muhammad Ali beat Sonny Liston in Miami Beach, Florida, and was crowned the Heavyweight Champion of the World
- Teamsters President Jimmy Hoffa was convicted by a federal jury of tampering with a federal jury in 1962
- In *New York Times Co. v. Sullivan*, the Supreme Court ruled that, under the First Amendment, speech criticizing political figures cannot be censored
- The first Ford Mustang rolled off the assembly line at Ford Motor Company
- A Dallas, Texas, jury found Jack Ruby guilty of killing John F. Kennedy's assassin Lee Harvey Oswald
- Merv Griffin's game show *Jeopardy!* debuted on NBC
- The Beatles dominated the top five positions in the Billboard Top 40 singles in America: "Can't Buy Me Love," "Twist and Shout," "She Loves You," "I Want to Hold Your Hand," and "Please Please Me"
- Three high school friends in Hoboken, New Jersey, opened the first BLIMPIE restaurant
- The Rolling Stones released their debut album, *The Rolling Stones*
- The New York World's Fair opened to celebrate the 300th anniversary of New Amsterdam being taken over by British forces and renamed New York in 1664
- John George Kemeny and Thomas Eugene Kurtz ran the first computer program written in BASIC (Beginners' All-purpose Symbolic Instruction Code), an easy-to-learn, high-level programming language

- College students marched through Times Square and San Francisco in the first major student demonstration against the Vietnam War
- President Johnson signed the Civil Rights Act of 1964 into law, legally abolishing racial segregation in the United States
- At the Republican National Convention in San Francisco, presidential nominee Barry Goldwater declared that "extremism in the defense of liberty is no vice," and "moderation in the pursuit of justice is no virtue"
- Cosmic microwave background radiation was discovered

- Dr. Farrington Daniels's book, *Direct Use of the Sun's Energy*, was published by Yale University Press
- The first Moog synthesizer was designed by Robert Moog
- Americans purchased $60 million worth of prescription weight-loss drugs, twice the dollar amount spent just five years earlier
- "Flower Power" was coined by Allen Ginsburg at a Berkeley antiwar rally
- Quaker Norman Morrison immolated himself on the steps of the Pentagon to protest the U.S. military buildup in Vietnam
- Unemployment, at 4.2 percent, was at its lowest point in eight years
- The U.S. Immigration Bill abolished national origin quotas
- Avis Rent-A-Car was acquired by International Telephone and Telegraph
- The Voting Rights Act, which eliminated literacy tests and provided federal oversight in elections, stimulated a dramatic increase in voting by African-Americans
- The robust American business expansion, begun in 1961, continued without interruption, representing the longest period of economic expansion in peacetime since 1854
- The U.S. Supreme Court struck down a Connecticut statute forbidding the use of contraceptives and eliminated state and local film censorship
- Pope Paul VI visited the United Nations headquarters and delivered a message of peace
- After extended hearings on cigarette smoking, Congress required that cigarette packages carry the warning, "Caution: Cigarette smoking may be hazardous to your health"
- The amount Americans paid for prepackaged food increased $7.5 billion from 1940
- The birth rate fell to 19 per 1,000 people, the lowest since 1940
- Cereal packaged with fruits preserved through freeze-drying was introduced
- Miniskirts, Cranapple, Diet Pepsi, the Sony home videotape recorder and all-news radio stations made their first appearance
- Work began on a 150-mile commuter rail transportation system around San Francisco and Oakland, California
- Kraft foods sponsored the first commercial television program transmitted between the U.S. and Switzerland via the *Early Bird* communications satellite
- More than 70 percent of the world's orchestras resided in the United States
- The production of soft-top convertible automobiles reached a record 507,000
- For the first time since 1962, the administration did not ask Congress for a fallout shelter construction program
- The Council on Religion and the Homosexual launched a gay Mardi Gras Ball in San Francisco that was raided by police
- In his State of the Union address, President Lyndon Johnson outlined the goals of his "Great Society" that included an attack on diseases, a doubling of the war on poverty, greater enforcement of the Civil Rights Law, immigration law reform and greater support of education
- Eighteen were arrested in Mississippi for the murder of three civil rights workers

- President Johnson ordered the bombing of North Vietnam known as "Rolling Thunder" and authorized commanders in Vietnam to commit U.S. ground forces to combat
- Fourteen Vietnam War protesters were arrested for blocking U.N. doors in New York
- The *Ranger 8* spacecraft crashed on the moon after sending back 7,000 photos of the lunar surface
- Former Black Muslim leader El-Hajj Malik El-Shabazz, known as Malcolm X, was shot to death in front of 400 people in New York by assassins identified as Black Muslims
- Julie Andrews starred in the film adaptation of the popular Broadway hit, *The Sound of Music*
- Neil Simon's play *The Odd Couple*, starring Walter Matthau as Oscar Madison and Art Carney as Felix Unger, opened on Broadway
- President Johnson ordered 4,000 troops to protect the Selma-Montgomery civil rights marchers
- Despite repeated acts of violence, Martin Luther King, Jr. and 25,000 civil rights activists successfully ended the four-day march from Selma, Alabama, to the Capitol of Montgomery; King and 770 of his followers were arrested
- Sixteen-year-old Lawrence Wallace Bradford, Jr. was appointed by New York Republican Jacob Javits to be the first Black page of the U.S. Senate
- The Rolling Stones recorded "Satisfaction"
- NASA successfully launched *Gemini 3*, America's first two-person spacecraft, into Earth's orbit
- Astronaut Edward White became the first American to "walk" in space during the flight of *Gemini 4*
- President Johnson signed the Voting Rights Act of 1965, which outlawed the literacy test for voting eligibility in the South
- Approximately 3,500 United States Marines arrived in South Vietnam, becoming the first official American combat troops there
- At the Academy Awards, *My Fair Lady* won Best Picture and Best Director; Julie Andrews won an Academy Award for Best Actress in *Mary Poppins*
- The West German parliament extended the statute of limitations on Nazi war crimes
- Charlie Brown and the *Peanuts* gang were featured on the cover of *Time* magazine
- The first Students for a Democratic Society (SDS)-sponsored march against the Vietnam War attracted 25,000 protestors to Washington, DC
- U.S. troops were sent to the Dominican Republic by President Johnson, "for the stated purpose of protecting U.S. citizens and preventing an alleged Communist takeover of the country," thus thwarting the possibility of "another Cuba"
- Jonathan Myrick Daniels, an Episcopal seminarian from Keene, New Hampshire, was murdered in Hayneville, Alabama, while working for the Civil Rights Movement
- The *Tom & Jerry* cartoon series made its world broadcast premiere on CBS
- The student-run National Coordinating Committee to End the War in Vietnam staged the first public burning of a draft card in the United States to result in arrest under the new law
- Pope Paul VI announced that the Ecumenical Council had decided that Jews were not collectively responsible for the killing of Christ
- In St. Louis, Missouri, the 630-foot-tall parabolic steel Gateway Arch was completed
- Pillsbury's mascot, the Pillsbury Doughboy, was created
- The soap opera *Days of our Lives* debuted on NBC
- Cosmonaut Aleksei Leonov left his spacecraft *Voskhod 2* for 12 minutes and became the first person to walk in space
- NASA launched the first two-person crew, Gus Grissom and John Young, into orbit around Earth
- The world's first space nuclear power reactor, *SNAP-10A*, was launched by the United States; the reactor operated for 43 days

- Forty men burned their draft cards at the University of California, Berkeley, and a coffin was marched to the Berkeley Draft Board
- Muhammad Ali knocked out Sonny Liston in the first round of their championship rematch with the "Phantom Punch" at the Central Maine Civic Center in Lewiston
- The U.S. spacecraft *Mariner 4* flew by Mars, becoming the first spacecraft to return 22 images from the Red Planet
- Bob Dylan elicited controversy among folk purists by "going electric" at the Newport Folk Festival
- President Johnson signed the Social Security Act of 1965 into law, establishing Medicare and Medicaid
- The racially motivated Watts Riots ripped through Los Angeles
- The Beatles performed the first stadium concert in the history of rock, playing before 55,600 people at Shea Stadium in New York City
- Congress passed a law penalizing the burning of draft cards with up to five years in prison and a $1,000 fine
- Cuba and the United States formally agreed to start an airlift for Cubans who wanted to come to America
- American generals called for an increase in the number of troops in Vietnam, from 120,000 to 400,000
- Blanket student deferments from the draft are abolished; draft calls reached 50,000 young men a month
- The largest year-to-year rise in the cost of living since 1958 was announced-2.8 percent
- The term "Black Power" was introduced into the Civil Rights movement, signifying the rift between the pacifist followers of Martin Luther King, Jr.'s SCLC and the militants following Stokely Carmichael, Student Nonviolent Coordinating Committee (SNCC) and Congress of Racial Equality (CORE)
- 41 percent of non-White families made less than $3,000 annually
- *New York World Journal & Tribune* closed; *Rolling Stone* magazine was founded
- 2.7 million Americans received food stamp assistance
- Nearly 10,000 farmers received more than $20,000 each in subsidies
- Annual per capita beef consumption reached 105.6 pounds
- Burger King Corporation was acquired by Pillsbury Corporation
- The Clean Waters Restoration Act allocated funds for preventing river and air pollution
- The National Association of Broadcasters instructed all disc jockeys to screen all records for hidden references to drugs or obscene meanings
- The U.S. population passed 200 million
- Per capita consumption of processed potato chips rose from 6.3 pounds a year in 1958 to 14.2 pounds a year
- The Rare and Endangered Species list was introduced by the Department of the Interior
- The phrase "Third World" for underdeveloped countries gained currency of usage
- The exquisite playing of Jimi Hendrix helped popularize the electric guitar
- The President's Commission on Food Marketing reported that consumers pay 29 percent more for nationally advertised brands than for high-quality local brands

- Jackie Robinson, the man who broke the color barrier in major league baseball, became the general manager of the Brooklyn Dodgers of the Continental Football League
- The International Days of Protest against the war in Vietnam took place in seven American and seven foreign cities
- The Fillmore Theater in San Francisco popularized strobe lights, liquid color blobs, glow paint, and psychedelic posters
- Boxing Heavyweight Champion Cassius Clay became a Muslim and changed his name to Muhammad Ali
- Civil Rights activist James Meredith was shot during a march from Memphis, Tennessee, to Jackson, Mississippi
- Haynes Johnson of the *Washington Star* won the Pulitzer for his coverage of the Selma, Alabama, Civil Rights conflict; the *Los Angeles Times* staff won the Pulitzer in the local reporting category for its coverage of the racially charged Watts riots
- Frank Robinson became the first baseball player to win a Most Valuable Player award in each league
- Los Angeles Dodger pitcher Sandy Koufax won his third Cy Young Award and retired
- *Time* named the "Twenty-five and Under Generation" its "Man of the Year"
- In a decision to end the chaos of touring, the Beatles played their last live concert on August 29 at Candlestick Park, San Francisco
- The top music hits of the year were "The Ballad of the Green Berets," "Born Free," "Good Vibrations," "The Impossible Dream," "Sunny," "What Now, My Love?", "Winchester Cathedral," "Alfie," "The Sounds of Silence" and "Georgy Girl"
- *Batman*, which aired twice weekly on television, became a national fad; villains included Art Carney as the Archer, Burgess Meredith as the Penguin and Cesar Romero as the Joker
- To combat the smog, California imposed car exhaust standards, to take effect in 1969
- Bestsellers included *In Cold Blood* by Truman Capote, *A Thousand Days* by Arthur M. Schlesinger, Jr., *Valley of the Dolls* by Jacqueline Susann, *Games People Play* by Eric Berne, *Capable of Honor* by Allen Drury and *All in the Family* by Edwin O'Connor
- Television premieres included *The Newlywed Game, Mission Impossible, Batman, Star Trek, The Avengers, The Monkees, That Girl, The Dating Game* and *The Smothers Brothers Comedy Hour*
- Stokely Carmichael was elected head of the Student Nonviolent Coordinating Committee
- The court case *Miranda v. Arizona* required law enforcement officers to inform defendants of their rights, including the right to remain silent and the right to an attorney
- The National Organization for Women was founded "to bring about equality for all women"
- Hewlett-Packard introduced its first computer, the HP 2116A
- The novel *Valley of the Dolls* by Jacqueline Susann sold over 20 million copies
- Xerox introduced the Magnafax Telecopier capable of transmitting a single-page letter in six minutes
- In Oakland, California, Bobby Seale and Huey Newton co-founded the Black Panthers, which promoted the use of violence as self-defense
- Martin Luther King, Jr. took a stand against the Vietnam War, fearing it was sapping resources from domestic social programs
- Soviet *Luna 9* became the first spacecraft to soft-land on the moon

- The U.S. *Lunar Orbiter 1* entered the moon's orbit and took the first picture of Earth from there
- U.S. troop strength in Vietnam grew from 200,000 in January to 400,000 by December
- The Cultural Revolution began in China
- President Lyndon Johnson signed the Freedom of Information Act
- Twenty-five thousand anti-Vietnam War demonstrators marched in New York City
- Fuel injection for cars was invented
- Popular music included "These Boots Were Made for Walking" by Nancy Sinatra, "The Sound of Silence" by Simon and Garfunkel, and "Monday, Monday" by the Mamas and the Papas
- Movie openings included *A Man for All Seasons*, *Who's Afraid of Virginia Woolf?*, *Blow-up*, *Fahrenheit 451*, and *Alfie*
- In professional baseball, The Major League Players Association was formed
- Cesar Chavez's National Farm Workers Union was recognized as the bargaining agent for farm workers
- Virginia Masters and William Johnson's book *Human Sexual Response* controversially asserted that women possess as much sexual energy as do men
- Frank Sinatra won a Grammy Award for his recording of "Strangers in the Night"
- Biodegradable liquid detergents were produced for the first time to reduce pollution
- Roman Catholic bishops ruled that except during Lent, American Catholics could eat meat on Friday
- Soviet space probe *Venera 3* crashed on Venus, becoming the first spacecraft to land on another planet
- The Texas Western Miners defeated the Kentucky Wildcats with five African-American starters, ushering in desegregation in athletic recruiting
- An artificial heart was implanted in the chest of Marcel DeRudder in a Houston, Texas, hospital
- Bob Dylan's album, *Blonde on Blonde* was released
- The final episode of *The Dick Van Dyke Show* aired
- Groundbreaking took place for the World Trade Center in New York City; Caesars Palace opened in Las Vegas
- The Beatles released their *Revolver* album; the Doors recorded their self-titled debut LP
- In the People's Republic of China, Mao Zedong began the brutal Cultural Revolution to purge and reorganize China's Communist Party
- The Metropolitan Opera House opened at Lincoln Center in New York City with the world premiere of Samuel Barber's opera, *Antony and Cleopatra*
- The Toyota Corolla automobile was introduced
- ABC-TV broadcast a 90-minute television adaptation of the musical *Brigadoon*, starring Robert Goulet, Peter Falk, and Sally Ann Howes
- Grace Slick joined the Jefferson Airplane
- The merger of the AFL-NFL in football was approved by Congress

Late 1960s

- The connection between a cholesterol-lowering diet and a reduced incidence of heart disease was shown in a five-year study
- Both CBS and NBC televised the Super Bowl
- A reported 100,000 hippies lived in the San Francisco area, principally around Haight-Ashbury
- The first rock festival was held at Monterey, California, featuring the Grateful Dead and Big Brother and the Holding Company starring Janis Joplin
- Heavyweight boxer Muhammad Ali was denied conscientious objector status after refusing induction in the Army and was stripped of his title
- George Lincoln Rockwell, president of the U.S. Nazi Party, was shot to death
- The United States revealed that an anti-ballistic missile defense plan had been developed against Chinese attack
- Hit songs included "Natural Woman," "Soul Man," "I Never Loved a Man," "Penny Lane," "By The Time I Get to Phoenix," and "Can't Take My Eyes Off You"
- When Army physician Captain Harold Levy refused to train Green Berets heading to Vietnam in the treatment of skin disease, he was court-martialed and sent to Fort Leavenworth prison
- Coed dorms opened at numerous colleges across the country for the first time
- *Sgt Pepper's Lonely Hearts Club Band* by the Beatles captured a Grammy award for best album
- Jogging, Mickey Mouse watches, protest buttons and psychedelic art were all important fads
- Thurgood Marshall became the first African American appointed to the U.S. Supreme Court
- Television premieres included *The Flying Nun, The Carol Burnett Show, Ironside* and *The Phil Donahue Show*
- Black leader Rap Brown said of the ghetto riots, "Violence is as American as apple pie"
- Journalist Bernard Fall was killed in Vietnam by a landmine
- The Doors' self-titled debut album was released
- Dr. James Bedford became the first person to be cryonically preserved with the intent of future resuscitation
- Louis Leakey announced the discovery of pre-human fossils in Kenya; he named the species *Kenyapithecus africanus*
- The Green Bay Packers defeated the Kansas City Chiefs 35-10 at the Super Bowl
- In Munich, Wilhelm Harster, accused of the murder of 82,856 Jews (including Anne Frank) when he led German security police during the German occupation of The Netherlands, was sentenced to 15 years in prison

TX 1326 • 60¢

Edited by CAROLYN BARNES

1. THE HIPPIE SCENE, Carolyn Barnes, editor. Who are they? More than that, WHY are they? News stories on various aspects of the hippie scene, including the tragic, prize-winning Linda Fitzpatrick story. (And great photos!)

~~60¢~~ YOU PAY **50¢**

- Astronauts Gus Grissom, Edward Higgins White, and Roger Chaffee were killed when a fire broke out in their *Apollo* spacecraft during a launch pad test
- The American Basketball Association was formed
- The Twenty-fifth Amendment to the Constitution concerning presidential succession and disability was ratified
- The song "Respect" was recorded by Aretha Franklin
- *A Man for All Seasons* was named Best Picture at the Academy Awards
- The Soviet Union ratified a treaty with the United States and the United Kingdom, banning nuclear weapons in outer space
- Israel occupied the West Bank, Gaza Strip, Sinai peninsula and the Golan Heights after defeating its Arab neighbors in the Six-Day War

- The Supreme Court declared unconstitutional all laws prohibiting interracial marriage
- In Detroit, Michigan, one of the worst riots in United States history began on 12th Street in the predominantly African-American inner city; 43 were killed
- The Doors defied CBS censors on *The Ed Sullivan Show* when Jim Morrison sang the word "higher" from their Number One hit "Light My Fire"
- Thirty-nine people, including singer-activist Joan Baez, were arrested in Oakland, California, for blocking the entrance of the city's military induction center
- The musical *Hair* opened off-Broadway
- Walt Disney's nineteenth full-length animated feature, *The Jungle Book*, was released, and was the last animated film personally supervised by Disney
- Tens of thousands of Vietnam War protesters marched in Washington, DC, where poet Allen Ginsberg symbolically called upon the protestors to "levitate" the Pentagon
- President Lyndon B. Johnson signed legislation establishing the Corporation for Public Broadcasting
- Robert Lehman bequeathed 3,000 works valued at more than $100 million to the Metropolitan Museum of Art
- Shirley Chisholm of New York became the first African-American woman elected to the U.S. House of Representatives
- Protestors at the Miss America Pageant threw bras, girdles, curlers, false eyelashes, and wigs into the Freedom Trash Can
- Celibacy of the priesthood became an issue in the Catholic Church; Pope Paul VI's ban on contraception was challenged by 800 U.S. theologians
- Yale University admitted women for the first time
- Film courses and Black Studies programs were developed at many colleges
- The Poor People's Campaign, led by the Reverend Ralph Abernathy, arrived in Washington, DC
- IBM stocks split again; 100 shares purchased in 1914 for $2,750 now totaled 59,320 shares valued at more than $20 million
- The American Medical Association formulated a new standard of death: "brain dead"
- Johnny Cash recorded *At Folsom Prison*

- The Green Bay Packers won Super Bowl II over the Oakland Raiders 33-14; quarterback Bart Starr was named Most Valuable Player
- *Rowan & Martin's Laugh-In* debuted on NBC
- North Korea seized the *USS Pueblo,* claiming the ship violated its territorial waters while spying
- A civil rights protest staged at a white-only bowling alley in Orangeburg, South Carolina, resulted in the deaths of three South Carolina State College students
- PBS televised the first episode of *Mister Rogers' Neighborhood*
- U.S. President Lyndon B. Johnson mandated that all computers purchased by the federal government support the ASCII character encoding
- President Johnson announced he would not run for re-election after edging out antiwar candidate Eugene J. McCarthy in the New Hampshire Democratic Primary, highlighting the deep divisions in the country over Vietnam
- Congress repealed the requirement for a gold reserve to back U.S. currency
- Howard University students protesting the Vietnam War, the ROTC program on campus and the draft, confronted Gen. Lewis Hershey, head of the U.S. Selective Service System, with cries of "America is the black man's battleground!"
- The Standard & Poor's 500 Index closed at 100.38, the first time it had ever closed above 100
- U.S. presidential candidate Robert F. Kennedy was shot and killed in Los Angeles, California, by Sirhan Sirhan shortly after winning the California Democratic primary
- The soap opera *One Life to Live* premiered on ABC
- The semiconductor company Intel was founded
- Police clashed with antiwar protesters in Chicago, Illinois, outside the 1968 Democratic National Convention, which nominated Hubert Humphrey for president and Edmund Muskie for vice president
- Mattel's Hot Wheels toy cars were introduced
- The Tet Offensive began in Vietnam, as Viet Cong forces launched a series of surprise attacks across South Vietnam, reducing American support for the war
- The Pennsylvania Railroad and the New York Central Railroad merged to form Penn Central, the largest-ever corporate merger up to that time
- The Florida Education Association (FEA) initiated a mass resignation of teachers to protest state funding of education, the first statewide teachers' strike in the United States
- In Vietnam, hundreds of civilians-children, women, and elderly-were raped, sodomized and killed by U.S. soldiers in what became known as the My Lai Massacre
- Folk singer Joan Baez married activist David Harris in New York
- The films *2001: A Space Odyssey* and *Planet of the Apes* were released in theaters
- Apollo-Saturn mission 502 (*Apollo* 6) was launched, as the second and last unmanned test-flight of the *Saturn V* launch vehicle

2. 2001: A SPACE ODYSSEY. Arthur C. Clarke. That wild, way-out movie, novelized by the famous science-fiction author who wrote the script. Sixteen pages of photos from the movie.

~~95¢~~ YOU PAY 75¢

- The Beatles announced the creation of Apple Records; James Taylor was the first non-British musician they signed on
- The Catonsville Nine entered the Selective Service offices in Catonsville, Maryland, took dozens of selective service draft records, and burned them with napalm as a protest against the Vietnam War
- Radical feminist Valerie Solanas shot Andy Warhol as he entered his studio, wounding him
- Pope Paul VI published the encyclical entitled *Humanae Vitae*, condemning birth control
- Television crime show *Hawaii 5-0* and *60 Minutes* both debuted on CBS
- Led Zeppelin performed their first live performance, at Surrey University in England
- In Mexico City, black American athletes Tommie Smith and John Carlos raised their arms in a Black Power salute after winning, respectively, the gold and bronze medals in the Olympic men's 200 meter race
- The Beatles released their self-titled album popularly known as *The White Album*
- The '68 *Comeback Special* marked the concert return of Elvis Presley
- The U.S. gross national product reached $861 billion
- The Vietnam War and student protests intensified across the nation
- Richard Nixon was elected president
- BankAmericard holders numbered 14 million, up 12 million in two years
- Civil Rights leader Rev. Martin Luther King, Jr., was assassinated at a Memphis, Tennessee, motel; riots occurred in over 199 cities nationwide
- In response to the Martin Luther King and President Kennedy assassinations, Sears & Roebuck removed toy guns from its Christmas catalog
- Automobile production reached 8.8 million
- Volkswagen captured 57 percent of the U.S. automobile import market
- Television advertising revenues hit $2 billion, twice that of radio
- First-class postage climbed to $0.06
- Inflation was now a worldwide issue
- The Uniform Monday Holiday Law was enacted by Congress, creating three-day holiday weekends
- The average farm subsidy from the government was $1,000; the average U.S. farm produced enough food for 47 people
- The average U.S. automobile wholesaled for $2,280
- Pantyhose production reached 624 million pairs in 1969, up from 200 million in 1968
- Blue Cross health insurance covered 68 million Americans
- *Penthouse* magazine began publication
- The National Association of Broadcasters began a cigarette advertising phase-out
- Richard Nixon's 43.3 percent victory was the lowest presidential margin since 1912
- Pope Paul VI's ban on contraception was challenged by 800 U.S. theologians
- The Vietnam War became the longest war in U.S. history

- Approximately 484,000 U.S. soldiers were fighting in the war in Vietnam
- President Richard Nixon introduced Vietnamization to reduce U.S. troops in Vietnam
- Rock and Pop concerts drew millions as artists such as the Rolling Stones, the Who, Joan Baez, Jimi Hendrix and the Jefferson Airplane launched tours
- A copy of the first printing of the Declaration of Independence sold for $404,000
- "The Johnny Cash Show," "Hee Haw" with Buck Owens and Roy Clark, and "The Bill Cosby Show" all premiered on television
- Following student protests, universities nationwide made ROTC voluntary, or abolished the program altogether
- The popularity of paperback novels detailing life in "today's easy-living, easy-loving playground called suburbia" skyrocketed
- Actor Richard Burton bought Elizabeth Taylor a 69.42-carat diamond from Cartier; the price was not revealed
- Beatle John Lennon and Yoko Ono married
- 448 Universities experienced strikes or were forced to close; student demands included revisions of admissions policies and the reorganization of academic programs
- The 17-point underdog New York Jets, led by quarterback Joe Namath, upset the Baltimore Colts to become the first AFL Super Bowl winner
- Bestsellers for the year included Philip Roth's *Portnoy's Complaint*, Jacqueline Susann's *The Love Machine*, Mario Puzo's *The Godfather*, and Penelope Ashe's *Naked Came the Stranger*
- The first draft lottery was held
- Lorraine Hansberry's *To Be Young, Gifted and Black* premiered in New York City
- Thirty thousand copies of the John Lennon/Yoko Ono album, *Two Virgins*, were confiscated by police in Newark, New Jersey, because the nude photo of John and Yoko on the cover violated pornography laws
- President Nixon approved the bombing of Cambodia
- A Los Angeles court convicted Robert Kennedy's assassin Sirhan Sirhan
- Mickey Mantle of the New York Yankees announced his retirement from baseball
- James Earl Ray pleaded guilty to the murder of Dr. Martin Luther King, Jr. in Memphis, Tennessee, and was sentenced to 99 years in prison
- Levi's began to sell bell-bottomed jeans
- The Supreme Court unanimously struck down laws prohibiting private possession of obscene material
- Eighty armed, militant black students at Cornell University took over Willard Straight Hall and demanded a black studies program and total amnesty for their actions
- American troop levels in Vietnam peaked at 543,000; over 33,000 had been killed
- Walt Disney World construction began in Florida
- The musical review *Oh! Calcutta!* opened in New York
- Patrons at the Stonewall Inn, a gay bar in New York City's Greenwich Village, clashed with police; the incident was considered the birth of the gay rights movement
- A car driven by Senator Edward M. Kennedy (Democrat-Massachusetts) plunged off a bridge on Chappaquiddick Island near Martha's Vineyard; his passenger, 28-year-old Mary Jo Kopechne, died
- Astronaut Neil Armstrong took "One small step for man, one giant leap for mankind" after he and Edwin "Buzz" Aldrin made the first successful landing of a manned vehicle on the moon
- The U.S. space probe *Mariner 7* flew by Mars, sending back photographs and scientific data
- The Food and Drug Administration issued a report calling birth control pills safe
- *Marcus Welby, MD* and *The Brady Bunch* both premiered on ABC-TV
- The federal government banned artificial sweeteners known as cyclamates

- President Richard M. Nixon announced the first withdrawal of 25,000 U.S. troops from South Vietnam; Vietnam casualties now exceeded the total for the Korean War
- Frosted Mini-Wheats, bank automated teller machines and a postage stamp depicting a living American-Neil Armstrong-all made their first appearance
- The largest national demonstration against the Vietnam War was held in Washington, DC, on November 15, when 250,000 people marched in protest
- DDT usage in residential areas was banned
- ARPANET, the precursor to the Internet, was created
- The Woodstock Festival, which attracted more than 300,000 music fans, was held in White Lake, New York
- The Boeing 747 jumbo jet was introduced
- The children's television program *Sesame Street* aired for the first time
- Bestsellers included *Portnoy's Complaint* by Philip Roth, *The Godfather* by Mario Puzo, *The Love Machine* by Jacqueline Susann, *Naked Came the Stranger* by Penelope Ash and *I Know Why the Caged Bird Sings* by Maya Angelou
- Led Zeppelin released their first album, *Led Zeppelin;* the Beatles released *Abbey Road*
- After 147 years, *The Saturday Evening Post* ceased publication
- Hit songs included "Good Morning Starshine," "Hair," "Lay Lady Lay," "Honky Tonk Women" and "Crimson and Clover"
- President Richard Nixon appointed Warren Burger Chief Justice of the Supreme Court
- The Soviet Union launched *Venera 5* toward Venus
- Elvis Presley recorded his landmark comeback albums *From Elvis in Memphis* and *Back in Memphis* that included the singles "Suspicious Minds," "In the Ghetto" and "Kentucky Rain"

- NASA launched *Apollo 9* (James McDivitt, David Scott, Rusty Schweickart) to test the lunar module
- Operation Breakfast, the secret bombing of Cambodia by American forces, began
- The Harvard University Administration Building was seized by close to 300 students, mostly members of the Students for a Democratic Society
- *Midnight Cowboy*, an X-rated, Oscar-winning John Schlesinger film, debuted
- "Give Peace a Chance" was recorded during the famous bed-in for peace by John Lennon and Yoko Ono
- *The New York Times* publicly took back its ridicule, published in 1920, of the rocket scientist Robert H. Goddard that spaceflight was impossible
- President Richard Nixon declared the Nixon Doctrine, stating that the United States now expected its Asian allies, including Vietnam, to take care of their own military defense

SECTION THREE: ECONOMY OF THE TIMES

Economy of the Times *defines the 1960s by three economic elements: Consumer Expenditures; Annual Income of Standard Jobs; and Selected Prices. We highlighted three specific years for each category—1961, 1966, and 1969—for easy comparison. For example, the largest jumps in what Americans paid for goods and services between 1961 and 1969 were in food, which increased by $181.69, and auto usage, which increased by $154.25. The smallest increases were in tobacco, at $9.70, and health insurance, which went up only $9.83 over the 8-year period. Of standard incomes reported, the annual income in the building trades increased the most, by $3,111, to $9,049.*

Consumer Expenditures

The numbers below are average per capita consumer expenditures in the years 1961, 1966, and 1969, for all workers nationwide.

Category	1961	1966	1969
Auto Parts	$14.15	$19.33	$26.64
Auto Usage	$207.41	$294.06	$361.66
Clothing	$125.21	$158.73	$189.96
Dentists	$11.43	$15.26	$21.22
Food	$462.19	$555.05	$643.88
Furniture	$26.13	$35.61	$41.45
Gas and Oil	$65.33	$81.40	$101.15
Health Insurance	$10.89	$15.26	$20.72
Housing	$278.73	$353.58	$428.27
Intercity Transport	$7.62	$11.70	$18.26
Local Transport	$10.89	$10.68	$13.32
New Auto Purchase	$65.87	$106.84	$123.84
Per Capita Consumption	$1,856.92	$2,450.14	$2,978.63
Personal Business	$65.87	N/A	$144.07
Personal Care	$33.21	$117.52	$54.77
Physicians	$32.12	$46.29	$61.18
Private Education and Research	$22.32	$39.68	$54.77
Recreation	$103.98	$156.69	$196.86
Religion/Welfare Activities	$29.94	$43.24	$54.27
Telephone and Telegraph	$26.13	$35.61	$45.89
Tobacco	$38.65	$43.24	$48.35
Utilities	$76.21	$93.10	$105.09

Annual Income, Standard Jobs

The numbers below are annual income for standard jobs across America in the years 1961, 1966, and 1969.

Category	1961	1966	1969
Average of all Industries, Excluding Farm Labor	N/A	N/A	N/A
Average of all Industries, Including Farm Labor	$4,961	N/A	N/A
Bituminous Coal Mining	$5,357	$7,398	$8,582
Building Trades	$5,938	$7,373	$9,049
Domestic Industries	N/A	N/A	$7,230
Domestics	$2,356	$2,780	$3,543
Farm Labor	$1,929	$2,923	$3,646
Federal Civilian	$6,451	$8,170	$9,969
Federal Employees, Executive Departments	$4,812	N/A	$7,010
Federal Military	$3,813	$4,650	$5,526
Finance, Insurance and Real Estate	$5,203	$6,239	$7,400
Gas and Electricity Employees	$6,390	$7,801	$9,316
Manufacturing, Durable Goods	$6,048	$7,228	$8,454
Manufacturing, Nondurable Goods	$5,250	$6,172	$7,257
Medical/Health Services Employees	$3,636	$4,565	$5,845
Miscellaneous Manufacturing	$4,753	$5,548	$6,620
Motion Picture Services	$5,871	$7,397	$8,318
Nonprofit Organization Employees	$3,684	$4,280	$5,138
Passenger Trans. Employees, Local and Highway	$4,966	$5,737	$6,623
Personal Services	$3,810	$4,551	$5,254
Private Industries, Including Farm Labor	N/A	$6,098	$7,237
Public School Educators	$4,991	$6,142	$7,623
Radio Broadcasting and Television Employees	$7,384	$8,833	$10,085
Railroad Employees	$6,440	$7,708	$9,317
State and Local Government Employees	$4,721	$5,834	$7,894
Telephone and Telegraph Employees	$5,793	$6,858	$8,044
Wholesale and Retail Trade Employees	$5,932	$7,345	$8,685

Selected Prices

1961

Air Conditioner, Admiral $158.00
American Flag Set, 3' x 5' Flag and Pole $3.95
Apples, Pound $0.10
Automobile, Corvair $2,850.00
BB Gun, Daisey $12.88
Barbie Doll Nighty-Negligee $3.00
Battery, Auto $7.88
Bedroom Set, Walnut $645.00
Bluebrook Margarine, per Pound $0.15
Boy's Life Magazine, monthly $0.25
Brassiere, Formfit $3.00
Briefcase $8.00
Can Opener, Electric $8.44
Chap-et Lip Balm $0.35
Charcoal, 20 Pounds $0.85
Child's Car Seat $6.95
Chrysler Newport Automobile $2,964.00
Coffee Maker, Percolator $16.88
Cold Medicine, Contac $1.49
Driving Lessons $46.88
Ethan Allen Desk, Four-Drawer $85.60
Flintstones Child's Feeding Set $1.99
Jif Peanut Butter, 18 Ounce Jar $0.51
Kelvinator Air Conditioner $169.00
Kodak Brownie Super 27 Camera $22.00
Kraft Miracle Whip Salad Dressing, Quart . . $0.43
Lipstick, Cashmere Bouquet $0.49
Little Star Dress for Teens $5.00
Lunch, Walgreen's $0.49
Magna-Lite Shop Light $6.95
Magnavox Broadway Stereo Theater $495.00
Mattress, Serta $79.50
McGregor Meteor Slacks $10.00
Movie Ticket $0.75
Nylons $1.00
Pakula Necklace $3.00
Paneling, 70 Panels $47.00
Pen, Parker-T-Ball Jotter $1.98
Pioneer Ebonetts Kitchen Gloves $0.98
RCA Victor Tape Recorder, Reel to Reel . . . $99.95
Refrigerator $259.00
Scott Tissues, Two Packages of 400 . . . . $0.39
Scripto Goldenglo Lighter $5.00
Slacks, Man's Wool $11.90
Smarteens Blouse for Girls, Cotton $3.00
Stereo $124.95

Subway Token, New York City $0.15
Tape Recorder $99.95
Tums Antacid, per roll $0.12
Typewriter, Smith-Corona, Electric $209.35
Ultra-Sheer Seamless Stockings, Box of Six. . $5.28
Vacuum Cleaner, Eureka. $69.95
Watch, Bulova. $59.50
Water Heater $229.95
Young Men's Caumet Shoes $9.99

1966

Acne Medicine, Clearasil $0.98
After Shave, English Leather $2.00
Aluminum Lawn Chair. $5.99
Antiques Magazine, Monthly for One Year . . $12.00
BB Gun $12.98
Beer, Schlitz, Six-Pack. $0.99
Black and Decker Drill, Electric. $19.95
Bloomcraft Art Nouveau Cloth, per Yard. . . . $3.50
Calculator, Electronic. $1,950.00
Camera, Kodak Instamatic S-10. . . . . $35.00
Car Seat. $6.95
Child's Magic Grow Slip, Package of Three . . $2.97
Coffee, Folger's Two-Pound Can. $1.27
Crib, Portable. $22.95
Culottes $8.00
Custom 7 Transistor Radio $12.95
Dance Concert, per Couple $4.50
Delta Airline Fare, Miami. $74.70
Deluxe Walker-Stroller $18.95
Doll, Mattel Teenage Barbie $2.29
Drill, Black & Decker $10.99
Drive-in Movie, per Car $1.50
Electric Scissors, Dritz. $7.45
Electric Shaver, Lady Kenmore. $13.97
Englander Mattress, Full Size $59.95
Film, 35 Millimeter Color Slide $2.49
Flight Bag. $39.47
Florient Disinfectant Spray. $0.59
Food Processor. $39.95
Fred Astaire Dance Lessons, Eight Lessons . $13.95
Friden Model 132 Electronic Calculator . $1,950.00
General Electric Alarm Clock. $5.98
Goldblatt's Air Conditioner $498.88
Hair Cream, Brylcreem $0.59
Hat, Pillbox $4.97
Honeywell Slide Projector. $149.50
Jarman Shoes. $22.00
Kutmaster, Two-Bladed Knife $1.00

Lawn Flamingo $3.69
Magazine, *Life*, Weekly $0.40
Magnavox Television. $650.00
Major League Warm-Up Jacket $12.95
Old Patina Polish, per Pint $2.25
Pepsi, Six-Pack. $0.59
Pittsburgh Plate Glass Mirror $7.00
Phonograph, Hi-Fi. $29.95
Polaroid Color Pack Camera. $50.00
Pool Table, Imperial. $334.50
Proctor Ice Cream Maker $16.95
Radio, Portable Transistor. $12.95
Recliner, King-Size, Plastic $59.95
Sheffield Candelabra, 22" High $425.00
Schlitz Beer, Six Pack $0.99
Shirt, Man's Arrow $7.50
Socket Set, 57-Piece $56.95
Stiffel Lamp, 22" Height $72.50
Simonize Car Wax. $0.99
Slide Projector, Kodak Carousel $80.00
Stereo. $499.95
Tape Player, 8-Track $67.95
Ticket, Newport Jazz Festival $6.50
Tru-dent Electric Toothbrush $12.50
Truetone Color Television. $629.95
Tuition, Augusta Military Academy, Year $1,300.00
Tyco Prairie Sante Fe Locomotive $16.77
Viking Chair $11.95
Watch, Timex $9.95
Water Skis, Wizard $19.95
West Bend Coffee Maker $9.95
Wizard Electric Dryer $169.95
Wizard Imperial Manual Typewriter $89.95
Wizard Set 'N' Spray Sprinkler $9.19

1969
Acne Solution $2.98
Air Conditioner, 8,000 btu $189.95
Airline Fare, Delta $74.70
Artificial Fingernails, Set of 10 . . . .$0.49
Beer, Six-Pack $0.99
Blender, Proctor. $13.49
Boots, Men's Cowboy $26.80
Bread, Loaf $0.20
Bunk Bed. $69.95
Camera, 8 mm. $129.95
Camera, Polaroid. $50.00
Car Battery $12.88
Car Wax, Simonize $0.99

Seagram's Crown Royal is the finest Canadian whisky in the world. If it weren't, it wouldn't cost you what it does.
About nine dollars!
That's a lot to put out for a fifth of whisky.
But Seagram has put a lot into Crown Royal.
Smoothness you find hard to believe. And good taste that will spoil you for anything else.
In a way what you're paying for is inspiration.
And that doesn't grow on trees.

Chaise, Redwood......................$25.95
Child's Sundress $12.00
Clock Radio.........................$62.95
Coffee, Folger's, Two Pounds............$1.27
Dancing Shoes, Child's Tap..............$5.77
Dinette Set, Five Pieces $119.88
Dishwasher $119.25
Drill, Electric.......................$10.99
Dryer $178.00
Electric Blanket.....................$19.35
Encyclopædia, World University.........$59.00
Flag Set $44.88
Food Processor......................$39.95
Gas, Gallon $0.35
Guitar $97.95
Guitar, Electric $199.95
Hair Spray $0.47
Ice Cream Maker, Electric..............$27.95
Lawn Mower $79.95
Living Room Suite, Seven Pieces $169.77
Locomotive, Tyco $16.77
Milk, Gallon $1.10
New House $40,000
New York City Ballet Ticket.............$4.95
Pepsi, Six 10-Ounce Bottles $0.59
Pool Table, 8' $334.50
Razor Blades, 10 ....$0.99
Rider Tractor.......................$352.95
Rod and Reel, Zebco..................$15.49
Sewing Machine, Kenmore.............$149.95
Shaving Cream, Gillette $0.59
Shoes, Women's Flats $6.97
Slide Projector, Kodak.................$80.00
Slide Viewer........................$2.45
Spray Paint.........................$1.49
Stroller............................$29.95
Tape Recorder, Four-Track, with Speakers . $198.95
Television, Magnavox $650.00
Tile, Vinyl Asbestos Floor...............$12.50
Vitamins, 100 Tablets $1.49

The Value of a Dollar, 1860-2012

Composite Consumer Price Index; 1860=1

Year	Amount	Year	Amount	Year	Amount	Year	Amount
1860	$1.00	1899	$1.00	1938	$1.69	1977	$7.33
1861	$1.06	1900	$1.03	1939	$1.69	1978	$7.89
1862	$1.22	1901	$1.03	1940	$1.69	1979	$8.78
1863	$1.53	1902	$1.03	1941	$1.78	1980	$9.97
1864	$1.89	1903	$1.06	1942	$1.97	1981	$11.00
1865	$1.97	1904	$1.08	1943	$2.08	1982	$11.67
1866	$1.92	1905	$1.06	1944	$2.14	1983	$12.06
1867	$1.78	1906	$1.08	1945	$2.17	1984	$12.58
1868	$1.72	1907	$1.14	1946	$2.36	1985	$13.03
1869	$1.64	1908	$1.11	1947	$2.69	1986	$13.25
1870	$1.58	1909	$1.11	1948	$2.92	1987	$13.75
1871	$1.47	1910	$1.14	1949	$2.89	1988	$14.31
1872	$1.47	1911	$1.14	1950	$2.92	1989	$15.00
1873	$1.44	1912	$1.17	1951	$3.14	1990	$15.81
1874	$1.39	1913	$1.19	1952	$3.19	1991	$16.47
1875	$1.33	1914	$1.22	1953	$3.22	1992	$16.97
1876	$1.31	1915	$1.22	1954	$3.25	1993	$17.47
1877	$1.28	1916	$1.31	1955	$3.25	1994	$17.92
1878	$1.22	1917	$1.56	1956	$3.28	1995	$18.44
1879	$1.22	1918	$1.83	1957	$3.39	1996	$18.97
1880	$1.22	1919	$2.08	1958	$3.50	1997	$19.42
1881	$1.22	1920	$2.42	1959	$3.53	1998	$19.72
1882	$1.22	1921	$2.17	1960	$3.58	1999	$20.17
1883	$1.22	1922	$2.03	1961	$3.61	2000	$20.83
1884	$1.19	1923	$2.06	1962	$3.67	2001	$21.42
1885	$1.17	1924	$2.06	1963	$3.69	2002	$21.78
1886	$1.14	1925	$2.11	1964	$3.75	2003	$22.25
1887	$1.14	1926	$2.14	1965	$3.81	2004	$22.86
1888	$1.14	1927	$2.11	1966	$3.92	2005	$23.64
1889	$1.11	1928	$2.06	1967	$4.03	2006	$24.39
1890	$1.11	1929	$2.06	1968	$4.22	2007	$25.08
1891	$1.11	1930	$2.03	1969	$4.44	2008	$26.06
1892	$1.11	1931	$1.83	1970	$4.69	2009	$25.94
1893	$1.08	1932	$1.67	1971	$4.89	2010	$26.39
1894	$1.03	1933	$1.58	1972	$5.06	2011	$27.22
1895	$1.03	1934	$1.61	1973	$5.36	2012	$27.78
1896	$1.03	1935	$1.67	1974	$5.97		
1897	$1.00	1936	$1.69	1975	$6.50		
1898	$1.00	1937	$1.75	1976	$6.89		

SECTION FOUR: ALL AROUND US

This section offers a ringside seat to the issues and attitudes that were 1960s America. Reminiscent of the "current events" homework assignment, these 48 documents are exact reprints from popular 1960 magazines, local and national newspapers, and political speeches. You will understand more about the 1960s as you read "Program for Non-White Jobs to Begin," "College 'Sex Revolution' Overstressed," "JFK Orders Start of Peace Corps," and "Computers May Enable Men to Farm by Phone." These documents also remind us that, while the details have changed, racism, education, technology, the economy, and foreign threats have been on the minds of Americans throughout history.

"New Grid League Has Troubles"
GRIT, November 27, 1960

Owners of clubs in the American Football League are discovering there are plenty of headaches connected with launching a new grid circuit, foremost of which is bucking the established National Football League to the box office. In the battle for the entertainment dollar, the NFL is way out in front.

Crowds of more than 50,000 are common in NFL games, whereas the AFL has few crowds of more than 25,000. On one Sunday alone, five NFL games featured cliffhanging action, out-rivaling any work of fiction. Less than one touchdown separated the rivals, and in just about every case the winning points were scored in the final minutes of play. That's tough competition for a new loop with few "name" players to attract fans.

Tune in to a broadcast of an NFL game and you hear the scores of other league games, but no scores of games in the rival loop. On an AFL broadcast, however, you get scores in both loops. It's a tipoff on which league has the clamp on the Pro football TV fans.

Commissioner Joe Foss, of the AFL, freely admits the new circuit will lose about $2 million this year. Other observers estimate losses will be even higher. And if it weren't for television, the league would lose close to $4 million in its first season. Under a five-year contract with the sponsors, each team in the AFL gets $225,000 yearly from TV. Without this fee, some of the teams might have folded already.

"Negro Singer to Wed White Actress Sunday"
The Danville Virginia Bee, November 12, 1960

The Sunday wedding of Sammy Davis, Jr., 34, and Swedish actress May Britt, 26, took on a formal note today with the following communiqué issued by the Negro performer's press representatives

"Following a private family wedding ceremony, Mr. and Mrs. Sammy Davis, Jr., will go to the Nordic Room of the Beverly Hills Hotel, arriving there at 4 p.m.

"They will remain in the Nordic Room posing for photographs and answering questions from the press for approximately 30 minutes. They will then depart for a private wedding which, for the convenience of their guests, Mr. and Mrs. Davis have requested to be closed to the press."

Newspapers as far away as Stockholm, Miss Britt's hometown, have sent reporters here to cover the rites.

The ceremony will be held at Davis's home above Sunset Strip and will be performed by a rabbi. Frank Sinatra will be Davis's best man and Miss Britt's bridesmaids will include the wives of Davis's business manager and his pianists.

Both Davis and his bride-to-be converted to the Jewish faith.

A wonderful place to work! Made wonderful by Steelcase office furniture. Each desk, each chair shares the responsibility of making this office a place where work can be handled quickly, deftly, almost effortlessly. This is the kind of office you should have — and can. Steelcase Inc., Grand Rapids, Michigan; Canadian Steelcase Co., Ltd., Don Mills, Ontario.

On request: A copy of our new full color 1300 Series brochure. Address Department B, or call your local Steelcase dealer. He's listed in the Yellow Pages.

STEELCASE INC

"The Revolution Nobody Noticed, Timid Taste Turned Bold"
Life Magazine, **December 26, 1960**

"The great revolution in the U.S. household took place so gradually, so close under everybody's nose, that most people did not notice it. The plain pot turned into a colored casserole. Big floral patterns diminished to small elegant patterns. Lace tablecloths gave way to straw mats. When the 25 years of change were added up, the American home had switched from muted to bright, from overstuffed to streamlined, from careful to carefree.

To show the vast difference between the homes of 25 years ago and those of today, a group of home furnishings that Macy's was selling in 1936 was gathered. During the Depression people chose safe, practical colors. Today, with better dyes and easier-to-clean fabrics, light colors are popular. The 1936 furnishings are almost all 18th century reproductions with only a modern chest and chair. Nineteen-sixty-one's furnishings are international in flavor; the hibachi is from Japan; the black chair with purple seat cushion is Swedish; the colored glasses are Belgian. Technological improvements have brought molded plastic for furniture, foam rubber for upholstery.

Other signs of the new taste of the '60s are easy to spot. A cheery bird has replaced yesterday's glum goldfish and the sansevieria plant is replaced by a big philodendron in a bright stand. Poodles have nosed out cocker spaniels and the master of the house has gone from a lumpy sofa to a cushion. The radio has taken on the appearance of a small book and the block has turned into a star. Bottles, glasses, pans, and even the garbage can have dressed-up-in-parlor splendor which is only fitting since, with servants scarce, the mistress of the house does the work."

❧❧❧❧❧❧❧❧

"Boom in Organized Bowling Continues, No End in Sight"
GRIT, **October 23, 1960**

If you are bowling in one or more leagues this year, you are a member of the fastest growing participant sport in the nation.

The boom in bowling is so swift that even those who are directing it have difficulty keeping pace with it today.

"Four years ago our membership showed a 10 percent gain," said Frank Baker, executive secretary of the American Bowling Congress. "The next year the gain went up about 12 percent. We look, then, for a leveling off. But for the last two years the surge reached 20 percent."

The progress, said Baker, has been almost incredible since the Second World War.

ABC membership in 1946 was 880,000. Today it is 3,500,000 and still growing. It's estimated the total will reach 5,000,000 by 1965.

The interest in the tenpins sport is tremendous. Bowling shows on lanes have contributed to the rapid growth of the sport.

Professional bowlers compete on one TV show for king-size stakes. Six straight strikes are worth from $25,000 up. Frank Clause, of old Forge, Pa., won a $40,000 jackpot on one recent show.

There also is a marked increase in the number of youngsters participating. It is estimated 11,300,000 boys and girls will be firing at tenpins during the new bowling year, most of them taking part in the junior bowling program of the ABC. This represents an increase of 4,000,000 young bowlers in the two-year period.

"Improving Textbooks"
Russell Kirk, *National Review*, September 10, 1960

Anyone who has bothered to save school and college textbooks over the past 40 or 50 years—or who will go to the trouble of turning over such textbooks as have accumulated in the attics of an old house—can see for himself there has been a dismaying deterioration of quality with the passing of the decades. The paper, binding, illustrations, and typeface all have improved; but in style and substance, the text itself, in nearly all disciplines, has been reduced to boring and deceptive generalizations. Really first-rate textbooks for high schools now are difficult to obtain: The educationist pressure-groups have persuaded every big publisher in the field to adopt his textbooks to "progressive" and "permissive" standards.

What is equally disheartening, there has crept into textbooks a sermonizing indoctrination in "socially approved attitudes," at the expense of straightforward instruction in the particular discipline. This is true not only of "social studies" textbooks, but of many in the humanities. "Socially approved attitudes" usually include enthusiasm (quite indiscriminating) for the United Nations Organization, zeal for promoting equality of economic condition, fondness for the centralized welfare state, a favorable view of federal aid to schools, and all that. Until very recent years, sweet sympathy for the aims of the Soviet peoples was on this list of approved attitudes in many textbooks, but in recent editions, that socially approved attitude has been stricken out or modified.

Sometimes the authors of these textbooks are so candid as to declare their aim of indoctrination. Take, for instance, the foreword "To Teachers" in a high school textbook entitled *Geography and World Affairs*, by Stephen Jones and Marion Fisher Murphy (Rand McNally and Company, 1957). Jones and Murphy declare roundly that "an important part of our objectives is the development of socially desirable understandings and attitudes. Evaluating these intangibles is more difficult. *Geography and World Affairs* sets up a series of subjective tests as one means by which the student's personal and social reactions can be gauged. These ... may be used in pre-testing as a legitimate part of the evaluation process..." In short, indoctrination and conditioning are fine and dandy with Prof. Jones and Mrs. Murphy. It should be said for them, however, that their "socially approved attitudes" toward world affairs and geography are merely part and parcel of a muddled and sentimental humanitarianism.

Distorted History
To effect some reform of substance and style in these textbooks, frank and fair criticism is necessary. Secondary school and high school textbooks are reviewed almost nowhere; college textbooks only in the journals of learned societies. Educational administrators, professors, teachers, school board members, and college trustees scarcely know where to turn for evaluation of textbooks, even when they are aware that the books used in their classrooms are anti-intellectual and propagandistic.

At a Michigan high school, a student's mother came to complain to the superintendent about the tenth-grade textbook in American history. Yes, the superintendent agreed, it was a superficial and opinionated book. About Benjamin Franklin, for instance, all the textbook authors said was that he was senile at the Constitutional Convention and had been over fond of women. The superintendent knew and regretted this. But where could one find a better one? He had tried and failed. The whole level of history textbooks was low, and textbooks used in the schools have to be in a list approved by the state educational authorities, so he was limited in his choice.

Lest I sink my readers irrecoverably deep in the Slough of Despond, I hasten to add that rescue is at hand: Two tax-exempt foundations are taking action in this matter and are about to make standard evaluation of standard textbooks...

If you, gentle reader, desire to aid in the improvement of textbooks, we suggest you give or lend copies of these evaluations to professors, teachers, school board members, and college trustees—aye, even unto administrators. Say not the struggle naught availeth.

"Franchise Selling Catches On" 1960

"We are witnessing a new surge of small, independent, enterprise. But, if we're going to be good, we've got to be good. That's why we're here."

Thus roughly you might paraphrase the thinking at a meeting in New York's Coliseum last week. Representatives of some 40 franchising corporations, blanketing 25,000 franchise holders, gathered to midwife and baptize the International Franchise Assn. According to A. I. Tunick, president of the Chicken Delight chain of carry-out and delivery dinner outlets, and first president of the association, the group has two chief aims: to win recognition for franchising as a major method of merchandising and to set up a code of ethics.

How It Works

The franchising formula varies from one operation to another. Basically, though, it's a system set up by a manufacturer or purveyor of services, which sets up under a single brand name a chain of small businessmen, who buy some of their equipment and supplies from the franchisers and run their own show—with some strings. To get a franchise, the dealer may pay a franchise fee—most of them under $10,000, some as low as $10—or he may simply make a down payment on the equipment or plan. Usually, too, he pays a fee or royalty on his own sales. Franchising as the association defines it, Tunick says, is not a one-shot deal. A continuing relationship between franchise and franchisee marks the operations of its members.

For the franchising company, this setup offers quick, assured distribution and expansion at relatively low cost—since the franchise holder himself puts up some of the investment. The franchiser keeps title to the name and basic product or service rights. Because the franchise holder runs the business himself, the franchiser gets a dealer who is both cost and sales conscious.

For the franchise holder, the setup gives him some independence with the security of a tested business. His capital investment is relatively small—and financing comes easier with a big concern backing him. In effect, he gets the buying edge of a big chain, the parent's promotion, and management knowhow. In some cases, he gets the plus of direct-from-manufacturer price. Sherwood estimates that bulk buying gives the dealer savings of anywhere from 30 percent to 50 percent. While he is subject to quality and other controls, he is basically a man on his own.

Postwar Spurt

The first big spurt in franchise selling came right after World War II. During the war, Tunick explains, GIs lived with two dreams: the little white cottage they were going to own, and the prospect of a job with no boss to hound them. With their bonuses in their pockets, they constituted a fine potential for the franchiser.

The 1957-58 recession gave franchising another boost. Men lost their jobs, or got scared. They wanted security—and they wanted it in an easy-to-handle package.

Expanded credit is now a major factor in contributing to franchising's growth, thinks J. J. Connolly, president of Roll-A-Grill Corp. of America, and a director of the association. Credit allows the little man to take part in the kind of enterprise that a Frank Woolworth built up for himself in the old days, he says.

In the last few months, several newcomers—large and small—have moved in. In November, Frank G. Shattuck Co. announced a new Franchise Div., for operation of Schrafft's restaurants, chiefly tied into new motel operations… And last week, an ad in *The New York Times* urged people to go into the Franchised Art Galleries business.

"Huge Salt Cavern in Kansas May Be U.S. Treasure Chest"
GRIT, November 27, 1960

A gigantic cavern deep in the Kansas earth is so far beneath the surface the most powerful nuclear bombs could not faze it, and so big that it could contain a whole small town. Some day it may become a vast subterranean fortress—filled with priceless treasures and perhaps even the nerve center that would keep the United States alive in the event of war or some national disaster.

The cavern is the workings of the Carey Salt Company, which for 37 years has been making rock salt out of the vein that runs 400 to 600 feet beneath the surface of the ground around Hutchinson, Kansas. It contains 50,000,000 cubic feet of space, more than triple the area of the Pentagon, the huge headquarters for the American forces at Washington.

First steps have already been taken toward converting this fantastic chamber into a national safety deposit vault.

❧❧❧❧❧❧❧❧

"This Is Coca-Cola?" *Business Week*, October 8, 1960

Last week, Coca-Cola Company made a brief announcement that it was test-marketing a new soft drink called Sprite. From many companies, such a new product announcement would pass as routine. But with Coke, the announcement has more than usual significance, especially for the soft drink industry and its suppliers.

Sprite is the latest sign of Coke's expansionist mode. Earlier signs include going to market with new soft drink products, diversifying into other kinds of beverages, and introducing new packaging to add to its familiar bottle.

Clearly, the industry giant (with 1959 sales of $342 million) is ending its long dependence on a single product—even one that is world-famous. To stay at the head of its industry, Coca-Cola Company is broadening its coverage of a market its executives described expansively as "liquid refreshments."

Along with announcing Sprite, Coca-Cola is now pushing domestic distribution of its Fanta line of flavored soft drinks, which it began selling overseas years ago. News of Sprite and Fanta follows Coke's proposal of a merger with Minute Maid Corp., which would mean diversification out of the carbonated beverage field into frozen juices and instant coffee and tea.

A few months ago, too, the company confirmed that it is reluctantly making Coke nationally available in cans. Now the company reportedly is thinking about putting the drink in a new throwaway bottle.

For the first 70 years or so of its history, Coca-Cola maintained a successful "one product in one size" policy, so these developments indicate a decided shift in management attitude. Coke executives will say little about it—they stress "evolution" and "continued progress"—but Coke bottlers and industry competitors are more vocal.

"I've never seen a company change its policies as drastically as Coca-Cola has done," said a leading distributor.

Coke's flavored soda drinks, Sprite and Fanta, illustrate the new directions in which the company is moving. Sprite, a lemon-like flavor, can be drunk either alone or as a mixer. Coke bottlers are testing it in two markets: Sandusky, Ohio, and Lansing, Michigan. The company says tests may continue for six months before the product is put into general distribution. Fanta is the label for a full line of soft drink flavors, plus ginger ale and club soda. The line, developed in Germany many years ago, is sold in 36 countries. Coke began testing Fanta in the U.S. in late 1958. According to the company, about 190 bottlers have taken steps to offer it.

With these drinks, Coca-Cola is going after a share of the soft-drink market that it has never exploited before. Flavored soda drinks account for about a third of the total soft-drink business, with cola-type drinks taking two-thirds. Pepsi-Cola Company, second biggest in the industry, which introduced the Patio line of flavored drinks last February in Kentucky on a regional basis, is now adding more regions, with 57 bottlers signed up.

Sprite, coming along as a separate product from the broad Fanta line of flavors, reveals Coke's determination to penetrate deeply in the non-cola market.

According to industry members, the demand for lemon-lime soda, such as Sprite, is distinct from that of flavored beverages generally. Consumers tend to ask for flavored sodas more or less by the flavor they want—such as orange or grape—but they ask for the lemon-lime soda by a brand name. The industry credits this habit to the success of 7-Up, probably the third leading soft drink, establishing a brand identity for its lemon-lime soda.

Most soft-drink companies sell a similar drink, such as Pepsi's Team and Royal Crown's Upper 10. Pepsi introduced Team in April 1959, in both bottles and cans, and now has 152 franchise bottlers.

Despite Coke's entry into this new field, company officials see no sharp departure from the past. They point out that Coke has always followed the policy of slow but steady evolution. It took Coke 25 years, for example, to move from fountain sales to the bottles.

"We've done many things in the past 75 years," says the vice president. "They haven't been years of status quo."

For the past few years, he continues, Coke has been occupied with establishing its larger 10- and 26-ounce bottles, after long holding fast to its six-ounce bottle-"Little Gem," as Coke men call it. Now, in the fullness of time, the company is ready for new moves forward…

Many observers say Coke's expansion into new products lies in large part in Coke's relations with its independent bottlers.

The economics of bottling increasingly demanded full product lines and packages.

Many bottlers, particularly those in Eastern states where the peak hot weather selling season for soft drinks is short, need additional lines to maintain their production facilities and help take care of overhead. Also, a lot of bottlers service vending machines, many of which now dispense several varieties of soda drinks. It makes sense for the bottler to be able to stock the machine completely.

For such reasons, many Coke bottlers have taken on product lines from other companies. Coke has now decided it ought to start selling its bottlers these products.

One bottler points out that, compared with the company's tremendous volume in Coke itself, the new products won't add much to the total volume, and not for a long time. He believes handling the new product right now is chiefly to keep bottlers happy. However, he goes on to say, many bottlers' "investment in glass may keep them from switching to the Fanta flavors," which come in a different container.

"Admirals Expect Polaris Sub Buildup to Enlarge Pearl Harbor Fleet, Jobs"
Honolulu Advertiser, **March 20, 1961**

"Top naval commanders headquartered in Hawaii agree that President Kennedy's decision to speed up the Polaris program will shortly have a major effect at Pearl Harbor.

They expect: 1) At least 12 Polaris-type nuclear submarines to be assigned to the Pacific Fleet, and all 12 to be home-ported at Pearl Harbor. That would mean an additional 3,000 submariners based here, a 75 percent increase in the present 4,000-man sub force now based at Pearl. 2) That as a result of basing Polaris subs here, there will be an 'appreciable buildup' in overhaul and maintenance at the Pearl Harbor shipyard. The shipyard presently employs 4,000 workers and channels about $12 million annually into Hawaii's economy.

Defense Department plans originally didn't call for Polaris submarines to be stationed in the Pacific until 1965. (The first 19 Polaris subs are tentatively earmarked for the Atlantic Fleet, with five already built and assigned to that fleet.) The reason was 'better target availability' in the Atlantic—in simple language, the nuclear tipped Polaris missiles were needed to help deter Russia from any idea of launching an atomic attack against the U.S.

Now, however, it is known that President Kennedy believes that more emphasis should be given to the Pacific, with Red China on the verge of acquiring nuclear capability. Although new Defense Department studies ordered by President Kennedy aren't yet complete, it is believed that the Pacific Fleet will now get its first Polaris submarines in 1963—perhaps even sooner, if the Chinese communists get atomic missiles this year. The 12 Polaris submarines to be based here—probably at Ford Island—won't replace any present Pacific subs but will be in addition to them."

ॐ∾ॐ∾ॐ∾ॐ∾ॐ∾

"Presley Due Tomorrow; Honolulu Airport Braced"
Honolulu Advertiser, **March 24, 1961**

"Thousands of Elvis Presley fans are expected to jam Honolulu Airport tomorrow when Presley arrives at 12:20 p.m. aboard a Pan American Airways plane for his USS Arizona War Memorial concert benefit. The police department has assigned 75 men to the airport.

All 27 Oahu high schools will send designated representatives to a press conference immediately following Elvis' arrival. Each school has a Presley fan club and most of these fans are expected to be at the airport to greet him. Presley will arrive with a party of 26 from Los Angeles.

At 8:30 p.m. tomorrow he will headline a benefit show at Bloch Arena to raise funds for the Arizona Memorial. There are still tickets available for the show. A telephone campaign was on yesterday in an effort to sell 104 remaining $100.00 tickets. A total of 196 $100.00 tickets already have been sold.

General admission sales have topped 18,000 with $4,500 worth of $10.00 and $5.00 tickets yet to be sold.

Radio station KPOI will cover Presley's arrival live, beginning at 9:00 a.m.

Among those to be on hand to greet the singer will be his manager Col. Tom Parker, who has been here for two weeks making arrangements. Also on hand at the airport will be representatives of the Pacific War Memorial Commission."

"JFK Orders Start of Peace Corps"
San Francisco Examiner, **May 2, 1961**

"President Kennedy today ordered the creation of a peace corps on a temporary basis and asked Congress to make it permanent. And he cautioned those who want to join that their life will not be easy and their pay will be low.

'The volunteer peace corps,' Kennedy said, 'will provide a pool of Americans, mostly young men and women, to go overseas and help a foreign country meet their urgent need for skilled manpower. Applicants will be screened carefully,' he said, 'to make sure that those who are selected can contribute to peace corps programs, and have the personal qualities which will enable them to represent the United States abroad with honor and dignity.'

Kennedy said he hopes to send the first members of the corps overseas by late fall and hopes to have 500 to 1,000 in the field by the end of the year. 'Within a few years,' the President said, 'I hope several thousand will be working in foreign lands. Each recruit will receive a training and orientation course varying from six weeks to six months, including instruction in the culture and language of the country to which the corps member is being sent.'"

"The Machines Are Taking Over, Computers Outdo Man at His Work Now and Soon May Outthink Him"
Life Magazine, **March 3, 1961**

"In the peaceful little town of Troy, Ohio, an epic battle was recently fought at the local sausage factory. Once a week for four months top officials of the Braun Brothers Packing Co., each a sausage expert in his own right, gathered in an office to figure furiously with sharp pencils and clicking desk calculators. The experts were pitting their formidable experience against an implacable rival and each time they found they were beaten before they had begun. A robot brain, in the form of an electronic digital computer, was proving that it could give shrewder orders about sausage-making than the most experienced sausage-master could.

Calculating how to blend a variety of slaughterhouse oddments such as beef lips and pork stomachs into a tasty, inexpensive, attractive, nourishing, and cohesive bologna is an intricate art. There are always thousands of possible combinations to consider. Only a very clever sausage-maker, often an old German who carefully turns his back before consulting a little black book, is normally entrusted with the task.

But Braun Brothers' human sausage maker had magnanimously taught the machine all the tricks he knew. When the computer was informed (by means of coded holes punched into 100 yellow, green, and brown cards) what meat cuts were on hand and their current prices, it hummed softly, its lights flickered, and it riffled the deck of cards over and over again for 36 minutes. Then it automatically punched out the most profitable bologna formula for that particular day. The machine's answer was invariably faster, surer, and cheaper than the answer of the human sausage experts. Braun Brothers now takes it for granted that the computer's decisions are correct, and today all its sausage is mixed by order of the computer."

"The Chosen Three for First Space Ride"
by Loudon S. Wainwright, *Life*, March 3, 1961

"Three men and their families stood on a beach near Cape Canaveral and waited to watch a rocket fired. In shorts and summer hats, carrying cameras and field glasses, the group looked like sightseers whose next stop might be Cypress Gardens or Marine land. But the men are not vacationers. They are astronauts from Project Mercury, the prime candidates for a violent, historic event.

Last week the world learned that one of these three would be chosen as the first American, and perhaps the first man, to be launched into space. Some time this spring either John Glenn or Virgil Grissom or Alan Shepard will climb into a small capsule on top of a redstone rocket and wait for the most awesome journey man has ever taken. It will be the same sort of dangerous mission on which, according to persistent and believable reports, one or more of Russia's cosmonauts have already died. The 15-minute ballistic flight will fling the chosen astronaut more than 100 miles high and then drop him and his capsule by parachute into the sea more than 200 miles away from the launching point. Though all three men will be ready to go, the one finally chosen will not be named until just before the flight.

Glenn, Grissom and Shepard were picked for the first launch team by Robert Gilruth, director of the National Aeronautics and Space Administration's Space Task Group. In announcing his decision, Gilruth made one point emphatically clear: the other two astronauts will still play a big part of Project Mercury. They will be candidates for future rides in the capsule, including the project's climactic mission, an orbital flight three times around the earth."

"Making the Tax Mess Worse"
Editorial, *Life Magazine*, March 3, 1961

"President Kennedy's program for federal aid to schools and colleges ($5.6 billion in five years) reminds us of nothing so much as the need for federal tax reform. We are really not trying to change the subject; there's a connection. For, once the federal tax structure is reformed, states and municipalities can have more ample tax sources of their own, and the chief excuse for massive federal school aid would vanish.

In contrast with 20 years ago, when the ratio was about 50-50, the federal government now collects about twice as much in taxes as all state and local governments together. It does this through a patchwork tax system that has become hopelessly complex and inequitable and requires drastic rewriting. This system has also pre-empted or crowded all tax sources except real estate, not virtually the sole source of local school taxes.

Despite their cramped resources, states and localities (as well as private institutions) have done a heroic job of keeping abreast of the need for more and better schools. Total expenditures on U.S. education have more than doubled since 1952. This was done with practically no federal aid or stimulus. After *Sputnik*, the people of the U.S. did not need to be told by Washington that their educational system was in trouble.

The unceasing strain on local money and the need for still further school improvement in the decade ahead have steamed up the lobbies for massive federal aid. More steam came from the unevenness of our recent progress—that the fact that Alabama, for example, is spending only $217 per pupil in public schooling, while New York spends $585. This gross inequity of educational opportunity is undemocratic and there is plenty of precedent for steps by the federal government to correct it. The simple way would be such a formula as the Committee for Economic Development proposed last year which confines federal aid to the poorer states. But the Kennedy plan subsidizes everybody—$30 extra per child in Alabama, but $15 extra in New York, and California, too.

White House Economist
WALTER W. HELLER

By moving massively into education, however, the federal government would compound the very problem—i.e., federal taxes—that keeps the chief and proper sources of school funds under such strain. The school Boards would become increasingly dependent on federal aid, as have the farmers, veterans, and aged, etc., before them. This is too bad, because if Kennedy would shift his legislative priorities, the traditional supports of American education could still prove strong enough to meet all foreseeable requirements. His administration is studded with experts who realize that the basic reform of our tax laws is an absolute must for the health of the whole U.S. economy. This reform is on Kennedy's agenda, but not for this year. His immediate "musts" are some 16 other bills, including school aid, most of which cost money and therefore tend to make the tax mess even worse. If tax reform came first, the problems behind these bills would be a lot easier to handle."

"Special Message to Congress on Urgent National Needs"
[excerpt], President John F. Kennedy, May 25, 1961

Finally, if we are to win the battle that is now going on around the world between freedom and tyranny, the dramatic achievements in space which occurred in recent weeks should have made clear to us all, as did *Sputnik* in 1957, the impact of this adventure on the minds of men everywhere, who are attempting to make a determination of which road they should take. Since early in my term, our efforts in space have been under review. With the advice of the Vice President, who is Chairman of the National Space Council, we have examined where we are strong and where we are not. Now it is time to take longer strides—time for a great new American enterprise—time for this nation to take a clearly leading role in space achievement, which in many ways may hold the key to our future on Earth...

I therefore ask the Congress, above and beyond the increases I have earlier requested for space activities, to provide the funds which are needed to meet the following national goals:

First, I believe that this nation should commit itself to achieving the goal, before this decade is out, of landing a man on the moon and returning him safely to the Earth. No single space project in this period will be more impressive to mankind, or more important for the long range exploration of space, and none will be so difficult or expensive to accomplish. We propose to accelerate the development of the appropriate lunar space craft. We propose to develop alternate liquid and solid fuel boosters, much larger than any now being developed, until certain which is superior. We propose additional funds for other engine development and for unmanned explorations—explorations which are particularly important for one purpose which this nation will never overlook: the survival of the man who first makes this daring flight. But in a very real sense, it will not be one man going to the moon—if we make this judgment affirmatively, it will be an entire nation. For all of us must work to put him there.

కాకాకాకాకాకాకా

"Your Life Easily May Depend on How Well You Are Prepared,
If an ATTACK Comes"
by John D. Hacket, *The Evening Sun*, Baltimore, Maryland, August 1961

Baltimore is a "critical target" for an enemy bomb.

It is the sixth-largest United States city, a principal railroad hub with the fourth-largest ocean port. The largest single steel mill, a major missile factory and a modern jet airport are next-door.

The area is a major production center for steel, copper, aluminum, chemicals, ships, missiles, electronics, automobiles, apparel, food and research.

Some 939,000 people live in Baltimore. You are one of them. If the enemy dropped an H-bomb in this area right now—could you come out alive...?

CONELRAD May Say: EVACUATE
There are 115 air raid sirens in Baltimore today.

They work.

They are checked out once a month by telephone company technicians.

The entire Baltimore area civil defense communications network, which includes police, fire, military, rescue, hospitals, factory and others, is tested every Monday.

These sirens are a part of the nationwide Civil Defense Warning System. They are set off only in an emergency. (However, these sirens do scream once a year in Baltimore, on "Operation Alert" day. They sounded last April....)

Possible Attack

The ALERT signal, the STEADY BLAST for three to five minutes, blares out only when the military and CD people feel planes or missiles are headed for the United States.

It means—PROBABLE ATTACK.

What is the other signal?

Sirens give off a WARBLING sound. It goes up and down, up and down, up and down in tone.

It is the UNDER ATTACK warning.

It screams for three minutes, then stops.

It means the Baltimore area is going to get it, but good—and soon, maybe in minutes.

"Working Girls Beat Living Cost"
San Francisco Examiner, March 2, 1961

"The working girl kept a skip and a jump ahead of the rise in the cost of living last year. In fact, she received the equivalent of an extra week's pay—enough to buy one good suit.

John Dana of the Department of Labor disclosed yesterday that the average office girl received a 4.3 percent raise in salary while the cost of living was going up 1.6 percent. This gave her a 1.9 percent increase in real earnings after allowing for high prices and taxes.

Her boyfriend received a somewhat smaller percentage increase, but about the same amount of cash if he worked the year 'round. One analyst remarked that the lower increase for the boyfriend was the more important statistic. The analyst, a woman, explained: 'After all, how is the poor working girl going to get married if her boyfriend can't earn more money?'

Dana, the department's assistant to the Regional Director of Labor Statistics, said local stenographers, with an average weekly salary of $84.00, have received a 47.3 percent boost in wages since January, 1952. In the same period, the cost of living has risen 18.5 percent, giving her a net increase in real spendable earnings of 21.5 percent.

The weekly salaries of women office workers ranged from an average $60.50 for file clerks to $96.50 for secretaries. The report showed that the average woman elevator operator receives $2.05 an hour, $0.22 more than the average male elevator

operator, while the average woman janitor or cleaner receives $2.08, $0.07 less than the male janitor. In most skilled occupations studied, men averaged more than $3.10 an hour, with tool and dye makers drawing $3.53, carpenters $3.22, and painters $3.15."

"World's Fair Poises for Start Today"
The Salt Lake Tribune, April 21, 1962

The Seattle World's Fair, packed with color, culture and science, will open Saturday with President Kennedy pressing a gold telegraph key at Palm Beach, Florida.

This is the same key made of gold nuggets gathered at the Klondike Gold Rush, which President William Howard Taft used to open the Alaska-Yukon-Pacific Exposition in Seattle in 1909.

The World's Fair not only tells the story of man's progress in the last half-century-it also projects man 38 years in the future with a bold forecast of how he'll be living in the year 2000....

A first-day crowd of 90,000 has been forecast by Mayor Gordon Clinton, who wants the entire city to celebrate the moment of the opening by ringing bells, blowing horns and whistles and generally acting as if it were New Year's Eve.

"JFK IS ASSASSINATED"
by Frank Cormier, *Associated Press*, November 23, 1963

A hidden gunman assassinated President Kennedy with a high-powered rifle Friday.

Three shots reverberated and blood sprang from the president's face. He fell face downward. *His* wife clutched his head crying, "Oh, no."

Within half an hour, John F. Kennedy was dead and the United States had a new president, Lyndon B. Johnson.

Within the hour, police arrested a 24-year-old man following the fatal shooting of a Dallas policeman. Homicide Capt. Will Fritz said Friday night witnesses had identified the man as the slayer of the policeman and he had been charged with murder.

Fritz said it had not been established that the man killed the president—but it had been established that he was in the building from which the shots were fired at the time of the assassination.

He is Harvey Lee Oswald [sic] of Fort Worth, who four years ago said he was applying for Soviet citizenship. He has a Russian wife.

Oswald denied that he had shot anybody.

"Education 1963"
Fred M. Hachinger, Education Editor,
The New York Times Encyclopedia Yearbook, 1964

In 1963 the battle between the two rival U.S. teacher organizations came to boiling point—with indications of important consequences to public education. The relatively small (80,000 members) American Federation of Teachers (AFL-CIO) in its public meetings attacked the giant (860,000 members) National Education Association. The AFT used as its major success story the tough stance of the New York City Local United Federation of Teachers, which, as the official bargaining agent for the city's 43,000 teachers, has taken credit for unprecedented increases. In fact, the country's largest city has, in collective bargaining and under the threat of teachers' strikes, given pay increases which give most teachers $1,500 more money over a three-year period in addition to their regular salary.

The NEA, under such pressure, stiffened its back. While opposing strikes in theory, it has put teeth into its substitute weapon—sanctions—to a point where it's hard to tell the instruments apart. The threat of sanctions against an entire state—Utah—gave the NEA a substantial victory, including both immediate pay increases and the promise of further improvements based on an impartial commission report. As for the general education scene, the contest between the labor union and the quasi-professional organization has had this important effect:

it has made teachers more aggressively determined to have a voice in local and state affairs related to school policy.

On a different level, the American teacher also became a matter of spirited debate: the question as to how well or badly today's teachers are prepared was aired in two publications. James D. Koerner, long a critic of teachers' colleges and a leading member of the Council for Basic Education, which is often identified with Adm. Rickover's approach to the schools, wrote an extensive critique, *Miseducation of American Teachers* (Houghton Mifflin Co.). He documented much shabby teaching in so-called education courses and called for substantial improvement of the teacher training curriculum.

After such rough treatment, it came as a major surprise when Dr. James D. Conant, usually a far more gentle critic of public education, presented a far more dramatic prescription for change in his long-awaited book *The Education of American Teachers* (McGraw-Hill Book Company). The former Harvard president, author of the already historic *Conant Report (1959) on The American High School Today*, asked for abolition of existing state certification rules. He urged substitution instead of three major control elements: direct responsibility for the quality of teachers on the part of colleges and universities which train them; greater responsibility for selection and on-the-job training of teachers on the part of local school boards; and supervision of what Conant wants to make the heart of teacher certification—practice teaching—on the part of state education authorities. In addition, Dr. Conant would not allow credits for salary increases based on completed "educational courses." He urged recruiting of teacher-training candidates among the upper third of each year's high school graduating class.

The third great controversy—integration—continued, but a new element was added when the issue shifted notably to the Northern cities and suburbs. The problem there-in contrast to legal segregation in the South—was that of de facto segregation in areas with Negro concentration in housing. In many cities, including New York and Chicago, the issue led to picketing and even school boycotts. Dr. James E. Allen, Jr., New York State education commissioner, asked all school districts to report to him on plans to deal with de facto segregation. He attempted to define the problem by warning that any school in which the

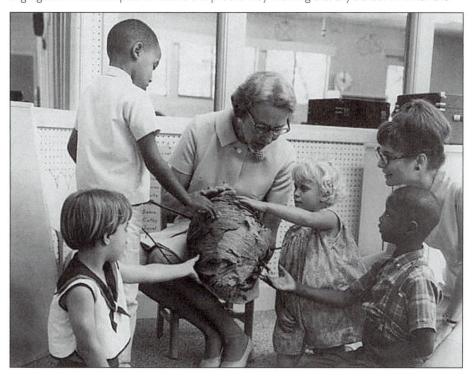

non-white population exceeds 50 per cent should be considered as being in danger of being segregated. The problem was particularly difficult to solve in some cities—Chicago, Washington, and at least the New York boroughs of Manhattan—where the total white enrollment represents a minority.

Finally, the year brought a somewhat milder controversy over the ruling of the Supreme Court, on June 17, that no state or locality may require Bible reading or the Lord's prayer as a religious exercise in the public schools. The controversial impact of this emotion-charged issue was somewhat softened by two factors: the court had prepared the ground with a decision, a year earlier, that it was unconstitutional for any state agency, such as a school board or Board of Regents, to write or prescribe a prayer for use in the schools; the court also made it clear that study of the Bible, with proper discussion, is a legitimate part of public education and should be encouraged.

ֆֆֆֆֆֆֆֆֆֆ

Computers May Enable Men To Farm By Phone

NEW YORK — "Farming by phone" may be the next big "brain" in his office or in the barn, which would automatically

"Computers May Enable Men to Farm by Phone"
The Greenville News (South Carolina), November 25, 1963

"Farming by phone" may be the next big innovation in agriculture, says a national farm magazine. The phone would be used by farmers to take advantage of centralized computer installations, according to an article, "Livestock Feeding of the Future," in the November issue of *Electricity on the Farm* magazine.

The computers can help the farmer make the many business decisions he has to, such as how much of which ingredients to feed his animals for the best meat and milk, or production at the lowest cost. It's being done on a limited scale right now in Washington State, and the idea is expected to spread.

Here's the way it would work: the farmer could pick up the phone, call a number, and read off the type of animal he wants to feed, types of feed ingredients available, and other such information. This information would be fed into a computer at the state university or other centralized computer location.

The farmer would then be instructed to take a certain computer-type punch card from a file on his desk. He would place this card into an electronic "brain" in his office or in the barn, which would automatically instruct feed-making machinery how much of which ingredients to use for the most efficient feeding ration.

Automatic equipment could then easily convey the feed to the cows, chickens, hogs, etc., in feeding areas around the farmstead. Automation and computerization are fast becoming common to most large industries in the U.S., and agriculture, America's largest industry, will be no exception.

"Building the Beatle Image"
by Vance Packard, *Saturday Evening Post*, March 21, 1964

"What causes an international craze like the current Beatlemania?

Press agentry can only swell a craze. To get one started you need to bring into fusion five ingredients. This is true whether the craze involves Davy Crockett, Liberace or Elvis Presley.

Only three years ago it is doubted that any observer of pop culture would have picked the Beatles to inspire madness on both sides of the Atlantic. In 1961 the Beatles affected a beatnik look. They wore black T-shirts, black leather jackets, blue jeans and disheveled hair. In one picture taken of them that year they scowled at the camera as good beatniks would.

Then, along came Brian Epstein, an aristocratic-looking young Englishman who ran a record shop and soon became their manager. First he made them scrub, comb their hair and get into civilized clothing. Then little by little, by a combination of hunch, luck and design, he began exploiting the five ingredients that will create a craze.

First, the Beatles needed a symbol that would make them stand out in people's minds, a symbol such as the coonskin cap that Walt Disney gave to his Davy Crockett creation. For a symbol it was decided to exploit their already overlong hair. The Beatles let it grow longer and bushier, combed it forward—and then had it immaculately trimmed. The result was not only eye catching but evocative. Such hairdos were common in the Middle Ages and the new coiffure suggested the ancient roots of England.

A second ingredient necessary for a craze is to fill some important subconscious need of teenagers. Youngsters see themselves as subjugated people constantly exposed to arbitrary edicts from adult authorities. The entertainment world has developed many strategies to offer youngsters a sense of escape from adult domination. Television producers of children's shows sometimes make adult figures either stupid or villainous. The press agents for some teen stars publicize the stars' defiance of their parents. Teenage crooners relate with amiable condescension their support of their parents.

Rock'n'roll music, of course, annoys most parents, which is one of the main reasons why millions of youngsters love it. But the Beatles couldn't possibly hope to outdo Elvis Presley in appalling parents. Instead of open opposition, the Beatles practice an amiable impudence and a generalized disrespect for just about everybody. They succeed, happily, in getting themselves denounced in some pretty high adult places. The Lord Privy Seal indicated his annoyance. And Field Marshal Lord Montgomery growled that the army would take care of those mop-top haircuts if the Beatles were ever conscripted.

But the Beatles—under Mr. Epstein's tutelage—also have put stress on filling other subconscious needs of teenagers. As restyled, they are no longer roughnecks but rather lovable, almost cuddly, imps. With their collarless jackets and boyish grins, they have succeeded in bringing out the mothering instinct in adolescent girls.

The subconscious need that they fill most expertly is in taking adolescent girls clear out of this world. The youngsters in the darkened audiences can let go all inhibitions in a quite primitive sense when the Beatles cut loose. They can retreat from rationality and individuality. Mob pathology takes over, and they are momentarily freed of all of civilization's restraints.

The Beatles have become peculiarly adept at giving girls this release. Their relaxed, confident manner, their wild appearance, their whooping and jumping, their electrified rock'n'roll pulsing out into the darkness makes the girls want to jump—and then scream. The more susceptible soon faint or develop twitching hysteria. (One reason why Russia's totalitarian leaders frown on rock'n'roll and jazz is that these forms offer people release from controlled behavior.)

A third ingredient needed to get a craze started—as Brian Epstein obviously knew—is an exciting sense of freshness. In an informal poll conducted through my offspring, who are at high school and college, I find that the fact that the Beatles are somewhat 'different'—something new in the musical world—made the deepest impression. Teenagers feel they are helping create something new that is peculiarly their own. And as my 15-year-old expert (feminine) explained, 'We were kind of at a lag with popular singers.'

The delivery, if not the music, is refreshingly different with the Beatles. Surliness is out, exuberance is in. Sloppiness is out, cleanliness is in. Self-pity is out, whooping with joy is in. Pomposity is out, humor is in.

A fourth ingredient needed to keep a craze rolling once it shows signs of starting is a carrying device, such as a theme song. The carrying device of the Beatles is found in their name. It playfully suggests beatnik, but it also suggests 'beat'—and the beat is the most conspicuous feature of the Beatles' music. It is laid on heavily with both drums and bass guitar. When the screaming starts, the beat still gets through.

Finally, a craze can succeed only if it meets the mood of the times. England, after centuries of cherishing the subdued, proper form of life, is bursting out of its inhibitions. There has been a growth of open sexuality, plain speaking and living it up. The Beatles came along at just the right time to help the bursting-out process.

What is the future of the Beatle craze in America? At this point it is hard to say. But the Beatles are so dependent upon their visual appeal that there is a question whether they can sustain the craze in their American territory from across the Atlantic. Another problem is that they are not really offensive enough to grownups to inspire youngsters to cling to them.

Frankly, if I were in the business of manufacturing mophead Beatle wigs, I would worry. Crazes tend to die a horribly abrupt death. It was not so long ago, after all, that a good many unwary businessmen got caught with warehouses full of coonskin caps when the Crockett craze stopped almost without warning."

"Strongest Rights Law Signed by President"
Roanoke Times (Virginia), July 3, 1964

President Johnson signed the strongest civil rights law in nearly a century Thursday night, only three hours after Congress approved it amid cheers, and called on Americans to "eliminate the last vestiges of injustice in America."

In a historic ceremony in the East Room of the White House, Johnson pledged himself to "faithful execution" of the statute and announced immediate steps to insure its enforcement.

Johnson delivered a conciliatory statement to the nation, by radio and television, to more than 200 lawmakers, civil rights leaders, and government officials on the spot who helped bring the sweeping legislation to enactment.

"We have come now to a kind of testing," Johnson said slowly and solemnly. "We must not fail. Let us close the springs of racial poison. Let us pray for wise and understanding hearts. Let us lay aside irrelevant differences and make our nation whole. Let us hasten that day when our unbounded spirit will be free to do the great works ordained for this nation by the just and wise God who is the Father of all."

Then dignitaries clustered around him, each to claim one of the 72 pens with which he put his signature to the bill delivered from the Capitol with extraordinary speed after the 289-126 House vote which ended long and bitter congressional debate.

He appealed for voluntary compliance and predicted it will be given "because most Americans are law-abiding citizens who want to do what is right."

In what was clearly an effort to calm the indignation of many Southerners and refute the objections of those who have denounced the measure as an invasion of states' rights, Johnson told the country: "It provides for the national authority to step in only when others cannot and will not do the job.

"I urge every public official, every religious leader, every business and professional man, every housewife—I urge every American—to join in this effort to bring justice and hope to all our people and peace to our land.…"

Although the founding fathers guaranteed all Americans the blessings of liberty, Johnson said, "millions are being deprived of those blessings not because of their own failures, but because of the color of their skin.

"The reasons are deeply imbedded in history and tradition and the nature of man. We can understand—without rancor or hatred—how this happened," he went on. "But it cannot continue. Our Constitution, the foundation of our republic, forbids it. The principles of our freedom forbid it. Morality forbids it. And the law I will sign tonight forbids it."

Johnson emphasized that the measure received the bipartisan support of more than two-thirds of the members of both House and Senate including "an overwhelming majority of Republicans as well as Democrats.

"It does not restrict the freedom of any American, so long as he respects the rights of others," he said, adding: "It does say that those who are equal before God shall now also be equal in the polling booths, in classrooms, in the factories, and in hotels, restaurants, movie theaters, and other places that provide service to the public."

Only an hour's debate preceded the House vote, and most speakers sounded the familiar themes that have been echoing through the House and Senate since last June. But one member produced a major surprise—a Georgia Democrat who supported the bill.

Rep. Charles L. Weltner of Atlanta, who voted against a similar bill when it passed the House last February, drew cheers and applause from the bill's supporters when he announced he was changing his vote.

"I would urge that we at home now move on to the unfinished task of building a new South. We must not remain forever bound to another lost cause," he said.

The Southern leaders of the opposition showed no weakening in their last fruitless opposition to the bill, however.

Rep. Howard W. Smith, (Democrat, Virginia), said it would loose upon the South "a second invasion of carpet-baggers." He predicted violence, bitterness and bloodshed would inevitably follow enactment of the bill, and ended his speech, "God save the United States of America."

"The Ku Klux Klan Is Moving Boldly into the Open in a Last-Ditch Fight against Integration; 'We Got Nothing to Hide,'" by Harold H. Martin and Kenneth Fairly, *The Saturday Evening Post*, January 30, 1965

"One starlit evening not long ago, in a tobacco patch near the little town of Hemingway, South Carolina, 29 robed and hooded men and women gathered in a circle around a 50-foot black-gum cross which had been wrapped in burlap and soaked in crankcase oil. Solemnly they set the towering shaft ablaze and marched around it singing, as a record player hitched up to a loudspeaker boomed into the darkness the opening strains of the 'The Old Rugged Cross.' Suddenly the needle stuck, and over the dark woods surrounding the little field, the speaker repeated over and over the phrase that ends the first line of the song, '… and shame'—'and shame'—'and shame.'

If the Klansmen who set the cross aflame felt any shame at this use of the symbol of Christian brotherhood to publicize an organization which thrives on racial hatred, they gave no sign of it. There was nothing clandestine about the meeting in the Masonic Hall in Hemingway; ladies of the Klan sold barbecue, slaw, cake, and soda pop, and passed out literature extolling the noble purposes of the order. At the rally itself, on a flatbed truck decorated with Confederate and American flags, the assembled Dragons, Titans, and Exalted Cyclopes of the two Carolinas sat proudly in their emerald, white, and crimson robes, waiting for 'his Lordship,' one Robert Shelton of Tuscaloosa, Alabama, Imperial Wizard of the United Klans of America Knights.

None wore a mask. 'We want you to see our faces,' bellowed Robert Scoggins, the Grand Dragon of South Carolina, to the crowd of 800 men, women, and barefoot children who stood before the speakers' platform in the glare of the burning cross. 'We want you to know who we are and what we are doing. We got nothing to hide…'

Passage of the Civil Rights Bill in June of 1964 brought the Klan boldly into the open. All over the South crosses blazed at public rallies. Fierce-eyed preachers, most of them self-ordained, began to shout in public the twisted doctrine they had proclaimed in the secrecy of the Klaverns—that Jesus Christ was not a Jew, that the Pope of Rome was anti-Christ, that the Negro was a beast who must be destroyed. 'Oh, God,' prayed one, 'please put grace and grit into the white race and let us wipe out this black-ape race before it is too late.'"

Civil Rights Timeline

1921   Race riots in Tulsa, Oklahoma, resulted in approximately 150 people killed, 800 injured, and 10,000 homeless.

1931   The Scottsboro Boys, nine African American boys accused of raping two White women, were arrested.

1940   The Supreme Court freed three Black men who were coerced into confessing to a murder.

1941   President Franklin Delano Roosevelt issued Executive Order 8802, the "Fair Employment Act."

1944   The United Negro College Fund was incorporated.

1947   Jackie Robinson became the first Black player in professional baseball.

1948   Hubert Humphrey spoke in favor of American civil rights at the Democratic National Convention.

President Harry S. Truman issued Executive Order 9981 ending segregation in the armed forces.

1950   In *McLaurin v. Oklahoma State Regents* the Supreme Court ruled that a public institution of higher learning cannot provide different treatment to students solely because of their race.

In *Sweatt v. Painter* the Supreme Court ruled that a "separate-but-equal" Texas law school was unequal.

1951   High school students in Farmville, Virginia, went on strike; the case *Davis v. County School Board of Prince Edward County* was heard by the Supreme Court in 1954 as part of *Brown v. Board of Education of Topeka, Kansas.*

1952   *Briggs v. Elliott:* after a district court ordered separate but equal school facilities in South Carolina, the Supreme Court agreed to hear the case as part of *Brown v. Board of Education.*

1954   The Supreme Court unanimously ruled in *Brown v. Board of Education* that segregation in public schools was unconstitutional.

The Supreme Court decided in *Hernandez v. Texas* that Mexican Americans and all other racial groups in the United States were entitled to equal protection under the Fourteenth Amendment to the U.S. Constitution.

1955   President Dwight D. Eisenhower signed Executive Order 10590, establishing the President's Committee on Government Policy to enforce a nondiscrimination policy in federal employment.

Fourteen-year-old Chicagoan Emmett Till was kidnapped, brutally beaten, shot, and dumped in the Tallahatchie River for allegedly whistling at a White woman in Mississippi.

NAACP member Rosa Parks refused to give up her seat at the front of a bus to a White passenger, sparking a bus boycott which lasted more than a year.

1957   Martin Luther King, Charles K. Steele and Fred L. Shuttlesworth established the Southern Christian Leadership Conference (SCLC), of which King was president.

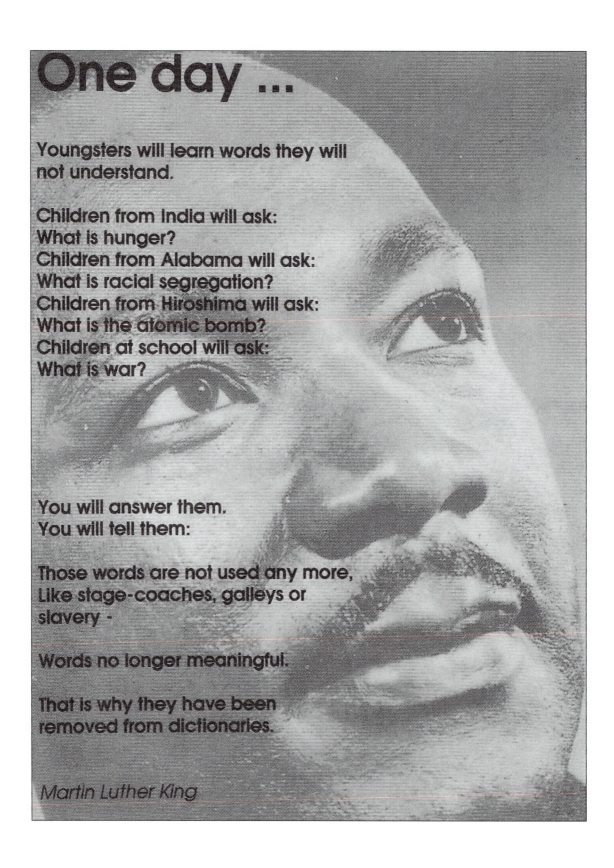

One day ...

Youngsters will learn words they will
not understand.

Children from India will ask:
What is hunger?
Children from Alabama will ask:
What is racial segregation?
Children from Hiroshima will ask:
What is the atomic bomb?
Children at school will ask:
What is war?

You will answer them.
You will tell them:

Those words are not used any more,
Like stage-coaches, galleys or
slavery -

Words no longer meaningful.

That is why they have been
removed from dictionaries.

Martin Luther King

In Little Rock, Arkansas, nine Black students were blocked from entering a school on the orders of Governor Orval Faubus; President Dwight Eisenhower ordered federal troops to intervene on behalf of the students.

The Civil Rights Act of 1957 was signed.

1958   The Supreme Court awarded the NAACP the right to continue operating in Alabama under *NAACP v. Alabama.*

1960   Four Black students from North Carolina Agricultural and Technical College began a sit-in at a segregated Woolworth's lunch counter, sparking a national movement to integrate parks, swimming pools, theaters, libraries, and other public facilities.

The Student Nonviolent Coordinating Committee (SNCC) was founded at Shaw University, providing young Blacks with a place in the civil rights movement.

The Civil Rights Act of 1960 was signed.

1961   The Congress of Racial Equality (CORE) began sending student volunteers on bus trips to test the implementation of laws prohibiting segregation in interstate travel facilities; a mob in Alabama set the riders' bus on fire.

James Meredith became the first Black student to enroll at the University of Mississippi; President John Kennedy was forced to send 5,000 federal troops to control the rioting.

1963   Martin Luther King was arrested and jailed during anti-segregation protests in Birmingham, Alabama, where he wrote his "Letter from Birmingham Jail," arguing that individuals have the moral duty to disobey unjust laws.

During civil rights protests in Birmingham, Alabama, Commissioner of Public Safety Eugene "Bull" Connor used fire hoses and police dogs on Black demonstrators; the images of brutality were televised and published widely.

Mississippi's NAACP field secretary Medgar Evers was murdered outside his home.

About 200,000 people gathered for the March on Washington, where Martin Luther King delivered his "I Have a Dream" speech.

Four young girls were killed when a bomb exploded at the Sixteenth Street Baptist church in Birmingham, Alabama, a popular location for civil rights meetings.

1964   The Twenty-fourth Amendment abolished the poll tax.

The Council of Federated Organizations (COFO), a network of civil rights groups that included CORE and SNCC, launched a massive effort to register Black voters.

President Johnson signed the Civil Rights Act of 1964, the most sweeping civil rights legislation since Reconstruction.

The bodies of three civil-rights workers—two White, one Black—were found in an earthen dam in Mississippi.

1965   Malcolm X, Black nationalist and founder of the Organization of Afro-American Unity, was shot to death in New York.

Congress passed the Voting Rights Act of 1965, making it easier for Southern Blacks to register to vote; literacy tests and other requirements were made illegal.

Race riots erupted in a Black section of Los Angeles.

Asserting that civil rights laws alone were not enough to remedy a history of discrimination, President Lyndon Johnson enforced affirmative action in hiring for the first time.

Selma, Alabama High School Black Student Bettie Mae Fikes and Her Involvement in the Movement in 1965

I didn't have a clue what was going on around me in the adult world. I could only deal with what I was seeing from my own eyes, and I knew, I could tell there was something wrong; I just didn't know what. My mother, being a gospel singer, we traveled a lot, and traveling you get a chance to see different areas. It seemed like in each state the people lived differently, which I didn't understand. I still did not know that there was an issue between Black and White in Selma, because the White community, as far as I was concerned, were friendly to us, my godfather was a White man....

When I got back to Selma, I didn't go right into the arms of the civil rights struggle, but I knew something was going on; I just didn't know what. And when my uncle and all of them would get together and talk about surrounding areas and things that were happening with the Blacks, that kind of scared me, because they were also talking about war. So I was just looking for another war or something to break out. I believe they were talking about 1925, and the soup lines, and things like that.

Around in the early sixties, I just needed an avenue to get out of the house to keep from going to church so much. This fellow here, Mr. Bonner, and my other dear friend Cle, was telling us about SNCC. And they got all of their friends that they knew involved. I was one of the friends they got involved. When it hit, it was like something that—you went to bed, like tonight, and you woke up the next day with a new world order.

All of a sudden these people are coming to town and they're talking about voters' rights. I didn't even know that was happening—that our parents didn't have the right to vote. There were a few Black people that were registered, mostly in Selma. Lowndes County and all these [surrounding] counties were unregistered. So these are the things that brought me into the Movement....

The first meeting was very tense, it was at night, we had never had a mass meeting before. We didn't know what a mass meeting was. There was a lot of singing, a lot of praise to Mr. Boynton, a lot of discussion of the need to organize, to challenge the segregation laws, the apartheid laws, but most importantly, the need to register people to vote. And it was energizing, and it motivated everyone, particularly the students, to get involved in the Movement and to really try to get Black people registered to vote.

"Broken Glass Marks Namath Success Trail"
Evening Independent (Massillon, Ohio), January 7, 1965

MOBILE, Alabama. The windows of the neighborhood laundry on Fourth Ave. in Beaver Falls, Pennsylvania, are carefully guarded by strong steel wire.

The wiring is Beaver Falls's monument to Joe Namath, who spent a good part of his errant youth smashing glass panes with well-aimed footballs, but went on to become the town's most famous and one of its richest citizens.

Now the townspeople, and the proprietors of the laundry most of all, look at the wired windows with pride and say "Little Joe, he was a card, wasn't he?"

"When Joe was a boy he busted every window in the place," recalls Joe's mother, Mrs. Rose Sznolnoki, who divorced Namath's steelworker father and remarried several years ago.

"The laundry people were very mad and they kept coming around to make us pay damages. Finally, they put up the steel wiring, and it's still there."

Today Joe is not only in a position to pay for all the broken windows, but could buy the laundry and half the town. Star quarterback of the national champion Alabama football team, he signed a week ago the largest contract ever offered a football rookie: a $400,000 salary and bonuses for three years with the New York Jets in the American Football League. He plays his last college game Saturday in the Senior Bowl here.

The contract, which also reportedly included a $5,000 a year pension for life, staggered the professional football world. Only Beaver Falls, a bustling little steel community of 30,000 30 miles from Pittsburgh, took the news in stride.

"Everything here is just the same," said Mrs. Sznolnoki. "Everyone knew Joe would make it good."

Joe, whose parents are Hungarian, was the youngest of five children: John, now 33, career soldier in Germany; Robert, 30, a mill hand; Frank, 27, a life insurance salesman, and Rita, 26, a sister living in Philadelphia.

"Joe was throwing the football when he was big enough to walk," the mother recalled.

"Bobby and Franklin always got up football games in the front yard. Joe was just five and too little to play, but the boys needed a quarterback. So Joe was it.

"Bobby and Franklin taught Joe to throw the ball over the telephone wires.

They agreed he shouldn't be tackled. Joe got so he could throw the ball out of sight and he could hit a stump from 40 yards away."

Namath was outstanding as a high school athlete, playing football, basketball and baseball. When he finished high school, the Baltimore Orioles tried to sign him to a baseball contract.

Joe liked football and wanted to go to college. Scores of big schools sent scouts to court him. His first choice was Notre Dame.

"Joe was flying out so much, I found myself washing and packing him out the door every day," Mrs. Sznolnoki said.

Namath failed to get into Notre Dame and finally chose Alabama. "I was responsible for that," his mother said. "I made him go to Alabama, and he never quit thanking me…"

Paul (Bear) Bryant, head coach of the Crimson Tide, said he hardly got to see Namath as a freshman.

"It was 1961 when we had our championship unbeaten team, and I was kept pretty busy," Bryant recall. "But the coaching staff kept telling me we had a fine prospect in Namath."

This was borne out the next year when, as a sophomore, Namath completed 76 of 146 passes for 1,192 yards and 12 touchdowns. In 1963, he hit 63 of 128 for 765 yards, although he was booted off the team for the last game of the season for breaking training.

"I knew Joe wasn't a bad boy," Bryant said. "I talked to him and he admitted he had broken training. He promised never to do it again, and he has been perfect—an inspirational leader ever since."

⚜⚜⚜⚜⚜⚜⚜

"The Unwanted Fight"
Arthur Daley, *The Winston-Salem Journal* (North Carolina),
May 11, 1965

The Cassius Clay–Sonny Liston fight is now in the same category as *Lady Chatterley's Lover* and other works of dubious distinction. It has been banned in Boston.

Like fugitive fighters of ancient days, they have taken it on the lam across state lines and will set up their tent in Lewiston, Maine, 130 miles to the north. It isn't far enough. Labrador would have been better. Then it could have been placed in a deep freeze.

The clock has been turned back half a century or more to the era when pugilists were scrambling to keep at least one step in front of the law.

Those were the days when they fought on barges in secret assembly points. It was a time that Nat Fleischer's *Ring Record Book* now lists with the parenthetical footnote: (police stopped bout). Clay and Liston have loused up a sport that already seemed much too pediculous for further contamination.

Clay could have saved it. When he was winning his Olympic championship in Rome in 1960, he was a likable young man of infinite charm and attractive personality, all the requisites for

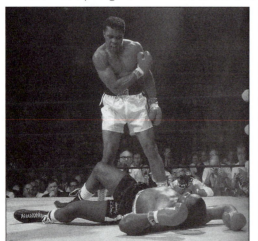

becoming as popular a heavyweight king as was Joe Louis.

Then he stepped out of character and became a loud-mouthed braggart with his I-am-the-greatest routine and alienated sports followers. It drew attention to him and it moved him up the ladder far faster than if he hadn't been in such a hurry. The worst of it was that his false front became part of his nature.

When Cassius fought Liston for the title in Miami a year ago last February, he should have had everyone rooting for him. Instead, at least half wanted to see Liston jam his big glove into Clay's big mouth.

Despite his surly arrogance, disagreeable personality and police record, Sonny-boy actually had people rooting for him.

At the end of the fifth round Clay wanted to quit when some irritating substance found its way into his eyes and blinded him. His seconds pushed him into the ring. At the end of the seventh round Liston wanted to quit, and did, sitting on a stool in abject surrender. His shoulder bothered him, he claimed.

Malodorous though the so-called fight was, the aftermath increased the stench. It was revealed that Clay had joined the Black Muslims and this further alienated the public. Another development was that the Liston camp secretly signed Clay to a return bout after his promotional aegis in the event that he won, a happenstance that didn't allay suspicions that hanky-panky of some sort was involved in the strange ending of their first bout.

When the heat grew intense at the peculiar setup of Intercontinental Promotions, Inc., Liston gave away half his stock to an erstwhile benefactor who just happened to be a friend of Frankie Carbo and a business partner of Blinky Palermo. Later the other half was sold to someone else. But Boston willingly agreed to stage the Clay–Liston rematch last November. On the virtual eve of the fight, Cassius had undergone an emergency hernia operation.

Eventually the match was rescheduled for the same Boston Garden on May 25.

However, a new governor was in the state house by then and the climate had changed. Garrett Byrne, the Boston district attorney, began some legal moves and local gendarmes

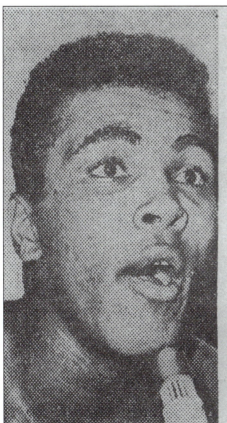

began harassment of Liston in his training camp. That was not too unusual. Liston always had troubles with cops.

Since the tail wags the dog in boxing's present method of doing business, the live gate is of minor consequence compared to the theater-TV. The closed-circuit boys took a stab at Cleveland, which wanted no part of it.

"We'll hold it on barges, if necessary," said the theater-TV boys.

This would have completed the cycle of a total throwback to yesteryear. Lewiston spared them this embarrassment.

The bold talk is that Lewiston, a depressed area with a 5,000-seat arena, might draw almost as much live gate as was expected in the Boston Garden, which is almost thrice its size. That's nonsense. The big thing still is theater-television, some $4 million of it.

Clay, now known as Muhammad Ali, will continue training in Chicopee, Massachusetts, while Liston, now laundered to Boy Scout respectability, will shift his camp on Wednesday to Poland Spring near Lewiston. So the fight game has gone tank town like a struggling road show.

"Congressmen Tap Outside Sources to Bolster Their $30,000 Salaries"
by Richard Harwood, *The Washington Post*, May 1, 1966

"A week ago in Thomas Corcoran's capacious backyard in Woodley Park, a sparse crowd of lawyers, lobbyists, and politicians gathered to celebrate the twenty-fifth wedding anniversary of Senator and Mrs. Thomas McIntyre of New Hampshire.

It was not a celebration in the traditional mold. The price of admission was $100. The party was not the idea of the host-a lawyer-lobbyist whose clients include the Tennessee Gas Transmission Company of Houston—but of a Chevy Chase housewife, Mrs. Esther Coopersmith, who has made a hobby of raising money for 'fine Democratic candidates.'

The turnout of about 150 people was smaller than expected. Not all the guests paid. The 'candidate'—Senator McIntyre—is not officially a candidate for anything, though his Senate term expires this year. And the proceeds from the affair will be used, the Senator has said, not for a political campaign, but to underwrite McIntyre's entertainment and office expenses during the next few months.

This pleasant gathering on a Sunday afternoon symbolized the ethic dilemmas and the financial problems confronting public men of every description in Washington today. They are reaching out into the private society in increasing numbers for financial help to subsidize the political way of life.

Rep. Morris Udall (D-Arizona) recently accepted a $30,000 testimonial dinner gift to underwrite various office expenses and his extensive travels back home. Rep. Paul J. Krebs (D-New Jersey) has set up the Paul J. Krebs Civic Association to collect funds for political purposes, including the purchase of tickets for 'political, social, and charitable affairs.'

Rep. William D. Hathaway (D-Maine) has created a Hathaway Newsletter and Public Information Committee to underwrite his publicity activities.

The DC Western Development Committee was created to subsidize the travels of Sen. Quentin Burdick (D-North Dakota).

Indiana's six Democratic Congressmen and two Democratic Senators received subsidies averaging $1,500 last year from the Indiana State Democratic Committee. The Committee's main sources of revenue are (1) a two-percent levy on the salaries of 14,000 Indiana state employees, and (2) a $0.04 tribute collected on every automobile license plate sold in the state....

These practices raise serious questions for the public and for the public men who benefit from them. Should Congressmen be subsidized by lobbyists, special interest groups, and other contributors whose careers often depend on their ability to influence public policy? Is the Washington lifestyle so lavish that a Senator or Congressman is unable to live on a $30,000 salary? Are his office allowances so niggardly he must seek charity to meet his obligations?

Precisely these questions are at the heart of the current controversy over Sen. Thomas J. Dodd's financial practices. The senatorial way of life, his associates have said, is so costly that Dodd was forced to accept somewhere between $100,000 and $200,000 in 'testimonial gifts' from constituents, political allies, and lobbyists.

'It is well known,' Dodd's friends have said, 'that a Senator's salary is inadequate and that for most men in Washington the "break-even" point on expenses is about $50,000 a year.... Unless a Senator has outside income he is in financial difficulty.... Testimonial dinners enable a poor man to remain in office. They are part of the American way of life.' "

"College 'Sex Revolution' Overstressed"
by Jean White, *The Washington Post*, May 1, 1966

"'Nice girls do, and that's that.' (Student at Reed College)

'I don't think there's been a sex revolution in what people are doing—just in the amount they talk about it.' (Radcliffe Co-ed)

'Promiscuity isn't a matter of the pill.... It may be easier to have an affair, but just because she's safe from pregnancy doesn't mean a girl is going to sleep with two dozen guys. Female psychology just doesn't work that way.' (University of Texas Co-ed)

'Who cares about a sex revolution? The thing is, how many dates do you have?' (Blonde at Ohio State University.) Perhaps no revolution in history has been so minutely and flamboyantly reported as the so called 'sexual revolution' of our time.

It has been debated in magazines and newspapers and on television panels. The scope of concern has ranged from the morality of it all to this fine point of etiquette raised in a question to an advice-to-the-lovelorn columnist: Should the man or woman pay for the pills for an affair?

The discussion has necessarily focused on the campus, where the first Post-Pill Generation has come of sexual age. Now even a best-selling book can be patched together from the quotes of 600 co-eds talking about their sex life on campus. On the other hand, 'I'm not at all

convinced that the activity matches the conversation,' says Clark E. Vincent, a family-life professor at the Bowman Gray School of Medicine at Winston-Salem.

Paul H. Gebhard, one of the authors of The Kinsey Report and Kinsey's successor as director of the Institute for Sex Research at Indiana University, agrees. He points to what he wryly calls the 'terrific amount of verbalization about sex' these days....

With all the present ferment about campus sex, Gebhard feels that there is a need for 'hard data' beyond talk to document any revolution that has occurred. He has applied for a quarter million-dollar federal grant to study sexual behavior on college campuses.

He shouldn't have any trouble collecting both views and experiences from the students, a survey of college correspondents of the *Washington Post* shows. They supplied most of the quotations and other material for this article, which was rounded out with observations from several specialists.

The survey report points to these conclusions:

The modern 'sexual revolution' has been inflated and over reported. One distortion has come from the overexposure of the sex life of the single student—and the brashest are always the most quotable.

'No one ever seems to write about the sex life of the 41-year-old truck driver or the 30-year old matron these days,' complains Gebhard, 'and whoever interviews the girl who sits around the dorm and studies?'

Sociologist Vincent points out that an interviewer could talk to a half-dozen girls at each of 20 colleges and conclude that the sex has broken wide open; then go back and choose sets of six other girls and conclude that this is an age of prudery.

Or as a 22-year-old English major at Harvard put it: 'It's not really the "new moralists" who are talking, but the "new blabbermouths."'

The 'sexual revolution' is not all talk, however. Campus sex morals have been changing, and these changes must be taken seriously in contrast to the sensationalism of the free-love exhibitionists whose dirty words match their discarded dirty clothes at naked sex orgies.

In sex ethics, as in many other areas, young men and women are honestly questioning the relevance of old codes to contemporary society. The move is from stern 'thou-shalt-not' morality to more permissiveness and self-determination.

These changes are evident in two main areas: (1) freer discussion of sex, and (2) more premarital sex between 'serious' couples and more open living together before marriage....

In a recent report on 'Sex and the College Student,' a committee of the Group for the Advancement of Psychiatry (GAP) has this to say about campus sex

'There is general agreement that premarital sexual relations among undergraduate college students are more frequent than they were a generation ago. Certain students are more open in their activities and more vocal in their prerogatives.'

The report goes on to note a tolerance of behavior that would have been censured a few decades ago and even now is questioned in many quarters. Only 25 years ago, the GAP committee points out, the college boy went into 'town' for a sexual experience. Today, his partner is likely to be a college girl on campus."

"The Inside Story of The NFL-AFL Merger"
by Bob Stewart, *Complete Sports*, November 1966

"Sonny Werblin relaxed over his coffee. His luncheon date with one of the New York newspapermen this Tuesday afternoon of May 24 had run quite a bit longer than he had intended. But then, such affairs always take up more time than you anticipate, and he had enjoyed the session. He had had yet one more opportunity to preach his gospel of unrelenting war with the National Football League, just so long as that league chose to fight, rather than talk on sensible, business-like terms.

Werblin's spectacular success with the New York team in the American Football League had altered all concepts of the pro-football world. It has been axiomatic that no league in any sport can succeed without a profitable, going concern in New York. Even the National League in baseball had rued its decision to pull the Giants and Dodgers from the big town, and recouped only by installing the ridiculous but rich Mets back in the United States' prime market.

Werblin, with a career of success behind him in showmanship, had seen the staggering possibilities of a New York Football League franchise. When the ill-fated, mismanaged Titans of the new league provided an albatross of staggering weight, he had stepped in, purchased its assets and, to some extent liabilities, and proceeded to provide the franchise with the magic touch—money.

It had taken two years of unrelenting labor, but the green-clad team through unlimited money had become the strongest entry in a league which had been hanging on, even without a premier showcase in New York.

Acceptable finally as a going, solid concern, the AFL had been assured of financial stability through a multi-million-dollar virtual sponsorship by the National Broadcasting Company, which, as always, was locked in its rating war with the Columbia Broadcasting System. Profootball had become as much an NBC-CBS struggle as an AFL-NFL battle for survival.

Over his coffee, Werblin now permitted himself a secret smile. He had, as ever, sounded off about the ultimate victory of his AFL and Jets over the NFL and the Giants. That that (sic) was even closer, he had not intimated. The newspapermen recapitulating his notes had not asked,

Sonny Werblin

nor could not know, that this very evening the owners of other AFL franchises were meeting in Werblin's apartment to hear what Lamar Hunt had to say about the peace terms being offered by Tex Schramm of the Dallas Cowboys, with the authority of Pete Rozelle and his NFL superiors.

Rozelle and his owners knew that continuation of the struggle was senseless. The AFL, through its TV package and the 50,000-plus attendance at Shea Stadium, as well as increased dates in its other cities—even those cities deemed 'bush'—could hold out for years, and in that time the savage cost could only lacerate those NFL teams that could not approach the blasé, happy circumstances which had made New York Giant season tickets an item for divorce settlements or last will and testament codicils.

Yet, the independence of the AFL owners could prove financially frightening. Wellington Mara of New York had signed Pete Gogolak, the astonishing field goal kicker who had played out his option with the Buffalo team of the AFL. This seemingly minor transaction in terms of cost had pried open the Pandora's Box, for now in retaliation the Werblins, the Wilsons, the Hunts of the AFL could and would go to NFL stars, offer them staggering contracts to be signed once said NFL greats had played out their options.

The college draft had been brutal, with All-Americans sitting back calmly with their attorneys while the two leagues bickered, bargained, and undercut each other. The bonus money proliferated, so much so that Joe Namath's $400,000 a year before was taken as the guideline to be surpassed."

⊱⊰⊱⊰⊱⊰⊱⊰

"Can She Boil a Pot or Water, Billy Boy?"
by Jeanne Lamb O'Neill, *American Home*, October 1966

I hope that with all the whoop-de-do about science in the schools today we're not forgetting about dowdy old domestic science. I hope that we're not too busy making our daughters physically fit to make them femininely fit. I'd hate to think we're raising a brand-new breed of eggheaded, ham-legged super girls who can't boil water.

Not that I think the schools are to blame. Most schools make some attempt to expose our children to the homely arts. Sean made cranberry relish in school one year. Cindy once "cooked" some sugar-coated dates. I hear that in our local junior high, girls get three hours of home economics a week (four, I believe, if they're not "gifted or superior" students selected for higher things). That may not be much, but I think we can be grateful Susie's getting any domestic education at all in school. Because I'm not sure Susie's even learning which end of the mop is up at home.

So far as I can see, some of today's young things may never be able to leave their mothers. Never mind if they can make a cherry pie. I know teenager girls who can't make a bed properly, professionally, with snappy hospital corners. I know teenage girls who can't peel a potato or iron a hanky. We've had babysitters who couldn't get the children's dinner if you put a can of spaghetti in their hands and opened it for them. Maybe I shouldn't talk about babysitters; it's possible they're perfect whizzes in their own homes but purposely helpless in mine. But I can't help wondering about the ever-so-willing dumb Doras who load the dirty dishes on top of my clean ones and scrub my antique Italian marble with scouring powder. Obviously, Dora missed a lesson somewhere. And think of all the Doras in our college dorms who blithely boil their cashmeres and wash their red things with white things—unless they ship the dirty laundry home to mom each week.

I don't mean to pick on teenagers. I've read that teenagers are generically good-for-nothing. (Okay, I remember that teenagers are good—for nothing.) Teenagers are supposed to rebel against responsibility and suddenly switch from mother's little helpers to Satan's little lounge-lizards. So let's grant that this, too, shall pass and half of today's helpless Hannahs will be tomorrow's crackerjack housekeepers—and let's pick on even littler kids. You just have to observe the young friends your children bring home for dinner or to spend the night. You can tell right away who's being brought up by mother and who's bringing mother up. Some children automatically swoop up their dishes when they leave the table and automatically tuck their pj's and trading cards back in the suitcase, and automatically make their bed. Other children wouldn't pick up a plate if they dropped it right in the middle of the kitchen floor. They're the ones, I'm sure, who couldn't cook a piece of toast or run water in the bathtub without screaming for mom. Interestingly enough, some of the best little table-cleaners who visit our house are boys. It's not surprising at all these days to hear of strapping young he-men who can cook and sew and iron as well as they can throw a pass or make a basket. In fact, a third of the junior contestants in the Pillsbury Bake-Off this year were boys. Ditto for the Delmarva Chicken Festival. Now wouldn't it be a pretty pickle if our girls start asking Billy Boy if he can bake a cherry pie?

෴෴෴෴෴෴෴෴

"The Talent for Listening, Help your Child Learn to Love Good Music" by André Previn, *American Home*, October 1966

I've never met a child who couldn't be interested in music—good music. That doesn't mean he must play an instrument. More often his innate talent is in the area of intensive listening pleasure. But to develop that talent, he needs exposure—and of all the art forms, good music is the most neglected in this matter of exposure. Some music pursues us everywhere—in elevators, airplanes, even supermarkets—but this is music designed for inattentive listening. How then can we expose our children to a real listening experience?

The Bernstein Young People's Concerts have proved that even very young children can be held by great music, especially when they hear it with other young people, accompanied by information given with authority and charm. In quite a few cities where I have conducted, I throw open the last rehearsal to young people only. They can come dressed as they like as long as they're quiet. (I occasionally mention they are enjoying the same program their elders will hear later at $7.50 a seat.) It is wonderful to see the astounding number of kids who come to these rehearsals, and even more thrilling to hear their intelligent, searching comments and questions afterward....

An important word about children's tastes belongs right here. From experience I have learned some startling facts. The old standard fare for "beginning musical appreciation" doesn't interest most young people today. What we adults consider easily assimilated melodies and harmonies are apt to be more difficult for them to grasp than complicated, contemporary dissonances. They are very likely to fall in love at first hearing with a lot of what we may have deemed to be "difficult" classical music. I have heard marvelous, instinctively knowledgeable comments from 12-year olds after performances of Stravinsky and Bartok—and conversely, admissions of boredom after Mozart and Haydn. To think that the purity and elegance of eighteenth-century music is easier than the complexities of today's output is to misunderstand today's children. They identify more thoroughly and quickly with a musical mirror of their time than with a remembrance.

"Things You Should Know About Harvest Aid Chemicals"
Harris H. Barnes, Jr., *Progressive Farmer*, July 1967

Cyanamid dust is still a good defoliant if plants are mature and weather conditions are good. The best method of application is to fly on 30 pounds of the material in the still of the evening, during periods you can be certain of dews.

Chlorates work well under the same conditions as the dust. The (cotton) plants must be mature with colors greenish yellow or gold tinged with red....

Some growers have added a desiccant to do the defoliant. This gives partial defoliation and partial desiccation, with mature leaves dropping and immature leaves drying up and remaining fastened to the tree plant. But growers and defoliation areas are getting away from this practice in order to cut down the amount of trash in cotton.

"Patent Protects Inventor Rights"
Charleston Daily Mail, November 16, 1967

Suppose you invent something that you think can make a lot of money for you. You don't want anyone to "steal" your idea, that is, have the right to copy it exactly.

The government protects you from having this happen by granting you a "patent." A patent is an agreement between the government, representing the public, and the inventor.

The government agrees that no one but the inventor will be allowed to manufacture, use, or sell his invention for 17 years without the inventor's permission. In return, the inventor files his new discovery in the patent office so that everyone will profit from it when the 17 years are over.

Any person who has invented or discovered a new and useful art, machine, manufacture, or composition of matter may obtain a patent for it. This also includes any new or useful improvement.

Application for a patent must be made by the inventor, but he is usually represented by a patent lawyer or agent. A written description and drawings of the invention, together with an application fee, must be submitted to the Patent Office.

If the patent examiners (experts who work for the government's Patent Office) find the invention is actually new, a patent is granted after the payment of an additional fee. The patent now becomes the inventor's own property, and he may sell or assign it.

If anyone disregards a patent, the inventor can force him to stop using it or sue him for the profits made.

The present U.S. Patent system was started in 1836. It laid down the principle, then new, that patents should be given only after inventions had been carefully examined and compared with earlier ones. Two questions were asked: "Is the invention useful?" and "Is it new?" This system was copied by the rest of the civilized world.

"King Charges U.S. Stifled War Dissent"
Delaware County Daily Times (Chester, Penn.), June 1, 1967

Dr. Martin Luther King has accused the Johnson administration of bringing the U.S. commander in Vietnam back to the United States to stifle antiwar dissent.

"It's a dark day in our nation when high-level authorities will seek to use every method to silence dissent," King declared Sunday.

Gen. William C. Westmoreland spoke before a joint session of Congress Friday.

In his sermon at the Ebenezer Baptist Church, where he is co-pastor with his father, the Rev. Martin Luther King, Sr., the civil rights leader said some "equate dissent with disloyalty."

King told the packed congregation he chose to preach in Vietnam "because conscience gives me no other choice."

Reiterating passages in a recent New York address, King deplored the downgrading of antipoverty programs which has coincided with increasing war expenditures, and charged that "a nation that continues year after year to spend more money on military defense than on programs of social uplift is approaching spiritual death."

In his impassioned sermon, King said America must repent from a "tragic, reckless adventure in Vietnam. This madness must stop. We must admit we've been wrong from the beginning of our adventure in Vietnam."

The Nobel Prize winner urged every young man who finds the war objectionable and unjust to file as a conscientious objector.

"It matters what you think of Mohammed Ali (heavyweight champion Cassius Clay's black Muslim name). You certainly have to admire his courage," King told the congregation, which included "Black Power" advocate Stokely Carmichael.

Cries of "Amen" greeted the mention of Clay, who refused to be inducted into the Army last week and was stripped of his heavyweight title.

"Here is a young man willing to give up millions of dollars to do what conscience tells him is right," King said.

"Will Lift-Skiing Spoil Snowmass?"
by John Henry Auran, *Skiing*, October 1967

"Rather than starting off with a list of facilities to establish Snowmass' 'big, big mountain' image, a much more telling clue to the mountain's character is the little service which will provide snowcat tours from the top of lift Number 4 to just below Baldy Mountain, the highest summit in the Snowmass complex.

Snowcat tours are no longer a novelty. In the case of Snowmass, however, these tours have a special purpose—to keep alive the spirit of adventure and the sense of personal involvement that have characterized the area since the skiing public first got a look at it—via snowcat tours—in 1962. 'Almost by accident the tours gave Snowmass a special excitement,' Bill Janss, the major mover of the project, says. 'It's the sort of excitement the people in the 1930s felt when they first discovered skiing. Once lost, you can never recapture it. We're going to preserve that excitement.'

The snowcat tours came about because the vehicle used by the Aspen Skiing Corporation for the exploration and evaluation of the mountain had room for 10 riders. Since the evaluation crews usually consisted of only three men, including the driver, why not, it was reasoned, take along a few paying passengers ($10 a head) to defray some of the costs, and why not get some feedback from those who would eventually pay for the privilege of skiing at Snowmass?

The tours were a sparkling success from the start. Each party of six to eight skiers, accompanied by a guide, would make two or three long runs in the morning, the object being to ski fresh, uncut powder on every run. At midday, there was time out for a leisurely lunch—a combination of All-American camp-out and Renoiresque picnic—at a hut on Sam's Knob, a shoulder in the midsection of the mountain. After lunch, there was more skiing, more powder, but this time with emphasis on moving around to catch the last of the sinking sun.

The powder, of course, was the big attraction. And so was the opportunity to be among the first to ski what was to be an important new area. But what gave the tours their special character was the camaraderie and single-mindedness they would engender in an otherwise highly diverse group of people. What you were and what you did for a living receded into nothing. The mountain was everything."

"Hippie Meccas, Sun-Soaked Beaches Are Top Attractions"
Columbus Daily Telegraph, July 19, 1967

Last month, students were today's summer nomads, pouring onto the sun-soaked beaches of the East and West Coast and into the hippie meccas of San Francisco and New York City by the hundreds of thousands.

A year ago, Southern California's beaches were the number one lure on the West Coast for young people who gathered to swim, surf and take the sun.

The big change is that this summer, the main draw is San Francisco's psychedelic resort, Haight-Ashbury. Spokesman for the hippies predicts before the summer is out, half a million people will stop in this "love" district. Worried city officials expect 50,000 to 100,000.

Says Linda Taylor, 23, from Stamford, Connecticut: "I've been to every resort on the East Coast, from Fire Island to Fort Lauderdale. But San Francisco tops them all. There's more to see here. You don't have to just lie in the sun or swim. San Francisco has sophistication."

SOUTH CAROLINA

Palmetto Tree State

Mitzy McKenna, a slim young brunette from the Los Angeles area, now making her home in San Francisco, sums it up: "Haight-Ashbury's what's happening."

This summer the hippie district is overshadowing the city's traditional attractions such as its European atmosphere, Golden Gate Park, an exciting cultural scene and Golden Gate Bridge. A bus tours Haight-Ashbury. Weekend traffic jams and police arrests for "mill-ins" are features of the district.

Jazz and rock music critic Ralph Gleason calls it "the second immigration to the West," and says it is a result "of the total environment of the city which has made it the rock capital.

Dozens of rock bands—Jefferson Airplane, the Grateful Dead, Big Brother and the Holding Company, The Sopwith Camel, Country Joe and the Fish, and the Steve Miller Blues Band, to name a few—make the city their home. The Fillmore Auditorium and the Avalon Ballroom regularly host big-name groups from all over the country.

ᕖᕖᕖᕖᕖᕖᕖᕖᕖ

"The Search for a Nexus—Vietnam and the Negroes"
William F. Buckley, Jr., *National Review*, August 22, 1967

There is a shift in the making—a shift in public opinion on the question of the Vietnam War, and in the strange way it relates to the Negro problem, or rather is being made to relate to

the Negro problem. There are signs everywhere, and from very important people. The most significant, in my judgment, is the recent declaration of Bishop Fulton Sheen that we should unilaterally pull out of Vietnam. Bishop Sheen is neither senile nor looseminded. His anti-Communism is unalloyed, and his knowledge of the strategic realities is unsentimental. I put off for another day an analysis of the bishop's reasoning—for the present purposes it is significant to note merely that he has taken that position, and that he is an enormously influential priest.

Moreover, a priest who is grimly engaged at the moment, as Bishop of Rochester, in attempting a substantive reconciliation between the Negro and white people in that tense city. Notwithstanding his great urbanity and learning, he is at heart an

evangelist—and he is asking for nothing less than reconciliation, between white and Negro, but also between white and yellow.

At this point, the mind sets out doggedly in search of a nexus. Is there one between the Negro problem and the Vietnam War? The effort is being made to find one, and we can trust to the ingenuity of the politician to discover one. During the weekend, Senator Robert Kennedy went on a paralogistic spree. The occasion was a Democratic fundraising dinner in San Francisco, the immediate purpose of which was to show the great big biceps of Speaker Jesse Unruh, who was recently worsted at the O.K. Corral by the deft gunmanship of Ronald Reagan. Senator Kennedy got his usual running ovation. But it was interrupted by a special ovation when he called on the American people to note the "monstrous disproportion of anyone willing to spend billions for the freedom of others while denying it to our own people." That is one of the political effusions which are the highest testimony to the moral and intellectual emptiness of the political idiom.

The costliest riot in United States history took place a few weeks ago in Detroit, whose Democratic mayor, a long-time hero of the National Association for the Advancement of Colored People, can hardly be said to have conspired against the freedom of the Negro people. But the senator was just warming up. "We cannot allow involvement in the name of independence and democracy in Vietnam to interfere with democracy for our own people." Another burst of applause, more testimony to non-thought. Who is asking that democracy for the Negroes be put off until the end of the Vietnam War? Lyndon Johnson? Ronald Reagan? Abigail Van Buren?

And then the old blackmail: "We must reject the counsel of those willing to pass laws against violence while refusing to eliminate rats." It's sentences like that one that discredit the democratic process. Sentences like that one plus the applause they receive.

But the outline emerges. Somehow, our commitment in Vietnam is one cause of the riots in the United States. Get it? Remember it: The one-two will be very prominent in the rhetoric to come. This is to begin with the sick-at-heartness over the Vietnam war of which Bishop Sheen's manifesto is the expression. Then there is the dazed American attitude towards the riots…. why? why? why? There are politicians around who think they can supply a viable answer.

"PROTEST: The Banners of Dissent"
Time, October 27, 1967

The Pentagon is the most formidable redoubt in official Washington. Squat and solid as a feudal fortress, it hunkers in a remote reclaimed Virginia swamp that used to be called Hell's Bottom, across the Potomac River from the spires, colonnades and domes of the federal city. Through its two tiers of sub-basements and five aboveground stories, windowless corridors weave like badger warrens. The bastion of America's military establishment not only houses the secretary of defense, the Joint Chiefs of Staff and a mint of high brass, but is also a beehive of bureaucracy where some 10,800 civilians shuffle routinely through the daily load of paperwork. It is actually five giant buildings, concentrically interconnected and braced one upon another.

Against that physically and functionally immovable object last week surged a self-proclaimed irresistible force of 35,000 ranting, chanting protestors who are immutably opposed to the U.S. commitment in Vietnam. By the time the demonstration had ended, more than 425 irresistibles had been arrested, 13 more had been injured, and the Pentagon had remained immobile. Within the tide of dissenters swarmed all the elements of dissent in 1967: hard-eyed revolutionaries and skylarking hippies; ersatz motorcycle gangs and all-too-real college professors; housewives, ministers and authors; black nationalists in African garb—but no real African nationalists; nonviolent pacifists and nonpacifist advocates of violence—some of them anti-anti-warriors and American Nazis spoiling for a fight.

Acid & Acrimony. The demonstration began under a crystalline noonday sky at the Lincoln Memorial. It took on special impact by climaxing a week of antiwar protests across the nation. Beneath the marbled gaze of Lincoln's statue, red and blue Viet Cong flags mingled with signs affirming that "Che Guevara Lives," posters proclaiming "Dump Johnson" and asking "Where is Oswald When We Need Him?" The meeting had hardly begun before three Nazis were arrested for jumping a British trade-union orator who criticized U.S. involvement in Vietnam. Speakers caterwauled in competition with blues and rock bands as the demonstrators jostled across the lawns. "The enemy is Lyndon Johnson; the war is disastrous in every way," cried baby doctor Benjamin Spock. Aroused by acrimony and acid-rock, the crowd moved exuberantly out across the Arlington Memorial Bridge toward the Pentagon. Inside the Pentagon, a siege mood prevailed. Defense Secretary Robert McNamara had entered his third-floor office at 8:15 a.m. and immersed himself in his customary workload. The skeleton staff of 3,000 that usually mans the Pentagon on Saturdays had been sharply pared by orders to all personnel to stay home unless their presence was absolutely necessary....

Abortive Assault. When the main force arrived, its good humor had begun to fray. An assault squad wielding clubs and ax handles probed the rope barrier in front of the Pentagon entrances, taunting and testing white-hatted federal marshals who stood in close ranks along the line. After 90-odd minutes of steadily rising invective and roiling around in the north parking lot of the Pentagon, flying wedges of demonstrators surged toward the less heavily defended press entrance.

A barrage of pop bottles and clubs failed to budge the outer ring of marshals, and military police were summoned from the bowels of the bastion to form a brace of backup rings. A final desperate charge actually breached the security lines, and carried a handful of demonstrators whirling into the rifle butts and truncheons of the rearmost guards at the Pentagon gate. At least 10 invaders managed to penetrate the building before they were hurled out—ahead of a counterattacking wave of soldiers vigorously wielding their weapons from port-arms. Handcuffs clicked as marshals corralled their captives, left behind in the abortive assault on the doors. Bloodstains clotted in rusty trails into the Pentagon, where prisoners had been dragged. Among them, uninjured, was Novelist Norman Mailer, who had tried to breach the police line after a wild build-up of booze and obscenity.

"Astros Object to Playing on U.S. Day of Mourning"
The New York Times, June 9, 1968

The Houston Astros baseball players threatened today to stay away from the ballpark tomorrow on the national day of mourning for Senator Robert F. Kennedy. Club officials said if the players carried out the threat, they might have to pay any refunds to the fans out of their salaries.

The player representative of the Astros, Dave Giusti, a pitcher, said the players voted unanimously not to play tomorrow against the Pittsburgh Pirates. He sent word to the Pittsburgh players and Marvin Miller, executive director of the Professional Baseball Players Association, to that effect.

H. B. (Spec) Richardson, the general manager of the Astros, said the game would be played.

At Cincinnati Friday night, the 25 players on the Reds' roster voted unanimously against playing a scheduled doubleheader with the St. Louis Cardinals Sunday at Crosley Field, but officials turned down the request and said the game would be played as planned.

"CONSERVATION, Reprieve for the Redwoods"
Time, September 27, 1968

The giant redwood tree, which grows only in the foggy climes of Northern California and Oregon, is one of the world's oldest and largest plants. Yet it is more than a plant and more than a relic. With huge trunks soaring hundreds of feet into the sky, a forest of *Sequoia sempervirens* is a life unto itself, binding a despoiled planet to its pristine past. As California naturalist Duncan McDuffie said: "To enter a grove of redwoods is to step within the portals of a cathedral more beautiful and more serene than any erected by the hands of man."

For 50 years, conservationists have been fighting a losing battle to save the redwoods. Their mahoganyhued, durable lumber (it virtually defies dry rot) is highly prized for its structural and decorative uses. To date, the battle has gone to the chainsaw. Where there were once two million acres of virgin redwoods, only 250,000 stand today. Last week, as Congress sent to President Johnson a bill establishing the nation's first Redwood National Forest, the conservationists won a significant victory....

Much of the credit for saving the redwoods belongs to the California-based Sierra Club and San Francisco's Save-the-Redwoods League, which was founded 50 years ago. Creation of the park comes none too soon. At the present rate of logging, the virgin stands of redwoods would last only another 20 years, a mere second in the lives of trees that were swaying in the Pacific breeze when Christ was born.

"What Those Draft Classifications Mean"
Good Housekeeping, June 1968

Current draft policy calls for the drafting first of oldest eligible men in the age group of 19 through 25, although under the law deferred men are liable for military induction until age 35.

All young men are required to register with the local draft board within five days after their 18th birthdays. This local board will retain jurisdiction, even if the man moves. The board

places him in one of 18 classifications on the basis of information about his dependents and from such sources as his employer, high school or college. The young man is required to report changes in his address and status, such as marriage, fatherhood or education, to his local board within 10 days of their occurrence....

Draft boards have been selecting single men from 19 through 25, or those married after August 26, 1965, first, with a priority given to delinquents, volunteers and oldest members of this group.... The average age of current draftees is about 20.5 years....

Starting in June, students graduating from college, who expected to attend graduate school, and those in their first year of graduate school, will no longer be deferred from the draft except for students in medicine and related fields such as dentistry.

"Beatles Still Tops in Poll"
San Antonio Light, February 27, 1969

The Beatles, Janis Joplin, Donovan, Jim Morrison, and Jimi Hendrix were among the top winners in *Eye Magazine*'s first annual nationwide rock 'n' roll poll. Some 6,800 teenagers in 50 states voted in the January issue of *Eye*, a monthly magazine geared to 18 to 20 year olds of both sexes.

Divided into 30 categories from Best Album to Most Exciting New Face, the poll revealed youngsters dig progressive rock (like Cream), but they put down teenybopper bubblegum rock (like the 1910 Fruit Gum Company).

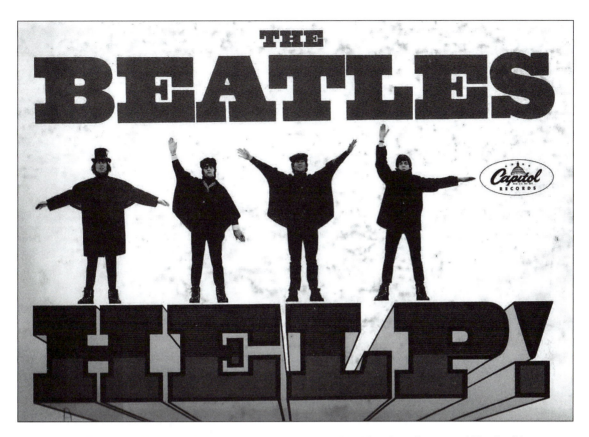

The Beatles walked off with three categories—Album of the Year, Best Group, and Top English Group—and "Hey Jude" by the Beatles won the Best Single and Best Lyrics awards.

The top American group was the Doors.

Tiny Tim took the 1968 Public Nuisance Award, and his album was voted runner-up to The Rolling Stones' *Their Satanic Majesties Request* as Bad-Trip Album of the Year.

Janis Joplin took Best Female Vocalist and also captured "Sexiest Woman in Rock 'n' Roll." Jim Morrison was Sexiest Man and runner-up to Donovan as Top Male Vocalist.

The sleeper in the poll was Frank Zappa, named as 1968 Private Delight ("I don't care what anyone says, I dig it.")

Cream was hailed as the Most Lamented Breakup of the Year and also runner-up as Top English Group.

The King and Queen of Soul were James Brown and Aretha Franklin.

"Program for Non-White Jobs to Begin"
New York Times, September 21, 1969

"Arthur A. Fletcher, Under Secretary of Labor, said today that the Nixon administration had decided to require contractors on federally financed projects to make specific commitments to hire non-whites.

Mr. Fletcher told West Coast Negro leaders that the new policy would be announced officially Monday in Philadelphia.

He said the strict federal requirements would first be applied to projects involving federal money in the Philadelphia area and would be implemented in the San Diego, Los Angeles and

San Francisco Bay areas 'within the next 30 to 60 days.'

Previously, the high-ranking Negro official said the Government required contractors to sign a nondiscrimination pledge but allowed them to arrive at the specific number of minority workers by themselves.

Under the new policy, supervisors of federal agencies that grant contracts will be required to make certain that sufficient non-white personnel are employed.

'We are using contract law to achieve a social end,' Mr. Fletcher told a news conference during the West Coast conference of the National Association for the Advancement of Colored People."

"The Game of the Name"
by William Zinsser, *Life*, November 7, 1969

"I keep losing American companies. Every week two or three more disappear, taking with them their names, their trademarks and my memories. It makes me nervous. Suddenly everyone is GAF or GAC or GCA. Or Dayco or Citgo or Armco. Or National General. National General what? Two adjectives and no noun. I miss the noun. I no longer know what business American businesses are in.

Remember Pittsburgh Plate Glass, the company that made plate glass in Pittsburgh? Now it's PPG Industries, presumably making ppg's. And where have you gone, Corn Products? I used to like to think of you making corn products. Now you're CPC International—unless that's somebody else—and I don't think of you at all. Or of any other company that took some commodity out of my life by burrowing into the alphabet. The shoe machinery went out of USM, the rubber out of Uniroyal. What can a man hang on to?

Is the Minneapolis and St. Louis Railway really MSL Industries, Inc.? And the Alaska Juneau Gold Mining Company really A.J. Industries, Inc.? Say it ain't so! Did railroaders push West and prospectors push north to die in a desert of initials? Did founders found businesses to serve real needs that would later be hidden behind fake names? Take the American Molasses Company. I doubt if there's a man or boy who doesn't like to picture a company that's sitting around all day making molasses. Well, that picture's over. The firm vanished, and when I found it again it was SuCrest. What's SuCrest to me, or me to SuCrest?

I don't even insist on knowing exactly what a company does—all I ask is a decent clue. I've never understood for instance, how the Air Reduction Company makes any money reducing air, but that's evidently what it does and I think of it with fondness. Not so the National Cylinder Gas Company, which I guess made gas, or cylinder gas. Now it's Chemetron. And I'm Apathy Industries, Inc."

"Gift for Nixon"
World Week, **January 31, 1969**

President Nixon received an unusual housewarming gift when he moved into the White House on January 20. Just a few days earlier, Congress increased the presidential salary by 100 percent. New salary: $200,000 a year.

Congress cannot increase the salary of a president while he is in office. Just before leaving office, President Johnson asked Congress to vote a pay raise that would take effect for the new president. The presidential pay raise is only the fourth in the nation's history. President Washington earned $25,000. Later the salary was increased to $50,000 (in 1873), then $75,000 (in 1909) and $100,000 (in 1949).

Members of Congress also are in line for a pay boost from the present $30,000 to $42,500 year. The increase was recommended by President Johnson and will take effect automatically unless vetoed by Congress.

Neither the President or the Congressmen will take home all of their higher pay, however. Federal income taxes will take a big bite. The President's $200,000 may be whittled down to something like $78,000 after taxes.

$\approx\ll\approx\ll\approx\ll\approx\ll$

"In the Round, Viet Talks Resume"
World Week, **January 31, 1969**

After 10 weeks of deadlock, delegates from the U.S., South Vietnam, Communist North Vietnam, and the Communist-led National Liberation Front (NLF) sat down for the first of their "expanded" four-party talks in Paris on January 18. The breakthrough came when all four agreed to negotiate across a round table.

The 10-week wrangle over the shape of the negotiating table gave cartoonists and humorists a field day—but the negotiators were deadly serious. They could point to historical precedents for their hassle over an apparently trivial point. In the seventeenth century, for example, negotiations to end a major war were stalled six months because French and Austrian delegates couldn't agree on who should enter the conference room first.

But there was a lot more than national pride involved in the Paris dispute over settling over seating arrangements. Since April 1968 U.S. and North Vietnamese negotiators had met regularly in Paris to try to launch meaningful peace talks. All agreed that such talks would eventually have to include the other two major combatants in the Vietnam War: the South Vietnamese government and the NLF (or Viet Cong). But how should these two be represented?

South Vietnam did not want any seating arrangements that might imply equality between itself and the NLF. In South Vietnam's view, the NLF is a guerrilla organization with no claim to be an equal to any actual government. Thus, South Vietnam wanted a table with two sides—one for the Allies (U.S. and South Vietnam) and one for the Communists.

North Vietnam and the NLF, on the other hand, wanted a table with no sides (a plain round table) or a square table with four sides. This, in their view, would emphasize equality of all four parties. In the end, it was decided to use a round table—but with two small rectangular tables (for secretaries) set just 18 inches away on opposite sides. This allowed each side to interpret seating arrangements in its own way. The U.S. and South Vietnam pointed out that the side tables formed a symbolic separation between them and the Communists—making a two-sided table. North Vietnam and the NLF pointed out that the main table was, after all, round. Said a senior U.S. spokesman: "It looks as if this show is getting back on the road."

SECTION FIVE: CENSUS DATA

This section begins with 16 state-by-state comparative tables that rank data from the 1960, 1970, and 2010 census, designed to help define the times during which the families profiled in Section One lived. Table topics are listed below. Following the state-by-state tables is General Demographic Trends for Metropolitan Areas, 1960 to 1970—a study by the U.S. Census of population and housing trends. Results are portrayed, nationally and state-by-state, by maps, tables and narrative, helping to visualize the environment of the 1960s, as well as how this tumultuous decade affected the years that followed.

State-by-State Comparative Tables

General Demographic Trends for Metropolitan Areas, 1960 to 1970

Total Population

Area	Population			1960		1970		2010	
	1960	1970	2010	Area	Rank	Area	Rank	Area	Rank
Alabama	3,266,740	3,444,165	4,779,736	New York	1	California	1	California	1
Alaska	226,167	300,382	710,231	California	2	New York	2	Texas	2
Arizona	1,302,161	1,770,900	6,392,017	Pennsylvania	3	Pennsylvania	3	New York	3
Arkansas	1,786,272	1,923,295	2,915,918	Illinois	4	Texas	4	Florida	4
California	15,717,204	19,953,134	37,253,956	Ohio	5	Illinois	5	Illinois	5
Colorado	1,753,947	2,207,259	5,029,196	Texas	6	Ohio	6	Pennsylvania	6
Connecticut	2,535,234	3,031,709	3,574,097	Michigan	7	Michigan	7	Ohio	7
Delaware	446,292	548,104	897,934	New Jersey	8	New Jersey	8	Michigan	8
D.C.	763,956	756,510	601,723	Massachusetts	9	Florida	9	Georgia	9
Florida	4,951,560	6,789,443	18,801,310	Florida	10	Massachusetts	10	North Carolina	10
Georgia	3,943,116	4,589,575	9,687,653	Indiana	11	Indiana	11	New Jersey	11
Hawaii	632,772	768,561	1,360,301	North Carolina	12	North Carolina	12	Virginia	12
Idaho	667,191	712,567	1,567,582	Missouri	13	Missouri	13	Washington	13
Illinois	10,081,158	11,113,976	12,830,632	Virginia	14	Virginia	14	Massachusetts	14
Indiana	4,662,498	5,193,669	6,483,802	Wisconsin	15	Georgia	15	Indiana	15
Iowa	2,757,537	2,824,376	3,046,355	Georgia	16	Wisconsin	16	Arizona	16
Kansas	2,178,611	2,246,578	2,853,118	Tennessee	17	Tennessee	17	Tennessee	17
Kentucky	3,038,156	3,218,706	4,339,367	Minnesota	18	Maryland	18	Missouri	18
Louisiana	3,257,022	3,641,306	4,533,372	Alabama	19	Minnesota	19	Maryland	19
Maine	969,265	992,048	1,328,361	Louisiana	20	Louisiana	20	Wisconsin	20
Maryland	3,100,689	3,922,399	5,773,552	Maryland	21	Alabama	21	Minnesota	21
Massachusetts	5,148,578	5,689,170	6,547,629	Kentucky	22	Washington	22	Colorado	22
Michigan	7,823,194	8,875,083	9,883,640	Washington	23	Kentucky	23	Alabama	23
Minnesota	3,413,864	3,804,971	5,303,925	Iowa	24	Connecticut	24	South Carolina	24
Mississippi	2,178,141	2,216,912	2,967,297	Connecticut	25	Iowa	25	Louisiana	25
Missouri	4,319,813	4,676,501	5,988,927	South Carolina	26	South Carolina	26	Kentucky	26
Montana	674,767	694,409	989,415	Oklahoma	27	Oklahoma	27	Oregon	27
Nebraska	1,411,330	1,483,493	1,826,341	Kansas	28	Kansas	28	Oklahoma	28
Nevada	285,278	488,738	2,700,551	Mississippi	29	Mississippi	29	Connecticut	29
New Hampshire	606,921	737,681	1,316,470	West Virginia	30	Colorado	30	Iowa	30
New Jersey	6,066,782	7,168,164	8,791,894	Arkansas	31	Oregon	31	Mississippi	31
New Mexico	951,023	1,016,000	2,059,179	Oregon	32	Arkansas	32	Arkansas	32
New York	16,782,304	18,236,967	19,378,102	Colorado	33	Arizona	33	Kansas	33
North Carolina	4,556,155	5,082,059	9,535,483	Nebraska	34	West Virginia	34	Utah	34
North Dakota	632,446	617,761	672,591	Arizona	35	Nebraska	35	Nevada	35
Ohio	9,706,397	10,652,017	11,536,504	Maine	36	Utah	36	New Mexico	36
Oklahoma	2,328,284	2,559,229	3,751,351	New Mexico	37	New Mexico	37	West Virginia	37
Oregon	1,768,687	2,091,385	3,831,074	Utah	38	Maine	38	Nebraska	38
Pennsylvania	11,319,366	11,793,909	12,702,379	Rhode Island	39	Rhode Island	39	Idaho	39
Rhode Island	859,488	946,725	1,052,567	D.C.	40	Hawaii	40	Hawaii	40
South Carolina	2,382,594	2,590,516	4,625,364	South Dakota	41	D.C.	41	Maine	41
South Dakota	680,514	665,507	814,180	Montana	42	New Hampshire	42	New Hampshire	42
Tennessee	3,567,089	3,923,687	6,346,105	Idaho	43	Idaho	43	Rhode Island	43
Texas	9,579,677	11,196,730	25,145,561	Hawaii	44	Montana	44	Montana	44
Utah	890,627	1,059,273	2,763,885	North Dakota	45	South Dakota	45	Delaware	45
Vermont	389,881	444,330	625,741	New Hampshire	46	North Dakota	46	South Dakota	46
Virginia	3,966,949	4,648,494	8,001,024	Delaware	47	Delaware	47	Alaska	47
Washington	2,853,214	3,409,169	6,724,540	Vermont	48	Nevada	48	North Dakota	48
West Virginia	1,860,421	1,744,237	1,852,994	Wyoming	49	Vermont	49	Vermont	49
Wisconsin	3,951,777	4,417,731	5,686,986	Nevada	50	Wyoming	50	D.C.	50
Wyoming	330,066	332,416	563,626	Alaska	51	Alaska	51	Wyoming	51
United States	179,323,175	203,211,926	308,745,538	United States	–	United States	–	United States	–

Source: U.S. Census Bureau, 1960 Census of Population; U.S. Census Bureau, 1970 Census of Population; U.S. Census Bureau, Census 2010

White Population

Area	Percent of Population			1960		1970		2010	
	1960	1970	2010	Area	Rank	Area	Rank	Area	Rank
Alabama	69.9	73.5	68.5	Vermont	1	Vermont	1	Vermont	1
Alaska	77.2	78.8	66.7	New Hampshire	2	New Hampshire	2	Maine	2
Arizona	89.8	90.6	73.0	Maine	3	Maine	3	New Hampshire	3
Arkansas	78.1	81.4	77.0	Iowa	4	Iowa	4	West Virginia	3
California	92.0	89.0	57.6	Minnesota	5	Minnesota	5	Iowa	5
Colorado	97.0	95.7	81.3	Idaho	6	Idaho	6	Wyoming	6
Connecticut	95.6	93.5	77.6	Utah	7	Utah	7	North Dakota	7
Delaware	86.1	85.1	68.9	North Dakota	8	Wyoming	8	Montana	8
D.C.	45.2	27.6	38.5	Oregon	9	Oregon	9	Idaho	9
Florida	82.1	84.2	75.0	Wyoming	10	North Dakota	10	Kentucky	10
Georgia	71.4	73.8	59.7	Massachusetts	11	Rhode Island	11	Wisconsin	11
Hawaii	32.0	38.7	24.7	Rhode Island	11	Nebraska	12	Utah	12
Idaho	98.5	98.0	89.1	Wisconsin	11	Wisconsin	13	Nebraska	12
Illinois	89.4	86.3	71.5	Nebraska	14	Massachusetts	14	South Dakota	14
Indiana	94.1	92.8	84.3	Colorado	15	West Virginia	15	Minnesota	15
Iowa	99.0	98.5	91.3	Washington	16	Colorado	16	Indiana	16
Kansas	95.4	94.4	83.8	Montana	16	Montana	17	Kansas	17
Kentucky	92.8	92.6	87.8	South Dakota	18	Washington	18	Oregon	18
Louisiana	67.9	69.8	62.6	Connecticut	19	South Dakota	19	Missouri	19
Maine	99.4	99.3	95.2	Kansas	20	Kansas	20	Ohio	20
Maryland	83.0	81.4	58.2	West Virginia	21	Connecticut	21	Pennsylvania	21
Massachusetts	97.6	96.2	80.4	Indiana	22	Indiana	22	Rhode Island	22
Michigan	90.6	88.2	78.9	Kentucky	23	Kentucky	23	Colorado	23
Minnesota	98.8	98.1	85.3	Pennsylvania	24	Nevada	24	Massachusetts	24
Mississippi	57.7	62.8	59.1	Nevada	25	Pennsylvania	25	Michigan	25
Missouri	90.8	89.3	82.8	New Mexico	26	Arizona	26	Connecticut	26
Montana	96.4	95.4	89.4	California	27	Ohio	27	Tennessee	26
Nebraska	97.4	96.5	86.1	Ohio	28	New Mexico	28	Washington	28
Nevada	92.3	91.7	66.2	New Jersey	29	Missouri	29	Arkansas	29
New Hampshire	99.6	99.3	93.9	New York	30	Oklahoma	30	Florida	30
New Jersey	91.3	88.5	68.6	Missouri	31	California	31	Arizona	31
New Mexico	92.1	90.1	68.4	Michigan	32	New Jersey	32	Oklahoma	32
New York	91.1	86.8	65.7	Oklahoma	33	Michigan	33	Illinois	33
North Carolina	74.6	76.7	68.5	Arizona	34	New York	34	Texas	34
North Dakota	98.0	97.0	90.0	Illinois	35	Texas	35	Delaware	35
Ohio	91.8	90.5	82.7	Texas	36	Illinois	36	New Jersey	36
Oklahoma	90.5	89.1	72.2	Delaware	37	Delaware	37	Virginia	36
Oregon	97.9	97.1	83.6	Tennessee	38	Florida	38	North Carolina	38
Pennsylvania	92.4	91.0	81.9	Maryland	39	Tennessee	39	Alabama	38
Rhode Island	97.6	96.6	81.4	Florida	40	Maryland	40	New Mexico	40
South Carolina	65.1	69.2	66.2	Virginia	41	Arkansas	41	Alaska	41
South Dakota	96.0	94.7	85.9	Arkansas	42	Virginia	42	Nevada	42
Tennessee	83.5	83.9	77.6	Alaska	43	Alaska	43	South Carolina	42
Texas	87.4	86.7	70.4	North Carolina	44	North Carolina	44	New York	44
Utah	98.1	97.4	86.1	Georgia	45	Georgia	45	Louisiana	45
Vermont	99.8	99.6	95.3	Alabama	46	Alabama	46	Georgia	46
Virginia	79.2	80.9	68.6	Louisiana	47	Louisiana	47	Mississippi	47
Washington	96.4	95.3	77.3	South Carolina	48	South Carolina	48	Maryland	48
West Virginia	95.1	95.9	93.9	Mississippi	49	Mississippi	49	California	49
Wisconsin	97.6	96.4	86.2	D.C.	50	Hawaii	50	D.C.	50
Wyoming	97.8	97.1	90.7	Hawaii	51	D.C.	51	Hawaii	51
United States	88.5	0.0	72.4	United States	–	United States	–	United States	–

Source: U.S. Census Bureau, 1960 Census of Population; U.S. Census Bureau, 1970 Census of Population; U.S. Census Bureau, Census 2010

Black Population

Area	Percent of Population			1960		1970		2010	
	1960	1970	2010	Area	Rank	Area	Rank	Area	Rank
Alabama	30.0	26.2	26.2	D.C.	1	D.C.	1	D.C.	1
Alaska	3.0	2.9	3.3	Mississippi	2	Mississippi	2	Mississippi	2
Arizona	3.3	3.0	4.1	South Carolina	3	South Carolina	3	Louisiana	3
Arkansas	21.8	18.3	15.4	Louisiana	4	Louisiana	4	Georgia	4
California	5.6	7.0	6.2	Alabama	5	Alabama	5	Maryland	5
Colorado	2.3	3.0	4.0	Georgia	6	Georgia	6	South Carolina	6
Connecticut	4.2	5.9	10.1	North Carolina	7	North Carolina	7	Alabama	7
Delaware	13.6	14.2	21.4	Arkansas	8	Virginia	8	North Carolina	8
D.C.	53.9	71.0	50.7	Virginia	9	Arkansas	9	Delaware	9
Florida	17.8	15.3	16.0	Florida	10	Maryland	10	Virginia	10
Georgia	28.5	25.8	30.5	Maryland	11	Tennessee	11	Tennessee	11
Hawaii	0.8	0.9	1.6	Tennessee	12	Florida	12	Florida	12
Idaho	0.2	0.3	0.6	Delaware	13	Delaware	13	New York	13
Illinois	10.3	12.8	14.5	Texas	14	Illinois	14	Arkansas	14
Indiana	5.8	6.8	9.1	Illinois	15	Texas	15	Illinois	15
Iowa	0.9	1.1	2.9	Michigan	16	New York	16	Michigan	16
Kansas	4.2	4.7	5.9	Missouri	17	Michigan	17	New Jersey	17
Kentucky	7.1	7.1	7.8	New Jersey	18	New Jersey	18	Ohio	18
Louisiana	31.9	29.8	32.0	New York	19	Missouri	19	Texas	19
Maine	0.3	0.2	1.2	Ohio	20	Ohio	20	Missouri	20
Maryland	16.7	17.8	29.4	Pennsylvania	21	Pennsylvania	21	Pennsylvania	21
Massachusetts	2.2	3.0	6.6	Kentucky	22	Kentucky	22	Connecticut	22
Michigan	9.2	11.1	14.2	Oklahoma	23	California	23	Indiana	23
Minnesota	0.7	0.9	5.2	Indiana	24	Indiana	24	Nevada	24
Mississippi	42.0	36.8	37.0	California	25	Oklahoma	25	Kentucky	25
Missouri	9.0	10.2	11.6	West Virginia	26	Connecticut	26	Oklahoma	26
Montana	0.2	0.2	0.4	Nevada	27	Nevada	27	Massachusetts	27
Nebraska	2.1	2.6	4.5	Connecticut	28	Kansas	28	Wisconsin	28
Nevada	4.7	5.6	8.1	Kansas	28	West Virginia	29	California	29
New Hampshire	0.3	0.3	1.1	Arizona	30	Massachusetts	30	Kansas	30
New Jersey	8.5	10.7	13.7	Alaska	31	Arizona	31	Rhode Island	31
New Mexico	1.8	1.9	2.1	Colorado	32	Colorado	31	Minnesota	32
New York	8.4	11.8	15.9	Massachusetts	33	Alaska	33	Nebraska	33
North Carolina	24.5	22.1	21.5	Rhode Island	34	Wisconsin	34	Arizona	34
North Dakota	0.1	0.4	1.2	Nebraska	34	Nebraska	35	Colorado	35
Ohio	8.1	9.1	12.2	Wisconsin	36	Rhode Island	36	Washington	36
Oklahoma	6.6	6.7	7.4	New Mexico	37	Washington	37	West Virginia	37
Oregon	1.0	1.2	1.8	Washington	38	New Mexico	38	Alaska	38
Pennsylvania	7.5	8.6	10.8	Oregon	39	Oregon	39	Iowa	39
Rhode Island	2.1	2.6	5.7	Iowa	40	Iowa	40	New Mexico	40
South Carolina	34.8	30.4	27.9	Hawaii	41	Hawaii	41	Oregon	41
South Dakota	0.2	0.2	1.3	Minnesota	42	Minnesota	42	Hawaii	42
Tennessee	16.5	15.8	16.7	Wyoming	42	Wyoming	43	South Dakota	43
Texas	12.4	12.4	11.8	Utah	44	Utah	44	Maine	44
Utah	0.5	0.6	1.1	New Hampshire	45	North Dakota	45	North Dakota	44
Vermont	0.1	0.1	1.0	Maine	45	New Hampshire	46	Utah	46
Virginia	20.6	18.5	19.4	Montana	47	Idaho	47	New Hampshire	46
Washington	1.7	2.0	3.6	South Dakota	47	Montana	48	Vermont	48
West Virginia	4.8	3.8	3.4	Idaho	47	Maine	49	Wyoming	49
Wisconsin	1.9	2.9	6.3	Vermont	50	South Dakota	50	Idaho	50
Wyoming	0.7	0.7	0.8	North Dakota	50	Vermont	51	Montana	51
United States	10.5	0.0	12.6	United States	–	United States	–	United States	–

Source: U.S. Census Bureau, 1960 Census of Population; U.S. Census Bureau, 1970 Census of Population; U.S. Census Bureau, Census 2010

American Indian/Alaska Native Population

Area	Percent of Population			1960		1970		2010	
	1960	1970	2010	Area	Rank	Area	Rank	Area	Rank
Alabama	0.0	0.0	0.6	Arizona	1	New Mexico	1	Alaska	1
Alaska	6.4	5.4	14.8	Alaska	1	Alaska	2	New Mexico	2
Arizona	6.4	5.4	4.6	New Mexico	3	Arizona	3	South Dakota	3
Arkansas	0.0	0.1	0.8	South Dakota	4	South Dakota	4	Oklahoma	4
California	0.2	0.4	1.0	Montana	5	Montana	5	Montana	5
Colorado	0.2	0.4	1.1	Oklahoma	6	Oklahoma	6	North Dakota	6
Connecticut	0.0	0.0	0.3	Nevada	7	North Dakota	7	Arizona	7
Delaware	0.1	0.1	0.5	North Dakota	8	Nevada	8	Wyoming	8
D.C.	0.1	0.1	0.3	Wyoming	9	Wyoming	9	Washington	9
Florida	0.1	0.1	0.4	Utah	10	Utah	10	Oregon	10
Georgia	0.0	0.0	0.3	Idaho	10	Washington	11	Idaho	10
Hawaii	0.1	0.1	0.3	North Carolina	10	Idaho	12	North Carolina	12
Idaho	0.8	0.9	1.4	Washington	13	North Carolina	13	Nevada	13
Illinois	0.0	0.1	0.3	Minnesota	14	Oregon	14	Utah	13
Indiana	0.0	0.0	0.3	Oregon	14	Minnesota	15	Colorado	15
Iowa	0.1	0.1	0.4	Wisconsin	16	California	16	Minnesota	15
Kansas	0.2	0.3	1.0	Nebraska	16	Nebraska	17	California	17
Kentucky	0.0	0.0	0.2	California	18	Wisconsin	18	Kansas	17
Louisiana	0.1	0.1	0.7	Maine	18	Colorado	19	Nebraska	17
Maine	0.2	0.2	0.6	Colorado	18	Kansas	20	Wisconsin	17
Maryland	0.0	0.1	0.4	Kansas	18	Maine	21	Arkansas	21
Massachusetts	0.0	0.0	0.3	New York	22	Michigan	22	Texas	22
Michigan	0.1	0.1	0.6	Hawaii	22	Mississippi	22	Louisiana	22
Minnesota	0.5	0.6	1.1	Rhode Island	22	New York	24	New York	24
Mississippi	0.1	0.1	0.5	Michigan	22	Texas	24	Rhode Island	24
Missouri	0.0	0.1	0.5	Florida	22	Hawaii	26	Michigan	24
Montana	3.1	3.9	6.3	D.C.	22	Rhode Island	26	Alabama	24
Nebraska	0.4	0.4	1.0	Delaware	22	Louisiana	26	Maine	24
Nevada	2.3	1.6	1.2	Texas	22	D.C.	29	Delaware	29
New Hampshire	0.0	0.0	0.2	Iowa	22	Delaware	30	Missouri	29
New Jersey	0.0	0.0	0.3	Virginia	22	Missouri	30	Mississippi	29
New Mexico	5.9	7.1	9.4	Louisiana	22	Maryland	32	Florida	32
New York	0.1	0.1	0.6	Mississippi	22	Iowa	32	Maryland	32
North Carolina	0.8	0.8	1.3	Massachusetts	34	Florida	34	Virginia	32
North Dakota	1.9	2.3	5.4	Connecticut	34	Illinois	34	South Carolina	32
Ohio	0.0	0.0	0.2	New Jersey	34	Virginia	34	Iowa	32
Oklahoma	2.8	3.8	8.6	New Hampshire	34	Arkansas	34	Vermont	32
Oregon	0.5	0.6	1.4	Illinois	34	South Carolina	38	New Jersey	38
Pennsylvania	0.0	0.0	0.2	Vermont	34	Massachusetts	39	Hawaii	38
Rhode Island	0.1	0.1	0.6	Pennsylvania	34	New Jersey	40	Massachusetts	38
South Carolina	0.0	0.0	0.4	Ohio	34	Connecticut	40	Illinois	38
South Dakota	3.8	4.8	8.8	Maryland	34	Indiana	40	Connecticut	38
Tennessee	0.0	0.0	0.3	Indiana	34	Alabama	40	D.C.	38
Texas	0.1	0.1	0.7	Missouri	34	Ohio	44	Georgia	38
Utah	0.8	1.0	1.2	West Virginia	34	Tennessee	44	Tennessee	38
Vermont	0.0	0.0	0.4	Georgia	34	New Hampshire	46	Indiana	38
Virginia	0.1	0.1	0.4	Kentucky	34	Vermont	46	Pennsylvania	47
Washington	0.7	0.9	1.5	South Carolina	34	Pennsylvania	46	New Hampshire	47
West Virginia	0.0	0.0	0.2	Alabama	34	Georgia	46	Ohio	47
Wisconsin	0.4	0.4	1.0	Arkansas	34	Kentucky	46	Kentucky	47
Wyoming	1.2	1.5	2.4	Tennessee	34	West Virginia	51	West Virginia	47
United States	0.2	0.0	0.9	United States	–	United States	–	United States	–

Source: U.S. Census Bureau, 1960 Census of Population; U.S. Census Bureau, 1970 Census of Population; U.S. Census Bureau, Census 2010

Asian Population

Area	Percent of Population			1960		1970		2010	
	1960	1970	2010	Area	Rank	Area	Rank	Area	Rank
Alabama	0.0	0.0	1.1	Hawaii	1	Hawaii	1	Hawaii	1
Alaska	0.8	0.8	5.4	California	2	California	2	California	2
Arizona	0.4	0.4	2.8	Washington	3	Washington	3	New Jersey	3
Arkansas	0.1	0.0	1.2	Alaska	4	Alaska	4	New York	4
California	2.0	2.6	13.0	D.C.	5	D.C.	5	Nevada	5
Colorado	0.5	0.4	2.8	Utah	5	New York	6	Washington	5
Connecticut	0.1	0.2	3.8	Nevada	7	Oregon	6	Maryland	7
Delaware	0.1	0.2	3.2	Oregon	7	Utah	8	Virginia	7
D.C.	0.6	0.6	3.5	Colorado	7	Nevada	9	Alaska	9
Florida	0.1	0.1	2.4	Arizona	10	Colorado	10	Massachusetts	10
Georgia	0.1	0.1	3.2	Idaho	10	Arizona	11	Illinois	11
Hawaii	65.3	47.2	38.6	New York	12	Idaho	11	Minnesota	12
Idaho	0.4	0.4	1.2	Massachusetts	13	Illinois	13	Texas	13
Illinois	0.2	0.4	4.6	Illinois	13	Maryland	14	Connecticut	13
Indiana	0.1	0.1	1.6	Montana	13	Massachusetts	15	Oregon	15
Iowa	0.0	0.0	1.7	Maryland	13	Rhode Island	15	D.C.	16
Kansas	0.1	0.1	2.4	Wyoming	13	Virginia	17	Georgia	17
Kentucky	0.0	0.0	1.1	New Mexico	13	New Jersey	18	Delaware	17
Louisiana	0.1	0.1	1.5	Connecticut	19	Wyoming	18	Rhode Island	19
Maine	0.1	0.1	1.0	New Jersey	19	Delaware	20	Arizona	20
Maryland	0.2	0.3	5.5	Rhode Island	19	Connecticut	21	Colorado	20
Massachusetts	0.2	0.3	5.3	New Hampshire	19	New Mexico	22	Pennsylvania	22
Michigan	0.1	0.1	2.4	Michigan	19	Florida	23	Florida	23
Minnesota	0.1	0.1	4.0	Maine	19	Michigan	24	Kansas	23
Mississippi	0.1	0.1	0.9	Florida	19	Minnesota	24	Michigan	23
Missouri	0.1	0.1	1.6	Pennsylvania	19	Montana	26	Wisconsin	26
Montana	0.2	0.1	0.6	Wisconsin	19	Texas	26	North Carolina	27
Nebraska	0.1	0.1	1.8	Minnesota	19	Kansas	26	New Hampshire	27
Nevada	0.5	0.5	7.2	Ohio	19	Wisconsin	29	Utah	29
New Hampshire	0.1	0.1	2.2	Delaware	19	Nebraska	29	Nebraska	30
New Jersey	0.1	0.2	8.3	Texas	19	Missouri	29	Oklahoma	31
New Mexico	0.2	0.1	1.4	Nebraska	19	Pennsylvania	32	Iowa	31
New York	0.3	0.6	7.3	Indiana	19	New Hampshire	33	Ohio	31
North Carolina	0.0	0.0	2.2	Missouri	19	Ohio	33	Indiana	34
North Dakota	0.0	0.1	1.0	Kansas	19	Oklahoma	35	Missouri	34
Ohio	0.1	0.1	1.7	Virginia	19	Indiana	36	Louisiana	36
Oklahoma	0.1	0.1	1.7	Louisiana	19	Mississippi	36	New Mexico	37
Oregon	0.5	0.6	3.7	Oklahoma	19	Maine	38	Tennessee	37
Pennsylvania	0.1	0.1	2.7	Georgia	19	North Dakota	38	South Carolina	39
Rhode Island	0.1	0.3	2.9	Mississippi	19	Louisiana	38	Vermont	39
South Carolina	0.0	0.1	1.3	Arkansas	19	Georgia	38	Idaho	41
South Dakota	0.0	0.0	0.9	Vermont	42	South Carolina	38	Arkansas	41
Tennessee	0.0	0.0	1.4	North Dakota	42	Iowa	43	Alabama	43
Texas	0.1	0.1	3.8	South Dakota	42	Tennessee	43	Kentucky	43
Utah	0.6	0.6	2.0	Iowa	42	Vermont	45	Maine	45
Vermont	0.0	0.0	1.3	West Virginia	42	West Virginia	45	North Dakota	45
Virginia	0.1	0.3	5.5	Kentucky	42	North Carolina	45	South Dakota	47
Washington	1.0	1.2	7.2	South Carolina	42	Arkansas	45	Mississippi	47
West Virginia	0.0	0.0	0.7	North Carolina	42	South Dakota	49	Wyoming	49
Wisconsin	0.1	0.1	2.3	Alabama	42	Alabama	49	West Virginia	50
Wyoming	0.2	0.2	0.8	Tennessee	42	Kentucky	49	Montana	51
United States	0.5	0.0	4.8	United States	–	United States	–	United States	–

Source: U.S. Census Bureau, 1960 Census of Population; U.S. Census Bureau, 1970 Census of Population; U.S. Census Bureau, Census 2010

Foreign-Born Population

Area	Percent of Population			1960		1970		2010	
	1960	1970	2010	Area	Rank	Area	Rank	Area	Rank
Alabama	0.5	0.5	3.4	New York	1	New York	1	California	1
Alaska	3.6	2.6	7.2	Massachusetts	2	Hawaii	2	New York	2
Arizona	5.4	4.3	14.2	Hawaii	3	New Jersey	3	New Jersey	3
Arkansas	0.4	0.4	4.3	Connecticut	3	California	4	Nevada	4
California	8.5	8.8	27.2	New Jersey	5	Massachusetts	5	Florida	5
Colorado	3.4	2.7	9.8	Rhode Island	6	Connecticut	6	Hawaii	6
Connecticut	10.9	8.6	13.2	California	7	Florida	7	Texas	7
Delaware	3.3	2.9	8.2	New Hampshire	8	Rhode Island	8	Massachusetts	8
D.C.	5.1	4.4	13.0	Michigan	9	Illinois	9	Arizona	9
Florida	5.5	8.0	19.2	Illinois	9	New Hampshire	10	Illinois	10
Georgia	0.6	0.7	9.6	Washington	11	Michigan	11	Maryland	11
Hawaii	10.9	9.8	17.7	Maine	12	Washington	12	Connecticut	11
Idaho	2.3	1.8	5.9	Vermont	13	D.C.	13	D.C.	13
Illinois	6.8	5.7	13.6	Florida	14	Maine	14	Washington	14
Indiana	2.0	1.6	4.4	Arizona	15	Arizona	14	Rhode Island	15
Iowa	2.0	1.4	4.1	Pennsylvania	16	Vermont	16	Virginia	16
Kansas	1.5	1.2	6.3	D.C.	17	Pennsylvania	17	Colorado	17
Kentucky	0.6	0.5	3.1	North Dakota	18	Nevada	18	New Mexico	18
Louisiana	0.9	1.1	3.6	Nevada	19	Oregon	19	Oregon	18
Maine	6.2	4.3	3.3	Montana	20	Maryland	19	Georgia	20
Maryland	3.0	3.2	13.2	Wisconsin	21	Ohio	21	Utah	21
Massachusetts	11.2	8.7	14.5	Minnesota	22	North Dakota	21	Delaware	21
Michigan	6.8	4.8	5.9	Ohio	23	Wisconsin	21	North Carolina	23
Minnesota	4.2	2.6	7.0	Oregon	24	Delaware	24	Alaska	24
Mississippi	0.4	0.4	2.2	Utah	25	Montana	25	Minnesota	25
Missouri	1.8	1.4	3.7	Alaska	25	Texas	25	Kansas	26
Montana	4.5	2.8	2.0	Colorado	27	Utah	25	Michigan	27
Nebraska	2.9	1.9	5.9	Delaware	28	Colorado	28	Idaho	27
Nevada	4.6	3.7	19.3	Texas	29	Minnesota	29	Nebraska	27
New Hampshire	7.4	5.0	5.3	Maryland	30	Alaska	29	Pennsylvania	30
New Jersey	10.1	8.9	20.3	Nebraska	31	New Mexico	31	New Hampshire	31
New Mexico	2.3	2.2	9.7	Wyoming	31	Wyoming	32	Oklahoma	32
New York	13.6	11.6	21.7	South Dakota	33	Nebraska	33	South Carolina	33
North Carolina	0.5	0.6	7.4	New Mexico	34	Idaho	34	Wisconsin	34
North Dakota	4.7	3.0	2.4	Idaho	34	Indiana	35	Tennessee	35
Ohio	4.1	3.0	3.8	Iowa	36	South Dakota	35	Indiana	35
Oklahoma	0.9	0.8	5.2	Indiana	36	Virginia	35	Arkansas	37
Oregon	4.0	3.2	9.7	Missouri	38	Iowa	38	Iowa	38
Pennsylvania	5.3	3.8	5.6	Kansas	39	Missouri	38	Vermont	39
Rhode Island	10.0	7.8	12.6	West Virginia	40	Kansas	40	Ohio	40
South Carolina	0.5	0.6	4.7	Virginia	41	Louisiana	41	Missouri	41
South Dakota	2.7	1.6	2.3	Louisiana	42	West Virginia	42	Louisiana	42
Tennessee	0.4	0.5	4.4	Oklahoma	42	Oklahoma	43	Alabama	43
Texas	3.1	2.8	16.1	Georgia	44	Georgia	44	Maine	44
Utah	3.6	2.8	8.2	Kentucky	44	North Carolina	45	Wyoming	45
Vermont	6.0	4.2	4.0	South Carolina	46	South Carolina	45	Kentucky	45
Virginia	1.2	1.6	10.8	North Carolina	46	Alabama	47	North Dakota	47
Washington	6.3	4.6	12.7	Alabama	46	Kentucky	47	South Dakota	48
West Virginia	1.3	1.0	1.3	Mississippi	49	Tennessee	47	Mississippi	49
Wisconsin	4.3	3.0	4.6	Arkansas	49	Mississippi	50	Montana	50
Wyoming	2.9	2.1	3.1	Tennessee	49	Arkansas	50	West Virginia	51
United States	5.4	4.7	12.7	United States	–	United States	–	United States	–

Source: U.S. Census Bureau, 1960 Census of Population; U.S. Census Bureau, 1970 Census of Population; U.S. Census Bureau, American Community Survey, 2006-2010 Five-Year Estimate

Urban Population

Area	Percent of Population			1960		1970		2010	
	1960	1970	2010	Area	Rank	Area	Rank	Area	Rank
Alabama	54.8	58.6	55.0	D.C.	1	D.C.	1	D.C.	1
Alaska	37.9	56.9	60.5	New Jersey	2	California	2	New Jersey	2
Arizona	74.5	79.6	86.7	Rhode Island	3	New Jersey	3	California	3
Arkansas	42.8	50.0	52.0	California	3	Rhode Island	4	Massachusetts	4
California	86.4	90.9	93.2	New York	5	New York	5	Rhode Island	5
Colorado	73.7	78.5	82.0	Massachusetts	6	Massachusetts	6	Nevada	6
Connecticut	78.3	78.4	87.9	Illinois	7	Illinois	7	Hawaii	7
Delaware	65.6	72.2	80.1	Connecticut	8	Hawaii	8	Florida	8
D.C.	100.0	100.0	100.0	Hawaii	9	Florida	9	Connecticut	9
Florida	73.9	81.7	89.3	Texas	10	Nevada	10	Illinois	10
Georgia	55.3	60.3	70.7	Utah	11	Utah	11	Arizona	11
Hawaii	76.5	83.1	90.0	Arizona	12	Texas	12	Maryland	12
Idaho	47.5	54.1	63.8	Florida	13	Arizona	13	New York	13
Illinois	80.7	83.2	87.3	Colorado	14	Colorado	14	Utah	14
Indiana	62.4	64.9	72.1	Michigan	15	Connecticut	15	Colorado	15
Iowa	53.0	57.2	61.4	Ohio	15	Maryland	16	Washington	16
Kansas	61.0	66.1	71.1	Maryland	17	Ohio	17	Texas	17
Kentucky	44.5	52.3	55.9	Pennsylvania	18	Michigan	18	Delaware	18
Louisiana	63.3	66.5	72.1	Nevada	19	Washington	19	Ohio	19
Maine	51.3	50.8	36.6	Washington	20	Delaware	20	Oregon	20
Maryland	72.7	76.6	86.4	Missouri	21	Pennsylvania	21	Pennsylvania	21
Massachusetts	83.6	84.6	91.1	New Mexico	22	Missouri	22	New Mexico	22
Michigan	73.4	74.0	72.2	Delaware	23	New Mexico	23	Michigan	23
Minnesota	62.2	66.5	68.3	Wisconsin	24	Oklahoma	24	Indiana	24
Mississippi	37.7	44.5	48.7	Louisiana	25	Oregon	25	Louisiana	24
Missouri	66.6	70.1	68.3	Oklahoma	26	Minnesota	26	Virginia	26
Montana	50.2	53.4	52.0	Indiana	27	Louisiana	26	Kansas	27
Nebraska	54.3	61.5	68.4	Minnesota	28	Kansas	28	Georgia	28
Nevada	70.4	80.9	90.6	Oregon	28	Wisconsin	29	Nebraska	29
New Hampshire	58.3	56.4	55.6	Kansas	30	Indiana	30	Minnesota	30
New Jersey	88.6	88.9	94.7	New Hampshire	31	Virginia	31	Missouri	30
New Mexico	65.9	69.8	73.7	Wyoming	32	Nebraska	32	Wisconsin	32
New York	85.4	85.7	85.6	Virginia	33	Wyoming	33	Oklahoma	33
North Carolina	39.5	45.5	59.1	Georgia	34	Georgia	34	Idaho	34
North Dakota	35.2	44.3	54.0	Alabama	35	Tennessee	35	Tennessee	35
Ohio	73.4	75.3	78.9	Nebraska	36	Alabama	36	Wyoming	36
Oklahoma	62.9	68.0	65.1	Iowa	37	Iowa	37	Iowa	37
Oregon	62.2	67.1	77.9	Tennessee	38	Alaska	38	South Carolina	38
Pennsylvania	71.6	71.5	76.4	Maine	39	New Hampshire	39	Alaska	39
Rhode Island	86.4	87.1	90.9	Montana	40	Idaho	40	North Carolina	40
South Carolina	41.2	48.3	61.2	Idaho	41	Montana	41	Kentucky	41
South Dakota	39.3	44.6	51.6	Kentucky	42	Kentucky	42	New Hampshire	42
Tennessee	52.3	59.1	63.6	Arkansas	43	Maine	43	Alabama	43
Texas	75.0	79.7	80.7	South Carolina	44	Arkansas	44	North Dakota	44
Utah	74.9	80.4	85.4	North Carolina	45	South Carolina	45	Arkansas	45
Vermont	38.5	32.2	33.6	South Dakota	46	North Carolina	46	Montana	45
Virginia	55.6	63.2	71.4	Vermont	47	South Dakota	47	South Dakota	47
Washington	68.1	73.4	81.3	West Virginia	48	Mississippi	48	Mississippi	48
West Virginia	38.2	39.1	46.4	Alaska	49	North Dakota	49	West Virginia	49
Wisconsin	63.8	65.9	65.8	Mississippi	50	West Virginia	50	Maine	50
Wyoming	56.8	60.5	62.4	North Dakota	51	Vermont	51	Vermont	51
United States	69.9	73.6	77.6	United States	–	United States	–	United States	–

Source: U.S. Census Bureau, 1960 Census of Housing; U.S. Census Bureau, 1970 Census of Housing; U.S. Census Bureau, Census 2010

Rural Population

Area	Percent of Population 1960	1970	2010	1960 Area	Rank	1970 Area	Rank	2010 Area	Rank
Alabama	45.2	41.4	45.0	North Dakota	1	Vermont	1	Vermont	1
Alaska	62.1	43.1	39.5	Mississippi	2	West Virginia	2	Maine	2
Arizona	25.5	20.4	13.3	Alaska	3	North Dakota	3	West Virginia	3
Arkansas	57.2	50.0	48.0	West Virginia	4	Mississippi	4	Mississippi	4
California	13.6	9.1	6.8	Vermont	5	South Dakota	5	South Dakota	5
Colorado	26.3	21.5	18.0	South Dakota	6	North Carolina	6	Arkansas	6
Connecticut	21.7	21.6	12.1	North Carolina	7	South Carolina	7	Montana	6
Delaware	34.4	27.8	19.9	South Carolina	8	Arkansas	8	North Dakota	8
D.C.	n/a	n/a	n/a	Arkansas	9	Maine	9	Alabama	9
Florida	26.1	18.3	10.7	Kentucky	10	Kentucky	10	New Hampshire	10
Georgia	44.7	39.7	29.3	Idaho	11	Montana	11	Kentucky	11
Hawaii	23.5	16.9	10.0	Montana	12	Idaho	12	North Carolina	12
Idaho	52.5	45.9	36.2	Maine	13	New Hampshire	13	Alaska	13
Illinois	19.3	16.8	12.7	Tennessee	14	Alaska	14	South Carolina	14
Indiana	37.6	35.1	27.9	Iowa	15	Iowa	15	Iowa	15
Iowa	47.0	42.8	38.6	Nebraska	16	Alabama	16	Wyoming	16
Kansas	39.0	33.9	28.9	Alabama	17	Tennessee	17	Tennessee	17
Kentucky	55.5	47.7	44.1	Georgia	18	Georgia	18	Idaho	18
Louisiana	36.7	33.5	27.9	Virginia	19	Wyoming	19	Oklahoma	19
Maine	48.7	49.2	63.4	Wyoming	20	Nebraska	20	Wisconsin	20
Maryland	27.3	23.4	13.6	New Hampshire	21	Virginia	21	Minnesota	21
Massachusetts	16.4	15.4	8.9	Kansas	22	Indiana	22	Missouri	21
Michigan	26.6	26.0	27.8	Minnesota	23	Wisconsin	23	Nebraska	23
Minnesota	37.8	33.5	31.7	Oregon	23	Kansas	24	Georgia	24
Mississippi	62.3	55.5	51.3	Indiana	25	Minnesota	25	Kansas	25
Missouri	33.4	29.9	31.7	Oklahoma	26	Louisiana	25	Virginia	26
Montana	49.8	46.6	48.0	Louisiana	27	Oregon	27	Indiana	27
Nebraska	45.7	38.5	31.6	Wisconsin	28	Oklahoma	28	Louisiana	27
Nevada	29.6	19.1	9.4	Delaware	29	New Mexico	29	Michigan	29
New Hampshire	41.7	43.6	44.4	New Mexico	30	Missouri	30	New Mexico	30
New Jersey	11.4	11.1	5.3	Missouri	31	Pennsylvania	31	Pennsylvania	31
New Mexico	34.1	30.2	26.3	Washington	32	Delaware	32	Oregon	32
New York	14.6	14.3	14.4	Nevada	33	Washington	33	Ohio	33
North Carolina	60.5	54.5	40.9	Pennsylvania	34	Michigan	34	Delaware	34
North Dakota	64.8	55.7	46.0	Maryland	35	Ohio	35	Texas	35
Ohio	26.6	24.7	21.1	Michigan	36	Maryland	36	Washington	36
Oklahoma	37.1	32.0	34.9	Ohio	36	Connecticut	37	Colorado	37
Oregon	37.8	32.9	22.1	Colorado	38	Colorado	38	Utah	38
Pennsylvania	28.4	28.5	23.6	Florida	39	Arizona	39	New York	39
Rhode Island	13.6	12.9	9.1	Arizona	40	Texas	40	Maryland	40
South Carolina	58.8	51.7	38.8	Utah	41	Utah	41	Arizona	41
South Dakota	60.7	55.4	48.4	Texas	42	Nevada	42	Illinois	42
Tennessee	47.7	40.9	36.4	Hawaii	43	Florida	43	Connecticut	43
Texas	25.0	20.3	19.3	Connecticut	44	Hawaii	44	Florida	44
Utah	25.1	19.6	14.6	Illinois	45	Illinois	45	Hawaii	45
Vermont	61.5	67.8	66.4	Massachusetts	46	Massachusetts	46	Nevada	46
Virginia	44.4	36.8	28.6	New York	47	New York	47	Rhode Island	47
Washington	31.9	26.6	18.7	Rhode Island	48	Rhode Island	48	Massachusetts	48
West Virginia	61.8	60.9	53.6	California	48	New Jersey	49	California	49
Wisconsin	36.2	34.1	34.2	New Jersey	50	California	50	New Jersey	50
Wyoming	43.2	39.5	37.6	D.C.	n/a	D.C.	n/a	D.C.	n/a
United States	30.1	26.4	22.4	United States	–	United States	–	United States	–

Source: U.S. Census Bureau, 1960 Census of Housing; U.S. Census Bureau, 1970 Census of Housing; U.S. Census Bureau, Census 2010

Males per 100 Females

Area	Males per 100 Females			1960		1970		2010	
	1960	1970	2010	Area	Rank	Area	Rank	Area	Rank
Alabama	95.0	93.3	94.3	Alaska	1	Alaska	1	Alaska	1
Alaska	132.3	119.1	108.5	Hawaii	2	Hawaii	2	Wyoming	2
Arizona	101.2	96.8	98.7	Nevada	3	Nevada	3	North Dakota	3
Arkansas	96.9	94.1	96.5	Wyoming	4	North Dakota	4	Nevada	4
California	99.4	96.8	98.8	North Dakota	5	Wyoming	5	Utah	5
Colorado	98.5	97.5	100.5	Montana	6	Montana	6	Montana	6
Connecticut	96.4	94.2	94.8	Idaho	7	Idaho	7	Colorado	7
Delaware	98.2	95.2	93.9	South Dakota	8	Washington	8	Idaho	8
D.C.	88.3	86.8	89.5	New Mexico	9	South Dakota	9	Hawaii	9
Florida	96.9	93.2	95.6	Washington	10	Virginia	10	South Dakota	10
Georgia	95.5	94.6	95.4	Arizona	10	Utah	11	Washington	11
Hawaii	114.8	108.1	100.3	Utah	12	Colorado	12	California	12
Idaho	102.9	99.7	100.4	Virginia	13	New Mexico	13	Arizona	13
Illinois	96.6	94.2	96.2	California	14	California	14	Minnesota	14
Indiana	97.2	95.1	96.8	Oregon	15	Arizona	14	Nebraska	14
Iowa	97.2	94.6	98.1	Wisconsin	16	South Carolina	16	Wisconsin	14
Kansas	98.6	96.2	98.4	Kansas	17	Wisconsin	17	Texas	17
Kentucky	98.6	96.3	96.8	Kentucky	17	Kentucky	17	Kansas	17
Louisiana	95.6	94.7	95.9	Michigan	19	Rhode Island	19	Iowa	19
Maine	97.7	94.8	95.8	Colorado	19	Kansas	19	Oregon	20
Maryland	97.8	95.5	93.6	Minnesota	21	Michigan	21	Oklahoma	20
Massachusetts	93.4	91.6	93.7	Nebraska	21	Minnesota	22	New Mexico	22
Michigan	98.5	96.1	96.3	Delaware	23	Oregon	23	New Hampshire	23
Minnesota	98.4	96.0	98.5	Texas	24	Texas	23	West Virginia	23
Mississippi	96.2	94.0	94.4	Maryland	25	North Carolina	23	Vermont	25
Missouri	95.3	93.2	96.0	Maine	26	New Hampshire	26	Indiana	26
Montana	103.8	99.9	100.8	South Carolina	27	Vermont	27	Kentucky	26
Nebraska	98.4	95.4	98.5	North Carolina	28	Maryland	28	Arkansas	28
Nevada	107.1	102.8	102.0	Iowa	29	Nebraska	29	Virginia	29
New Hampshire	96.5	95.7	97.3	Indiana	29	Delaware	30	Michigan	29
New Jersey	96.0	93.7	94.8	Oklahoma	29	Indiana	31	Illinois	31
New Mexico	101.8	97.2	97.7	Florida	32	Oklahoma	32	Missouri	32
New York	93.8	91.5	93.8	Arkansas	32	Maine	33	Louisiana	33
North Carolina	97.3	95.9	95.0	Vermont	34	Louisiana	34	Maine	34
North Dakota	104.5	101.8	102.1	West Virginia	34	Iowa	35	Florida	35
Ohio	96.4	94.1	95.4	Illinois	36	Georgia	35	Georgia	36
Oklahoma	97.2	94.9	98.0	New Hampshire	37	Connecticut	37	Ohio	36
Oregon	99.0	95.9	98.0	Connecticut	38	Illinois	37	Pennsylvania	38
Pennsylvania	94.8	92.4	95.1	Rhode Island	38	Ohio	39	Tennessee	38
Rhode Island	96.4	96.2	93.4	Ohio	38	Arkansas	39	North Carolina	40
South Carolina	97.4	96.5	94.7	Mississippi	41	Mississippi	41	New Jersey	41
South Dakota	102.4	98.4	100.1	New Jersey	42	West Virginia	42	Connecticut	41
Tennessee	95.3	93.7	95.1	Louisiana	43	New Jersey	43	South Carolina	43
Texas	98.1	95.9	98.4	Georgia	44	Tennessee	43	Mississippi	44
Utah	99.8	97.6	100.9	Missouri	45	Alabama	45	Alabama	45
Vermont	96.8	95.6	97.1	Tennessee	45	Florida	46	Delaware	46
Virginia	99.6	97.7	96.3	Alabama	47	Missouri	46	New York	47
Washington	101.2	98.7	99.3	Pennsylvania	48	Pennsylvania	48	Massachusetts	48
West Virginia	96.8	93.9	97.3	New York	49	Massachusetts	49	Maryland	49
Wisconsin	98.9	96.3	98.5	Massachusetts	50	New York	50	Rhode Island	50
Wyoming	104.9	100.7	104.1	D.C.	51	D.C.	51	D.C.	51
United States	97.1	94.8	96.7	United States	–	United States	–	United States	–

Source: U.S. Census Bureau, 1960 Census of Population; U.S. Census Bureau, 1970 Census of Population; U.S. Census Bureau, Census 2010

High School Graduates

Area	Percent of Population			1960		1970		2010	
	1960	1970	2010	Area	Rank	Area	Rank	Area	Rank
Alabama	30.3	41.3	82.1	Utah	1	Utah	1	Wyoming	1
Alaska	54.7	66.7	91.0	Alaska	2	Alaska	2	Minnesota	2
Arizona	45.7	58.1	85.6	Nevada	3	Nevada	3	Montana	3
Arkansas	28.9	39.9	82.9	Colorado	4	Colorado	4	New Hampshire	4
California	51.5	62.6	80.7	Wyoming	4	Washington	5	Alaska	5
Colorado	52.0	63.9	89.7	California	6	Wyoming	6	Vermont	5
Connecticut	43.8	56.0	88.6	Washington	6	California	7	Utah	7
Delaware	43.3	54.6	87.7	Idaho	8	Hawaii	8	Iowa	7
D.C.	47.8	55.2	87.4	Oregon	9	Oregon	9	Nebraska	9
Florida	42.6	52.6	85.5	Kansas	10	Kansas	10	Maine	10
Georgia	32.0	40.6	84.3	D.C.	11	Idaho	11	North Dakota	10
Hawaii	46.1	61.9	89.9	Montana	11	Nebraska	12	Wisconsin	12
Idaho	48.6	59.5	88.3	Nebraska	13	Montana	13	Hawaii	13
Illinois	40.4	52.6	86.9	Massachusetts	14	Iowa	14	Washington	14
Indiana	41.8	52.9	87.0	Iowa	15	Massachusetts	15	Colorado	15
Iowa	46.3	59.0	90.6	Hawaii	16	Arizona	16	South Dakota	16
Kansas	48.2	59.9	89.2	Arizona	17	New Hampshire	17	Kansas	17
Kentucky	27.6	38.5	81.9	New Mexico	18	Minnesota	17	Massachusetts	18
Louisiana	32.3	42.2	81.9	Minnesota	19	Vermont	19	Oregon	19
Maine	43.2	54.7	90.3	Connecticut	20	Connecticut	20	Michigan	20
Maryland	40.0	52.3	88.1	Delaware	21	D.C.	21	Connecticut	21
Massachusetts	47.0	58.5	89.1	Maine	22	New Mexico	21	Pennsylvania	22
Michigan	40.9	52.8	88.7	New Hampshire	23	Maine	23	Idaho	23
Minnesota	43.9	57.6	91.8	Vermont	23	Delaware	24	Maryland	24
Mississippi	29.8	41.0	81.0	Florida	25	Wisconsin	25	Ohio	24
Missouri	36.6	48.8	86.9	South Dakota	26	South Dakota	26	New Jersey	26
Montana	47.8	59.2	91.7	Ohio	27	Ohio	27	Delaware	27
Nebraska	47.7	59.3	90.4	Indiana	28	Indiana	28	D.C.	28
Nevada	53.3	65.2	84.7	Wisconsin	29	Michigan	29	Indiana	29
New Hampshire	42.9	57.6	91.5	New York	30	New York	30	Illinois	30
New Jersey	40.7	52.5	88.0	Michigan	30	Florida	31	Missouri	30
New Mexico	45.5	55.2	83.3	New Jersey	32	Illinois	31	Virginia	32
New York	40.9	52.7	84.9	Oklahoma	33	New Jersey	33	Oklahoma	33
North Carolina	32.3	38.5	84.7	Illinois	34	Maryland	34	Arizona	34
North Dakota	38.9	50.3	90.3	Maryland	35	Oklahoma	35	Florida	35
Ohio	41.9	53.2	88.1	Texas	36	North Dakota	36	New York	36
Oklahoma	40.5	51.6	86.2	North Dakota	37	Pennsylvania	37	Nevada	37
Oregon	48.4	60.0	88.8	Pennsylvania	38	Missouri	38	North Carolina	37
Pennsylvania	38.1	50.2	88.4	Virginia	39	Virginia	39	Georgia	39
Rhode Island	35.0	46.4	83.5	Missouri	40	Texas	40	South Carolina	40
South Carolina	30.4	37.8	84.1	Rhode Island	41	Rhode Island	41	Tennessee	41
South Dakota	42.2	53.3	89.6	Louisiana	42	Louisiana	42	Rhode Island	42
Tennessee	30.4	41.8	83.6	North Carolina	42	Tennessee	43	New Mexico	43
Texas	39.5	47.4	80.7	Georgia	44	West Virginia	44	West Virginia	44
Utah	55.8	67.3	90.6	West Virginia	45	Alabama	45	Arkansas	45
Vermont	42.9	57.1	91.0	South Carolina	46	Mississippi	46	Alabama	46
Virginia	37.9	47.8	86.5	Tennessee	46	Georgia	47	Louisiana	47
Washington	51.5	63.5	89.8	Alabama	48	Arkansas	48	Kentucky	47
West Virginia	30.6	41.6	83.2	Mississippi	49	North Carolina	49	Mississippi	49
Wisconsin	41.5	54.5	90.1	Arkansas	50	Kentucky	49	California	50
Wyoming	52.0	62.9	92.3	Kentucky	51	South Carolina	51	Texas	50
United States	41.1	52.3	85.6	United States	–	United States	–	United States	–

Note: Figures cover the population 25 years old and over.
Source: U.S. Census Bureau, 1960 Census of Population; U.S. Census Bureau, 1970 Census of Population; U.S. Census Bureau, American Community Survey, 2010 One-Year Estimate

College Graduates

Area	Percent of Population			1960		1970		2010	
	1960	1970	2010	Area	Rank	Area	Rank	Area	Rank
Alabama	5.7	7.8	21.9	D.C.	1	D.C.	1	D.C.	1
Alaska	9.5	14.1	27.9	Colorado	2	Colorado	2	Massachusetts	2
Arizona	9.1	12.6	25.9	Utah	3	Alaska	3	Colorado	3
Arkansas	4.8	6.7	19.5	Delaware	4	Hawaii	4	Maryland	4
California	9.8	13.4	30.1	California	5	Utah	4	Connecticut	5
Colorado	10.7	14.9	36.4	New Mexico	5	Maryland	6	New Jersey	6
Connecticut	9.5	13.7	35.5	Connecticut	7	Connecticut	7	Virginia	7
Delaware	10.1	13.1	27.8	Alaska	7	California	8	Vermont	8
D.C.	14.3	17.8	50.1	Washington	9	Delaware	9	New Hampshire	9
Florida	7.8	10.3	25.8	Maryland	9	Washington	10	New York	10
Georgia	6.2	9.2	27.3	Arizona	11	New Mexico	10	Minnesota	11
Hawaii	9.0	14.0	29.5	Hawaii	12	Massachusetts	12	Washington	12
Idaho	7.2	10.0	24.4	New York	13	Arizona	12	Illinois	13
Illinois	7.3	10.3	30.8	Massachusetts	14	Virginia	14	Rhode Island	14
Indiana	6.3	8.3	22.7	Wyoming	15	New York	15	California	15
Iowa	6.4	9.1	24.9	Oregon	16	New Jersey	16	Kansas	16
Kansas	8.2	11.4	29.8	New Jersey	17	Oregon	16	Hawaii	17
Kentucky	4.9	7.2	20.5	Virginia	17	Wyoming	16	Utah	18
Louisiana	6.7	9.0	21.4	Nevada	19	Vermont	19	Oregon	19
Maine	5.5	8.4	26.8	Kansas	20	Kansas	20	Montana	19
Maryland	9.3	13.9	36.1	Texas	21	Minnesota	21	Nebraska	21
Massachusetts	8.8	12.6	39.0	Oklahoma	22	Montana	22	Alaska	22
Michigan	6.8	9.4	25.2	Florida	23	New Hampshire	23	Delaware	23
Minnesota	7.5	11.1	31.8	Montana	24	Texas	23	North Dakota	24
Mississippi	5.6	8.1	19.5	Minnesota	24	Nevada	25	Georgia	25
Missouri	6.2	9.0	25.6	Illinois	26	Florida	26	Pennsylvania	26
Montana	7.5	11.0	28.8	Vermont	26	Illinois	26	Maine	27
Nebraska	6.8	9.6	28.6	Idaho	28	Idaho	28	North Carolina	28
Nevada	8.3	10.8	21.7	New Hampshire	29	Oklahoma	28	Wisconsin	29
New Hampshire	7.1	10.9	32.8	Ohio	30	Wisconsin	30	South Dakota	29
New Jersey	8.4	11.8	35.4	South Carolina	31	Nebraska	31	Texas	31
New Mexico	9.8	12.7	25.0	Michigan	32	Rhode Island	32	Arizona	31
New York	8.9	11.9	32.5	Nebraska	32	Michigan	32	Florida	33
North Carolina	6.3	8.5	26.5	Wisconsin	34	Ohio	34	Missouri	34
North Dakota	5.6	8.4	27.6	Louisiana	34	Georgia	35	Michigan	35
Ohio	7.0	9.3	24.6	Rhode Island	36	Iowa	36	New Mexico	36
Oklahoma	7.9	10.0	22.9	Pennsylvania	37	Missouri	37	Iowa	37
Oregon	8.5	11.8	28.8	Iowa	37	Louisiana	37	Ohio	38
Pennsylvania	6.4	8.7	27.1	Indiana	39	South Carolina	37	South Carolina	39
Rhode Island	6.6	9.4	30.2	North Carolina	39	Pennsylvania	40	Idaho	40
South Carolina	6.9	9.0	24.5	Missouri	41	South Dakota	41	Wyoming	41
South Dakota	5.7	8.6	26.3	Georgia	41	North Carolina	42	Tennessee	42
Tennessee	5.5	7.9	23.1	South Dakota	43	Maine	43	Oklahoma	43
Texas	8.0	10.9	25.9	Alabama	43	North Dakota	43	Indiana	44
Utah	10.2	14.0	29.3	North Dakota	45	Indiana	45	Alabama	45
Vermont	7.3	11.5	33.6	Mississippi	45	Mississippi	46	Nevada	46
Virginia	8.4	12.3	34.2	Maine	47	Tennessee	47	Louisiana	47
Washington	9.3	12.7	31.1	Tennessee	47	Alabama	48	Kentucky	48
West Virginia	5.2	6.8	17.5	West Virginia	49	Kentucky	49	Arkansas	49
Wisconsin	6.7	9.8	26.3	Kentucky	50	West Virginia	50	Mississippi	49
Wyoming	8.7	11.8	24.1	Arkansas	51	Arkansas	51	West Virginia	51
United States	7.7	10.7	28.2	United States	–	United States	–	United States	–

Note: Figures cover the population 25 years old and over.
Source: U.S. Census Bureau, 1960 Census of Population; U.S. Census Bureau, 1970 Census of Population; U.S. Census Bureau, American Community Survey, 2010 One-Year Estimate

One-Person Households

Area	Percent of Population			1960		1970		2010	
	1960	1970	2010	Area	Rank	Area	Rank	Area	Rank
Alabama	9.5	14.6	27.4	D.C.	1	D.C.	1	D.C.	1
Alaska	16.2	13.7	25.6	Nevada	2	California	2	North Dakota	2
Arizona	13.6	16.5	26.1	California	3	New York	3	Montana	3
Arkansas	12.6	17.2	27.1	Washington	4	Montana	4	Rhode Island	4
California	17.9	21.0	23.3	Montana	5	Washington	5	South Dakota	5
Colorado	15.5	18.0	27.9	Oregon	6	Nevada	6	New York	6
Connecticut	11.6	16.0	27.3	Alaska	6	Nebraska	7	Ohio	7
Delaware	10.9	15.3	25.6	New York	8	Missouri	7	Massachusetts	8
D.C.	27.0	32.1	44.0	Colorado	8	Oregon	9	Nebraska	8
Florida	14.5	18.7	27.2	Oklahoma	8	Oklahoma	10	Pennsylvania	10
Georgia	10.1	14.4	25.4	Missouri	11	Massachusetts	11	Maine	10
Hawaii	12.1	12.8	23.3	Florida	12	Florida	12	Iowa	12
Idaho	13.3	16.5	23.8	Illinois	13	Illinois	13	West Virginia	12
Illinois	14.4	18.5	27.8	Wyoming	14	Iowa	13	Missouri	14
Indiana	12.3	16.5	26.9	Massachusetts	15	Kansas	15	Wisconsin	15
Iowa	13.8	18.5	28.4	Nebraska	15	Rhode Island	16	Vermont	15
Kansas	14.0	18.4	27.8	Kansas	17	South Dakota	17	New Mexico	17
Kentucky	10.6	15.2	27.5	Iowa	18	Colorado	18	Minnesota	17
Louisiana	12.3	16.0	26.9	Rhode Island	19	Wyoming	18	Wyoming	17
Maine	12.6	16.8	28.6	Minnesota	19	Minnesota	20	Colorado	20
Maryland	10.1	14.9	26.1	Arizona	21	Pennsylvania	21	Michigan	20
Massachusetts	14.2	18.8	28.7	Idaho	22	Arkansas	22	Illinois	22
Michigan	11.6	15.5	27.9	New Hampshire	23	New Hampshire	23	Kansas	22
Minnesota	13.7	17.7	28.0	South Dakota	24	North Dakota	23	Oklahoma	24
Mississippi	10.7	15.4	26.3	Maine	25	Wisconsin	25	Kentucky	24
Missouri	15.2	19.3	28.3	Texas	25	Maine	26	Oregon	26
Montana	16.8	19.8	29.7	Arkansas	25	Vermont	26	Alabama	26
Nebraska	14.2	19.3	28.7	Vermont	28	Ohio	28	Connecticut	28
Nevada	18.9	19.4	25.7	Indiana	29	Arizona	29	Florida	29
New Hampshire	13.1	17.0	25.6	Louisiana	29	Idaho	29	Washington	29
New Jersey	11.3	15.8	25.2	Wisconsin	31	Indiana	29	Arkansas	31
New Mexico	10.7	14.9	28.0	Hawaii	32	Texas	32	North Carolina	32
New York	15.5	20.2	29.1	Ohio	32	Connecticut	33	Tennessee	33
North Carolina	8.3	13.3	27.0	Utah	34	Louisiana	33	Indiana	33
North Dakota	11.9	17.0	31.5	Pennsylvania	35	West Virginia	33	Louisiana	33
Ohio	12.1	16.6	28.9	North Dakota	35	New Jersey	36	South Carolina	36
Oklahoma	15.5	19.1	27.5	Connecticut	37	Michigan	37	Mississippi	37
Oregon	16.2	19.2	27.4	Michigan	37	Mississippi	38	Arizona	38
Pennsylvania	11.9	17.3	28.6	New Jersey	39	Delaware	39	Maryland	38
Rhode Island	13.7	18.2	29.6	Delaware	40	Kentucky	40	Virginia	40
South Carolina	9.4	13.8	26.5	New Mexico	41	Maryland	41	Nevada	41
South Dakota	12.8	18.1	29.4	Mississippi	41	New Mexico	41	Delaware	42
Tennessee	9.7	14.4	26.9	Kentucky	43	Alabama	43	Alaska	42
Texas	12.6	16.3	24.2	Maryland	44	Utah	44	New Hampshire	42
Utah	12.0	14.4	18.7	West Virginia	44	Virginia	44	Georgia	45
Vermont	12.5	16.8	28.2	Georgia	44	Georgia	44	New Jersey	46
Virginia	9.4	14.4	26.0	Tennessee	47	Tennessee	44	Texas	47
Washington	17.6	19.6	27.2	Alabama	48	South Carolina	48	Idaho	48
West Virginia	10.1	16.0	28.4	Virginia	49	Alaska	49	California	49
Wisconsin	12.2	16.9	28.2	South Carolina	49	North Carolina	50	Hawaii	49
Wyoming	14.3	18.0	28.0	North Carolina	51	Hawaii	51	Utah	51
United States	13.3	17.6	26.7	United States	–	United States	–	United States	–

Source: U.S. Census Bureau, 1960 Census of Housing; U.S. Census Bureau, 1970 Census of Housing; U.S. Census Bureau, Census 2010

Homeownership

Area	Percent of Population			1960		1970		2010	
	1960	1970	2010	Area	Rank	Area	Rank	Area	Rank
Alabama	59.7	66.7	69.7	Michigan	1	Michigan	1	West Virginia	1
Alaska	48.3	50.3	63.1	Minnesota	2	Indiana	2	Minnesota	2
Arizona	63.9	65.3	66.0	Utah	3	Iowa	2	Michigan	3
Arkansas	61.4	66.7	66.9	Indiana	4	Minnesota	4	Iowa	3
California	58.4	54.9	56.0	Idaho	5	Maine	5	Delaware	5
Colorado	63.8	63.4	65.5	Oregon	6	Idaho	5	Maine	6
Connecticut	61.9	62.5	67.5	Iowa	7	South Dakota	7	New Hampshire	7
Delaware	66.9	68.0	72.0	Kansas	8	Utah	8	Vermont	8
D.C.	30.0	28.2	42.0	Wisconsin	9	Oklahoma	9	Utah	9
Florida	67.5	68.6	67.3	Washington	10	Vermont	10	Idaho	10
Georgia	56.2	61.1	65.7	North Dakota	11	Wisconsin	10	Indiana	11
Hawaii	41.1	46.9	57.7	Pennsylvania	12	Kansas	10	Alabama	12
Idaho	70.5	70.1	69.9	Florida	13	West Virginia	13	Pennsylvania	13
Illinois	57.8	59.4	67.4	Ohio	14	Pennsylvania	14	Mississippi	13
Indiana	71.1	71.7	69.8	South Dakota	15	Florida	15	South Carolina	15
Iowa	69.1	71.7	72.1	Oklahoma	16	North Dakota	16	Wyoming	15
Kansas	68.9	69.1	67.7	Delaware	17	New Hampshire	17	Missouri	17
Kentucky	64.3	66.9	68.7	Maine	18	Delaware	18	Kentucky	18
Louisiana	59.0	63.1	67.3	Vermont	19	Ohio	19	New Mexico	19
Maine	66.5	70.1	71.3	New Mexico	20	Missouri	20	Tennessee	20
Maryland	64.5	58.8	67.5	New Hampshire	21	Kentucky	21	Wisconsin	21
Massachusetts	55.9	57.5	62.3	Texas	22	Washington	22	South Dakota	21
Michigan	74.4	74.4	72.1	Nebraska	22	Alabama	23	Montana	23
Minnesota	72.1	71.5	73.1	Maryland	24	Tennessee	23	Kansas	24
Mississippi	57.7	66.3	69.6	Missouri	25	Arkansas	23	Ohio	25
Missouri	64.3	67.2	68.8	West Virginia	25	New Mexico	26	Maryland	26
Montana	64.0	65.7	68.0	Kentucky	25	Wyoming	26	Connecticut	26
Nebraska	64.8	66.4	67.2	Montana	28	Nebraska	26	Illinois	28
Nevada	56.3	58.5	58.8	Arizona	29	Mississippi	29	Florida	29
New Hampshire	65.1	68.2	70.9	Colorado	30	Oregon	30	Oklahoma	29
New Jersey	61.3	60.9	65.4	Tennessee	31	South Carolina	30	Louisiana	29
New Mexico	65.3	66.4	68.5	Wyoming	32	Montana	32	Virginia	32
New York	44.8	47.3	53.3	Connecticut	33	North Carolina	33	Nebraska	32
North Carolina	60.1	65.4	66.7	Arkansas	34	Arizona	34	Arkansas	34
North Dakota	68.4	68.4	65.4	New Jersey	35	Texas	35	North Carolina	35
Ohio	67.4	67.7	67.6	Virginia	35	Colorado	36	Arizona	36
Oklahoma	67.0	69.2	67.3	North Carolina	37	Louisiana	37	Georgia	37
Oregon	69.3	66.1	62.1	Alabama	38	Connecticut	38	Colorado	38
Pennsylvania	68.3	68.8	69.6	Louisiana	39	Virginia	39	New Jersey	39
Rhode Island	54.5	57.9	60.7	California	40	Georgia	40	North Dakota	39
South Carolina	57.3	66.1	69.3	Illinois	41	New Jersey	41	Washington	41
South Dakota	67.2	69.6	68.1	Mississippi	42	Illinois	42	Texas	42
Tennessee	63.7	66.7	68.2	South Carolina	43	Maryland	43	Alaska	43
Texas	64.8	64.7	63.7	Nevada	44	Nevada	44	Massachusetts	44
Utah	71.7	69.3	70.5	Georgia	45	Rhode Island	45	Oregon	45
Vermont	66.0	69.1	70.7	Massachusetts	46	Massachusetts	46	Rhode Island	46
Virginia	61.3	62.0	67.2	Rhode Island	47	California	47	Nevada	47
Washington	68.5	66.8	63.9	Alaska	48	Alaska	48	Hawaii	48
West Virginia	64.3	68.9	73.4	New York	49	New York	49	California	49
Wisconsin	68.6	69.1	68.1	Hawaii	50	Hawaii	50	New York	50
Wyoming	62.2	66.4	69.3	D.C.	51	D.C.	51	D.C.	51
United States	61.9	62.9	65.1	United States	–	United States	–	United States	–

Source: U.S. Census Bureau, 1960 Census of Housing; U.S. Census Bureau, 1970 Census of Housing; U.S. Census Bureau, Census 2010

Median Home Value

Area	Median Home Value ($)			1960		1970		2010	
	1960	1970	2010	Area	Rank	Area	Rank	Area	Rank
Alabama	8,600	12,200	123,900	Hawaii	1	Hawaii	1	Hawaii	1
Alaska	9,100	22,700	241,400	Connecticut	2	Connecticut	2	D.C.	2
Arizona	11,100	16,300	168,800	New Jersey	3	New Jersey	3	California	3
Arkansas	6,700	10,500	106,300	D.C.	4	California	4	New Jersey	4
California	15,100	23,100	370,900	New York	5	Alaska	5	Massachusetts	5
Colorado	12,300	17,300	236,600	Nevada	6	New York	6	Maryland	6
Connecticut	16,700	25,500	288,800	California	7	Nevada	7	New York	7
Delaware	12,400	17,100	243,600	Illinois	8	D.C.	8	Connecticut	8
D.C.	15,400	21,300	426,900	Massachusetts	9	Massachusetts	9	Washington	9
Florida	11,800	15,000	164,200	Ohio	10	Illinois	10	Rhode Island	10
Georgia	9,500	14,600	156,200	Minnesota	11	Maryland	11	Virginia	11
Hawaii	20,900	35,100	525,400	Wisconsin	12	Washington	12	Oregon	12
Idaho	10,600	14,100	165,100	Utah	12	Rhode Island	13	Delaware	13
Illinois	14,700	19,800	191,800	Delaware	14	Minnesota	14	New Hampshire	14
Indiana	10,200	13,800	123,300	Rhode Island	15	Ohio	15	Alaska	15
Iowa	9,900	13,900	123,400	Colorado	15	Michigan	16	Colorado	16
Kansas	9,300	12,100	127,300	Wyoming	15	Wisconsin	17	Utah	17
Kentucky	8,800	12,600	121,600	Michigan	18	Colorado	17	Vermont	18
Louisiana	10,700	14,600	137,500	Maryland	19	Delaware	19	Minnesota	19
Maine	8,800	12,800	179,100	Florida	20	Virginia	19	Illinois	20
Maryland	11,900	18,700	301,400	Washington	21	Utah	21	Montana	21
Massachusetts	13,800	20,600	334,100	Arizona	22	New Hampshire	22	Wyoming	22
Michigan	12,000	17,500	123,300	Montana	23	Vermont	22	Maine	23
Minnesota	12,800	18,000	194,300	Missouri	23	Arizona	24	Nevada	24
Mississippi	7,900	11,200	100,100	Virginia	25	Oregon	25	Wisconsin	25
Missouri	10,900	14,400	139,000	New Hampshire	26	Wyoming	26	Arizona	26
Montana	10,900	14,000	181,200	New Mexico	26	Florida	27	Pennsylvania	27
Nebraska	9,400	12,400	127,600	Louisiana	26	Louisiana	28	Idaho	28
Nevada	15,200	22,400	174,800	Idaho	29	Georgia	28	Florida	29
New Hampshire	10,700	16,400	243,000	Oregon	30	Missouri	30	New Mexico	30
New Jersey	15,600	23,400	339,200	Pennsylvania	31	Idaho	31	Georgia	31
New Mexico	10,700	13,000	161,200	Indiana	31	Montana	32	North Carolina	32
New York	15,300	22,500	296,500	Iowa	33	Iowa	33	Tennessee	33
North Carolina	8,000	12,800	154,200	North Dakota	34	Indiana	34	Missouri	33
North Dakota	9,800	13,000	123,000	Vermont	35	Pennsylvania	35	South Carolina	35
Ohio	13,400	17,600	134,400	Georgia	36	North Dakota	36	Louisiana	36
Oklahoma	7,900	11,100	111,400	Nebraska	37	New Mexico	36	Ohio	37
Oregon	10,500	15,400	244,500	Kansas	38	South Carolina	36	South Dakota	38
Pennsylvania	10,200	13,600	165,500	Alaska	39	Maine	39	Texas	39
Rhode Island	12,300	18,200	254,500	Maine	40	North Carolina	39	Nebraska	40
South Carolina	7,500	13,000	138,100	Texas	40	Kentucky	41	Kansas	41
South Dakota	8,800	11,400	129,700	South Dakota	40	Tennessee	42	Alabama	42
Tennessee	8,300	12,500	139,000	Kentucky	40	Nebraska	43	Iowa	43
Texas	8,800	12,000	128,100	Alabama	44	Alabama	44	Michigan	44
Utah	12,600	16,800	217,200	Tennessee	45	Kansas	45	Indiana	44
Vermont	9,700	16,400	216,800	North Carolina	46	Texas	46	North Dakota	46
Virginia	10,800	17,100	249,100	Oklahoma	47	South Dakota	47	Kentucky	47
Washington	11,700	18,500	271,800	Mississippi	47	West Virginia	48	Oklahoma	48
West Virginia	7,600	11,300	95,100	West Virginia	49	Mississippi	49	Arkansas	49
Wisconsin	12,600	17,300	169,400	South Carolina	50	Oklahoma	50	Mississippi	50
Wyoming	12,300	15,300	180,100	Arkansas	51	Arkansas	51	West Virginia	51
United States	11,900	17,000	179,900	United States	–	United States	–	United States	–

Source: U.S. Census Bureau, 1960 Census of Housing; U.S. Census Bureau, 1970 Census of Housing; U.S. Census Bureau, American Community Survey, 2010 One-Year Estimate

Median Gross Rent

Area	Median Gross Rent ($/month)			1960		1970		2010	
	1960	1970	2010	Area	Rank	Area	Rank	Area	Rank
Alabama	45	69	667	Alaska	1	Alaska	1	Hawaii	1
Alaska	126	189	981	Nevada	2	Nevada	2	D.C.	2
Arizona	69	109	844	Illinois	3	Hawaii	3	California	3
Arkansas	47	71	638	D.C.	4	Connecticut	4	Maryland	4
California	79	126	1,163	New Jersey	5	Maryland	4	New Jersey	5
Colorado	72	110	863	California	6	New Jersey	6	New York	6
Connecticut	77	127	992	Wisconsin	6	California	6	Virginia	7
Delaware	77	111	952	Maryland	8	Illinois	8	Massachusetts	8
D.C.	81	119	1,198	Connecticut	9	D.C.	9	Connecticut	9
Florida	71	112	947	Michigan	9	Massachusetts	10	Alaska	10
Georgia	51	86	819	Delaware	9	Minnesota	10	Nevada	11
Hawaii	72	132	1,291	Massachusetts	12	Michigan	12	Delaware	11
Idaho	65	92	683	Ohio	12	Virginia	12	New Hampshire	13
Illinois	85	124	848	New York	14	Washington	14	Florida	14
Indiana	70	105	683	Hawaii	15	Wisconsin	14	Washington	15
Iowa	68	99	629	Minnesota	15	Florida	16	Rhode Island	16
Kansas	66	94	682	Colorado	15	New York	17	Colorado	17
Kentucky	55	83	613	Washington	18	Delaware	17	Illinois	18
Louisiana	53	81	736	Florida	18	Colorado	19	Arizona	19
Maine	64	90	707	North Dakota	18	Arizona	20	Vermont	20
Maryland	78	127	1,131	New Mexico	18	Oregon	21	Georgia	21
Massachusetts	75	117	1,009	Virginia	18	Ohio	22	Oregon	22
Michigan	77	115	730	Oregon	23	Indiana	22	Texas	23
Minnesota	72	117	764	Indiana	23	New Hampshire	24	Utah	24
Mississippi	43	65	672	Arizona	25	Iowa	24	Minnesota	25
Missouri	65	96	682	Iowa	26	Vermont	26	Pennsylvania	26
Montana	66	89	642	Nebraska	27	North Dakota	27	Louisiana	27
Nebraska	67	95	669	Wyoming	27	Utah	27	North Carolina	28
Nevada	91	141	952	South Dakota	27	Missouri	29	Michigan	29
New Hampshire	65	99	951	Montana	30	Texas	30	South Carolina	30
New Jersey	80	126	1,114	Utah	30	Nebraska	30	Wisconsin	31
New Mexico	71	88	699	Kansas	30	Kansas	32	Maine	32
New York	74	111	1,020	New Hampshire	33	Rhode Island	33	New Mexico	33
North Carolina	55	86	731	Idaho	33	Pennsylvania	33	Tennessee	34
North Dakota	71	97	583	Missouri	33	Idaho	35	Wyoming	35
Ohio	75	105	685	Maine	36	Maine	36	Ohio	36
Oklahoma	57	82	659	Pennsylvania	36	Montana	37	Idaho	37
Oregon	70	107	816	Rhode Island	38	New Mexico	38	Indiana	37
Pennsylvania	64	93	763	Vermont	38	South Dakota	38	Kansas	39
Rhode Island	62	93	868	Texas	40	Wyoming	40	Missouri	39
South Carolina	49	77	728	Oklahoma	41	Georgia	41	Mississippi	41
South Dakota	67	88	591	Kentucky	42	North Carolina	41	Nebraska	42
Tennessee	52	82	697	North Carolina	42	Kentucky	43	Alabama	43
Texas	60	95	801	West Virginia	44	Oklahoma	44	Oklahoma	44
Utah	66	97	796	Louisiana	44	Tennessee	44	Montana	45
Vermont	62	98	823	Tennessee	46	Louisiana	46	Arkansas	46
Virginia	71	115	1,019	Georgia	47	South Carolina	47	Iowa	47
Washington	71	113	908	South Carolina	48	West Virginia	48	Kentucky	48
West Virginia	53	72	571	Arkansas	49	Arkansas	49	South Dakota	49
Wisconsin	79	113	715	Alabama	50	Alabama	50	North Dakota	50
Wyoming	67	87	693	Mississippi	51	Mississippi	51	West Virginia	51
United States	71	108	855	United States	–	United States	–	United States	–

Source: U.S. Census Bureau, 1960 Census of Housing; U.S. Census Bureau, 1970 Census of Housing; U.S. Census Bureau, American Community Survey, 2010 One-Year Estimate

Households Lacking Complete Plumbing

Area	Percent of Households			1960		1970		2010	
	1960	1970	2010	Area	Rank	Area	Rank	Area	Rank
Alabama	38.5	16.9	3.6	Mississippi	1	Mississippi	1	Alaska	1
Alaska	29.4	17.2	11.9	Arkansas	2	Kentucky	2	West Virginia	2
Arizona	13.4	5.2	2.3	Kentucky	3	South Carolina	3	Maine	3
Arkansas	43.2	18.4	4.3	South Carolina	4	Arkansas	4	New Mexico	4
California	5.1	2.1	1.1	Alabama	4	West Virginia	5	Arkansas	5
Colorado	14.1	5.0	1.3	North Carolina	6	Alaska	6	Mississippi	5
Connecticut	7.3	2.7	1.1	Tennessee	7	Alabama	7	Montana	7
Delaware	12.4	5.1	1.6	Georgia	8	North Carolina	8	Louisiana	8
D.C.	7.7	2.3	2.2	North Dakota	9	Maine	9	Alabama	9
Florida	15.0	5.1	1.4	West Virginia	10	Tennessee	10	Kentucky	10
Georgia	33.7	13.2	2.2	Maine	11	North Dakota	11	Oklahoma	11
Hawaii	16.8	5.6	1.5	South Dakota	12	South Dakota	12	Michigan	12
Idaho	14.7	5.3	1.6	Louisiana	13	Virginia	13	Indiana	12
Illinois	13.4	4.8	2.1	Alaska	14	Georgia	14	Missouri	12
Indiana	17.3	6.5	3.1	Virginia	15	Louisiana	15	South Dakota	12
Iowa	19.8	7.5	1.7	Missouri	16	New Mexico	16	Pennsylvania	16
Kansas	15.9	5.6	2.3	Minnesota	17	Missouri	17	Texas	17
Kentucky	39.7	20.8	3.5	Oklahoma	18	Montana	18	South Carolina	17
Louisiana	29.5	11.5	3.9	Montana	19	Vermont	19	Vermont	17
Maine	30.5	15.4	4.7	New Mexico	19	Minnesota	20	North Carolina	20
Maryland	10.5	4.4	1.5	Texas	21	Texas	21	Tennessee	21
Massachusetts	9.6	3.6	1.0	Iowa	22	Iowa	22	North Dakota	21
Michigan	11.7	4.4	3.1	Vermont	23	Wisconsin	23	Arizona	23
Minnesota	22.1	8.2	2.1	Nebraska	24	Oklahoma	24	Kansas	23
Mississippi	47.8	24.3	4.3	Indiana	25	New Hampshire	25	Ohio	23
Missouri	25.9	9.7	3.1	Wisconsin	26	Indiana	26	D.C.	26
Montana	20.4	9.0	4.1	Hawaii	27	Nebraska	27	Georgia	26
Nebraska	17.5	6.1	2.2	New Hampshire	28	Wyoming	28	Nebraska	26
Nevada	9.8	3.2	1.2	Kansas	29	Hawaii	29	Illinois	29
New Hampshire	16.7	7.0	1.6	Wyoming	30	Kansas	29	Minnesota	29
New Jersey	6.5	2.5	1.2	Florida	31	Idaho	31	Virginia	31
New Mexico	20.4	10.6	4.6	Idaho	32	Arizona	32	Rhode Island	32
New York	8.0	3.2	1.6	Colorado	33	Ohio	32	Wyoming	32
North Carolina	35.6	15.6	2.5	Rhode Island	34	Florida	34	Wisconsin	34
North Dakota	33.1	13.8	2.4	Illinois	35	Pennsylvania	34	Iowa	35
Ohio	12.8	5.2	2.3	Arizona	35	Delaware	34	New York	36
Oklahoma	20.8	7.1	3.2	Ohio	37	Colorado	37	Delaware	36
Oregon	9.9	3.6	1.3	Delaware	38	Illinois	38	Idaho	36
Pennsylvania	11.3	5.1	2.7	Michigan	39	Michigan	39	New Hampshire	36
Rhode Island	13.6	3.1	1.9	Pennsylvania	40	Maryland	39	Hawaii	40
South Carolina	38.5	18.6	2.6	Maryland	41	Massachusetts	41	Maryland	40
South Dakota	30.3	13.6	3.1	Oregon	42	Oregon	41	Washington	40
Tennessee	34.9	14.8	2.4	Washington	43	Washington	43	Florida	43
Texas	19.9	7.7	2.6	Nevada	43	New York	44	Colorado	44
Utah	6.1	2.7	1.2	Massachusetts	45	Nevada	44	Oregon	44
Vermont	18.7	8.4	2.6	New York	46	Rhode Island	46	New Jersey	46
Virginia	27.4	13.4	2.0	D.C.	47	Connecticut	47	Nevada	46
Washington	9.8	3.4	1.5	Connecticut	48	Utah	47	Utah	46
West Virginia	32.3	18.3	5.2	New Jersey	49	New Jersey	49	California	49
Wisconsin	17.2	7.2	1.8	Utah	50	D.C.	50	Connecticut	49
Wyoming	15.8	5.9	1.9	California	51	California	51	Massachusetts	51
United States	16.8	6.9	2.2	United States	–	United States	–	United States	–

Note: Complete plumbing facilities are defined as hot and cold piped water, a bath- tub or shower, and a flush toilet. In earlier censuses, these facilities must have been for exclusive use of a housing unit's inhabitants; this requirement was dropped in 1990.
Source: U.S. Census Bureau, 1960 Census of Housing; U.S. Census Bureau, 1970 Census of Housing; U.S. Census Bureau, American Community Survey, 2010 One-Year Estimate

Analytical Text

POPULATION GROWTH AND DISTRIBUTION
United States

During the 1960-70 decade the total population of the United States grew from 179,323,000 to 203,235,000.[1] The rate of increase for this period, 13.3 percent, was lower than at any other time in the Nation's history except for the 1930-40 decade.

As for several decades past, population growth between 1960 and 1970 was overwhelmingly metropolitan. While the population living in metropolitan areas grew by 20 million persons (an increase of 16.6 percent since 1960) the population living outside them grew by less than 4 million (an increase of 6.5 percent). Metropolitan growth thus accounted for nearly 85 percent of the entire increase in the United States population in the 1960's.

By far the largest part of metropolitan growth occurred outside the central cities—an area which includes the densely-settled territory close in to central cities which is generally acknowledged to be "suburban", as well as the more lightly-populated areas which make up the remainder of the metropolitan counties.[2]

---

[1]The population shown in the tables of this report adds to 203,166,000. Revisions in totals for certain States were made after the tabulations used for this report had been completed. See correction note, page 24.

[2]This entire territory—inside metropolitan areas, but outside central cities—is, for convenience's sake, referred to as "suburban."

During the 1960-70 decade the population living in metropolitan areas outside central cities increased by 16.8 million persons, or by 28 percent over the population in the same areas in 1960. By contrast, central cities, which had an increase in population of 3.2 million, show the lowest rate of growth for the decade—of only 5 percent (see table 1).

As extensive as these changes were, they nonetheless represent a slowing down of the metropolitan growth of the previous decade. Between 1950 and 1960, rates of increase for both central city and suburban populations were twice as high as in the recent period.

In 1960, the population of the United States was divided almost equally among central cities, suburbs, and nonmetropolitan areas, each of which contained approximately 60 million persons. By 1970, the population of nonmetropolitan areas had grown to 63 million and that of central cities to 64 million (each comprising 31 percent), but the population of the suburbs exceeded 76 million and made up 38 percent of the Nation's total.

The metropolitan area definition used to gauge 1960-70 population change is consistent. For SMSA's which expanded their boundaries during the decade, 1960 population has been reconstructed within 1970 limits. Population within metropolitan areas are not as easily compared. Between 1960 and 1970, a great many central cities annexed suburban populations. In some parts of the country, this was a major element in central city growth (table A). For all central cities having annexations except three (Indianapolis, Jacksonville, and

Table A.   Change in Population of Central Cities Through Annexation: 1960 to 1970

United States Regions	1970 population			1960 population	Change		Percent change	
	Total	In 1960 area	In annexed area		With annexation	Without annexation	With annexation	Without annexation
UNITED STATES	63,824,480	60,953,566	2,870,914	60,630,027	3,194,453	323,539	5.3	0.5
Northeast....	17,233,001	17,203,734	29,267	17,575,505	-342,504	-371,771	-1.9	-2.1
North Central	17,076,663	16,336,425	740,238	17,120,788	-44,125	-784,363	-0.3	-4.6
South........	17,954,993	16,654,236	1,300,757	16,139,342	1,815,651	514,894	11.2	3.2
West........	11,559,823	10,759,171	800,652	9,794,392	1,765,431	964,779	18.0	9.9

NOTE: In this report central city change for Indianapolis, Jacksonville, and Nashville is shown in terms of 1970 boundaries. Hence annexations by these three central cities are not included in table A.

Nashville; see "Definitions and Explanations"), detailed population change had to be based on 1960 population within 1960 boundaries and 1970 population within 1970 boundaries.

By including annexed territories in central city population change, the growth of these cities is overstated in general, and in particular in the Southern and Western States, where annexations have been most numerous and most extensive. At the same time, the considerable growth of metropolitan areas outside central cities is understated.

Regions

In all four regions of the United States—the Northeastern and North Central States, the South and the West—metropolitan population trends in the 1960-70 decade were much the same. Metropolitan population growth in each region was heavily concentrated in areas outside the central cities, while central city populations grew at much lower rates or were diminished (see table 1). In every region, consequently, the central city population declined as a proportion of total population, and the "suburban" population increased.

In the North, which historically has had the Nation's largest central city and "suburban" populations, total metropolitan growth over the past decade was below the national average. The metropolitan populations of the South and the West grew more than twice as fast as those of the Northeastern and North Central States, and their absolute increases were considerably higher. Between 1960 and 1970 there was an increase in population of 7.6 million (or 11 percent) in the metropolitan areas of the Northeastern and North Central States combined, compared to an increase of 6.3 million (or 22 percent) in the South and 6 million (28 percent) in the West alone.

In the Northeast and North Central Regions, metropolitan population growth was due wholly to increases in the "suburban" areas; their central cities show slight losses for the decade. By contrast, in the South and the West, central cities increased at rates well above the national average and accounted for 30 percent of total metropolitan growth in each region.

Within regions, the percentage of total population living in central cities is somewhat similar—roughly one-third of the population of each region. In spite of the rapid advances made by the South, the percentage of its population living in central cities in 1970 was lowest of any region (29 percent) and shows least change over the decade. In the Northeast, where central cities are declining, the proportion of total population living in them in 1970 was still highest (35 percent).

Considerable differences are apparent in the distribution of the remainder of the population of each region, however. The extremes are again represented by the South and the Northeast. Less than 28 percent of the population of the South was suburban in 1970, but over 46 percent of the total population of the Northeastern States lived in metropolitan areas outside central cities.

RACIAL CHANGE

United States

During the 1960-70 decade the white population of the United States increased by 18.8 million persons, the Negro population by 3.8 million, and other races by 1.3 million. About 80 percent of white growth was concentrated in metropolitan areas. Negroes, however, increased only in metropolitan areas. The black population of nonmetropolitan areas declined in the last decade by more than one quarter of a million persons.

Metropolitan growth in the United States overall was produced largely by a natural increase of 14.9 million, at a rate of 12.3 percent for the decade (see table 7). Net inmigration (which includes net immigration from abroad) added 5.3 million persons (3 percent of 1960 population).[3]

Inmigration was of less importance to the increase of the white population than of other races in metropolitan areas. Only one-fifth of the growth of whites, but 40 percent of the growth of other races was due to net inmigration. The natural increase rate, as well as the net inmigration rate for whites, was much below those for other races. Negro and other races had a metropolitan rate of natural increase of 22 percent, twice that of the white population, but their net inmigration rate was 5 times as great.

The moderate growth of the Nation's central cities was due almost entirely to black population increases; while blacks increased by 3.2 million and the population of other races by more than one half of a million, the white population of central cities declined over the decade by 600,000. The great population expansion in metropolitan areas outside central cities, on the other hand, was overwhelmingly the result of white growth; the large white population already established in the

---

[3] International immigration was of great importance to migration gains in the metropolitan areas, particularly in the Northeast Region. An overwhelming proportion of the 3.3 million immigrants admitted to the United States between 1960 and 1970 gave urban areas as their place of intended permanent residence; one-fourth had as their destination Northeastern cities of 100,000 or more population.

suburbs in 1960 increased over the decade by close to 30 percent, or 15 and a half million persons. The number of blacks in the suburbs grew at about the same rate as whites (by 29.2 percent compared to the white rate of 27.5 percent), but their numerical increase was much lower—only 800,000, or about 5 percent of the total population increase there.

As a result of these changes, blacks increased considerably as a proportion of the Nation's total central city population, from 16 percent in 1960 to 21 percent in 1970. But in the suburbs, their position did not change at all: in 1970 as in 1960, blacks comprised just under 5 percent of all suburban residents (table B).

Table B.   Percent White and Negro in the Total Population, by Metropolitan and Nonmetropolitan Residence: 1970 and 1960

United States Regions	1970		1960	
	White	Negro	White	Negro
Total..............................	87.4	11.2	88.6	10.5
Metropolitan residence[1]...................	86.5	12.0	88.5	10.7
Inside central cities....................	77.5	20.6	82.6	16.3
Outside central cities[1]..................	94.1	4.8	94.6	4.8
Nonmetropolitan residence...................	89.4	9.3	88.7	10.3
Northeast................................	90.4	8.9	92.9	6.8
Metropolitan residence[1]...................	88.7	10.5	91.8	7.9
Inside central cities....................	79.0	19.5	86.3	13.2
Outside central cities[1]..................	96.0	3.6	96.9	3.0
Nonmetropolitan residence...................	97.8	1.8	98.2	1.6
North Central............................	91.3	8.1	93.0	6.7
Metropolitan residence...................	88.0	11.4	90.2	9.6
Inside central cities....................	77.4	21.7	83.3	16.3
Outside central cities..................	96.8	2.8	97.4	2.5
Nonmetropolitan residence...................	97.8	1.5	98.2	1.4
South...................................	80.1	19.2	79.1	20.6
Metropolitan residence...................	80.2	19.1	80.2	19.6
Inside central cities....................	71.7	27.6	74.6	25.1
Outside central cities..................	89.0	10.3	87.2	12.6
Nonmetropolitan residence...................	80.1	19.3	77.9	21.7
West....................................	90.2	4.9	92.1	3.9
Metropolitan residence...................	89.5	5.9	91.7	4.8
Inside central cities....................	84.3	9.7	87.6	7.6
Outside central cities..................	93.3	3.2	95.2	2.4
Nonmetropolitan residence...................	92.7	1.0	93.3	1.0

[1]Includes Middlesex and Somerset Counties in New Jersey.

The effect of these growth patterns on the distribution of the two racial groups by area of residence has also been substantial. In 1960, one-third of the total white population of the United States lived in central cities; by 1970, this proportion had dropped to 28 percent. In contrast, the proportion of the black population living in central cities rose from 53 percent in 1960 to 58 percent by 1970. During the same period the percentage of total white population in the suburbs grew appreciably (from 35 to 40 percent), but the proportion of all blacks living in suburbs shows virtually no change, increasing from 15 to only 16 percent.

Regions

As a result of differential growth patterns of the white and Negro populations by region, Negroes now comprise slightly higher proportions of the populations of the northern and western regions and a lower percentage of the population of the South (table B).

In the Northeastern and North Central States where Negroes grew at very rapid rates (43 percent and 33 percent, respectively), significant proportions of overall population increases during the 1960-70 decade were black: 30 percent of the growth of population in the Northeastern States (1.3 million out of 4.3 million) and 23 percent of the growth in the North Central States (1.1 million out of 5 million) were produced by the Negro population. By contrast, in the South, which contains more than one-half of the Nation's total black population, the Negro growth rate was low (7 percent). The black population of this region accounted for less than 10 percent of the total population increase there (753,000 out of 7.8 million), and dropped as a percentage of the total (from 21 to 19 percent). In the West, which contains the smallest number of blacks of any region, the growth rate of this population was highest in the Nation (56 percent). Their contribution to total growth, however, was small (609,000 out of 6.8 million).

Numerically and in terms of rates, the white population shows strongest growth in the South (6.9 million, or an increase of 16 percent) and in the West (5.5 million, or 22 percent). White rates of growth in the Northeast (7 percent) and North Central States (8 percent) were well below those of the rest of the country. In combination the two northern regions gained a white population of only 6.4 million. Thus, nearly 37 percent of the total white population increase in the Nation was produced by the South, about 30 percent by the West and one-third by the Northeast and North Central Regions combined.

With the exception of the South, the black population of every region is more metropolitan than the white population (see table 1). More than 94 percent of all blacks in the North and the West are concentrated in metropolitan areas, contrasted with two-thirds to four-fifths of the white population of these regions. In the South, the proportions are equal: 56 percent of each racial group is metropolitan. Within metropolitan areas of every region, including the South, whites are found in largest numbers in the suburbs, while blacks are concentrated in central cities.

In all sections of the country blacks now comprise higher percentages of central city populations than they did a decade ago. Change was greatest in the central cities of the Northeastern and North Central States: the percentage of total population represented by Negroes in central cities of the North rose from 14 percent in 1960 to 21 percent in 1970. In central cities of the West, where Negroes are increasing fastest, their representation in the total population is still small and shows least change over the decade, growing from 8 percent in 1960 to 10 percent in 1970.

By contrast, in spite of very rapid rates of growth, black population increases in suburban areas in every section of the country were dwarfed by white gains. In the suburbs of the North and the West, Negro proportions rose very slightly (by less than 1 percentage point), but in southern suburbs there was a decline in the proportion represented by Negroes, from nearly 13 percent in 1960 to 10 percent in 1970.

POPULATION CHANGE WITHIN REGIONS

Northeastern States: New England and Middle Atlantic Divisions

The Middle Atlantic States of the Northeast Region (New York, New Jersey, and Pennsylvania) contain the largest concentration of metropolitan population in the United States (see table 2). In 1970, 31,385,000 persons lived in the metropolitan areas of these States, or 84 percent of their combined populations. The metropolitan population of New England is only about one-fourth that of the Middle Atlantic States (8,540,000 in 1970), and comprises a somewhat lower percentage of total population (72 percent).

Rates of metropolitan growth for both New England (11.1 percent) and the Middle Atlantic States (8.5 percent) were lowest among the nine divisions, while nonmetropolitan rates of growth were among the highest in the Nation (16.9 percent in New England and 10.2 percent in the Middle Atlantic States).

In New England, States with highest proportions of population in metropolitan areas show least growth in these areas: Massachusetts and Rhode Island each had an increase in metropolitan population of about 8 percent, while growth in nonmetropolitan areas was more than twice as great. Connecticut's metropolitan growth rate of 17.4 percent was also much below the nonmetropolitan increase of 31.2 percent.

Of the three Middle Atlantic States, New Jersey shows the most rapid growth for the 1960-70 decade, in both metropolitan and nonmetropolitan areas. The metropolitan population of New Jersey increased by 15 percent, but the nonmetropolitan population's rate of increase, 47 percent, greatly exceeded that of any other State in the Nation. At the other extreme is Pennsylvania, with very low rates of growth in both metropolitan (5 percent) and nonmetropolitan areas (1.4 percent).

Metropolitan growth in the Northeast Region was chiefly suburban. In the entire Northeast only two States gained central city populations: Connecticut, where central cities increased by 5.2 percent, and New Hampshire, where central city populations increased by 12.7 percent. Elsewhere in the Northeast, rates of central city loss varied from a low of 0.8 percent in New York to 5.9 percent in Pennsylvania. Suburban gains, on the other hand, had a wide range, from 12.7 percent (Pennsylvania) to 70.9 percent (New Hampshire). As a result of central city-suburban changes, all States in the Northeast Region recorded higher proportions of metropolitan population living in suburban areas in 1970 than in 1960. In 1970 more than one-half of the total population of New Jersey, Massachusetts, and Pennsylvania was found in suburban areas. Only one State—New York—had a majority of its population living in central cities.

At the time of the 1970 Census, 90.4 percent of the population of the Northeast Region was white, down from 92.9 percent in 1960 (table B). Rates of growth for the black population were higher in all areas: they were twice as high in nonmetropolitan areas, but nine times the white rate in metropolitan areas. While whites in the central cities of the Northeast declined 10 percent, Negroes there increased by 45 percent. In central cities, the white share of the total population consequently dropped, from 86 percent in 1960 to 70 percent by 1970.

In the Northeast Region the black population is more highly concentrated in metropolitan areas than elsewhere in the Nation (see table 1). At the time of both censuses, about 96 percent of this population lived in metropolitan areas, contrasted with 80 percent of the total white population. To a much greater extent than the white population also, Negroes in the Northeast are city dwellers: 78 percent of Negroes, but less than one-third of whites live in these central cities.

The growth of population in the Northeast Region was a function primarily of natural increase, in metropolitan and nonmetropolitan areas alike (see table 6). Net inmigration (including net immigration from abroad) added only 100,000 persons to metropolitan areas,[3] out of a total increase of 3.5 million. The role of net inmigration was considerably more important in nonmetropolitan areas, where it accounted for one-fourth of the total increase in population.

Patterns of population change by race differ greatly. The entire white population increase in metropolitan areas of the Northeast was due to natural increase. There was a net outmigration of 728,000 white persons from these areas over the decade (see table 7). On the other hand, net inmigration was more important to the growth of other races. Between 1960 and 1970 this population group had an excess of births over deaths of 689,000 (23 percent of 1960 population) while net inmigration added an additional 835,000 persons (28 percent of 1960 population). In contrast, in nonmetropolitan areas a considerable portion of white population growth, but only a minor part of the growth of other races, was produced by net inmigration.

The Negro population of the Northeast is considerably more youthful than the white population (see tables 8 and C). In 1970, one out of every three Negroes living in both metropolitan and nonmetropolitan areas of the Northeast Region was under 15 years of age, and 6 percent were 65 years old and over. By contrast, the age structure of the white population is older in every area, particularly in the central cities, where in 1970 only 22 percent of the white population was under 15 years of age but 14 percent was 65 and over.

Table C. Percent Negro of Metropolitan and Nonmetropolitan Populations, by
          Age: 1970

United States Regions	Total	Metropolitan			Non-metropolitan
		Total	Inside central cities	Outside central cities	
UNITED STATES					
All ages...................	11.2	12.0	20.6	4.8	9.1
Under 15 years..................	13.8	14.8	27.0	5.7	11.6
15 to 44 years..................	11.2	12.2	21.0	4.9	8.8
45 to 64 years..................	8.9	9.6	16.2	3.7	7.4
65 years and over..............	7.8	8.0	11.9	3.7	7.3
NORTHEAST					
All ages...................	8.9	10.6	19.5	3.5	2.0
Under 15 years..................	11.1	13.4	27.0	4.1	2.3
15 to 44 years..................	9.7	11.5	21.3	3.8	2.3
45 to 64 years..................	6.6	7.9	14.0	2.8	1.4
65 years and over..............	4.8	5.7	8.8	2.5	1.1
NORTH CENTRAL					
All ages...................	8.1	11.4	21.7	2.8	1.5
Under 15 years..................	9.8	13.8	28.4	3.2	1.7
15 to 44 years..................	8.4	11.5	22.2	2.9	1.6
45 to 64 years..................	6.5	9.2	17.1	2.2	1.5
65 years and over..............	5.0	7.7	12.0	2.3	1.1
SOUTH					
All ages...................	19.2	19.1	27.6	10.3	19.1
Under 15 years..................	23.7	23.1	34.2	12.5	24.5
15 to 44 years..................	18.2	18.4	27.0	9.8	17.9
45 to 64 years..................	16.0	16.3	23.3	8.5	15.6
65 years and over..............	15.7	15.4	20.3	9.0	15.9
WEST					
All ages...................	4.9	5.9	9.7	3.2	1.0
Under 15 years..................	6.0	7.3	12.9	3.8	1.2
15 to 44 years..................	5.1	6.0	9.7	3.4	1.2
45 to 64 years..................	3.8	4.9	7.8	2.2	0.7
65 years and over..............	2.6	3.3	5.0	1.5	0.6

North Central States: East North Central and West North Central Divisions

The North Central Region comprises the five States of the East North Central Division and seven States in the West North Central Division. The East North Central Division contains the second largest concentration of metropolitan population in the Nation. In 1970, 29,738,000 persons, or 74 percent of the total population of this division, lived in metropolitan areas, and 10,514,000 in nonmetropolitan areas. The metropolitan population of the West North Central Division is only about one-fourth that of the East North Central States (7,920,000) and comprises a much lower percentage of total population (48 percent). In 1970, the nonmetropolitan population of this division was 8,399,000.

Unlike the Northeast Region, the growth of all States in the North Central Region was predominantly metropolitan. Highest rates of metropolitan growth were registered in the 1960-70 decade by Minnesota (19 percent), Nebraska (17), Wisconsin (15), and Michigan (14). In all States in this region except for North and South Dakota, metropolitan growth was predominantly or exclusively suburban. The central cities of only one State—Nebraska—show a significant increase (of 15 percent). In States with largest central cities—Illinois, Ohio, and Michigan—there were losses of central city population, in spite of very substantial annexations during the decade.

There were appreciable gains in the nonmetropolitan population only of Michigan (11 percent), Indiana (9), and Wisconsin (8).

In both 1960 and 1970 over 90 percent of the region's population was white. While two out of three whites lived in metropolitan areas in 1970, 94 percent of blacks were located there. Over the decade Negroes increased their representation in central cities of the region from 16 to 22 percent of the population, but in suburban and nonmetropolitan areas their proportions scarcely changed (table B).

Between 1960 and 1970 there was a net outmigration of 843,000 persons from the nonmetropolitan areas of the North Central States, and a much smaller net inmigration of 86,000 persons into metropolitan areas. The nonmetropolitan loss was produced mainly by the West North Central Division (672,000), but virtually every State in the Region suffered net outmigration from nonmetropolitan areas.

Rates of white population growth in the North Central States in the 1960-70 decade were below those for Negro and other races. In both metropolitan and nonmetropolitan areas white rates of natural increase were much lower than those for other races (see table 7); but in addition, the white population of both areas was

depleted by net outmigration (of 450,000 persons from metropolitan areas and 821,000 from nonmetropolitan areas). The metropolitan population of other races, by contrast, grew considerably through a net inmigration of 536,000 persons (equivalent to 16 percent of their 1960 metropolitan population) which accounted for more than 40 percent of the growth of this population.

Both white and Negro populations of the North Central States are somewhat more youthful than those in the Northeast, but present the same differences with respect to one another (see table 8). In the central cities of this region, 36 percent of the Negro population is under 15 years of age, and 6 percent is 65 and over; in the same areas, 25 percent of whites are under 15 and 12 percent are 65 and over.

The South: The South Atlantic, East South Central, and West South Central Divisions

Numerically, the South's contribution to metropolitan growth exceeded that of any other region (see table 1). Between 1960 and 1970 the metropolitan population of the South grew by 6.3 million or 22 percent, a higher rate of increase than for the United States as a whole (16.6 percent). Nine States in the South had rates of metropolitan increase higher than the U.S. average. Nearly all these fast-growing metropolitan areas are in the South Atlantic Division: Florida, which increased by 37 percent, Maryland (30 percent), Virginia (28), Georgia and Delaware (26), North Carolina (24), and South Carolina (19). Texas and Oklahoma in the West South Central Division also had high rates of metropolitan growth (24 percent and 20 percent, respectively).

In contrast to the pattern in the Northeast and North Central States, increases in central city populations were an important component of metropolitan growth in the South: 29 percent of the increase in metropolitan areas (1.8 million population) occurred in these cities. Most of this gain was due to annexation of suburban territory, however. Between 1960 and 1970 the central cities of the entire South Region annexed a population of 1.3 million (table A).

Within 1970 boundaries, the central cities of the South contain a population of nearly 18 million, the largest of any of the four regions. Most of the South's central city population is found in the six States of Texas (5.4 million), Florida (2 million), Tennessee (1.4 million), Louisiana (1.1 million), Virginia (1.1 million), and Georgia (1 million). Together these States contain two-thirds of all central city residents in the South. Texas alone holds 30 percent of the total.

The fastest-growing central city populations are found in Florida (22 percent), Tennessee (20), and

Oklahoma (19), where annexations were of major importance. Among Southern States, Florida also has the fastest growing suburban population which increased by just over 50 percent in the 1960-70 decade.

Central cities of the Upper South were the only ones in the region to lose population. Delaware had the highest rate of loss from its only central city, Wilmington (16 percent), while its suburbs grew rapidly, by 44 percent. Maryland (Baltimore), the District of Columbia, and the central cities of West Virginia likewise lost population. Virginia's central cities grew moderately, however, by 8 percent. The suburban populations of Maryland and Virginia also had very high rates of growth (49 percent and 46 percent, respectively). In Maryland this was due in large measure to the location within the State of part of the suburbs of the Wilmington, Del-N.J.-Md. SMSA and the Washington, D.C.-Md.-Va. SMSA. Virginia's suburban growth similarly was affected by its inclusion in the Washington SMSA.

In addition to having the largest central city population of any region, the South also has the Nation's largest nonmetropolitan population. In 1970, 27.6 million persons lived in nonmetropolitan areas, 44 percent of the region's total population. The rate of growth for this sector was one of the lowest in the Nation, however (6 percent). In relation to metropolitan growth within the South, nonmetropolitan growth was also low. Central cities grew twice as fast over the decade and suburban areas six times as fast.

In 1970 as in 1960, about 80 percent of the South's population was white. As elsewhere in the Nation, a higher proportion of suburban (89 percent in 1970) than of central city population (72 percent) was white (table B).

The rapid growth of the South's metropolitan areas was due in large part to a high rate of natural increase (15 percent) as well as to a substantial net inmigration of more than 2 million persons (at a rate of 7 percent). The natural increase of the nonmetropolitan population on the other hand was cut in half by a net outmigration of nearly one and one-half million.

The white rate of inmigration into southern metropolitan areas was considerably higher than (almost 4 times) that of other races (see table 7). While white net inmigration amounted to 1,960,000 (8 percent), that of Negro and other races added only 124,000 (2 percent). In nonmetropolitan areas, on the other hand, there was a minor net outmigration of whites amounting to 154,000 (or 1 percent), but a very considerable net outmigration of 1.3 million persons of other races, equivalent to 23 percent of their 1960 nonmetropolitan population. The nonmetropolitan South was the only major area of the Nation to show a black population loss between 1960 and 1970.

Every State in the South grew considerably more through natural increase than through net inmigration, with the exception of Florida and Maryland. In Florida approximately three-fourths of the growth of both metropolitan (920,000 of 1.3 million) and nonmetropolitan areas (407,000 of 576,000) was produced by net inmigration (see table 6). In Maryland about one-half of the growth of metropolitan areas was due to net inmigration (377,000 of 757,000).

There was substantial net inmigration into the metropolitan areas of other States as well: Texas (403,000), Virginia (262,000), Georgia (160,000), and North Carolina (134,000). On the other hand, there were large migratory losses from the metropolitan areas of Alabama (107,000), West Virginia (79,000), and from the District of Columbia (100,000).

The white population of southern central cities tends to be more youthful than in other regions (see table 8). More than 25 percent of this population was under 15 in 1970 (the highest percentage among the four regions) and only 10 percent was 65 years old and over (the lowest among the regions). Conversely, the white population of nonmetropolitan areas of the South tends to be older than in other regions.

As elsewhere in the Nation, the black population of the South is considerably younger than the white population: 34 to 37 percent of Negroes in the South are under age 15, but only 7 to 9 percent are 65 and over. Children and the elderly comprise a particularly high proportion (more than 46 percent) of the black population of southern nonmetropolitan areas. Outmigration of blacks from the rural South in the recent, as in previous decades, has tended to remove young adults from this population.

The West: The Mountain and Pacific Divisions

The fastest-growing metropolitan areas and central cities in the Nation are located in the West Region. Between 1960 and 1970 the metropolitan population of the Pacific Division increased by 4.8 million or 27 percent, while the metropolitan population of the Mountain Division grew by 1.2 million, or 34 percent. As a result of this increase, the proportion of the Mountain Division population living in metropolitan areas rose from 51 percent in 1960 to 57 percent in 1970, but this percentage is still among the lowest in the Nation. In contrast, the population of the Pacific Division is more highly concentrated in metropolitan areas than elsewhere in the Nation, having surpassed the Middle Atlantic Division during the decade.

Nonmetropolitan growth rates were moderate by comparison with those of metropolitan areas (6 percent in the Mountain States and 14 percent in the Pacific), but nationally the nonmetropolitan growth rate of the West Region ranks second.

With the exception of Montana, every State in the West[4] had metropolitan increases of 20 percent or more. States with the fastest-growing metropolitan areas in the Nation are the Mountain States of Nevada (where the metropolitan population increased by 86 percent) and Arizona (which had a metropolitan increase of 42 percent). The State of Colorado, with a metropolitan growth rate of 33 percent, is in fourth place nationally. (See table 2 and table D.)

Central city growth, which was an important feature of metropolitan increases, was due in good part to annexations of suburban populations during the decade. In the West as a whole, central cities gained a population of 1.8 million, more than 800,000 of which was through annexation (see table A). Numerically, the largest transfers of population were made in California (423,000 in annexed areas), Colorado (101,000) and Arizona (87,000).

The population of the West is predominantly white: 90 percent of the metropolitan population and 93 percent of the nonmetropolitan population were white in 1970.

Negroes in the West comprise a smaller proportion of races other than white than elsewhere in the Nation (see table 1). The balance of this population group is mainly American Indian. As in the Northeastern and North

[4]Excluding Alaska and Wyoming which have no SMSA's.

Central States, Negroes in the West are overwhelmingly concentrated in metropolitan areas. In 1970, over 95 percent of the black population in the West lived in metropolitan areas. A much smaller proportion of American Indians and other races is found in metropolitan areas (73 percent).

Net inmigration over the 1960-70 decade was of much greater significance to population growth in the West than elsewhere in the Nation. In metropolitan areas the population increase of 6 million was due almost equally to net inmigration and to natural increase, but the nonmetropolitan areas experienced a small net outmigration. The white net inmigration of 2.4 million into metropolitan areas (see table 7) was equivalent to 12 percent of the total white population living in those areas in 1960, while net inmigration of other races amounted to nearly 650,000 and was equivalent to 36 percent of their 1960 population.

The greatest attractor of migrants in the Nation is California which between 1960 and 1970 acquired a population of over 2 million as a result of net inmigration. Nearly all this gain was experienced in metropolitan areas, where net inmigration was equivalent to 14 percent of 1960 population. Other States in the West with large metropolitan net inmigration are Washington (with 240,000 or 13 percent of 1960 population), and Arizona (with 235,000 or 25 percent of 1960 population). In terms of rates, Nevada's gain through net inmigration was greatest: 132,000 net inmigrants to the metropolitan areas of the State were equivalent to 62 percent of the 1960 population in those areas.

Table D.   Percent Change in Population of 25 Fastest-Growing SMSA's: 1960 to 1970

Standard Metropolitan Statistical Areas	Percent change	Standard Metropolitan Statistical Areas	Percent change
1. Las Vegas, Nev.	115.2	13. Danbury, Conn.[1]	44.3
2. Anaheim-Santa Ana-Garden Grove, Calif.	101.8	14. Reno, Nev.	42.9
		15. Fayetteville, N.C.	42.9
3. Oxnard-Ventura, Calif.	89.0	16. Gainesville, Fla.[1]	41.4
4. Fort Lauderdale-Hollywood, Fla.	85.7	17. San Bernardino-Riverside-Ontario, Calif.	41.2
5. San Jose, Calif.	65.8	18. Houston, Tex.	40.0
6. Colorado Springs, Colo.	64.2	19. Austin, Tex.	39.3
7. Santa Barbara, Calif.	56.4	20. Dallas, Tex.	39.0
8. West Palm Beach, Fla.	52.9	21. Santa Rosa, Calif.[1]	39.0
9. Huntsville, Ala.	48.3	22. Tallahassee, Fla.	38.8
10. Nashua, N.H.[1]	47.8	23. Washington, D.C.	37.8
11. Columbia, Mo.[1]	46.6	24. Atlanta, Ga.	36.7
12. Phoenix, Ariz.	46.0	25. Ann Arbor, Mich.	35.8

[1]SMSA's created as a result of the 1970 Census.

Natural increase was also an important factor in the growth of the Western States. In virtually every State and in both metropolitan and nonmetropolitan areas, the natural increase rates were higher than the national averages for the corresponding areas. Western rates of natural increase for races other than white are highest among the four regions (26 percent).

The age structure of metropolitan and nonmetropolitan areas of the West Region is more youthful than in other regions. Although the State of Arizona over the decade had a large inmigration of retired persons, the West Region as a whole has the lowest percentage of elderly population in the Nation. Only 9 percent of the white population and 5 percent of other races were 65 years old and over in 1970 (see table 8).

In all areas the black population is substantially younger than the white population. Inside central cities the differences between the two races are greatest. Here children under 15 comprise nearly 35 percent of the total black population, compared to 25 percent of all whites; the elderly population makes up about 5 percent of the black population of central cities, but 11 percent of the white population.

POPULATION CHANGE WITHIN METROPOLITAN AREAS

Patterns of population change show considerable differences from national or regional averages when metropolitan areas are grouped by size. White and Negro population growth are in even greater contrast when looked at in this way.

The decline in the white population of central cities (a loss of 1 percent in the Nation as a whole) was produced by very heavy losses from central cities of the largest metropolitan areas together with small gains from metropolitan areas of intermediate size, and fairly large gains from smaller metropolitan areas (see table 9 and table E).

Table E.   Population Change by Size of Standard Metropolitan Statistical Areas in 1970 and Race: 1960 to 1970

SMSA's Inside and Outside Central Cities	Total		White		Negro	
	Number	Per-cent	Number	Per-cent	Number	Per-cent
SMSA's[1]...............	19,792,666	16.6	14,694,538	13.9	4,054,070	31.8
2,000,000 or more........	5,589,745	12.0	2,773,303	6.8	2,302,084	40.3
1,000,000 to 1,999,999...	5,965,813	26.6	4,940,277	24.4	819,660	38.8
500,000 to 999,999.......	3,345,937	18.0	2,766,758	17.0	437,592	22.3
250,000 to 499,999.......	2,768,837	16.3	2,337,358	15.3	320,165	20.0
Less than 250,000........	2,122,334	14.2	1,876,842	13.9	174,569	12.9
Inside central cities	3,194,453	5.3	−606,747	−1.2	3,233,937	32.6
2,000,000 or more........	−423,343	−1.8	−2,488,654	−13.4	1,755,568	36.7
1,000,000 to 1,999,999...	1,034,263	9.7	294,730	3.3	637,693	39.1
500,000 to 999,999.......	763,114	7.6	298,812	3.6	407,044	25.9
250,000 to 499,999.......	767,542	9.6	462,466	6.7	248,007	23.8
Less than 250,000........	1,052,877	12.5	825,899	11.0	185,675	21.0
Outside central cities[1].............	16,598,213	28.2	15,301,285	27.5	820,133	29.0
2,000,000 or more........	6,013,088	26.1	5,261,957	23.9	546,516	58.9
1,000,000 to 1,999,999...	4,931,550	41.7	4,645,547	41.1	181,967	37.8
500,000 to 999,999.......	2,582,823	30.2	2,467,946	30.7	30,548	7.9
250,000 to 499,999.......	2,001,295	22.2	1,874,892	22.3	72,158	12.9
Less than 250,000........	1,069,457	16.4	1,050,943	17.4	−11,056	−2.4

[1]Excludes Middlesex and Somerset Counties in New Jersey.

Source: Table 9.

The white population loss from central cities of the 12 largest metropolitan areas in 1970 amounted to 2 and one half million between 1960 and 1970—a drop of more than 13 percent since 1960. The cities of New York, Chicago, and Detroit account for more than one-half of this loss (1.5 million). Among the central cities of the largest SMSA's, white rates of loss were highest in Washington, D.C. (39 percent), St. Louis (32), Detroit (29), and Cleveland (27). Rates of loss from Chicago (19 percent) and New York (9 percent) were relatively moderate. Los Angeles was the one city in this group to experience a white population gain (of 5 percent). (See table 10.)

Two factors combined to produce the white population losses from these cities—very low natural increase and heavy outmigration (see table 12). Washington, D.C. provides the extreme case, with one of the lowest rates of natural increase and the highest white net outmigration rate in the Nation. The natural increase of Washington's white population for the entire decade was only 2,300, a rate of less than 1 percent. Net outmigration at the same time removed 138,000 persons, 40 percent of the total white population in the city in 1960.[5] In addition to Washington, D.C., three other central cities in this size class had white net outmigration of 30 percent or more: St. Louis (34 percent), Cleveland (33), and Detroit (33).

The central cities of metropolitan areas of one-half to 2 million population in 1970 had a gain of about 600,000 whites altogether, equivalent to 3 percent of their combined 1960 population. Only one-half of the central cities of the 54 SMSA's in this size class gained white population over the decade. Rates of increase were highest in Fort Lauderdale (128 percent), San Jose (111), Riverside (66), and Anaheim (58). In each of these cities annexation of suburban territory was an important component of population growth.

Heaviest white losses were sustained by Newark (37 percent), Wilmington (37), Buffalo (21), and Atlanta (20). Low natural increase was a factor which affected the population change of comparatively few central cities of this intermediate metropolitan size class. In Newark, Wilmington, and Buffalo only, low natural increase (1 to 3 percent) and high outmigration (24 to 40 percent) operated together to produce declines in white population (see table 12). Other central cities had heavy white outmigration but natural increase was moderate or substantial, e.g., in Atlanta, Cincinnati, Gary, Dayton, and Louisville.

The central cities of metropolitan areas with populations under 500,000 in 1970 gained a white population

of 1.3 million altogether, an increase of 9 percent since 1960. In virtually every one of these cities natural increase was a strong force in favor of white population growth. Only in West Palm Beach and Trenton were white rates of natural increase very low (1 percent and 3 percent, respectively), while Atlantic City had a white natural decrease of 9 percent.

Suburban white growth was spread over metropolitan areas of all sizes, but was strongest in those areas having population of one-half to 2 million in 1970. Here the white suburban population increased by 7.1 million, or 37 percent. In contrast, whites in the suburban areas of the largest SMSA's increased by 5.3 million, or 24 percent.

In central cities and suburbs alike, black gains were highly concentrated in metropolitan areas of the largest size class. More than one-half of the total black increase in metropolitan areas occurred in the 12 largest SMSA's. Between 1960 and 1970, 1.8 million blacks were added to these central cities and 550,000 to these suburban areas.

One-half of the black increase in central cities of the largest SMSA's was concentrated in the two cities of New York (600,000), and Chicago (300,000). Rates of increase were highest in Boston (66 percent), with New York second (53), followed by Los Angeles (52), San Francisco and Oakland combined (40), and Detroit (37).

In most of the central cities of the largest SMSA's, the growth of races other than white was accounted for primarily by natural increase. In the five cities where this population increased most rapidly, however, net inmigration was responsible for most of the growth. In New York City, which was by far the largest attractor of black migrants in the Nation, net inmigration accounted for 62 percent of the city's increase in Negro and other races. New York City's net inmigration of this population group (436,000) exceeded the combined migration gains of Los Angeles (128,000), Chicago (113,000), Detroit (98,000) and San Francisco-Oakland (67,000).

Black suburban increases in the 1960-70 decade were concentrated in the SMSA's of Los Angeles (123,000), Washington (82,000), and New York (77,000), which together account for more than one-half of the gain. Rates of increase vary greatly, from lows of 7 percent in the Pittsburgh suburbs and 16 percent in Baltimore to 453 percent in Cleveland and 105 percent in Los Angeles. Only in the suburbs of Detroit, Pittsburgh, and Baltimore was natural increase of primary importance to black growth.

In metropolitan areas of 1 to 2 million, blacks in central cities increased by only 638,000, but at a somewhat faster rate than in the largest size class (by 39.1 percent compared with 36.7 percent). This growth was concentrated in four of the central cities in this

---

[5] Newark, which is in the next metropolitan size class, had a white net outmigration equal to Washington, D.C.'s.

class. Houston (with a black population increase of 102,000), Dallas (81,000), Newark and Atlanta (each with 69,000), account for one-half of black central city growth. The primary source of population change varies greatly among the central cities of these metropolitan areas, but in general natural increase tends to be more important.

In SMSA's of smaller size, Negro rates of increase drop off rather sharply. In SMSA's of one-half to 1 million population, blacks grew most rapidly in the cities of Sacramento (by 15,000, or 125 percent), Rochester (26,000, or 111 percent), Syracuse (10,000, or 91 percent), and Hartford (19,000, or 77 percent).

In contrast to the white trend, the lowest rate of black increase was experienced in central cities of smallest metropolitan areas. As a result of the changes by race which occurred in metropolitan areas over the 1960-70 decade, the vast majority of central cities had an increase in the Negro proportion of their populations, but suburbs show little change in racial composition. Nearly all the cities which had declines in Negro percentages are located in the South and are in SMSA's of less than 500,000 population.

The greatest increases in percent Negro were in central cities in the largest metropolitan size class, where the overall change was from 20 to 28 percent. Cities in which the Negro population shows the largest relative gains between 1960 and 1970 are: Washington, where the increase was from 54 percent in 1960 to 71 percent by 1970; Detroit, from 29 to 44 percent; St. Louis, from 29 to 41 percent; and Baltimore, from 35 to 46 percent. In this group of SMSA's Boston has the lowest Negro proportion, which between 1960 and 1970 grew from 9 percent to only 16 percent.

Whereas in 1960 only Washington, D.C. and Charleston, S.C. had Negro majorities, by 1970 several other central cities has passed the 50 percent mark. Newark over the decade increased its black population percentage from 34 to 54 percent, which was the greatest change in any city in the Nation. In addition, Atlanta in 1970 had a Negro majority of 51 percent (up from 38 percent in 1960) as did Gary (53 percent, from 39 percent in 1960), and Petersburg (55 percent in 1970 and 47 percent in 1960). Augusta, Georgia in 1970 was about evenly divided.

Several other central cities are now close to having a Negro majority. Between 1960 and 1970 the Negro population of New Orleans rose from 37 to 45 percent, in Wilmington it increased from 26 to 44 percent, and in Savannah from 36 to 45 percent of the total. Charleston, on the other hand, shows a reverse trend: the black population here declined from 51 to 45 percent of the city's total.

Other cities in which Negroes are rapidly increasing in proportion to total population are in Northern States: Trenton (22 to 38 percent), Hartford (15 to 28 percent), Harrisburg (19 to 31 percent), New Haven (14 to 26 percent) and Flint (18 to 28 percent) are a few.

Black increases in the suburbs of SMSA's of all sizes have been very large. Nonetheless, there has been little change in the proportions represented by Negroes. Only the largest metropolitan size class (2 million or more population) registered an increase in blacks as a proportion of their total suburban population (from 4.0 in 1960 to 5.1 in 1970). Among areas of this size, Detroit and Pittsburgh show virtually no change and Baltimore shows a decline, but in the other largest SMSA's the percentage of blacks in suburbs was increased. In Washington, D.C. and St. Louis, which in 1970 had the highest proportions of Negroes in suburbs, blacks increased from 6 percent of both areas in 1960 to 8 percent in the Washington, D.C. suburbs and 7 percent in the St. Louis suburbs.

HOUSING TRENDS

United States

The total number of housing units in the United States in 1970 was 68,631,000.[6] Between 1960 and 1970 housing increased more rapidly than did population. While population grew by 23,912,000, or 13.3 percent, housing units increased by 10,305,000, or 17.7 percent (table F).

The metropolitan area growth of housing overshadowed the nonmetropolitan increase. The number of housing units in metropolitan areas rose from 38,633,000 to 46,496,000 over the decade, an increase of 7,863,000, or 20 percent. In comparison, the increase in nonmetropolitan areas was 2,438,000, or 12 percent. About 68 percent of all housing units in 1970 were in the metropolitan areas and these areas accounted for 76 percent of the total United States increase between 1960 and 1970.

Within the metropolitan areas of the country, much greater housing growth occurred in the suburban areas than in the central cities. Housing units in the suburbs, which comprised 51 percent of the metropolitan housing in 1970, increased by 5,712,000 units, or 31 percent. In contrast, housing in the combined central cities increased by 2,151,000 units, or 11 percent. Although central city housing comprised 49 percent of metropolitan housing, this area accounted for only 27 percent of the metropolitan housing growth in the 1960's. By 1970, there were 23,905,000 housing units in the suburbs and 22,591,000 units in the central cities.

The number of housing units in multiunit structures in the Nation increased at a faster rate during the decade

[6] The housing units shown in the tables of this report add to 68,627,366. Revisions in totals for certain States were made after the tabulations for this report had been completed. The revised 1970 count for the United States is 68,631,428.

than did one-family units, 37 percent compared with 7 percent. The corresponding increase in occupied mobile homes or trailers was 141 percent. In the suburban areas (where housing growth was the greatest), units in multiunit structures almost doubled, while structures with one unit rose 17 percent. By 1970, the proportion of one-unit structures in the United States was 69 percent. It was higher in the nonmetropolitan areas (83 percent) than in the metropolitan areas (63 percent).

The number of units lacking some or all plumbing facilities in the United States declined from 9,778,000 to 4,678,000, a 52-percent decrease since 1960. In 1970, the proportion of such units was 7 percent of all year-round units compared with 17 percent in 1960. The proportion of units lacking complete plumbing in 1970 was 4 percent in metropolitan areas (also 4 percent in the central cities and the suburbs) and 14 percent in nonmetropolitan areas.

Approximately 1,050,000, or 17 percent, of Negro-occupied units in the United States lacked some or all plumbing in 1970, compared with 41 percent in 1960. The 1970 proportions for inside and outside the metropolitan areas were 7 percent and 49 percent, respectively. About 5 percent of the Negro-occupied units in the central cities and 17 percent in the suburbs lacked complete plumbing facilities in 1970.

Households were smaller in 1970 than in 1960. The relative drop in the average household size over the decade was greatest in the nonmetropolitan areas, 3.4 persons in 1960 to 3.1 persons in 1970. In the metropolitan areas household size declined from 3.3 in 1960 to 3.1 in 1970. The suburban areas continued to have a higher average household size (3.5 in 1960 and 3.3 in 1970) than the central cities (3.1 in 1960 and 2.9 in 1970).

One-person households increased by 57 percent in the Nation, while households with five or more persons gained only 7 percent. The increase in the number of

Table F.   Housing Units by Metropolitan and Nonmetropolitan Residence: 1970 and 1960

United States Metropolitan and Nonmetropolitan Residence	Housing units					Population percent change
	Total		Change			
	1970	1960	Number	Percent		
Total................	68,627,366	58,326,357	10,301,009	17.7		13.3
Metropolitan residence....	46,495,892	38,632,900	7,862,992	20.4		16.6
Inside central cities...	22,590,910	20,440,217	2,150,693	10.5		5.3
Outside central cities..	23,904,982	18,192,683	5,712,299	31.4		28.2
Nonmetropolitan residence.	22,131,474	19,693,457	2,438,017	12.4		6.5

one-person households was about the same in the suburbs as in the central cities; in relative terms, such households increased 93 percent in the suburban areas, as against 43 percent in central cities.

The median number of rooms in housing units increased in the 10-year period both inside and outside metropolitan areas—4.9 rooms in 1960 to 5.0 rooms in 1970 in each area. In the suburban areas the median number of rooms increased from 5.1 to 5.3, whereas in the central cities the median rose from 4.6 to 4.7 rooms.

The proportion of small units (one-to-three-room units) in the inventory decreased during the decade, especially in the nonmetropolitan areas of the United States. In 1960, housing units with one to three rooms comprised 21 percent of metropolitan housing, and by 1970, 18 percent. For nonmetropolitan housing, the decrease was from 18 to 13 percent.

In 1970, the largest proportion of small units was found in central cities, about 25 percent. Suburban units with one to three rooms comprised 12 percent of the 1970 inventory. Larger housing units, i.e., those with six or more rooms, comprised 44 percent of the inventory in the suburban areas, 30 percent in the central cities, and 38 percent in the nonmetropolitan areas.

Number of persons per room is often used as a measure of crowding. In the United States, both the number and the proportion of housing units with 1.01 or more persons per room decreased during the decade. In 1960, 10 percent of all occupied units in metropolitan areas and 14 percent in nonmetropolitan areas had 1.01 or more persons per room. By 1970, the proportion of such units decreased to 8 percent inside standard metropolitan statistical areas (SMSA's) and 9 percent outside SMSA's. Housing units with more than one person per room also decreased in the central cities (11 to 9 percent) as well as in the suburbs (10 to 7 percent) (table G).

About 63 percent of the households in the United States owned their homes in 1970 compared with 62 percent in 1960. The homeownership rate remained at 60 percent in metropolitan areas and rose from 67 to 70 percent in nonmetropolitan areas. Of the 39,862,000 owner-occupied units in the country, 26,237,000, or 66 percent, were inside metropolitan areas and 13,625,000, or 34 percent, were outside these areas in 1970. Homeownership continued to be noticeably more prevalent in the suburbs than in the central cities. About 70 percent of occupied units in the suburban areas and 48 percent in the central cities were owner-occupied.

Negro homeownership rose from 38 percent in 1960 to 42 percent in 1970. In 1970, about 38 percent of the Negro households in metropolitan areas (36 percent in 1960) and 52 percent in nonmetropolitan areas (45 percent in 1960) owned their homes. The Negro-homeownership rate rose from 52 to 54 percent in the suburbs and from 32 to 35 percent in the central cities. Of the 2,578,000 Negro-homeowner households in the country, 1,832,000, or 71 percent, lived inside SMSA's (1,337,000 inside central cities and 495,000 in the suburbs) and 746,000 lived outside SMSA's.

Property values and rents increased during the last decade. The median value in metropolitan areas increased 42 percent, from $13,400 to $19,000, while in nonmetropolitan areas the median rose from under $10,000 to $12,200. In central cities the median value of owner-occupied housing was $16,500 ($12,500 in 1960) compared with $20,800 ($14,200 in 1960) in the suburbs. About 20 percent of the owner-occupied housing in the central cities was valued at $25,000 or more, compared with 34 percent in the suburbs.

In metropolitan areas, median contract rent in 1970 was 54 percent higher than in 1960, rising from $63 to $97. In nonmetropolitan areas rent increased 48 percent, from $42 to $62. In the central cities the rise was from

Table G. Plumbing Facilities and Persons Per Room by Metropolitan and Nonmetropolitan Residence: 1970 and 1960

United States Metropolitan and Nonmetropolitan Residence	Percent of housing units			
	Lacking some or all plumbing facilities		With 1.01 or more persons per room[1]	
	1970[2]	1960[3]	1970	1960
Total......................	6.9	16.8	8.2	11.5
Metropolitan residence.............	3.5	[4]9.1	7.8	10.5
Inside central cities...........	3.5	9.6	8.5	10.7
Outside central cities..........	3.5	[4]8.6	7.1	10.3
Nonmetropolitan residence.........	14.3	[4]31.8	9.3	13.7

[1]Percent of all occupied units.   [2]Percent of all year-round housing units.
[3]Percent of all housing units.   [4]Estimated by proportionate adjustments to reflect metropolitan boundary changes between 1960 and 1970.

$61 to $91 (49 percent) and in the suburban areas from $67 to $113 (69 percent). About 29 percent of the units in central cities rented for $120 or more, compared with 46 percent in the suburbs.

Value and rent are expressed in current dollars (the value at the time of the respective censuses). Thus, any comparison must take into account the general rise in the cost of living during the 10-year period, as well as changes in the characteristics of the housing inventory.

The homeowner vacancy rate in the United States dropped over the decade from 1.6 to 1.2 percent. The rental vacancy rate decreased from 6.7 to 6.5 percent.

Regions

Although in all four regions the total supply of housing units increased more rapidly than population, housing gains in the West and South approximately doubled those of the other two regions (table H).

California led the States in number of additional housing units with a 1,531,000-unit increase, or 28 percent, and replaced New York as the State with the greatest number of housing units (6,997,000) in the country. Large numbers of housing units were added to the inventory in Florida (745,000 units), Texas (670,000), and New York (580,000).

In the West, housing units in Nevada increased by 70 percent with the addition of 71,000 units. Other fast-growing States in the West were Arizona (40 percent), Alaska (35), and Hawaii (31), these four States accounted for only 13 percent of the total housing increase in the West. In the South, Florida led the region with a 42-percent gain in its housing inventory. The fastest growing States in the South after Florida were Maryland (34 percent) and Virginia (28), but these three States accounted for 36 percent of the region's total housing increase.

In all regions except the Northeast, housing growth was concentrated in the metropolitan areas. The greatest increases in metropolitan areas were in the West and South, 30 percent and 29 percent, respectively. Housing units in the metropolitan areas of the North Central Region increased 16 percent. In the Northeast, the metropolitan areas gained only 12 percent, compared with 14 percent in the nonmetropolitan areas.

While 78 percent of the housing units in 1970 in the West were inside SMSA's, these areas accounted for 88 percent of the total regional increase between 1960 and 1970. About 55 percent of the housing units in the South were inside SMSA's, but 68 percent of the increase from 1960 to 1970 occurred in its metropolitan areas.

Within the metropolitan areas of the four regions, the suburban areas experienced much greater growth in housing than did the central cities (table I). Suburban

Table H. Housing Units by Regions

(Numbers in millions)

Regions	1970 total	Increase from 1960		Population percent increase
		Number	Percent	
United States..............	68.6	10.3	17.7	13.3
Northeast....................	16.6	1.8	12.3	9.7
North Central...............	19.0	2.2	13.0	9.6
South.......................	21.0	3.8	22.3	14.2
West........................	12.0	2.5	25.9	24.1

Table I. Housing Growth Inside SMSA's: 1960 to 1970

(Numbers in thousands)

Regions	Central cities		Suburbs		Suburban units as percent of SMSA total 1970 units
	Number	Percent	Number	Percent	
United States..............	2,151	10.5	5,712	31.4	51.4
Northeast....................	190	3.2	1,219	20.9	53.2
North Central...............	284	5.0	1,410	29.3	51.0
South.......................	954	18.3	1,639	42.6	47.1
West........................	722	20.4	1,444	39.0	54.7

housing, which comprised about half of the metropolitan housing in each region in 1970, accounted for 86 percent of the metropolitan housing increase in the Northeast, 83 percent in the North Central, 67 percent in the West, and 63 percent in the South.

As housing units in multiunit structures and mobile homes or trailers both increased faster than one-unit structures, the proportion of single-family units in each of the four regions decreased over the decade. The South had the greatest increase in multiunit structures of any region—1.6 million units, or 69 percent. One-unit structures also increased by 1.6 million units in the South, but the relative increase was only 11 percent. By 1970 the distribution of housing units in the South was 78 percent in one-unit structures (compared with 85 percent in 1960), 18 percent in multiunit structures, and 4 percent in mobile homes or trailers.

Units in multiunit structures increased much faster in the suburban areas than in the central cities or in the nonmetropolitan areas. For example, in the South, units in multiunit structures in the suburban areas more than doubled, from 390,000 in 1960 to 1,009,000 in 1970, compared with a 43-percent increase (1,366,000 to 1,958,000 units) in the central cities and a 71-percent increase (496,000 to 846,000 units) in nonmetropolitan areas.

Although each region shared in the decrease in the number of units lacking some or all plumbing facilities, the greatest numerical decline occurred in the South (2,301,000 units, or a 48-percent decrease). By 1970, the proportion of units lacking some or all plumbing was 3 percent for the West, 4 percent for the Northeast, 6 percent for the North Central, and 12 percent for the South.

Within the metropolitan areas of each region, except in the South, the central cities had higher proportions of units without complete plumbing facilities than the suburban areas. The proportions of such units in the central cities in the North Central and in the South regions were 4 percent and the Northeast and West, 3 percent. The central cities in the South had the largest percentage decrease during the decade, 66 percent (a 435,000-unit decline), dropping the proportion of units without complete plumbing from 13 percent in 1960 to 4 percent in 1970. For the suburban areas, the largest percentage of units lacking complete plumbing was in the South (7 percent) and the smallest proportion in the West (2 percent).

The State in each region with the largest proportion of housing units lacking some or all plumbing facilities was Mississippi (24 percent) in the South, Alaska (17) in the West, Maine (15) in the Northeast, and North Dakota (14) in the North Central Region. The State with the smallest proportion of such units in each region was California (2 percent), New Jersey (3), Michigan (4), and Maryland (4).

Approximately 913,000, or 29 percent of the Negro-occupied units in the South, lacked some or all plumbing in 1970 compared with 60 percent in 1960. The 1970 proportions for inside and outside metropolitan areas were 12 percent and 52 percent, respectively. About 7 percent of the Negro-occupied units in the central cities of the South and 31 percent in the suburbs lacked complete plumbing facilities in 1970. In all areas of the other regions, the proportions of Negro households lacking complete plumbing were considerably smaller (table J).

Table J. Percent of Negro-Occupied Housing Units Lacking Some or All Plumbing Facilities: 1970

Metropolitan and Nonmetropolitan Residence	United States	Northeast	North Central	South	West
Total.....................	16.9	4.4	5.2	29.1	2.6
Metropolitan residence........	7.2	4.4	4.4	12.3	2.4
Inside central cities.......	4.8	4.2	4.1	6.5	2.7
Outside central cities......	17.1	5.3	7.1	31.3	1.7
Nonmetropolitan residence.....	48.8	7.0	19.0	52.3	7.7

Households were smaller in 1970 than in 1960. The region experiencing the greatest change was the South, where average household size dropped from 3.5 to 3.2 persons. The smallest change was in the households of the Northeast, down from an average of 3.2 to 3.1 persons. Within the metropolitan areas of each of the four regions, suburban households were larger than those in central cities, the smallest averages being found in the central cities of the Northeast and the West, 2.8 persons each.

The number of one-person households increased much more rapidly than households with five or more persons throughout the four regions. The greatest gain was in the South, where over the decade 1.3 million one-person households were added (a 72-percent increase) and, of this number, 60 percent was added to the metropolitan areas. Although the suburban areas of the South had a greater percentage increase in one-person households (120 percent) than the central cities (58 percent), the numerical increase was greater in the cities. The percentage increase in the number of households with five or more persons was greatest in the West (17 percent). Within this region, the greatest increase in large households was in the suburban areas (30 percent).

The median number of rooms in housing units increased during the decade in the four regions. The South showed the greatest increase in the metropolitan areas (4.7 to 5.0 rooms). The medians were higher in the suburban areas in each region than in the central cities, especially in the Northeast where the median was 4.4 for the central cities and 5.6 for the suburbs.

The proportion of the housing inventory in small units (one to three rooms) decreased over the decade in all regions of the United States except in the Northeast, where they remained approximately the same.

The proportion of the larger units, i.e., six or more rooms, increased in all regions and was greatest in the Northeast, with 29 percent in the central cities and 53 percent in the suburbs having six or more rooms in 1970. Large units increased most sharply in the suburbs of the West, from 28 percent in 1960 to 36 percent of the total housing inventory in 1970.

Number of persons per room is often used as a measure of crowding. In the Northeast, North Central, and South Regions, both the number and proportion of housing units with 1.01 or more persons per room decreased during the decade. In the West, although both metropolitan and nonmetropolitan areas also recorded decreases in the proportion of such units from 1960 to 1970, the number of these units in central cities increased from 280,000 to 302,000 and in the suburbs from 379,000 to 384,000.

Units with 1.01 or more persons per room were most prevalent in the South (10 percent), but this region showed the greatest change over the decade, down from 16 percent in 1960. The smallest proportion of units with more than one person per room was found in the Northeast Region (7 percent). In this region the corresponding proportions were 8 percent in the central cities, 5 percent in its suburban areas, and 6 percent in its nonmetropolitan areas.

The homeownership rate was highest in the North Central Region in 1970—68 percent, a slight increase from 67 percent in 1960. The Northeast had the smallest proportion of homeowners (58 percent in 1970), an increase of 2 percentage points since 1960. The central cities of the Northeast had a much smaller proportion of homeowners than the central cities of the other regions—36 percent in both 1960 and 1970. Homeownership decreased in the West from 53 to 50 percent in the central cities and from 67 to 63 percent in the suburban areas.

The North Central Region recorded a 59-percent increase in Negro homeownership from 1960 to 1970. By 1970, the homeownership rate was 42 percent. In the metropolitan areas of the North Central Region the Negro-homeownership rate rose from 34 percent in 1960 to 41 percent in 1970 with the percentage of Negro homeownership reaching 59 percent in the suburbs.

In the South, the proportion of Negro-homeowner households in the nonmetropolitan areas increased from 44 percent in 1960 to 52 percent in 1970. In the suburban areas of the South, Negro owners increased from 51 to 57 percent; the corresponding increase in the central cities was from 36 to 39 percent.

In the Northeast, the proportion of Negro-owner-occupied units rose from 27 percent in 1960 to 29 percent in 1970. In the West, this proportion declined from 45 to 40 percent.

The Northeast had the lowest metropolitan area proportion of Negro-homeowner households, 28 percent. Almost half the Negro households in the suburbs owned homes, but slightly less than one-fourth in the central cities were homeowners.

In all regions, property values and rents increased during the last decade. The West experienced the largest relative increase in median value, from $13,700 to $20,500, or 50 percent. In 1970, 33 percent of all owner-occupied housing units in the West were valued at $25,000 or more, as compared with only 10 percent in 1960. The North Central Region showed the smallest increase, from $12,100 to $16,700, or 38 percent. The West had the highest median value in both 1960 and 1970, $13,700 and $20,500, respectively. In the South, median value was lowest in both 1960 ($9,500) and 1970 ($13,600).

In each region, median value in 1970 was greater in metropolitan areas than in nonmetropolitan areas. In the

West, for example, the median value in metropolitan areas was $21,900, and in nonmetropolitan areas, $14,300.

Within SMSA's in each region, median value was greater in suburban areas than in central cities. In the West, the median value in the suburban areas was $22,700, as compared with $20,700 in the central cities.

As with value, the West showed the largest relative increase in median contract rent, 61 percent. In 1970, 20 percent of all renter-occupied housing units in the West rented for $150 or more, as compared with only 2 percent in 1960. The North Central Region underwent the smallest increase in median rent, from $62 to $90, or 45 percent. The West had the highest median contract rent in both 1960 and 1970, $66 and $106, respectively. In the South median contract rent was lowest in both 1960 ($46) and in 1970 ($73).

Median contract rent in each region was greater in metropolitan areas than in nonmetropolitan areas. In the Northeast, for example, median contract rent was $95 in metropolitan areas and $74 in nonmetropolitan areas. Within metropolitan areas, median contract rent was greater in suburban areas than in the central cities. The suburban areas in the Northeast had a median contract rent of $109, while the central cities had a median of $90.

Population Change for Counties: 1960 to 1970

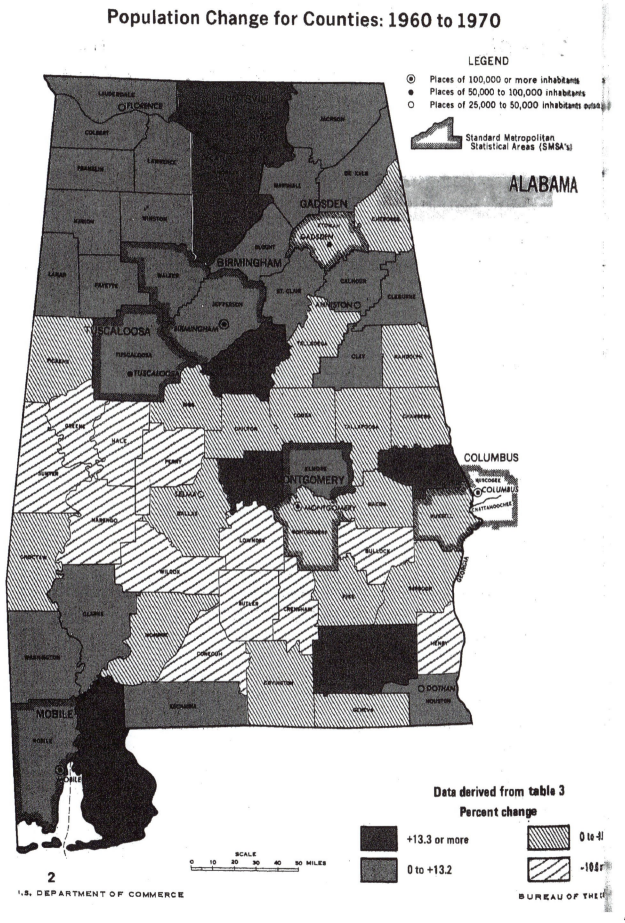

LEGEND

⊙ Places of 100,000 or more inhabitants

● Places of 50,000 to 100,000 inhabitants

○ Places of 25,000 to 50,000 inhabitants outside

Standard Metropolitan
Statistical Areas (SMSA's)

ALABAMA

Data derived from table 3

Percent change

+13.3 or more

0 to +13.2

0 to +1

-10 or

SCALE
0   10   20   30   40   50 MILES

2

U.S. DEPARTMENT OF COMMERCE   BUREAU OF THE C

Analytical Text

POPULATION TRENDS

General

Between 1960 and 1970 the population of Alabama grew from 3,267,000 to 3,444,000, an increase of 177,000, or 5.4 percent. This rate of increase is substantially below the rate of increase in the entire United States (13.3 percent) and in the South region (14.2 percent) in which Alabama is located.

The total number of households in Alabama in 1970 was 1,034,000 or 150,000 more than in 1960. The population living in households increased more slowly than the rate at which new households were formed,

with the result that average household size dropped from 3.7 to 3.3 persons per unit.

During the 1960 to 1970 decade, the population of metropolitan areas increased by 111,000 persons. The growth rates of the metropolitan and nonmetropolitan populations in Alabama were about the same, and, as a result, the proportion of the total population living in metropolitan areas remained at 52 percent. In the nation as a whole about two-thirds of the population live in metropolitan areas. Less than 10 percent of the increase in the metropolitan population occurred in central cities or a total of 10,000 persons (table A). All central cities in the State annexed territory during the decade; if the populations in these annexed territories are excluded,

Table A. Population by Race and Metropolitan and Nonmetropolitan Residence: 1970 and 1960

The State Metropolitan and Non-metropolitan Residence	Population		Change		Percent Distribution	
	1970	1960	Number	Percent	1970	1960
Total..............	3,444,165	3,266,740	177,425	5.4	100.0	100.0
Metropolitan residence...	1,801,095	1,690,569	110,526	6.5	52.3	51.8
Inside central cities..	881,825	871,882	9,943	1.1	25.6	26.7
Outside central cities.	919,270	818,687	100,583	12.3	26.7	25.1
Nonmetropolitan residence	1,643,070	1,576,171	66,899	4.2	47.7	48.2
White..............	2,528,983	2,283,609	245,374	10.7	73.4	69.9
Metropolitan residence...	1,297,450	1,173,239	124,211	10.6	37.7	35.9
Inside central cities..	595,573	581,971	13,602	2.3	17.3	17.8
Outside central cities.	701,877	591,268	110,609	18.7	20.4	18.1
Nonmetropolitan residence	1,231,533	1,110,370	121,163	10.9	35.8	34.0
Negro and other races	915,182	983,131	-67,949	-6.9	26.6	30.1
Metropolitan residence...	503,645	517,330	-13,685	-2.6	14.6	15.8
Inside central cities..	286,252	289,911	-3,659	-1.3	8.3	8.9
Outside central cities.	217,393	227,419	-10,026	-4.4	6.3	7.0
Nonmetropolitan residence	411,537	465,801	-54,264	-11.6	11.9	14.3

he central cities would show a net population loss of 23,000, instead of a gain (table B).

The rates of population change by race differed sharply in Alabama between 1960 and 1970. The white population increased 10.7 percent while the population of other races (which is overwhelmingly Negro) decreased by 6.9 percent. As a result the proportion of Negro and other races in the total population declined from 30 to 27 percent. Among whites the rates of increase in metropolitan and nonmetropolitan areas were about equal. Among Negro and other races, there were decreases of 3 percent in metropolitan areas and 12 percent in nonmetropolitan areas.

The population increase of 117,000 in Alabama in the 1960 to 1970 decade was the result of a natural increase (births minus deaths) of 410,000 and a net outmigration of 233,000. The net outmigration was equivalent to about 7 percent of the 1960 population. The net outmigration of whites was negligible while the net outmigration of Negro and other races was 228,000. This figure is equivalent to 23 percent of the 1960 population of Negro and other races.

The age composition of the Alabama population changed significantly between 1960 and 1970. The greatest decline occurred among the population under 5 years old and was due largely to the decline in birth rates which occurred throughout the United States during the 1960's. The greatest increase occurred in the 15 to 24 age group and was due to the entry of the large number of persons born during the post–World War II "baby boom" into this age group. As a result of these changes, the proportion of the total population in the under 5 group declined from 12 to 9 percent, and the proportion in the 15 to 24 group increased from 15 to 18 percent.

Standard Metropolitan Statistical Areas

In 1970, there were seven Standard Metropolitan Statistical Areas (SMSA's) in Alabama, including six SMSA's located entirely within Alabama and one SMSA located partially in Alabama (the Columbus, Ga.-Ala. SMSA). The following discussion refers only to the metropolitan population in Alabama.[1]

Between 1960 and 1970, the metropolitan population of Alabama increased by 111,000. Two-thirds of this increase occurred in the Huntsville SMSA which grew rapidly because of heavy inmigration inspired by the Redstone Arsenal facility. The Huntsville SMSA had a 48 percent increase in population during the decade and passed the Montgomery SMSA in population to become the third largest metropolitan area in the State.

If the Huntsville SMSA is excluded, the patterns of population change in the remaining six SMSA's in Alabama were similar. During the 1960 to 1970 decade, each of the six metropolitan areas experienced a small rate of population change ranging from an increase of 6 percent in the Tuscaloosa SMSA to a decrease of 3 percent in the Gadsden SMSA.

The Birmingham SMSA (an important manufacturing center) and the Mobile SMSA (an important transportation center) had the lowest growth rates among the 25 largest SMSA's in the South region of the United States. The Birmingham SMSA, which was one of the 10 largest SMSA's in the South in 1960, had a growth rate of only 2.5 percent, while the other nine largest SMSA's had

---

[1] For a discussion of the entire Columbus, Ga.-Ala. SMSA, see 1970 Census Report, PHC(2)-12.

Table B.   Change in Population of Central Cities Through Annexation: 1960 to 1970

Central Cities	1970 population			1960 population	Change 1960 to 1970 in 1960 area
	Total	In 1960 area	In annexed area		
Birmingham..................	300,910	298,440	2,470	340,887	-42,447
Mobile.....................	190,026	189,594	432	194,856	-5,262
Montgomery.................	133,386	118,498	14,888	134,393	-15,895
Huntsville.................	137,802	120,436	17,366	72,365	48,071
Tuscaloosa.................	65,773	60,554	5,219	63,370	-2,816
Gadsden....................	53,928	53,179	749	58,088	-4,909

growth rates ranging from 14 to 40 percent. The Montgomery SMSA had a growth rate of less than 1 percent. In contrast, the metropolitan areas of the other 10 State capitals in the Deep South had growth rates ranging from 17 to 39 percent.

In the Birmingham, Mobile, Montgomery, Tuscaloosa, and Gadsden SMSA's, the rates of population change were lower in the central cities than in the remainder of the SMSA's. Each one of these five central cities lost population within its 1960 boundaries (table B). Tuscaloosa was the only one of these five central cities in which the 1970 population of the area annexed between 1960 and 1970 was greater than the population loss within the 1960 boundaries, and thus Tuscaloosa was the only one of these cities to increase in population between 1960 and 1970. In contrast, the city of Huntsville gained population within its 1960 boundaries. One-fourth of Huntsville's growth was due to annexation.

With the exception of the Huntsville SMSA, each of the other six metropolitan areas in Alabama had a net outmigration between 1960 and 1970, among both the white population and the population of Negro and other races. The rates of net outmigration of Negro and other races in these six metropolitan areas ranged from 16 to 30 percent.

Counties

Of the 67 counties in Alabama, 35 gained population and 32 lost population between 1960 and 1970. Ten counties had rates of growth above the national average of 13.3 percent, and 12 counties experienced population declines exceeding 10 percent.

Every county in Alabama had a natural increase (i.e., births outnumbered deaths) during the decade. In 32 counties (those losing population), net outmigration was greater than natural increase. Only nine counties gained population through both natural increase and net inmigration, and only two of these counties had substantial amounts of net inmigration.

One was Madison County (where Huntsville is located) which had a net inmigration of 38,000. The other was Dale County (where Ft. Rucker is located) which had a net inmigration of 14,000. In most of the other seven counties experiencing a net inmigration, the major cause was the extension of suburban development beyond the county in which the central city of the metropolitan area is located.

At the other extreme, in the 12 counties which had population declines exceeding 10 percent, the demographic changes can best be portrayed by treating the 12 counties as an aggregate. These counties are located mostly in the southwestern quarter of the State and are dominantly rural. Between 1960 and 1970, the population of these counties fell from 218,000 to 188,000, and they had a net outmigration of 56,000. The patterns of population change in the counties differed greatly by race. The white population remained unchanged at 82,000 and had a net outmigration of only 4,000. The population of Negro and other races fell from 136,000 to 105,000 and experienced a net outmigration of 52,000, which was equivalent to 38 percent of the 1960 population.

HOUSING TRENDS

General

Between 1960 and 1970 the total supply of housing units in Alabama increased more rapidly than population. While the population grew by 177,000, or 5 percent, housing units increased by 151,500, or 16 percent (table C).

Table C. Housing Units by Metropolitan and Nonmetropolitan Residence: 1970 and 1960

The State Metropolitan and Nonmetropolitan Residence	Housing units				Popula- tion percent change
	Total		Change		
	1970	1960	Number	Percent	
Total.................	1,118,948	967,466	151,482	15.7	5.4
Metropolitan residence.....	584,187	504,283	79,904	15.8	6.5
Inside central cities....	293,961	268,740	25,221	9.4	1.1
Outside central cities...	290,226	235,543	54,683	15.5	12.3
Nonmetropolitan residence..	534,761	463,183	71,578	15.5	4.2

Housing units in Alabama were about evenly distri-uted between metropolitan and nonmetropolitan areas t 584,200 units (52 percent) and 534,800 (48 percent), espectively. The 10-year increase for metropolitan areas vas 16 percent; for nonmetropolitan, it was 15 percent.

About 83 percent of the housing in Alabama con-isted of one-unit structures in 1970. The number of inits in multiunit structures, however, increased at a nuch faster rate than one-unit structures during the lecade, 35 percent and 9 percent, respectively.

The size of housing units increased between 1960 and 1970. The median number of rooms rose from 4.7 to 5.1 n metropolitan areas and from 4.6 to 5.0 in nonmetro-olitan areas. Units with one to three rooms declined, vhereas those with five or more rooms had large ercentage increases over the decade.

Households were smaller in 1970 than in 1960. In the netropolitan areas of the State, average household size leclined from 3.6 persons in 1960 to 3.2 in 1970, and in ionmetropolitan areas, from 3.7 in 1960 to 3.3 in 1970. There were large percentage increases in one-person iouseholds, 79 percent in the metropolitan areas, and 81 ercent in nonmetropolitan areas. Households with five or more persons showed decreases in both areas.

The number of units in the State lacking some or all olumbing facilities declined from 372,400 to 188,100, a 19-percent decrease since 1960. In 1970, the proportion of such units was 10 percent in metropolitan areas and 24 percent in nonmetropolitan areas.

Number of persons per room is often used as a measure of crowding. In Alabama, both the number and proportion of housing units with 1.01 or more persons per room decreased during the decade. In 1960, 18 percent of all occupied housing units in metropolitan areas and 21 percent in nonmetropolitan areas had 1.01 or more persons per room. By 1970, the proportion of such units decreased to 10 percent in metropolitan areas and 12 percent in nonmetropolitan areas (table D).

Homeownership in the State increased from 60 percent in 1960 to 67 percent in 1970. In metropolitan areas there was an increase from 60 percent to 66 percent, while in nonmetropolitan areas the proportion rose from 59 to 67 percent.

Property values and rents increased in the last decade. The median value in metropolitan areas increased by 43 percent from $9,600 in 1960 to $13,700 in 1970, while in the nonmetropolitan areas value increased 51 percent, from $6,900 to $10,400. In metropolitan areas, median contract rent in 1970 was 46 percent higher than in 1960, rising from $37 to $54.

Value and rent are expressed in current dollars (the value at the time of the respective censuses). Thus, any comparison must take into account the general rise in the cost of living during the 10-year period, as well as changes in the characteristics of the housing inventory.

Standard Metropolitan Statistical Areas

The increase in the housing supply for the metropolitan area total of the State during the decade was 79,900 housing units, from 504,300 in 1960 to 584,200 in 1970.

able D.   Plumbing Facilities and Persons Per Room by Metropolitan and Nonmetro-politan Residence: 1970 and 1960

he State etropolitan and Nonmetropolitan Residence	Percent of housing units			
	Lacking some or all plumbing facilities		With 1.01 or more persons per room[1]	
	1970[2]	1960[3]	1970	1960
Total.........................	16.9	38.5	11.1	19.4
etropolitan residence...........	10.1	(NA)	10.3	18.1
Inside central cities..........	3.9	18.4	9.3	15.5
Outside central cities........	16.5	(NA)	11.3	21.2
onmetropolitan residence........	24.3	(NA)	12.1	20.7

[1]Percent of all occupied units.
[2]Percent of all year-round housing units.
[3]Percent of all housing units.

Average household size for the metropolitan area total of the State declined during the decade. In the central cities, the average decreased from 3.4 persons to 3.1, and in the suburbs from 3.8 persons to 3.4.

The rate of homeownership was greater in the suburban areas than in the central cities. About 73 percent of occupied units in the suburbs were owner-occupied, compared with 59 percent in the central cities.

In 1970, 58,700 housing units in metropolitan areas, or 10 percent of all year-round units, lacked some or all plumbing facilities. The corresponding proportion was 4 percent in the central cities and 16 percent in the suburbs.

Of all occupied units in metropolitan areas, 55,800 units, or 10 percent, reported more than one person per room in 1970, compared with 18 percent in 1960. In 1970, the proportion of such units was 9 percent in the central cities and 11 percent in the suburbs (table D).

The homeowner vacancy rate for metropolitan areas decreased during the decade from 2.1 percent to 1.4 percent. The rental vacancy rate increased from 7.9 to 8.3.

Annexations

Annexations occurred in the central cities of Birmingham, Mobile, Montgomery, Huntsville, Tuscaloosa, and Gadsden during the decade (see "Population Trends" and text table B). Such annexations affect changes in the characteristics for these central cities and their suburbs.

Analytical Text

POPULATION TRENDS

Between 1960 and 1970, the population of Alaska grew by 74,000 persons from 226,000 to 300,000, an increase of 33 percent since 1960. The largest city in the State, Anchorage, had a population of 48,000 in 1970.

During the decade, Alaska's white population grew more rapidly than the population of other races. While the white population grew by 62,000 persons or 36 percent, other races increased by 12,000 persons or 23 percent. There was a small increase in the proportion of the total population which is white, from 77.2 percent in 1960 to 78.8 percent in 1970.

Total population change in the State was due primarily to a natural increase of 60,000 (made up of 73,000 births and 13,000 deaths), and less importantly, to a net inmigration of 14,000 persons. The role of these components varies considerably by race. About two-thirds of white population growth is due to natural increase (40,000) and the remainder to a net inmigration of 22,000 persons. The population of other races, however, which also had a substantial natural increase (of 20,000), experienced a net outmigration of 8,000 persons, equivalent to 15 percent of its 1960 population.

Changes in the age composition of Alaska's population during the 1960-70 decade have produced a somewhat younger population. Although the number of children under 5 years of age was diminished slightly (by 6 percent), the population 5 to 24 years of age increased by more than half, or by 47,000 persons. The population 45 to 64 years of age also shows a very large increase, amounting to 45 percent; while the elderly population and that 25 to 44 years old grew more slowly. These changes characterize both the white population and the population of other races, but to different degrees. A significant difference between the two racial groups is the rate at which the elderly population grew during the decade: in the white population, this is the age group which shows least growth (22 percent); whereas in the population of other races it is the fastest growing age group, increasing by 43 percent in the intercensal period.

Similar changes are found in other sections of the country and are the product in part of changing birth rates and in part are due to migration which is highly selective by age. Low birth rates during the 1960's contribute to the diminution of the population under 5 years of age, whereas the post-World War II "baby boom" is currently reflected in the large size of the population 5 to 24 years old.

Persons living in group quarters (military barracks, college dormitories, extended stay hospitals, and the like) make up a large part of Alaska's population. In 1970, there were over 22,000 persons in group quarters, representing 7.4 percent of the total population of the State. Persons in this category comprise a still larger proportion of the population of particular census divisions. Highest percentages are found in the Aleutian Islands (41 percent), Bristol Bay Borough (36 percent), and Upper Yukon (23 percent) Census Divisions.

Population change is not shown for the territorial subdivisions of Alaska. The electoral districts used at the time of the 1960 census do not match the census divisions used in 1970; valid comparisons cannot, therefore, be made.

HOUSING TRENDS

During the decade the total supply of housing units in Alaska increased by 23,500, or 35 percent, while population increased by 74,000, or 33 percent. The average household size was 3.5 persons in both 1970 and 1960.

Housing units in Alaska are almost evenly divided between owner- and renter-occupied units in 1970. Large increases occurred in both owner-occupied and renter-occupied housing over the decade. There were net gains of 12,100 and 9,700 units, respectively.

During the decade the median value of owner-occupied housing rose sharply in Alaska, from $9,100 in 1960 to $22,700 in 1970, or 150 percent. Median contract rent rose 55 percent, from $110 in 1960 to $171 in 1970. Value and rent data are expressed in current dollars (the dollar value at the time of the respective censuses). Thus, any comparison between the two dates must take into account the general rise in the cost of living in the 10-year period as well as changes in the characteristics of the housing inventory.

Number of persons per room is often used as a measurement of crowding. In Alaska, occupied housing units with 1.01 or more persons per room comprised about 20 percent of all occupied housing units in 1970, compared with 28 percent in 1960. The number of all such units in 1970 was 15,500, a decrease of 600, or 4 percent, between 1960 and 1970, with an even greater drop in the percentage having 1.51 or more persons per room.

Homeowner vacancy rates dropped from 1.8 in 1960 to 1.4 in 1970. Rental vacancies, however, remained at about the same level, 6.8 percent in 1960 and 6.9 percent in 1970.

Population Change for Counties: 1960 to 1970

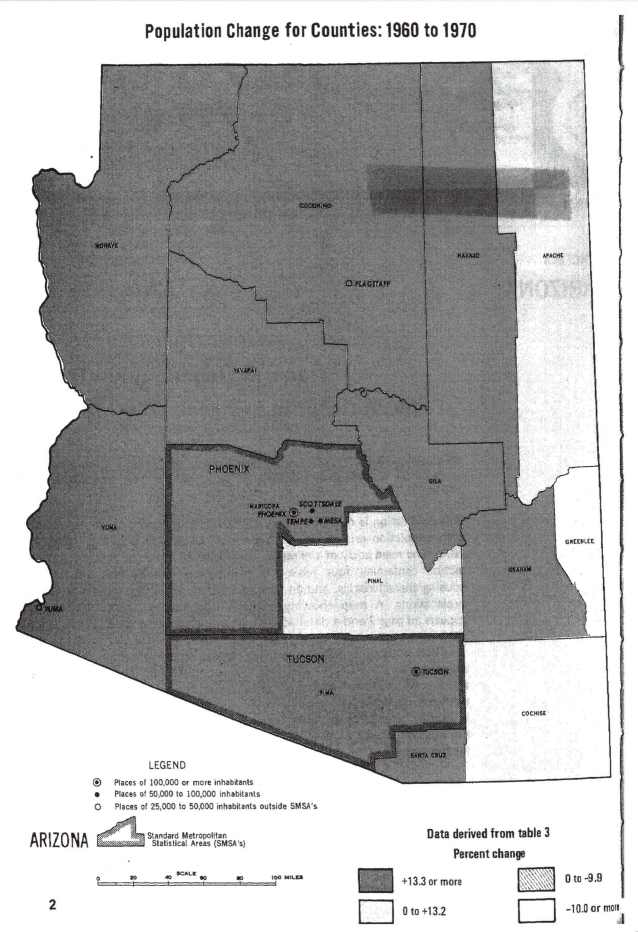

LEGEND

⊙   Places of 100,000 or more inhabitants
●   Places of 50,000 to 100,000 inhabitants
○   Places of 25,000 to 50,000 inhabitants outside SMSA's

ARIZONA   Standard Metropolitan
                 Statistical Areas (SMSA's)

SCALE
0   20   40   60   80   100 MILES

Data derived from table 3

Percent change

+13.3 or more	0 to -9.9
0 to +13.2	-10.0 or more

2

Analytical Text

POPULATION TRENDS

General

Between 1960 and 1970 the total population of Arizona grew by 469,000 persons, from 1,302,000 to 1,771,000, an increase of 36 percent over the population living in the State in 1960 (table A). This increase was highly concentrated in the two metropolitan areas of Phoenix and Tucson, which together accounted for 83 percent of the total State growth (390,000 persons). The increase in the population of nonmetropolitan areas was also substantial, amounting to 21 percent for the decade. As a result of these changes, the proportion of Arizona's population living in metropolitan areas rose between 1960 and 1970. At present three out of four persons in the State live in metropolitan areas, compared with a national average of two out of three.

The total number of households in Arizona in 1970 was 539,000, or 173,000 more than in 1960. The population living in households increased more slowly than the rate at which new households were formed, with the result that average household size dropped, from 3.4 to 3.2 persons per unit.

At the time of both censuses, 94 percent of Arizona's metropolitan population and about 80 percent of its nonmetropolitan population were white. The majority of the State's population of other races is American Indian; the balance is mainly Negro. Much different proportions are found in the central cities of the two SMSA's where, in 1970, Negroes comprised 70 percent of races other than white.

The rapid growth of Arizona over the 1960-70 decade was due almost equally to natural increase (the excess of births over deaths) and to net inmigration. A natural increase of 243,000 recorded for the State during this

Table A. Population by Race and Metropolitan and Nonmetropolitan Residence: 1970 and 1960

The State Metropolitan and Non-metropolitan Residence	Population		Change		Percent Distribution	
	1970	1960	Number	Percent	1970	1960
Total...............	1,770,900	1,302,161	468,739	36.0	100.0	100.0
Metropolitan residence...	1,319,189	929,170	390,019	42.0	74.5	71.4
Inside central cities..	844,495	652,062	192,433	29.5	47.7	50.1
Outside central cities.	474,694	277,108	197,586	71.3	26.8	21.3
Nonmetropolitan residence	451,711	372,991	78,720	21.1	25.5	28.6
White...............	1,604,948	1,169,517	435,431	37.2	90.6	89.8
Metropolitan residence...	1,243,742	876,133	367,609	42.0	70.2	67.3
Inside central cities..	791,809	617,133	174,676	28.3	44.7	47.4
Outside central cities.	451,933	259,000	192,933	74.5	25.5	19.9
Nonmetropolitan residence	361,206	293,334	67,822	23.1	20.4	22.5
Negro and other races	165,952	132,644	33,308	25.1	9.4	10.2
Metropolitan residence...	75,447	53,037	22,410	42.3	4.3	4.1
Inside central cities..	52,686	34,929	17,757	50.8	3.0	2.7
Outside central cities.	22,761	18,108	4,653	25.7	1.3	1.4
Nonmetropolitan residence	90,505	79,607	10,898	13.7	5.1	6.1

period was supplemented by a net inmigration of 226,000 persons. Within the State only the metropolitan areas gained population as a result of inmigration. Nonmetropolitan areas show a small net outmigration equivalent to 2 percent of their 1960 population.

Arizona's migratory gain was wholly white. Other races show a net outmigration of 22,000 persons, equivalent to more than 16 percent of their 1960 population.

Throughout Arizona there were large increases in the populations of two broad age groups: 15 to 24 years old and 45 years of age and over (see table 4). The fastest growing age group in metropolitan and nonmetropolitan areas alike was the elderly population, 65 years of age and over. In the State as a whole, this age group increased by 71,000 persons, or by 79 percent over the decade. In the metropolitan areas, the rate of growth for this group was slightly higher, 88 percent. The bulk of the increase in the State's elderly population was due to net inmigration, perhaps as much as 50,000 of the 71,000 increase. Young adults 15 to 24 years of age grew at slightly lower rates, but their numerical increases were much greater than those of the elderly population. The growth of the 45 to 64 year old population was also substantial in all parts of Arizona, particularly in the suburban rings of the two SMSA's. The number of young children under 5 years of age was diminished in both metropolitan and nonmetropolitan areas during the decade, to only a minor extent in the metropolitan areas, but by more than 13 percent in the nonmetropolitan areas. Schoolchildren and adults 25 to 44 years of age show moderate increases for the period.

Changes in the age composition of the population are the product in part of changing birth rates and in part are due to migration which is highly selective by age. Low birth rates during the 1960's contribute to the diminution of the population under 5 years of age, whereas the post-World War II "baby boom" is currently reflected in the large size of the population 15 to 24 years old.

Standard Metropolitan Statistical Areas

At the time of both censuses slightly more than one-half of Arizona's total population lived in the Phoenix SMSA. During the decade Phoenix grew more rapidly than any other metropolitan or nonmetropolitan area in the State, increasing by 304,000 persons, or by 46 percent. In 1970, the population of the SMSA was 968,000. The Tucson SMSA, with a population one-third as large as that of Pheonix, also grew very rapidly during the decade, from 266,000 to 352,000, or by 32 percent. The growth of both SMSA's was based to a larger extent on net inmigration than on natural increase (see table 3).

The fastest growing areas within the two SMSA's were the suburban rings, which had growth rates more than twice as high as the central cities. Nonetheless, there were very large increases in the populations of both central cities over the decade, amounting to 142,000 in Phoenix and 50,000 in Tucson. Between 1960 and 1970 each of these cities annexed suburban territory containing substantial populations (table B). More than 50 percent of the growth of Phoenix city and Tucson city alike was produced by population gained as a result of such annexations. As presently constituted, the major portion of the population of each SMSA resides in the central city: in 1970, 60 percent of the Phoenix's population and 75 percent of Tucson's population was found in the central city.

The age composition of the populations of both Phoenix and Tucson were altered over the decade in the same ways as in the State as a whole: increases in the population 15 to 24 years old and 45 years old and over outweigh all other age changes. In Tucson city, the young adult population and the elderly population 65 and over grew at almost identical rates (by more than 60 percent), but the numerical increase of the 15 to 24 year old population was twice as great. In the city of Phoenix, young adults increased by 77 percent, and the

Table B.   Change in Population of Central Cities Through Annexation: 1960 to 1970

Central Cities	1970 population			1960 population	Change 1960 to 1970 in 1960 area
	Total	In 1960 area	In annexed area		
Phoenix.............	581,562	517,084	64,478	439,170	77,914
Tucson.............	262,933	240,710	22,223	212,892	27,818

elderly population by 50 percent; here 45 to 64 year olds also show a very large gain, of 41 percent.

The dominant feature of population growth in the suburbs of each SMSA was the very rapid rate at which the populations 45 years of age and over grew during the decade. The elderly populations of the suburbs tripled during this period, and the 45 to 64 year old population was doubled. Together their increase accounted for about 40 percent of the total decennial growth of each suburban area.

Counties

Arizona's 14 counties range in population size from 10,000 (Greenlee County) to nearly 1,000,000 in metropolitan Maricopa County (Phoenix SMSA). The second most populous county in the State is Pima, which makes up the Tucson SMSA and has a population of over 350,000. The largest nonmetropolitan counties, with populations over 50,000, are Pinal, Cochise, and Yuma. These five counties, in which 85 percent of the population of Arizona is located, occupy most of the southern half of the State.

All counties in Arizona grew in population size with the exception of the smallest county, Greenlee. Over the decade Greenlee's population was reduced by 10 percent, in consequence of a large outmigration. Ten counties grew at rates exceeding the 13.3 percent increase for the nation as a whole. Only three of the five largest counties grew this rapidly—the two metropolitan counties and Yuma County. The fastest growing county in Arizona and in the Nation was Mohave, which, as a result of substantial inmigration, more than tripled in population size between 1960 and 1970, from 8,000 to 26,000.

Among the nonmetropolitan counties which show large population gains are Yuma and Coconino, each of which contains a fast-growing city. Between 1960 and 1970 the population of Yuma city (Yuma County) increased by 21 percent, from 24,000 to 29,000, and the population of Flagstaff city (Coconino County) increased by 43 percent, from 18,000 to 26,000.

Every county had considerably more births than deaths during the decade. In nine of the 13 counties which show population growth for the period, natural increase was of much greater importance than inmigration. Most of these counties grew in spite of net migratory losses equivalent to as much as 42 percent of 1960 population (Apache County). In only the four fastest-growing counties—the two metropolitan counties, Yuma and Mohave—were significant population gains made as a result of large-scale net inmigration.

In addition to the two metropolitan counties, there are six counties in Arizona which contain a large enough population of races other than white (mainly Indian) to have this population shown separately in the table on county components of change (see "Definitions and Explanations"). In each of these counties, the Indian population grew over the decade; in five of the nonmetropolitan counties, there was growth in spite of substantial net outmigration.

HOUSING TRENDS

General

During the decade, the total supply of housing units in Arizona increased faster than population. While housing units increased by 168,300, or 40 percent, the population increased by 469,000, or 36 percent (table C).

Table C. Housing Units by Metropolitan and Nonmetropolitan Residence: 1970 and 1960

The State Metropolitan and Nonmetropolitan Residence	Housing units				Population percent change
	Total		Change		
	1970	1960	Number	Percent	
Total.................	584,171	415,834	168,337	40.5	36.0
Metropolitan residence.....	437,337	297,081	140,256	47.2	42.0
Inside central cities....	284,345	212,124	72,221	34.0	29.5
Outside central cities...	152,992	84,957	68,035	80.1	71.3
Nonmetropolitan residence..	146,834	118,753	28,081	23.6	21.1

The metropolitan areas of the State experienced the greatest relative growth in housing, as in population. The number of housing units in the metropolitan areas increased from 297,081 to 437,337 over the decade, an increase of 140,256, or 47 percent; this compares with an increase of 28,100 units, or 24 percent, in the nonmetropolitan areas. Almost three out of four housing units were located in the Phoenix and Tucson SMSA's; these areas accounted for more than 83 percent of the total State increase between 1960 and 1970.

A trend toward smaller households is evident in the State. Households consisting of one or two persons experienced large gains, while the number of larger households grew more slowly.

Homeownership rates in Arizona were slightly higher in 1970 than in 1960, about 65 percent and 64 percent, respectively. Estimated value of housing increased during the decade from a median of $11,100 in 1960 to $16,400 in 1970, with substantial increases in homes valued at $15,000 or more. In the State, rents increased by more than one-half (about 54 percent) with large increases in the number of units renting at $80 or more.

Value and rent are expressed in current dollars (the dollar value at the time of the respective censuses). Thus, any comparison must take into account the general rise in the cost of living during the 10-year period, as well as changes in the characteristics of the housing inventory.

The number of units in the State lacking some or all plumbing facilities declined from 55,800 to 30,200, a 46-percent decrease since 1960. In 1970, the proportion of such units was 5 percent of all year-round units.

Number of persons per room is often used as a measure of crowding. In Arizona as a whole, units with 1.01 or more persons per room comprised less than 13 percent of all occupied housing units in 1970, compared with 19 percent in 1960 (table D). The number of all such units in 1970 was 68,200, a decrease of about 1,700, or 2 percent, between 1960 and 1970; virtually all of the decline occurred in nonmetropolitan areas.

Standard Metropolitan Statistical Areas

The increase in the housing supply in the two SMSA's during the decade was 140,300 housing units, of which more than three-fourths (106,800) was in the Phoenix area. This produced a 50-percent increase in the Phoenix SMSA and 39 percent in the Tucson SMSA.

Average household size (population per occupied unit) declined in both SMSA's during the decade. Population per occupied unit for both Phoenix and Tucson was 3.1 in 1970, compared with 3.4 and 3.3, respectively, in 1960.

The two SMSA's revealed similarities in homeownership patterns. Rates of homeownership in the central cities in 1970 were nearly identical (63.8 percent in Phoenix and 64.2 in Tucson); likewise in the suburban rings, Phoenix showed a rate of 70.4 and Tucson 69.3.

The median value of owner-occupied housing in the Phoenix and Tucson SMSA's increased between 1960 and 1970, from $11,700 to $17,500 in Phoenix and

Table D. Plumbing Facilities and Persons Per Room by Metropolitan and Nonmetropolitan Residence: 1970 and 1960

The State Metropolitan and Nonmetropolitan Residence	Percent of housing units			
	Lacking some or all plumbing facilities		With 1.01 or more persons per room[1]	
	1970[2]	1960[3]	1970	1960
Total.....................	5.2	13.4	12.7	19.1
Metropolitan residence...........	2.8	8.4	10.1	15.6
Inside central cities..........	2.0	5.8	9.5	13.3
Outside central cities........	4.2	14.7	11.3	21.7
Nonmetropolitan residence........	12.7	26.1	21.0	28.5

[1]Percent of all occupied units.
[2]Percent of all year-round housing units.
[3]Percent of all housing units.

from $11,600 to $16,700 in Tucson. The Phoenix SMSA showed a decrease in the number of units valued below $15,000, while the Tucson SMSA showed a decrease in the number of units valued below $10,000, with a small increase (about 4 percent) in the $10,000 to $14,999 value range. Both SMSA's reflected large percentage increases in the number of units valued above $15,000, with greater increases in number of units valued at $20,000 or more. Median contract rent rose from $64 to $105 in the Phoenix SMSA and from $63 to $92 in the Tucson SMSA.

In both the Phoenix and the Tucson SMSA's, 3 percent of the housing units lacked some or all plumbing facilities in 1970 compared with 8 percent in 1960.

The proportion of housing units in the Phoenix SMSA with 1.01 or more persons per room in 1970 was 10 percent, compared with 16 percent in 1960. The comparable percentages for Tucson were 11 percent in 1970 and 16 percent in 1960.

The homeowner vacancy rates for the SMSA's decreased from 2.6 to 0.9 percent for Phoenix and from 2.8 to 1.4 for Tucson. Rental vacancy rates for the Phoenix SMSA decreased from 11.1 to 7.2 and for Tucson from 11.1 to 8.0.

Annexation

Annexations occurred in the central cities of Phoenix and Tucson during the decade (see "Population Trends" and text table B). Such annexations affect changes in the characteristics for these central cities and their suburbs.

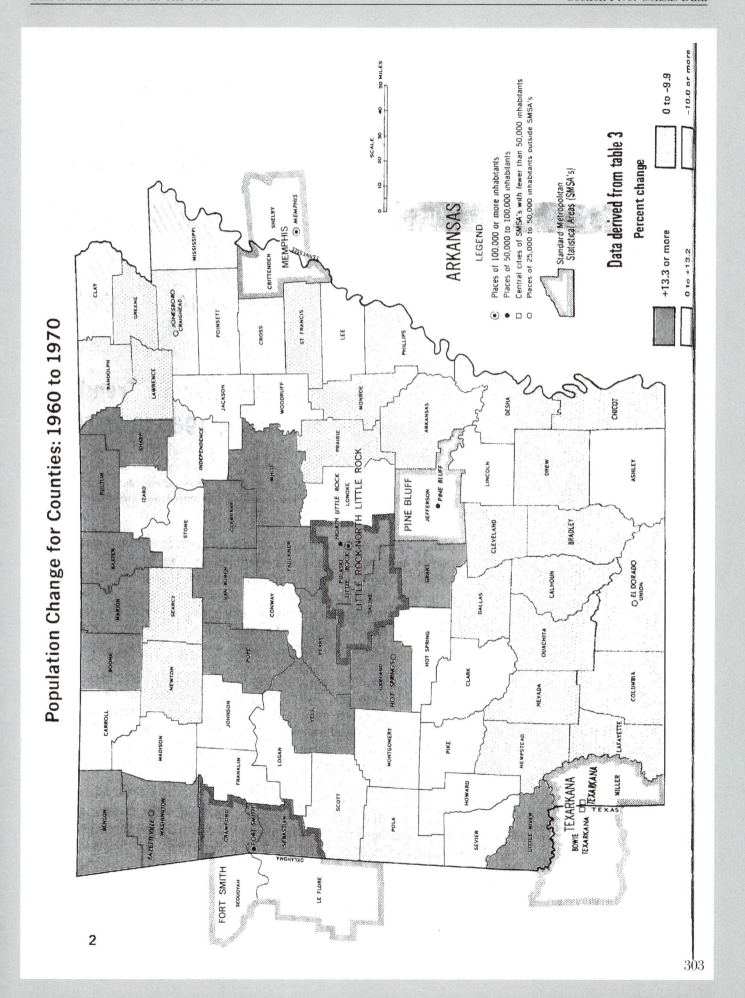

Population Change for Counties: 1960 to 1970

Analytical Text

POPULATION TRENDS

General

Between 1960 and 1970, the total population of Arkansas grew by 137,000, from 1,786,000 to 1,923,000, an increase of 7.7 percent over the population living in the State in 1960 (table A). This rate of increase is only about half that for the United States as a whole (13.3 percent). The increase in the population of metropolitan areas was somewhat higher than that of nonmetropolitan areas (74,000 compared with 63,000). Rates of gain show considerable differences, however. The nonmetropolitan areas, which contain 69 percent of the State's population, grew by only 5 percent, while metropolitan areas grew by 14 percent.

The total number of households in the State in 1970 was 614,000, or 91,000 more than in 1960. The population living in households increased less rapidly than the rate at which households increased with the result that average household size decreased from 3.4 to 3.1 persons.

The effect of these changes on population distribution by metropolitan-nonmetropolitan residence was very small. The proportion of the total population living in metropolitan areas increased by only 2 percentage points during the decade. Only three out of 10 persons in Arkansas now live in metropolitan areas compared with a national average of two out of three.

In 1970, the white population accounted for 78 percent of the metropolitan area population, a somewhat higher proportion than in 1960. Similarly, in nonmetropolitan areas the white population comprised a greater proportion of the total in 1970 (83 percent) than in 1960 (80 percent). Within metropolitan areas, the white population increased its share only in suburban areas; in the central cities their position remained the same.

All areas of the State experienced significant changes in age composition. There was a decline in the number of children under 5 years of age during the 1960-70 decade, from 194,000 to 159,000, a loss of 18 percent for this age group. Only small gains were registered by the 5-14 and 25-44 age groups, but all other age groups

Table A. Population by Race and Metropolitan and Nonmetropolitan Residence: 1970 and 1960

The State Metropolitan and Non-metropolitan Residence	Population		Change		Percent Distribution	
	1970	1960	Number	Percent	1970	1960
Total..............	1,923,295	1,786,272	137,023	7.7	100.0	100.0
Metropolitan residence...	595,030	520,562	74,468	14.3	30.9	29.1
Inside central cities..	334,396	282,661	51,735	18.3	17.4	15.8
Outside central cities.	260,634	237,901	22,733	9.6	13.6	13.3
Nonmetropolitan residence	1,328,265	1,265,710	62,555	4.9	69.1	70.9
White..............	1,561,108	1,395,703	165,405	11.9	81.2	78.1
Metropolitan residence...	461,441	389,584	71,857	18.4	24.0	21.8
Inside central cities..	256,223	216,332	39,891	18.4	13.3	12.1
Outside central cities.	205,218	173,252	31,966	18.5	10.7	9.7
Nonmetropolitan residence	1,099,667	1,006,119	93,548	9.3	57.2	56.3
Negro and other races	362,187	390,569	-28,382	-7.3	18.8	21.9
Metropolitan residence...	133,589	130,978	2,611	2.0	6.9	7.3
Inside central cities..	78,173	66,329	11,844	17.9	4.1	3.7
Outside central cities.	55,416	64,649	-9,233	-14.3	2.9	3.6
Nonmetropolitan residence	228,598	259,591	-30,993	-11.9	11.9	14.5

grew substantially. The 15-24 year old population shows greatest growth (nearly 30 percent).

Similar changes are found in other sections of the country and are due in part to changing birth rates and in part to migration, which is highly selective by age. Low birth rates during the depression years and in the 1960's contribute to the diminution of age groups 25-44 and under 5, whereas the post-World War II "baby boom" is currently reflected in the large size of the population 15-24 years old.

Standard Metropolitan Statistical Areas

There are two Standard Metropolitan Statistical Areas (SMSA's) entirely within Arkansas: Little Rock North Little Rock and Pine Bluff. Three other SMSA's are only partially in Arkansas: Fort Smith, Ark.-Okla., Texarkana, Tex.-Ark., and Memphis, Tenn.-Ark.

The Little Rock-North Little Rock SMSA had a population of 323,000 in 1970 compared with 272,000 in 1960, an increase of 19 percent over the decade. Little Rock is the capital of Arkansas. Situated in the center of the State it provides trade, service and financial assistance to the rest of the State. It also has significant primary metals production. Pine Bluff is a much smaller SMSA (85,000 population). It carries on some primary metals manufacturing.

Both SMSA's had significant numbers of Negroes. In Little Rock-North Little Rock, 20 percent of the population was black in 1970 and in Pine Bluff, 41 percent. In the other metropolitan counties in the State, the Negro proportion varied substantially. In 1970, 5 percent of the Arkansas portion of the Fort Smith SMSA was Negro, 47 percent of the Arkansas portion of the Memphis SMSA, and 23 percent of the Arkansas portion of the Texarkana SMSA.

Annexation of territory during the decade was responsible for additions to the five central cities in Arkansas. The addition to Fort Smith was very minor. However, the city's own growth resulted in an 18 percent increase in population. The annexations for Little Rock, North Little Rock, Pine Bluff and Texarkana added populations of about 35,000, 6,000, 14,000, and 3,000 to these cities, respectively. Without annexation, these central cities would have shown population losses for the decade (table B).

Generally, the age distribution of the metropolitan population shows the same tendencies as for the State as a whole. Children under 5 years of age declined, but all other age groups increased.

Counties

Between 1960 and 1970 46 of the 75 counties in Arkansas increased in population. These counties are located in the central part of the State and on its western and northern borders (see map). Twenty-one of these growing counties registered an increase above the Nation's average of 13.3 percent. Those with the most rapid growth were: Baxter (54 percent); Benton (39); Washington (39); Pope (35); Sharp (30); and Faulkner (30). The largest county, Pulaski, with a population of 287,000 in 1970, had an 18 percent growth rate for the decade. Of the 29 counties with losses (located chiefly on Arkansas' borders with Louisiana and Mississippi), seven had declines of 10 percent or more. They were: Clay, Jackson, Lee, Lincoln, Mississippi, Poinsett and Woodruff.

Every county had more births than deaths during the decade. However, 41 of the counties had net outmigration and 26 of these suffered a population decline as the excess of births over deaths did not offset net outmigra-

Table B. Change in Population of Central Cities Through Annexation: 1960 to 1970

Central Cities	1970 population			1960 population	Change 1960 to 1970 in 1960 area
	Total	In 1960 area	In annexed area		
Fort Smith	62,802	62,207	595	52,991	9,216
Little Rock	132,483	97,572	34,911	107,813	-10,241
North Little Rock	60,040	53,718	6,322	58,032	-4,314
Pine Bluff	57,389	43,042	14,347	44,037	-995
Texarkana	21,682	18,979	2,703	19,788	-809

tion. The counties with net inmigration generally were the fast growing ones in the central part of the State and those on the western and northern borders.

Thirty-eight counties in the State contained a large enough population of Negro and other races to have this group shown separately in the table on county components of change (see "Definitions and Explanations"). Only five counties had increases in the population of Negro and other races: Faulkner (16 percent), Pulaski (15), Garland (7), Little River (7), and Howard (6). The increases were achieved despite net outmigration. Twenty-five counties had declines in Negro population which exceeded 10 percent or more. Among these 25, the highest declines were in Woodruff (29 percent), Poinsett (28), St. Francis (23), Lincoln (22), and Cleveland (22).

HOUSING TRENDS

General

During the decade the total supply of housing units in Arkansas increased by 87,500, or 15 percent, while population grew by 137,000, or 8 percent (table C).

The metropolitan areas of the State experienced greater relative growth in housing (as in population), than did the nonmetropolitan part. The number of housing units in metropolitan areas rose from 166,000 to 201,200 over the decade, an increase of 35,200 units, or 21 percent; this compares with an increase of 52,300 units, or 12 percent, in nonmetropolitan areas. While the metropolitan areas contained 30 percent of the housing

in Arkansas, the additions to the housing supply in these areas accounted for 40 percent of Arkansas' total housing increase between 1960 and 1970.

About 86 percent of the housing in Arkansas consisted of one-unit structures in 1970. The number of units in multiunit structures, however, increased at a much faster rate than one-unit structures during the decade, 65 percent and 7 percent, respectively.

The size of housing units increased between 1960 and 1970. The median number of rooms rose from 4.5 to 4.8 in metropolitan areas and from 4.4 to 4.7 in nonmetropolitan areas. Units with one to four rooms declined or had only small relative gains, whereas those with five rooms or more had large percentage increases over the decade.

Households were smaller in 1970 than in 1960. In both metropolitan and nonmetropolitan areas, average household size declined from 3.4 persons in 1960 to 3.1 in 1970. The largest percentage increases in household size for Arkansas were in one-person households—67 percent in metropolitan areas and 58 percent in nonmetropolitan areas. Households with five or more persons showed relatively small gains in metropolitan areas and losses in nonmetropolitan areas.

The number of units lacking some or all plumbing facilities declined from 253,300 to 124,000, a 51-percent decrease since 1960. In 1970, the proportion of such units was 18 percent of all year-round units.

Number of persons per room is often used as a measure of crowding. In Arkansas, both the number and proportion of housing units with 1.01 or more persons per room decreased during the decade. In 1960, 18 percent of all occupied housing units had more than one

Table C. Housing Units by Metropolitan and Nonmetropolitan Residence: 1970 and 1960

The State Metropolitan and Nonmetropolitan Residence	Housing units					Population percent change
	Total		Change			
	1970	1960	Number	Percent		
Total..............	674,059	586,552	87,507	14.9		7.7
Metropolitan residence.....	201,196	165,985	35,211	21.2		14.3
Inside central cities....	119,643	95,957	23,686	24.7		18.3
Outside central cities...	81,553	70,028	11,525	16.5		9.6
Nonmetropolitan residence..	472,863	420,567	52,296	12.4		4.9

person per room. By 1970, the proportion of such units had decreased to 11 percent (table D).

Homeownership in Arkansas increased from 61 percent in 1960 to 67 percent in 1970. In metropolitan areas there was an increase from 61 to 65 percent, while in nonmetropolitan areas the proportion rose from 62 to 67 percent.

Estimated value of housing increased during the 10-year period from a median $6,700 in 1960 to $10,600 in 1970, with large percentage increases in homes valued at $10,000 or more. Rents increased from $34 to $52, or 53 percent, with substantial increases in the number of units rented at $60 or more.

Value and rent are expressed in current dollars (the value at the time of the respective censuses). Thus, any comparison must take into account the general rise in the cost of living during the 10-year period as well as changes in the characteristics of the housing inventory.

Standard Metropolitan Statistical Areas

Average household size for the metropolitan area declined during the decade. In the central cities, the average was 2.9 persons in 1970, and, in the suburbs, 3.4.

In 1970, 21,600 housing units in metropolitan areas, or 11 percent of all year-round units, lacked some or all plumbing facilities. The corresponding proportion in the central cities was 5 percent, compared with 19 percent in the suburbs.

Of all occupied units in metropolitan areas, 19,100 units, or 10 percent, reported more than one person per room in 1970, compared with 17 percent in 1960. In 1970, the proportion of such units was 8 percent in the central cities and 14 percent in the suburbs.

The homeowner vacancy rate for metropolitan areas was recorded at 1.8 percent in 1970 as in 1960. The rental vacancy rate increased from 8.4 to 8.7 percent.

Annexations

Annexations occurred in the central cities of Little Rock, North Little Rock, and Pine Bluff during the decade (see "Population Trends" and text table B). Such annexations affect changes in the characteristics for these central cities and their suburbs.

Table D. Plumbing Facilities and Persons Per Room by Metropolitan and Nonmetropolitan Residence: 1970 and 1960

The State Metropolitan and Nonmetropolitan Residence	Percent of housing units			
	Lacking some or all plumbing facilities		With 1.01 or more persons per room[1]	
	1970[2]	1960[3]	1970	1960
Total......................	18.5	43.2	10.8	17.8
Metropolitan residence...........	10.7	(NA)	10.2	16.8
Inside central cities..........	5.0	14.8	7.8	12.5
Outside central cities.........	19.2	(NA)	13.8	22.7
Nonmetropolitan residence........	21.8	(NA)	11.0	18.2

NA Not available.
[1]Percent of all occupied units.
[2]Percent of all year-round housing units.
[3]Percent of all housing units.

Population Change for Counties: 1960 to 1970

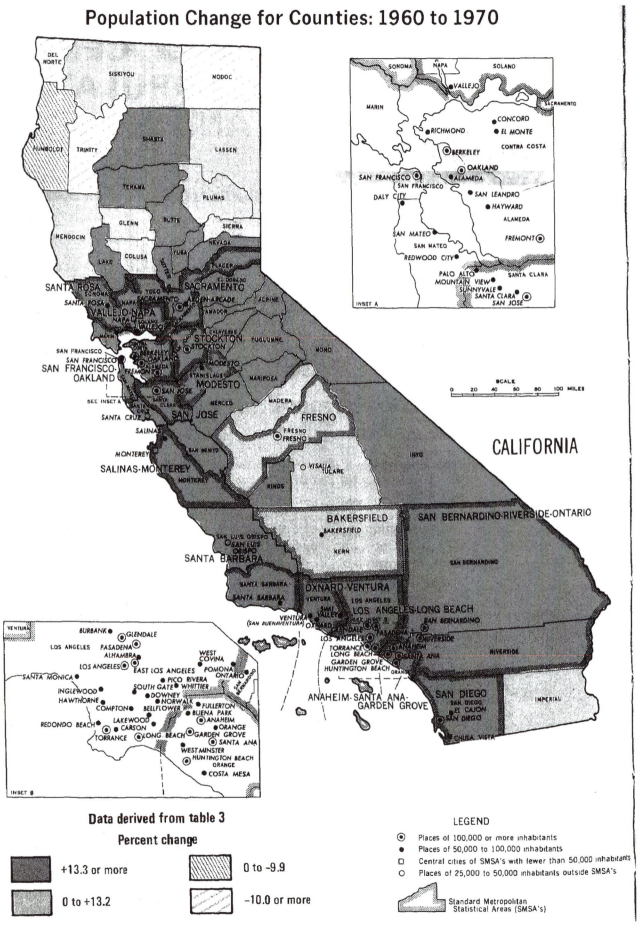

Data derived from table 3

Percent change

+13.3 or more

0 to +13.2

0 to -9.9

-10.0 or more

LEGEND

⊙ Places of 100,000 or more inhabitants

● Places of 50,000 to 100,000 inhabitants

□ Central cities of SMSA's with fewer than 50,000 inhabitants

○ Places of 25,000 to 50,000 inhabitants outside SMSA's

Standard Metropolitan Statistical Areas (SMSA's)

Analytical Text

POPULATION TRENDS

General

Between 1960 and 1970, the population of California grew from 15,717,000 to 19,953,000, an increase of 4,236,000 or 27.0 percent. This rate of increase is double the rate for the entire United States (13.3 percent) and is above the rate for the other 12 States in the West region (20.4 percent). In its rate of increase California ranked fifth behind Nevada, Florida, Arizona, and Alaska. The total number of households in California in 1970 was 6,574,000, or 1,593,000 more than in 1960. The population living in households increased more slowly than the rate at which households increased with the result that average household size dropped from 3.1 to 2.9 persons. In the Nation as a whole there was an average of 3.1 persons per household in 1970.

The census of 1970 was the first one to show California as the most populous State in the Nation. New York ranked first in censuses from 1820 through 1960. In each decade since 1900, the rate of population growth in California has been two to four times the national average. During the 1900 to 1970 period, California's population increased from 1.5 million to nearly 20 million while the national population increased from 76 million to 203 million. Between 1940 and 1970, California's population grew by 13 million which is more than the 1970 population of any other State except New York. During the 30-year period, nearly one-fifth of the population growth in the United States occurred in California. In 1900, California ranked 21st in population among the States. In 1970, California's population was larger than the combined population of the 20 least populous States.

Between 1960 and 1970, the metropolitan population in California grew by 28 percent from 14,482,000 to 18,500,000 and the nonmetropolitan population grew by 18 percent from 1,236,000 to 1,453,000 (table A). In 1970, 93 percent of the population lived in metropolitan areas, a higher percentage than in any other State. In the Nation as a whole, two-thirds of the population live in metropolitan areas.

Table A. Population by Race and Metropolitan and Nonmetropolitan Residence: 1970 and 1960

The State Metropolitan and Non-metropolitan Residence	Population		Change		Percent Distribution	
	1970	1960	Number	Percent	1970	1960
Total................	19,953,134	15,717,204	4,235,930	27.0	100.0	100.0
Metropolitan residence...	18,500,006	14,481,594	4,018,412	27.7	92.7	92.1
Inside central cities..	7,243,169	6,019,256	1,223,913	20.3	36.3	38.3
Outside central cities.	11,256,837	8,462,338	2,794,499	33.0	56.4	53.8
Nonmetropolitan residence	1,453,128	1,235,610	217,518	17.6	7.3	7.9
White................	17,761,032	14,455,230	3,305,802	22.9	89.0	92.0
Metropolitan residence...	16,384,623	13,272,051	3,112,572	23.5	82.1	84.4
Inside central cities..	5,925,579	5,222,513	723,066	13.9	29.7	33.1
Outside central cities.	10,459,044	8,069,538	2,389,506	29.6	52.4	51.3
Nonmetropolitan residence	1,376,409	1,183,179	193,230	16.3	6.9	7.5
Negro and other races	2,192,102	1,261,974	930,128	73.7	11.0	8.0
Metropolitan residence...	2,115,383	1,209,543	905,840	74.9	10.6	7.7
Inside central cities..	1,317,590	816,743	500,847	61.3	6.6	5.2
Outside central cities.	797,793	392,800	404,993	103.1	4.0	2.5
Nonmetropolitan residence	76,719	52,431	24,288	46.3	0.4	0.3

Within metropolitan areas, the population of central cities grew by 20 percent from 6,019,000 to 7,243,000, and the population outside central cities grew by 33 percent from 8,462,000 to 11,257,000. One-third of the growth in central cities was due to annexation (table B).

The population of Negro and other races (about two-thirds of which is Negro) increased from 1,262,000 in 1960 to 2,192,000, or by 74 percent. In 1970, 11 percent of California's population was comprised of Negro and other races, up from 8 percent in 1960. Three-fifths of the population of Negro and other races lived in the central cities of metropolitan areas compared to one-third of the white population.

The population increase of 4,236,000 in California in the 1960 to 1970 decade was divided equally between natural increase (births minus deaths) and net inmigra-

tion. In each decade from 1880 to 1960, over half of California's population growth was due to net inmigration. The net inmigration of 2,113,000 between 1960 and 1970 was equivalent to 13 percent of the 1960 population. The amount of net inmigration was larger than in any other State. In its rate of net inmigration, California ranked fourth behind Nevada, Florida, and Arizona. Among Negro and other races in California, net inmigration during the decade was 585,000, which accounted for three-fifths of the population growth in this group.

The age structure of the California population changed significantly between 1960 and 1970. The only decline occurred among the population under 5 years old and was due largely to the decline in birth rates which occurred throughout the United States during the

Table B. Change in Population of Central Cities Through Annexation: 1960 to 1970

Central Cities	1970 population			1960 population	Change 1960 to 1970 in 1960 area
	Total	In 1960 area	In annexed area		
Los Angeles	2,816,061	2,805,768	10,293	2,479,015	326,753
Long Beach	358,633	350,827	7,806	344,168	6,659
Oakland	361,561	360,842	719	367,548	-6,706
San Diego	696,769	686,824	9,945	573,224	113,600
San Bernardino	104,251	98,159	6,092	91,922	6,237
Riverside	140,089	96,643	43,446	84,332	12,331
Ontario	64,118	60,409	3,709	46,617	13,792
San Jose	445,779	365,798	79,981	204,196	161,602
Sacramento	254,413	190,531	63,882	191,667	-1,136
Anaheim	166,701	151,464	15,237	104,184	47,280
Santa Ana	156,601	143,037	13,564	100,350	42,687
Garden Grove	122,524	110,969	11,555	84,238	26,731
Fresno	165,972	138,499	27,473	133,929	4,570
Bakersfield	69,515	56,353	13,162	56,848	-495
Stockton	107,644	102,026	5,618	86,321	15,705
Vallejo	66,733	64,276	2,457	60,877	3,399
Napa	35,978	27,028	8,950	22,170	4,858
Santa Barbara	70,215	68,465	1,750	58,768	9,697
Oxnard	71,225	45,839	25,386	40,265	5,574
Ventura (San Buenaventura)	55,797	33,625	22,172	29,114	4,511
Salinas	58,896	43,405	15,491	28,957	14,448
Monterey	26,302	26,224	78	22,618	3,606
Modesto	61,712	40,074	21,638	36,585	3,489
Santa Rosa	50,006	37,394	12,612	31,027	6,367

1960's. The greatest increase (71 percent) occurred in the 15 to 24 age group and was due largely to the entry of the large number of persons born during the post-World War II "baby boom" into this age group. As a result of these changes, the proportion of the total population in the under 5 group declined from 11 to 8 percent and the proportion in the 15 to 24 group increased from 13 to 18 percent.

The population of Negro and other races in California has a young age structure. Among the total population of California in 1970, 46 percent were under age 25 and 9 percent were age 65 and over. Among Negro and other races, 52 percent were under age 25 and only 5 percent were age 65 and over.

Standard Metropolitan Statistical Areas

In 1970, there were 16 standard metropolitan statistical areas (SMSA's) in California, including six of the Nation's 33 SMSA's with populations exceeding 1 million.

Between 1960 and 1970, the population of the six SMSA's in Southern California increased by 29 percent.

The Los Angeles-Long Beach SMSA, which is the largest in California and the second largest in the Nation behind the New York City SMSA, grew from 6,039,000 to 7,032,000, or by 16 percent, during the decade. Negro and other races constitute about one-seventh of the population of the Los Angeles-Long Beach SMSA. Los Angeles, which with a 1970 population of 2,816,000 is the third largest city in the Nation, is a leading national manufacturing commercial, transportation, and maritime center as well as the hub of an area known for its movie industry and mild climate. In 1900, the Los Angeles-Long Beach SMSA had a population of only 170,000, and the city of Los Angeles was only the 36th largest city in the Nation.

The population of the Anaheim-Santa Ana-Garden Grove SMSA grew from 704,000 in 1960 to 1,420,000 in 1970, or by 102 percent, making it one of two of the 243 SMSA's in the Nation in 1970 that doubled in population during the decade. The Anaheim-Santa Ana-Garden Grove SMSA, which previously was part of the Los Angeles-Long Beach SMSA and which still has close economic ties, had a population in 1940 less than one-tenth as large as in 1970.

The San Diego SMSA grew from 1,033,000 to 1,358,000, or by 31 percent during the 1960 to 1970 decade. Part of the area's growth is attributable to the United States Navy and Marine Corps, the two largest facilities being the San Diego Navy Base and Camp Pendleton Marine Corps Base. San Diego is also an important port and food processing center. In each decade from 1910 to 1960, the rate of population

growth in the San Diego SMSA was at least four times as high as in the Nation as a whole.

The population of the San Bernardino-Riverside SMSA increased from 810,000 in 1960 to 1,143,000 in 1970, or by 41 percent. The vast area of the SMSA (27,000 square miles) is deceptive because more than four-fifths of the population live within 25 miles of the "twin" cities of San Bernardino and Riverside. The area's diversified economy includes food processing and heavy industry as well as desert spas for which it is noted (e.g., Palm Springs).

The Oxnard-Ventura SMSA and the Santa Barbara SMSA are characterized by fruit and vegetable farming, light industry, resort activites, and prosperous residential areas. Oxnard-Ventura, also an oil-producing area, began to experience suburbanization from Los Angeles after 1960. Santa Barbara is the site of a rapidly growing State university. Between 1960 and 1970, the population of the Oxnard-Ventura SMSA increased 89 percent to 376,000, and the population of the Santa Barbara SMSA increased 56 percent to 264,000. In each decade since 1910, the rate of population growth in the Oxnard-Ventura SMSA was at least triple the national average.

The population of the four SMSA's in the San Francisco Bay area increased by 27 percent between 1960 and 1970.

The San Francisco-Oakland SMSA, which is the second largest in California and the sixth largest in the Nation, grew from 2,649,000 to 3,110,000, or by 17 percent, during the decade. Negro and other races constitute about one-sixth of the population in the SMSA. The population in the two central cities, dropped from 1,108,000 to 1,077,000 while the population in the balance of the SMSA increased by nearly one-third from 1,541,000 to 2,032,000. As is the case in Los Angeles, San Francisco and Oakland represent the nucleus of a major national manufacturing, commercial, transportation, and maritime center. In addition the area is noted for its mild climate, cultural activities, and ethnic diversity.

The population of the San Jose SMSA grew from 642,000 in 1960 to 1,065,000 in 1970, or by 66 percent. In 1940 the population was less than one-sixth as large as in 1970. Prior to World War II, the area's economy was based largely on food canning; however, during the last two decades, the San Jose area has become a leading national producer of electronic equipment.

During the 1960 to 1970 decade, the population of the Vallejo-Napa SMSA increased by 24 percent to 249,000, and the population of the Santa Rosa SMSA increased by 39 percent to 205,000. While the population growth in each of these SMSA's is due in part to suburban expansion from the San Francisco-Oakland

MSA, poultry and dairy farming, horticulture, and the remost vineyards in the Nation underlie the economy these two SMSA's. Vallejo is a port on San Francisco ay and the location of a Navy shipyard.

Between 1960 and 1970, the population of the five MSA's in the California Central Valley increased by 20 ercent.

The Sacramento SMSA had a population of 801,000 1970, an increase of 28 percent since 1960. In each ecade since 1920, the rate of population growth has een at least double the national average. Expanded overnmental activity in the capital city of Sacramento nderlies this growth along with the goods and services acramento provides to its rich agricultural hinterland.

In 1970, the Fresno SMSA had a population of 13,000, and the Bakersfield SMSA had a population of 29,000. Both are located in the Upper San Joaquin alley and had population increases of only 13 percent etween 1960 and 1970 after more than doubling in opulation between 1940 and 1960. The processing of ruits and cotton are included in Fresno's diversified conomy while Bakersfield is the focal point of California's petroleum industry.

In 1970, the Stockton SMSA had a population of 90,000, an increase of 16 percent since 1960, and the Modesto SMSA had a population of 195,000, up 24 ercent from 1960. The economies of Stockton and Modesto are centered on processing the agricultural roduction of the Lower San Joaquin Valley.

The Salinas-Monterey SMSA, located on the coast etween the San Francisco Bay area and Southern California, had a 1970 population of 250,000, an ncrease of 26 percent over 1960. Vegetable farming, ood processing, and the tourist trade of the Monterey Peninsula have contributed to the area's steady growth during the past 50 years. Fort Ord, a large army base, is ocated near the city of Monterey.

Counties

Of the 58 counties in California, 53 gained population and five lost population between 1960 and 1970. Forty-one counties had rates of growth above the national average of 13.3 percent and three counties experienced population declines of 10 percent or more. In the Nation as a whole, slightly more than half of all counties gained population during the decade.

With the exception of Lake County, every county in California had a natural increase (i.e., births outnumbered deaths) between 1960 and 1970. Lake County is a retirement center and has an "old" age structure. In 1970, 52 percent of Lake County's population was aged 45 and over compared to only 29 percent in the State as a whole.

Forty-two of California's 58 counties had a net inmigration during the 1960 to 1970 decade. In the Nation as a whole, less than one-third of all counties experienced net inmigration. The largest net inmigration (551,000) and the highest rate of net inmigration (equivalent to 78 percent of the 1960 population) occurred in Orange County, which constitutes the Anaheim-Santa Ana-Garden Grove SMSA. Seven counties had a net inmigration exceeding 100,000, and with the exception of Santa Clara County, which constitutes the San Jose SMSA, these counties are in Southern California. The net inmigration in Orange County was larger than in any other county in the Nation.

In 1970, nearly three-fifths of California's population lived in the eight counties in Southern California. Between 1960 and 1970, the population of these eight counties increased by 29 percent while the population of the remainder of the State increased by 23 percent. During most previous decades since 1900, the rate of population growth was much higher in Southern California than in the remainder of the State. In 1900, only one-fifth of California's population lived in these eight southern counties.

The population of the 16 counties in the predominantly rural Eastern and Northern California mountain and valley area increased by 23 percent to 299,000 between 1960 and 1970. Much of the growth is attributable to increased recreational activities for the State's metropolitan population.

The population of the four counties along the Northern California Coast Area (Del Norte, Humboldt, Mendocino, and Lake counties) declined slightly during the decade to 185,000 in 1970. Lumber production, the basic activity in this area, fell off after 1960.

The population of San Francisco County, which is coextensive with the city of San Francisco, declined by 3 percent to 716,000 in 1970.

HOUSING TRENDS

General

Between 1960 and 1970, the total supply of housing units in California increased at about the same rate as population. The population grew by 4,236,000, or 27 percent, and housing units increased by 1,531,100, or 28 percent (table C).

The metropolitan areas of the State experienced greater relative growth in housing, as in population, than did the nonmetropolitan part. The number of housing units in metropolitan areas rose over the decade to 6,456,600, an increase of 1,447,200 units, or 29 percent; this compares with an increase of 83,900 units, or 18 percent, in the nonmetropolitan areas. Approximately 92 percent of all housing units were in metropolitan areas; these areas accounted for 95 percent of the total State increase between 1960 and 1970.

About 67 percent of the housing in California consisted of one-unit structures in 1970. The corresponding proportions in metropolitan and nonmetropolitan areas were 66 percent and 82 percent, respectively.

In 1970, about 143,700, or 2 percent, of the housing units in the State lacked some or all plumbing facilities. The proportion of housing units lacking plumbing facilities was smaller in the State's metropolitan areas (2 percent) than in the nonmetropolitan areas (4 percent). Approximately 9,500, or 2 percent, of the Negro-occupied units in the State lacked some or all plumbing in 1970. Inside metropolitan areas, 2 percent of the Negro-occupied housing lacked such plumbing, compared with 7 percent outside the metropolitan areas.

Households were smaller in 1970 than in 1960. In the metropolitan areas, average household size declined from 3.0 persons in 1960 to 2.9 in 1970 and in nonmetropolitan areas, from 3.2 to 3.0 persons. The number of one-person households increased by 56 percent in metropolitan areas and by 41 percent in nonmetropolitan areas. In comparison, households with five or more persons increased 25 percent in metropolitan areas and 8 percent in nonmetropolitan areas.

The median number of rooms was 4.7 in the metropolitan areas and 4.6 in nonmetropolitan areas. About 31 percent of the metropolitan housing units had six or more rooms, compared with 25 percent of the nonmetropolitan housing.

Number of persons per room is often used as a measure of crowding. In California, the proportion of housing units with 1.01 or more persons per room decreased during the decade. In 1960, 9 percent of all occupied housing units in metropolitan areas and 14 percent in nonmetropolitan areas had 1.01 or more

Table C. Housing Units by Metropolitan and Nonmetropolitan Residence: 1970 and 1960

The State Metropolitan and Nonmetropolitan Residence	Housing units				Population percent change
	Total		Change		
	1970	1960	Number	Percent	
Total.................	6,996,990	5,465,870	1,531,120	28.0	27.0
Metropolitan residence.....	6,456,555	5,009,330	1,447,225	28.9	27.7
Inside central cities....	2,699,218	2,228,304	470,914	21.1	20.3
Outside central cities...	3,757,337	2,781,026	976,311	35.1	33.0
Nonmetropolitan residence..	540,435	456,540	83,895	18.4	17.6

persons per room. By 1970, the proportion of such units decreased to 8 percent in metropolitan areas and 10 percent in nonmetropolitan areas (table D).

The homeownership rate decreased in metropolitan areas from 58 percent in 1960 to 54 percent in 1970. In nonmetropolitan areas, the homeownership rate was about the same (61.7 percent in 1960 and 61.4 percent in 1970). Of the 3,611,300 owner-occupied units in California, 3,324,900 were inside metropolitan areas and the remainder were outside these areas.

About 39 percent of the Negro households in metropolitan areas and 44 percent in nonmetropolitan areas owned their homes in 1970. Of the 166,300 Negro-homeowner households in the State, 163,200 lived inside SMSA's and 3,100 lived outside SMSA's.

Property values and rents increased during the decade. The median value of owner-occupied housing in metropolitan areas increased by 54 percent, from $15,300 in 1960 to $23,500 in 1970, while in the nonmetropolitan areas the median increased 45 percent, from $11,000 to $16,000. In metropolitan areas, median contract rent was 62 percent higher in 1970 than in 1960, rising from $71 to $115 over the decade. In nonmetropolitan areas rent increased 50 percent, from $52 to $78.

Value and rent are expressed in current dollars (the value at the time of the respective censuses). Thus, any comparison must take into account the general rise in the cost of living during the 10-year period, as well as changes in the characteristics of the housing inventory.

Standard Metropolitan Statistical Areas

In the metropolitan areas of the State, the housing supply increased by 1,447,200 units, or 29 percent. The Los Angeles-Long Beach SMSA, the largest in the State, contained 39 percent of the housing units in the metropolitan areas and accounted for 27 percent of the increase. The San Francisco-Oakland SMSA, second largest, had 18 percent of the State's metropolitan housing and accounted for 13 percent of the increase. The Anaheim-Santa Ana-Garden Grove SMSA, third largest, with 7 percent of the metropolitan housing, accounted, however, for 16 percent of the increase.

About 66 percent of the housing units in the State's metropolitan areas consisted of one-unit structures in 1970. The number of units in multiunit structures, however, increased at a much faster rate than one-unit structures during the decade, 63 percent and 16 percent, respectively.

In 1970, 124,200 housing units in metropolitan areas, or 1.9 percent of all year-round units, lacked some or all plumbing facilities. The corresponding proportions for the central cities and the suburbs were 2.5 percent and 1.5 percent, respectively. Approximately 7,200, or 2.4 percent, of the Negro households in central cities occupied units which lacked some or all plumbing facilities in 1970; in suburban areas, 1,800 Negro households, or 1.5 percent, lacked such plumbing facilities.

Table D.   Plumbing Facilities and Persons Per Room by Metropolitan and Nonmetropolitan Residence: 1970 and 1960

The State Metropolitan and Nonmetropolitan Residence	Percent of housing units			
	Lacking some or all plumbing facilities		With 1.01 or more persons per room[1]	
	1970[2]	1960[3]	1970	1960
Total......................	2.1	5.1	7.9	9.5
Metropolitan residence...........	1.9	(NA)	7.8	9.2
Inside central cities..........	2.5	5.4	7.7	7.8
Outside central cities.........	1.5	(NA)	7.8	10.4
Nonmetropolitan residence........	3.7	(NA)	9.9	13.6

NA Not available.
[1] Percent of all occupied units.
[2] Percent of all year-round housing units.
[3] Percent of all housing units.

Housing units in the central cities were smaller in size than in the suburbs. In 1970, the median number of rooms in the central cities was 4.4 and in the suburbs 4.9. While 30 percent of the housing in the central cities had one to three rooms, 19 percent of the housing units in the suburbs were in this category. At the same time, 26 percent of the units in the central cities had six or more rooms, compared with 34 percent in the suburbs.

Of all occupied units in metropolitan areas, 475,800, or 8 percent, reported more than one person per room in 1970; this proportion was 9 percent in 1960. The proportion of such units in the central cities and in the suburbs was the same in 1970, about 8 percent (table D).

Homeownership in 1970 was greater in the suburban areas than in the central cities. About 60 percent of occupied units in the suburbs and 46 percent in the central cities were owner-occupied. The Negro-home-ownership rate in the suburbs was 50 percent, compared with 35 percent in the central cities. Of the 163,200 Negro-homeowner households in the metropolitan areas of the State, 103,200 lived in the central cities and 60,000 in the suburbs.

Median value of owner-occupied housing was $23,300 in the central cities and $23,600 in the suburbs. About 17 percent of the owner-occupied housing units in the central cities and 19 percent in the suburbs were valued at $35,000 or more. Median contract rent was $111 in the central cities, compared with $120 in the suburbs. Renter-occupied units renting for $150 or more con-stituted 22 percent of rental housing in the central cities and 27 percent in the suburbs.

The homeowner vacancy rate for metropolitan areas decreased during the decade from 2.2 to 1.3 percent. The rental vacancy rate decreased from 8.5 to 5.5 percent.

Annexations

Annexations occurred in each of the central cities except the city of San Francisco, during the decade, (see "Population Trends" and text table B). Such annexa-tions affect changes in the characteristics for these central cities and their suburbs.

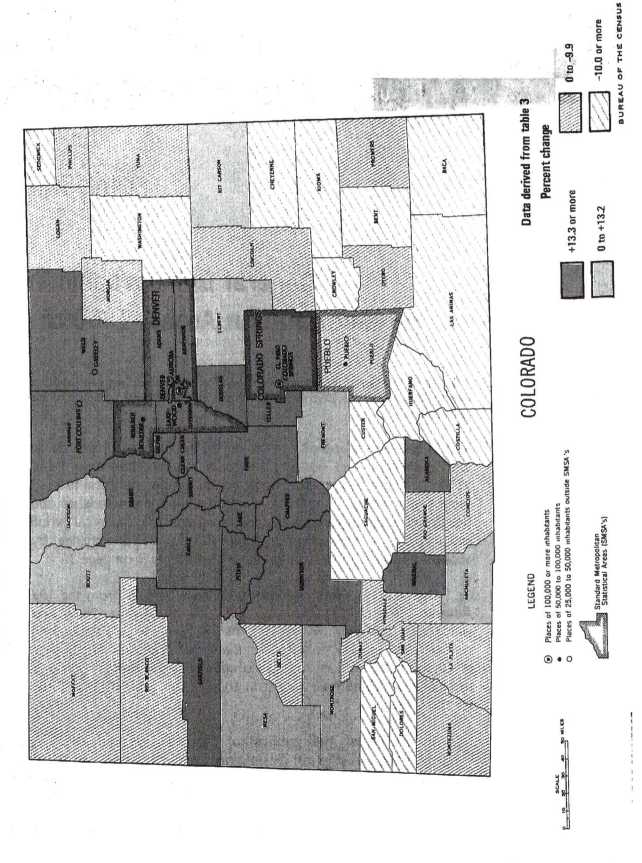

Population Change for Counties: 1960 to 1970

COLORADO

LEGEND

⊙ Places of 100,000 or more inhabitants
● Places of 50,000 to 100,000 inhabitants
○ Places of 25,000 to 50,000 inhabitants outside SMSA's

Standard Metropolitan
Statistical Areas (SMSA's)

Data derived from table 3

Percent change

+13.3 or more

0 to +13.2

0 to −9.9

−10.0 or more

BUREAU OF THE CENSUS

Analytical Text

POPULATION TRENDS

General

Between 1960 and 1970 the total population of Colorado grew by nearly 453,000, from 1,754,000 to 2,207,000, an increase of 26 percent over the population living in the State in 1960 (table A). This rate of increase is almost double the national rate of 13.3 percent. About 86 percent of Colorado's growth occurred in the State's three SMSA's (Denver, Colorado Springs, and Pueblo). While the population of metropolitan areas increased by 390,000, or 33 percent, the population of nonmetropolitan areas increased by only 63,000 persons, or 11 percent. As a result, the proportion of the total population living in metropolitan areas increased during the decade, from 68 percent to almost 72 percent, a somewhat higher proportion than in the Nation as a whole (69 percent).

The total number of households in the State in 1970 was 691,000, or 162,000 more than in 1960. The population living in households increased less rapidly than the rate at which households increased, with the result that average household size decreased slightly, from 3.2 to 3.1 persons.

The population of Colorado and each of its three metropolitan areas is predominantly white—94 percent or more (see table 1). The proportion is somewhat lower inside central cities (91 percent). The population of other races, which is mostly Negro, is concentrated in the central cities: in 1970, 71 percent of the State's population of Negro and other races lived in central cities, but only 32 percent of Colorado's white population.

Substantial growth occurred in the State as a whole and in both metropolitan and nonmetropolitan areas as a result of the excess of births over deaths. There was also a very substantial inmigration to the State. The State's population gain of 453,000 consisted of a natural increase of 238,000 and a net inmigration of 215,000.

During the decade, there were significant changes in the age composition of the population of both metropolitan and nonmetropolitan areas. Each area experienced a decline in the population under 5 years of age and very large increases in the population 15 to 24 years

Table A.   Population by Race and Metropolitan and Nonmetropolitan Residence: 1970 and 1960

The State Metropolitan and Non-metropolitan Residence	Population		Change		Percent Distribution	
	1970	1960	Number	Percent	1970	1960
Total.................	2,207,259	1,753,947	453,312	25.8	100.0	100.0
Metropolitan residence...	1,581,739	1,191,832	389,907	32.7	71.7	68.0
Inside central cities..	747,191	655,262	91,929	14.0	33.9	37.4
Outside central cities.	834,548	536,570	297,978	55.5	37.8	30.6
Nonmetropolitan residence	625,520	562,115	63,405	11.3	28.3	32.0
White.................	2,112,352	1,700,700	411,652	24.2	95.7	97.0
Metropolitan residence...	1,496,687	1,144,020	352,667	30.8	67.8	65.2
Inside central cities..	679,376	614,156	65,220	10.6	30.8	35.0
Outside central cities.	817,311	529,864	287,447	54.2	37.0	30.2
Nonmetropolitan residence	615,665	556,680	58,985	10.6	27.9	31.7
Negro and other races	94,907	53,247	41,660	78.2	4.3	3.0
Metropolitan residence...	85,052	47,812	37,240	77.9	3.9	2.7
Inside central cities..	67,815	41,106	26,709	65.0	3.1	2.3
Outside central cities.	17,237	6,706	10,531	157.0	0.8	0.4
Nonmetropolitan residence	9,855	5,435	4,420	81.3	0.4	0.3

old. All other age groups increased, but at rates well below those for young adults.

Similar changes are found in other sections of the country and are due in part to changing birth rates and in part to migration, which is highly selective by age. Low birth rates during the 1960's contribute to the diminution of the age group under 5 years, whereas the post-World War II "baby boom" is currently reflected in the large size of the population 15 to 24 years old.

Standard Metropolitan Statistical Areas

Denver, which had a population of 1,228,000 in 1970, is the largest standard metropolitan statistical area (SMSA) in Colorado and is the 27th largest SMSA in the Nation. Denver is the capital of Colorado, a tourist center, the site of large military installations and many schools of higher education, the locale of an important meat products industry and the commercial, wholesale, and financial center for a large region in the West.

The two other metropolitan areas in Colorado are Colorado Springs (236,000 population) and Pueblo (118,000 population). Colorado Springs is the site of the U.S. Air Force Academy. Pueblo is the site of an institution of higher learning and also has significant Federal Government employment.

The Denver SMSA registered substantial population growth during the decade, increasing by nearly 300,000 persons, or 32 percent. Almost all this growth occurred outside the central city, where population increased by 64 percent over the decade. Population increased very little in Denver city proper (by only 21,000) as a result of significant net outmigration.

The Colorado Springs SMSA, which grew by 64 percent over the decade, is the site of the U.S. Air Force Academy. The rate of growth was particularly rapid (92 percent) inside the central city because of extensive annexation and markedly less (37 percent) outside the central city.

The Pueblo SMSA, in contrast to Denver and Colorado Springs, just held its own over the decade. Annexation of territory during the decade was responsible for additions to all three central cities of Colorado Springs, Denver and Pueblo (table B). The annexation for Colorado Springs (38,000 persons) resulted in a population increase over the 1960-70 period that more than doubled what would have been the increase without the annexation.

Counties

Between 1960 and 1970 about half (31) of the 63 counties in Colorado increased in population. Twenty-two of these counties had a rate of growth that exceeded the national average of 13.3 percent. Among these were counties comprising the Denver and Colorado Springs metropolitan areas and counties surrounding these areas in the central part of Colorado. The fastest growing counties in this group were Gilpin (86 percent), Jefferson (83), Boulder (78), Douglas (75), Clear Creek (73), Larimer (69), and El Paso (64).

Thirty-two counties had population losses, 14 of these of 10 percent or more. The highest loss was suffered by San Miguel County in Southwest Colorado, whose population dropped from 2,900 to 1,900, by 34 percent. Four counties touching on the Pueblo metropolitan areas also had losses. These were Custer (-14 percent), Huerfano (16), Las Animas (21) and Crowley (22). Looking at the map of Colorado, one can see that those counties losing population form a big "U" around the central part of Colorado which contains the growing counties.

Every county had more births than deaths during the decade except for Hinsdale. In the case of the 32 counties with losses, net outmigration more than offset natural increase. In respect to net inmigration, the counties comprising "suburban" Denver, i.e., Adams, Arapahoe, Boulder and Jefferson, all had significant net inmigra-

Table B. Change in Population of Central Cities Through Annexation: 1960 to 1970

| Central Cities | 1970 population | | | 1960 population | Change 1960 to 1970 in 1960 area |
	Total	In 1960 area	In annexed area		
Colo Springs................	135,060	97,560	37,500	70,194	27,366
Denver.....................	514,678	457,806	56,872	493,887	-36,081
Pueblo.....................	97,453	90,730	6,723	91,181	-451

tion. Denver County had a net outmigration of 29,000, a loss equivalent to 6 percent of the 1960 population and El Paso County (U.S. Air Force Academy) had a net inmigration of 71,000, equivalent to 49 percent of 1960 population. Larimer County (site of Colorado State University) had a net inmigration of 28,000, equivalent to 53 percent of its 1960 population reflecting the tripling of student enrollment at the University. Other counties with high inmigration rates were very small in population.

Only two counties in the State contain a large enough population of races other than white to have this population group shown separately in table 3 on county components of change (see "Definition and Explanations"). The counties are Denver and San Miguel. Denver had 56,000 Negroes and other races in 1970 compared to 35,000 in 1960. The number of Negroes and other races in San Miguel County in 1970 numbered less than 500.

HOUSING TRENDS

General

During the decade the total supply of housing units in Colorado increased by 162,500, or 27 percent, and the population grew by 453,000, or 26 percent (table C).

The metropolitan areas of the State experienced greater relative growth in housing, as in population, than did the nonmetropolitan part. The number of housing units in metropolitan areas rose over the decade to 521,900, an increase of 131,700 units, or 34 percent;

this compares with an increase of 30,800 units, or 15 percent, in nonmetropolitan areas. While the metropolitan areas contained 69 percent of the housing in Colorado, the additions to the housing supply in these areas accounted for 81 percent of Colorado's total housing increase between 1960 and 1970.

The size of housing units in the State increased between 1960 and 1970. The median number of rooms rose from 4.7 to 5.0 in metropolitan areas and from 4.5 to 4.7 in nonmetropolitan areas.

Households were smaller in 1970 than in 1960. In metropolitan areas, average household size declined from 3.2 persons in 1960 to 3.1 in 1970, and in nonmetropolitan areas, from 3.3 persons in 1960 to 3.1 in 1970. During the same period, there were large percentage increases in the number of one-person households, 56 percent in metropolitan areas, and 43 percent in the nonmetropolitan areas. Households with five or more persons showed relatively smaller gains in the metropolitan areas, and losses in the nonmetropolitan areas.

About 72 percent of the housing in Colorado consisted of one-unit structures in 1970, compared with 79 percent in 1960. The proportion lacking some or all plumbing facilities declined from 14 percent in 1960 to 5 percent in 1970.

Number of persons per room is often used as a measure of crowding. In Colorado, both the number and proportion of housing units with 1.01 or more persons per room decreased during the decade. In 1960, 10 percent of all occupied housing units in metropolitan areas and 14 percent of all occupied housing units in nonmetropolitan areas had 1.01 or more persons per

Table C.   Housing Units by Metropolitan and Nonmetropolitan Residence: 1970 and 1960

The State Metropolitan and Nonmetropolitan Residence	Housing units				Popula- tion percent change
	Total		Change		
	1970	1960	Number	Percent	
Total.................	757,070	594,522	162,548	27.3	25.8
Metropolitan residence.....	521,855	390,144	131,711	33.8	32.7
Inside central cities....	271,304	226,743	44,561	19.7	14.0
Outside central cities...	250,551	163,401	87,150	53.3	55.5
Nonmetropolitan residence..	235,215	204,378	30,837	15.1	11.3

room. By 1970, the proportion of such units had decreased to 6 percent in metropolitan areas and 9 percent in nonmetropolitan areas (table D).

Homeownership in the State decreased from 64 percent in 1960 to 63 percent in 1970. In metropolitan areas there was a decrease from 63 percent to 62 percent, while in nonmetropolitan areas the proportion increased from 66 to 67 percent.

Property values and rents increased in the last decade. The median value in metropolitan areas increased by 39 percent from $13,300 in 1960 to $18,500 in 1970, while in the nonmetropolitan areas, value increased 45 percent from $8,800 to $12,800. In metropolitan areas, median contract rent in 1970 was 53 percent higher than in 1960, rising from $68 to $104. In nonmetropolitan areas, the increase was 48 percent, from $50 in 1960 to $74 in 1970.

Value and rent are expressed in current dollars (the value at the time of the respective censuses). Thus, any comparison must take into account the general rise in the cost of living in the 10-year period, as well as changes in the characteristics of the housing inventory.

Standard Metropolitan Statistical Areas

Average household size in the metropolitan area total of the State declined during the decade. The average was 3.1 persons in 1970, compared with 3.2 in 1960.

The rate of homeownership was greater in the suburban areas than in the central cities. About 71 percent of occupied units in the suburbs were owner-occupied, compared with 54 percent in the central cities.

In 1970, 16,100 housing units in metropolitan areas, or 3 percent of all year-round units, lacked some or all plumbing facilities. The corresponding proportion was 4 percent in the central cities and 2 percent in the suburbs.

Of all occupied units in metropolitan areas, 30,000 units, or 6 percent, reported more than one person per room in 1970, compared with 10 percent in 1960. In 1970, the proportion of such units was 6 percent both in the central cities and in the suburban areas.

The homeowner vacancy rate for metropolitan areas decreased during the decade from 1.7 to 1.1 percent. Similarly, the rental vacancy rate decreased from 8.1 to 5.9 percent.

Annexations

Annexations occurred in the central cities of Colorado Springs, Denver, and Pueblo during the decade (see "Population Trends" and text table B). Such annexations affect changes in the characteristics for these central cities and their suburbs.

Table D. Plumbing Facilities and Persons Per Room by Metropolitan and Nonmetropolitan Residence: 1970 and 1960

The State Metropolitan and Nonmetropolitan Residence	Percent of housing units			
	Lacking some or all plumbing facilities		With 1.01 or more persons per room[1]	
	1970[2]	1960[3]	1970	1960
Total.........................	5.0	14.1	6.9	11.6
Metropolitan residence...........	3.1	9.1	6.1	10.3
Inside central cities.........	3.8	9.8	6.2	8.8
Outside central cities........	2.3	8.1	5.9	12.5
Nonmetropolitan residence........	9.3	23.7	9.2	14.3

[1]Percent of all occupied units.
[2]Percent of all year-round housing units.
[3]Percent of all housing units.

Population Change for Counties: 1960 to 1970

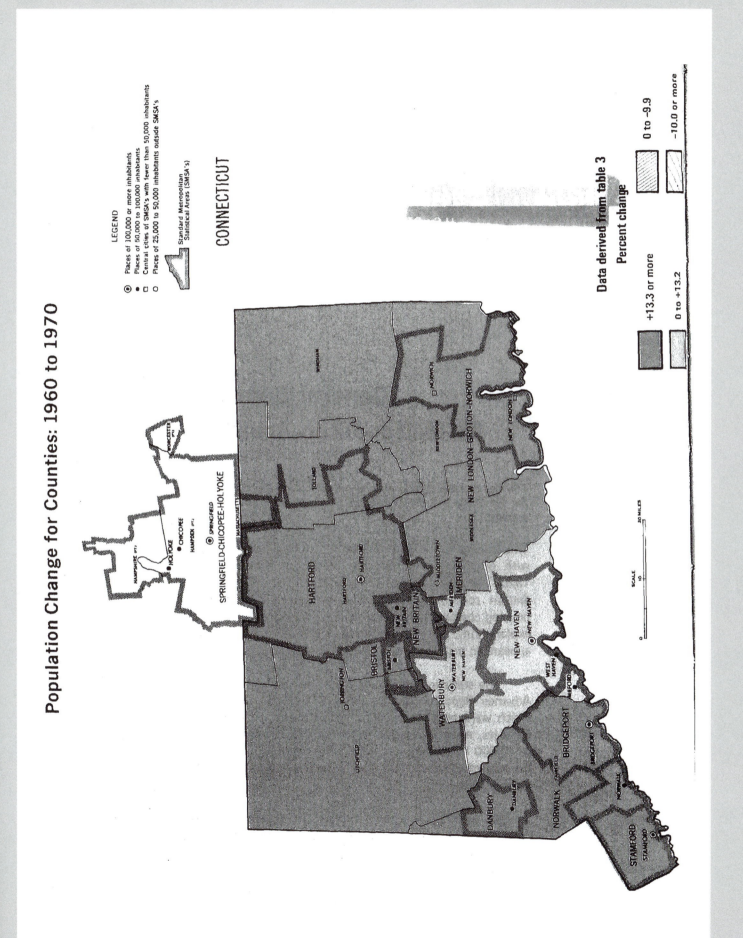

LEGEND

⊙ Places of 100,000 or more inhabitants
● Places of 50,000 to 100,000 inhabitants
◻ Central cities of SMSA's with fewer than 50,000 inhabitants
○ Places of 25,000 to 50,000 inhabitants outside SMSA's

Standard Metropolitan
Statistical Areas (SMSA's)

CONNECTICUT

Data derived from table 3

Percent change

+13.3 or more

0 to +13.2

0 to −9.9

−10.0 or more

Analytical Text

POPULATION TRENDS

General

Between 1960 and 1970, the population of Connecticut grew from 2,535,000 to 3,032,000, an increase of 496,000 or 19.6 percent. This rate of increase was well above the rates of increase for the entire United States (13.3 percent) and for the Northeast region (9.7 percent) in which Connecticut is located. Connecticut ranked 13th among the 50 states in rate of population growth during the decade.

The total number of households in Connecticut in 1970 was 933,000 or 181,000 more than in 1960. The population living in households increased more slowly than the rate at which households increased, with the result that average household size dropped from 3.3 to 3.2 persons.

The metropolitan population of Connecticut increased by 17 percent from 2,134,000 in 1960 to 2,505,000 in 1970 while the nonmetropolitan population increased by 31 percent from 402,000 to 527,000 (see table A-1). In 1970, five-sixths of the population lived in metropolitan areas. In the Nation as a whole, more than two-thirds of the population lived in metropolitan areas.

Within the metropolitan areas, the population of the central cities grew by 5 percent from 1,014,000 to 1,067,000 and the population in the balance of the metropolitan areas grew by 28 percent from 1,020,000 to 1,438,000. Of the 371,000 population increase in metropolitan areas between 1960 and 1970, nearly 90 percent occurred outside central cities.

The population of Negro and other races (more than nine-tenths of which is Negro) in Connecticut increased from 111,000 in 1960 to 196,000 in 1970, or by 76 percent and, as a result, increased from 4 to 6 percent of the total population. In 1970, 95 percent of the population of Negro and other races lived in metropolitan areas and 86 percent lived in the central cities of metropolitan areas.

The population increase of 496,000 in Connecticut in the 1960 to 1970 decade resulted from a natural increase (births minus deaths) of 283,000 and a net inmigration of 214,000, which was equivalent to 8 percent of the 1960 population. Forty-three percent of the population increase in Connecticut between 1960 and 1970 was due to net inmigration (see table 3).

The net inmigration of Negro and other races in Connecticut during the decade totaled 48,000, which was equivalent to 43 percent of the 1960 population.

More than one-half of the population growth among Negro and other races between 1960 and 1970 was due to net inmigration.

The age structure of the Connecticut population changed significantly between 1960 and 1970. The only decline occurred among the population under 5 years old and was due largely to the decline in birth rates which occurred throughout the United States during the 1960's. The greatest increase (62 percent) occurred in the 15 to 24 age group and was due mostly to the entry of the large number of persons born during the post-World War II "baby boom" into this age group. As a result of these changes, the proportion of the total population in the under 5 group declined from 11 to 8 percent, and the proportion in the 15 to 24 group increased from 12 to 16 percent (see table 4).

The population of Negro and other races in Connecticut has a young age structure. In 1970, 55 percent were under age 25, and only 4 percent were over age 65. Among the total population of the State, 44 percent were under age 25, and 10 percent were over age 65.

Standard Metropolitan Statistical Areas

In 1970, there were 12 standard metropolitan statistical areas (SMSA's) in Connecticut, including 11 SMSA's located entirely in Connecticut and one SMSA located partly in Connecticut, the Springfield-Chicopee-Holyoke, Mass.-Conn. SMSA.[1] Only 1 percent of the population in this SMSA is in the Connecticut portion (see table A-2).

Each of the 11 metropolitan areas located entirely in Connecticut increased in population between 1960 and 1970 with the rates of growth ranging from a high of 44 percent in the Danbury SMSA to a low of 8 percent in the Meriden SMSA (see table A-3).

The Hartford SMSA, which is the largest metropolitan area in Connecticut, grew from 549,000 in 1960 to 664,000 in 1970, or by 21 percent. The city of Hartford, which is the State capital and a major financial center, had a population loss of 3 percent while the population in the balance of the Hartford SMSA increased by 32 percent.

---

[1] In the population tables in this report and other reports for States in New England, data are shown for two types of metropolitan areas: standard metropolitan statistical areas (SMSA's) and State economic areas (SEA's). See "Definitions and Explanations" for a discussion of the differences between the two types of metropolitan areas. SMSA tables are shown in the Appendix to this text.

The Bridgeport SMSA grew from 338,000 to 389,000, or by 15 percent between 1960 and 1970. The population in the city of Bridgeport remained unchanged while the population in the balance of the Bridgeport SMSA increased by 28 percent. Both the Bridgeport SMSA and the New Haven SMSA, which are the second and third largest metropolian areas in Connecticut, respectively, are major manufacturing centers.

The New Haven SMSA grew from 321,000 in 1960 to 356,000 in 1970, or by 11 percent. The rates of population changed differed greatly in the central city and in the remainder of the metropolitan area. The city of New Haven experienced a population loss of 9 percent while the population in the balance of the SMSA increased by 29 percent. Over one-half of the population increase in the New Haven SMSA during the 1960 and 1970 decade occurred among Negro and other races.

The Waterbury SMSA, a leading center of the chemicals industry, grew from 186,000 to 209,000, or by 13 percent, between 1960 and 1970. The population in the city of Waterbury increased by 1 percent while the population in the balance of the SMSA increased by 29 percent.

The New London-Groton-Norwich SMSA, which is the site of the New London Submarine Base and which is the only one of Connecticut's 11 SMSA's in the eastern portion of the State, grew from 171,000 in 1960 to 208,000 in 1970, or by 22 percent. The central city portion of the SMSA, which is comprised of New London city and Norwich city, had a population increase of less than 1 percent while the population in the balance of the SMSA increased by 39 percent.

The Stamford SMSA and the Norwalk SMSA are located between New York City and Bridgeport and combine light manufacturing with their suburban functions. Between 1960 and 1970, the population of the Stamford SMSA grew from 178,000 to 206,000, or by 16 percent, and the population of the Norwalk SMSA grew from 97,000 to 120,000, or by 24 percent.

The New Britain SMSA, which is a manufacturing center, grew from 129,000 in 1960 to 145,000 in 1970, or by 12 percent. The population in the city of New Britain increased by 2 percent while the population in the remainder of the SMSA increased by 31 percent.

There are three metropolitan areas in Connecticut with populations in 1970 of less than 100,000. Between 1960 and 1970, the Danbury SMSA grew from 54,000 to 78,000, or by 44 percent; the Bristol SMSA grew from 54,000 to 66,000, or by 21 percent; and the Meriden SMSA grew from 52,000 to 56,000, or by 8 percent. The rapid growth in the Danbury SMSA was due primarily to the movement of several light industries into the Danbury area. Most of the population growth in the city of Danbury was due to annexation (table A).

Counties

All eight counties in Connecticut gained population between 1960 and 1970. Seven counties gained at rates above the national average of 13.3 percent while the eighth—New Haven County—recorded a 12.8 percent increase. During the decade, every county gained population through net inmigration, making Connecticut the only one of the 50 States in which this occurred.

In the New England States, SMSA's are comprised of cities and towns (rather than of counties as in the remainder of the Nation), and thus a county may be partly metropolitan and partly nonmetropolitan (see "Definitions and Explanations"). The populations of Fairfield, Hartford, New Haven, and New London Counties are largely metropolitan; the populations of Litchfield, Middlesex, and Windham Counties are largely nonmetropolitan; and the population of Tolland County is about evenly divided with most of its metropolitan population belonging to the Hartford SMSA.

The highest rate of growth among the eight counties occurred in Tolland County in which the population increased 50 percent from 69,000 in 1960 to 103,000 in 1970. Two-thirds of the increase was due to net

Table A.   Change in Population of Central Cities Through Annexation: 1960 to 1970

Central Cities	1970 population			1960 population	Change 1960 to 1970 in 1960 area
	Total	In 1960 area	In annexed area		
Danbury....................	50,781	23,761	27,020	22,928	833

inmigration which was attributable to the expansion of the University of Connecticut and to suburban expansion east of Hartford. Net inmigration into Tolland County during the decade was equivalent to 34 percent of the 1960 population.

The three largely nonmetropolitan counties—Litchfield, Middlesex, and Windham—had rates of population growth ranging from 20 to 29 percent during the decade. In each county, net inmigration accounted for more than one-half of the increase.

Fairfield County (including the Bridgeport, Stamford, Norwalk, and Danbury SMSA's) grew from 654,000 in 1960 to 793,000 in 1970, or by 21 percent. The population increase of 139,000, which was the largest for any county in Connecticut, was about evenly divided between natural increase (births minus deaths) and net inmigration.

In Hartford County (including the Hartford, New Britain, and Bristol SMSA's), the most populous county in the State, the population grew from 690,000 to 817,000, or by 18 percent. About one-third of the increase was due to net inmigration.

New Haven County (including the New Haven, Waterbury and Meriden SMSA's) grew from 660,000 in 1960 to 745,000 in 1970. Less than one-fourth of the growth was due to net inmigration, and the rate of net inmigration which was equivalent to 3 percent of the 1960 population was the lowest among the eight counties in Connecticut.

In New London County (including the New London-Groton-Norwich SMSA), the population increased from 186,000 in 1960 to 230,000 in 1970, or by 24 percent. One-third of the growth was due to net immigration.

HOUSING TRENDS

General

During the decade the population in Connecticut grew by 496,000, or 20 percent, and the total supply of housing units increased 162,600, also 20 percent (table B).

The metropolitan areas of the State experienced about the same relative growth in housing as did the nonmetropolitan part. The number of housing units in metropolitan areas rose from 674,000 to 808,500 over the decade, an increase of 134,500 units, or 20 percent; the increase in nonmetropolitan areas was 28,100 units, or 19 percent.

About 59 percent of the housing in Connecticut consisted of one-unit structures in 1970. The proportion of such units was 57 percent in metropolitan areas and 70 percent in nonmetropolitan areas.

Table B.   Housing Units by Metropolitan and Nonmetropolitan Residence: 1970 and 1960

The State Metropolitan and Nonmetropolitan Residence	Housing units				Population percent change
	Total		Change		
	1970	1960	Number	Percent	
Total..................	981,158	818,544	162,614	19.9	19.6
Metropolitan residence.....	808,529	674,001	134,528	20.0	18.1
Inside central cities....	365,538	333,696	31,842	9.5	5.9
Outside central cities...	442,991	340,305	102,686	30.2	29.1
Nonmetropolitan residence..	172,629	144,543	28,086	19.4	29.1

The number of units in the State lacking some or all plumbing facilities in 1970 was 25,800 units, or 3 percent. The proportion of such units was 2 percent in metropolitan areas and 4 percent in nonmetropolitan areas (table C).

Approximately 1,800, or 4 percent, of the Negro-occupied units inside metropolitan areas lacked some or all plumbing in 1970, compared with 90, or 5 percent, of Negro housing outside metropolitan areas.

Households were smaller in 1970 than in 1960. In metropolitan areas average household size declined from 3.3 persons in 1960 to 3.1 in 1970, and in nonmetropolitan areas, from 3.3 persons in 1960 to 3.2 in 1970. There were large percentage increases in one-person households, 68 percent in metropolitan areas, and 85 percent in nonmetropolitan areas. Households with five or more persons increased 18 percent in metropolitan areas, and 30 percent in nonmetropolitan areas.

The median number of rooms in housing units in Connecticut was 5.2 in 1970. In metropolitan areas the median was 5.2, compared with 5.4 in nonmetropolitan areas. About 42 percent of the metropolitan housing units and 47 percent of units in nonmetropolitan areas had six or more rooms.

Number of persons per room is often used as a measure of crowding. In Connecticut, the proportion of housing units with 1.01 or more persons per room decreased during the decade. In 1960, 8 percent of all occupied housing units in metropolitan areas and 7 percent in nonmetropolitan areas had more than one person per room. By 1970, the proportion of such units had decreased to 6 percent in both metropolitan and nonmetropolitan areas (table C).

The homeownership rate in Connecticut was 63 percent in 1970, compared with 62 percent in 1960. The proportion of owner-occupied units remained at 61 percent in metropolitan areas and increased from 69 to 70 percent in nonmetropolitan areas.

About 23 percent of the Negro households in metropolitan areas owned their homes in 1970, compared with 31 percent in nonmetropolitan areas. Of the 11,500 Negro-homeowner households in the State, 10,900 lived inside SMSA's and 600 lived outside SMSA's.

Property values and rents increased during the last decade. The median value of owner-occupied homes in the State increased by 53 percent, from $16,700 in 1960 to $25,500 in 1970. Median contract rent rose by 78 percent, from $59 to $105.

Value and rent are expressed in current dollars (the value at the time of the respective censuses). Thus, any comparison must take into account the general rise in the cost of living during the 10-year period, as well as changes in the characteristics of the housing inventory.

Standard Metropolitan Statistical Areas

The suburban areas of the State experienced greater growth in housing than did the central cities. Housing units in the suburbs increased by 102,700 units, or 30 percent; while housing in the central cities increased by 31,800, or 10 percent. By 1970, there were 443,000 housing units in the suburbs and 365,500 units in the central cities.

The proportion of the housing inventory in one-unit structures declined in both the central cities and their

Table C. Plumbing Facilities and Persons Per Room by Metropolitan and Nonmetropolitan Residence: 1970 and 1960

The State Metropolitan and Nonmetropolitan Residence	Percent of housing units			
	Lacking some or all plumbing facilities		With 1.01 or more persons per room[1]	
	1970[2]	1960[3]	1970	1960
Total......................	2.7	7.3	6.2	7.4
Metropolitan residence..........	2.5	6.6	6.3	7.6
Inside central cities.........	3.5	8.9	8.1	8.6
Outside central cities........	1.6	4.3	4.8	6.5
Nonmetropolitan residence.......	3.6	10.7	5.9	6.8

[1]Percent of all occupied units.
[2]Percent of all year-round housing units.
[3]Percent of all housing units.

suburbs. In the central cities, the proportion of such units declined from 36 percent in 1960 to 34 percent in 1970 and, in the suburban areas, from 83 to 76 percent.

In the central cities the proportion of year-round housing units lacking some or all plumbing facilities declined during the decade from 9 to 3 percent. Such units in the suburban areas declined from 4 to 2 percent.

Average household size for metropolitan areas declined during the decade. In the central cities, the average decreased from 3.1 persons to 2.9 and, in the suburbs, from 3.5 persons to 3.3.

The median number of rooms for the suburban housing units in the State increased from 5.5 in 1960 to 5.7 in 1970. In the central cities the median remained at 4.7 rooms during the decade. While 8 percent of the housing in the suburbs had one to three rooms in 1970, 20 percent of the housing units in central cities were in this category. At the same time, 54 percent of suburban housing had six or more rooms, compared with 28 percent in the central cities.

Of all occupied units in the suburbs, 20,400 units, or 5 percent, reported more than one person per room, compared with 7 percent in 1960. In the central cities of the State, such units declined during the decade from 9 to 8 percent.

Homeownership in the central cities remained at 43 percent during the decade. In the suburbs, however, the homeownership rate declined from 78 percent in 1960 to 75 percent in 1970. About 18 percent of the Negro households in the central cities owned their homes in 1970, as in 1960. In the suburban areas, the proportion of Negro homeowners increased from 58 percent in 1960 to 63 percent in 1970. Of the 10,900 Negro-homeowner households in the State's metropolitan areas, 7,600 lived in the central cities and the remainder in the suburbs.

In the central cities of Connecticut, the median value of owner-occupied housing rose 44 percent ($16,700 in 1960 to $24,100 in 1970) and, in the suburbs, the median increased by 54 percent ($17,500 to $26,900). About 21 percent of the owner-occupied housing was valued in 1970 at $35,000 or more in the central cities, compared with 27 percent in the suburbs.

In 1970, median contract rent in the central cities was $101 and, in the suburbs, $126. Approximately 34 percent of the renter-occupied units in the central cities and 54 percent of the suburban units had rents of $120 or more in 1970.

The homeowner vacancy rate decreased from 1.0 percent in 1960 to 0.6 percent in 1970 in the central cities and from 1.7 to 0.7 in the suburbs. The rental vacancy rate also decreased in these areas, from 4.9 to 4.4 percent in the central cities, and from 4.8 to 3.9 in the suburbs.

Annexation

Annexation occurred in the central city of Danbury during the decade (see "Population Trends" and text table A). Such annexation affects changes in the characteristics for this central city and its suburbs.

Population Change for Counties: 1960 to 1970

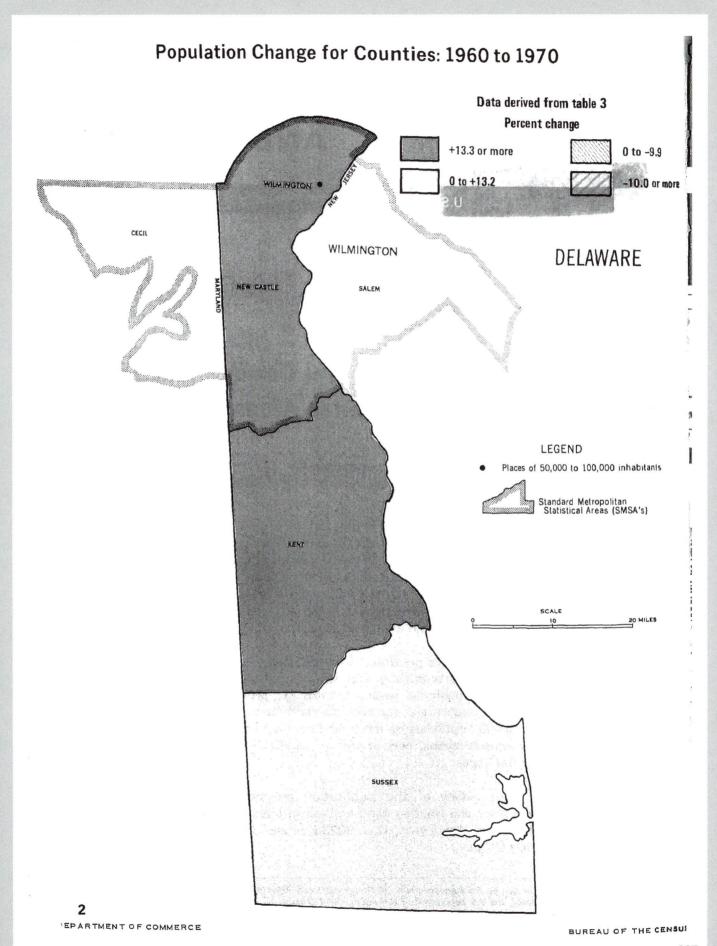

Data derived from table 3
Percent change

+13.3 or more

0 to +13.2

0 to -9.9

-10.0 or more

DELAWARE

WILMINGTON

CECIL

MARYLAND

NEW CASTLE

NEW JERSEY

SALEM

KENT

SUSSEX

LEGEND

● Places of 50,000 to 100,000 inhabitants

Standard Metropolitan
Statistical Areas (SMSA's)

SCALE
0   10   20 MILES

2

Analytical Text

POPULATION TRENDS

General

Between 1960 and 1970 the total population of Delaware grew by more than 100,000, from 446,000 to 548,000, an increase of 23 percent over the population living in the State in 1960 (table A). Most of the increase (77 percent) was recorded in the State's only standard metropolitan statistical area (SMSA), Wilmington.

The total number of households in the State in 1970 was 165,000, or 36,000 more than in 1960. The population living in households increased less rapidly than the rate at which households increased with the result that average household size decreased slightly from 3.4 to 3.2 persons.

The effect of the changes on population distribution by metropolitan-nonmetropolitan residence was very small. The proportion in the metropolitan area increased by only one and one-half percentage points during the decade. In 1970, just over 70 percent of the population of Delaware was metropolitan, about the same as the national average (69 percent).

The State's growth was produced by a natural increase of 64,000 and a net inmigration of 38,000 persons. Both metropolitan and nonmetropolitan populations increased substantially over the decade, but only in the metropolitan area was net inmigration of significance. While the metropolitan area gained 36,000 inmigrants (equivalent to 12 percent of its 1960 population), the nonmetropolitan areas of Delaware had a net inmigration of only 2,000 (equivalent to less than 2 percent of its 1960 population).

The State as a whole experienced significant changes in age composition (see table 4). The population under 5 years of age declined by more than 12 percent, while all other age groups increased. Least growth was shown by the 25 to 44 year old population (7 percent) and the greatest growth by 15 to 24 year olds (66 percent).

Similar changes are found in other sections of the country and are due in part to changing birth rates and in part to migration, which is highly selective by age.

Table A. Population by Race and Metropolitan and Nonmetropolitan Residence: 1970 and 1960

The State Metropolitan and Non-metropolitan Residence	Population		Change		Percent Distribution	
	1970	1960	Number	Percent	1970	1960
Total...............	548,104	446,292	101,812	22.8	100.0	100.0
Metropolitan residence...	385,856	307,446	78,410	25.5	70.4	68.9
Inside central cities..	80,386	95,827	-15,441	-16.1	14.7	21.5
Outside central cities.	305,470	211,619	93,851	44.3	55.7	47.4
Nonmetropolitan residence	162,248	138,846	23,402	16.9	29.6	31.1
White...............	466,459	384,327	82,132	21.4	85.1	86.1
Metropolitan residence...	335,246	271,025	64,221	23.7	61.2	60.7
Inside central cities..	44,901	70,752	-25,851	-36.5	8.2	15.9
Outside central cities.	290,345	200,273	90,072	45.0	53.0	44.9
Nonmetropolitan residence	131,213	113,302	17,911	15.8	23.9	25.4
Negro and other races	81,645	61,965	19,680	31.8	14.9	13.9
Metropolitan residence...	50,610	36,421	14,189	39.0	9.2	8.2
Inside central cities..	35,485	25,075	10,410	41.5	6.5	5.6
Outside central cities.	15,125	11,346	3,779	33.3	2.8	2.5
Nonmetropolitan residence	31,035	25,544	5,491	21.5	5.7	5.7

Low birth rates during the 1960's contribute to the diminution of the age group under 5 years, whereas the post-World War II "baby boom" is currently reflected in the large size of the population 15-24 years old.

Standard Metropolitan Statistical Areas

The Wilmington SMSA comprises three counties: New Castle in Delaware; Salem in New Jersey; and Cecil in Maryland. Their 1970 populations were 386,000, 60,000 and 53,000, respectively. The total SMSA population in 1970 was 499,000, compared to 415,000 in 1960. This was a gain of 85,000 or 20 percent over the 10-year period. The gain resulted from a natural increase of 57,000 combined with a net inmigration of 28,000.

The Wilmington SMSA's growth is related closely to the vast chemical plants that operate in the area. The SMSA also carries on transportation equipment manufacturing and services a large market area.

Within the SMSA, there were differing population trends by residence and by race. Inside the central city of Wilmington population declined over the decade, from 96,000 to 80,000, or by 16 percent. This decrease was produced by a loss of 26,000 white population and a gain of over 10,000 persons of other races (mostly Negro). The white population loss was produced by a substantial net outmigration of 26,000 persons, equivalent to 37 percent of the total white population of Wilmington city in 1960. The natural increase of the white population at the same time was minimal, amounting to only 500 for the decade. The growth of Wilmington city's population of other races was due in almost equal part to natural increase (5,500) and net inmigration (5,000). As a result of these changes, the black population increased from 26 to 44 percent of Wilmington city's total population.

In the suburban areas outside the central city, blacks increased by 21 percent mainly as a result of natural increase. By contrast, the white population in these areas, which increased by 36 percent, grew more through net inmigration (52,000) than through natural increase (39,000).

The Wilmington SMSA as a whole had age trends much like those for the State: a decline in the population under 5, a small increase in the 25 to 44 year old population, and a substantial increase in the population 15 to 24 years of age. Inside the central city, the white population registered significant declines in every age group, but the Negro population in each age group increased.

Counties

Between 1960 and 1970, the three Delaware counties recorded population increases. The metropolitan county, New Castle, had an increase of 26 percent, with population increasing from 307,000 to 386,000; Kent County, just south of New Castle, had a comparable increase of 25 percent with population increasing from 66,000 to 82,000; and Sussex had a slower growing population with a 10 percent gain and a population increase from 73,000 to 80,000. Each county had more births than deaths during the decade. In only one county, Sussex, was there net outmigration (see table 3).

HOUSING TRENDS

General

During the decade the population in Delaware grew by 102,000, or 23 percent, while the total supply of housing units increased by 36,500, or 25 percent (table B).

Table B. Housing Units by Metropolitan and Nonmetropolitan Residence: 1970 and 1960

The State Metropolitan and Nonmetropolitan Residence	Housing units				Population percent change
	Total		Change		
	1970	1960	Number	Percent	
Total................	180,233	143,725	36,508	25.4	22.8
Metropolitan residence.....	120,704	94,688	26,016	27.5	25.5
Inside central cities....	29,971	33,190	-3,219	-9.7	-16.1
Outside central cities...	90,733	61,498	29,235	47.5	44.3
Nonmetropolitan residence..	59,529	49,037	10,492	21.4	16.9

The metropolitan area of the State (the Delaware portion of the Wilmington, Del.-N.J.-Md. SMSA) experienced greater relative growth in housing, as in population, than did the nonmetropolitan part. The number of housing units in the metropolitan area rose from 94,700 to 120,700 over the decade, an increase of 26,000 units, or 27 percent; this compares with an increase of 10,500 units, or 21 percent, in nonmetropolitan areas. The metropolitan area contained 67 percent of the housing in Delaware and additions to the housing supply in this area accounted for 71 percent of the State's total housing increase between 1960 and 1970.

About 76 percent of the housing in Delaware consisted of one-unit structures in 1970. The corresponding proportions in the Delaware part of the Wilmington metropolitan area and in the nonmetropolitan areas were 75 percent and 78 percent, respectively.

The median number of rooms in housing units in Delaware was 5.7 in 1970. In the metropolitan area the median number of rooms was 5.9, compared with 5.4 in nonmetropolitan areas. While 59 percent of the metropolitan housing units in Delaware had six or more rooms, 48 percent of the nonmetropolitan housing units were in this category.

Households were smaller in 1970 than in 1960. In the Delaware part of the Wilmington SMSA average household size declined from 3.4 persons in 1960 to 3.2 in 1970, and in nonmetropolitan areas, from 3.3 persons in 1960 to 3.2 in 1970. There were large percentage increases in one-person households, 87 percent in the metropolitan area, and 64 percent in nonmetropolitan areas. Households with two or more persons in the

Wilmington SMSA showed moderate increases in both metropolitan and nonmetropolitan areas.

In 1970, the proportion of housing units in Delaware lacking some or all plumbing facilities was 5 percent. For the metropolitan area, the proportion of units without complete plumbing facilities was 2 percent, compared with 13 percent for nonmetropolitan areas.

Approximately 600, or 4 percent, of the Negro-occupied units inside the State's metropolitan area lacked some or all plumbing facilities in 1970, compared with 3,100, or 42 percent, of Negro housing outside the metropolitan area.

Number of persons per room is often used as a measure of crowding. In Delaware, both the number and proportion of housing units with 1.01 or more persons per room decreased during the decade. In 1960, 7 percent of all occupied housing units in the Delaware part of the Wilmington SMSA and 10 percent in nonmetropolitan areas had more than one person per room. By 1970, the proportion of such units had decreased to 5 percent in the State's metropolitan area and 8 percent in the nonmetropolitan areas (table C).

Homeownership in the State increased from 67 percent in 1960 to 68 percent in 1970. In the metropolitan area there was a decrease from 69 to 68 percent, while in nonmetropolitan areas the proportion increased from 63 to 68 percent.

About half the Negro households in both the metropolitan and nonmetropolitan areas owned their homes in 1970. Of the 10,300 Negro-homeowner households in the State, 6,700 lived in the Delaware part of the Wilmington SMSA and 3,600 lived outside the metropolitan area.

Table C. Plumbing Facilities and Persons Per Room by Metropolitan and Nonmetropolitan Residence: 1970 and 1960

The State Metropolitan and Nonmetropolitan Residence	Percent of housing units			
	Lacking some or all plumbing facilities		With 1.01 or more persons per room[1]	
	1970[2]	1960[3]	1970	1960
Total......................	5.1	12.4	5.6	7.9
Metropolitan residence..........	1.7	5.3	4.8	6.9
Inside central cities..........	1.5	6.7	6.6	7.9
Outside central cities........	1.8	4.5	4.2	6.4
Nonmetropolitan residence........	12.6	26.1	7.7	10.0

[1]Percent of all occupied units.
[2]Percent of all year-round housing units.
[3]Percent of all housing units.

Property values and rents increased during the last decade. The median value of owner-occupied housing in the metropolitan area increased by 36 percent ($13,200 in 1960 to $18,000 in 1970), while in the nonmetropolitan areas value increased 53 percent ($9,700 in 1960 to $14,800 in 1970). In the metropolitan area, median contract rent in 1970 was 48 percent higher than in 1960, rising from $66 to $98. In nonmetropolitan areas, rent increased from $49 to $68, or 39 percent.

Value and rent are expressed in current dollars (the value at the time of the respective censuses). Thus, any comparison must take into account the general rise in the cost of living during the 10-year period, as well as changes in the characteristics of the housing inventory.

Standard Metropolitan Statistical Area

The number of housing units in the Delaware suburbs of the Wilmington, Del.-N.J.-Md. SMSA increased by 48 percent during the decade, while housing in the central city (Wilmington) decreased 10 percent. By 1970, there were 90,700 housing units in the suburbs and 30,000 in the central city.

Average household size for the metropolitan area declined during the decade. In the central city, the average decreased from 3.1 persons to 2.9 and, in the suburbs, from 3.6 persons to 3.4.

The proportion of the housing inventory in one-unit structures declined in both Wilmington city and its suburbs in Delaware during the decade. In the central city, the proportion of such units declined from 72 percent in 1960 to 67 percent in 1970 and, in the suburban areas, from 87 to 78 percent.

The median number of rooms in the suburban housing units in the State increased from 5.8 in 1960 to 6.0 in 1970. In Wilmington central city the median number of rooms remained at 5.6 during the decade.

The number of units with seven or more rooms increased by 86 percent in the suburban areas; in the central city there were relatively large decreases in the smallest and largest units, i.e., those with one or two rooms and units with seven or more rooms.

In the central city the proportion of year-round housing units lacking some or all plumbing facilities declined during the decade from 7 to 2 percent. Such units in the suburban areas declined from 5 to 2 percent.

Of all occupied units in Wilmington city, 1,800 units, or 7 percent, reported more than one person per room in 1970, compared with 8 percent in 1960. In the suburban areas of the SMSA, such units declined during the decade from 6 to 4 percent.

Homeownership in the central city remained at 52 percent during the decade. In its Delaware suburbs, however, the homeownership rate declined from 78 percent in 1960 to 73 percent in 1970. About 45 percent of the Negro households in Wilmington city owned their homes in 1970, compared with 32 percent in 1960. In the suburban areas, the proportion of Negro homeowners increased from 61 percent in 1960 to 66 percent in 1970.

In the central city of Wilmington, the median value of owner-occupied housing rose 9 percent ($10,400 in 1960 to $11,300 in 1970), while in its suburbs in Delaware the median increased by 38 percent ($14,200 in 1960 to $19,600 in 1970). Median contract rent in the central city in 1970 was 23 percent higher than in 1960, rising from $62 to $76. Rent increased in the suburban areas from $72 to $114, or 58 percent.

The homeowner vacancy rate increased from 1.6 to 2.9 percent in the central city and decreased from 2.2 in 1960 to 0.6 in 1970 in its suburban areas in the State. The rental vacancy rate changed slightly in the central city, from 8.6 in 1960 to 8.0 in 1970 and decreased from 9.6 to 4.7 in the suburbs.

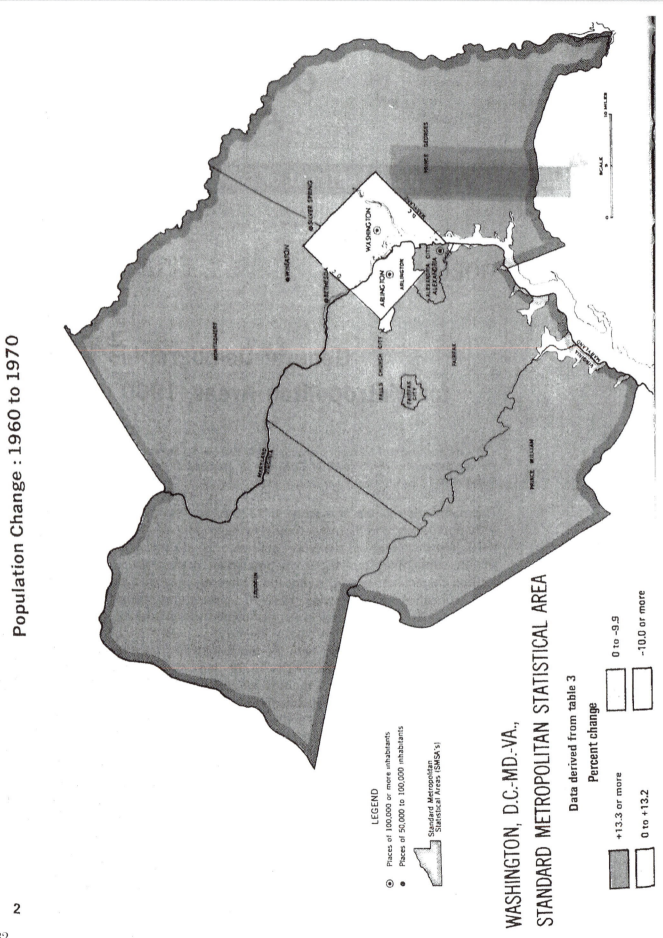

Population Change : 1960 to 1970

WASHINGTON, D.C.-MD.-VA., STANDARD METROPOLITAN STATISTICAL AREA

Data derived from table 3

Percent change

+13.3 or more

0 to +13.2

0 to -9.9

-10.0 or more

LEGEND

Places of 100,000 or more inhabitants

Places of 50,000 to 100,000 inhabitants

Standard Metropolitan Statistical Areas (SMSA's)

SCALE

0   5   10 MILES

Analytical Text

POPULATION TRENDS

The Standard Metropolitan Statistical Area

Between 1960 and 1970, the population of the Washington, D.C.-Md.-Va. Standard Metropolitan Statistical Area (SMSA) grew from 2,064,000 to 2,861,000—an increase of 797,000 or 38.6 percent[1] (table A). As a result, the Washington SMSA, which ranked 10th in population in 1960, moved past the Boston, Pittsburgh, and St. Louis SMSA's to become the seventh most populous metropolitan area in the Nation. Only the New York and Los Angeles-Long Beach SMSA's had population increases in the 1960 to 1970 decade larger than that which occurred in the Washington SMSA. In contrast to the growth rate of nearly 39 percent in the Washington SMSA, the other nine largest metropolitan areas in the Nation had rates of population change ranging from a small decrease in the Pittsburgh SMSA to an increase of 17 percent in the San Francisco-Oakland SMSA.

In 1970, the Washington SMSA was comprised of the city of Washington, D.C., the counties of Montgomery and Prince Georges in Maryland, the counties of Arlington, Fairfax, Loudoun, and Prince William in Virginia, and the independent cities of Alexandria, Fairfax, and Falls Church in Virginia.[2]

The population of Washington, D.C. declined from 764,000 to 757,000, or by 1 percent, between 1960 and 1970. At both dates Washington, D.C. was the ninth largest city in the Nation. Of the 10 largest cities in the United States in 1960, only three experienced population growth between 1960 and 1970.

---

[1] In the remainder of this text, "the Washington SMSA" refers to the entire metropolitan area (the Washington, D.C.-Md.-Va. SMSA).

[2] In the remainder of this text, "the central city," "the Maryland suburbs," and "the Virginia suburbs" refer to the city of Washington, D.C., the Maryland portion of the SMSA, and the Virginia portion of the SMSA, respectively.

Table A.   Population by Race and Inside and Outside Central City: 1970 and 1960

The District Metropolitan Residence	Population		Change		Percent Distribution	
	1970	1960	Number	Percent	1970	1960
Washington, D.C.-Md.-Va. SMSA, total......	2,861,123	2,064,090	797,033	38.6	100.0	100.0
Inside central city.......	756,510	763,956	-7,446	-1.0	26.4	37.0
Outside central city......	2,104,613	1,300,134	804,479	61.9	73.6	63.0
White...............	2,124,534	1,557,842	566,692	36.4	100.0	100.0
Inside central city.......	209,272	345,263	-135,991	-39.4	9.9	22.2
Outside central city......	1,915,262	1,212,579	702,683	57.9	90.1	77.8
Negro and other races.	736,589	506,248	230,341	45.5	100.0	100.0
Inside central city.......	547,238	418,693	128,545	30.7	74.3	82.7
Outside central city......	189,351	87,555	101,796	116.3	25.7	17.3

The total number of households in Washington, D.C. in 1970 was 263,000 or 10,000 more than in 1960. The population living in households declined slightly with the result that average household size dropped from 2.9 to 2.7 persons. In the entire Washington SMSA in 1970, there were 899,000 households and an average of 3.1 persons per household.

While the population of Washington, D.C. declined, the population in the balance of the Washington SMSA increased from 1,300,000 to 2,105,000, or by 62 percent, between 1960 and 1970. The Maryland suburbs grew from 698,000 to 1,183,000, or by 70 percent, and the Virginia suburbs grew from 602,000 to 921,000, or by 53 percent. Whereas 37 percent of the population of the Washington SMSA lived in the central city in 1960, the figure was down to 26 percent in 1970.

Between 1960 and 1970, the white population of the Washington SMSA increased from 1,558,000 to 2,125,000 or by 36 percent. The population of Negro and other races (over 95 percent of which is Negro) increased from 506,000 to 737,000, or by 45 percent, but despite this more rapid rate of growth, the proportion of Negro and other races in the total population increased only slightly from 25 to 26 percent. The population increase of 797,000 in the Washington SMSA between 1960 and 1970 was divided nearly equally between natural increase (births minus deaths) and net inmigration. The net inmigration of 417,000 was equivalent to 20 percent of the 1960 population.

During the 1960 to 1970 decade, the population of Negro and other races in Washington, D.C. grew from 419,000 to 547,000, or by 31 percent while the white population declined from 345,000 to 209,000, or by 39 percent. As a result the proportion of Negro and other races in the city's population increased from 55 percent to 72 percent. (In the other nine of the 10 largest cities in the United States in 1970, the proportion of Negro and other races in the total population ranged from 23 percent in New York City and Los Angeles to 47 percent in Baltimore.)

The population of Negro and other races in the Maryland and Virginia suburbs more than doubled from 88,000 in 1960 to 189,000 in 1970, but because the white population also increased rapidly from a much larger base—from 1,213,000 to 1,915,000 or by 58 percent—the proportion of Negro and other races in the suburban population increased only slightly from 7 to 9 percent. In 1970, 74 percent of Negro and other races in the Washington SMSA lived in the central city compared with 83 percent in 1960. In 1970, only 10 percent of

whites in the Washington SMSA lived in the central city compared with 22 percent in 1960.

While population growth in the Washington SMSA during the 1960 to 1970 decade was about equally divided between natural increase and net immigration, both among whites and among Negro and other races, patterns of population change by race and by source of change varied greatly between the central city and the remainder of the metropolitan area. In the central city the natural increase of 93,000 was more than offset by net out-migration which totaled 100,000 and which was equivalent to 13 percent of the 1960 population. Among whites the population decline of 136,000 was due to a natural increase of only 1,000 and a net outmigration of 137,000. Among Negro and other races, the population gain of 129,000 resulted from a natural increase of 91,000 and a net immigration of 37,000. In the Maryland and Virginia suburbs, net immigration of 517,000 accounted for nearly two-thirds of the population increase of 804,000 between 1960 and 1970.

Between 1960 and 1970, the population in each age group increased in the Washington SMSA. The rates of growth ranged from 4 percent in the under 5 group to 87 percent in the 15 to 24 group. The small increase in the under 5 group reflects the offsetting effects of the decline in birth rates which occurred throughout the United States during the 1960's and the sizable increase in the population in the childbearing ages in the Washington SMSA. The large increase in the 15 to 24 group reflects the combined effects of the entry of the large number of persons born during the post-World War II "baby boom" into this age group and the sizable net immigration of persons in this age group in 1970 into the Washington SMSA during the 1960's. As a result of these changes, the proportion of the total population in the under 5 group declined from 12 to 9 percent, and the proportion in the 15 to 24 group increased from 14 to 18 percent. In 1970, only 6 percent of the population was age 65 and over compared to 10 percent in the Nation as a whole.

In the central city, the population under 5 years old declined by 24 percent and the population in the 15 to 24 group increased by 33 percent. The proportion of the city's population in the 15 to 24 group increased from 14 to 19 percent. The population of Negro and other races is much younger than the white population. In 1970, 50 percent of Negro and other races and only 29 percent of whites were under age 25. Six percent of Negro and other races and 19 percent of whites were in the age group 65 and over.

HOUSING TRENDS

Between 1960 and 1970, population decreased by 7,400, or 1 percent, while the total supply of housing units in Washington, D.C. (central city of Washington, D.C.-Md.-Va. SMSA) increased by 15,800, or 6 percent. The SMSA, however, experienced growth in both housing and population. The number of housing units in the metropolitan area rose over the decade to 937,900, an increase of 298,900, or 47 percent. While the District of Columbia contained 30 percent of the housing in the SMSA, the additions to the housing supply in the city accounted for only 5 percent of the total housing increase in the SMSA between 1960 and 1970.

About 54 percent of the housing in the SMSA consisted of one-unit structures in 1970. The corresponding proportions for the District of Columbia and the suburbs were 37 percent and 61 percent, respectively. However, the number of units in multiunit structures increased at a much faster rate than one-unit structures during the decade. In the District of Columbia housing units in multiunit structures increased 12 percent and one-unit structures decreased 3 percent. In the suburbs corresponding figures were increases of 163 percent for multiunit structures and 46 percent for one-unit structures.

The size of housing units increased in the SMSA between 1960 and 1970. The median number of rooms was unchanged at 3.9 for the District of Columbia, but rose from 5.3 to 5.5 in the suburbs. In the District of Columbia, units with one, two, and five rooms showed large percentage increases, whereas, units with six or more rooms declined. In the suburbs the large increases occurred in units with one, two, and seven or more rooms.

Households were smaller in 1970 than in 1960. In the SMSA, the average number of persons in housing units decreased from 3.3 in 1960 to 3.1 in 1970. In the District of Columbia the decline was from 2.9 to 2.7 and in the suburbs from 3.5 to 3.2. During the same period the District of Columbia showed an increase of 24 percent in one-person households and a decline in households having two or more persons. In the suburbs, the number of one-person households more than tripled, two-person households doubled, and three-or-more-person households increased 55 percent.

In the District of Columbia, the number of units lacking some or all plumbing facilities declined from 20,300 to 6,400, or by 68 percent since 1960. In 1970, the proportion of such units in the city was 2 percent. The corresponding proportion in the suburbs was the same—2 percent.

Approximately 3,700, or 2 percent, of the Negro-occupied units in the District of Columbia lacked some or all plumbing facilities in 1970. In the suburbs, 3,400 units, or 8 percent, were in this category.

Number of persons per room is often used as a measure of crowding. In the suburbs, the proportion of housing units with 1.01 or more persons per room decreased from 8 percent in 1960 to 5 percent in 1970. In the District of Columbia the proportion remained unchanged, 12 percent.

Homeownership in the SMSA declined from 49 percent in 1960 to 46 percent in 1970. In the District of Columbia there was a decrease from 30 to 28 percent, while in the suburban areas the decline was from 63 to 53 percent.

About 31 percent of the Negro households in the SMSA owned their homes in 1970. Corresponding percentages for the District of Columbia and the suburbs were 27 percent and 46 percent, respectively.

The homeowner vacancy rate for the metropolitan area dropped from 1.9 percent in 1960 to 1.3 percent in 1970. The corresponding rate for the District of Columbia was 1.2 percent in both 1960 and 1970. In the suburbs, the homeowner vacancy rate declined from 2.2 to 1.4 percent. Rental vacancy rates for the SMSA remained unchanged at 4.4 percent. However, the rental vacancy rate for the District of Columbia increased from 3.8 to 5.3 percent and for the suburbs decreased from 5.2 to 3.8 percent.

Estimated value of housing in the city increased during the 10-year period from a median of $15,400 in 1960 to $21,300 in 1970, with large percentage increases in homes valued at $20,000 or more. In the suburbs, the median value increased from $17,600 to $29,300, with large increases in homes valued at $25,000 or more. Rents increased from $82 to $135, or 65 percent in the SMSA. In the District of Columbia rents increased 47 percent ($75 to $110), while in the suburbs the increase was 63 percent ($91 to $148), with large percentage increases in both areas in units renting at $100 or more.

Value and rent are expressed in current dollars (the value at the time of the respective censuses). Thus, any comparison must take into account the general rise in the cost of living during the 10-year period as well as changes in the characteristics of the housing inventory.

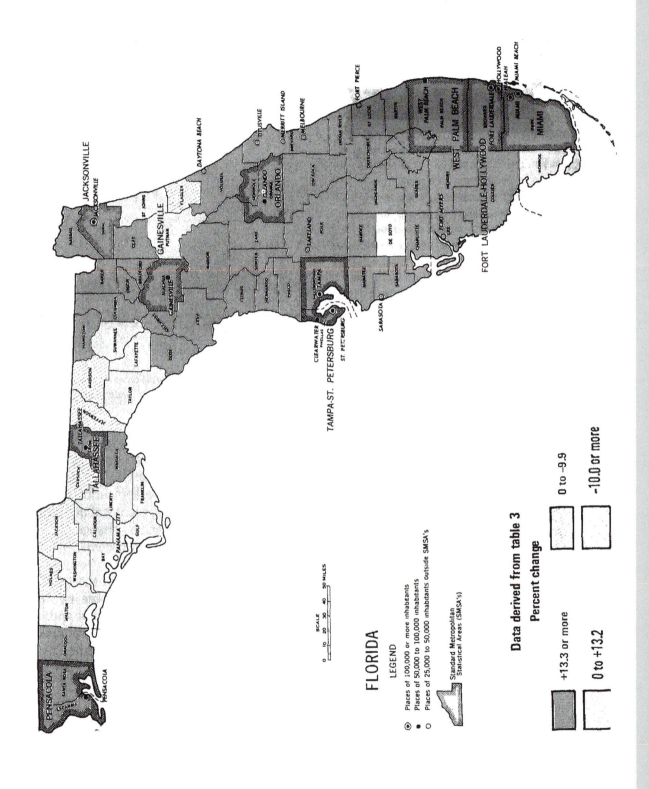

Population Change for Counties: 1960 to 1970

FLORIDA

LEGEND

⊙ Places of 100,000 or more inhabitants

● Places of 50,000 to 100,000 inhabitants

○ Places of 25,000 to 50,000 inhabitants outside SMSA's

Standard Metropolitan
Statistical Areas (SMSA's)

SCALE

0 10 20 30 40 50 MILES

Data derived from table 3

Percent change

+13.3 or more

0 to +13.2

0 to –9.9

–10.0 or more

Analytical Text

POPULATION TRENDS

General

One of the fastest growing States in the Nation, Florida increased in population between 1960 and 1970 from 4,952,000 to 6,789,000, a gain of 1,838,000, or 37 percent (table A). Unlike most States, rapid growth occurred in both metropolitan and nonmetropolitan areas, each of which increased by 37 percent. This widespread growth reflects the State's many functions: vacation and retirement areas; military and space activities; fruit and vegetable growing; and many kinds of manufacturing operations.

The total number of households in the State in 1970 was 2,282,000 or 732,000 more than in 1960. The population living in households increased less rapidly than the rate at which households increased with the result that average household size decreased, from 3.1 to 2.9 persons.

Population distribution by metropolitan-nonmetropolitan residence remained unchanged as a result of the similar growth of these two areas. As in the Nation as a whole, about 69 percent of Florida's residents live in metropolitan areas.

Between 1960 and 1970, Florida's white population increased its share of the total population of both metropolitan and nonmetropolitan areas. In 1970, 84 percent of the population of each area was white.

Florida's population growth stemmed from a substantial natural increase (excess of births over deaths) of 512,000 and a very large net inmigration of 1,326,000.

Table A.   Population by Race and Metropolitan and Nonmetropolitan Residence: 1970 and 1960

The State Metropolitan and Non-metropolitan Residence	Population		Change		Percent Distribution	
	1970	1960	Number	Percent	1970	1960
Total..............	6,789,443	4,951,560	1,837,883	37.1	100.0	100.0
Metropolitan residence...	4,656,993	3,395,125	1,261,868	37.2	68.6	68.6
Inside central cities...	1,849,608	1,601,222	248,386	15.5	27.2	32.3
Outside central cities.	2,807,385	1,793,903	1,013,482	56.5	41.3	36.2
Nonmetropolitan residence	2,132,450	1,556,435	576,015	37.0	31.4	31.4
White..............	5,711,411	4,063,881	1,647,530	40.5	84.1	82.1
Metropolitan residence...	3,928,230	2,817,524	1,110,706	39.4	57.9	56.9
Inside central cities..	1,446,393	1,258,755	187,638	14.9	21.3	25.4
Outside central cities.	2,481,837	1,558,769	923,068	59.2	36.6	31.5
Nonmetropolitan residence	1,783,181	1,246,357	536,824	43.1	26.2	25.2
Negro and other races	1,078,032	887,679	190,353	21.4	15.9	17.9
Metropolitan residence...	728,763	577,601	151,162	26.2	10.7	11.7
Inside central cities..	403,215	342,467	60,748	17.7	5.9	6.9
Outside central cities.	325,548	235,134	90,414	38.5	4.8	4.7
Nonmetropolitan residence	349,269	310,078	39,191	12.6	5.1	6.3

The white population accounted for all of Florida's net inmigration (1,340,000). The population of other races had a net outmigration of 13,000 persons.

Metropolitan areas recorded a natural increase of 342,000 and a net-inmigration of 920,000, for a total increase of 1,262,000. The nonmetropolitan area had a natural increase of 169,000 and a net inmigration of 407,000, for a total increase of 576,000.

All areas of the State experienced significant changes in age composition (see table 4). The number of children under 5 declined. All other age groups increased. The smallest increase was registered by 25-44 year olds (18 percent) and the largest by the population 65 and over (79 percent), followed by 15 to 24 year olds (69 percent).

These changes were in part due to changing birth rates and in part to migration, which is highly selective by age. Low birth rates during the depression years and in the 1960's contribute to the diminution of age groups 25-44 and under 5 years of age, whereas the post-World War II "baby boom" is currently reflected in the large size of the population 15-24 years old. The rapid growth in the population aged 65 and over is the result of the State's attraction of large numbers of retirees from all over the Nation. The State had a net inmigration of roughly 350,000 persons in this age group during the decade.

Standard Metropolitan Statistical Areas

The State of Florida in 1970 had nine standard metropolitan statistical areas (SMSA's), scattered throughout the State. All areas benefit economically from the State's excellent climate, but they vary greatly in size and in primary functions.

Three SMSA's are primarily vacation areas. These are on the Gold Coast, located in the southeastern corner of the State: West Palm Beach, Fort Lauderdale-Hollywood, and Miami.

The Miami SMSA is the largest and southernmost SMSA in the State. In 1970, its population numbered 1,268,000, up 333,000, or about 36 percent from the 1960 level of 935,000. It functions as a vacation resort. It also carries on diversified manufacturing activities and is an important air transportation center. The influx of a large Cuban population added considerably to the area's growth during the 1960's.

The Fort Lauderdale-Hollywood and the West Palm Beach SMSA's are the third and sixth largest metro-

politan areas in the State. Fort Lauderdale-Hollywood's population increased from 334,000 in 1960 to 620,000 in 1970, a gain of 286,000 or 86 percent. West Palm Beach population increased from 228,000 in 1960 to 349,000 in 1970, a gain of 121,000, or 53 percent. Both these SMSA's are primarily vacation resort areas.

Tampa-St. Petersburg on the west coast of Florida in the central part of the State is the second largest metropolitan area in the State. Population increased from 772,000 to 1,013,000 in 1970, a gain of 240,000, or 31 percent. Tampa has major manufacturing activities such as canning and preserving of fruits and tobacco manufacturing. It also carries on port activity and wholesaling for its hinterland. St. Petersburg is Florida's leading retirement center and a major resort.

Orlando, the fifth largest metropolitan area in Florida, is located in central Florida. Between 1960 and 1970 its population increased from 318,000 to 428,000, a gain of 110,000, or about 34 percent. It functions as a transportation, trade, and finance center, servicing the nearby Cape Kennedy Space Center.

Gainesville is the most recently designated SMSA in Florida and the next to the smallest in population size. Its population increased from 74,000 to 105,000, a gain of 31,000 or 41 percent. The University of Florida is located here.

Jacksonville SMSA, located in the northeastern corner of the State, is the fourth largest SMSA in Florida. It is a port and transportation hub, servicing the southeastern United States and is the largest industrial center in Florida. Tourist and vacation activities are also carried on. Several naval installations are located in the area.

Tallahassee, the smallest metropolitan area in the State, is located in north Florida. Its population increased from 74,000 in 1960 to 103,000 in 1970, a gain of 29,000, or 39 percent. This rapid growth relates to its function as capital of the State and to the location in the area of Florida State and Florida A and M Universities.

The Pensacola SMSA, the seventh largest in Florida, is located at the extreme northwestern corner of the State. Its population increased from 203,000 in 1960 to 243,000 in 1970, a gain of 40,000 or almost 20 percent. This is the smallest relative gain of any SMSA except Jacksonville. Pensacola has a major naval installation and chemical industries.

Annexation of territory during the decade was responsible for some of the population increases of all central cities except Miami and West Palm Beach, which did not have annexations (table B). Jacksonville, at the other extreme. during the 1960-70 decade consolidated with Duval County, thus becoming the largest city in area in the United States and absorbing virtually all of its suburbs in the process.

Counties

Sixty-one of Florida's 67 counties registered population increases during the 1960-70 decade. The six that declined had decreases below 10 percent. Five of the six are located in north Florida along the Alabama and Georgia State lines.

Many counties recorded very substantial population gains, with several nonmetropolitan West Coast resort counties showing the largest percent increases. Collier, Charlotte, Citrus, and Pasco Counties all more than doubled in size, with Lee, Sarasota, and Hernando Counties experiencing somewhat smaller gains. The largest increase on the East Coast was 106 percent registered by Brevard County (the Cape Kennedy Space Center). Other fast growing counties on the East Coast were Broward, Martin, and Palm Beach and interior counties with rapid growth were Okeechobee, Clay, and Seminole. All of these had at least 50 percent growth during the 10-year period.

There were six counties which had an excess of deaths over births, best known of which is Pinellas County (St. Petersburg), with 16,000 more deaths than births. The other five are Charlotte, Manatee, Osceola, Pasco, and Sarasota Counties. All are retirement areas, and all but Osceola are along the Gulf coast. Osceola is in central Florida. All of the six counties had large population increases as the result of substantial net inmigration. The percent of the migration to the 1960 population was for Charlotte. 129; Sarasota, 58; Manatee, 41; and Osceola, 33.

All but 20 counties had net inmigration. Of the 20 with net outmigration, 18 are located in a strip that runs between Pensacola and Gainesville (see map), which is less of a vacation and resort area than the rest of the State and also has less of industrial and space activities.

In 61 counties 10 percent or more of the population was of Negro and other races. Forty-four of these counties had declines in Negro population. Of the six counties which declined in total population, five had Negro outmigration as the probable primary cause.

Significant Negro growth and net inmigration occurred in resort areas such as Fort Lauderdale-Hollywood, Miami and Tampa-St. Petersburg and in Brevard County where space activities are carried on.

Table B.   Change in Population of Central Cities Through Annexation: 1960 to 1970

Central Cities	1970 population			1960 population	Change 1960 to 1970 in 1960 area
	Total	In 1960 area	In annexed area		
Tampa	277,767	263,852	13,915	274,970	−11,118
St. Petersburg	216,232	214,710	1,522	181,298	33,412
Fort Lauderdale	139,590	110,746	28,844	83,648	27,098
Hollywood	106,873	81,059	25,814	35,237	45,822
Orlando	99,006	86,784	12,222	88,135	−1,351
Pensacola	59,507	55,033	4,474	56,752	−1,719
Tallahassee	71,897	55,561	16,336	48,174	7,387
Gainesville	64,510	28,940	35,570	29,701	−761

HOUSING TRENDS

General

Between 1960 and 1970 the total supply of housing units in Florida increased more rapidly than population. The population grew by 1,838,000, or 37 percent, while housing units increased by 745,100, or 42 percent (table C).

About 68 percent of all housing units in the State were in its standard metropolitan statistical areas. The metropolitan areas experienced less relative growth in housing than did the nonmetropolitan areas. The number of housing units in SMSA's rose to 1,709,200 over the decade, an increase of 489,300 units, or 40 percent; this compares with an increase outside SMSA's of 255,900 units, or 46 percent.

About 70 percent of the housing in Florida consisted of one-unit structures in 1970. The proportion of such units in metropolitan areas was 67 percent and in nonmetropolitan areas, 76 percent.

The number of units in the State lacking some or all plumbing facilities in 1970 was 129,500 units, or 5 percent; the proportion of units in this category was 4 percent in metropolitan areas and 9 percent in nonmetropolitan areas (table D). Approximately 59,800, or 21 percent, of the Negro-occupied units in the State lacked some or all plumbing facilities in 1970. The corresponding proportions for inside and outside metropolitan areas were 14 percent and 37 percent, respectively.

Table C. Housing Units by Metropolitan and Nonmetropolitan Residence: 1970 and 1960

The State Metropolitan and Nonmetropolitan Residence	Housing units				Population percent change
	Total		Change		
	1970	1960	Number	Percent	
Total..................	2,522,080	1,776,961	745,119	41.9	37.1
Metropolitan residence.....	1,709,229	1,219,979	489,250	40.1	37.2
Inside central cities....	730,887	582,840	148,047	25.4	15.5
Outside central cities...	978,342	637,139	341,203	53.6	50.5
Nonmetropolitan residence..	812,851	556,982	255,869	45.9	37.0

Table D. Plumbing Facilities and Persons Per Room by Metropolitan and Nonmetropolitan Residence: 1970 and 1960

The State Metropolitan and Nonmetropolitan Residence	Percent of housing units			
	Lacking some or all plumbing facilities		With 1.01 or more persons per room[1]	
	1970[2]	1960[3]	1970	1960
Total......................	5.2	15.0	9.0	12.4
Metropolitan residence...........	3.7	(NA)	9.1	11.4
Inside central cities..........	4.1	12.8	9.6	10.4
Outside central cities........	3.3	(NA)	8.7	12.4
Nonmetropolitan residence........	8.5	(NA)	8.9	14.4

NA Not available.
[1]Percent of all occupied units.
[2]Percent of all year-round housing units.
[3]Percent of all housing units.

Households were smaller in 1970 than in 1960. In the metropolitan areas, the average household size declined from 3.1 persons in 1960 to 2.9 in 1970 and in nonmetropolitan areas, from 3.2 to 2.9 persons. The number of one- and two-person households in metropolitan areas increased by 88 percent and 55 percent, respectively; in nonmetropolitan areas one- and two-person households increased 91 percent and 68 percent, respectively. In comparison, the number of households with five or more persons increased 28 percent in metropolitan areas and 24 percent in nonmetropolitan areas.

The 1970 median number of rooms was 4.7 in both metropolitan and nonmetropolitan areas. One- and two-room units comprised a very small proportion of the year-round housing, 9 percent in metropolitan areas and 7 percent in nonmetropolitan areas. About 31 percent of the metropolitan housing units and 29 percent of units in nonmetropolitan areas had six or more rooms.

Number of persons per room is often used as a measure of crowding. In Florida, the proportion of housing units with 1.01 or more persons per room decreased during the decade. In 1960, about 11 percent of all occupied housing units in metropolitan areas and 14 percent in nonmetropolitan areas had 1.01 or more persons per room. By 1970, the proportion of such units had decreased to 9 percent in both metropolitan and nonmetropolitan areas (table D).

The homeownership rate in the State's metropolitan areas decreased slightly from 67 percent in 1960 to 66 percent in 1970, while in nonmetropolitan areas the proportion rose from 69 to 73 percent. Of the 1,564,100 owner-occupied units in the State, 1,043,500 were inside metropolitan areas and 520,600 were outside these areas.

About 47 percent of the Negro households in metropolitan areas owned their homes in 1970, compared with 53 percent in nonmetropolitan areas. Of the 135,800 Negro-homeowner households in the State, 88,700 lived inside SMSA's and 47,100 lived outside SMSA's.

Property values and rents increased during the last decade. The median value in metropolitan areas increased by 28 percent, from $12,400 in 1960 to $15,900 in 1970, while in nonmetropolitan areas the median increased 32 percent, from $10,000 to $13,200. In metropolitan areas, median contract rent in 1970 was 59 percent higher than in 1960, rising from $64 to $102. In nonmetropolitan areas rent increased by 45 percent, from $49 to $71.

Value and rent are expressed in current dollars (the value at the time of the respective censuses). Thus, any comparison must take into account the general rise in the cost of living during the 10-year period, as well as changes in the characteristics of the housing inventory.

Standard Metropolitan Statistical Areas

In the metropolitan areas of the State, the housing supply increased by 489,300 units, or 40 percent. The Miami SMSA, the largest in the State, contained 27 percent of the housing in the metropolitan areas and accounted for 21 percent of the increase. The Tampa-St. Petersburg SMSA, second largest, had 23 percent of the State's metropolitan housing and accounted for 20 percent of the increase. The Fort Lauderdale-Hollywood SMSA, third largest, with 15 percent of the metropolitan housing accounted, however, for 25 percent of the increase.

The suburban areas of the State experienced greater growth in housing than did the central cities. Housing units in the suburbs increased by 341,200, or 54 percent, while housing in the combined central cities increased by 148,000, or 25 percent. By 1970, there were 978,300 housing units in the suburbs and 730,900 units in the central cities.

In 1970, 61,600 housing units in the metropolitan areas, or 4 percent of all year-round units, lacked some or all plumbing facilties. The proportion of such units in the central cities was 4 percent, and in the suburbs, 3 percent. Approximately 12,800, or 11 percent, of the Negro households in central cities occupied units which lacked some or all plumbing facilities in 1970, compared with 13,600, or 18 percent, of Negro households in suburban areas.

Household size in the metropolitan areas declined during the decade. In the central cities, the average decreased from 3.0 to 2.8 persons, and in the suburbs, from 3.2 to 3.0 persons. One-person households constituted 22 percent of occupied housing units in the central cities and 17 percent in the suburbs.

In 1970, the median number of rooms was 4.6 in the central cities and 4.7 in the suburbs. While 11 percent of the housing in central cities had one or two rooms in 1970, 8 percent of the housing units in the suburbs were in this category. At the same time, 29 percent in the central cities had six or more rooms, compared with 31 percent in the suburbs.

Of all occupied units in the central cities, 10 percent reported 1.01 or more persons per room in 1970, as in 1960. In the suburban areas, the proportion was 9 percent in 1970, compared with 12 percent in 1960.

Homeownership in 1970 was greater in the suburban areas than in the central cities. About 71 percent of occupied units in the suburbs and 60 percent in the central cities were owner-occupied. The Negro-home-ownership rate in the suburbs was 53 percent, compared with 43 percent in the central cities.

In the central cities of Florida, the median value of owner-occupied housing rose 18 percent ($11,800 in 1960 to $13,900 in 1970) and in the suburbs, the median increased by 35 percent ($13,000 to $17,500). About 14 percent of the owner-occupied housing was valued in 1970 at $25,000 or more in the central cities, compared with 24 percent in the suburbs.

In 1970, median contract rent in the central cities was $89 and in the suburbs, $120. Approximately 16 percent of the renter-occupied units in the central cities and 32 percent of the suburban units had rents of $150 or more in 1970.

The homeowner vacancy rate decreased from 2.7 percent in 1960 to 1.6 percent in 1970 in the central cities, and from 4.7 to 1.6 percent in the suburbs. The rental vacancy rate decreased from 11.5 to 8.9 percent in the central cities, and from 15.0 to 9.2 percent in the suburbs.

Annexations

Annexations occurred in the central cities of Tampa, St. Petersburg, Fort Lauderdale, Hollywood, Orlando, Pensacola, Tallahassee, and Gainesville during the decade (see "Population Trends" and text table B). Such annexations affect changes in the characteristics for these central cities and their suburbs.

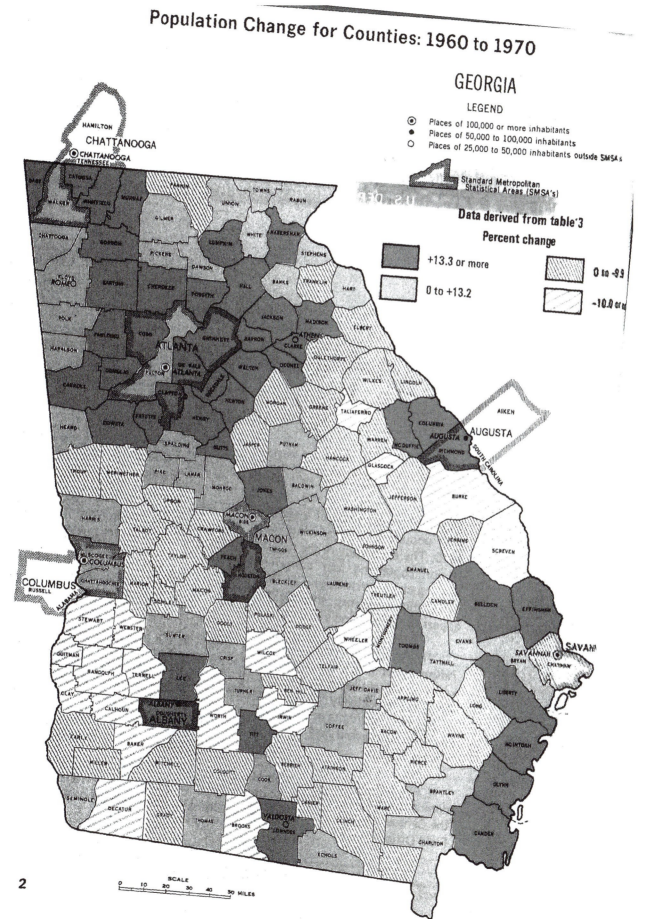

Population Change for Counties: 1960 to 1970

GEORGIA

LEGEND

⊙ Places of 100,000 or more inhabitants
• Places of 50,000 to 100,000 inhabitants
○ Places of 25,000 to 50,000 inhabitants outside SMSA's

Standard Metropolitan Statistical Areas (SMSA's)

Data derived from table 3

Percent change

+13.3 or more

0 to +13.2

0 to -9.9

-10.0 or more

Analytical Text

POPULATION TRENDS

General

Between 1960 and 1970, the population of Georgia increased by 646,000 or 16 percent, the highest decennial rate of increase since 1900. Nearly 73 percent of the increase, or about 466,000 persons, were added to the metropolitan population (table A). By far the largest part of this increase occurred in suburban areas which gained 391,000 persons over the decade. The population of the central cities on the other hand increased by only 75,000 or 8 percent. Annexation of suburban territory contributed to this modest growth; without it the central cities would have lost a population of 65,000 (table B).

Table A. Population by Race and Metropolitan and Nonmetropolitan Residence: 1970 and 1960

The State Metropolitan and Non-metropolitan Residence	Population		Change		Percent Distribution	
	1970	1960	Number	Percent	1970	1960
Total...............	4,589,575	3,943,116	646,459	16.4	100.0	100.0
Metropolitan residence...	2,280,230	1,814,069	466,161	25.7	49.7	46.0
Inside central cities..	1,024,400	949,759	74,641	7.9	22.3	24.1
Outside central cities.	1,255,830	864,310	391,520	45.3	27.4	21.9
Nonmetropolitan residence	2,309,345	2,129,047	180,298	8.5	50.3	54.0
White...............	3,387,516	2,817,223	570,293	20.2	73.8	71.4
Metropolitan residence...	1,709,509	1,349,306	360,203	26.7	37.2	34.2
Inside central cities..	570,472	594,993	-24,521	-4.1	12.4	15.1
Outside central cities.	1,139,037	754,313	384,724	51.0	24.8	19.1
Nonmetropolitan residence	1,678,007	1,467,917	210,090	14.3	36.6	37.2
Negro and other races	1,202,059	1,125,893	76,166	6.8	26.2	28.6
Metropolitan residence...	570,721	464,763	105,958	22.8	12.4	11.8
Inside central cities..	453,928	354,766	99,162	28.0	9.9	9.0
Outside central cities.	116,793	109,997	6,796	6.2	2.5	2.8
Nonmetropolitan residence	631,338	661,130	-29,792	-4.5	13.8	16.8

Table B. Change in Population of Central Cities Through Annexation: 1960 to 1970

Central Cities	1970 population			1960 population	Change 1960 to 1970 in 1960 area
	Total	In 1960 area	In annexed area		
Atlanta...................	496,973	493,542	3,431	487,455	6,087
Columbus..................	154,168	106,203	47,965	116,779	-10,576
Savannah..................	118,349	118,207	142	149,245	-31,038
Macon.....................	122,423	52,035	70,388	69,764	-17,729
Albany....................	72,623	54,692	17,931	55,890	-1,198

Georgia's rate of growth was higher than the growth rates for the Nation (13 percent) and for the South Region (14 percent). Georgia ranks fifth among the States in the South with regard to growth.

The total number of households in Georgia in 1970 was 1,672,000, or 602,000 more than in 1960. The population living in households increased less rapidly than the rate at which households increased with the result that the average household size decreased, from 3.3 to 3.1 persons.

The majority of Georgia's population (54 percent) in 1960 lived in nonmetropolitan areas. However, between 1960 and 1970, the metropolitan rate of growth, 26 percent, was almost triple the nonmetropolitan rate (9 percent), resulting in a higher proportion of the population living in metropolitan areas by the end of the decade. The proportion rose from 46 percent in 1960 to 50 percent in 1970. In the country as a whole, about two out of three Americans live in metropolitan areas.

The white population of central cities declined between 1960 and 1970 by 25,000, or 4 percent, while the white population in the suburban areas gained about 384,000, or 51 percent. The decline in the white population in central cities was more than offset by the increase in persons of Negro and other races of 99,000 or 28 percent.

Georgia's intercensal population increase was due overwhelmingly to natural increase (the excess of births over deaths). About 92 percent of the growth (595,000) was due to natural increase, and the remainder to net inmigration of 51,000 persons.

The pattern of migration change in Georgia for white and other races is in sharp contrast. Since 1940, there has been an unabated pattern of outmigration for the population of Negro and other races. By contrast, the white population shifted from a migration loss of 49,000 during the 1940's to a gain of 198,000 persons during the last decade. A similar pattern was evident in other States in the South.

As with most States in the Nation, Georgia's age structure changed significantly during the decade. The population under age 5 declined almost 11 percent while other age groups showed modest increases. The population under 5 now makes up only 9 percent of the population. Ten years ago, the group was nearly 12 percent of the State's total.

The greatest increase occurred in the 15 to 24 age group and was due for the most part to the entry of the large number of persons born during the post-World War II "baby boom" into this age group.

The population of Negro and other races is somewhat younger than the white population. Only 44 percent of the former is over age 25 while 54 percent of the white population is over 25.

Standard Metropolitan Statistical Areas

In 1970, there were seven standard metropolitan statistical areas (SMSA's) in Georgia. Three of these, Augusta, Ga.-S.C., Chattanooga, Tenn.-Ga., and Columbus, Ga.-Ala. are partially located in other States. The SMSA's range in size from 1,390,000 persons for Atlanta to 90,000 for Albany.

Of the 2,280,000 people living in metropolitan areas in Georgia, 61 percent live in the Atlanta SMSA, which is an important commercial and financial center in the southeast. Between 1960 and 1970, the population of the Atlanta SMSA increased by 37 percent, making it not only the most rapidly growing SMSA in Georgia but one of the fastest-growing large SMSA's in the United States. The area's growth was nearly evenly distributed between natural increase and net inmigration. Net inmigration was equivalent to about 20 percent of the 1960 population. The central city of Atlanta, which is the State capital, grew from 487,000 to 497,000, part of which can be attributed to the annexation of suburban territory between 1960 and 1970. Atlanta grew from the 24th largest SMSA in the country in 1960 to the 20th largest in 1970.

The Augusta, Ga.-S.C. SMSA had a population increase of 37,000. Natural increase was the primary factor contributing to population growth; more than 90 percent of the growth was accounted for by the excess of births over deaths. The central city of Augusta suffered a population loss of 11,000 persons or 15 percent between 1960 and 1970 and an outmigration equivalent to 31 percent of its 1960 population.

The South Carolina portion of the Augusta SMSA grew from 81,000 to 91,000, at half the rate of the Georgia portion which increased by 20 percent.

The Columbus, Ga.-Ala. SMSA had a population increase of 21,000 in the entire SMSA with a net migration loss of 23,000. Chattahoochee, the smallest suburban county, almost doubled its population between 1960 and 1970 as a result of the expansion of Fort Benning. The central city, Columbus, grew from 117,000 to 154,000 while the balance of the SMSA lost 17,000. However, the 1970 population of the area annexed to the city of Columbus between 1960 and 1970 was 48,000. Without annexation the city would have shown a loss of 11,000 population.

The Macon SMSA grew from 180,000 in 1960 to 206,000 in 1970, or by 14 percent. Natural increase was responsible for all the growth in this SMSA.

The Savannah SMSA was the only metropolitan area in the State to experience a population loss between 1960 and 1970; natural increase failed to offset net outmigration. The central city of Savannah lost a population of 31,000 between 1960 and 1970 despite annexation of suburban territory.

The Albany SMSA, the smallest in the State, grew from 76,000 in 1960 to 90,000 in 1970, or by 18 percent. The growth in the SMSA was due to natural increase which was partially offset by a small net outmigration.

Counties

Georgia's 159 counties range in population size from 2,000 in Echols County (located along the State's southern border) to 608,000 in Fulton County (Atlanta SMSA), one of the State's 13 metropolitan counties. De Kalb County, the second most populous in the State, is also part of the Atlanta SMSA. Third in population is Chatham County (the Savannah SMSA). The largest nonmetropolitan counties in Georgia with 1970 population exceeding 50,000 are: Floyd, Whitfield, and Glynn.

Of the 159 counties in Georgia, 46 exceeded the U.S. average growth rate of 13.3 percent, 47 counties grew more slowly, and 66 counties lost population during the 1960-70 period. During the decade, 93 counties gained population. All counties had more births than deaths. Of the 66 counties which show population losses for the decade, nearly all (62 counties) lost 10 percent or more of their 1960 totals.

Excepting Chatham County (Savannah SMSA) each of the metropolitan counties experienced population growth and four of these, De Kalb, Houston, Chattahoochee and Clayton, had inmigration rates of 30 percent or more. Clayton County (a suburban county of the Atlanta SMSA) experienced heavy inmigration (82 percent). The county had the largest relative increase experienced by any Georgia county (111 percent). Chattahoochee County, whose population was 26,000 in 1970, had the second highest rate of increase for the

decade, 98 percent. The county population growth was due principally to the addition of military personnel to Fort Benning. Nearly two-thirds of Chattahoochee County's 1970 population was living in group quarters, i.e. military barracks.

Of the 133 counties for which data are available by race, all but four showed heavy to moderate loss of black population through net outmigration. The counties showing black population gains through inmigration were De Kalb, Fulton, Douglas, and Richmond.

HOUSING TRENDS

General

Between 1960 and 1970, the total supply of housing units in Georgia increased more rapidly than population. The population grew by 646,000, or 16 percent, while housing units increased by 298,800, or 26 percent (table C).

The metropolitan areas of the State experienced greater relative growth in housing, as in population, than did the nonmetropolitan part. The number of housing units in the metropolitan areas rose from 541,000 to 728,500 over the decade, an increase of 187,500 units, or 35 percent; this compares with an increase of 111,300 units, or 18 percent, in the nonmetropolitan areas. While 50 percent of all housing units were in the metropolitan areas, these areas accounted for 63 percent of the total State increase between 1960 and 1970.

About 75 percent of the housing in Georgia consisted of one-unit structures in 1970. The number of units in multiunit structures, however, increased at a much faster rate than one-unit structures during the decade, 65 percent and 13 percent, respectively.

Table C. Housing Units by Metropolitan and Nonmetropolitan Residence: 1970 and 1960

The State Metropolitan and Nonmetropolitan Residence	Housing units				Population percent change
	Total		Change		
	1970	1960	Number	Percent	
Total.................	1,468,858	1,170,039	298,819	25.5	16.4
Metropolitan residence.....	728,468	540,968	187,500	34.7	25.7
Inside central cities....	348,046	297,331	50,715	17.1	7.9
Outside central cities...	380,422	243,637	136,785	56.1	45.3
Nonmetropolitan residence..	740,390	629,071	111,319	17.7	8.5

The size of housing units increased between 1960 and 1970. The median number of rooms rose from 4.8 to 5.0 in metropolitan areas and from 4.7 to 4.9 in nonmetropolitan areas. Units with one to three rooms declined in both metropolitan and nonmetropolitan areas.

Households were smaller in 1970 than in 1960. In the metropolitan areas, average household size declined from 3.5 persons in 1960 to 3.2 in 1970 and in nonmetropolitan areas, from 3.7 persons to 3.3. The number of one- and two-person households in metropolitan areas increased by 94 percent and 47 percent, respectively; in nonmetropolitan areas, one- and two-person households increased 72 percent and 38 percent, respectively. The number of households with five or more persons increased 13 percent in metropolitan areas and declined 7 percent in nonmetropolitan areas.

The number of units in the State lacking some or all plumbing facilities declined from 393,700 to 194,100, a 51-percent decrease since 1960. In 1970, the proportion of such units was 4 percent in metropolitan areas and 22 percent in nonmetropolitan areas.

Approximately 16,700, or 11 percent, of the Negro-occupied units inside SMSA's lacked some or all plumbing in 1970, compared with 85,600, or 57 percent, of the Negro housing outside SMSA's.

Number of persons per room is often used as a measure of crowding. In Georgia, both the number and proportion of housing units with 1.01 or more persons per room decreased during the decade. In 1960, 16 percent of all occupied housing units in metropolitan areas and 21 percent in nonmetropolitan areas had 1.01 or more persons per room. By 1970, the proportion of

such units decreased to 9 percent in metropolitan areas and 13 percent in nonmetropolitan areas (table D).

Homeownership in the State increased from 56 percent in 1960 to 61 percent in 1970. In metropolitan areas there was an increase from 56 to 57 percent, while in nonmetropolitan areas the proportion rose from 56 to 65 percent.

About 39 percent of the Negro households in metropolitan areas owned their homes in 1970, compared with 43 percent in the nonmetropolitan areas. Of the 125,300 Negro-homeowner households in the State, 59,700 lived inside SMSA's and 65,600 lived outside SMSA's.

Property values and rents increased in the last decade. The median value in metropolitan areas increased by 55 percent from $11,500 in 1960 to $17,800 in 1970, while in the nonmetropolitan areas value increased 54 percent, from $6,800 to $10,500. In metropolitan areas, median contract rent in 1970 was 71 percent higher than in 1960, rising from $48 to $82. In nonmetropolitan areas rent increased from $26 to $43, or 65 percent.

Value and rent are expressed in current dollars (the value at the time of the respective censuses). Thus, any comparison must take into account the general rise in the cost of living during the 10-year period, as well as changes in the characteristics of the housing inventory.

Standard Metropolitan Statistical Areas

In the metropolitan areas of the State, the housing supply increased by 187,500 units, or 35 percent. The Atlanta SMSA, which contained 62 percent of the

Table D. Plumbing Facilities and Persons Per Room by Metropolitan and Nonmetropolitan Residence: 1970 and 1960

The State Metropolitan and Nonmetropolitan Residence	Percent of housing units			
	Lacking some or all plumbing facilities		With 1.01 or more persons per room[1]	
	1970[2]	1960[3]	1970	1960
Total......................	13.3	33.7	10.9	18.4
Metropolitan residence...........	4.3	17.3	8.8	15.7
Inside central cities..........	4.3	18.3	11.2	16.9
Outside central cities.........	4.2	16.2	6.7	14.2
Nonmetropolitan residence........	22.1	47.7	13.0	20.8

[1]Percent of all occupied units.
[2]Percent of all year-round housing units.
[3]Percent of all housing units.

housing units in metropolitan areas, accounted for 76 percent of the increase.

In 1970, about 67 percent of the housing units in the State's metropolitan areas consisted of one-unit structures. The number of units in multiunit structures, however, increased at a much faster rate than one-unit structures during the decade, 70 percent and 21 percent, respectively.

Housing units increased in size in the metropolitan areas during the decade. The median number of rooms increased from 4.8 to 5.0. In 1970, the median number of rooms in the central cities was 4.7 and in the suburbs 5.3.

Average household size for the metropolitan areas of the State declined during the decade. In 1970, the combined central cities had an average of 3.0 persons per household and the suburbs, 3.3 persons.

Homeownership in 1970 was greater in the suburbs than in the central cities. About 68 percent of occupied units in the suburbs and 46 percent in the central cities were owner-occupied. The Negro homeownership rate in the central cities was 36 percent, compared with 54 percent in the suburbs.

In 1970, 31,000 housing units in metropolitan areas, or 4 percent of all year-round units, lacked some or all plumbing facilities. The proportion of such units in the central cities and the suburbs was the same, 4 percent.

Approximately 9,900, or 8 percent, of the Negro households in central cities occupied units which lacked some or all plumbing facilities in 1970, compared with 6,800, or 27 percent, of Negro households in the suburban areas.

Of all occupied units in metropolitan areas, 60,600 units, or 9 percent, reported more than one person per room in 1970, compared with 16 percent in 1960. In 1970, the proportion of such units was 11 percent in the central cities and 7 percent in the suburban areas (table D).

The homeowner vacancy rate for metropolitan areas decreased during the decade from 2.3 to 1.6 percent. The rental vacancy rate increased from 6.1 to 7.3 percent.

Annexations

Annexations occurred in each of the central cities except Augusta during the decade (see "Population Trends" and text table B). Such annexations affect changes in the characteristics for these central cities and their suburbs.

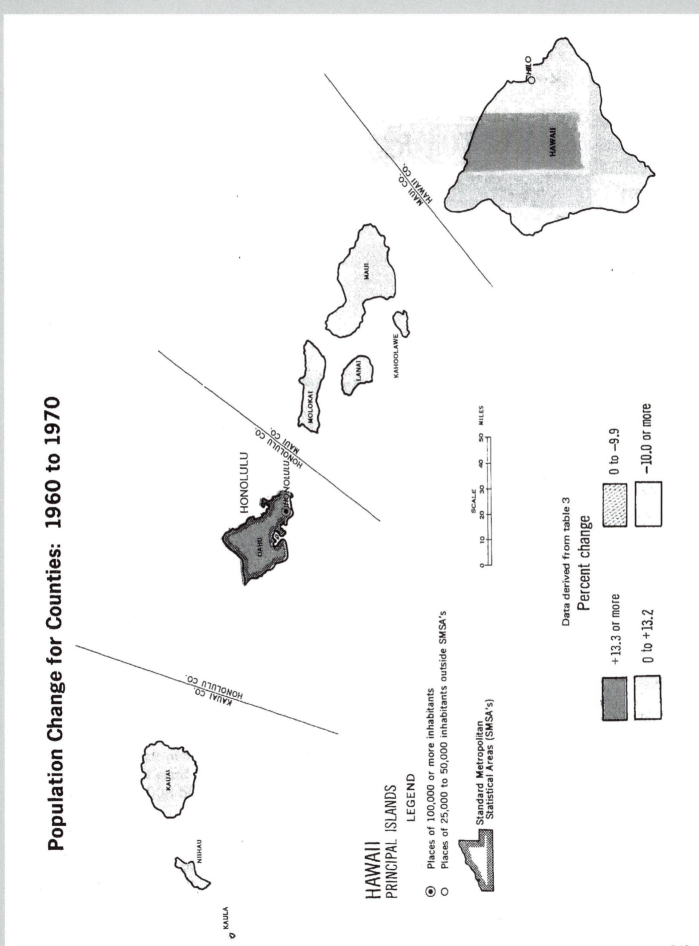

Population Change for Counties: 1960 to 1970

HAWAII
PRINCIPAL ISLANDS

LEGEND

⦿ Places of 100,000 or more inhabitants
◯ Places of 25,000 to 50,000 inhabitants outside SMSA's

Standard Metropolitan
Statistical Areas (SMSA's)

Data derived from table 3

Percent change

+13.3 or more

0 to +13.2

0 to −9.9

−10.0 or more

SCALE

0   10   20   30   40   50   MILES

Analytical Text

POPULATION TRENDS

General

Between 1960 and 1970 the total population of Hawaii grew by 136,000 persons, from 633,000 to 769,000, an increase of 21.5 percent over the population living in the State in 1960. This growth was highly concentrated in Hawaii's single SMSA, Honolulu, which accounted for 94 percent of the total intercensal population increase of the State (table A). At the time of both censuses, about four out of five persons in Hawaii lived in the SMSA. In the nation as a whole, two out of three persons are residents of metropolitan areas.

The rapid growth of the Honolulu SMSA between 1960 and 1970 was largely due to increases in the population of the suburban ring. While the suburban population grew by 98,000 persons, or by 48 percent, the population of the central city increased by 31,000 persons, or by 10 percent.

The total number of households in Hawaii in 1970 was 203,000, or 50,000 more than in 1960. The population living in households increased less rapidly than the rate at which new households were formed, however, with the result that average household size decreased, from 3.9 to 3.6 persons per unit.

The State has a large group quarters population (residents of military barracks, college dormitories, extended stay hospitals, and the like), consisting of 38,000 persons in 1970. More than 90 percent of this population is located in the Honolulu SMSA which is the site of University of Hawaii, several colleges, and the Pearl Harbor Naval Base. The growth and characteristics of Honolulu's suburbs in particular are affected by the

Table A. Population by Race and Metropolitan and Nonmetropolitan Residence:
1970 and 1960

The State Metropolitan and Non-metropolitan Residence	Population		Change		Percent Distribution	
	1970	1960	Number	Percent	1970	1960
Total..............	768,561	632,772	135,789	21.5	100.0	100.0
Metropolitan residence...	629,176	500,409	128,767	25.7	81.9	79.1
Inside central cities..	324,871	294,194	30,677	10.4	42.3	46.5
Outside central cities.	304,305	206,215	98,090	47.6	39.6	32.6
Nonmetropolitan residence	139,385	132,363	7,022	5.3	18.1	20.9
White..............	298,160	202,230	95,930	47.4	38.8	32.0
Metropolitan residence...	259,519	178,861	80,658	45.1	33.8	28.3
Inside central cities..	110,097	80,274	29,823	37.2	14.3	12.7
Outside central cities.	149,422	98,587	50,835	51.6	19.4	15.6
Nonmetropolitan residence	38,641	23,369	15,272	65.4	5.0	3.7
Negro and other races	470,401	430,542	39,859	9.3	66.2	68.0
Metropolitan residence...	369,657	321,548	48,109	15.0	48.1	50.8
Inside central cities..	214,774	213,920	854	0.4	27.9	33.8
Outside central cities.	154,883	107,628	47,255	43.9	20.2	17.0
Nonmetropolitan residence	100,744	108,994	-8,250	-7.6	13.1	17.2

resence of a large military population attached to the laval Base. In 1970, 9 percent of the total population of he suburban ring (26,000 persons) were residents of roup quarters, but there were in addition many military amilies living outside barracks.

Over the decade, Hawaii's white population grew ioth in size and as a proportion of the total populations of the metropolitan and nonmetropolitan areas. In the Honolulu SMSA, where the white growth rate was three imes that of other races, whites increased as a proportion of total population, from 36 percent in 1960 to 41 iercent in 1970. In the nonmetropolitan areas, there was a large percentage increase in the white population at the same time that there was a loss of population of other races; in these areas, the representation of whites was raised from 18 percent to 28 percent.

Hawaii's population growth in the 1960-70 decade was due primarily to natural increase and only to a minor degree to net inmigration (see table 3). Between 1960 and 1970, there was a very substantial excess of births over deaths amounting to 127,000, while net inmigration contributed only an additional 9,000 persons. Although all races contributed to the State's natural increase, the entire gain in population due to net inmigration was produced by the white population. White inmigration over the decade amounted to 58,000 persons, equivalent to 29 percent of the white population living in the State in 1960. At the same time, other races experienced a net outmigration of 49,000 persons, equivalent to 11 percent of their 1960 population.

Within the State, there was considerably more births than deaths during the decade in the SMSA and nonmetropolitan areas alike, but only one area grew as a result of net inmigration. The rapidly growing suburban ring of the Honolulu SMSA shows a net migratory gain of 41,000 persons of all races. The State's greatest migratory loss, on the other hand, was experienced by Honolulu city, which had a total net outmigration of 24,000 persons over the decade. The city's loss was the product of an extensive outmigration of races other than white (42,000) and a moderate white inmigration (17,000).

Changes in the age composition of Hawaii's population over the decade reflect the distinct migration experiences of the State's two racial groups and the greater tendency of young people to migrate. In the State as a whole, the white population—which grew greatly through net inmigration—over the decade became somewhat younger; but the population of other races—which suffered an extensive outmigration—is appreciably older now (see table 4).

In all areas of the State there were significant gains in populations 5 to 24 years of age and 45 years of age and over. While the increases at younger ages were produced mainly by the white population, other races contributed more to the growth of populations at older ages. These differences by race are noted particularly in Honolulu city.

Because of its large military component, the population of the Honolulu suburbs is predominantly youthful. In 1970, as well as in 1960, close to 60 percent of the suburban population was under 25 years of age, and only about 15 percent was 45 years of age and over. By contrast, a declining proportion of the central city population is under 25 years of age, and a sharply increasing proportion is 45 years old and over. In 1970, the central city population under 25 years of age comprised 45 percent of the total, but the population 45 and over accounted for nearly 30 percent of the city's population.

Counties

Hawaii's four counties are Kauai (30,000 population), Maui (46,000 population), Hawaii (63,000 population), and the metropolitan county of Honolulu (629,000 population). Between 1960 and 1970 each county had an increase in population, ranging from 3.5 percent in Hawaii County to 25.7 percent in Honolulu County.

Although the white populations of the three nonmetropolitan counties are comparatively small, comprising 30 percent or less of county totals in 1970, white population growth is responsible for the entire intercensal increase of these counties. While the populations of races other than white declined by 5 to 10 percent over the decade, the white populations grew rapidly, by 50 to 70 percent.

In all counties both racial groups had more births than deaths during the decade. The great variation in patterns of population change by race was produced by net migration. White population growth in the nonmetropolitan counties was overwhelmingly due to inmigration. Net inmigration rates for this population amounted to 45 percent in Kauai County, 68 percent in Maui County, and 64 percent in Hawaii County. At the same time, races other than white suffered large population losses as a result of net outmigration equivalent in the nonmetropolitan counties to 17 percent to 22 percent of their 1960 populations.

HOUSING

General

Between 1960 and 1970 the total supply of housing units in Hawaii increased faster than population. While housing units increased by 50,600 or 31 percent, the population grew by 136,000 or 22 percent (table B). Similarly, the number of households increased at a greater rate than the population, resulting in lower average household size.

Housing trends in Hawaii, like population trends, are dominated by the Honolulu SMSA, which contains four-fifths of the State's housing stock. During the decade, about 96 percent (48,400) of Hawaii's housing increase occurred in the SMSA.

Almost two-thirds of the housing in Hawaii consisted of one-unit structures. In both the metropolitan and nometropolitan areas, however, multiunit structures increased at much faster rates. The proportion of housing units in multiunit structures accordingly increased from 32 percent to 41 percent in the Honolulu SMSA and from 5 to 10 percent in the nonmetropolitan areas.

The size of housing units increased slightly between 1960 and 1970. The median number of rooms rose from 4.4 to 4.5 in the Honolulu SMSA and from 4.7 to 4.8 in the nonmetropolitan areas.

Households were smaller in 1970 than in 1960. In the Honolulu SMSA, the median number of persons per housing unit declined from 3.7 in 1960 to 3.3 in 1970, and in the nonmetropolitan areas of the State from 3.4 persons in 1960 to 3.2 in 1970. The number of one- and two-person households in the Honolulu SMSA increased by 66 percent and 77 percent, respectively; in the

nonmetropolitan areas two-person households showed the greatest increase, 47 percent.

Number of persons per room is often used as a measure of crowding. In Hawaii, the total number of housing units with 1.01 or more persons per room increased slightly during the decade, while the proportion of such units decreased noticeably. In 1960, 27 percent of all occupied housing units in the Honolulu SMSA and 21 percent of all occupied housing units in nonmetropolitan areas had 1.01 or more persons per room. By 1970, the proportion of such units decreased to 20 percent for both metropolitan and nonmetropolitan areas (table C). Although the number of housing units with 1.01 or more persons per room increased by 3 percent in both metropolitan and nonmetropolitan areas, the number of units with 1.51 or more persons per room showed a marked increase of 18 percent in the SMSA and a 33-percent increase in nonmetropolitan areas.

Less than half (47 percent) of Hawaii's housing was owner-occupied in 1970. Large increases in homeownership occurred over the decade, however. In the Honolulu SMSA, there was an increase of 55 percent in the number of owner-occupied units, and of nearly 40 percent in the nonmetropolitan areas. Renter-occupied units in the nonmetropolitan areas decreased by 2,800 units, or 14 percent, but in the metropolitan area increased by almost 30 percent.

Property values and rents increased markedly in the last decade. The median value of owner-occupied homes for the Honolulu SMSA increased by 64 percent from $23,200 in 1960 to $38,100 in 1970 while in the nonmetropolitan areas, value more than doubled, from $11,700 to $24,600.

Table B. Housing Units by Metropolitan and Nonmetropolitan Residence: 1970 and 1960

The State Metropolitan and Nonmetropolitan Residence	Housing units					Population percent change
	Total		Change			
	1970	1960	Number	Percent		
Total..............	216,170	165,506	50,579	30.6		21.5
Metropolitan residence.....	174,170	125,795	48,375	38.5		25.7
Inside central cities....	103,002	80,758	22,244	27.5		10.4
Outside central cities...	71,168	45,037	26,131	58.0		47.6
Nonmetropolitan residence..	41,915	39,711	2,204	5.6		5.3

In the SMSA, median contract rent in 1970 was 81 percent higher than in 1960, rising from $72 to $130. In the nonmetropolitan areas, rent doubled in the 10-year period, from $24 to $47.

Value and rent are expressed in current dollars (the value at the time of the respective censuses). Thus, any comparison must take into account the general rise in the cost of living during the 10-year period as well as changes in the characteristics of the housing inventory.

Honolulu SMSA

Within the Honolulu SMSA, the overall supply of housing grew twice as fast relatively in the suburbs as in the central city. The housing supply of the central city increased by 22,200 units, or 28 percent; housing in the suburbs increased by 26,100 units, or 58 percent. In 1970, 59 percent of the SMSA's housing was in the central city, compared with 64 percent in 1960.

The number of households and the population living in them grew at different rates over the decade. While the number of households in Honolulu city increased by 27 percent during the decade, population living in households grew by only 10 percent. In the suburbs, households increased 64 percent and the population in them 56 percent. Population per household decreased as a result; in the city of Honolulu, average household size declined from 3.7 to 3.2 persons, while in the suburbs, it declined less, from 4.3 to 4.1 persons.

The number of housing units in multiunit structures increased far more rapidly in both the central city and in the suburbs than one-unit structures. Units in multiunit structures increased by more than half (58 percent) in the central city and almost tripled in the suburban ring. In contrast, one-unit structures increased by 4 percent in the city and 40 percent in the suburbs.

The median number of rooms increased from 4.7 to 5.0 in the suburbs, but decreased from 4.1 to 4.0 in the city. The largest increases in the city were noted in housing units having only one and two rooms (56 percent), while in the suburbs by far the largest increases were in units having six or more rooms, which more than doubled over the decade.

Between 1960 and 1970 the number of housing units having 1.01 or more persons per room declined in the city of Honolulu by 2,000 units, or 10 percent. In the suburban ring, by contrast, there was a 25-percent increase in the number of units so occupied (2,900 units), and a still greater relative increase in housing units having 1.51 or more persons per room. The proportion of all housing units represented by units with 1.01 or more persons per room nonetheless declined over the decade in both the suburbs and in the city (table C).

There is a trend toward more homeownership in both areas. In 1970, approximately 41 percent of the city's housing and 51 percent of suburban housing were owner-occupied. In 1960, the corresponding homeownership rates were 39 percent and 44 percent, respectively.

Both value of property and contract rent showed large increases between 1960 and 1970, particularly in the central city. Median value of owner-occupied housing in Honolulu city increased by 73 percent, from $25,000 in 1960 to $43,200 in 1970. In the suburbs, value of

Table C.   Plumbing Facilities and Persons Per Room by Metropolitan and Nonmetro-
           politan Residence: 1970 and 1960

The State Metropolitan and Nonmetropolitan Residence	Percent of housing units			
	Lacking some or all plumbing facilities		With 1.01 or more persons per room[1]	
	1970[2]	1960[3]	1970	1960
Total......................	5.6	16.8	19.9	25.7
Metropolitan residence...........	3.3	9.4	19.9	27.1
Inside central cities..........	3.7	9.2	19.0	26.7
Outside central cities.........	2.7	9.9	21.2	27.8
Nonmetropolitan residence........	15.0	40.1	19.9	21.1

[1]Percent of all occupied units.
[2]Percent of all year-round housing units.
[3]Percent of all housing units.

housing increased by 64 percent during the decade, from $20,500 to $33,700. There was a much greater concentration of units at upper price levels. In 1970, 70 percent of owner-occupied housing in the city was valued at $35,000 or more, compared with 23 percent in 1960. In the suburbs in 1970, 45 percent of owner-occupied housing units reported values of $35,000 or more; in 1960 the corresponding proportion was 10 percent. Contract rent increased even faster than value in Honolulu city, almost doubling over the decade, from $70 to $132. In the suburbs, contract rent increased by 62 percent.

The homeowner vacancy rate for the Honolulu SMSA increased over the decade (1.4 percent for 1970 and 1.1 percent for 1960). These rates represent an increase in the city (0.9 and 1.6) and a decrease in the suburbs (1.5 to 1.2). Similarly rental vacancy rates increased from 4.1 to 4.5 percent for the SMSA representing an increase in the city (3.6 to 4.9) and a decrease in the suburbs (5.1 to 3.9).

Population Change for Counties: 1960 to 1970

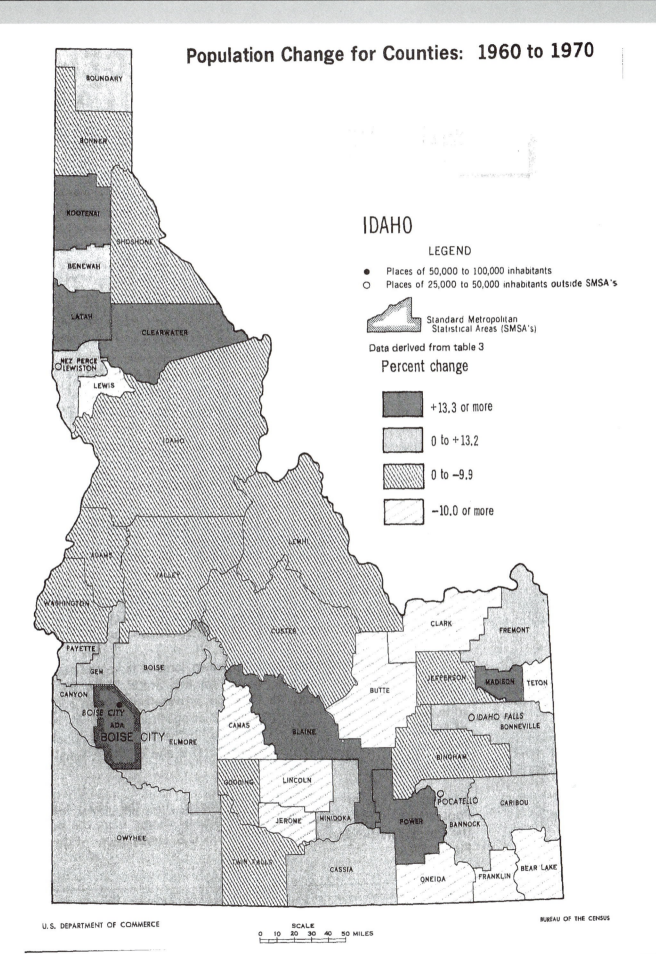

IDAHO

LEGEND

● Places of 50,000 to 100,000 inhabitants

○ Places of 25,000 to 50,000 inhabitants outside SMSA's

Standard Metropolitan Statistical Areas (SMSA's)

Data derived from table 3

Percent change

+13.3 or more

0 to +13.2

0 to −9.9

−10.0 or more

U.S. DEPARTMENT OF COMMERCE

SCALE

0   10   20   30   40   50 MILES

BUREAU OF THE CENSUS

Analytical Text

POPULATION TRENDS

General

Between 1960 and 1970 the population of Idaho grew by 45,000 persons, from 667,000 to 713,000, an increase of approximately 7 percent since 1960. Two-fifths of this increase was added to the State's single SMSA, Boise, which had a population of 93,000 in 1960 and 112,000 in 1970. Nonmetropolitan areas, which contained about 85 percent of the population in 1970 as in 1960, showed only moderate growth during this period (table A).

All metropolitan growth during the decade was concentrated in the central city of Boise, which more than doubled its population, while the suburban population was diminished by more than one-third. These changes were produced in large part as a result of annexation by the city of Boise of suburban territory containing a population of 44,000. Had this annexation not taken place, Boise city, instead of gaining, would have lost a population of several thousand, and the

Table A.   Population by Race and Metropolitan and Nonmetropolitan Residence: 1970 and 1960

The State Metropolitan and Non-metropolitan Residence	Population		Change		Percent Distribution	
	1970	1960	Number	Percent	1970	1960
Total..............	[1]712,567	667,191	45,376	6.8	100.0	100.0
Metropolitan residence...	112,230	93,460	18,770	20.1	15.8	14.0
Inside central cities..	74,990	34,481	40,509	117.5	10.5	5.2
Outside central cities.	37,240	58,979	-21,739	-36.9	5.2	8.8
Nonmetropolitan residence	600,337	573,731	26,606	4.6	84.2	86.0
White..............	698,802	657,383	41,419	6.3	98.1	98.5
Metropolitan residence...	111,079	92,795	18,248	19.7	15.6	13.9
Inside central cities..	74,130	34,113	40,017	117.3	10.4	5.1
Outside central cities.	36,949	58,682	-21,733	-37.0	5.2	8.8
Nonmetropolitan residence	587,723	564,588	23,135	4.1	82.5	84.6
Negro and other races	13,765	9,808	13,957	40.3	1.9	1.5
Metropolitan residence...	1,151	665	486	73.1	0.2	0.1
Inside central cities..	860	368	492	133.7	0.1	0.1
Outside central cities.	291	297	-6	-2.0	-	-
Nonmetropolitan residence	12,614	9,143	3,471	38.0	1.8	1.4

[1]See correction note on page 8.

suburbs would have increased (table B). The result of the changes which did occur, however (i.e., including the effects of annexation of territory by the central city), was to increase the share of the total SMSA population living in Boise city from approximately one-third in 1960 to two-thirds in 1970.

The population of Idaho and of the Boise SMSA is overwhelmingly white; in 1970 less than 2 percent of State and SMSA populations belonged to Negro and other races. While races other than white grew at much faster rates during the decade (by 40 percent, compared with the white rate of 6 percent), numerically this racial group was so small that its growth was not significant in producing changes in distribution by residence. Less than 10 percent of the entire group was found to be living in the Boise SMSA at the time of both censuses.

Although the population of the State increased by more than 45,000 persons between 1960 and 1970, there was a much greater natural increase of 87,000 (see table 3). The difference between these two figures implies a net outmigration from the State amounting to 42,000 persons for the decade. The entire Boise SMSA, on the other hand, grew as a result of both natural increase and net inmigration.

In 1970 as in 1960, approximately one-half of the population of Idaho was under 25 years of age. There were, nonetheless, marked changes in the size of particular age groups during the decade. As in many other sections of the country, there were large reductions in the number of children under 5 years of age and more than offsetting gains in young adults aged 15 to 24 years. While the State's population under 5 was diminished by 18,000, or 22 percent, the number of 15 to 24 year olds increased by 33,000, or 35 percent. By contrast, the number of children of school age, 5 to 14 years old, hardly changed, increasing by only 2 percent. In 1970, as in 1960, children of this age constituted the largest 10-year age group, comprising more than 20 percent of the total population of the State.

The population at middle and older ages increased during this period by more than 16 percent, while the number of adults 25 to 44 years old declined slightly.

Age changes in the Boise SMSA parallel those in the State as a whole, but differ in degree. The reduction in the size of the age group under 5 years is less (14 percent) and the increase in ages 15 to 24 is more prominent (57 percent). Unlike the State, however, the 25 to 44 year old population of the SMSA shows an increase of 12 percent. As a consequence of the large population loss suffered by the suburban portion of the SMSA, every age group there was diminished, while inside the city of Boise all ages except the youngest and the oldest more than doubled.

These changes are in part the product of changing birth rates and are in part due to migration which is highly selective by age. Low birth rates during the late 1960's contribute to the diminution of the population under 5 years old, whereas the post-World War II "baby boom" is currently reflected in the large size of the population 15 to 24 years old.

Counties

Idaho's 44 counties range in population size from a few hundred to over 100,000 persons in the State's single metropolitan county (Ada). Three nonmetropolitan counties had more than 50,000 inhabitants in 1970: Canyon (adjacent to the Boise SMSA), Bannock (site of Idaho State University and the city of Pocatello, in which four-fifths of the County's population is concentrated), and Bonneville (containing the city of Idaho Falls, with a population of 36,000).

Seven counties in Idaho increased at rates equivalent to or faster than the 13.3 percent increase for the nation as a whole (see table 3). With the exception of Ada County, the State's most populous counties were not among the fastest-growing. Madison County (13,500 population) had by far the highest rate of increase: between 1960 and 1970, its population grew by 4,000 persons, or 43 percent. It also had the highest rate of net inmigration in the State, equivalent to 25 percent of its total 1960 population. Madison County's growth is associated with a very substantial increase in enrollment at Ricks College during the decade. In 1970, population

Table B.   Change in Population of Central Cities Through Annexation: 1960 to 1970

Central Cities	1970 population			1960 population	Change 1960 to 1970 in 1960 area
	Total	In 1960 area	In annexed area		
Boise City................	74,990	30,533	44,457	34,481	-3,948

living in group quarters (defined as residents of college dormitories, military barracks, and the like) comprised 20 percent of the total population of the County, compared with less than 4 percent of the total population in 1960.

Other fast-growing nonmetropolitan counties, with rates of increase ranging from 18 percent to 27 percent, are: Clearwater (11,000 population), Blaine (5,700 population), Kootenai (35,300 population), Power (4,900 population), and Latah (25,000 population; this county is the seat of the University of Idaho). The metropolitan county of Ada, whose population increase amounted to 20 percent, ranks fourth among all counties in rate of growth.

Four of the fastest-growing nonmetropolitan counties also had high rates of net inmigration, that is, exceeding 10 percent. However, in Latah and Power Counties, as well as in Ada County, natural increase was a distinctly more important component of population change than net inmigration.

Four-fifths of Idaho's counties show net outmigration for the decade, including the largest nonmetropolitan counties. In spite of the attraction of a State University and the rapidly growing city of Pocatello, Bannock County suffered a net outmigration equivalent to 12 percent of its 1960 population. Bonneville County and Canyon County had net out-migration rates of 13 percent and 4 percent, respectively.

HOUSING TRENDS

General

During the decade, the total supply of housing units in Idaho increased relatively more than population. While housing units increased by 21,200 or over 9 percent, the population grew by almost 7 percent (table C). Similarly, the number of households increased at a greater rate than the population, resulting in lower average household size.

The metropolitan area of the State (Boise SMSA) experienced greater relative growth in housing, as in population, than did the nonmetropolitan part. The number of housing units in the metropolitan area rose to 37,100 over the decade, an increase of 6,400 units, or 21 percent; this compares with an increase of 14,800 units, or 8 percent, in the nonmetropolitan areas. While only 15 percent of the housing units were located in the Boise SMSA, this area accounted for about 30 percent of the total State increase between 1960 and 1970.

A trend toward smaller households is evident in the State. Households of one or two persons had large gains, while the number of larger households grew slowly or even declined. Nonmetropolitan areas provide an example of this trend. There the number of households with one or two persons increased by 20,300, while those containing three or more persons decreased by about 2,500.

Homeownership rates in Idaho were 70.1 percent in 1970 and 70.5 percent in 1960. Estimated value of housing increased during the same period from a median of $10,600 in 1960 to $14,200 in 1970. Metropolitan-nonmetropolitan differentials remained about the same over the decade. In 1960, median value was $12,200 in the Boise SMSA, about 20 percent higher than the $10,200 median in nonmetropolitan areas. Similarly in 1970, the $16,500 median for the SMSA was 20 percent higher than the $13,700 median in the nonmetropolitan territory.

In the State, rents increased by almost two-fifths, with very large increases in the number of units priced at $100 and above.

Table C. Housing Units by Metropolitan and Nonmetropolitan Residence: 1970 and 1960

The State Metropolitan and Nonmetropolitan Residence	Housing units				Population percent change
	Total		Change		
	1970	1960	Number	Percent	
Total...............	244,695	223,533	21,162	9.5	6.8
Metropolitan residence.....	37,145	30,782	6,363	20.7	20.1
Inside central cities....	25,992	13,383	12,609	94.2	117.5
Outside central cities...	11,153	17,399	6,246	-35.9	-36.9
Nonmetropolitan residence..	207,550	192,751	14,799	7.7	4.6

Value and rent are expressed in current dollars (the dollar value at the time of the respective censuses). Thus, any comparison must take into account the general rise in the cost of living during the 10-year period as well as changes in the characteristics of the housing inventory.

Number of persons per room is often used as a measure of crowding. In Idaho, units with 1.01 or more persons per room comprised about 9 percent of all occupied housing units in 1970, compared with 15 percent in 1960 (table D). The number of all such units in 1970 was 20,200, a decrease of about 9,700, or 32 percent, between 1960 and 1970, with an even greater relative drop in the number having 1.51 or more persons per room. The decline occurred in metropolitan and nonmetropolitan areas alike, but in nonmetropolitan areas the improvement was greater.

Boise SMSA

The housing supply in the Boise SMSA increased by 6,400 units, or 21 percent, between 1960 and 1970. Paralleling the population changes, housing in Boise increased by 94 percent in the city, compared with a decrease of 36 percent in the suburbs. A component of

housing and population change in the Boise SMSA is annexation of territory by the central city (see "Population Trends" and text table B). Such annexation affects to an unknown extent changes in housing characteristics for the central city and suburbs.

Average household size declined in the SMSA during the decade. Population per occupied unit was 3.1 in 1970, compared with 3.3 in 1960.

Homeownership in the SMSA declined from 72.9 percent in 1960 to 71.2 percent in 1970. The median value of owner-occupied homes increased from $12,200 to $16,500, or a 35-percent increase over the decade. Median contract rent rose from $56 in 1960 to $84 in 1970—a 50-percent increase.

In 1970, 800 housing units in the SMSA, or 2 percent of all year-round units, lacked some or all plumbing facilities. Of all occupied units in the metropolitan area, 2,200 units, or 6 percent, reported more than one person per room in 1970, compared with 10 percent in 1960.

The homeowner vacancy rate for the SMSA decreased for the decade from 2.2 to 1.0 percent. Similarly, the rental vacancy rate decreased from 10.5 to 4.3 percent.

Table D. Plumbing Facilities and Persons Per Room by Metropolitan and Nonmetropolitan Residence: 1970 and 1960

The State Metropolitan and Nonmetropolitan Residence	Percent of housing units			
	Lacking some or all plumbing facilities		With 1.01 or more persons per room[1]	
	1970[2]	1960[3]	1970	1960
Total......................	5.3	14.7	9.2	15.5
Metropolitan residence...........	2.2	(NA)	6.0	10.2
Inside central cities..........	2.2	(NA)	4.8	6.9
Outside central cities.........	2.1	(NA)	8.9	12.7
Nonmetropolitan residence........	5.9	(NA)	9.9	16.4

NA Not available.
[1]Percent of all occupied units.
[2]Percent of all year-round housing units.
[3]Percent of all housing units.

Population Change for Counties: 1960 to 1970

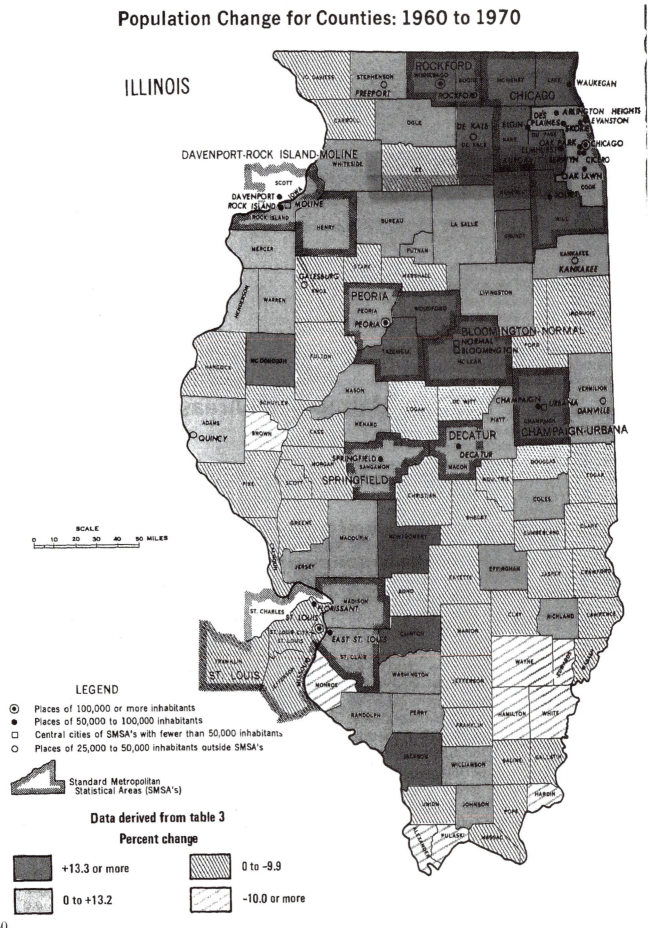

ILLINOIS

DAVENPORT-ROCK ISLAND-MOLINE

SCALE

0   10   20   30   40   50 MILES

LEGEND

⊙ Places of 100,000 or more inhabitants
● Places of 50,000 to 100,000 inhabitants
□ Central cities of SMSA's with fewer than 50,000 inhabitants
○ Places of 25,000 to 50,000 inhabitants outside SMSA's

Standard Metropolitan
Statistical Areas (SMSA's)

Data derived from table 3

Percent change

▓ +13.3 or more	▨ 0 to -9.9	
░ 0 to +13.2	⬜ -10.0 or more	

Analytical Text

POPULATION TRENDS

General

Between 1960 and 1970, the population of the State of Illinois increased from 10,081,000 to 11,114,000, a gain of 1,033,000, or 10 percent. Metropolitan areas increased by more than 12 percent, from 7,933,000 to 8,903,000, while nonmetropolitan areas grew by only 3 percent (table A). The Chicago Standard Metropolitan Statistical Area (SMSA) alone accounted for about 70 percent of the State's population increase and about the same share in metropolitan areas. All metropolitan gain was in the suburban areas which increased by 1,057,000 persons, or 28 percent. The central cities of the State lost a population of 87,000 over the decade, or 2 percent of their 1960 total.

The proportion of total State population living in metropolitan areas increased only slightly as a result of decennial changes, from 79 percent in 1960 to 80 percent in 1970. In the Nation as a whole, 69 percent of the population is metropolitan.

The total number of households in Illinois in 1970 was 3,502,000, or 417,000 more than in 1960. The population living in households increased less rapidly than the rate at which households increased, with the result that average household size decreased slightly, from 3.2 to 3.1 persons.

In 1970, 84 percent of Illinois' metropolitan population was white, down from 87 percent in 1960. This drop reflected the rapid growth of Negro and other races which increased by 434,000 (42 percent) and the much slower growth of the white population which increased by 536,000 (8 percent). The nonmetropolitan population of Illinois was more than 97 percent white in both 1960 and 1970.

The decrease in population of Illinois' central cities was produced by a loss of 434,000 whites and a gain of 347,000 persons of other races. Suburban growth, by contrast, was due overwhelmingly to a white population

Table A.   Population by Race and Metropolitan and Nonmetropolitan Residence: 1970 and 1960

The State Metropolitan and Non-metropolitan Residence	Population		Change		Percent Distribution	
	1970	1960	Number	Percent	1970	1960
Total...............	11,113,976	10,081,158	1,032,818	10.2	100.0	100.0
Metropolitan residence...	8,903,065	7,933,031	970,034	12.2	80.1	78.7
Inside central cities..	4,075,563	4,162,620	-87,057	-2.1	36.7	41.3
Outside central cities.	4,827,502	3,770,411	1,057,091	28.0	43.4	37.4
Nonmetropolitan residence	2,210,911	2,148,127	62,784	2.9	19.9	21.3
White...............	9,600,381	9,010,252	590,129	6.5	86.4	89.4
Metropolitan residence...	7,443,285	6,907,378	535,907	7.8	67.0	68.5
Inside central cities..	2,853,078	3,287,002	-433,924	-13.2	25.7	32.6
Outside central cities.	4,590,207	3,620,376	969,831	26.8	41.3	35.9
Nonmetropolitan residence	2,157,096	2,102,874	54,222	2.6	19.4	20.9
Negro and other races	1,513,595	1,070,906	442,689	41.3	13.6	10.6
Metropolitan residence...	1,459,780	1,025,653	434,127	42.3	13.1	10.2
Inside central cities..	1,222,485	875,618	346,867	39.6	11.0	8.7
Outside central cities.	237,295	150,035	87,260	58.2	2.1	1.5
Nonmetropolitan residence	53,815	45,253	8,562	18.9	0.5	0.4

gain of 970,000. The population of Negro and other races in the suburban rings increased by only 87,000 persons. The proportion of central city population which is white consequently declined, from 79 percent in 1960 to 70 percent in 1970. In the suburban rings, however, there was practically no change in the racial distribution; races other than white increased their representation from 4 percent in 1960 to only 5 percent in 1970.

In the State as a whole and in both metropolitan and nonmetropolitan areas there were substantially more births than deaths. Net outmigration was sufficient in some instances to offset natural increase and result in only small increases or a decline in population. From the central cities of metropolitan areas, there was a net outmigration of more than 500,000 persons, but a natural increase of 417,000. Suburban areas, by contrast, grew equally through natural increase and net inmigration. In nonmetropolitan areas, a natural increase of 125,000 was sharply cut back by a net outmigration of 62,000, to produce a population gain of only 63,000.

While both white and other races showed substantial natural increase for the 1960-70 decade, their migration trends differed. The white population of the State experienced a natural increase of 805,000, but a net outmigration of 215,000. In sharp contrast was the heavy net inmigration of 170,000 persons of races other than white which augmented a natural increase of 270,000 (see table 3).

All areas of the State experienced significant changes in age composition (see table 4). In both metropolitan and nonmetropolitan areas, the population under 5 years of age was diminished between 1960 and 1970, by 16 percent in metropolitan areas and 22 percent in nonmetropolitan areas. In nonmetropolitan areas the age group 25 to 44 years was also reduced, by 6 percent. All other age groups increased, notably the 15 to 24 year old group which grew by 49 percent in metropolitan areas and 35 percent in nonmetropolitan areas of the State.

Inside central cities, the substantial white population loss affected every age group except for the 15 to 24 year olds, which increased by 14 percent. The population of other races, by contrast, which had a large net inmigration, shows gains at all ages except under 5 years, which declined only slightly. The fastest growing group in this population was 15 to 24 years old, which increased by 90 percent. Schoolchildren, 5 to 14 years of age, and elderly persons, 65 and over, also grew very rapidly, by 66 percent and 57 percent, respectively.

Outside central cities, where the population of both races grew most rapidly, all age groups increased substantially except for the white population under 5 years of age.

Similar age changes are found in other sections of the country. They are due in part to changing birth rates and in part to migration, which is highly selective by age. Low birth rates during the depression years and in the 1960's contribute to the diminution of age groups 25 to 44 and under 5 years, whereas the post-World War II "baby boom" is currently reflected in the large size of the population 15 to 24 years of age.

Standard Metropolitan Statistical Areas

There are seven standard metropolitan statistical areas (SMSA's) completely within the borders of Illinois. They are concentrated in the central and northeastern sections of the State. In addition, two SMSA's are located partially within the State: St. Louis, Mo.-Ill. and Davenport-Rock Island-Moline, Iowa-Ill.

The Chicago SMSA, in the northeast corner of the State, dominates the State of Illinois. It is among the five largest industrial concentrations in the country. Accounting for 63 percent of the State's population, its activities largely influence population and economic trends in the State and much of the middle West. The Chicago SMSA has a broad industrial base and provides metropolitan services to its residential population and to a large population outside its environs. Between 1960 and 1970, its population increased from 6,221,000 to 6,979,000, a gain of 758,000, or 12 percent.

The population of the city of Chicago was reduced over the decade by 183,000, or 5 percent, while the suburbs increased by 941,000 persons, or 35 percent. In 1960, 57 percent of the SMSA's population lived in the central city, but by 1970 this proportion had dropped to 48 percent. The central city's decrease was produced by a loss of 505,000 whites and a gain of 322,000 persons of other races. The natural increase of the white population amounted to 141,000 for the decade, but at the same time there was a net outmigration of 646,000, equivalent to 24 percent of the total white population of the city in 1960. Most of the gain in population of other races was due to a natural increase of 208,000; net inmigration added 113,000 persons. As a result of these changes, the white population of Chicago declined as a proportion of the total, from 76 percent in 1960 to 66 percent in 1970.

In the Chicago suburbs races other than white grew more than twice as fast as the white population (by 79 percent, compared to 34 percent for the white population). Numerically, persons of Negro and other races remained a small minority, comprising less than 5 percent of the total suburban population at the time of both censuses. A larger part of the suburban growth of both racial groups was due to net inmigration than to natural increase.

The Peoria SMSA, an important manufacturing area specializing in machinery and transportation equipment, is Illinois' second largest SMSA. Between 1960 and 1970, the population of this SMSA rose from 313,000 to 342,000, or by 9 percent. Nearly all of the SMSA's population increase occurred in the central city, which grew by 24,000, while the suburban population increased by only 5,000. The central city's population growth was produced by annexation of a suburban population of 33,000; without this annexation, Peoria city would have shown a population loss of 9,000 (table B).

The Rockford SMSA is a manufacturing center which specializes in the production of machine tools. Its population increased by 18 percent over the decade, from 230,000 to 272,000. This increase was distributed almost equally between the central city and the suburban ring. A very large part of the central city's gain was due to annexation of a suburban population of 19,000.

The Champaign-Urbana SMSA, the site of the University of Illinois, had one of the highest rates of population growth in the State, 23 percent. Between 1960 and 1970, the population of this SMSA grew from 132,000 to 163,000. The two central cities in combination accounted for 40 percent of this gain. However, during the decade both Champaign and Urbana annexed surburban populations. Without these annexations, the population growth of both cities would have been reduced substantially.

The Springfied SMSA, which is the capital of Illinois, had a population gain of 10 percent over the decade, growing from 147,000 to 161,000. The city of Springfield grew moderately during this period, from 83,000 to 92,000 as a result of annexation of a population of nearly 12,000. Without this addition, the population of the city would have shown a loss.

The lowest metropolitan growth rate was registered by the Decatur SMSA, a manufacturing center. Between 1960 and 1970 this SMSA increased by less than 6 percent, from 118,000 to 125,000. All growth was concentrated in the central city which grew from 78,000 to 90,000, and the suburbs show a loss of population. This situation is the result of annexation of suburban territory by the central city. Without it, the city would have shown a population loss.

The fastest-growing SMSA in Illinois, Bloomington-Normal, is the site of northern Illinois State University and Illinois Wesleyan. The combined enrollments at these schools tripled over the decade. Between 1960 and 1970, the population of the SMSA grew 25 percent, from 84,000 to 104,000. More than 64 percent of this increase took place in the city of Normal, which nearly doubled in population over the decade. More than half of the growth occurred at ages 15 to 24. In 1970, 44 percent of the total population of Normal consisted of young adults 15 to 24 years of age, compared to 28 percent in 1960. Virtually all of Bloomington's moderate increase in population (less than 4,000 persons, or 10 percent) was produced by annexation.

Table B.   Change in Population of Central Cities Through Annexation: 1960 to 1970

Central Cities	1970 population			1960 population	Change 1960 to 1970 in 1960 area
	Total	In 1960 area	In annexed area		
Chicago..........................	3,366,957	3,362,220	4,737	3,550,404	-188,184
Rock Island......................	50,166	48,829	1,337	51,863	-3,034
Moline...........................	46,237	42,992	3,245	42,705	287
Peoria...........................	126,963	93,979	32,984	103,162	-9,183
Rockford.........................	147,370	128,567	18,803	126,706	1,861
Springfield......................	91,753	80,148	11,605	83,271	-3,123
Champaign........................	56,532	50,581	5,951	49,583	998
Urbana...........................	32,800	28,563	4,237	27,294	1,269
Decatur..........................	90,397	75,284	15,113	78,004	-2,720
Bloomington......................	39,992	36,304	3,688	36,271	33
Normal...........................	26,396	24,780	1,616	13,357	11,423

More than 60 percent of the total population of the Davenport-Rock Island-Moline SMSA is in Illinois (Henry and Rock Island Counties). Between 1960 and 1970, the population of the Illinois portion increased by 10 percent, from 200,000 to 220,000. The population of Rock Island city was reduced over the decade by 3 percent (from 52,000 to 50,000) while Moline's population increased moderately by 8 percent (from 43,000 to 46,000). The suburbs, which have a population larger than both cities combined, grew by 17 percent during this period.

Approximately one-fourth of the population of the St. Louis, Mo.-Ill. SMSA is in the State of Illinois (Madison and St. Clair Counties). During the 1960-70 decade this population increased from 487,000 to 536,000, or by 10 percent. The Illinois portion of the St. Louis SMSA is the second most populous metropolitan area in Illinois.

Counties

Between 1960 and 1970, 53 of the 102 counties in Illinois recorded increases in population (see map). Eighteen of these counties grew at rates equivalent to or faster than the 13.3 percent rate of increase for the United States as a whole. Nearly all counties with highest rates of growth (above 30 percent) were in the Chicago SMSA or adjacent to it (Du Page, which increased by 57 percent; Kendall, by 50; De Kalb, by 39; McHenry, by 33; Lake and Will, each by 30). The only exception was Jackson County, located in the extreme southwestern portion of the State and site of Southern Illinois State University, which grew by 31 percent.

Counties losing population were scattered throughout the State, but seven of the eight counties with heavy losses (10 percent or more of their 1960 populations) were concentrated in the southern part of the State.

There were five counties, all in Southern Illinois, which had a natural decrease (excess of deaths over births) during the decade. Two of these counties had large populations: Franklin, with 38,000 population, and Saline, with 26,000 population. Franklin's small population loss (1,000) was produced almost entirely by the natural decrease. There was a neglible net inmigration to the county. Saline's population loss (500) was also due entirely to natural decrease which was great enough to counteract the county's small net inmigration.

There were 30 counties in Illinois which had net inmigration between 1960 and 1970. Of these, 12 had rates of net inmigration of 10 percent or more. In nearly every case, the county with large-scale inmigration was metropolitan or adjacent to a metropolitan area. In the two counties not associated with a metropolitan area—Jackson and McDonough—there were rapidly growing universities (University of Southern Illinois and Western Illinois, respectively).

There was heavy net outmigration from nine counties located in Southern Illinois and three counties scattered through the western portion of the State. These include all eight counties experiencing population losses of 10 percent or more, and in addition, Union and Wabash Counties in Southern Illinois, and Stark County, which is midway between the SMSA's of Peoria and Davenport-Rock Island-Moline.

HOUSING TRENDS

General

Between 1960 and 1970 the total supply of housing units in Illinois increased more rapidly than population. The population grew by 1,033,000, or 10 percent, while housing units increased by 427,600, or 13 percent (table C).

Table C. Housing Units by Metropolitan and Nonmetropolitan Residence: 1970 and 1960

The State Metropolitan and Nonmetropolitan Residence	Housing units				Population percent change
	Total		Change		
	1970	1960	Number	Percent	
Total................	3,703,367	3,275,799	427,568	13.1	10.2
Metropolitan residence.....	2,926,977	2,542,289	384,688	15.1	12.2
Inside central cities....	1,453,850	1,419,753	34,097	2.4	-2.1
Outside central cities...	1,473,127	1,122,536	350,591	31.2	28.0
Nonmetropolitan residence..	776,390	733,510	42,880	5.8	2.9

The metropolitan areas of the State experienced greater relative growth in housing, as in population, than did the nonmetropolitan part. The number of housing units in metropolitan areas rose over the decade to 2,927,000, an increase of 384,700 units, or 15 percent; this compares with an increase of 42,900 units, or 6 percent, in nonmetropolitan areas. Metropolitan areas contained 79 percent of the housing in Illinois, and additions to the housing supply in these areas accounted for 90 percent of the State's total housing increase between 1960 and 1970.

About 59 percent of the housing in the State consisted of one-unit structures in 1970. The proportion of such units in metropolitan areas was 53 percent and in nonmetropolitan areas, 85 percent.

The number of units in Illinois lacking some or all plumbing facilities declined from 440,300 to 177,000, a 60-percent decrease since 1960. By 1970, 5 percent of the housing in the State lacked plumbing facilities. The proportion of such units was 3 percent in metropolitan areas and 10 percent in nonmetropolitan areas. Approximately 22,300, or 6 percent, of the Negro-occupied units in the State lacked some or all plumbing in 1970. The corresponding proportion for inside metropolitan areas was 5 percent, compared with 23 percent outside metropolitan areas.

Households were smaller in 1970 than in 1960. In the metropolitan areas, average household size declined from 3.2 persons in 1960 to 3.1 in 1970, and in nonmetropolitan areas, from 3.1 to 3.0 persons. The number of one-person households increased by 46 percent in metropolitan areas and by 43 percent in nonmetropolitan areas. In comparison, households with five or more persons increased 13 percent in metropolitan areas and decreased 1 percent in nonmetropolitan areas.

The median number of rooms increased from 4.8 to 4.9 in metropolitan areas and decreased from 5.1 to 5.0 in nonmetropolitan areas. Housing units with one and two rooms declined by 20 percent in metropolitan areas and by 17 percent in nonmetropolitan areas. Units with seven or more rooms increased by 51 percent in metropolitan areas and decreased by 7 percent in nonmetropolitan areas.

Number of persons per room is often used as a measure of crowding. In Illinois, the proportion of housing units with 1.01 or more persons per room decreased during the decade. In 1960, 11 percent of all occupied housing units in metropolitan areas and 8 percent in nonmetropolitan areas had 1.01 or more persons per room. By 1970, the proportion of such units decreased to 8 percent in metropolitan areas and to 6 percent in nonmetropolitan areas (table D).

The homeownership rate increased in metropolitan areas from 54 percent in 1960 to 56 percent in 1970. In nonmetropolitan areas homeownership increased from 70 to 72 percent. Of the 2,081,100 owner-occupied units in the State, 1,566,400 were inside metropolitan areas and 514,700 were outside these areas.

About 28 percent of the Negro households in metropolitan areas and 55 percent in nonmetropolitan

Table D. Plumbing Facilities and Persons Per Room by Metropolitan and Nonmetropolitan Residence: 1970 and 1960

The State Metropolitan and Nonmetropolitan Residence	Percent of housing units			
	Lacking some or all plumbing facilities		With 1.01 or more persons per room[1]	
	1970[2]	1960[3]	1970	1960
Total......................	4.8	13.4	7.8	10.0
Metropolitan residence..........	3.3	(NA)	8.2	10.6
Inside central cities..........	4.3	11.6	9.2	11.1
Outside central cities........	2.4	(NA)	7.1	9.9
Nonmetropolitan residence.......	10.3	(NA)	6.4	8.1

NA Not available.
[1]Percent of all occupied units.
[2]Percent of all year-round housing units.
[3]Percent of all housing units.

areas owned their homes in 1970. Approximately 108,400 Negro-homeowner households lived inside SMSA's and 6,800 lived outside SMSA's.

Property values and rents increased during the decade. The median value in metropolitan areas increased by 32 percent, from $16,700 in 1960 to $22,100 in 1970, while in nonmetropolitan areas value increased 51 percent, from $8,000 to $12,100. In metropolitan areas, median contract rent in 1970 was 45 percent higher than in 1960, rising from $77 to $112. In nonmetropolitan areas, rent increased by 51 percent, from $45 to $68.

Value and rent are expressed in current dollars (the value at the time of the respective censuses). Thus, any comparison must take into account the general rise in the cost of living during the 10-year period, as well as changes in the characteristics of the housing inventory.

Standard Metropolitan Statistical Areas

In the metropolitan areas of the State, the housing supply increased 384,700 units, or 15 percent. The Chicago SMSA, the largest in the State, contained 78 percent of the housing units in the metropolitan areas and accounted for 77 percent of the increase.

Approximately 53 percent of the housing units in the State's metropolitan areas consisted of one-unit structures in 1970. The corresponding proportions in the central cities and suburban areas were 31 percent and 75 percent, respectively.

In 1970, about 97,100 units in metropolitan areas, or 3 percent of all year-round units, lacked some or all plumbing facilities. The proportions of such units in the central cities and the suburbs were 4 percent and 2 percent, respectively. Approximately 15,100, or 5 percent, of the Negro households in central cities occupied units which lacked some or all plumbing facilities in

1970, compared with 4,300, or 8 percent, of the Negro households in suburban areas.

Average household size in 1970 was 2.9 persons in the central cities and 3.3 persons in the suburbs. One-person households constituted 24 percent of all households in the central cities and 13 percent in the suburbs.

Of all occupied units in metropolitan areas, 227,600, or 8 percent, reported more than one person per room in 1970, compared with 11 percent in 1960. In 1970, the proportion of such units was 9 percent in the central cities and 7 percent in the suburban areas (table D).

Homeownership in 1970 was greater in the suburbs than in the central cities. About 73 percent of occupied units in the suburbs and 39 percent in the central cities were owner-occupied. The Negro-homeownership rate in the suburbs was 50 percent, compared with 25 percent in the central cities.

Median value of the owner-occupied housing was $20,000 in the central cities, compared with $23,200 in the suburbs. About 27 percent of the owner-occupied housing in the central cities was valued at $25,000 or more compared with 43 percent in the suburbs. Median contract rent in the central cities and in the suburbs was $107 and $129, respectively. In the central cities 16 percent of renter-occupied units rented for $150 or more, compared with 35 percent in the suburbs.

The homeowner vacancy rate for metropolitan areas decreased during the decade from 1.2 to 0.9 percent. The rental vacancy rate increased, however, from 5.4 to 6.5 percent.

Annexations

Annexations occurred in each of the central cities during the decade (see "Population Trends" and text table B). Such annexations affect changes in the characteristics for these central cities and their suburbs.

Population Change for Counties: 1960 to 1970

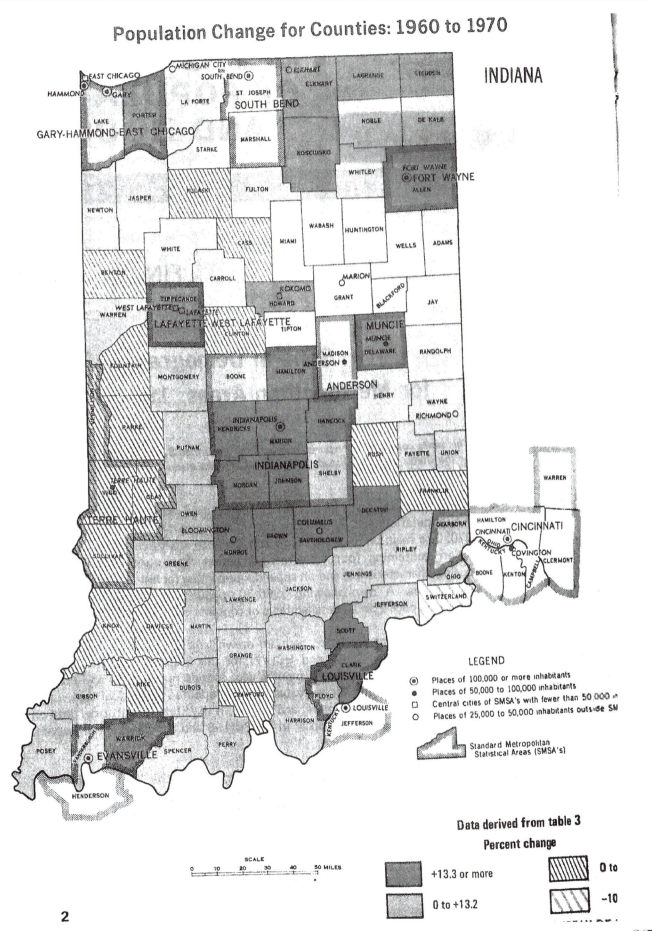

INDIANA

LEGEND

⊙ Places of 100,000 or more inhabitants
● Places of 50,000 to 100,000 inhabitants
□ Central cities of SMSA's with fewer than 50,000 in
○ Places of 25,000 to 50,000 inhabitants outside SM

Standard Metropolitan
Statistical Areas (SMSA's)

Data derived from table 3

Percent change

+13.3 or more

0 to

0 to +13.2

-10

SCALE

0   10   20   30   40   50 MILES

2

Analytical Text

POPULATION TRENDS

General

Between 1960 and 1970 the population of Indiana grew from 4,662,000 to 5,194,000, an increase of 531,000, or 11.4 percent. This rate of increase is slightly below the rate of increase in the entire United States (13.3 percent) and virtually the same as the rate in the East North Central States (11.1 percent), which in addition to Indiana include Ohio, Illinois, Michigan, and Wisconsin. Indiana ranked 11th in population among the 50 States in 1960 and in 1970.

The total number of households in Indiana in 1970 was 1,609,000, or 222,000 more than in 1960. The population living in households increased less rapidly than the rate at which households increased, with the result that the average household size decreased slightly, from 3.3 to 3.1 persons.

The patterns of population change in Indiana by type of residence differed little during the 1960 to 1970 decade. The metropolitan population increased by 13 percent from 2,851,000 to 3,214,000, and the non-metropolitan population increased by 9 percent from 1,811,000 to 1,980,000. In 1970, 62 percent of Indiana's population lived in metropolitan areas (table A). In the Nation as a whole, about two-thirds of the population live in metropolitan areas.

Table A.   Population by Race and Metropolitan and Nonmetropolitan Residence: 1970 and 1960

The State Metropolitan and Non-metropolitan Residence	Population		Change		Percent Distribution	
	1970	1960	Number	Percent	1970	1960
Total..............	5,193,669	4,662,498	531,171	11.4	100.0	100.0
Metropolitan residence...	3,213,598	2,851,461	362,137	12.7	61.9	61.2
Inside central cities..	1,838,766	1,726,192	112,574	6.5	35.4	37.0
Outside central cities.	1,374,832	1,125,269	249,563	22.2	26.5	24.1
Nonmetropolitan residence	1,980,071	1,811,037	169,034	9.3	38.1	38.9
White..............	4,820,324	4,388,554	431,770	9.8	92.8	94.1
Metropolitan residence...	2,877,761	2,602,682	275,079	10.6	55.4	55.8
Inside central cities..	1,520,607	1,489,947	30,660	2.1	29.3	32.0
Outside central cities.	1,357,154	1,112,735	244,419	22.0	26.1	23.9
Nonmetropolitan residence	1,942,563	1,785,872	156,691	8.8	37.4	38.2
Negro and other races	373,345	273,944	99,401	36.3	7.2	5.9
Metropolitan residence...	335,837	248,779	87,058	35.0	6.5	5.3
Inside central cities..	318,159	236,245	81,914	34.7	6.2	5.1
Outside central cities.	17,678	12,534	5,144	41.0	0.3	0.3
Nonmetropolitan residence	37,508	25,165	12,343	49.0	0.7	0.5

Nearly one-third of the increase in Indiana's metropolitan population occurred in central cities. If annexations during the decade are excluded, the proportion was only one-sixth (table B).[1]

The population of Negro and other races in Indiana increased by 36 percent during the 1960's while the white population increased by 10 percent. As a result, Negro and other races rose from 6 to 7 percent of the total population. In 1970, 85 percent of the population of Negro and other races lived in the central cities of metropolitan areas. The corresponding figure for the white population was 32 percent.

The population increase of 531,000 in Indiana in the 1960-70 decade was due to a natural increase (births minus deaths) of 547,000 and a net outmigration of 16,000. Net outmigration was equivalent to less than 1 percent of the 1960 population. The rates of net migration differed by race. Among whites, the net outmigration of 58,000 was equivalent to 1 percent of the 1960 population. Among Negro and other races, the net inmigration of 42,000 was equivalent to 15 percent of the 1960 population. Net inmigration accounted for about two-fifths of the population increase among Negro and other races (see table 3).

The age distribution of the Indiana population changed significantly between 1960 and 1970. The only decrease occurred among the population under 5 years

old and was due largely to the fall in the birth rates which occurred throughout the United States during the 1960's. The greatest increase occurred in the 15 to 24 age group and was due to the entry of the large number of persons born during the post-World War II "baby boom" into this age group (see table 4). As a result of these changes, the proportion of the total population in the under 5 group declined from 12 to 9 percent and the proportion in the 15 to 24 group increased from 13 to 18 percent.

The population of Negro and other races has a young age structure. Among the total population of Indiana in 1970, 47 percent were under age 25 and 10 percent were age 65 and over; however, among the population of Negro and other races, 55 percent were under age 25 and only 6 percent were age 65 and over.

Standard Metropolitan Statistical Areas

In 1970, there were 11 standard metropolitan statistical areas (SMSA's) in Indiana, including eight SMSA's located entirely within Indiana. Three SMSA's crossed State lines: the Cincinnati, Ohio-Ky.-Ind. SMSA; the Evansville, Ind.-Ky. SMSA; and the Louisville, Ky.-Ind. SMSA. Of these three SMSA's, only the Evansville SMSA is located mostly in Indiana and is discussed in its entirety in the text.

The population of the Indianapolis SMSA, the largest metropolitan area in Indiana, grew from 944,000 in 1960 to 1,110,000 in 1970, or by 18 percent. Although the Indianapolis SMSA is now one of the Nation's 33 metropolitan areas with populations exceeding 1,000,000, its rank dropped from 25th in 1960 to 29th

---

[1] For purposes of this discussion, Indianapolis is not included among the central cities which annexed population between 1960 and 1970. The 1960 population has been recomputed to represent the 1970 area. See "Definitions and Explanations."

Table B.   Change in Population of Central Cities Through Annexation: 1960 to 1970

Central Cities	1970 population			1960 population	Change 1960 to 1970 in 1960 area
	Total	In 1960 area	In annexed area		
Anderson....................	70,787	43,646	27,141	49,061	−5,415
Evansville..................	138,764	136,854	1,910	141,543	−4,689
Fort Wayne..................	177,671	163,608	14,063	161,776	1,832
Gary.......................	175,415	173,057	2,358	178,320	−5,263
Lafayette..................	44,955	40,110	4,845	42,330	−2,220
West Lafayette.............	19,157	14,329	4,828	12,680	1,649
Muncie.....................	69,080	68,134	946	68,603	−469
South Bend.................	125,580	124,596	984	132,445	−7,849
Terre-Haute................	70,286	69,699	587	72,500	−2,801

in 1970. The city of Indianapolis, which is the capital of Indiana, has a diversified economy. About one-fifth of the population increase in the Indianapolis SMSA was due to net inmigration, which was equivalent to 4 percent of the 1960 population. In 1970, one-eighth of the population was of Negro and other races.

The Gary-Hammond-East Chicago SMSA, a major center of heavy industry and the second largest metropolitan area in Indiana, grew from 574,000 in 1960 to 633,000 in 1970, or by 10 percent. The net outmigration of 26,000 from the Gary-Hammond-East Chicago SMSA, which was equivalent to 4 percent of the 1960 population, was due to the net outmigration of whites. In 1970, Negro and other races constituted about one-sixth of the total population in the SMSA, and slightly more than one-half of the total population in the central city of Gary.

In 1970, the Fort Wayne SMSA and the South Bend SMSA each had a population of 280,000. The Fort Wayne SMSA grew by 21 percent between 1960 and 1970, and one-fourth of this growth was due to net inmigration. The South Bend SMSA, recovering from the closing of the Studebaker automobile plant, grew by only 3 percent during the decade as net outmigration was equivalent to 7 percent of the 1960 population.

The population of the Evansville, Ind.-Ky. SMSA grew from 223,000 in 1960 to 233,000 in 1970, or by 4 percent. Net outmigration during the decade totaled 10,000 and was equivalent to 4 percent of the 1960 population. The Indiana portion of the Evansville SMSA grew from 189,000 to 197,000, or by 4 percent, while the Kentucky portion (Henderson County) grew from 34,000 to 36,000, or by 7 percent.

The population of the Terre Haute SMSA grew from 172,000 in 1960 to 175,000 in 1970, or by 2 percent, which was the lowest growth rate among the 11 SMSA's in Indiana. The low growth rate occurred in spite of the rapid expansion of Indiana State University. The population of Vigo County, which includes the city of Terre Haute, grew from 108,000 in 1960 to 115,000 in 1970, or by 6 percent. Each of the other three counties included in the Terre Haute SMSA lost population between 1960 and 1970. In 1970, the population of these three counties was predominantly rural.

Between 1960 and 1970, the Anderson SMSA grew from 126,000 to 138,000, or by 10 percent. Net outmigration was 3,000 which was equivalent to 2 percent of the 1960 population. Rapid growth in the city of Anderson (from 49,000 to 71,000) was due to annexation.

The population of the Muncie SMSA grew from 111,000 in 1960 to 129,000 in 1970, or by 16 percent. One-fifth of the growth was due to net inmigration, which was equivalent to 3 percent of the 1960 population.

The most rapid rate of population growth during the decade among Indiana's metropolitan areas occurred in the Lafayette-West Lafayette SMSA which grew by 23 percent from 89,000 to 109,000. Net inmigration accounted for over one-fourth of the growth and was equivalent to 6 percent of the 1960 population. The rapid growth was inspired by the increased enrollment at Purdue University.

The Indiana portion of the Louisville SMSA (Clark and Floyd Counties) grew from 114,000 in 1960 to 131,000 in 1970, or by 15 percent, which was close to the rate of increase for the entire SMSA. Net inmigration accounted for nearly one-fourth of this growth. In 1970, 16 percent of the population in the Louisville SMSA lived in the Indiana portion.

The population of the Indiana portion of the Cincinnati SMSA (Dearborn County) was 29,000 in both 1960 and 1970. In 1970, only 2 percent of the population in the Cincinnati SMSA lived in the Indiana portion.

Counties

Of the 92 counties in Indiana, 76 gained population and 16 lost population between 1960 and 1970. Twenty-two counties had growth rates above the national average of 13.3 percent, and only one county had a population decline exceeding 10 percent. Of the 25 counties in metropolitan areas in 1970, 12 counties gained at rates above the national average and three counties, all of which are in the Terre Haute SMSA, lost population. Vermillion County in the Terre Haute SMSA was the only county in Indiana that had a natural decrease (deaths exceeded births) during the decade.

Between 1960 and 1970, six counties had growth rates exceeding 30 percent. The population of Porter County, which is in the Gary-Hammond-East Chicago SMSA, grew by 45 percent from 60,000 to 87,000. Two-thirds of the growth was due to net inmigration. Lake County, which includes the three central cities of the SMSA, had a net outmigration of 43,000, suggesting a sizable migration from Lake County to Porter County.

The population of Monroe County increased by 43 percent from 59,000 in 1960 to 85,000 in 1970. At the latter date half the population lived in the city of Bloomington. The rapid growth in the county was due largely to increased enrollment at Indiana University.

The Indianapolis SMSA is comprised of Marion County, which includes the city of Indianapolis, and the seven counties bordering on Marion County. Between 1960 and 1970, four of these counties—Hamilton, Hancock, Hendricks, and Johnson—had rates of growth ranging from 30 to 40 percent. In each of these four counties, net inmigration accounted for most of the population growth.

During the 1960 to 1970 decade, 33 of Indiana's 92 counties experienced net inmigration. Four counties—Allen, Johnson, Monroe, and Porter—gained more than 10,000 population through net inmigration. Monroe County is the only one of the four that is not in a metropolitan area. Three counties lost more than 10,000 population through net outmigration. Each of these counties includes one or more central cities of metropolitan areas: Lake County (Gary-Hammond-East Chicago); St. Joseph County (South Bend); and Vanderburgh County (Evansville).

Between 1960 and 1970, five counties in Indiana had rates of net outmigration equivalent to 10 percent or more of their 1960 populations: Benton, Fountain, Martin, Miami, and Switzerland Counties. In 1970, more than one-half of the population in each of these counties lived in rural areas. The highest rate of population loss among Indiana's counties occurred in Switzerland County which had a decrease of 11 percent.

HOUSING TRENDS

General

Between 1960 and 1970, the total number of housing units in Indiana increased more rapidly than population. The population grew by 531,000, or 11 percent, while housing units increased by 227,000, or 15 percent (table C).

The metropolitan areas of the State experienced greater relative growth in housing, as in population, than did the nonmetropolitan part. The number of housing units in metropolitan areas rose over the decade to 1,047,800, an increase of 148,700 units, or 17 percent; this compares with an increase of 78,200 units, or 13 percent, in the nonmetropolitan areas. While 61 percent of all housing units were in the metropolitan areas, these areas accounted for 66 percent of the total State increase between 1960 and 1970.

About 78 percent of the housing in Indiana consisted of one-unit structures in 1970. The corresponding proportions in metropolitan and nonmetropolitan areas were 75 percent and 83 percent, respectively.

In 1970, about 110,700, or 6 percent, of the housing units in the State lacked some or all plumbing facilities. The proportion of housing units lacking plumbing facilities was smaller in the metropolitan areas of the State than in the nonmetropolitan areas, 5 percent compared with 9 percent.

Approximately 6,200, or 6 percent, of the Negro-occupied units in the State lacked some or all plumbing in 1970. The corresponding proportions for inside and outside the metropolitan areas were 6 percent and 9 percent, respectively.

Households were smaller in 1970 than in 1960. In the metropolitan areas, average household size declined from 3.3 persons in 1960 to 3.2 in 1970 and in nonmetropolitan areas, from 3.3 persons to 3.1. The number of one-person households increased by 57 percent in metropolitan areas and by 52 percent in nonmetropolitan areas. In comparison, households with five or more persons increased 9 percent in metropolitan areas and 5 percent in nonmetropolitan areas.

The median number of rooms in the metropolitan areas was 5.0, compared with 5.1 in nonmetropolitan areas. About 34 percent of all units in metropolitan areas had six or more rooms, compared with 40 percent of all units in nonmetropolitan areas.

Number of persons per room is often used as a measure of crowding. In Indiana, both the number and proportion of housing units with 1.01 or more persons per room decreased during the decade. In 1960, 12 percent of all occupied housing units in metropolitan

Table C. Housing Units by Metropolitan and Nonmetropolitan Residence: 1970 and 1960

The State Metropolitan and Nonmetropolitan Residence	Housing units					Popula-tion percent change
	Total		Change			
	1970	1960	Number	Percent		
Total.................	1,730,099	1,503,148	226,951	15.1		11.4
Metropolitan residence.....	1,047,752	899,015	148,737	16.5		12.7
Inside central cities....	607,149	544,034	63,115	11.6		6.5
Outside central cities...	440,603	354,981	85,622	24.1		22.2
Nonmetropolitan residence..	682,347	604,133	78,214	12.9		9.3

areas and 10 percent in nonmetropolitan areas had 1.01 or more persons per room. By 1970, the proportion of such units decreased to 8 percent in metropolitan areas and 7 percent in nonmetropolitan areas (Table D).

The homeownership rate remained about the same in the metropolitan areas, 69.6 percent in 1960 and 69.4 percent in 1970. In the nonmetropolitan areas, however, the proportion rose from 73 to 75 percent. Of the 1,153,000 owner-occupied units in the State, 688,000 were inside metropolitan areas and 465,000 were outside these areas.

About 50 percent of the Negro households in metropolitan areas and 59 percent in nonmetropolitan areas owned their homes in 1970. About 44,600 Negro-homeowner households lived inside SMSA's and 4,700 lived outside SMSA's.

Property values and rents increased during the decade. The median value in metropolitan areas increased by 32 percent, from $11,100 in 1960 to $14,600 in 1970, while in the nonmetropolitan areas value increased 48 percent, from $8,400 to $12,400. In metropolitan areas, median contract rent in 1970 was 47 percent higher than in 1960, rising from $60 to $88. In nonmetropolitan areas rent increased from $48 to $73, or 52 percent.

Value and rent are expressed in current dollars (the value at the time of the respective censuses). Thus, any comparison must take into account the general rise in the cost of living during the 10-year period, as well as changes in the characteristics of the housing inventory.

Standard Metropolitan Statistical Areas

In the metropolitan areas of the State, the housing supply increased by 148,700 units, or 17 percent. The Indianapolis SMSA (the largest SMSA), contained 35 percent of the housing units in metropolitan areas and accounted for 45 percent of the increase. The Gary-Hammond-East Chicago SMSA (the second largest SMSA), with 18 percent of the State's metropolitan housing, accounted for 16 percent of the increase.

In 1970, about three-fourths of the housing units in the State's metropolitan areas consisted of one-unit structures. The number of units in multiunit structures, however, increased at a much faster rate than one-unit structures during the decade, 55 percent and 7 percent, respectively.

In 1970, approximately 47,500 housing units in metropolitan areas, or 5 percent of all year-round units, lacked some or all plumbing facilities. The proportion of such units in the central cities was 4 percent, and in the suburbs, 6 percent. About 4,900, or 6 percent, of the Negro households in central cities occupied units which lacked some or all plumbing facilities in 1970, compared with 600, or 18 percent, of Negro households in suburban areas.

Housing units increased in size in the metropolitan areas during the decade. The median number of rooms increased from 4.8 to 5.0. In 1970, the median number of rooms in the central cities was 4.8, and in the suburbs, 5.1.

Table D. Plumbing Facilities and Persons Per Room by Metropolitan and Nonmetro-politan Residence: 1970 and 1960

The State Metropolitan and Nonmetropolitan Residence	Percent of housing units			
	Lacking some or all plumbing facilities		With 1.01 or more persons per room [1]	
	1970 [2]	1960 [3]	1970	1960
Total......................	6.5	17.3	8.0	11.4
Metropolitan residence...........	4.5	(NA)	8.4	12.2
Inside central cities..........	3.8	10.7	8.5	11.8
Outside central cities.........	5.6	(NA)	8.2	12.7
Nonmetropolitan residence........	9.5	(NA)	7.5	10.2

NA Not available.
[1] Percent of all occupied units.
[2] Percent of all year-round housing units.
[3] Percent of all housing units.

Of all occupied units in metropolitan areas, 83,100, or 8 percent, reported more than one person per room in 1970, compared with 12 percent in 1960. In 1970, the proportion of such units was 9 percent in the central cities and 8 percent in the suburban areas (table D).

Homeownership in 1970 was greater in the suburban areas than in the central cities. About 78 percent of occupied units in the suburbs and 63 percent in the central cities were owner-occupied. The Negro homeownership rate in the suburbs was 64 percent, compared with 50 percent in the central cities.

In 1970, median value in the central cities was $14,000, compared with $15,600 in the suburbs. About 22 percent of the owner-occupied housing in the central cities was valued at $20,000 or more, compared with 30 percent in the suburbs. Median contract rent in both the central cities and the suburbs was $88.

The homeowner vacancy rate for metropolitan areas decreased during the decade from 1.4 to 1.2 percent. The rental vacancy rate, however, increased from 7.1 to 8.5 percent.

Annexations

Annexations occurred in each of the central cities during the decade, except for East Chicago and Hammond (see "Population Trends" and text table B). Such annexations affect changes in the characteristics for these central cities and their suburbs. Indianapolis is not included among the central cities which had annexations, as 1960 data have been recomputed to represent the 1970 area.

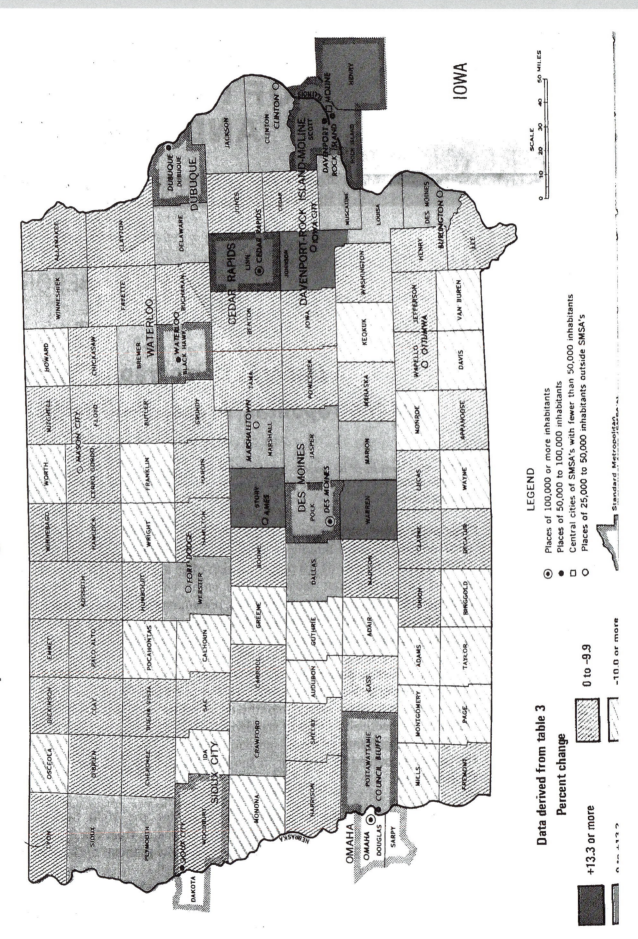

Population Change for Counties: 1960 to 1970

IOWA

SCALE

0   10   20   30   40   50 MILES

LEGEND

⊙ Places of 100,000 or more inhabitants

● Places of 50,000 to 100,000 inhabitants

□ Central cities of SMSA's with fewer than 50,000 inhabitants

○ Places of 25,000 to 50,000 inhabitants outside SMSA's

Standard Metropolitan

Data derived from table 3

Percent change

+13.3 or more

0 to -9.9

-10.0 or more

POPULATION TRENDS

General

Between 1960 and 1970 the population of Iowa increased from 2,758,000 to 2,825,000, an increase of 67,000. Iowa's rate of increase, 2.4 percent, was less than one-fifth of the United States' growth rate of 13.3 percent. Only five States had slower rates of increase during the decade. Iowa currently ranks 25th in size among the States, having been passed by Connecticut during the last 10 years.

Iowa experienced a net outmigration of 184,000 during the 1960's. This was somewhat smaller than the outmigration which occurred during the 1940's (196,000) and 1950's (233,000). Despite the fact that net outmigration in the last decade was actually 50,000 less than in the 1950's, a sharp decrease in the number of births coupled with a moderate increase in the

number of deaths cut the total growth from 136,000 in the 1950-60 period to 67,000 in the 1960-70 period. Iowa's growth has been below the national average each decade since 1880. At that time its population stood at 1,625,000 or 3.2 percent of the national total. Today only 1.4 percent of the Nation's population resides in Iowa.

The number of households in Iowa in 1970 was 896,000, or 55,000 more than in 1960. The population living in households increased less rapidly than the rate at which households increased with the result that the average household size decreased slightly from 3.2 to 3.0 persons.

The population of Negro and other races increased by over 40 percent in the past 10 years but the total number, 42,000, is still only 1.5 percent of the State's population (table A). As is generally true in the North, this group is much more concentrated in the central cities of metropolitan areas than is the white population.

Table A. Population by Race and Metropolitan and Nonmetropolitan Residence: 1970 and 1960

The State Metropolitan and Non-metropolitan Residence	Population		Change		Percent Distribution	
	1970	1960	Number	Percent	1970	1960
Total................	2,824,376	2,757,537	66,839	2.4	100.0	100.0
Metropolitan residence...	1,005,569	915,762	89,807	9.8	35.6	33.2
Inside central cities..	633,465	607,518	25,947	4.3	22.4	22.0
Outside central cities.	372,104	308,244	63,860	20.7	13.2	11.2
Nonmetropolitan residence	1,818,807	1,841,775	-22,968	-1.2	64.4	66.8
White...............	2,782,762	2,728,709	54,053	2.0	98.5	99.0
Metropolitan residence...	975,282	893,727	81,555	9.1	34.5	32.4
Inside central cities..	605,479	586,873	18,606	3.2	21.4	21.3
Outside central cities.	369,803	306,854	62,949	20.5	13.1	11.1
Nonmetropolitan residence	1,807,480	1,834,982	-27,502	-1.5	64.0	66.5
Negro and other races	41,614	28,828	12,786	44.4	1.5	1.0
Metropolitan residence...	30,287	22,035	8,252	37.4	1.1	0.8
Inside central cities..	27,986	20,645	7,341	35.6	1.0	0.7
Outside central cities.	2,301	1,390	911	65.5	0.1	0.1
Nonmetropolitan residence	11,327	6,793	4,534	66.7	0.4	0.2

[1]See correction note on page 8.

About two-thirds of this group live in the six central cities of standard metropolitan statistical areas (SMSA's) while only one-fourth of the State's white population live in the same six cities.

The contrast in the rate of growth between the seven metropolitan counties and the 92 nonmetropolitan counties is striking. The metropolitan counties increased 90,000, or 10 percent. On the other hand, the nonmetropolitan portion registered a population loss of 23,000, or one percent of its 1960 population.

The differential rate of growth is accounted for almost equally by differences in natural increase and migration. Iowa historically has had an age distribution considerably older than the Nation as a whole and this is especially so in the rural farming areas of the State. Thirty-five percent of the nonmetropolitan portion of Iowa is aged 45 or older while only 29 percent of metropolitan Iowa's population is age 45 or older. As a result of the disparity in the age structure, the natural increase (births minus deaths) was 13 percent in the metropolitan areas while it amounted to only 7 percent in the nonmetropolitan remainder of the State.

Iowa's age distribution underwent the same drastic change during the last decade as did the Nation. The population under 5 decreased 24 percent, mainly because of the large downward trend in births in the late 1960's as compared to the late 1950's. On the other hand the 15 to 24 year old group, which was the product of the post-World War II "baby boom," increased by 33 percent. The change in the other broad age categories was quite small.

Standard Metropolitan Statistical Areas

Iowa contains four standard metropolitan statistical areas (SMSA's) wholly within its borders—Des Moines, Cedar Rapids, Waterloo, and Dubuque. In addition, the main portion of the Sioux City, Iowa-Nebr. SMSA is in Iowa and the largest city in the Davenport-Rock Island-Moline, Iowa-Ill. SMSA is located in Iowa. Pottawattamie County, which is a part of the Omaha, Nebr. SMSA, is also in the State.

The Davenport-Rock Island-Moline SMSA containing three counties with a total population of 363,000 ranks 81st among all SMSA's in size. Its three central cities are well situated for trade. They are situated on the Mississippi River, giving them north-south access, and on the main east-west thoroughfare of some of the Nation's major railroads. As a whole, the SMSA increased by 43,000 or 14 percent, with nearly all the growth the result of natural increase. Scott County, the Iowa portion of the SMSA, increased its population by 20 percent, which was twice the rate of increase of the two Illinois counties. Although Davenport city increased by 9,000 or 11 percent, the major area of growth was in the suburban ring, which increased by 14,000, or 47 percent.

The Des Moines SMSA, coextensive with the State's largest county, Polk, had a population increase of 20,000 or over 7 percent. The central city, which is the capital of the State, experienced a population decline of 8,000 contrasted with a population increase of 28,000 or 49 percent in the remainder of the county. The city experienced net outmigration of 30,000 but this was in part counteracted by a 19,000 net inmigration to the remainder of the county.

Three of the remaining four metropolitan areas—Dubuque, Cedar Rapids, and Waterloo—are arranged in a triangle in the eastern portion of the State. Each of the three gained their prominence as a distribution center of farm produce and farming machinery. The Cedar Rapids SMSA, the largest of the three, had a population increase of 26,000 or 19 percent, larger than any other county in the State. Dubuque's population increase of 13 percent was exactly the same as the United States average and Waterloo had an increase of 10,000 or 9 percent. The growth of the central cities of these three SMSA's was due to a considerable extent to annexation of suburban territory (table B).

Table B. Change in Population of Central Cities Through Annexation: 1960 to 1970

Central Cities	1970 population			1960 population	Change 1960 to 1970 in 1960 area
	Total	In 1960 area	In annexed area		
Des Moines...............	200,587	200,215	372	208,982	-8,767
Cedar Rapids.............	110,642	99,970	10,672	92,035	7,935
Davenport................	98,469	98,153	316	88,981	9,172
Waterloo.................	75,533	70,357	5,176	71,755	-1,398
Dubuque..................	62,309	57,219	5,090	56,606	613

Iowa's remaining SMSA, Sioux City, which is shared with Nebraska, had a population decrease of nearly 4,000. All of the loss was confined to the Iowa portion (Woodbury County). The county had an outmigration of 15,000 equivalent to 14 percent of its 1960 population. This SMSA was one of 22 in the Nation which had a population decline between 1960 and 1970.

Counties

Seventy-four of Iowa's 99 counties lost population between 1960 and 1970. This is not an isolated happening as 59 of the counties have less population than in 1930 with 29 of them showing continuous losses for each decade since 1930. Going back still further in time, 44 of the State's counties registered their largest population in 1900 or earlier.

Only five of the State's counties had population increases in excess of the national average of 13.3 percent. Two of them, Linn, (Cedar Rapids) and Scott (Davenport) with increases of almost precisely 20 percent, were metropolitan. The counties with the largest and third largest percentage increases, Johnson and Story, contain the two largest centers of higher learning in the State, the University of Iowa and Iowa State University. The cities in which they are located, Iowa City and Ames, respectively, accounted for most of the growth in the county.

The remaining nonmetropolitan county, Warren, which had a high rate of growth, is located directly south of Des Moines. Warren, which is just beginning to receive population spillover from Des Moines, increased its population 6,600 or 32 percent. Sixty percent of the growth in the county was the result of net inmigration.

HOUSING TRENDS

General

Between 1960 and 1970, the total supply of housing units in Iowa increased more rapidly than population. The population grew by 66,800, or 2 percent, while housing units increased 58,800, or 6 percent (table C).

The metropolitan areas of the State experienced greater relative growth in housing than did the non-metropolitan part. The number of housing units in metropolitan areas rose from 291,000 to 328,900 over the decade, an increase of 37,900 units, or 13 percent; this compares with an increase of 20,900 units, or 3 percent, in nonmetropolitan areas. While metropolitan areas contained 34 percent of the housing in Iowa, the additions to the housing supply in these areas accounted for 65 percent of the State's total housing increase between 1960 and 1970.

Table C.   Housing Units by Metropolitan and Nonmetropolitan Residence: 1970 and 1960

The State Metropolitan and Nonmetropolitan Residence	Housing units				Population percent change
	Total		Change		
	1970	1960	Number	Percent	
Total.................	964,060	905,295	58,765	6.5	2.4
Metropolitan residence.....	328,900	290,991	37,909	13.0	9.8
Inside central cities....	216,322	198,471	17,851	9.0	4.3
Outside central cities...	112,578	92,520	20,058	21.7	20.7
Nonmetropolitan residence..	635,160	614,304	20,856	3.4	−1.2

About 82 percent of the housing in Iowa consisted of one-unit structures in 1970. The number of units in multiunit structures, however, increased 41.2 percent during the decade, while the number of one-unit structures declined 0.6 percent.

The number of units in the State lacking some or all plumbing facilities declined from 179,700 in 1960 to 71,800 in 1970, a decrease of 60 percent. In 1970, the proportion of such units was 5 percent in metropolitan areas and 9 percent in nonmetropolitan areas (table D).

Approximately 800, or 9 percent, of the Negro-occupied housing units in the State lacked some or all plumbing in 1970. The corresponding proportions for inside and outside the metropolitan areas were 8 percent and 16 percent, respectively.

Households were smaller in 1970 than in 1960. In metropolitan areas average household size declined from 3.2 persons in 1960 to 3.1 in 1970, and in nonmetropolitan areas, from 3.2 to 3.0 persons. There were large percentage increases in one-person households, 41 percent in metropolitan areas and 44 percent in nonmetropolitan areas. Households with five or more persons increased 7 percent in metropolitan areas and decreased 10 percent in nonmetropolitan areas.

The median number of rooms in housing units in Iowa was 5.3 in 1970. In metropolitan areas the median was 5.0, and in nonmetropolitan areas, 5.5. About 36 percent of the housing units in metropolitan areas had six or more rooms, compared with 49 percent in the nonmetropolitan areas.

Number of persons per room is often used as a measure of crowding. In Iowa, the proportion of housing units with 1.01 or more persons per room decreased during the decade. In 1960, 10 percent of all occupied housing units in metropolitan areas and 7 percent in nonmetropolitan areas had more than one person per room. By 1970, the proportion of such units had decreased to 7 percent inside metropolitan areas and to 5 percent outside metropolitan areas (table D).

The homeownership rate in Iowa was 72 percent in 1970 and 69 percent in 1960. The proportion of owner-occupied units rose slightly in metropolitan areas, from 70 to 71 percent, and in nonmetropolitan areas, owner-occupied units increased from 69 to 72 percent.

About 56 percent of the Negro households in metropolitan areas owned their homes in 1970, compared with 51 percent in nonmetropolitan areas. Of the 4,900 Negro-homeowner households in the State, 4,100 lived inside SMSA's and 800 lived outside SMSA's.

Property values and rents increased during the last decade. The median value of owner-occupied homes in metropolitan areas increased by 37 percent ($12,000 in 1960 to $16,400 in 1970) and in nonmetropolitan areas, value increased 45 percent ($8,500 in 1960 to $12,300 in 1970). In metropolitan areas, median contract rent in 1970 was 47 percent higher than in 1960, rising from $62 to $91. In nonmetropolitan areas, rent increased during the 10-year period from $49 to $70, or 43 percent.

Value and rent are expressed in current dollars (the value at the time of the respective censuses). Thus, any comparison must take into account the general rise in the cost of living during the 10-year period, as well as changes in the characteristics of the housing inventory.

Table D. Plumbing Facilities and Persons Per Room by Metropolitan and Nonmetropolitan Residence: 1970 and 1960

The State Metropolitan and Nonmetropolitan Residence	Percent of housing units			
	Lacking some or all plumbing facilities		With 1.01 or more persons per room[1]	
	1970[2]	1960[3]	1970	1960
Total......................	7.5	19.8	5.9	8.0
Metropolitan residence...........	5.0	14.1	7.3	10.4
Inside central cities..........	4.9	12.7	6.8	9.5
Outside central cities........	5.1	17.1	8.4	12.3
Nonmetropolitan residence........	8.8	22.6	5.1	6.8

[1]Percent of all occupied units.
[2]Percent of all year-round housing units.
[3]Percent of all housing units.

Standard Metropolitan Statistical Areas

The suburban areas in the State experienced greater growth in housing than did the central cities. Housing units in the suburbs increased by 20,100 units, or 22 percent, while housing in the central cities increased by 17,900, or 9 percent. By 1970, there were 112,600 housing units in the suburbs and 216,300 in the central cities.

In 1970, about 76 percent of the housing units in the State's metropolitan areas consisted of one-unit structures. The proportion of single-family units was 72 percent in the central cities and 83 percent in the suburbs.

In 1970, 16,400 housing units in metropolitan areas, or 5 percent, of all year-round units, lacked some or all plumbing facilities. The proportion of such units in the central cities and the suburbs was the same, 5 percent. Approximately 500, or 7 percent, of the Negro households in central cities occupied units which lacked some or all plumbing facilities in 1970, compared with 70, or 18 percent, of Negro households in suburban areas.

Of all occupied units in metropolitan areas, 22,900, or 7 percent, reported more than one person per room in 1970, compared with 10 percent in 1960. In 1970, the proportion of such units was 7 percent in the central cities and 8 percent in the suburban areas (table D).

Homeownership in 1970 was greater in the suburban areas than in the central cities. About 77 percent of occupied units in the suburbs and 68 percent in the central cities were owner-occupied. The Negro-homeownership rate was 69 percent in the suburbs, and 56 percent in the central cities.

Median value of owner-occupied housing in the central cities was $16,100, compared with $17,000 in the suburbs. About 29 percent of owned homes in the central cities were valued at $20,000 or more, compared with 36 percent in the suburban areas. Median contract rent in the central cities and the suburbs was $91 and $92, respectively. In the central cities 26 percent of renter-occupied units and in the suburban areas 30 percent of such units rented for $120 or more.

The homeowner vacancy rate for the metropolitan areas decreased slightly during the decade, from 1.2 to 1.1 percent. The rental vacancy rate increased from 5.9 to 8.5.

Annexations

Annexations occurred in each of the central cities of Iowa except Sioux City during the decade (see "Population Trends" and text table B). Such annexations affect changes in the characteristics for these central cities and their suburbs.

Population Change for Counties: 1960 to 1970

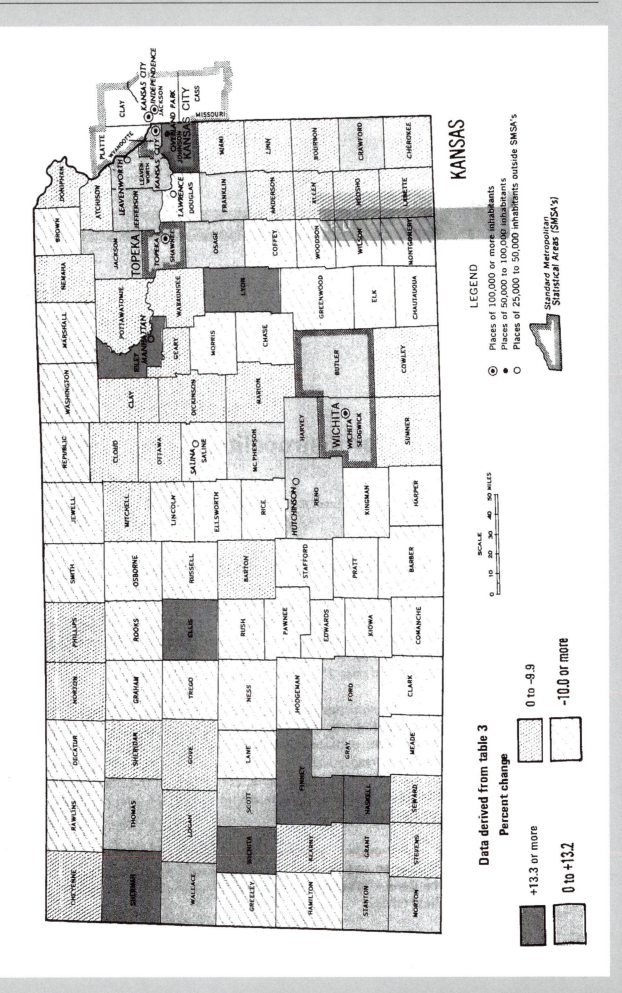

KANSAS

LEGEND

⊙ Places of 100,000 or more inhabitants
● Places of 50,000 to 100,000 inhabitants
○ Places of 25,000 to 50,000 inhabitants outside SMSA's

Standard Metropolitan Statistical Areas (SMSA's)

SCALE

0 10 20 30 40 50 MILES

Data derived from table 3

Percent change

+13.3 or more

0 to +13.2

0 to -9.9

-10.0 or more

Analytical Text

POPULATION TRENDS

General

Between 1960 and 1970 the total population of Kansas grew by only 68,000 persons, from 2,179,000 to 2,247,000, an increase of 3 percent over the population living in the State in 1960 (table A). This growth resulted from an increase of 97,000 in metropolitan areas and a decline of 29,000 in nonmetropolitan areas. Within metropolitan areas, central cities had an increase in population of 27,000, or 7 percent, while the areas outside central cities grew twice as fast, by 70,000 persons, or nearly 15 percent.

Over the decade, the metropolitan population of Kansas increased as a proportion of total population, from 39 percent in 1960 to 42 percent in 1970. In the Nation as a while, nearly 70 percent of the population is metropolitan.

The total number of households in Kansas in 1970 was 727,000, or 54,000 more than in 1960. The population living in households increased more slowly than the rate at which households increased, with the result that average household size declined from 3.2 to 3.0 persons.

At the time of the 1960 and 1970 Censuses, the population of Kansas was about 95 percent white. Whites constitute 92 percent of the population in metropolitan areas and 97 percent in nonmetropolitan areas.

The growth of the State and metropolitan area populations was produced by natural increase (the excess of births over deaths) which more than offset their net outmigration (see Table 3). This was not true of the nonmetropolitan areas where a substantial net outmigration more than offset the natural increase.

The State's white population grew slowly over the decade, by only 2 percent. The substantial natural increase of this group (182,000) was cut back sharply by a net outmigration of 139,000 persons, equivalent to 7 percent of the white population of Kansas in 1960. The population of other races, by contrast, grew very

Table A. Population by Race and Metropolitan and Nonmetropolitan Residence: 1970 and 1960

The State Metropolitan and Non-metropolitan Residence	Population		Change		Percent Distribution	
	1970	1960	Number	Percent	1970	1960
Total................	2,246,578	2,178,611	67,967	3.1	100.0	100.0
Metropolitan residence...	949,181	852,199	96,982	11.4	42.3	39.1
Inside central cities..	401,565	374,182	27,383	7.3	17.9	17.2
Outside central cities.	547,616	478,017	69,599	14.6	24.4	21.9
Nonmetropolitan residence	1,297,397	1,326,412	−29,015	−2.2	57.7	60.9
White................	2,122,068	2,078,666	43,402	2.1	94.5	95.4
Metropolitan residence...	865,929	787,298	78,631	10.0	38.5	36.1
Inside central cities..	360,005	343,226	16,779	4.9	16.0	15.8
Outside central cities.	505,924	444,072	61,852	13.9	22.5	20.4
Nonmetropolitan residence	1,256,139	1,291,368	−35,229	−2.7	55.9	59.3
Negro and other races	124,510	99,945	24,565	24.6	5.5	4.6
Metropolitan residence...	83,252	64,901	18,351	28.3	3.7	3.0
Inside central cities..	41,560	30,956	10,604	34.3	1.8	1.4
Outside central cities.	41,692	33,945	7,747	22.8	1.9	1.6
Nonmetropolitan residence	41,258	35,044	6,214	17.7	1.8	1.6

rapidly, by 25 percent over the decade, as a result of both natural increase (19,000) and net inmigration (6,000).

All areas of the State experienced significant changes in age composition. In metropolitan areas there were declines in the number of persons under 5 and 25 to 44 years of age. All other age groups increased, natably 15-24 year olds, which grew by 54 percent. In non-metropolitan areas, which suffered an overall loss, every age group was diminished except the young adult group, 15-24, which grew by 32 percent, and the elderly population 65 and over, which increased by 6 percent.

These changes are due in part to changing birth rates and in part to migration, which is highly selective by age. Low birth rates during the depression years and in the 1960's contribute to the diminution of age groups 25-44 and under 5 years, whereas the post-World War II "baby boom" is currently reflected in the large size of the population 15-24 years old.

Standard Metropolitan Statistical Areas

The two standard metropolitan statistical areas (SMSA's) entirely within Kansas are Wichita and Topeka. About one-third of the Kansas City, Mo.-Kans. SMSA is in Kansas also. The Wichita SMSA (consisting of Butler and Sedgwick Counties) had a population of 389,000 in 1970, up from 382,000 in 1960. This small increase, of only 2 percent, reflects substantial net outmigration. The central city of Wichita in Sedgwick County shows a population increase of 9 percent. This gain was produced by annexation of a suburban population of 39,000. Without it, Wichita city would have shown a population loss (table B). The SMSA carries out service functions for its market area in Kansas and Oklahoma. It also specializes in mining and aircraft production activities.

The Topeka SMSA (consisting of Shawnee County) had a population of 155,000 in 1970 and 141,000 in 1960, an increase of 10 percent. The city of Topeka shows a 5 percent increase in population, in part as a result of annexation. In addition to being the capital of Kansas, Topeka is also a financial and transportation center for Northeast Kansas. Reductions in the military installation in Shawnee County contributed to the metropolitan area's below average growth rate.

The Kansas portion of the Kansas City, Mo.-Kans. SMSA, which is made up of Johnson and Wyandotte Counties, contains a larger population than either the Topeka or Wichita SMSA's. Between 1960 and 1970 the population of these two counties increased from 329,000 to 405,000, by 23 percent. In 1970, this population comprised 43 percent of the total metropolitan population of the State.

Counties

Between 1960 and 1970 only 30 of the 105 counties in Kansas increased in population. These were largely located in the eastern half of the State (see map). Eight of these counties had percentage increases above the 13.3 percent national average. Those with the largest gains were: Johnson (a part of the Kansas City SMSA) with 51 percent; Riley (site of a military installation and college) with 36 percent; Douglas (site of the University of Kansas and adjoins Memphis SMSA) with 33 percent; Haskell with 23 percent; and Lyon (site of a college) with 19 percent. Among the fast growing counties, the fastest growing, Johnson, had the second largest population (218,000) in 1970. Next in size was Riley with 57,000. The remaining counties were substantially lower in population size.

Nineteen counties had an excess of deaths over births. The natural decrease in population combined with net outmigration resulted in a population loss for these counties over the decade. These counties are located in the north central and southeastern parts of the State. The proportion of the population over 65 in these counties ranged from 19 to 26 percent, significantly higher percentages than the State average of 12.

Table B.   Change in Population of Central Cities Through Annexation: 1960 to 1970

| Central Cities | 1970 population | | | 1960 population | Change 1960 to 1970 in 1960 area |
	Total	In 1960 area	In annexed area		
Kansas City	168,213	104,288	63,925	121,901	-17,613
Wichita	276,554	237,372	39,182	254,698	-17,326
Topeka	125,011	121,100	3,831	119,484	1,696

In the remaining 86 counties, net outmigration was sufficient in all but 17 cases to wipe out the gains contributed by natural increase. Only three counties had substantial net inmigration and these were the fastest growing counties mentioned above, i.e., Johnson, Douglas, and Riley.

Only four counties in Kansas contain a large enough population of races other than white to have this group shown separately in the table of county components of change (see "Definitions and Explanations"). In one county Geary, the population remained stable as net outmigration offset the natural increase. The three metropolitan counties of Sedgwick, Shawnee and Wyandotte had rapidly growing Negro populations. In Sedgwick, a very substantial natural increase and a small net inmigration produced a growth of 41 percent in the population of races other than white. This population in Shawnee County increased by 25 percent and in Wyandotte County by 19 percent.

HOUSING TRENDS

General

Between 1960 and 1970, the total supply of housing units in Kansas increased more rapidly than population. The population grew by 68,000, or 3 percent, while housing units increased by 48,900, or 7 percent (table C).

The metropolitan areas of the State experienced greater relative growth in housing than did the non-metropolitan part, while population increased in metropolitan areas and declined in nonmetropolitan areas. The number of housing units in metropolitan areas rose from 275,300 to 317,400 over the decade, an increase of 42,100 units, or 15 percent; this compares with an increase of 6,800 units, or 1 percent, in the nonmetropolitan areas. While 40 percent of all housing units were in the metropolitan areas, these areas accounted for 86 percent of the total State increase between 1960 and 1970.

About 82 percent of the housing in Kansas consisted of one-unit structures in 1970. The number of units in multiunit structures, however, increased 45.6 percent during the decade while the number of one-unit structures declined 0.4 percent.

The number of units in the State lacking some or all plumbing facilities declined from 117,500 to 43,900, a 63-percent decrease since 1960. In 1970, the proportion of such units was 3 percent in metropolitan areas and 8 percent in nonmetropolitan areas.

Approximately 1,700, or 6 percent, of the Negro-occupied units in the State lacked some or all plumbing in 1970. The corresponding proportions for inside and outside the metropolitan areas were 5 percent and 9 percent, respectively.

Households were smaller in 1970 than in 1960. In the metropolitan areas, average household size declined from 3.3 persons in 1960 to 3.1 in 1970 and in nonmetropolitan areas, from 3.1 persons to 2.9. The number of one- and two-person households in metropolitan areas increased by 61 percent and 26 percent, respectively; in nonmetropolitan areas one- and two-person households increased 34 percent and 8 percent, respectively. The number of households with five or more persons increased 2 percent in metropolitan areas and declined 12 percent in nonmetropolitan areas.

The median number of rooms rose from 4.9 to 5.1 in metropolitan areas and remained unchanged at 5.1 in nonmetropolitan areas. Units with one to three rooms declined in both metropolitan and nonmetropolitan areas, while units with seven or more rooms increased 65.5 percent in metropolitan areas and declined 0.1 percent in nonmetropolitan areas.

Table C.   Housing Units by Metropolitan and Nonmetropolitan Residence: 1970 and 1960

The State Metropolitan and Nonmetropolitan Residence	Housing units				Population percent change
	Total		Change		
	1970	1960	Number	Percent	
Total.................	789,196	740,335	48,861	6.6	3.1
Metropolitan residence.....	317,397	275,305	42,091	15.3	11.4
Inside central cities....	143,620	128,426	15,194	11.8	7.3
Outside central cities...	173,776	146,879	26,897	18.3	14.6
Nonmetropolitan residence..	471,800	465,030	6,770	1.5	-2.2

Number of persons per room is often used as a measure of crowding. In Kansas, both the number and proportion of housing units with 1.01 or more persons per room decreased during the decade. In 1960, 11 percent of all occupied housing units in metropolitan areas and 9 percent in nonmetropolitan areas had 1.01 or more persons per room. By 1970, the proportion of such units decreased to 6 percent in both metropolitan and nonmetropolitan areas (table D).

Changes in the trend of homeownership varied by location. In the metropolitan areas there was a decrease from 70 to 67 percent, while in nonmetropolitan areas the proportion rose from 68 to 70 percent. Of the 502,600 owner-occupied units in the State, 202,700 were inside metropolitan areas and 299,900 were outside these areas.

About 54 percent of the Negro households in both metropolitan and nonmetropolitan areas owned their homes in 1970. Of the 16,300 Negro-homeowner households in the State, 11,900 lived inside SMSA's and 4,400 lived outside SMSA's.

Property values and rents increased in the last decade. The median value in metropolitan areas increased by 31 percent from $11,400 in 1960 to $14,900 in 1970, while in the nonmetropolitan areas value increased 32 percent, from $7,300 to $9,600. In metropolitan areas, median contract rent in 1970 was 38 percent higher than in 1960, rising from $64 to $88. In nonmetropolitan areas rent increased from $49 to $65, or 33 percent.

Value and rent are expressed in current dollars (the value at the time of the respective censuses). Thus, any comparison must take into account the general rise in the cost of living during the 10-year period, as well as changes in the characteristics of the housing inventory.

Standard Metropolitan Statistical Areas

In the metropolitan areas of the State, the housing supply increased by 42,100 units, or 15 percent. The Kansas portion of the Kansas City, Mo.-Kans. SMSA, which contained 41 percent of the housing units in metropolitan areas, accounted for 69 percent of the increase. The Wichita SMSA, with 42 percent of the State's metropolitan housing, accounted for 17 percent of the increase.

In 1970, about 78 percent of the housing units in the State's metropolitan areas consisted of one-unit structures. The number of units in multiunit structures, however, increased at a much faster rate than one-unit structures during the decade, 52 percent and 8 percent, respectively.

In 1970, 8,100 housing units in metropolitan areas, or 3 percent of all year-round units, lacked some or all plumbing facilities. The proportion of such units in the central cities and the suburbs was the same, 3 percent.

Approximately 300, or 3 percent, of the Negro households in central cities occupied units which lacked some or all plumbing facilities in 1970, compared with 700, or 6 percent, of Negro households in suburban areas.

Housing units increased in size in the metropolitan areas during the decade. The median number of rooms

Table D: Plumbing Facilities and Persons Per Room by Metropolitan and Nonmetropolitan Residence: 1970 and 1960

The State Metropolitan and Nonmetropolitan Residence	Percent of housing units			
	Lacking some or all plumbing facilities		With 1.01 or more persons per room[1]	
	1970[2]	1960[3]	1970	1960
Total...............	5.6	15.9	5.9	9.4
Metropolitan residence...........	2.6	(NA)	6.5	10.8
Inside central cities........	2.5	8.3	6.1	10.1
Outside central cities........	2.6	(NA)	6.8	11.4
Nonmetropolitan residence.........	7.6	(NA)	5.5	8.6

(NA) Not available.
[1]Percent of all occupied units.
[2]Percent of all year-round housing units.
[3]Percent of all housing units.

increased from 4.9 to 5.1. In 1970, the median number of rooms in the central cities was 4.9 and in the suburbs, 5.3.

Of all occupied units in metropolitan areas, 19,500, or 6 percent, reported more than one person per room in 1970, compared with 11 percent in 1960. In 1970, the proportion of such units was 6 percent in the central cities and 7 percent in the suburban areas (table D).

Homeownership in 1970 was greater in the suburban areas than in the central cities. About 72 percent of occupied units in the suburbs and 62 percent in the central cities were owner-occupied. The Negro home-ownership rate in the suburbs was 58 percent, compared with 50 percent in the central cities.

Median value in the central cities was $13,800 compared with $16,300 in the suburbs. About 22 percent of the owner-occupied housing in the central cities was valued at $20,000 or more compared with 35 percent in the suburbs. Median contract rent in the central cities and the suburbs was $85 and $95, respectively. In the central cities 33 percent of renter-occupied units rented for $100 or more, compared with 46 percent in the suburbs.

The homeowner vacancy rate for metropolitan areas decreased during the decade from 2.2 to 1.3 percent. The rental vacancy rate decreased from 11.7 to 9.1.

Annexations

Annexations occurred in each of the central cities during the decade (see "Population Trends" and text table B). Such annexations affect changes in the characteristics for these central cities and their suburbs.

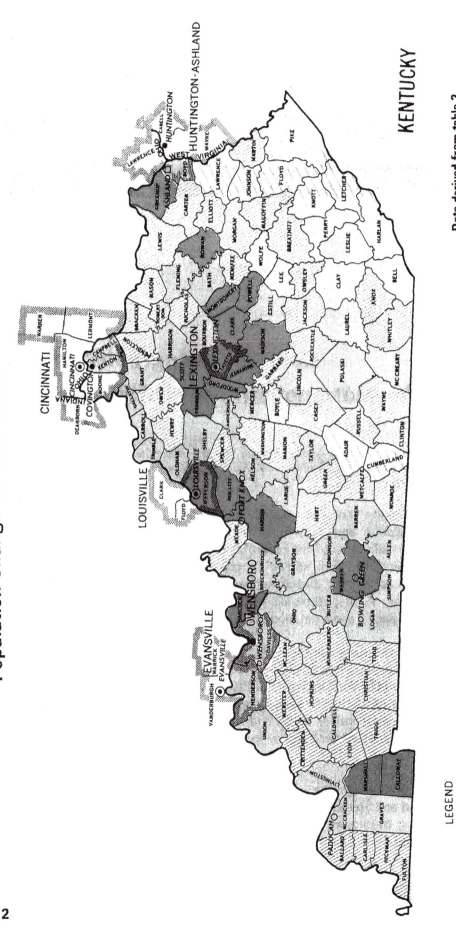

Population Change for Counties: 1960 to 1970

KENTUCKY

Data derived from table 3
Percent change

+13.3 or more

0 to +13.2

0 to -9.9

-10.0 or more

LEGEND

Places of 100,000 or more inhabitants
Places of 50,000 to 100,000 inhabitants
Central cities of SMSA's with fewer than 50,000 inhabitants
Places of 25,000 to 50,000 inhabitants outside SMSA's

Standard Metropolitan
Statistical Areas (SMSA's)

SCALE

0 10 20 30 40 50 MILES

Analytical Text

POPULATION TRENDS

General

Between 1960 and 1970, the population of Kentucky increased by 181,000 to reach a total of 3,219,000. This was an increase of 6 percent or a little less than half the national rate of 13 percent. Nearly 88 percent' of the increase, or about 159,000 persons, were added to the metropolitan population (table A). By far the largest share of the metropolitan increase occurred in the population of suburban areas which grew by 137,000 persons, or 23 percent, while the population of the central cities increased by only 22,000 persons, or 4 percent. Annexation of suburban territory contributed to the modest growth; without it central cities would have lost a total of 48,000 (table B).

The total number of households in Kentucky in 1970 was 983,000, or 131,000 more than in 1960. The population living in households increased less rapidly than the rate at which households increased, with the result that the average household size decreased slightly, from 3.5 to 3.2 persons.

As is typical of States in the South, the majority of Kentucky's population in the past has lived outside metropolitan areas. However, between 1960 and 1970, the metropolitan rate of growth was 14 percent, while the nonmetropolitan areas grew by only 1 percent. As a result, the proportion of the total population living in metropolitan areas rose from 37 percent in 1960 to 40 percent in 1970. This increased metropolitanization has been noted in other States in the South. In the Nation as a whole, about 2 out of 3 persons live in metropolitan areas.

The population of Negro and other races (almost entirely Negro) comprised 8 percent of Kentucky's total population, and 10 percent of the State's metropolitan population. As in the Nation as a whole, most whites in Kentucky's metropolitan areas tend to reside in the suburban ring, while the overwhelming majority of blacks were central city residents. In 1970, 38 percent of the white metropolitan population, but 83 percent of the black metropolitan population were residents of central cities (see table 1).

For the decade, the State experienced a natural increase of 334,000, and an outmigration of 153,000, equivalent to 5 percent of the 1960 population (see table 3). Only in metropolitan areas was there a net inmigration. Metropolitan areas gained 21,000 net inmigrants and had a natural increase of 138,000; nonmetro-

politan areas experienced a net outmigration of 174,000 and a natural increase of 196,000.

Kentucky's white population had a substantial net outmigration of 158,000 persons. This is a continuation of a long-term outmigration of the white population from the State, but the amount of net outmigration was much reduced from the previous two decades. A reduction in outmigration or reversal from outmigration to inmigration in the last decade occurred in many States in the South. The State's population of Negro and other races had a small net inmigration of 4,000 persons during this period.

As in other parts of the Nation, Kentucky's age structure changed significantly during the decade. There was a large decrease among the population under 5 years old of age which was due largely to falling birth rates which occurred throughout the United States during the 1960's. The greatest increase occurred in the 15 to 24 age group and was due for the most part to the entry of the large number of persons born during the post-World War II "baby boom." As a result of these changes, the total population under 5 declined from 11 to 8 percent; and the proportion in the 15 to 24 group increased from 15 to 18 percent.

Age changes in the metropolitan and nonmetropolitan areas show some dissimilarities. In the metropolitan population, the age group 5 to 14 grew by 18 percent while the nonmetropolitan population in the same age group declined by 7 percent. The metropolitan population showed substantial gains in the 15 to 24 age group (54 percent) and 65 years old and over (20 percent). This compares with 19 and 13 percent, respectively, for the nonmetropolitan population.

The population of Negro and other races is somewhat younger than the white population. Only 48 percent of the former is over age 25 while 54 percent of the white population is over 25.

Standard Metropolitan Statistical Areas

In 1970 there were six standard metropolitan statistical areas (SMSA's) in Kentucky. Four of these, Cincinnati, Ohio-Ky.-Ind., Evansville, Ind.-Ky., Huntington-Ashland, W. Va.-Ky.-Ohio, and Louisville, Ky.-Ind. are partially located in other States. The discussion of the Cincinnati, Evansville, and Huntington-Ashland SMSA's relate to the portion in Kentucky only. The SMSA's located entirely in Kentucky are Lexington and Owensboro. Each of the SMSA's gained population over the decade.

Table A. Population by Race and Metropolitan and Nonmetropolitan Residence: 1970 and 1960

The State Metropolitan and Non-metropolitan Residence	Population		Change		Percent Distribution	
	1970	1960	Number	Percent	1970	1960
Total................	[1]3,218,706	3,038,156	180,550	5.9	100.0	100.0
Metropolitan residence...	1,288,024	1,128,566	159,458	14.1	40.0	37.1
Inside central cities..	549,183	527,203	21,980	4.2	17.1	17.4
Outside central cities.	738,841	601,363	137,478	22.9	23.0	19.8
Nonmetropolitan residence	1,930,682	1,909,590	21,092	1.1	60.0	62.9
White................	2,971,232	2,820,083	151,149	5.4	92.3	92.8
Metropolitan residence...	1,155,531	1,017,076	138,455	13.6	35.9	33.5
Inside central cities..	439,148	436,770	2,378	0.5	13.6	14.4
Outside central cities.	716,383	580,306	136,077	23.4	22.3	19.1
Nonmetropolitan residence	1,815,701	1,803,007	12,694	0.7	56.4	59.3
Negro and other races	247,474	218,073	29,401	13.5	7.7	7.2
Metropolitan residence...	132,493	111,490	21,003	18.8	4.1	3.7
Inside central cities..	110,035	90,433	19,602	21.7	3.4	3.0
Outside central cities.	22,458	21,057	1,401	6.7	0.7	0.7
Nonmetropolitan residence	114,981	106,583	8,398	7.9	3.6	3.5

[1]See correction note on page 9.

Table B. Change in Population of Central Cities Through Annexation: 1960 to 1970

Central Cities	1970 population			1960 population	Change 1960 to 1970 in 1960 area
	Total	In 1960 area	In annexed area		
Louisville...............	361,472	348,752	12,720	390,639	-41,887
Ashland..................	29,245	28,856	389	31,283	-2,427
Lexington................	108,137	63,299	44,838	62,810	489
Owensboro................	50,329	38,172	12,157	42,471	-4,299

Of the 1,288,000 persons living in metropolitan areas in Kentucky, 695,000 (54 percent) lived in the Louisville SMSA. Louisville has long been one of the most important ports, marketing and industrial centers in the South. Between 1960 and 1970, the population of the entire Louisville SMSA increased from 725,000 to 827,000, or by 14 percent. Net inmigration contributed only a small proportion of this growth (15,000). The city of Louisville lost population between 1960 and 1970 in spite of annexation of suburban territory. The 1970 population of the area annexed to the city was 13,000. If annexation is excluded, the city would have lost 42,000 persons. The number of whites in the city of Louisville declined by 46,000 over the decade, while the population of Negro and other races increased by 17,000, a trend common to many large cities over the last decade.

The Lexington SMSA, with 174,000 population, had a population increase of 42,000 during the decade. The area is the site of the University of Kentucky, the market center of the Blue Grass region, and a rapidly developing research center. The area's growth was nearly evenly distributed between net inmigration and natural increase. Net inmigration was equivalent to 17 percent of the 1960 population. The central city of Lexington grew from 63,000 to 108,000, most of which can be attributed to the annexation of suburban territory between 1960 and 1970.

The Owensboro SMSA, which was designated an SMSA in 1970, includes Daviess County. The population grew from 71,000 to 79,000, or by 13 percent. The central city (Owensboro) grew from 42,000 to 50,000, while the balance of the SMSA gained 1,000 persons. The central city's growth is due to the annexation of a suburban population of 12,000. Within the 1960 boundary, the city lost 4,000 population.

In 1970, 251,000 persons, or 18 percent of the population of the Cincinnati SMSA resided in Kentucky. Between 1960 and 1970 the Kentucky portion (Campbell, Kenton, and Boone Counties) grew at the same rate as the SMSA as a whole (9 percent). Population change was made up of a natural increase of 26,000 (52,000 births minus 25,000 deaths) and a net outmigration of 5,000.

Only 15 percent of the entire Evansville SMSA population resided in Kentucky in 1970 (Henderson County). The population of the Kentucky portion of this SMSA grew from 34,000 to 36,000, at a rate of 7.5 percent, almost twice as fast as the entire SMSA.

In 1970 the Kentucky portion of the Huntington-Ashland SMSA contained 21 percent of the total population of the SMSA, or 52,000 persons. This population scarcely changed between 1960 and 1970. Natural increase (10,000 births minus 5,000 deaths) was offset by net outmigration.

Counties

The population of Kentucky's 120 counties ranges from 2,000 for Robertson County to 695,000 for Jefferson County. Of the 120 counties in Kentucky, 59 gained population and 61 lost population between 1960 and 1970. Between 1950 and 1960, 87 counties in Kentucky lost population. In the Nation as a whole, slightly more than half of the counties gained population during the decade.

Nineteen counties had growth rates above the national average of 13 percent, and 11 counties had a population decline exceeding 10 percent. Each of the eight metropolitan counties gained population, and three—Boone, Fayette (Lexington) and Jefferson (Louisville)—counties had rates exceeding the national average. Boone (Cincinnati SMSA), the smallest metropolitan county, was the fastest growing (49 percent), while Bullitt County, contiguous to metropolitan Jefferson County, was the fastest growing nonmetropolitan county (67 percent). During the 1960 to 1970 decade, 25 counties experienced net inmigration. Only four counties—Boone, Bullitt, Hancock, and Calloway (Murray State University)—had an inmigration rate exceeding 20 percent. Boone County is the only one of the four that is in a metropolitan area. The sudden influx of migrants into Hancock County, which is the smallest of the four, can be attributed to the location of several factories outside Lewisport city in recent years.

Between 1960 and 1970, 49 counties in Kentucky had rates of outmigration equivalent to 10 percent or more of their 1960 population; 45 of these counties had more than half of their populations living in rural areas. The highest rate of net outmigration (43 percent) among Kentucky's counties occurred in predominantly rural Perry County, located in the southeast sector of the State. The Appalachian Counties generally were sources of heavy net outmigration as in the previous two decades. Rural Carlisle County located in the southwestern corner of the State was the only county in Kentucky where deaths exceeded births during the decade.

HOUSING TRENDS

General

Between 1960 and 1970 the total supply of housing units in Kentucky increased more rapidly than population. The population grew by 181,000, or 6 percent, while housing units increased by 137,400, or 15 percent (table C).

The metropolitan areas of the State experienced greater relative growth in housing, as in population, than did the nonmetropolitan part. The number of housing units in metropolitan areas rose from 348,100 to 421,700 over the decade, an increase of 73,600 units, or 21 percent; the increase in nonmetropolitan areas was 63,800 units, or 11 percent. While 40 percent of all housing units were in the metropolitan areas, these areas accounted for 54 percent of the total State increase between 1960 and 1970.

About 80 percent of the housing in Kentucky consisted of one-unit structures in 1970. The number of units in multiunit structures, however, increased at a much faster rate than one-unit structures during the decade, 54 percent and 6 percent, respectively.

The number of units in the State lacking some or all plumbing facilities declined from 367,400 to 219,700, a 40-percent decrease since 1960. In 1970, the proportion of such units was 5 percent in metropolitan areas and 31 percent in nonmetropolitan areas. Approximately 14,400, or 21 percent, of the Negro-occupied units in the State lacked some or all plumbing in 1970. The corresponding proportions for inside and outside the metropolitan areas were 7 percent and 39 percent, respectively.

Households were smaller in 1970 than in 1960. In the metropolitan areas, the average household size declined from 3.4 persons in 1960 to 3.2 in 1970 and, in nonmetropolitan areas, from 3.6 to 3.2 persons. The number of one-person households increased by about 66 percent while two-person households increased by 25 percent. Households with five or more persons increased 8 percent in metropolitan areas and decreased 14 percent in nonmetropolitan areas.

The median number of rooms rose from 4.7 to 4.9 both inside and outside SMSA's. Units with one and two rooms declined in metropolitan and nonmetropolitan areas (21 percent and 30 percent, respectively), while units with seven or more rooms increased 59 percent in metropolitan areas and 10 percent in nonmetropolitan areas.

Number of persons per room is often used as a measure of crowding. In Kentucky, both the number and the proportion of housing units with 1.01 or more persons per room decreased during the decade. In 1960, 15 percent of all occupied housing units in metropolitan areas and 19 percent in nonmetropolitan areas had 1.01 or more persons per room. By 1970, the proportion of

Table C. Housing Units by Metropolitan and Nonmetropolitan Residence: 1970 and 1960

The State Metropolitan and Nonmetropolitan Residence	Housing units				Population percent change
	Total		Change		
	1970	1960	Number	Percent	
Total................	1,062,953	925,572	137,381	14.8	5.9
Metropolitan residence.....	421,686	348,113	73,573	21.1	14.1
Inside central cities....	196,251	172,589	23,662	13.7	4.2
Outside central cities...	225,435	175,524	49,911	28.4	22.9
Nonmetropolitan residence..	641,267	577,457	63,810	11.0	1.1

such units decreased to 9 percent in metropolitan areas and to 12 percent in nonmetropolitan areas (table D).

The homeownership rate rose slightly in metropolitan areas, from 63 percent in 1960 to 64 percent in 1970. In the nonmetropolitan areas, the owner-occupancy rate rose from 65 to 68 percent. Of the 657,000 owner-occupied units in the State, 257,500 were inside metropolitan areas and 399,500 were outside these areas.

About 45 percent of the Negro households in metropolitan areas and 52 percent in nonmetropolitan areas owned their homes in 1970; both percentages are higher than the corresponding percentages in 1960. About 17,400 Negro-homeowner households lived inside SMSA's and 15,600 lived outside SMSA's.

Property values and rents increased during the last decade. The median value in metropolitan areas increased by 33 percent, from $11,700 in 1960 to $15,600 in 1970, while in nonmetropolitan areas the median increased 67 percent, from $5,700 to $9,500. In metropolitan areas, median contract rent in 1970 was 45 percent higher than in 1960, rising from $53 to $77. In nonmetropolitan areas rent increased by 62 percent, from $29 to $47.

Value and rent are expressed in current dollars (the value at the time of the respective censuses). Thus, any comparison must take into account the general rise in the cost of living during the 10-year period, as well as changes in the characteristics of the housing inventory.

Standard Metropolitan Statistical Areas

In the metropolitan areas of the State, the housing supply increased by 73,600 units, or 21 percent. Housing units in the suburbs, which comprised more than half the metropolitan housing in 1970, increased by 49,900 units, or 28 percent; in comparison, housing in the central cities increased by 23,700, or 14 percent. The Kentucky portion of the Louisville, Ky.-Ind. SMSA, which contained 54 percent of the housing units in metropolitan areas, accounted for 52 percent of the increase.

In 1970, about 71 percent of the housing units in the State's metropolitan areas consisted of one-unit structures. The proportion of such units was 62 percent in the central cities and 80 percent in the suburbs.

About 20,200 housing units in metropolitan areas, or 5 percent of all year-round units, lacked some or all plumbing facilities in 1970. The proportion of such units in the central cities was 4 percent and in the suburbs, 6 percent. Approximately 1,600, or 5 percent, of the Negro households in central cities occupied units which lacked some or all plumbing facilities in 1970, compared with 1,200, or 20 percent, of Negro households in suburban areas.

Households were smaller in the central cities than in the suburbs. In the central cities, household size was 2.9 persons compared with 3.4 persons in the suburbs. The proportion of occupied units with one-person house-

Table D.   Plumbing Facilities and Persons Per Room by Metropolitan and Nonmetro-
           politan Residence: 1970 and 1960

The State Metropolitan and Nonmetropolitan Residence	Percent of housing units			
	Lacking some or all plumbing facilities		With 1.01 or more persons per room[1]	
	1970[2]	1960[3]	1970	1960
Total......................	20.8	39.7	10.7	17.1
Metropolitan residence...........	4.8	(NA)	9.3	14.8
Inside central cities..........	3.9	14.3	9.2	14.9
Outside central cities.........	5.6	(NA)	9.4	14.7
Nonmetropolitan residence........	31.3	(NA)	11.6	18.6

NA Not available.
[1]Percent of all occupied units.
[2]Percent of all year-round housing units.
[3]Percent of all housing units.

holds was 22 percent in the central cities and 12 percent in the suburban areas.

Of all occupied units in metropolitan areas, 37,200, or 9 percent reported more than one person per room in 1970, compared with 15 percent in 1960. In 1970, the proportion of such units was 9 percent in both the central cities and the suburban areas (table D).

Homeownership in 1970 was greater in the suburbs than in the central cities. About 74 percent of occupied units in the suburban areas and 54 percent in the central cities were owner-occupied. The Negro-homeownership rate in the suburbs was 62 percent, compared with 42 percent in the central cities.

Median value of owner-occupied housing was $13,900 in the central cities compared with $16,700 in the suburbs. About 22 percent of the owner-occupied housing in the central cities was valued at $20,000 or more, compared with 31 percent in the suburbs. Median contract rent in the central cities and the suburbs was $74 and $85, respectively. In the central cities 26 percent of renter-occupied units rented for $100 or more, compared with 37 percent in the suburbs.

The homeowner vacancy rate for metropolitan areas decreased during the decade from 1.6 to 1.1 percent. The rental vacancy rate increased from 6.8 to 8.3.

Annexations

Annexations occurred in the central cities of Louisville, Ashland, Lexington, and Owensboro during the decade (see ''Population Trends'' and text table B). Such annexations affect changes in the characteristics for these central cities and their suburbs.

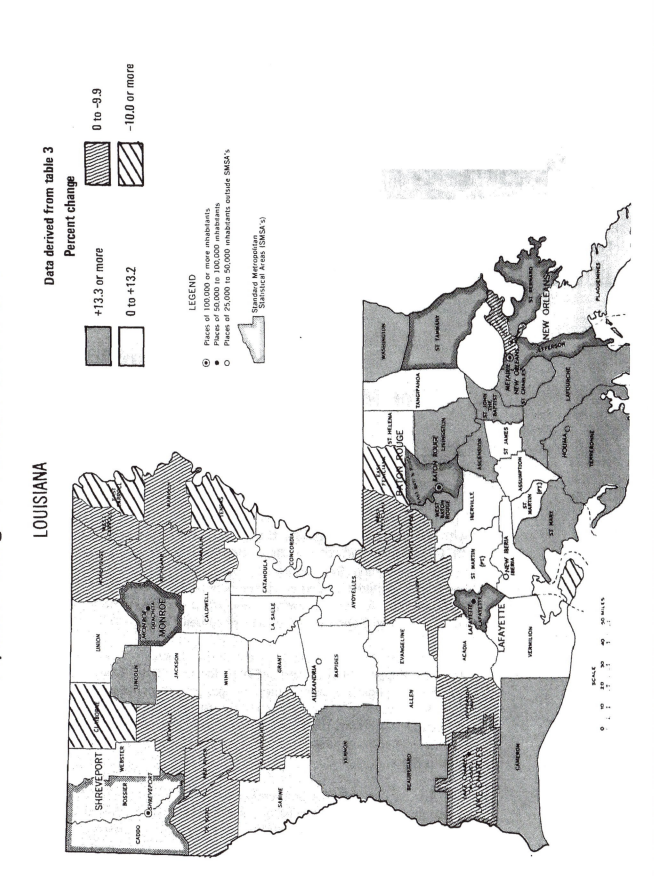

Population Change for Parishes: 1960 to 1970

LOUISIANA

Data derived from table 3

Percent change

+13.3 or more

0 to +13.2

0 to -9.9

-10.0 or more

LEGEND

◉ Places of 100,000 or more inhabitants
● Places of 50,000 to 100,000 inhabitants
○ Places of 25,000 to 50,000 inhabitants outside SMSA's

Standard Metropolitan
Statistical Areas (SMSA's)

Analytical Text

POPULATION TRENDS

General

Between 1960 and 1970 the total population of Louisiana grew by nearly 385,000, from 3,257,000 to 3,641,000, an increase of 11.8 percent over the population living in the State in 1960 (table A). This moderate increase is the average of metropolitan and nonmetropolitan rates of increase which vary considerably; while nonmetropolitan areas grew by 9 percent, central cities grew by only 4 percent and areas outside central cities by 31 percent.

The total number of households in the State in 1970 was 1,052,000, or 160,000 more than in 1960. The population living in households increased less rapidly than the rate at which new households were formed with the result that average household size decreased slightly, from 3.6 to 3.4 persons per unit.

The effect of these changes on population distribution by metropolitan-nonmetropolitan residence was very small. The proportion of the total population living in metropolitan areas increased by only 1 percent during the decade. About one out of every two persons in Louisiana now lives in metropolitan areas, compared with the national average of two out of three.

The proportion of whites in the nonmetropolitan areas increased from 66 to 69 percent between 1960 and 1970, but in metropolitan areas the white proportion was constant (70 percent). However, within metropolitan areas, there was a significant shift. In areas outside central cities, the proportion of whites rose from 77 to 82 percent between 1960 and 1970; collaterally, their proportion inside central cities declined from 65 to 61 percent.

The excess of births over deaths between 1960 and 1970 assured the State of population growth despite a net outmigration of 132,000. Diverse trends underlie

Table A. Population by Race and Metropolitan and Nonmetropolitan Residence: 1970 and 1960

The State Metropolitan and Non-metropolitan Residence	Population		Change		Percent Distribution	
	1970	1960	Number	Percent	1970	1960
Total...............	[1]3,641,306	3,257,022	384,284	11.8	100.0	100.0
Metropolitan residence...	1,996,197	1,750,456	245,741	14.0	54.8	53.7
Inside central cities..	1,144,778	1,100,327	44,451	4.0	31.4	33.8
Outside central cities.	851,419	650,129	201,290	31.0	23.4	20.0
Nonmetropolitan residence	1,645,109	1,506,566	138,543	9.2	45.2	46.3
White...............	2,539,547	2,211,715	327,832	14.8	69.7	67.9
Metropolitan residence...	1,399,786	1,217,932	181,854	14.9	38.4	37.4
Inside central cities..	701,878	715,041	-13,163	-1.8	19.3	22.0
Outside central cities.	697,908	502,891	195,017	38.8	19.2	15.4
Nonmetropolitan residence	1,139,761	993,783	145,978	14.7	31.3	30.5
Negro and other races	1,101,759	1,045,307	56,452	5.4	30.3	32.1
Metropolitan residence...	596,411	532,524	63,887	12.0	16.4	16.4
Inside central cities..	442,900	385,286	57,614	15.0	12.2	11.8
Outside central cities.	153,511	147,238	6,273	4.3	4.2	4.5
Nonmetropolitan residence	505,348	512,783	-7,435	-1.4	13.9	15.7

[1]See correction note on page 8.

this net outmigration. Over the decade, there was a net inmigration of whites amounting to 26,000 and a net outmigration of Negroes of 158,000. Net losses of population were registered outside metropolitan areas and inside the central cities of metropolitan areas, but net gains were registered in metropolitan areas outside central cities (see table 3).

Throughout the State both whites and Negroes experienced significant changes in age composition over the 1960-70 decade. The age group 15-24 registered the largest numerical gains (see table 4). On the other hand, declines or only small gains were registered by the under 5 and the 25 to 44 groups. Similar changes are found in other sections of the country and are due in part to changing birth rates and in part to migration, which is highly selective by age. Low birth rates during the depression years and in the 1960's contribute to the diminution of age groups 25 to 44, and under 5, whereas the post-World War II "baby boom" is currently reflected in the large size of the population 15-24 years old.

Standard Metropolitan Statistical Areas

The Standard Metropolitan Statistical Areas (SMSA's) in Louisiana while different in size and certain other characteristics, are closely alike in the proportion of the population that is Negro. New Orleans is the largest SMSA with a population of more than one million. It is a port and has substantial trade and financial functions. Shreveport is next in size with a population of 295,000; it is an oil and gas extraction area and contains a significant military establishment. Baton Rouge, which is third in size (285,000 population) is characterized by the functions of a State capital; it is also the site of a chemical manufacturing industry, and growing university

(Louisiana State University). The three smaller areas, Lafayette, Monroe and Lake Charles, range in population from 109,000 to 145,000. They carry out trade and financial functions in their areas.

Annexation of territory during the decade was responsible for additions to the population of central cities in five of Louisiana's metropolitan areas (table B). These annexations enabled the central cities to show an increase over the 1960-70 period. Without them, only Lafayette would have shown an increase in its central city population. Baton Rouge, Monroe and New Orleans all showed significant gains in their suburbs over the 1960-70 period. On the other hand, Lafayette, Lake Charles and Shreveport registered declines in their suburbs due to de-annexation.

Changes in the population by age for each of the six SMSA's in Louisiana show the same tendencies noted for the State as a whole: losses or small increases for age groups under 5 and 25 to 44 years, accompanied by large gains in age groups 15 to 24 and 45 to 64 years (see table 4).

Parishes

Between 1960 and 1970, 44 of the 64 parishes in Louisiana increased in population. Nineteen of these grew at rates which exceeded the 13.3 percent rate of population increase for the nation as a whole. This latter group for the most part consists either of metropolitan parishes or of parishes neighboring metropolitan areas. They are concentrated in the southeastern part of the State. Two parishes with populations over 200,000, East Baton Rouge and Jefferson, had increases of 24 percent and 62 percent, respectively. The parish showing the largest gain, Vernon, is on the central west border of the State. It grew at the rate of 194 percent. This large gain reflected the reactivation of Fort Polk in the parish.

Table B.   Change in Population of Central Cities Through Annexation: 1960 to 1970

Central Cities	1970 population			1960 population	Change 1960 to 1970 in 1960 area
	Total	In 1960 area	In annexed area		
Baton Rouge................	165,963	145,442	20,521	152,419	-6,977
Lafayette.................	68,908	43,879	25,029	40,400	3,479
Lake Charles.............	77,995	60,319	17,679	63,392	-3,073
Monroe....................	56,374	50,928	5,446	52,219	-1,291
Shreveport................	182,064	156,538	25,526	164,372	-7,834

Of the 20 parishes that showed losses in population between 1960 and 1970, only four showed losses of 10 percent or more. Most of the parishes showing losses are located in the northern section of the State. The two parishes showing losses and having large populations are Orleans (-5.4%) with a population of 593,000 and St. Landry (-1.4%) with a population of 80,000.

Every parish had more births than deaths during the decade (see table 3). In 20 parishes, however, net outmigration was more than sufficient to wipe out the gains contributed by natural increase of the total population. Large parishes with substantial outmigration were Orleans and St. Landry. All parishes, except two, contained a large enough population of races other than white to have this population group shown separately in table 3. Thirty-three of these 62 parishes had sufficient net outmigration to more than wipe out the gains from the excess of births over deaths.

Only seven parishes had substantial net inmigration which amounted to more than 10 percent of their 1960 population. They were the fastest growing parishes over the 1960-70 decade. Chief among these are Vernon Parish, mentioned above, with an overall growth rate of 194 percent and a net inmigration rate of 180 percent; and the suburban New Orleans parishes of Jefferson, with a growth rate of 62 percent and a net inmigration rate of 38 percent, of St. Tammany with a growth rate of 65 percent and a net inmigration rate of 46 percent, and of St. Bernard with a growth rate of 59 percent and a net inmigration rate of 38 percent.

HOUSING TRENDS

General

During the decade, the total supply of housing units in Louisiana increased more rapidly than population. While the population grew by 384,000, or 12 percent, the number of housing units increased by 170,600, or 17 percent (table C).

The metropolitan areas of the State experienced greater relative growth in housing, as in population, than did the nonmetropolitan part. The number of housing units in metropolitan areas rose from 539,100 to 647,300 over the decade, an increase of 108,200 units, or 20 percent; this compares with an increase of 62,300 units, or 14 percent, in nonmetropolitan areas. While 56 percent of all housing units were in metropolitan areas, these areas accounted for 63 percent of the total State increase between 1960 and 1970.

About 78 percent of the housing in Louisiana consisted of one-unit structures in 1970. The number of units in multiunit structures, however, increased at a faster rate than one-unit structures during the decade, 36 percent and 10 percent, respectively.

The size of housing units increased between 1960 and 1970. Median number of rooms rose from 4.5 to 4.8 in both metropolitan and nonmetropolitan areas. Units with one to three rooms declined, whereas those with five rooms or more had large percentage increases over the decade.

Table C. Housing Units by Metropolitan and Nonmetropolitan Residence: 1970 and 1960

The State Metropolitan and Nonmetropolitan Residence	Housing units				Population percent change
	Total		Change		
	1970	1960	Number	Percent	
Total..................	1,149,033	978,452	170,581	17.4	11.8
Metropolitan residence.....	647,334	539,090	108,244	20.1	14.0
Inside central cities....	391,624	350,586	41,038	11.7	4.0
Outside central cities...	255,710	188,504	67,206	35.7	31.0
Nonmetropolitan residence..	501,699	439,362	62,337	14.2	9.2

Households were smaller in 1970 than in 1960. In metropolitan areas, population per housing unit occupied declined from 3.5 in 1960 to 3.3 in 1970, and in nonmetropolitan areas, from 3.8 in 1960 to 3.5 in 1970. There were large percentage increases in one-person households, 55 percent in metropolitan areas and 52 percent in nonmetropolitan areas. Households with five or more persons showed relatively small gains in metropolitan areas and losses in nonmetropolitan areas.

The proportion of housing units lacking some or all plumbing facilities decreased from 30 to 12 percent during the decade in Louisiana. For metropolitan areas the proportion of units without complete plumbing facilities in 1970 was 5 percent as compared with 20 percent for nonmetropolitan areas.

Number of persons per room is often used as a measure of crowding. For the State, units with 1.01 or more persons per room comprised 15 percent of all occupied units in 1970, compared with 21 percent in 1960 (table D). The number of all such units in 1970 was 152,800, a decrease of about 35,300, or 19 percent, between 1960 and 1970. The decline occurred in metropolitan and nonmetropolitan areas alike, but in nonmetropolitan areas the improvement was somewhat greater.

Homeownership in the State increased from 59 percent in 1960 to 63 percent in 1970. In metropolitan areas there was an increase from 55 to 59 percent, while in nonmetropolitan areas the proportion increased from 64 to 69 percent.

Property values and rents increased during the last decade. The median value of owner-occupied housing in metropolitan areas increased by 33 percent ($13,200 in 1960 to $17,500 in 1970), while in nonmetropolitan areas value increased by 44 percent ($7,200 in 1960 to $10,400 in 1970). In metropolitan areas, median contract rent in 1970 was 38 percent higher than in 1960, rising from $50 to $69. In nonmetropolitan areas rent increased during the 10-year period from $26 to $43, or 65 percent.

Value and rent are expressed in current dollars (the value at the time of the respective censuses). Thus, any comparison must take into account the general rise in the cost of living during the 10-year period as well as changes in the characteristics of the housing inventory.

Standard Metropolitan Statistical Areas

Average household size for the metropolitan area total of the State decreased during the decade. Population per occupied unit in the central cities was 3.1 in 1970, compared with 3.6 in the suburbs.

The rate of homeownership was greater in the suburban areas than in the central cities. About 72 percent of occupied units in the suburbs were owner-occupied, compared with 49 percent in the central cities.

Table D. Plumbing Facilities and Persons Per Room by Metropolitan and Nonmetropolitan Residence: 1970 and 1960

The State Metropolitan and Nonmetropolitan Residence	Percent of housing units			
	Lacking some or all plumbing facilities		With 1.01 or more persons per room[1]	
	1970[2]	1960[3]	1970	1960
Total......................	11.6	29.5	14.5	21.1
Metropolitan residence...........	5.5	(NA)	12.8	18.6
Inside central cities..........	4.3	17.0	12.8	17.2
Outside central cities........	7.2	(NA)	12.7	21.3
Nonmetropolitan residence........	19.6	(NA)	16.8	24.2

NA Not available.
[1]Percent of all occupied units.
[2]Percent of all year-round housing units.
[3]Percent of all housing units.

In 1970, 4 percent of all year-round housing units lacked some or all plumbing facilities in the central cities, compared with 7 percent in the suburbs. Of all occupied units in metropolitan areas, 76,200 units, or 13 percent, reported more than one person per room in 1970, compared with 19 percent in 1960. In 1970, the proportion of such units was approximately the same in both the central cities and the suburbs.

The homeowner vacancy rate for metropolitan areas declined during the decade, from 2.4 percent in 1960 to 1.7 percent in 1970. The rental vacancy rate increased, however, from 7.3 to 9.8 percent.

Annexations

Annexations occurred in each of the central cities during the decade (see "Population Trends" and text table B). Such annexations affect changes in the characteristics for these central cities and their suburbs.

Population Change for Counties: 1960 to 1970

MAINE

LEGEND

- ● Places of 50,000 to 100,000 inhabitants
- □ Central cities of SMSA's with fewer than 50,000 inhabitants
- ○ Places of 25,000 to 50,000 inhabitants outside SMSA's

Standard Metropolitan Statistical Areas (SMSA's)

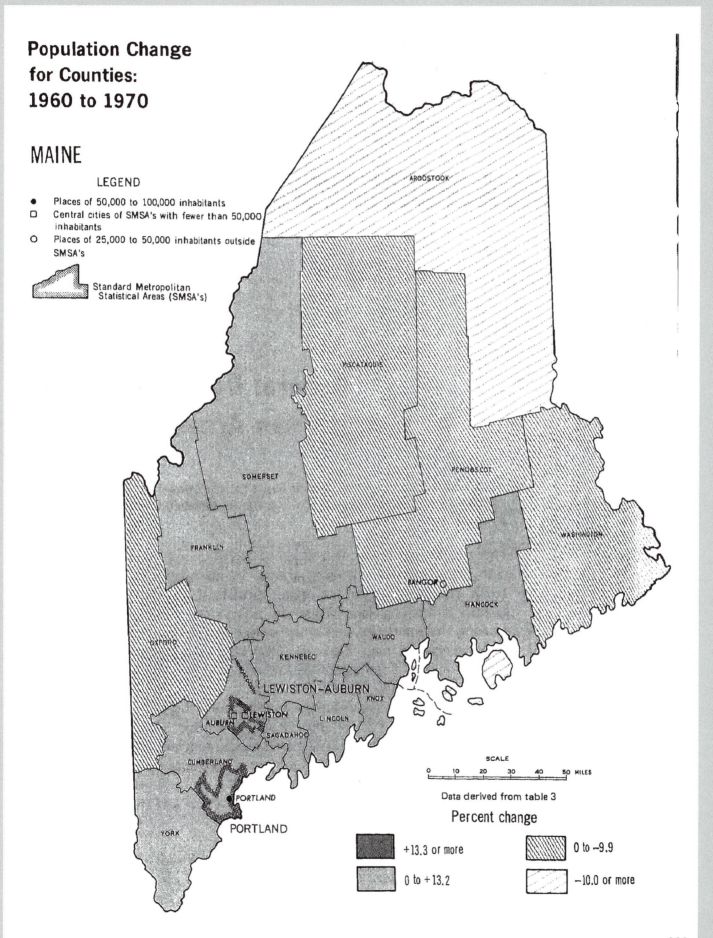

AROOSTOOK

PISCATAQUIS

SOMERSET

PENOBSCOT

FRANKLIN

WASHINGTON

OXFORD

BANGOR ○

HANCOCK

WALDO

KENNEBEC

LEWISTON-AUBURN

KNOX

□ □ LEWISTON

AUBURN

LINCOLN

SAGADAHOC

CUMBERLAND

● PORTLAND

YORK

PORTLAND

SCALE

0   10   20   30   40   50 MILES

Data derived from table 3

Percent change

+13.3 or more	0 to −9.9
0 to +13.2	−10.0 or more

399

Analytical Text

POPULATION TRENDS

General

Between 1960 and 1970 the population of Maine grew by 23,000 persons, from 969,000 to 992,000,[1] an increase of 2.4 percent since 1960. This was the lowest decennial rate of increase in nearly a century. The State is predominantly nonmetropolitan: in 1970, as in 1960, less than 30 percent of the total population was found to be living in the two metropolitan areas of Portland and Lewiston-Auburn. The population of the metro-

[1] The corrected 1970 population for the State is 993,663. Detailed distributions shown in this report have not been revised to reflect this correction because the errors were discovered after the tabulations were made. Further information will be provided in the PC(1)-B final report for this State.

politan areas, however, grew five times as fast as that of the nonmetropolitan areas, by 5.5 percent, compared with 1 percent in nonmetropolitan areas (table A).

The total number of households in the State in 1970 was 303,000, or 23,000 more than in 1960. The population living in households increased less rapidly than the rate at which new households were formed, however, with the result that average household size decreased from 3.4 to 3.2 persons per unit.

The small increase in the population of the State between 1960 and 1970 was produced by the difference between a natural increase of almost 100,000 and a net outmigration of 71,000 (see table 3). This net migration loss is equivalent to more than 7 percent of the State's total population in 1960. As the white population comprises 99 percent of the State total, its patterns of growth and distribution are practically identical with

Table A.   Population by Race and Metropolitan and Nonmetropolitan Residence: 1970 and 1960

The State Metropolitan and Non-metropolitan Residence	Population		Change		Percent Distribution	
	1970	1960	Number	Percent	1970	1960
Total.................	992,048	969,265	22,783	2.4	100.0	100.0
Metropolitan residence[1]..	283,807	269,063	14,744	5.5	28.6	27.8
Inside central cities..	131,046	137,819	−6,773	−4.9	13.2	14.2
Outside central cities.	152,761	131,244	21,517	16.4	15.4	13.5
Nonmetropolitan residence	708,241	700,202	8,039	1.1	71.4	72.2
White...............	985,276	963,291	21,985	2.3	99.3	99.4
Metropolitan residence[1]..	282,197	268,074	14,123	5.3	28.4	27.7
Inside central cities..	130,154	137,242	−7,088	−5.2	13.1	14.2
Outside central cities.	152,043	130,832	21,211	16.2	15.3	13.5
Nonmetropolitan residence	703,079	695,217	7,862	1.1	70.9	71.7
Negro and other races	6,772	5,974	798	13.4	0.7	0.6
Metropolitan residence[1]..	1,610	989	621	62.8	0.2	0.1
Inside central cities..	892	577	315	54.6	0.1	0.1
Outside central cities.	718	412	306	74.3	0.1	...
Nonmetropolitan residence	5,162	4,985	177	3.6	0.5	0.5

[1] State economic areas.

State trends. Although the population of Negro and other races increased overall at a much higher rate than the white population (13 percent compared with 2 percent), it also had a much higher net outmigration rate, amounting to 25 percent for the decade.

In 1970 as in 1960, approximately 45 percent of the population of Maine was under 25 years of age. There were, nonetheless, significant changes in the size of particular age groups during the decade (see table 4). As in other sections of the country, there were large reductions in the number of children under 5 years of age (24,000, or 22 percent less), and more than offsetting gains in young adults aged 15 to 24 years (35,000, or 26 percent more). By contrast, the population of school age, 5 to 14 years old—which constitutes the largest 10-year age group in the State—showed very little change for the period, increasing by somewhat less than 5 percent.

The population 25 years of age and older experienced only moderate changes over the decade. The age group 25 to 44 years old shows a reduction of 16,000 persons, or 7 percent, while the population of middle and older ages increased by 6 percent and 8 percent, respectively.

These changes are in part the product of changing birth rates and in part due to migration which is highly selective by age. Low birth rates during the depression years and in the 1960's contribute to the diminution of age groups under 5 and 25 to 44, whereas the post-World War II "baby boom" is currently reflected in the large size of the population 15 to 24 years old.

Metropolitan Areas

The populations of Maine's two metropolitan areas[2] increased at comparable rates during the decade. The Portland metropolitan area (Cumberland County), whose population is twice as great as that of the Lewiston-Auburn metropolitan area (Androscoggin County), had an intercensal population increase of 5.3 percent, compared with a rate for Lewiston-Auburn of 5.8 percent. Within the two metropolitan areas, however, considerable differences in distribution and change are apparent. While the population of the Portland metropolitan area is scattered throughout the county, the population of the Lewiston-Auburn metropolitan

area is heavily concentrated in the two central cities.

Between 1960 and 1970, the suburban populations of both metropolitan areas increased and the share of their populations living in central cities declined. This development is particularly marked in the Portland area, where the central city lost 10 percent of its population in the intercensal period, declining from 73,000 in 1960 to 65,000 in 1970. At the time of the earlier census, Portland city contained 40 percent of the population of the entire metropolitan area; by 1970 this proportion had dropped to 34 percent. The population of Portland's suburban ring increased during this time by 17,000 persons, or nearly 16 percent.

By contrast, very little change occurred within the Lewiston-Auburn metropolitan area. The two central cities—whose combined populations equal 72 percent of the area's total—show virtually no change over the intercensal period. Lewiston's population grew only slightly, from 41,000 to 42,000, or by 2.5 percent. Auburn, the smaller of the two cities, had a slight population loss amounting to just 1 percent of its 1960 total; in 1970 Auburn's population just exceeded 24,000.[3] Suburban increases, although much larger, were not great enough to alter overall patterns of population distribution.

Both metropolitan areas and central cities lost population as a result of net outmigration. Only the suburban areas show some inmigration, which, was not sufficient to overcome the losses sustained by the cities. Portland city, which was most affected by this movement, had a net outmigration of 12,000 persons, amounting to more than 16 percent of its 1960 population. The losses to Lewiston and Auburn cities were comparable: there were 2,800 net outmigrants from Lewiston, equivalent to 7 percent of its 1960 population, and 2,100 from Auburn, representing 8.5 percent of its 1960 population figure.

Portland city's total population loss is reflected in every age group with the sole exception of young adults 15 to 24 years old, which increased by 21 percent over the decade. In the city of Auburn, age changes closely resemble the State pattern, showing large percentage losses at ages under 5 and 25 to 44 and a marked gain at 15 to 24 amounting to 32 percent of the 1960 population of that age. Lewiston city presents a different picture in that only two age groups gained at all, and in the same degree: young adults, 15 to 24, and the elderly population, 65 and over, each increased by 26 percent.

[2] In the tables of this report and other reports for New England, the metropolitan areas shown are of two kinds: the standard metropolitan statistical area (SMSA) and the metropolitan state economic area (SEA). While the housing analysis in this report uses the SMSA, in the section on population trends reference is made only to the metropolitan SEA (see appendix A).

[3] A small portion of Auburn city is considered rural. In 1970, 1,800 residents of the city were classified as rural out of a total population of 24,200. See "Extended Cities" under "Definitions and Explanations."

Additions to particular age groups in the central cities were not great enough to affect the trend towards suburbanization of all age groups evident in Maine's two metropolitan areas. In the Portland area, there were increases in the proportions living in the suburbs at every age. The same shifts are noted in the Lewiston-Auburn area except for the elderly population, which is more highly concentrated in Lewiston city in 1970 than in 1960.

Counties

Population size of Maine's 16 counties extends from a low of 16,000 in Piscataquis County to a high of 193,000 in Cumberland County (Portland SEA). Decennial population changes were moderate throughout the State; of the 11 counties which show growth for this period, none increased at a rate equivalent to or higher than the national average of 13.3 percent.

The nonmetropolitan counties of the State had the highest rate of growth. The five fastest growing counties are York (112,000 population), Franklin (22,000 population), Lincoln (21,000 population), Hancock (35,000 population), and Kennebec (95,000 population). Androscoggin and Cumberland counties, the State's two metropolitan areas, rank sixth and seventh in rate of growth.

All counties in Maine had more births than deaths during the decade, but only four gained population through net inmigration. All four are among the fastest growing nonmetropolitan counties.

Heaviest population and net migration losses over the decade were sustained by Aroostook County, which lost a population of 14,000 representing 13 percent of its 1960 total. Population loss due to net outmigration amounted to 31,000 persons, equivalent to more than one-fourth of the population living in the county in 1960. A decrease in the number of military personnel stationed in Aroostook County appears to be significant in producing some part of the county's migratory loss.

Penobscot County, containing the city of Bangor, is second largest in Maine. This county is also the site of the University of Maine which had a substantial increase in enrollment over the decade. Nevertheless, Penobscot County shows a slight overall population loss produced by a net outmigration of more than 17,000 persons, equivalent to 14 percent of total 1960 population. This outmigration is largely associated with a decline in the size of the county's military population.

HOUSING TRENDS

General

During the decade, the total supply of housing units in Maine increased faster than population. While housing increased by almost 32,600 units, or 9 percent, the population grew by 23,000, or only 2.4 percent (table B). Similarly, the number of households increased at a faster rate than the population in housing units, resulting in lower average household size.

The nonmetropolitan areas of the State experienced the greatest growth in housing, as in population. Although one in five housing units was located in the two SMSA's, additions to the housing supply of these areas accounted for only about 10 percent of Maine's total housing increase between 1960 and 1970.

Table B. Housing Units by Metropolitan and Nonmetropolitan Residence: 1970 and 1960

The State Metropolitan and Nonmetropolitan Residence	Housing units				Population percent change
	Total		Change		
	1970	1960	Number	Percent	
Total................	397,169	364,617	32,552	8.9	2.4
Metropolitan residence.....	74,941	71,540	3,401	4.8	2.2
Inside central cities....	48,198	48,159	39	0.1	-4.9
Outside central cities...	26,743	23,381	3,362	14.4	16.0
Nonmetropolitan residence..	322,228	293,077	29,151	9.9	2.4

402

A trend toward smaller households is evident throughout the State. The number of households consisting of only one or two persons grew, while the number of all larger households declined. One-person households showed the greatest growth; the number in metropolitan areas increased by 31 percent, and in nonmetropolitan areas by 51 percent.

Homeownership in both 1970 and 1960 was more prevalent in the nonmetropolitan than in the metropolitan areas of Maine. During the decade, owner occupancy increased at about the same rate in metropolitan and nonmetropolitan areas (14 percent), while the number of renter-occupied units declined 3 to 4 percent. In 1970, as a result, 58 percent were owner occupied in the two SMSA's, compared with 54 percent in 1960; in nonmetropolitan areas, nearly 74 percent of housing units were owner occupied, compared with 70 percent in 1960.

Estimated value of Maine's housing increased during the decade by almost half, from a median of $8,800 to $13,000. At the same time, metropolitan-nonmetropolitan differentials narrowed. The median value of metropolitan housing was 53 percent higher than the nonmetropolitan median in 1960, but only 39 percent higher in 1970. In the State as a whole, rents increased faster than estimated value of housing; the median contract rent in 1970 was $71, or 54 percent higher than the 1960 median of $46. Value and rent are expressed in current dollars (the dollar value at the time of the respective censuses). Thus, any comparison must take into account the general rise in the cost of living in the 10-year period as well as changes in the characteristics of the housing inventory.

Number of persons per room is often used as a measurement of crowding. In Maine as a whole, housing units with 1.01 or more persons per room comprised about 8 percent of all occupied units in 1970, compared with 10 percent in 1960 (table C). The number of all such units in 1970 was 22,800; between 1960 and 1970 this number decreased by 6,100, or 21 percent. The decline occurred in metropolitan and nonmetropolitan areas alike, but in nonmetropolitan areas the improvement was somewhat greater. In 1960, 11 percent of nonmetropolitan housing units had an average of 1.01 or more persons per room; by 1970 this percentage was down to 8 percent. Corresponding percentages for the metropolitan areas were 8 percent in 1960, and 6 percent in 1970.

Standard Metropolitan Statistical Areas

Portland

Housing changes within the Portland SMSA parallel population trends. While there was a reduction in the housing supply of the central city of 900 units, or 3.4 percent, the population declined by 10 percent. At the same time, suburban housing increased by 3,000 units, or 14 percent, but population grew faster, by nearly

Table C. Plumbing Facilities and Persons Per Room by Metropolitan and Nonmetropolitan Residence: 1970 and 1960

The State Metropolitan and Nonmetropolitan Residence	Percent of housing units			
	Lacking some or all plumbing facilities		With 1.01 or more persons per room[1]	
	1970[2]	1960[3]	1970	1960
Total.....................	15.4	30.5	7.5	10.3
Metropolitan residence...........	6.5	13.5	6.1	7.9
Inside central cities..........	7.7	14.3	6.4	8.0
Outside central cities........	4.4	11.9	5.7	7.6
Nonmetropolitan residence........	17.9	34.6	7.9	11.1

[1]Percent of all occupied units.
[2]Percent of all year-round housing units.
[3]Percent of all housing units.

10,000 persons, or 15 percent. In 1970, Portland's housing supply was about evenly distributed between central city and suburb, compared with 1960 when 55 percent of the total stock in the SMSA was located in the city.

A trend toward smaller households is apparent throughout the SMSA. In Portland city, between 1960 and 1970, the number of one-person households increased by 17 percent, while the number of all larger households decreased. In the suburbs, where households of every size gained during the decade, the highest percentage increase (67 percent) was also registered by one-person households. The median number of persons per household was consequently lower in 1970 than in 1960; in the city, the median dropped from 2.5 to 2.3 persons per unit, and in the suburbs it declined from 3.1 to 2.9.

Homeownership patterns were substantially different in the central city and suburbs of this SMSA. In 1970, in Portland city, where approximately 40 percent of all year-round housing units were in single-unit structures, the homeownership rate was at its lowest (44 percent). In the suburbs, on the other hand, where single-unit structures predominated, 77 percent of housing units were owner occupied. In both the central city and the suburbs, the proportion of housing represented by owner-occupied units increased during the decade. In Portland city, however, the absolute number of such units stayed the same. The city's net loss of households reflected a decline in renter-occupied units of 1,100, or 8 percent. In the suburbs, the absolute number of both owner-occuped and renter-occupied units increased in the intercensal period by 3,300 and 300 units, respectively. The entire growth of both owner-occupied and renter-occupied housing in the Portland SMSA was thus due to suburban gains.

There was little difference in reported value of housing between the central city and suburbs in Portland. In 1960, the median value of owner-occupied housing in the two parts of the SMSA was identical ($11,900). Increases in value which occurred between 1960 and 1970 were nearly the same: the median for the city rose 40 percent to $16,700, and for the suburbs by 43 percent, to $17,000. Median contract rent in 1970 was likewise about the same in the two areas: $79 in the central city and $77 in the suburbs.

The number of housing units with 1.01 or more persons per room declined in Portland during the decade, by 24 percent in the central city and by 15 percent in the suburban ring. The proportions represented by such units also dropped, from 8 percent in 1960 to 6 percent in 1970, in both the city and suburbs.

Homeowner vacancy rates decreased from 1960 to 1970 in the central city and in the suburbs. Rental vacancies decreased over the decade in Portland city from 7.9 to 6.8, but rose in the suburbs from 4.4 to 5.3.

Lewiston-Auburn

Housing changes in the Lewiston-Auburn SMSA, like population changes, were dominated by developments in the two central cities, particularly by those in the larger city of Lewiston. Only 8 percent of the SMSA's total housing supply was located in the suburban ring. Suburban housing, however, grew at a much faster rate than housing in either of the two central cities. While Lewiston's housing grew by 6 percent and Auburn's by 1.5 percent, units in the suburbs increased by 22 percent.

A trend toward smaller households is evident in each of the central cities. The number of one-person households increased by 37 percent in Lewiston and 29 percent in Auburn, while the number of all larger households grew more slowly or declined. The median number of persons per household was reduced during the decade from 2.7 to 2.5 in Lewiston and from 2.8 to 2.6 in Auburn. There was no change in the median of 3.1 for the suburbs, where households of every size showed gains.

Within this SMSA there were considerable differences in structural characteristics of housing units and in homeownership patterns. In Lewiston city, at the time of both censuses, approximately two-thirds of all housing units were found in multiunit structures. Lewiston also had the highest rate of renter occupancy in the SMSA, exceeding 50 percent in both 1960 and 1970. In the suburbs, on the other hand, two out of three housing units were in single-unit structures and owner occupancy was the predominant form of tenure (75 percent). Auburn city occupied an intermediate position. At the time of both censuses, its housing stock was about evenly divided between 1-unit and multiunit structures, and owner-occupied units comprised about 60 percent of all occupied housing.

Median value of owner-occupied housing rose in all parts of the SMSA during the decade. The greatest increase occurred in the suburbs, where values were lowest at the time of both censuses; median value of housing here increased by 28 percent, from $10,600 in 1960 to $13,600 in 1970. Medians in the two cities increased at the same rate, 22 percent, from $13,700 to $16,700 in Lewiston, and from $12,000 to $14,600 in Auburn. Median contract rent, on the other hand, was highest in the suburban ring, where only one-fourth of all housing units were renter occupied. In 1970, median contract rent in the suburbs was $81, compared with $70 in Lewiston and $67 in Auburn.

In each of the two central cities, units with 1.01 or more persons per room comprised 7 percent of the units in 1970 compared with 8 to 9 percent in 1960. Corresponding percentages for the suburbs were 8 percent in 1970 and 7 percent in 1960. During the decade the number of housing units with 1.01 or more persons per room decreased 22 percent in Lewiston and 9 percent in Auburn. The suburbs had a large percentage increase in the number of units in this category, but the absolute number was small.

Homeowner vacancy rates decreased from 1960 to 1970 in each of the two central cities and in the suburbs. Rental vacancies, however, rose from 7.0 percent in 1960 to 7.7 percent in 1970 for the SMSA. Although the rate increased in both Lewiston city and Auburn city, it decreased in the suburbs.

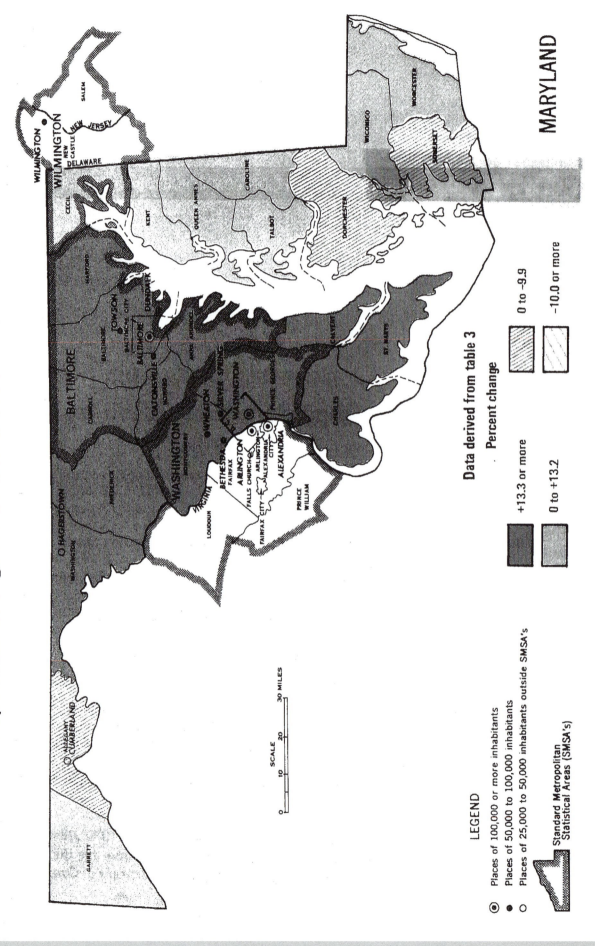

Population Change for Counties: 1960 to 1970

MARYLAND

LEGEND

⊙ Places of 100,000 or more inhabitants

● Places of 50,000 to 100,000 inhabitants

○ Places of 25,000 to 50,000 inhabitants outside SMSA's

Standard Metropolitan Statistical Areas (SMSA's)

Data derived from table 3

Percent change

+13.3 or more

0 to +13.2

0 to -9.9

-10.0 or more

SCALE

0 10 20 30 MILES

Analytical Text

POPULATION TRENDS

General

Between 1960 and 1970 the population of Maryland increased from 3,101,000 to 3,922,000, an increase of over 800,000. The rate of increase, 26.5 percent, was twice that of the United States and was exceeded by only five States. Maryland now ranks 18th in population among the States, having passed Alabama, Louisiana, and Minnesota during the decade (table A).

Maryland's growth was almost evenly divided between natural increase (births minus deaths) and net migration. The net inmigration of nearly 400,000 was exceeded only by California, Florida and New Jersey. Net inmigration of races other than white amounted to nearly 100,000. The rate of inmigration of this group (equivalent to 18 percent of their 1960 population) was slightly greater than the rate of inmigration of the white population. Maryland was the only Southern State to experience any appreciable Negro net inmigration during the decade.

The total number of households in Maryland in 1970 was 1,175,000 or 312,000 more than in 1960. The population living in households increased less rapidly than the rate at which households increased with the result that average household size decreased slightly from 3.5 to 3.2 persons.

The State can logically be divided into four distinct groups. The southern part bordering on the Chesapeake Bay contains 11 small rural counties comprising 8 percent of the State's population. The western part extending into Appalachia takes in four rural northern counties and contains 7 percent of the population. At the center of the State is the important port of Baltimore which is a stereotype of an old northern industrial city and contains 23 percent of the State's population. Finally there is an elliptically shaped eight county suburban area around Baltimore stretching from Washington, D.C. in the south to Wilmington, Del. in the north, which now holds 61 percent of Maryland's population.

The nonmetropolitan southern and western sections experienced population increase at a rate close to that of

Table A.   Population by Race and Metropolitan and Nonmetropolitan Residence: 1970 and 1960

The State Metropolitan and Non-metropolitan Residence	Population		Change		Percent Distribution	
	1970	1960	Number	Percent	1970	1960
Total...............	3,922,399	3,100,689	821,710	26.5	100.0	100.0
Metropolitan residence...	3,307,337	2,550,476	756,861	29.7	84.3	82.3
Inside central cities..	905,759	939,024	−33,265	−3.5	23.1	30.3
Outside central cities.	2,401,578	1,611,452	790,126	49.0	61.2	52.0
Nonmetropolitan residence	615,062	550,213	64,849	11.8	15.7	17.7
White...............	3,193,021	2,573,919	619,102	24.1	81.4	83.0
Metropolitan residence...	2,674,668	2,111,100	563,568	26.7	68.2	68.1
Inside central cities..	479,837	610,608	−130,771	−21.4	12.2	19.7
Outside central cities.	2,194,831	1,500,492	694,339	46.3	56.0	48.4
Nonmetropolitan residence	518,353	462,819	55,534	12.0	13.2	14.9
Negro and other races	729,378	526,770	202,608	38.5	18.6	17.0
Metropolitan residence...	632,669	439,376	193,293	44.0	16.1	14.2
Inside central cities..	425,922	328,416	97,506	29.7	10.9	10.6
Outside central cities.	206,747	110,960	95,787	86.3	5.3	3.6
Nonmetropolitan residence	96,709	87,394	9,315	10.7	2.5	2.8

the United States. Net migration was negligible for both areas, but the southern area, which is about 25 percent Negro, had a substantially higher birth rate than the western sector which is almost 100 percent white. Baltimore city had a population loss of over 30,000 and a net outmigration of nearly 120,000. The State's eight suburban counties (of the Baltimore, Washington, D.C.-Md.-Va., and Wilmington Del.-N.J.-Md. SMSA's) grew from 1,611,000 to 2,402,000 to acccount for 95 percent of the State's growth. These eight counties had a net inmigration of almost one-half million.

As in the Nation generally, Maryland's age structure changed significantly in the decade. The population under age 5 declined 6 percent while every other broad age group showed a significant increase. The loss of population under 5 is the result of the greatly reduced number of births in the period 1965 to 1969 relative to the period 1955 to 1959. The 15 to 24 age group which contains the post-World War II "baby boom" cohort expanded from 414,000 to 682,000 an increase of over 60 percent in this period. The age structure of Negro and other races exhibited the same pattern as for whites although the increments were somewhat larger age group by age group.

Standard Metropolitan Statistical Areas

Maryland has one standard metropolitan statistical area (SMSA), Baltimore, lying wholly within the State borders. In addition there are two metropolitan areas partially within the State. That part of the Washington, D.C. SMSA in Maryland consists of two suburban counties with nearly 1.2 million persons. A small part of the Wilmington, SMSA with slightly over 50,000 persons falls in Maryland.

The Baltimore SMSA is made up of the independent city of Baltimore, plus Anne Arundel, Baltimore, Carroll, Howard, and Harford counties. The Baltimore SMSA contains nearly 2.1 million persons and ranks 11th among all SMSA's in the county. The rate of population increase in the SMSA was 14.8 percent, slightly below the overall United States metropolitan growth of 16.6 percent. However, of the Nation's 12 metropolitan areas containing over two million persons, Baltimore ranked 4th in growth, trailing neighboring Washington, D.C. and two California areas, San Francisco-Oakland and Los Angeles-Long Beach.

The growth within the SMSA was mainly the result of natural increase, which amounted to over 200,000 while net inmigration was responsible for only 52,000. Within the SMSA there was a considerable contrast in growth rates. Baltimore city had an absolute population loss of over 30,000 with a net outmigration of nearly 120,000, which was one-eighth of its 1960 population. On the

other hand, the five suburban counties experienced a growth of 300,000 or 35 percent. Nearly 60 percent of the growth in the suburban areas was the result of net inmigration. The five suburban counties now contain 56 percent of the population in the SMSA compared with 48 percent in 1960.

The population of Negro and other races (primarily Negro) increased more than twice as fast as did the white population. Negro and other races increased by 111,000 or 28 percent while the white population increase of 156,000 was only 11 percent. Almost 90 percent of the increase in Negro and other races was confined to Baltimore city, where they now amount to 47 percent of the city's population. In 1960 Baltimore's population was almost two-thirds white. The change in the white-Negro proportion in the city was mainly caused by the white exodus from the city. White net outmigration amounted to 150,000, equivalent to 25 percent of the white 1960 population. Negro inmigration during the decade amounted to 30,000, equivalent to 10 percent of its 1960 population. Baltimore's five suburban counties are predominantly white (94 percent in 1970). The white rate of growth was considerably above that of Negro and other races, 36 percent as opposed to 22 percent in the past decade.

Counties

Maryland consists of 23 counties and the independent city of Baltimore. Twelve of the counties had population increases greater than the national average of 13.3 percent. Seven of the eight suburban metropolitan counties fell into this category, while only five of the remaining 16 nonmetropolitan counties could make this claim.

Prince Georges County in the Washingon SMSA had the greatest growth in terms of both absolute numbers and percentage increase. The county had a population increase of over 300,000 for a rate of growth of 85 percent. Only 20 of the more than 3,000 counties in the country had a greater rate of increase. Montgomery County, the other suburban county in the Washington SMSA, had an increase of over 180,000 for a 50-percent growth rate. Prince Georges and Montgomery Counties together accounted for nearly three-fifths of the State's growth and nearly five-sixths of the net inmigration experienced by the State.

All five of the Baltimore suburban counties had growth rates of at least 25 percent during the decade. Howard County with its new city of Columbia led the group with a growth of 71 percent, and Baltimore County trailed with a rate of 26 percent. Every one of these counties had net inmigration amounting to at least 10 percent of their 1960 populations.

Among the nonmetropolitan counties, Charles County which is less than 20 miles from the District of Columbia had a growth of 46 percent, half of which was the result of net inmigration. Three of the four remaining nonmetropolitan counties within 50 miles of Washington, D.C. had net inmigration, and the fourth, St. Mary's, increased its 1960 population by over 20 percent although it experienced slight net outmigration.

Not one of the remaining 10 counties, eight of them on the eastern side of Chesapeake Bay and the other two in the western reaches of the State, increased by as much as the national rate.

The increase in the population of Negro and other races was most pronounced in Prince Georges County, where the population of this group tripled in the past decade. The major area of Negro growth in the county was adjacent to the northeast tip of Washington, D.C. The county had a net inmigration of Negro and other races of 55,000 and together with Baltimore city was responsible for five-sixths of the Negro migration within the State.

HOUSING TRENDS

General

Between 1960 and 1970, the total supply of housing units in Maryland increased more rapidly than population. While the population grew by 822,000, or 27 percent, housing units increased by 314,000, or 34 percent (table B).

The metropolitan areas of the State experienced greater relative growth in housing, as in population, than did the nonmetropolitan areas. The number of housing units in metropolitan areas rose from 753,500 to 1,034,700 over the decade, an increase of 281,200 units, or 37 percent; this compares with an increase of 32,800 units, or 18 percent, in nonmetropolitan areas. While the metropolitan areas contained 83 percent of the housing in Maryland, additions to the housing supply in these areas accounted for about 90 percent of the State's total housing increase between 1960 and 1970.

About 69 percent of the housing in Maryland consisted of one-unit structures in 1970. Corresponding proportions of such units were 67 percent in metropolitan areas and 79 percent in the nonmetropolitan areas.

Households were smaller in 1970 than in 1960. In the metropolitan areas of the State, average household size declined from 3.5 persons in 1960 to 3.3 in 1970 and in nonmetropolitan areas, from 3.4 persons in 1960 to 3.2 in 1970. There were large percentage increases in one- and two-person households in metropolitan areas, 112 percent and 52 percent, respectively; in nonmetropolitan areas, one- and two-person households increased at 61 percent and 23 percent, respectively.

The number of units in the State lacking some or all plumbing was 55,000 in 1970, or 4 percent of all year-round units. About 2 percent of the units in metropolitan areas lacked some or all plumbing compared with 15 percent in nonmetropolitan areas.

Approximately 7,200, or 5 percent, of the Negro-occupied units inside SMSA's lacked some or all plumbing in 1970, compared with 10,900, or 46 percent, of the Negro housing outside SMSA's.

Number of persons per room is often used as a measure of crowding. In Maryland both the number and proportion of housing units with 1.01 or more persons decreased during the decade. In 1960, 9 percent of all occupied housing units in metropolitan areas and 11

Table B. Housing Units by Metropolitan and Nonmetropolitan Residence: 1970 and 1960

The State Metropolitan and Nonmetropolitan Residence	Housing units				Population percent change
	Total		Change		
	1970	1960	Number	Percent	
Total................	1,248,564	934,552	314,012	33.6	26.5
Metropolitan residence.....	1,034,703	753,517	281,186	37.3	29.7
Inside central cities....	305,521	290,155	15,366	5.3	-3.5
Outside central cities...	729,182	463,362	265,820	57.4	49.0
Nonmetropolitan residence..	213,861	181,035	32,826	18.1	11.8

percent in nonmetropolitan areas had 1.01 or more persons per room. By 1970, the proportion of such units decreased to 6 percent in metropolitan areas and 8 percent in nonmetropolitan areas (table C).

Homeownership in the State decreased from 64 percent in 1960 to 59 percent in 1970. In metropolitan areas there was a decrease from 65 to 57 percent, while in nonmetropolitan areas the proportion rose from 63 to 67 percent.

About 36 percent of the Negro households in metropolitan areas owned their homes in 1970, compared with 52 percent in the nonmetropolitan areas. Of the 68,900 Negro homeowner households in the State, 56,700 lived inside SMSA's and 12,200 lived outside SMSA's.

Property values and rents increased during the last decade. The median value in metropolitan areas increased by 58 percent from $12,400 in 1960 to $19,600 in 1970, while in the nonmetropolitan areas value increased 70 percent, from $8,400 to $14,300. In metropolitan areas, median contract rent in 1970 was 62 percent higher than in 1960, rising from $71 to $115. In nonmetropolitan areas rent increased from $42 to $63, or 50 percent.

Value and rent are expressed in current dollars (the value at the time of the respective censuses). Thus, any comparison must take into account the general rise in the cost of living during the 10-year period, as well as changes in the characteristics of the housing inventory.

Standard Metropolitan Statistical Areas

In the metropolitan areas of the State, the housing supply increased by 281,200 units, or 37 percent. The metropolitan areas are comprised of the Baltimore SMSA with 656,700 housing units, the Maryland portion of the Washington, D.C.-Md.-Va. SMSA with 361,600 units, and the Maryland portion of the Wilmington, Del.-N.J.-Md. SMSA with 16,400.

The Baltimore SMSA, which contained 63 percent of the metropolitan housing units in the State, accounted for 41 percent of the metropolitan area increase, whereas the Maryland portion of the Washington, D.C. metropolitan area with 35 percent of the housing units accounted for 59 percent of the increase.

In the Baltimore SMSA, the suburbs experienced greater relative growth in housing than did the central city. Housing units in the suburbs increased by 39 percent during the decade and housing in the central city increased 5 percent. In comparison, the increase in housing units in the Maryland portion of the Washington, D.C. metropolitan area was 84 percent.

The proportion of one-unit structures decreased from 71 percent in 1960 to 61 percent in 1970 in Baltimore city and from 86 to 78 percent in its suburbs. In the Maryland portion of the Washington, D.C. metropolitan area, the proportion of one-unit structures declined from 77 percent in 1960 to 61 percent in 1970.

Housing units decreased in size in Baltimore central city and increased in size in the suburbs. In the city the median number of rooms declined from 5.5 in 1960 to 5.3 in 1970 and in the suburbs increased from 5.5 to 5.7. In the Washington suburbs the median remained unchanged at 5.5.

Average household size for the Baltimore metropolitan area declined during the decade. In the central city, the average decreased from 3.3 persons to 3.1, and in the

Table C.   Plumbing Facilities and Persons Per Room by Metropolitan and Nonmetropolitan Residence: 1970 and 1960

The State Metropolitan and Nonmetropolitan Residence	Percent of housing units			
	Lacking some or all plumbing facilities		With 1.01 or more persons per room[1]	
	1970[2]	1960[3]	1970	1960
Total......................	4.5	10.5	6.6	9.7
Metropolitan residence...........	2.4	6.0	6.4	9.4
Inside central cities..........	1.8	3.0	8.7	10.2
Outside central cities........	2.7	7.9	5.4	8.9
Nonmetropolitan residence........	14.8	29.4	7.8	10.9

[1]Percent of all occupied units.
[2]Percent of all year-round housing units.
[3]Percent of all housing units.

suburbs from 3.6 persons to 3.4. Similarly, average household size decreased from 3.7 persons to 3.3 for the Washington, D.C. suburbs.

The proportion of housing units lacking some or all plumbing facilities declined from 3 to 2 percent during the decade in Baltimore city and from 9 to 4 percent in its suburban areas. The proportion of such units in the Maryland suburbs of the District of Columbia declined from 5 to 1 percent.

Approximately 1,700, or 2 percent, of Negro households in central cities occupied units which lacked some or all plumbing facilities in 1970, compared with 3,200, or 20 percent, of Negro households in the Baltimore suburbs. In the Maryland suburbs of the District of Columbia 2,000 Negro households, or 7 percent, occupied such units.

There was a slight decrease in the proportion of units with more than one person per room in Baltimore city from 10 to 9 percent. The proportion of the Baltimore suburban units in this category decreased from 9 to 6 percent. Similarly, a decrease from 9 to 5 percent occurred in the Maryland suburbs of the Washington, D.C. metropolitan area.

Homeownership decreased in the Baltimore SMSA as well as in the Maryland suburbs of the District of Columbia. In Baltimore city, homeownership decreased from 54 percent in 1960 to 45 percent in 1970 and in the suburbs from 75 to 70 percent. In the Maryland portion of the Washington, D.C. suburbs, the decrease was from 69 to 55 percent.

Three out of 10 Negro households in the city of Baltimore owned their homes in 1970, compared with one out of two in both the Baltimore suburbs and the Maryland suburbs of the District of Columbia.

In Baltimore central city, the median value of owner-occupied homes increased by 11 percent ($9,000 in 1960 to $10,000 in 1970), in contrast to the 51 percent increase in its suburbs ($12,500 in 1960 to $18,900 in 1970). Median contract rent in the central city in 1970 was 41 percent higher than in 1960, rising from $64 to $90. Rent increased in the Baltimore suburban area from $69 to $111, or 61 percent. Median value for homes in the Maryland suburbs of the Washington, D.C. metropolitan area increased 60 percent ($17,300 in 1960 to $27,700 in 1970) while median contract rent increased 67 percent (from $90 to $150).

The homeowner vacancy rate decreased from 1.4 to 0.9 percent in Baltimore city and from 2.4 to 0.8 percent in its suburbs. The rental vacancy rate decreased from 6.4 to 5.8 percent in the central city, and from 6.2 to 4.5 percent in the suburban areas. Decreases in the homeowner and rental vacancy rates also occurred in the Maryland suburbs of the Washington, D.C. metropolitan area.

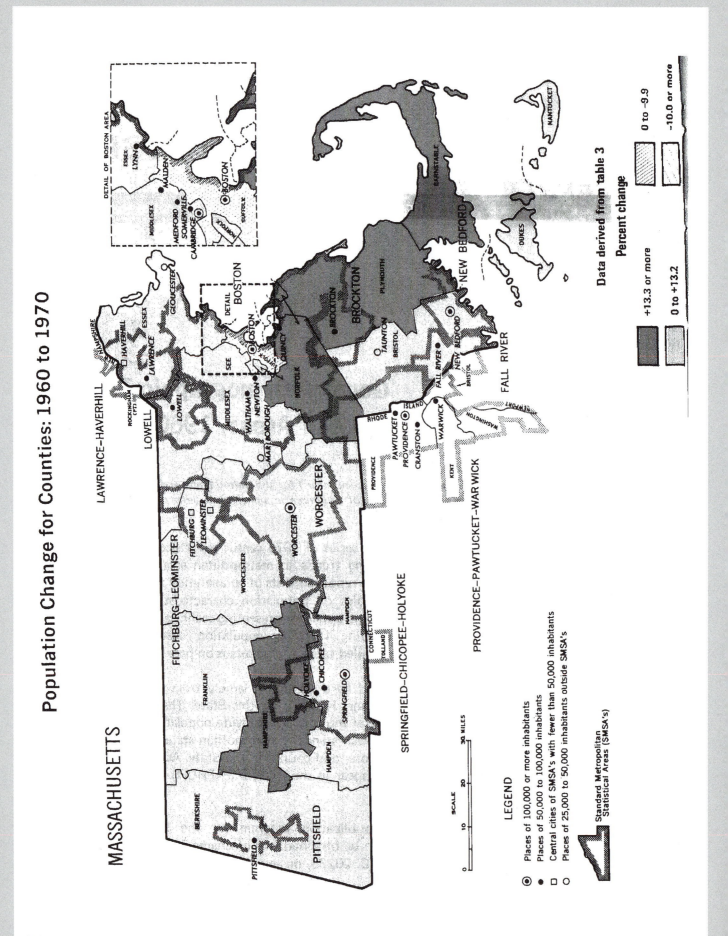

Population Change for Counties: 1960 to 1970

MASSACHUSETTS

Data derived from table 3

Percent change

- +13.3 or more
- 0 to +13.2
- 0 to -9.9
- -10.0 or more

LEGEND

- ⊙ Places of 100,000 or more inhabitants
- ● Places of 50,000 to 100,000 inhabitants
- □ Central cities of SMSA's with fewer than 50,000 inhabitants
- ○ Places of 25,000 to 50,000 inhabitants outside SMSA's

Standard Metropolitan Statistical Areas (SMSA's)

SCALE
0   10   20   30 MILES

Analytical Text

POPULATION TRENDS

General

Between 1960 and 1970, the population of Massachusetts grew from 5,149,000 to 5,689,000, an increase of 541,000, or 10.5 percent. This rate of increase was below the rate of increase for the entire United States (13.3 percent) but slightly above the rate for the Northeast region (9.7 percent) in which Massachusetts is located. Massachusetts ranks 10th in population among the 50 States.

The total number of households in Massachusetts in 1970 was 1,760,000, or 225,000 more than in 1960. The population living in households increased more slowly than the rate at which households increased, with the result that average household size dropped from 3.2 to 3.1 persons. In the Nation as a whole in 1970, the average was 3.1 persons.

The metropolitan population of Massachusetts increased by 8 percent from 4,441,000 in 1960 to 4,818,000 in 1970 while the nonmetropolitan population increased by 23 percent from 707,000 to 871,000 (see table A-1). In 1970, 85 percent of the population lived in metropolitan areas compared to about two-thirds of the population in the Nation as a whole. In most States the rate of growth was higher in metropolitan areas than in nonmetropolitan areas, due in part to the decline in the farm population. In Massachusetts, however, the rural farm population was already so low in 1960 (less than 1 percent of the State's population) that the potential for further decline was negligible. Another factor contributing to the higher growth rate in the nonmetropolitan population in Massachusetts as in other New England States is the spread of suburban development beyond the present boundaries of the metropolitan areas, which are defined in terms of towns rather than counties.

Within the metropolitan areas, the population living in the central cities declined by 3 percent from 1,786,000 to 1,727,000 while the population in the balance of the metropolitan areas grew by 16 percent from 2,655,000 to 3,091,000. More than one-half of Massachusetts' population lives in the portion of metropolitan areas outside central cities.

The population of Negro and other races (which is predominantly Negro) in Massachusetts increased from 125,000 in 1960 to 212,000 in 1970, or by 69 percent, and, as a result, increased from 2 to 4 percent of the total population. In 1970 three-fourths of the population of Negro and other races lived in the central cities of metropolitan areas (less than 30 percent of the white population lived in central cities), and slightly over half lived in the city of Boston alone.

The population increase of 541,000 in Massachusetts in the 1960 to 1970 decade resulted from a natural increase (births minus deaths) of 466,000 and a net inmigration of 74,000. Net inmigration accounted for one-seventh of the growth and was equivalent to 1.4 percent of the 1960 population. Among the population of Negro and other races, net inmigration was 51,000 and accounted for three-fifths of the population growth.

The population loss of 59,000 in the central cities of metropolitan areas resulted from a natural increase of 131,000 and a net outmigration of 190,000. The net outmigration was equivalent to 11 percent of the central city population in 1960.

The age structure of the Massachusetts population changed significantly between 1960 and 1970. The largest decline (14 percent) occurred among the population under 5 years old and was due largely to the decline in birth rates which occurred throughout the United States during the 1960's. The greatest increase (49 percent) occurred in the 15 to 24 age group and was due mostly to the entry of the large number of persons born during the post-World War II "baby boom" into this age group. As a result of these changes, the proportion of the total population in the under 5 group declined from 11 to 8 percent and the proportion in the 15 to 24 group increased from 13 to 17 percent.

Standard Metropolitan Statistical Areas

In 1970, there were 11 standard metropolitan statistical areas (SMSA's) in Massachusetts, including seven SMSA's located entirely in Massachusetts and four SMSA's located partly in Massachusetts.[1] Of the four SMSA's that cross State lines, three are located mostly in Massachusetts and are discussed in their entirety in this report.

The population of the Boston SMSA, which includes nearly one-half of Massachusetts' population and which is the eighth largest metropolitan area in the Nation, increased from 2,595,000 in 1960 to 2,754,000 in 1970, or by 6 percent. Of the 33 SMSA's with 1970 populations exceeding 1,000,000, only the Pittsburgh SMSA (which had a small loss) and the Buffalo SMSA had lower rates of population growth. In addition to being the State capital, Boston is one of the Nation's leading ports and a major financial and manufacturing center. The Boston area is also one of the Nation's leading centers of higher education.

---

[1] In the population tables in this report and other reports for States in New England, data are shown for two types of metropolitan areas: standard metropolitan statistical area (SMSA's) and metropolitan State economic areas (SEA's). See "Definitions and Explanations" for a discussion of the differences between the two types of metropolitan areas. SMSA table are shown in the Appendix to this text.

The population of the city of Boston declined from 801,000 in 1950 to 697,000 in 1960 and 641,000 in 1970. In 1970, Boston was the 16th largest city in the Nation. (With a population of 671,000 in 1910, Boston was the fifth largest city in the Nation.) Between 1960 and 1970, the population in Boston city declined 8 percent while the population in the balance of the SMSA increased by 11 percent. Boston city's decline in population was the product of a white population loss of 104,000 and a gain of 48,000 persons of other races. In 1970, races other than white constituted 18 percent of Boston's population, compared with 10 percent in 1960.

The Springfield-Chicopee-Holyoke SMSA grew from 494,000 in 1960 (including 4,000 in Connecticut) to 530,000 in 1970 (including 7,000 in Connecticut) or by 7 percent. As in the case of Boston, the Springfield-Chicopee-Holyoke SMSA is an important manufacturing center. Several institutions of higher learning are located in or adjacent to the SMSA. During the past decade, the population loss in Springfield and Holyoke exceeded the gain in Chicopee, and thus all of the growth in the SMSA occurred outside the central cities.

The population of the Worcester SMSA, also a manufacturing center, increased from 329,000 in 1960 to 344,000 in 1970, or by 5 percent. The population in the city of Worcester declined by 5 percent while the population in the balance of the SMSA increased by 17 percent.

Between 1960 and 1970, the population of the Lawrence-Haverhill SMSA grew 17 percent to 232,000 (including 27,000 in New Hampshire), and the population of the Lowell SMSA grew 30 percent to 213,000. These rates of growth are the highest experienced by these areas in several decades and reflect the change from economies based largely on textiles to diversified manufacturing, including electronic equipment. The population growth in these two SMSA's occurred outside the central cities.

The Brockton SMSA, which borders the Boston SMSA and which is a leading producer of footwear, had a population of 190,000 in 1970, up 27 percent since 1960. The population in the city of Brockton increased 22 percent, which was easily the highest growth rate of any central city in Massachusetts during the past decade.

The population of the New Bedford SMSA increased 7 percent to 153,000 in 1970, and the population of the Fall River SMSA increased 9 percent to 150,000 (including 13,000 in Rhode Island). New Bedford, most noted for its maritime history and Fall River, most noted for its textiles and apparel industry, each lost population during the past decade as all the growth in the two SMSA's occurred outside the central cities.

There are two SMSA's in Massachusetts with populations under 100,000. In 1970, the population of the Fitchburg-Leominister SMSA was 97,000, up 8 percent

since 1960, and the population of the Pittsfield SMSA was 80,000, up 4 percent since 1960.

The population in the Massachusetts portion of the Providence-Pawtucket-Warwick SMSA was 122,000 in 1970, a 35 percent increase over 1960. In 1970, about 13 percent of the SMSA's total population of 911,000 lived in Massachusetts.

Counties

Thirteen of the 14 counties in Massachusetts gained population between 1960 and 1970. Four counties gained at rates above the national average of 13.3 percent, and the one county losing population (Suffolk County) experienced a decline of 7 percent. In the Nation as a whole, slightly more than one-half of all counties gained population between 1960 and 1970.

Ten of Massachusetts' 14 counties experienced net inmigration between 1960 and 1970. In the Nation as a whole, less than one-third of all counties experienced net inmigration during the decade.

In the New England States, SMSA's are comprised of cities and towns (rather than of counties as in the remainder of the Nation), and thus a county may be partly metropolitan and partly nonmetropolitan (see "Definitions and Explanations"). The population of Suffolk County is entirely metropolitan; the populations of Bristol, Essex, Hampden, Middlesex, Norfolk, Plymouth, and Worcester Counties are largely metropolitan; the population of Berkshire and Hampshire Counties are about one-half metropolitan; the remaining counties are entirely nonmetropolitan.

Two of the State's counties had rates of population growth more than twice the national average during the 1960 to 1970 decade. In Barnstable County, which comprises the resort area of Cape Cod, the population increased 38 percent. Six-sevenths of the growth was due to net inmigration. The population of Plymouth County, which includes most of the Brockton SMSA and a suburban portion of the Boston SMSA, increased by 34 percent. Three-fifths of the growth was due to net inmigration.

In Middlesex County, the most populous county in the State, the population grew from 1,239,000 in 1960 to 1,397,000 in 1970, or by 13 percent. One-eighth of the growth was due to net inmigration. Three-fourths of Middlesex County's population is in the Boston SMSA and another 15 percent is in the Lowell SMSA.

Suffolk County, which is comprised largely of the city of Boston (87 percent of the County's 1970 population), had a population of 791,000 in 1960 and 735,000 in 1970. Net outmigration from the county during the decade was 110,000, equivalent to 14 percent of the 1960 population.

HOUSING TRENDS

General

Between 1960 and 1970 the total supply of housing units in Massachusetts increased more rapidly than population. The population grew by 541,000, or 10 percent, while housing units increased by 199,400, or 12 percent (table A).

About 82 percent of all housing units in the State were in its standard metropolitan statistical areas. The metropolitan areas experienced less relative growth than did the nonmetropolitan areas, in housing as well as in population. The number of housing units in metropolitan areas rose from 1,407,700 to 1,559,100 over the decade, an increase of 151,400 units, or 11 percent; this

compares with an increase of 48,000 units, or 17 percent, in nonmetropolitan areas.

About 50 percent of the housing in Massachusetts consisted of one-unit structures in 1970. The proportion of such units in metropolitan areas was 47 percent, and in nonmetropolitan areas, 67 percent.

The number of units in the State lacking some or all plumbing facilities in 1970 was 65,700 units, or 4 percent. The proportions of units in this category were 3 percent in metropolitan areas and 4 percent in nonmetropolitan areas (table B). Approximately 2,200, or 4 percent, of the Negro-occupied units in the State lacked some or all plumbing in 1970. The corresponding proportions for inside and outside the metropolitan areas were 4 percent and 6 percent, respectively.

Table A. Housing Units by Metropolitan and Nonmetropolitan Residence: 1970 and 1960

The State Metropolitan and Nonmetropolitan Residence	Housing units				Population percent change
	Total		Change		
	1970	1960	Number	Percent	
Total..................	1,890,400	1,690,998	199,402	11.8	10.5
Metropolitan residence.....	1,559,077	1,407,682	151,395	10.8	10.2
Inside central cities....	602,367	599,440	2,927	0.5	-3.3
Outside central cities...	956,710	808,242	148,468	18.4	17.6
Nonmetropolitan residence..	331,323	283,316	48,007	16.9	23.2

Table B. Plumbing Facilities and Persons Per Room by Metropolitan and Nonmetropolitan Residence: 1970 and 1960

The State Metropolitan and Nonmetropolitan Residence	Percent of housing units			
	Lacking some or all plumbing facilities		With 1.01 or more persons per room[1]	
	1970[2]	1960[3]	1970	1960
Total......................	3.6	9.6	6.0	6.7
Metropolitan residence..........	3.4	(NA)	6.0	6.7
Inside central cities..........	5.0	13.4	6.9	7.3
Outside central cities........	2.4	(NA)	5.5	6.3
Nonmetropolitan residence........	4.3	(NA)	5.7	6.6

NA Not available.   [1]Percent of all occupied units.   [2]Percent of all year-round housing units.   [3]Percent of all housing units.

Households were smaller in 1970 than in 1960. In both metropolitan and nonmetropolitan areas the average household size declined from 3.2 to 3.1 persons over the decade. There were large percentage increases in one-persons households, 49 percent in metropolitan areas and 70 percent in nonmetropolitan areas. In comparison, households with five or more persons increased 8 percent in metropolitan areas, and 23 percent in nonmetropolitan areas.

The median number of rooms in 1970 was 5.2 in metropolitan areas and 5.3 in nonmetropolitan areas. One- to three-rooms units comprised 15 percent of the year-round housing in metropolitan areas and 11 percent in nonmetrpolitan areas. About 43 percent of the metropolitan housing units and 46 percent of the nonmetropolitan units had six or more rooms.

Number of persons per room is often used as a measure of crowding. In Massachusetts, the proportion of housing units with 1.01 or more persons per room decreased during the decade. In 1960, 7 percent of all occupied housing units in both metropolitan and non-metropolitan areas had 1.01 or more persons per room. By 1970, the proportion of such units had decreased to 6 percent in these areas (table B).

Homeownership in the State increased from 56 to 58 percent over the decade. In the metropolitan areas homeownership rose from 54 to 56 percent and in nonmetropolitan areas from 67 to 69 percent. Of the 1,012,200 owner-occupied units in the State, 830,400 were inside metropolitan areas and 181,800 were outside these areas.

About 24 percent of the Negro households in metropolitan areas owned their homes in 1970, compared with 50 percent in nonmetropolitan areas. Of the 12,700 Negro-homeowner households in the State, 11,700 lived inside SMSA's and the remainder lived outside SMSA's.

Property values and rents increased during the last decade. The median value of owner-occupied homes in metropolitan areas rose 49 percent, from $14,200 to $21,100, while in the nonmetropolitan areas, the median increased 61 percent, from $11,700 to $18,800. In metropolitan areas, median contract rent in 1970 was $92 and in nonmetropolitan areas $78.

Value and rent are expressed in current dollars (the value at the time of the respective censuses). Thus, any comparison must take into account the general rise in the cost of living during the 10-year period, as well as changes in the characteristics of the housing inventory.

Standard Metropolitan Statistical Areas

In the metropolitan areas of the State, the housing supply increased by 151,400 units, or 11 percent. The Boston SMSA, the largest in the State, contained 57 percent of the housing units in the metropolitan areas and accounted for 53 percent of the increase.

The suburban areas of the State experienced greater growth in housing than did the central cities. Housing units in the suburbs increased by 148,500, or 18.4 percent, while housing in the combined central cities increased by 2,900, or 0.5 percent. By 1970, there were 956,700 housing units in the suburbs and 602,400 units in the central cities.

The proportion of the housing inventory in one-unit structures declined in both the central cities and their suburbs. In the central cities the proportion of such units declined from 28 percent in 1960 to 27 percent in 1970 and in the suburban areas from 66 to 60 percent.

In 1970, about 53,300 housing units in metro-politan areas, or 3 percent of all year-round units, lacked some or all plumbing facilities. The corresponding proportions for the central cities and the suburbs were 5 percent and 2 percent, respectively. Approximately 4 percent of the Negro households in central cities and in the suburbs occupied units which lacked some or all plumbing facilities in 1970. There were about 1,800 such units in the central cities and 300 in the suburban areas.

Household size in the metropolitan areas declined during the decade. In the central cities the average decreased from 3.0 to 2.9 persons and in the suburbs, from 3.4 to 3.3 persons. One-person households constituted 25 percent of the occupied units in the central cities and 16 percent in the suburbs.

The median number of rooms in the central cities declined slightly from 4.9 in 1960 to 4.8 in 1970. In the suburban areas, the median remained 5.5 rooms. While 20 percent of the housing in central cities had one to three rooms in 1970, 12 percent of the housing units in the suburbs were in this categroy. At the same time, 31 percent of the housing in the central cities had six or more rooms, compared with 50 percent in the suburbs.

Of all occupied units in the central cities 7 percent reported 1.01 or more persons per room, as in 1960. In the suburban areas, the proportions were 5 percent in 1970 and 6 percent in 1960.

Homeownership in 1970 was greater in the suburban areas than in the central cities. About 66 percent of occupied units in the suburbs and 39 percent in the central cities were owner-occupied. The Negro-home-ownership rate in the suburbs was 43 percent, compared with 20 percent in the central cities.

In the central cities of Massachusetts, the median value of owner-occupied housing rose 40 percent, from $12,500 in 1960 to $17,500 in 1970; in the suburbs, the median increased 51 percent, from $14,800 to $22,300. About 14 percent of the owner-occuped housing was valued in 1970 at $25,000 or more in the central cities, compared with 37 percent in the suburbs.

In 1970, median contract rent in the central cities was $81 and in the suburbs, $106. Approximately 21 percent of the renter-occupied units in the central cities and 39 percent of the suburban units had rents of $120 or more.

The homeowner vacancy rate decreased in the central cities from 1.0 percent in 1960 to 0.7 percent in 1970 and in the suburbs from 1.1 to 0.5 percent. The rental vacancy rate increased slightly from 5.4 to 5.5 percent in the central cities, and decreased from 3.6 to 3.3 in the suburbs.

Population Change for Counties: 1960 to 1970

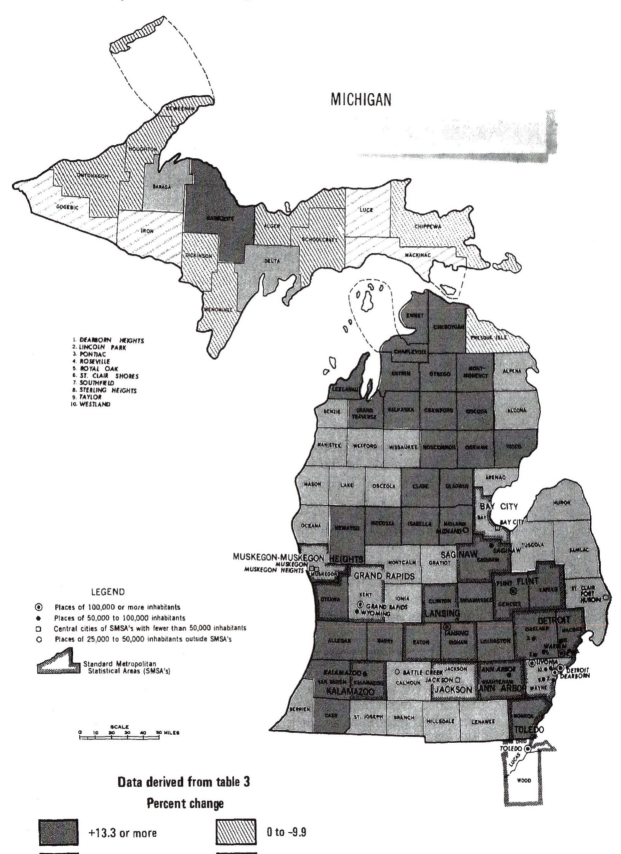

MICHIGAN

1. DEARBORN HEIGHTS
2. LINCOLN PARK
3. PONTIAC
4. ROSEVILLE
5. ROYAL OAK
6. ST. CLAIR SHORES
7. SOUTHFIELD
8. STERLING HEIGHTS
9. TAYLOR
10. WESTLAND

LEGEND

⊙ Places of 100,000 or more inhabitants
● Places of 50,000 to 100,000 inhabitants
□ Central cities of SMSA's with fewer than 50,000 inhabitants
○ Places of 25,000 to 50,000 inhabitants outside SMSA's

Standard Metropolitan
Statistical Areas (SMSA's)

SCALE
0 10 20 30 40 50 MILES

Data derived from table 3

Percent change

+13.3 or more	0 to -9.9
0 to +13.2	-10.0 or more

Analytical Text

POPULATION TRENDS

General

Between 1960 and 1970 the population of Michigan grew from 7,823,000 to 8,875,000, at the same rate as the United States population overall, 13 percent. Nearly all the State's growth occurred in the suburban parts of metropolitan areas, which grew by 946,000 persons to a population of 4,338,000 in 1970 (table A). Nonmetropolitan areas, which in 1970 had a population of 2,069,000, accounted for only one-tenth of the State's growth during the decade (208,000). In contrast, the central cities of metropolitan areas lost population between 1960 and 1970. Although nearly all central cities annexed some suburban territory over the decade

Table A.   Population by Race and Metropolitan and Nonmetropolitan Residence: 1970 and 1960

The State Metropolitan and Non-metropolitan Residence	Population		Change		Percent Distribution	
	1970	1960	Number	Percent	1970	1960
Total...............	8,875,083	7,823,194	1,051,889	13.4	100.0	100.
Metropolitan residence...	6,806,151	5,962,457	843,694	14.2	76.7	76.
Inside central cities..	2,468,063	2,570,259	-102,196	-4.0	27.8	32.
Outside central cities.	4,338,088	3,392,198	945,890	27.9	48.9	43.
Nonmetropolitan residence	2,068,932	1,860,737	208,195	11.2	23.3	23.
White...............	7,833,474	7,085,865	747,609	10.6	88.3	90.
Metropolitan residence...	5,830,583	5,272,394	558,189	10.6	65.7	67.
Inside central cities..	1,639,350	1,983,241	-343,891	-17.3	18.5	25.
Outside central cities.	4,191,233	3,289,153	902,080	27.4	47.2	42.
Nonmetropolitan residence	2,002,891	1,813,471	189,420	10.4	22.6	23
Negro and other races	1,041,609	737,329	304,280	41.3	11.7	9
Metropolitan residence...	975,568	690,063	285,505	41.4	11.0	8
Inside central cities..	828,713	587,018	241,695	41.2	9.3	7
Outside central cities.	146,855	103,045	43,810	42.5	1.7	1
Nonmetropolitan residence	66,041	47,266	18,775	39.7	0.7	0

(table B), their combined population declined, from 2,570,000 in 1960 to 2,468,000 in 1970.

The proportion of the State's population which lives in metropolitan areas was hardly affected by these changes, rising by less than one percentage point. In 1970, nearly 77 percent of Michigan's population was metropolitan, compared to 69 percent in the Nation as a whole. The proportion of Michigan's population living in central cities was reduced, on the other hand, from 33 percent in 1960 to 28 percent in 1970, and the suburban share rose correspondingly, to 49 percent by 1970.

The total number of households in Michigan in 1970 was 2,653,000, or 414,000 more than in 1960. The population living in households increased less rapidly than the rate at which households increased, with the result that average household size decreased slightly, from 3.4 to 3.3 persons.

In 1970, 88 percent of Michigan's population was white (7,833,000 persons), down from 91 percent in 1960. Over the decade, the population of other races (1,042,000 persons), which is predominantly Negro, grew four times as fast as the white population (by 41 percent compared to less than 11 percent). While there was a small net outmigration of whites between 1960 and 1970 (124,000 persons), half of the growth of races other than white was due to net inmigration (151,000).

Both racial groups are found in largest numbers in metropolitan areas. At the time of both censuses, 74 percent of the white population and 94 percent of the State's population of other races were in metropolitan areas. Within metropolitan areas, there are considerable differences in growth patterns by race. While the white population of central cities declined (by 344,000 persons, or 17 percent), Negroes and other races in the

central cities show substantial growth (of 242,000 persons, or 41 percent). By contrast, although growing at the same rate as in the cities, the population of Negro and other races contributed little to the growth of the suburbs during the decade (44,000 or less than 5 percent of the total increase there), but the number of whites in the suburbs grew faster than in any other area of the State (by 902,000, or 27 percent). As a result of these developments, whites decreased as a proportion of all central city residents, from 77 percent in 1960 to 66 percent in 1970, but continued to comprise 97 percent of all suburban residents.

The growth of both metropolitan and nonmetropolitan areas in Michigan was due mainly to the natural increase of the population (the excess of births over deaths) and only to a very minor extent to net inmigration (see table 3). Net migration was a more powerful force within metropolitan areas, however. Central cities show a loss of 367,000 persons as a result of net outmigration over the decade, equivalent to 14 percent of their total 1960 population. Suburban areas, at the same time, gained 385,000 net inmigrants, which accounted for 40 percent of total suburban growth.

The age distribution of Michigan's population changed significantly between 1960 and 1970. In metropolitan and nonmetropolitan areas, the population under 5 years of age was reduced 17 percent. Least change was experienced by the 25 to 44 age group, which increased by less than 1 percent in the State as a whole. All other age groups grew substantially, particularly the population 15 to 24, which had an increase of 56 percent. Similar changes are found in other sections of the country and are due in part to changing birth rates and in part to migration, which is highly selective by age.

Table B. Change in Population of Central Cities Through Annexation: 1960 to 1970

| Central Cities | 1970 population | | | 1960 population | Change 1960 to 1970 in 1960 area |
	Total	In 1960 area	In annexed area		
Grand Rapids...............	197,649	158,694	38,955	177,313	-18,619
Flint......................	193,317	193,131	186	196,940	-3,809
Lansing....................	131,546	111,054	20,492	107,807	3,247
Saginaw....................	91,849	91,675	174	98,265	-6,590
Ann Arbor..................	99,797	88,505	11,292	67,340	21,165
Kalamazoo..................	85,555	85,538	17	82,089	3,449
Muskegon...................	44,631	40,404	4,227	46,485	-6,081
Bay City...................	49,449	49,408	41	53,604	-4,196

Low birth rates during the depression years and in the 1960's contribute to the diminution or slow growth of the population 25-44 and under 5 years, whereas the post-World War II "baby boom" is currently reflected in the large size of the population 15 to 24 years old.

Standard Metropolitan Statistical Areas

In 1970, there were 11 standard metropolitan statistical areas (SMSA's) in Michigan, all concentrated in the southern part of the State. One, the Toledo, Ohio-Mich. SMSA' is located mainly in Ohio: less than one-fifth of the population of this SMSA is in Michigan.

Between 1960 and 1970, the population of the Detroit SMSA, the largest metropolitan area in Michigan, grew from 3,762,000 to 4,200,000, or by 12 percent. The Detroit SMSA ranks fifth in population among all metropolitan areas in the Nation. Detroit is the center of America's automotive industry, and is the headquarters of the General Motors Corporation, Chrysler Corporation and the Ford Motor Company. It is a major port on the Great Lakes and an important commercial and financial center. The city's population was reduced by 159,000 over the decade (10 percent of its 1960 population) while the suburban population gained 596,000 (or 28 percent). The city's decline resulted from an extensive loss of white population (344,000) and a much smaller increase in the population of Negro and other races (185,000).

Detroit's white population loss was caused largely by a net outmigration of 387,000, equivalent to 33 percent of the city's white population in 1960. In common with other very large cities, however, the natural increase of Detroit's white population was very low: there was an excess of births over deaths of only 43,000 for this ppoulation group, a rate of less than 4 percent. Nationwide, the white rate of natural increase between 1960 and 1970 exceeded 10 percent, but in the central cities of the 12 largest SMSA's (with populations of 2 million or more) the white natural increase rate was under 5 percent.

By contrast, the growth of other races was founded almost equally on natural increase and net inmigration. As a result of these changes the population of Negro and other races in the city of Detroit increased its share of the total population, from 29 percent in 1960 to 45 percent in 1970.

The white population loss from Detroit city affected every age group (see table 4). Conversely, the growth of other races was spread across all age groups, but the population 15-24 and 65 and over grew most rapidly (by 121 percent and 88 percent, respectively).

In spite of the rapid rate of growth of Negroes and other races in the Detroit suburbs (from 80,000 to 108,000, or by 35 percent), their representation in the suburban population scarcely changed. In 1970 as in 1960, races other than white comprised 4 percent of Detroit's suburban population.

Michigan's second most populous metropolitan area, the Grand Rapids SMSA, grew from 462,000 to 539,000, or by 17 percent. The city of Grand Rapids is a manufacturing and wholesale trade center. It is nationally famous for its furniture manufacture. Between 1960 and 1970, the city grew from 177,000 to 198,000, a 12 percent increase. This increase is attributable to annexation of suburban territory. Without it, the city would have lost 19,000 population (table B).

The population of the Flint SMSA grew from 416,000 in 1960 to 497,000 in 1970, or by 19 percent. Virtually all population growth in this area was due to the natural increase of the population. Flint is second to Detroit in volume of automotive production and parts manufacturing. There was a slight reduction in the population of Flint city over the decade, from 197,000 to 193,000. The loss affected the white population only, which declined by 24,000, or 15 percent; other races increased by 20,000 persons, or 59 percent.

The population of the Lansing SMSA, which grew from 299,000 to 378,000, or by 27 percent, was the second fastest growing SMSA in the State. Lansing is one of the very few SMSA's in Michigan where net inmigration was of significance to population growth. Net inmigration in this area was equivalent to 10 percent of its 1960 population and account for one-third of overall growth. A large share of this growth is the result of increased enrollment at Michigan State University. More than one-half of the SMSA's total population increase occurred in the age group 15 to 24 years. The large increase in the population of Lansing city, the State capital (from 108,000 to 132,000), was produced mainly by annexation of a suburban population of 20,000.

The most rapid rate of growth during the decade occurred in the Ann Arbor SMSA, which grew by 36 percent, from 172,000 to 234,000. The area's growth was produced in equal part by natural increase and net inmigration. The net inmigration rate of 18 percent was the highest among the State's metropolitan areas. The city of Ann Arbor, the site of the University of Michigan, grew from 67,000 to 100,000. A large part of this growth was due to annexation of suburban territory. Due mainly to the presence of the University, both central city and suburban population growth was concentrated at age 15 to 24; more than one-half of the total SMSA increase (32,000) occurred at this age.

Between 1960 and 1970 the population of the Saginaw SMSA grew from 191,000 to 220,000, or by 15 percent. The central city declined by 7 percent; its loss was made up of a substantial decrease in white population (13,000) and a smaller gain in other races (6,000)

The proportion of the city's population which is of Negro and other races consequently grew, from 17 percent in 1960 to 25 percent in 1970, one of the highest percentages among Michigan's SMSA's.

The population of the Kalamazoo SMSA grew from 170,000 in 1960 to 202,000 in 1970, or by 19 percent. It was one of the few SMSA's in Michigan to grow as a result of net inmigration. The city of Kalamazoo which is midway between Chicago and Detroit, is an industrial center and the site of Western Michigan University. The population of the city increased over the decade by only 4 percent, or 3,500 persons. Only one age group in the city shows an increase for this period, however: the 15 to 24 year old population--reflecting increased enroll-ment at the university as well as the high birth rate following World War II--grew by 11,000, or 68 percent over 1960.

The Muskegon-Muskegon Heights SMSA had the lowest rate of population increase and the highest rate of net outmigration of any metropolitan area in Michigan. Between 1960 and 1970 it grew from 150,000 to 157,000, by 5 percent. Net outmigration was equivalent to 9 percent of the total 1960 population of the SMSA. Both central cities lost population due to declines in the white population amounting to 11 percent in Muskegon and 32 percent in Muskegon Heights. The population of other races, by contrast, grew rapidly, by 76 percent in Muskegon and 20 percent in Muskegon Heights, although their numbers remain small in both cities (7,000 in Muskegon, or 15 percent of the total popu-lation, and 9,000 in Muskegon Heights, or 53 percent of the total population).

The Jackson and Bay City SMSA's are the two smallest metropolitan areas entirely within the State of Michigan, with 143,000 and 117,000 population, re-spectively. Their growth rates for the period were similar (9 percent and 10 percent). Each suffered a small net outmigration equivalent to 3 to 4 percent of their 1960 populations. Similarly, the populations of both central cities were reduced as a result of white population losses.

Counties

Of the 83 counties in Michigan, 70 gained and 13 lost population between 1960 and 1970. Of the 13 counties that lost population, all but one, Presque Isle County, were located in Michigan's Upper Peninsula. Thirty-nine counties had growth rates exceeding the national average of 13.3 percent and four counties had population declines exceeding 10 percent. Of the 17 counties in metropolitan areas in 1970, 12 gained at rates above the national average. Wayne County (Detroit SMSA), the third largest in the Nation, had almost no population change during the decade, however. The decline in the white population in Wayne County was offset by an increase in the population of Negro and other races.

During the 1960-70 decade, 12 counties had growth rates exceeding 30 percent. The population of Living-ston County and Macomb County (Detroit SMSA) both grew 54 percent, respectively. More than 73 percent of the growth in Livingston County and 56 percent of the growth in Macomb County was due to net inmigration.

Iosco County located on Lake Huron, grew by 51 percent, the county's greatest relative increase since 1890. Net inmigration accounted for half the growth. The rapid growth in the county was due to the location in recent years of a Strategic Air Command Unit in the county.

During the 1960 to 1970 period, 50 counties experi-enced net inmigration. Only five counties--Clare, Livingston, Macomb, Oscado and Roscommon-- had an inmigration rate exceeding 30 percent. Macomb County is the only one of the five that is in a metropolitan area.

Between 1960 and 1970, 10 counties in Michigan had rates of outmigration equivalent to 10 percent or more of their 1960 population. Six of these--Alger, Huron, Iron, Luce, Mackinac and Presque Isle--had more than half of their populations living in rural areas. The highest rate of net outmigration (20 percent) occurred in Chippewa County, located in Michigan's Upper Penin-sula.

HOUSING TRENDS

General

Between 1960 and 1970 the total supply of housing units in Michigan increased more rapidly than population. The population grew by 1,052,000 or 13 percent, while housing units increased by 405,800 or 16 percent (table C).

The standard metropolitan statistical areas of the State experienced greater relative growth in housing, as in population, than did the nonmetropolitan part. The number of housing units in metropolitan areas rose over the decade to 2,126,400, an increase of 301,600 units, or 17 percent; this compares with an increase of 104,200 units, or 14 percent, in the nonmetropolitan areas. About 72 percent of all housing units were in the SMSA's; these areas accounted for 74 percent of the total State increase between 1960 and 1970.

Approximately 76 percent of the housing in Michigan consisted of one-unit structures in 1970. The proportion of such units in metropolitan areas was 73 percent, and in nonmetropolitan areas, 85 percent.

The number of units in the State lacking some or all plumbing facilities in 1970 was 123,800 units, or 4 percent. The corresponding proportions in metropolitan and nonmetropolitan areas were 2 percent and 10 percent, respectively (table D). About 8,000 or 3

Table C.   Housing Units by Metropolitan and Nonmetropolitan Residence: 1970 and 1960

The State Metropolitan and Nonmetropolitan Residence	Housing units				Population percent change
	Total		Change		
	1970	1960	Number	Percent	
Total..................	2,954,570	2,548,792	405,778	15.9	13.4
Metropolitan residence.....	2,126,398	1,824,792	301,606	16.5	14.2
Inside central cities....	850,266	840,999	9,267	1.1	-4.0
Outside central cities...	1,276,132	983,793	292,339	29.7	27.9
Nonmetropolitan residence..	828,172	724,000	104,172	14.4	11.2

Table D.   Plumbing Facilities and Persons Per Room by Metropolitan and Nonmetropolitan Residence: 1970 and 1960

The State Metropolitan and Nonmetropolitan Residence	Percent of housing units			
	Lacking some or all plumbing facilities		With 1.01 or more persons per room[1]	
	1970[2]	1960[3]	1970	1960
Total.....................	4.4	11.7	7.6	9.8
Metropolitan residence...........	2.5	(NA)	7.6	9.9
Inside central cities..........	2.8	4.9	7.2	8.5
Outside central cities........	2.2	(NA)	8.0	11.1
Nonmetropolitan residence........	9.9	(NA)	7.5	9.7

NA Not available.
[1]Percent of all occupied units.
[2]Percent of all year-round housing units.
[3]Percent of all housing units.

percent, or the Negro-occupied units in the State lacked some or all plumbing in 1970. Inside metropolitan areas, 3 percent of the Negro-occupied housing lacked such plumbing, compared with 9 percent outside the metropolitan areas.

Households were smaller in 1970 than in 1960. In the metropolitan areas, average household size declined from 3.4 persons in 1960 to 3.3 in 1970 and in nonmetropolitan areas, from 3.4 to 3.2 persons. The number of one-person househeolds increased by 62 percent in metropolitan areas and by 47 percent in nonmetropolitan areas. In comparison, households with five or more persons increased 10 percent in metropolitan areas and 5 percent in nonmetropolitan areas.

The median number of rooms in housing units for the State and for the metropolitan and nonmetropolitan areas was 5.2 in 1970. About 19 percent of the metropolitan housing units and 23 percent of units in nonmetropolitan areas had seven or more rooms.

Number of persons per room is often used as a measure of crowding. In Michigan, the proportion of housing units with 1.01 or more persons per room decreased during the decade. In 1960, 10 percent of all occupied housing units in both metropolitan and nonmetropolitan areas had 1.01 or more persons per room. By 1970, the proportion of such units had decreased to 8 percent in both areas.

The homeownership rate in Michigan remained at 74 percent during the decade. As in 1960, homeownership was more prevalent in nonmetropolitan areas. About 79 percent of the households in nonmetropolitan areas owned their homes, compared with 73 percent in metropolitan areas. Of the 1,974,500 owner-occupied units in the State, 1,481,000 were inside metropolitan areas and 493,500 were outside these areas.

About 53 percent of the Negro housholds in metropolitan areas and 61 percent in nonmetropolitan areas owned their homes in 1970. Of the 148,100 Negro-homeowner households in the State, 139,700 lived inside SMSA's and 8,400 lived outside SMSA's.

Property values and rents increased during the last decade. The median value of owner-occupied housing in metropolitan areas rose 47 percent, from $12,600 to $18,500, while in the nonmetropolitan areas value increased 43 percent, from $9,000 to $12,900. In metropolitan areas, median contract rent in 1970 was 48 percent higher than in 1960, rising from $66 to $98. In nonmetropolitan areas, the increase was 54 percent, from $50 in 1960 to $77 in 1970.

Value and rent are expressed in current dollars (the value at the time of the respective censuses). Thus, any comparison must take into account the general rise in the cost of living during the 10-year period, as well as changes in the characteristics of the housing inventory.

Standard Metropolitan Statistical Areas

In the metropolitan areas of the State, the housing supply increased by 301,600 units, or 17 percent. The Detroit SMSA, the largest in the State, contained 62 percent of the housing units in the metropolitan areas and accounted for 56 percent of the increase.

The suburban areas of the State experienced greater growth in housing than did the central cities. Housing units in the suburbs increased by about 30 percent, while housing in the combined central cities showed little change. By 1970, there were 1,276,100 housing units in the suburbs and 850,300 units in the central cities.

About 73 percent of the housing units in the State's metropolitan areas consisted of one-unit structures in 1970. The number of units in multiunit structures, however, increased at a much faster rate than one-unit structures during the decade, 38 percent and 9 percent, respectively.

In 1970, 52,000 housing units in metropolitan areas, or 2 percent of all year-round units, lacked some or all plumbing facilities. The corresponding proportions for the central cities and the suburbs were 3 percent and 2 percent, respectively. Approximately 5,600, or 2 percent of the Negro households in the central cities, occupied units which lacked some or all plumbing facilities in 1970; in suburban areas, 1,100 Negro households, or 3 percent, lacked such plumbing facilities.

Average household size in 1970 was 3.0 persons in the central cities and 3.5 persons in the suburbs. One-person households constituted 22 percent of all households in the central cities and 11 percent in the suburbs.

Housing units in the central cities were smaller in size than in the suburbs. In 1970, the median number of rooms in the central cities was 5.1, and in the suburbs, 5.3. While 17 percent of the housing in the central cities had one to three rooms, 8 percent of the housing units in the suburbs were in this category. At the same time, 16 percent of the units in the central cities had seven or more rooms, compared with 21 percent in the suburbs.

Of all occupied units in metropolitan areas, 155,100 or 8 percent reported more than one person per room in 1970; the corresponding figure was 10 percent in 1960. In 1970, the proportion of such units was 7 percent in the central cities and 8 percent in the suburbs.

Homeownership in 1970 was more prevalent in the suburban areas than in the central cities. About 80 percent of occupied units in the suburbs and 62 percent in the central cities were owner-occupied. The Negro-homeownership rate in the suburbs was 63 percent, compared with 52 percent in the central cities.

In the central cities of Michigan, the median value of owner-occupied housing rose 30 percent, from $11,800 in 1960 to $15,300 in 1970; in the suburbs, the median increased 55 percent, from $13,300 to $20,600. In 1970, about 10 percent of the owner-occupied housing in the central cities was valued at $25,000 or more, compared with 32 percent in the suburbs. Median contract rent in the central cities and the suburbs was $87 and $126, respectively. In the central cities, 10 percent of renter occupied units rented for $150 or more, compared with 34 percent in the suburbs.

The homeowner vacancy rate for metropolitan areas decreased during the decade from 1.4 to 0.9 percent. The rental vacancy rate decreased from 9.9 to 7.6 percent.

Annexations

Annexations occurred in each of the central cities except the cities of Detroit, Muskegon Heights, and Jackson (see "Population Trends" and text table B). Such annexations affect changes in the characteristics for these central cities and their suburbs.

Population Change for Counties: 1960 to 1970

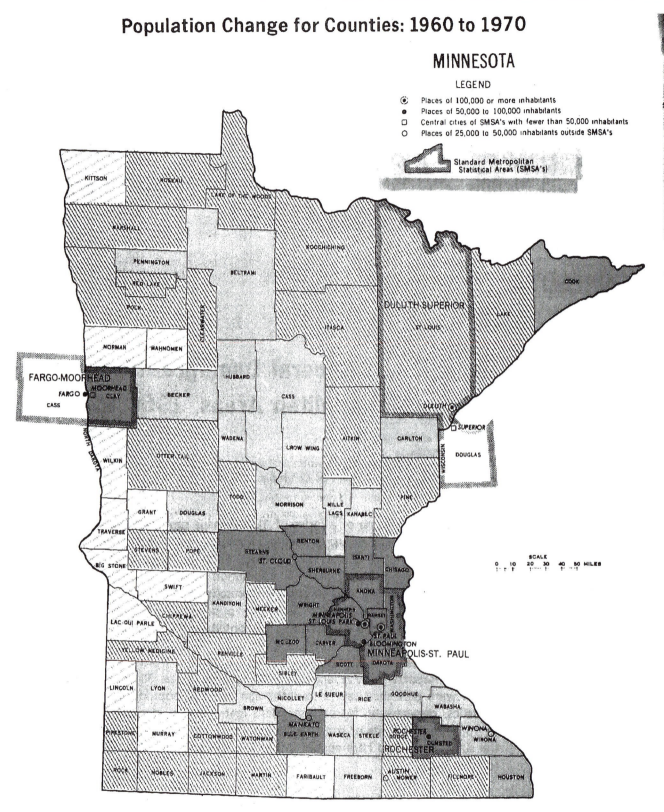

MINNESOTA

LEGEND

- ⊙ Places of 100,000 or more inhabitants
- ● Places of 50,000 to 100,000 inhabitants
- ☐ Central cities of SMSA's with fewer than 50,000 inhabitants
- ○ Places of 25,000 to 50,000 inhabitants outside SMSA's

Standard Metropolitan Statistical Areas (SMSA's)

SCALE

0   10   20   30   40   50 MILES

Data derived from table 3

Percent change

 +13.3 or more   0 to -9.9

0 to +13.2   -10.0 or more

Analytical Text

POPULATION TRENDS

General

Between 1960 and 1970 the total population of Minnesota grew by 391,000, from 3,414,000 to 3,805,000, an increase of 11.5 percent over the population living in the State in 1960 (table A). While the metropolitan areas of the State grew by 19 percent, nonmetropolitan areas increased by only 3 percent. Nearly 90 percent of the total State increase (347,000 persons) was accounted for by the metropolitan areas.

Within Minnesota's metropolitan areas, all growth occurred in the suburban rings, where population increased by 385,000 or 45 percent. Central cities show a slight loss of 38,000 population, or 4 percent.

As a result of these changes, there was a rise in the proportion of total State population living in metropolitan areas. In 1960, metropolitan areas accounted for 53 percent of the population; by 1970, this had increased to 57 percent. In the Nation as a whole nearly 70 percent of the population is metropolitan.

The total number of households in the State in 1970 was 1,154,000 or 162,000 more than in 1960. The population living in households increased less rapidly than the rate at which households increased, with the result that average household size decreased slightly, from 3.4 to 3.2 persons.

In both 1960 and 1970, more than 98 percent of Minnesota's population was white. Other races (slightly more than half of which are Negro) increased far more rapidly than the white population: while the white population grew by 11 percent, other races increased by 63 percent. Nearly 80 percent of races other than white lived in the metropolitan areas of the State in 1970, a considerably higher proportion than in 1960 (71 percent).

Table A.   Population by Race and Metropolitan and Nonmetropolitan Residence: 1970 and 1960

The State Metropolitan and Non-metropolitan Residence	Population		Change		Percent Distribution	
	1970	1960	Number	Percent	1970	1960
Total...............	[1]3,804,981	3,413,864	391,117	11.5	100.0	100.0
Metropolitan residence...	2,165,018	1,818,230	346,788	19.1	56.9	53.3
Inside central cities..	928,402	966,764	-38,362	-4.0	24.4	28.3
Outside central cities.	1,236,616	851,466	385,150	45.2	32.5	24.9
Nonmetropolitan residence	1,639,963	1,595,634	44,329	2.8	43.1	46.7
White...............	3,736,050	3,371,603	364,447	10.8	98.2	98.8
Metropolitan residence...	2,111,138	1,788,386	322,752	18.0	55.5	52.4
Inside central cities..	883,527	940,482	-56,955	-6.1	23.2	27.5
Outside central cities.	1,227,611	847,904	379,707	44.8	32.3	24.8
Nonmetropolitan residence	1,624,912	1,583,217	41,695	2.6	42.7	46.4
Negro and other races	68,931	42,261	26,670	63.1	1.8	1.2
Metropolitan residence...	53,880	29,844	24,036	80.5	1.4	0.9
Inside central cities..	44,875	26,282	18,593	70.7	1.2	0.8
Outside central cities.	9,005	3,562	5,443	152.8	0.2	0.1
Nonmetropolitan residence	15,051	12,417	2,634	21.2	0.4	0.4

[1]See correction note on page 8.

The growth of the State reflected an excess of births over deaths (natural increase) of 417,000, and a small net outmigration of 25,000 persons. In metropolitan areas, population growth was the result of both natural increase (268,000) and net inmigration (79,000). The central cities' loss was produced by a substantial outmigration of 132,000 persons, equivalent to 14 percent of the population of the cities in 1960. By contrast, net inmigration was of great importance to the growth of the suburbs, which gained 211,000 persons from this source, equivalent to 25 percent of 1960 population.

All areas of the State experienced significant changes in age composition (see table 4). The population under 5 years of age declined by 14 percent in metropolitan areas and by 28 percent in nonmetropolitan areas. The most rapidly growing group was 15 to 24 years of age, which increased by 62 percent in metropolitan areas and 34 percent in nonmetropolitan areas.

The central cities' population loss was felt by all age groups except for 15 to 24 years and 65 years of age and over, while the suburbs show gains at all ages except the youngest (under 5).

Age changes similar to those which occurred in the State as a whole are found in other sections of the country. They are due in part to changing birth rates and in part to migration, which is highly selective by age. Low birth rates during the 1960's contribute to the diminution of the population under 5, whereas the post-World War II "baby boom" is currently reflected in the large size of the population 15-24 years old.

Standard Metropolitan Statistical Areas

The Minneapolis-St. Paul Standard Metropolitan Statistical Area (SMSA) is the 15th largest metropolitan area in the Nation. Between 1960 and 1970, its population increased from 1,482,000 to 1,814,000. In 1970, the SMSA as a whole accounted for 48 percent of Minnesota's total population and 84 percent of the entire metropolitan population of the State.

The SMSA provides services of various kinds to a regional market area. St. Paul is the capital of Minnesota. Minneapolis has a broad manufacturing base, especially in nonelectric machinery.

The other SMSA's in Minnesota are small and limited in function. The Duluth-Superior, Minn.-Wis. SMSA is the next largest in Minnesota. It is a mining and manufacturing area which has been declining. Between 1960 and 1970, its population dropped from 277,000 to 265,000 (the Minnesota portion declined from 232,000 to 221,000). Next in size is the newly-created Rochester SMSA. In 1960 its population numbered 66,000; by 1970 it had increased to 84,000. The area is widely known for its medical facilities.

Nearly 40 percent of the Fargo-Moorhead, N. Dak.-Minn. SMSA is located in Minnesota. Between 1960 and 1970, the Minnesota portion of this SMSA increased from 39,000 to nearly 47,000.

Between 1960 and 1970, the cities of Minneapolis and St. Paul both lost population as a result of outmigration. Minneapolis suffered an overall reduction in population of more than 48,000 (10 percent) and a net outmigration of 87,000 persons. St. Paul's loss was smaller, amounting to 3,400 overall (1 percent) with a net outmigration of 38,000 persons. The suburban ring, by contrast, gained a population of 384,000, a large part of which was produced by net inmigration (see table 3).

Duluth city's population was likewise reduced over the decade, by 6,300 persons, or 6 percent. This loss was also produced by outmigration (15,000 persons).

Annexation of territory during the decade played a significant role in the growth of Rochester city, where it accounted for more than 50 percent of the city's increase of 13,000 (table B). In Moorhead annexation was also a factor in producing part of the central city's growth (1,300 of the city's increase of 6,800).

Table B. Change in Population of Central Cities Through Annexation: 1960 to 1970

Central Cities	1970 population			1960 population	Change 1960 to 1970 in 1960 area
	Total	In 1960 area	In annexed area		
Minneapolis..................	434,400	434,359	41	482,872	-48,513
Duluth......................	100,578	100,568	10	106,884	-6,316
Moorhead....................	29,687	28,372	1,315	22,934	5,438
Rochester...................	53,766	46,723	7,043	40,663	6,060

Counties

Between 1960 and 1970, 45 of the 87 counties in Minnesota increased in population. Fifteen of the 45 registered larger population increases than the 1960-70 percentage of 13.3 for the Nation. Five of the counties comprised the Minneapolis-St. Paul SMSA and the others were adjoining counties. The counties with the largest gains were: Anoka (80 percent), Dakota (79), Washington (58), Scott (48), Sherburne (43), Carver (33), Chisago (30), and Wright (30).

The 42 counties with declining populations are spread throughout the State with the exception of one segment. This is a belt of growing counties running North-South and through the Minneapolis-St. Paul area. Twelve of the declining counties had decreases of more than 10 percent. These were located on the western border of the State. Some of the counties with the largest losses were: Kittson (18 percent), Traverse (17), Lac qui Parle (16), Lincoln (16), and Murray (15).

Every county had more births than deaths during the decade. In the 42 counties with declining population, net outmigration over the decade was large enough to offset the excess of births over deaths. The counties with the largest net outmigration were relatively small. They tend to be concentrated along the western border of Minnesota. These included Murray, Traverse, Mahnomen, Wilkin and Lincoln. Counties with largest net inmigration are part of the Minneapolis-St. Paul SMSA, or adjoin it. These counties were Dakota, Anoka, Washington, Sherburne, Scott, and Chisago.

HOUSING TRENDS

General

Between 1960 and 1970, the total supply of housing units in Minnesota increased somewhat more rapidly than population. The population grew by 391,000, or 11 percent, while housing units increased by 156,900, or 14 percent (table C).

The metropolitan areas of the State experienced greater relative growth in housing, as in population, than did the nonmetropolitan part. The number of housing units in metrpolitan areas rose over the decade to 698,300, an increase of 122,500 units, or 21 percent; this compares with an increase of 34,500 units, or 6 percent, in nonmetropolitan areas. While the metropolitan areas contained 55 percent of the housing in Minnesota, the additions to the housing supply in these areas accounted for 78 percent of the State's total housing increase between 1960 and 1970.

About 73 percent of the housing in Minnesota consisted of one-unit structures in 1970. Corresponding proportions of such units were 65 percent in metropolitan areas and 85 percent in nonmetropolitan areas.

Households were smaller in 1970 than in 1960. In the metropolitan areas of the State, average household size declined from 3.3 persons in 1960 to 3.2 in 1970, and in nonmetropolitan areas, from 3.5 persons in 1960 to 3.2 in 1970. During the same period, in Minnesota, there were large percentage increases in one- and two-persons households, 51 percent and 22 percent, respectively,

Table C. Housing Units by Metropolitan and Nonmetropolitan Residence: 1970 and 1960

The State Metropolitan and Nonmetropolitan Residence	Housing units				Population percent change
	Total		Change		
	1970	1960	Number	Percent	
Total.................	1,276,198	1,119,271	156,927	14.0	11.5
Metropolitan residence.....	698,336	575,865	122,471	21.3	19.1
Inside central cities....	336,212	331,288	4,924	1.5	-4.0
Outside central cities...	362,124	244,577	117,547	48.1	45.2
Nonmetropolitan residence..	577,862	543,406	34,456	6.3	2.8

with relatively small gains in households with three or more persons.

The number of units in the State lacking plumbing was 99,500 in 1970, or 8 percent of all year-round units. This compares with 4 percent in metropolitan areas and 13 percent in nonmetropolitan areas.

Number of persons per room is often used as a measure of crowding. In Minnesota both the number and proportion of housing units with 1.01 or more persons per room decreased during the decade. In 1960, 10 percent of all occupied housing units in metropolitan areas and 11 percent in nonmetropolitan areas had 1.01 or more persons per room. By 1970, the proportion of such units decreased to 7 percent in metropolitan areas and 8 percent in nonmetropolitan areas (table D).

Homeownership in the State decreased from 72 percent in 1960 to 71 percent in 1970. In metropolitan areas there was a decrease from 69 percent to 66 percent, while in nonmetropolitan areas the proportion rose from 76 to 78 percent.

Property values and rents increased in the last decade. The median value in metropolitan areas increased by 44 percent from $14,300 in 1960 to $20,600 in 1970, while in the nonmetropolitan areas value increased 33 percent, from $9,800 to $13,000. In metropolitan areas, median contract rent in 1970 was 76 percent higher than in 1960, rising from $66 to $116. In nonmetropolitan areas rent increased from $47 to $70, or 49 percent.

Value and rent are expressed in current dollars (the value at the time of the respective censuses). Thus, any comparison must take into account the general rise in the cost of living during the 10-year period, as well as changes in the characteristics of the housing inventory.

Standard Metropolitan Statistical Areas

In the metropolitan areas of the State (Duluth-Superior, Minn.-Wis., Fargo-Moorhead, N. Dak.-Minn., Minneapolis-St. Paul, and Rochester), the housing supply increased by 122,500 units, or 21 percent. The Minneapolis-St. Paul SMSA which contained 83 percent of the housing accounted for 93 percent of the increase. The Duluth-Superior and Fargo-Moorhead metropolitan areas have central cities in adjoining States.

Average household size for the total metropolitan area of the State declined during the decade. The average in the central cities declined from 2.9 persons in 1960 to 2.7 in 1970, and in the suburbs from 3.8 persons to 3.6.

The rate of homeownership in 1970 was greater in the suburban areas than in the central cities. About 78 percent of occupied units in the suburbs were owner-occupied, compared with 54 percent in the central cities.

In 1970, 30,100 housing units in metropolitan areas, or 4 percent of all units, lacked some or all plumbing facilities. The corresponding proportion was 6 percent in the central cities and 3 percent in the suburbs. In the

Table D. Plumbing Facilities and Persons Per Room by Metropolitan and Nonmetropolitan Residence: 1970 and 1960

The State Metropolitan and Nonmetropolitan Residence	Percent of housing units			
	Lacking some or all plumbing facilities		With 1.01 or more persons per room[1]	
	1970[2]	1960[3]	1970	1960
Total.....................	8.2	22.0	7.4	10.4
Metropolitan residence...........	4.4	(NA)	6.8	10.0
Inside central cities..........	5.6	11.7	5.2	7.6
Outside central cities.........	3.2	(NA)	8.4	13.5
Nonmetropolitan residence........	13.1	(NA)	8.1	10.7

NA Not available.
[1]Percent of all occupied units.
[2]Percent of all year-round housing units.
[3]Percent of all housing units.

Minnesota part of the Duluth-Superior, Minn.-Wis. SMSA, and in the Rochester SMSA, however, the percentage of such units was lower in the central cities than in the suburbs, i.e., in Duluth, 8 percent in the central city lacked some or all plumbing facilities compared with 15 percent in its suburbs in Minnesota. Likewise, in Rochester the percentages were 4 and 6, respectively.

Of all occupied units in metropolitan areas, 45,500 units, or 7 percent, reported more than one person per room in 1970 compared with 10 percent in 1960. In 1970, the proportion of such units was 5 percent in the central cities and 8 percent in the suburbs.

The homeowner vacancy rate for metropolitan areas decreased during the decade from 1.1 to 0.5 percent. The rental vacancy rate decreased from 6.1 to 5.5 percent.

Annexations

Annexations occurred in the central cities of Minneapolis, Duluth, Moorhead, and Rochester, during the decade (see "Population Trends" and text table B). Such annexations affect changes in the characteristics for these central cities and their suburbs.

Population Change for Counties: 1960 to 1970

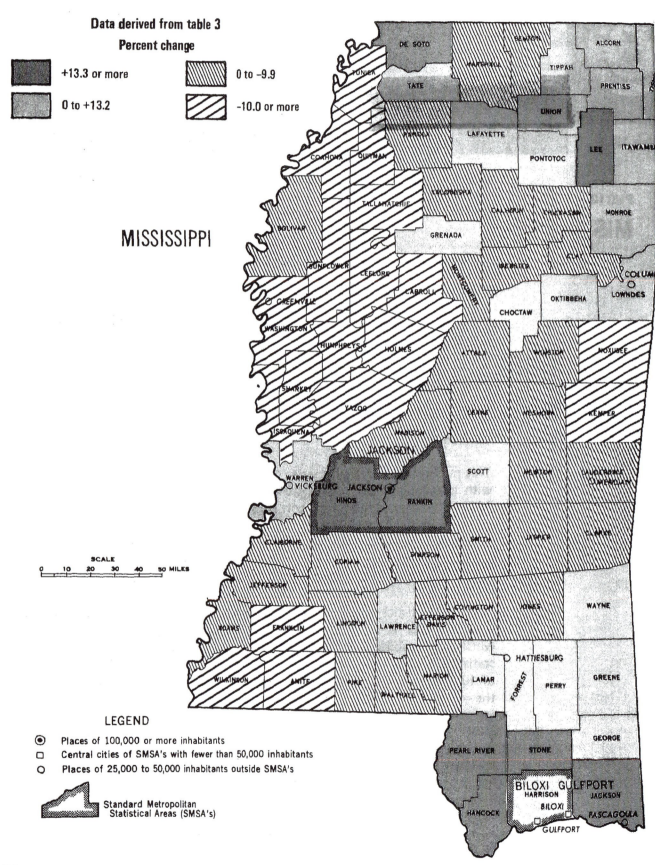

Data derived from table 3
Percent change

+13.3 or more

0 to +13.2

0 to -9.9

-10.0 or more

MISSISSIPPI

SCALE
0 10 20 30 40 50 MILES

LEGEND

⊙ Places of 100,000 or more inhabitants
□ Central cities of SMSA's with fewer than 50,000 inhabitants
○ Places of 25,000 to 50,000 inhabitants outside SMSA's

Standard Metropolitan
Statistical Areas (SMSA's)

Analytical Text

POPULATION TRENDS

General

Between 1960 and 1970 the total population of Mississippi grew from 2,178,000 to 2,217,000, an increase of only 1.8 percent over the population living in the State in 1960 (table A). This rather small increase reflects the outmigration of Negroes (who constituted 37 percent of the population in 1970) from the State. While the white population had a growth of 10.7 percent, the Negro population had a loss of 10.5 percent. As a result of extensive outmigration from nonmetropolitan areas, there was a very slight loss of population from these areas of about 1 percent. In metropolitan areas, there was a population gain of 15.4 percent.

The total number of households in the State in 1970 was 637,000 or 69,000 more than in 1960. The population living in households increased less rapidly than the rate at which households increased with the result that average household size decreased from 3.8 to 3.4 persons per unit.

The effect of these changes on population distribution by metropolitan-nonmetropolitan residence was very small. The proportion of the total population living in the State's two Standard Metropolitan Statistical Areas (SMSA's), Jackson and Biloxi-Gulfport, increased by only 2 percent during the decade from 15.6 to 17.7. Less than one in five persons in Mississippi lives in metropolitan areas compared with a national average of two out of three.

Similar changes are found in other sections of the country and are due in part to changing birth rates and in part to migration, which is highly selective by age. Low birth rates during the depression years and in the 1960's contribute to the diminution of age groups 25 to 44 and under 5, whereas the post-World War II "baby boom" is currently reflected in the large size of the population 15 to 24 years old.

Table A.   Population by Race and Metropolitan and Nonmetropolitan Residence: 1970 and 1960

The State Metropolitan and Non-metropolitan Residence	Population		Change		Percent Distribution	
	1970	1960	Number	Percent	1970	1960
Total................	2,216,912	2,178,141	38,771	1.8	100.0	100.0
Metropolitan residence...	393,488	340,856	52,632	15.4	17.7	15.6
Inside central cities..	243,245	218,679	24,566	11.2	11.0	10.0
Outside central cities.	150,243	122,177	28,066	23.0	6.8	5.6
Nonmetropolitan residence	1,823,424	1,837,285	-13,861	-0.8	82.3	84.4
White..............	1,393,283	1,257,546	135,737	10.8	62.8	57.7
Metropolitan residence...	273,182	233,942	39,240	16.8	12.3	10.7
Inside central cities..	167,304	154,980	12,324	8.0	7.5	7.1
Outside central cities.	105,878	78,962	26,916	34.1	4.8	3.6
Nonmetropolitan residence	1,120,101	1,023,604	96,497	9.4	50.5	47.0
Negro and other races	823,629	920,595	-96,966	-10.5	37.2	42.3
Metropolitan residence...	120,306	106,914	13,392	12.5	5.4	4.9
Inside central cities..	75,941	63,699	12,242	19.2	3.4	2.9
Outside central cities.	44,365	43,215	1,150	2.7	2.0	2.0
Nonmetropolitan residence	703,323	813,681	-110,358	-13.6	31.7	37.4

Standard Metropolitan Statistical Areas

Mississippi has two SMSA's: Jackson and Biloxi-Gulfport. The former has about twice the population of the latter. Jackson is the capital of Mississippi, a financial, commercial and trade center for the State which has diversified manufacturing industry. About one-third of its population is Negro. Biloxi-Gulfport, a recently recognized metropolitan area, sits on the Gulf of Mexico. It has oil and gas mining and carries on some port activities. Its population in 1970 was 135,000 with about 17 percent Negro.

Annexation of territory during the decade was responsible for additions to the cities of Biloxi and Gulfport of 11,800 and 9,900 (table B). Biloxi would have declined in population if not for the annexation. Gulfport, however, was little affected.

The change in the pattern of age distribution over the decade for Jackson and Biloxi-Gulfport was generally similar to that for the State as a whole. It consisted of losses for age groups under 5 and 25 to 44 and substantial increases in age groups 15 to 24, 45 to 64, and 65 and over. In the entire Biloxi-Gulfport SMSA, there was an increase from 23,500 to 31,000 in the 15 to 24 year group. For Jackson, the increase for this group was from 34,000 to 48,000.

Counties

Between 1960 and 1970, 33 of Mississippi's 82 counties increased in population size. Only eight of these counties had growth rates of 13.3 percent (the national average) or more. Four of these counties (Pearl River, Hancock, Stone and Jackson) were in the southeastern corner of

Mississippi bordered by the Mississippi River, the Gulf of Mexico and the Mobile SMSA in Alabama. Jackson County, on the border with Mobile, had a 58 percent growth rate, highest in the State.

Another county bordering an SMSA, De Soto, alongside the Memphis, Tennessee SMSA, had the second highest growth rate—50.2 percent. Hinds and Rankin Counties, which comprise the Jackson SMSA, had growth rates of 15 percent and 28 percent, respectively. Another fast-growing county, Lee, is in the northeastern part of the State and had a 13.7 percent growth rate.

In only seven of the 82 counties did Negroes register gains in population. Five of these are the adjoining counties of Stone, George, Hancock, Harrison and Jackson, located in the rapidly growing southeastern part of the State. Negroes increased also in Hinds County (part of the Jackson SMSA) and in Prentiss County in the northwestern part of the State.

Every county had more births than deaths during the decade. In most cases, however, net outmigration was more than sufficient to offset the natural increase. Only nine counties had net immigration and only five of these had a significant inflow. They were: De Soto, Rankin, Pearl River, Hancock and Jackson.

The net outmigration included both whites and Negroes. The incidence was much heavier for the latter. There were 12 counties in which net outmigration of Negroes and other races amounted to more than 40 percent of their 1960 population. These counties were largely on the central and eastern boundary of the State, bordering on the Mississippi River (see Map). These counties are: Tunica, Quitman, Tallahatchie, Bolivar, Sunflower, Leflore, Humphreys, Sharkey, Issaquena, Tate, Madison, and Carroll.

Table B.   Change in Population of Central Cities Through Annexation: 1960 to 1970

Central Cities	1970 population			1960 population	Change 1960 to 1970 in 1960 area
	Total	In 1960 area	In annexed area		
Biloxi........................	48,486	36,689	11,797	44,053	-7,364
Gulfport......................	40,791	30,883	9,908	30,204	679
Jackson.......................	-	-	-	-	-

HOUSING TRENDS

General

During the decade, the total supply of housing units in Mississippi increased more rapidly than population. While the population grew by 39,000, or 2 percent, the number of housing units increased by 70,200, or 11 percent (table C).

The metropolitan areas of the State experienced greater relative growth in housing, as in population, than did the nonmetropolitan part. The number of housing units in metropolitan areas rose from 97,300 to 120,900 over the decade, an increase of 23,600 units, or 24 percent; this compares with an increase of 46,600 units, or 9 percent, in nonmetropolitan areas. While the metropolitan areas contained 17 percent of the housing in Mississippi, additions to the housing supply in these areas accounted for about 34 percent of the State's total housing increase between 1960 and 1970.

About 86 percent of the housing in Mississippi consisted of one-unit structures in 1970. The number of units in multiunit structures, however, increased at a faster rate than one-unit structures during the decade, 34 percent and 5 percent, respectively.

The size of housing units increased between 1960 and 1970. The median number of rooms rose from 4.7 to 5.0 in metropolitan areas and from 4.5 to 4.9 in nonmetropolitan areas. Units with one to three rooms declined in the State, whereas those with five rooms or more had relatively large percentage increases over the decade.

Households were smaller in 1970 than in 1960. In metropolitan areas, population per occupied unit declined from 3.6 in 1960 to 3.3 in 1970, and in nonmetropolitan areas, from 3.8 in 1960 to 3.4 in 1970. There were large percentage increases in one-person households, 72 percent in metropolitan areas and 59 percent in nonmetropolitan areas. Households with five or more persons showed relatively small gains in metropolitan areas and losses in nonmetropolitan areas.

The proportion of housing units lacking some or all plumbing facilities decreased from 48 to 24 percent during the decade in Mississippi. For metropolitan areas the proportion of units without complete plumbing facilities in 1970 was 8 percent as compared with 28 percent for nonmetropolitan areas.

Number of persons per room is often used as a measure of crowding. In Mississippi units with 1.01 or more persons per room comprised 15 percent of all occupied units in 1970, compared with 23 percent in

Table C. Housing Units by Metropolitan and Nonmetropolitan Residence: 1970 and 1960

The State Metropolitan and Nonmetropolitan Residence	Housing units				Population percent change
	Total		Change		
	1970	1960	Number	Percent	
Total..................	699,150	628,945	70,205	11.2	1.8
Metropolitan residence.....	120,899	97,322	23,577	24.2	15.4
Inside central cities....	78,015	63,292	14,723	23.3	11.2
Outside central cities...	42,884	34,030	8,854	26.0	23.0
Nonmetropolitan residence..	578,251	531,623	46,628	8.8	-0.8

1960 (table D). The number of all such units in 1970 was 96,300, a decrease of about 37,100, or 28 percent, between 1960 and 1970. The decline occurred in metropolitan and nonmetropolitan areas alike.

Homeownership in the State increased from 58 percent in 1960 to 66 percent in 1970. In metropolitan areas there was an increase from 60 to 64 percent, while in nonmetropolitan areas the proportion increased from 57 to 67 percent.

Property values and rents increased during the last decade. The median value of owner-occupied homes in metropolitan areas increased by 33 percent ($10,500 in 1960 to $14,000 in 1970), while in nonmetropolitan areas value increased 48 percent ($7,100 in 1960 to $10,500 in 1970). In metropolitan areas, median contract rent in 1970 was 35 percent higher than in 1960, rising from $49 to $66.

Value and rent are expressed in current dollars (the value at the time of the respective censuses). Thus, any comparison must take into account the general rise in the cost of living during the 10-year period as well as changes in the characteristics of the housing inventory.

Standard Metropolitan Statistical Areas

Of the two metropolitan areas in the State (Jackson and Biloxi-Gulfport), the Jackson SMSA accounted for about two-thirds of the housing in these areas in 1970. The increase in the housing supply in these SMSA's during the decade was 23,600 units, of which nearly three-fourths (17,300) was in the Jackson area. This produced a 28-percent increase in the Jackson SMSA and 18 percent in the Biloxi-Gulfport SMSA.

Average household size for the total metropolitan area of the State declined during the decade. Population per occupied unit in the central cities was 3.1 in 1970, compared with 3.6 in the suburbs.

The rate of homeownership was greater in the suburban areas than in the central cities. About 77 percent of occupied units in the suburbs were owner-occupied, compared with 58 percent in the central cities.

In 1970, 2 percent of all year-round units lacked some or all plumbing facilities in the central cities, compared with 17 percent in the suburbs. Of all occupied units in metropolitan areas, 14,000 units, or 13 percent, reported more than one person per room in 1970, compared with 18 percent in 1960. In 1970, the proportion of such units was 11 percent in the central cities and 15 percent in the suburbs.

The homeowner vacancy rate for metropolitan areas decreased during the decade, from 2.1 percent in 1960 to 1.7 percent in 1970. The rental vacancy rate increased, however, from 7.7 to 9.2 percent.

Annexations

Annexations occurred in the central cities of Biloxi and Gulfport during the decade (see "Population Trends" and text table B). Such annexations affect changes in the characteristics for these central cities and their suburbs.

Table D.   Plumbing Facilities and Persons Per Room by Metropolitan and Nonmetropolitan Residence: 1970 and 1960

The State Metropolitan and Nonmetropolitan Residence	Percent of housing units			
	Lacking some or all plumbing facilities		With 1.01 or more persons per room[1]	
	1970[2]	1960[3]	1970	1960
Total.....................	24.3	47.8	15.1	23.5
Metropolitan residence..........	7.6	(NA)	12.5	18.4
Inside central cities..........	2.4	11.7	11.4	15.9
Outside central cities........	17.0	(NA)	14.6	23.3
Nonmetropolitan residence........	27.8	(NA)	15.7	24.4

NA Not available.
[1]Percent of all occupied units.
[2]Percent of all year-round housing units.
[3]Percent of all housing units.

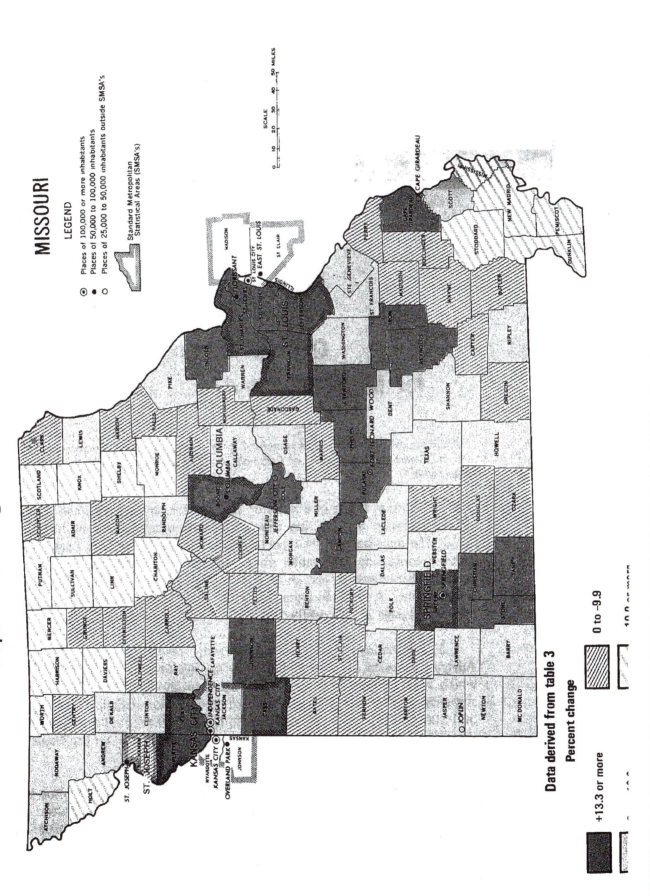

Population Change for Counties: 1960 to 1970

MISSOURI

LEGEND

⊙ Places of 100,000 or more inhabitants
● Places of 50,000 to 100,000 inhabitants
○ Places of 25,000 to 50,000 inhabitants outside SMSA's

Standard Metropolitan
Statistical Areas (SMSA's)

Data derived from table 3

Percent change

+13.3 or more

0 to -9.9

10.0 or more

Analytical Text

POPULATION TRENDS

General

Population in Missouri grew only moderately over the 1960-70 decade. It rose from 4,320,000 to 4,766,000, an increase of 357,000, or 8 percent over the population living in the State in 1960 (table A). In the Nation as a whole population increased by 13 percent over the decade. Missouri's population gain was highly concentrated in the metropolitan areas. Within metropolitan areas, only the suburban rings grew, increasing by over 400,000 persons, or 33 percent; central cities show a population loss of 57,000 for the decade, equivalent to 4 percent of their 1960 population. In the nonmetropolitan areas, which contain 36 percent of the State's total population, there was virtually no change in population between 1960 and 1970.

The proportion of the total population living in metropolitan areas rose over the decade, from 61 to 64 percent. In the Nation as a whole, nearly 70 percent of the population is metropolitan.

The total number of households in the State in 1970 was 1,521,000, or 161,000 more than in 1960. The population living in households increased less rapidly than the rate at which households increased, with the result that average household size decreased slightly, from 3.1 to 3.0 persons.

Although a "border" State, Missouri's white-Negro distribution in metropolitan and nonmetropolitan areas resembles that of many northern States. Negroes, who constitute 97 percent of all races other than white, are concentrated in metropolitan areas. In 1970, nearly 90 percent of this population group was found in the metropolitan areas of the State, compared to 60 percent of the white population. Within metropolitan areas, Negroes are found in largest numbers in the central cities, and whites in the suburban rings. Negroes account for about 27 percent of all residents of central cities in Missouri (up from 21 percent in 1960), but only 3 percent of all residents of the suburbs.

Missouri's substantial population growth was due entirely to the natural increase of the population (see table 3). Net migration overall played no part in this

Table A. Population by Race and Metropolitan and Nonmetropolitan Residence: 1970 and 1960

The State Metropolitan and Non-metropolitan Residence	Population		Change		Percent Distribution	
	1970	1960	Number	Percent	1970	1960
Total...............	[1]4,676,501	4,319,813	356,688	8.3	100.0	100.0
Metropolitan residence...	2,997,071	2,652,788	344,283	13.0	64.1	61.4
Inside central cities..	1,380,914	1,437,753	-56,839	-4.0	29.5	33.3
Outside central cities.	1,616,157	1,215,035	401,122	33.0	34.6	28.1
Nonmetropolitan residence	1,679,430	1,667,025	12,405	0.7	35.9	38.6
White...............	4,177,495	3,922,967	254,528	6.5	89.3	90.8
Metropolitan residence...	2,557,288	2,319,172	238,116	10.3	54.7	53.7
Inside central cities..	997,902	1,129,557	-131,655	-11.7	21.3	26.1
Outside central cities.	1,559,386	1,189,615	369,771	31.1	33.3	27.5
Nonmetropolitan residence	1,620,207	1,603,795	16,412	1.0	34.6	37.1
Negro and other races	499,006	396,846	102,160	25.7	10.7	9.2
Metropolitan residence...	439,783	333,616	106,167	31.8	9.4	7.7
Inside central cities..	383,012	308,196	74,816	24.3	8.2	7.1
Outside central cities.	56,771	25,420	31,351	123.3	1.2	0.6
Nonmetropolitan residence	59,223	63,230	-4,007	-6.3	1.3	1.5

[1]See correction note on page 9.

growth. A white outmigration of 25,000 was counterbalanced by a net inmigration of 26,000 persons of other races. Similarly net migration gains in metropolitan areas (50,000) were countered by migration losses from nonmetropolitan areas.

The population of races other than white grew 4 times as fast as the white population of Missouri, by 26 percent compared to less than 7 percent for the white population. White outmigration was equivalent to less than 1 percent of the white population of the State in 1960, but the inmigration of other races was equivalent to 6.5 percent of their 1960 population.

All areas of the State experienced significant changes in age composition. In both metropolitan and nonmetropolitan areas there were declines in the number of children under 5 years of age, by 19 percent in metropolitan areas and 24 percent in nonmetropolitan areas. In nonmetropolitan areas, 25-44 year olds were also reduced in number over the decade (by 5 percent). All other age groups increased, by notably 15 to 24 year olds (by 53 percent in metropolitan areas and 21 percent in nonmetropolitan areas).

Similar changes are found in other sections of the country and are due in part to changing birth rates and in part to migration, which is highly selective by age. Low birth rates during the depression years and in the 1960's contribute to the diminution of age groups 25-44 and under 5, whereas the post-World War II "baby boom" is currently reflected in the large size of the population 15-24 years old.

Standard Metropolitan Statistical Areas

Missouri has five standard metropolitan statistical areas (SMSA's). Two are among the largest in the United States. The entire St. Louis, Mo.-Ill. SMSA had a population of 2,363,000 in 1970 and ranked 10th among all SMSA's. The Missouri portion of the SMSA contained 1,827,000 persons in 1970. The Kansas City,

Mo.-Kans. SMSA ranks 26th among the Nation's SMSA's, with a population in 1970 of 1,254,000. The Missouri portion of this SMSA had a population of 849,000.

The Kansas City SMSA is heavily involved in meat production and other food processing activities. It is a major wholesale and retail center. It is also a major transportation hub. The St. Louis SMSA has a highly diversified set of manufacturing industries. It is also a large wholesaler and is an important transportation center.

The smaller three SMSA's are Springfield, St. Joseph and Columbia. The Springfield SMSA (153,000 population) is the capital of Missouri. It also has some higher education facilities. The St. Joseph SMSA (87,000 population) adjoins the Kansas City SMSA and is a manufacturing area. The Columbia SMSA (81,000 population) has some manufacturing activity and is the site of the University of Missouri.

Decennial rates of growth for the two largest SMSA's in Missouri are close to the national average of 13 percent. The population of the entire St. Louis SMSA increased over the decade by one-quarter of a million persons, or 12 percent. Nearly all this growth occurred in the Missouri portion (209,000). The increase in the population of the entire Kansas City SMSA which amounted to 161,000 or 13 percent, was more evenly distributed between the Missouri (86,000) and the Kansas portions (75,000). Over the decade, the population of St. Louis city declined from 750,000 to 622,000. This population loss was the result of an extensive outmigration of 183,000 persons, equivalent to 24 percent of the city's 1960 population. Kansas City, which annexed a substantial population over the decade (70,000) shows only moderate growth for the decade, increasing from a population of 476,000 to 507,000, or by 7 percent. Without such annexation, Kansas City would have shown a significant population loss, and a very extensive outmigration (table B).

Table B.   Change in Population of Central Cities Through Annexation: 1960 to 1970

Central Cities	1970 population			1960 population	Change 1960 to 1970 in 1960 area
	Total	In 1960 area	In annexed area		
Columbia................	58,804	43,558	15,246	36,650	6,908
Kansas City.............	507,087	437,143	69,944	475,539	-38,396
Springfield.............	120,096	100,066	20,030	95,865	4,201

Two of the three smaller SMSA's in Missouri show population increases for the decade. The Columbia SMSA grew very rapidly, by 47 percent, as a result of inmigration. Practically all growth in the SMSA shows up in the central city. Columbia city annexed a substantial suburban population over the decade, however; without it, the city's gain would have been cut back appreciably.

The Springfield SMSA shows a moderate population increase for the decade (21 percent), which was due in large part to net inmigration. As in the case of Columbia, the central city appears to have had the greatest share of the SMSA's growth, but annexation of suburban territory is largely responsible for this appearance.

The St. Joseph SMSA was the only one in the State to show a population loss for the 1960-70 decade. The population of this SMSA dropped by 4 percent (4,000 persons) due to net outmigration. This loss was produced by St. Joseph city which decreased by 7,000 persons, or 9 percent, and had a net outmigration of 11,000 persons, equivalent to 13 percent of the city's 1960 population.

In 1970 as in 1960, about 85 percent of the population of the entire St. Louis SMSA was white. In St. Louis city, however, the white proportion dropped sharply over the decade, from 71 percent in 1960 to 59 percent in 1970. In the entire Kansas City SMSA, 87 to 89 percent of the total population was white at the time of both censuses, but in the central city the white proportion fell from 82 to 77 percent.

St. Louis city's population changes by race were compounded of an extensive loss of whites (169,000, or 32 percent) and a moderate gain of persons of other races (41,000, or 19 percent). Kansas City's white population did not change over the decade, but other races show a gain of 31,000 persons, or 37 percent. Whites in the suburbs of both SMSA's show considerable growth, on the other hand, by 307,000 (36 percent) in St. Louis and 54,000 (19 percent) in Kansas City. Other races in the suburbs grew at even higher rates, but their numerical increases were much below white increases, and their representation in these areas scarcely changed (see table 1).

Counties

Between 1960 and 1970, 90 of the 114 counties in Missouri had increases in population. Twenty-two of these counties had increases above the national rate of 13.3 percent. The counties were located in the metropolitan areas and in the central and southern parts of the State (see map).

The fastest growing counties were in the SMSA's. Some of these were St. Charles (76 percent); Jefferson (59); Boone (47); Clay (41); Platte (37); St. Louis (35); and Cass (33).

There were 24 counties which lost population. These counties were concentrated in the north and in the southeastern corner. Of the 24 counties, 18 had declines of 10 percent or more. Some of those with the heaviest declines were: Pemiscot (31 percent); New Madrid (25); Mississippi (20); Holt (16); and Putnam (16).

There were 34 counties with an excess of deaths over births. Of these, eight had sufficient net inmigration to achieve a population increase. A large proportion of the population of all 34 counties was 65 years of age and over. This porportion ranged from 17 to 23 percent of the population. In the State as a whole only 11 percent of the population is in this age group. The counties were all relatively small in total population.

Only six counties in the State and an independent city, St. Louis, contain a large enough population of races other than white to have this population group shown separately in the table on county components of change (see "Definitions and Explanations"). In four counties the population of races other than white declined. In the two metropolitan counties of Jackson (Kansas City SMSA) and St. Louis (St. Louis SMSA) this population made very significant gains. In Jackson County, the population of Negro and other races grew by 37 percent, and in St. Louis County by 148 percent. In St. Louis city this population grew by 19 percent.

HOUSING TRENDS

General

During the decade the total supply of housing units in Missouri increased more rapidly than population. While the population grew by 357,000, or 8 percent, housing units increased by 182,000, or 12 percent (table C).

The metropolitan areas of the State experienced greater relative growth in housing, as in population, than did the nonmetropolitan part. The number of housing units in metropolitan areas rose from 887,900 to 1,029,600, an increase of 141,700 units or 16 percent; this compares with an increase of 40,300 units, or 7 percent, in nonmetropolitan areas. While the metropolitan areas contained 62 percent of the housing in Missouri, the additions to the housing supply in these areas accounted for about 78 percent of the State's total housing increase between 1960 and 1970.

Almost three-fourths of the housing in Missouri consisted of one-unit structures in 1970. The number of units in multiunit structures, however, increased at a faster rate than one-unit structures, 19 percent and 7 percent, respectively.

The size of housing units increased betwen 1960 and 1970. The median number of rooms rose from 4.6 to 4.8 in metropolitan areas and from 4.7 to 4.8 in nonmetro-politan areas. Units with one to three rooms declined in both the metropolitan and nonmetropolitan areas of the State.

Households were smaller in 1970 than in 1960. The average household size decreased from 3.1 persons in 1960 to 3.0 in 1970 for the State as a whole, remained at 3.1 persons in metropolitan areas, and declined from 3.1 persons to 2.9 in nonmetropolitan areas. There were large percentage increases in one-person households, 43 percent in metropolitan areas and 41 percent in non-metropolitan areas. Households with three or more persons showed relatively small gains in the metropolitan areas and losses in nonmetropolitan areas.

The proportion of units lacking some or all plumbing facilities decreased from 26 to 10 percent during the decade in Missouri. For metropolitan areas the propor-tion without complete plumbing facilities in 1970 was 4 percent as compared with 18 percent for nonmetro-politan areas.

Approximately 8,300 Negro-occupied units, or 7 percent, of the Negro-occupied units inside SMSA's lacked some or all plumbing in 1970, compared with 5,700, or 40 percent, of the Negro housing outside SMSA's.

Number of persons per room is often used as a measure of crowding. In Missouri, units with 1.01 or more persons per room comprised 8 percent of all

Table C.   Housing Units by Metropolitan and Nonmetropolitan Residence: 1970 and 1960

The State Metropolitan and Nonmetropolitan Residence	Housing units				Popula-tion percent change
	Total		Change		
	1970	1960	Number	Percent	
Total.................	1,673,361	1,491,397	181,964	12.2	8.3
Metropolitan residence.....	1,029,642	887,942	141,700	16.0	13.0
Inside central cities....	519,931	514,284	5,647	1.1	-4.0
Outside central cities...	509,711	373,658	136,053	36.4	33.0
Nonmetropolitan residence..	643,719	603,455	40,264	6.7	0.7

occupied units in 1970, compared with 12 percent in 1960 (table D). The number of all such units in 1970 was 124,200, a decrease of about 36,900, or 23 percent, between 1960 and 1970. The decline occurred in metropolitan and nonmetropolitan areas alike.

Homeownership in the State increased from 64 percent in 1960 to 67 percent in 1970. In metropolitan areas there was an increase from 61 to 63 percent, and in nonmetropolitan areas the proportion increased from 70 to 74 percent.

About 42 percent of the Negro households in metropolitan areas owned their homes in 1970, compared with 51 percent in the nonmetropolitan areas. Of the 59,100 Negro-homeowner households in the State, 51,900 lived inside SMSA's and 7,200 lived outside SMSA's.

Property values and rents increased during the last decade. The median value of owner-occupied housing in metropolitan areas increased by 28 percent ($12,800 in 1960 to $16,400 in 1970), while in nonmetropolitan areas value increased 48 percent ($6,300 in 1960 to $9,300 in 1970). In metropolitan areas, median contract rent in 1970 was 40 percent higher than in 1960, rising from $58 to $81. In nonmetropolitan areas, rent increased during the 10-year period from $36 to $53, or 47 percent.

Value and rent are expressed in current dollars (the value at the time of the respective censuses). Thus, any comparison must take into account the general rise in the cost of living during the 10-year period as well as changes in the characteristics of the housing inventory.

Standard Metropolitan Statistical Areas

In the metropolitan areas of the State, there were 1,029,600 housing units in 1970. The housing supply in these areas is dominated by the Missouri part of the St. Louis, Mo.-Ill. SMSA, with 611,900 housing units, and the Missouri part of the Kansas City, Mo.-Kans. SMSA, with 305,500 housing units.

In 1970, about 66 percent of the housing units in the State's metropolitan areas consisted of one-unit structures. The corresponding proportions in the central cities and suburban areas were 50 percent and 81 percent, respectively.

Housing units increased in size in the metropolitan areas during the decade. The median number of rooms increased from 4.6 to 4.8. In 1970, the median number of rooms in the central cities was 4.4 and in the suburbs 5.1.

Homeownership in 1970 was greater in the suburbs than in the central cities. About 76 percent of occupied units in the suburbs and 51 percent in the central cities were owner-occupied. The Negro homeownership rate in the suburbs was 71 percent, compared with 39 percent in the central cities.

About 27,000 housing units, or 5 percent, lacked some or all plumbing facilities in the central cities. In the suburban areas, 19,200 units, or 4 percent, lacked plumbing. Approximately 7,200, or 7 percent of Negro households in central cities occupied units which lacked some or all plumbing facilities in 1970, compared with 1,100, or 9 percent, of Negro households in the suburbs.

Table D.   Plumbing Facilities and Persons Per Room by Metropolitan and Nonmetro-
            politan Residence: 1970 and 1960

The State Metropolitan and Nonmetropolitan Residence	Percent of housing units			
	Lacking some or all plumbing facilities		With 1.01 or more persons per room[1]	
	1970[2]	1960[3]	1970	1960
Total......................	9.7	25.9	8.2	11.8
Metropolitan residence...........	4.5	(NA)	8.3	12.0
Inside central cities..........	5.2	16.8	9.2	12.8
Outside central cities........	3.8	(NA)	7.5	10.9
Nonmetropolitan residence........	18.2	(NA)	7.9	11.6

NA Not available.
[1]Percent of all occupied units.
[2]Percent of all year-round housing units.
[3]Percent of all housing units.

Of all occupied units in metropolitan areas, 80,200 units, or 8 percent, reported more than one person per room in 1970, compared with 12 percent in 1960. In 1970, the proportion of such units was 9 percent in the central cities and 7 percent in the suburbs.

The homeowner vacancy rate for metropolitan areas decreased during the decade from 1.8 to 1.3 percent. The rental vacancy rate increased from 6.8 to 10.0 percent.

Annexations

Annexations occurred in the central cities of Columbia, Kansas City, and Springfield during the decade (see "Population Trends" and text table B). Such annexations affect changes in the characteristics for these central cities and their suburbs.

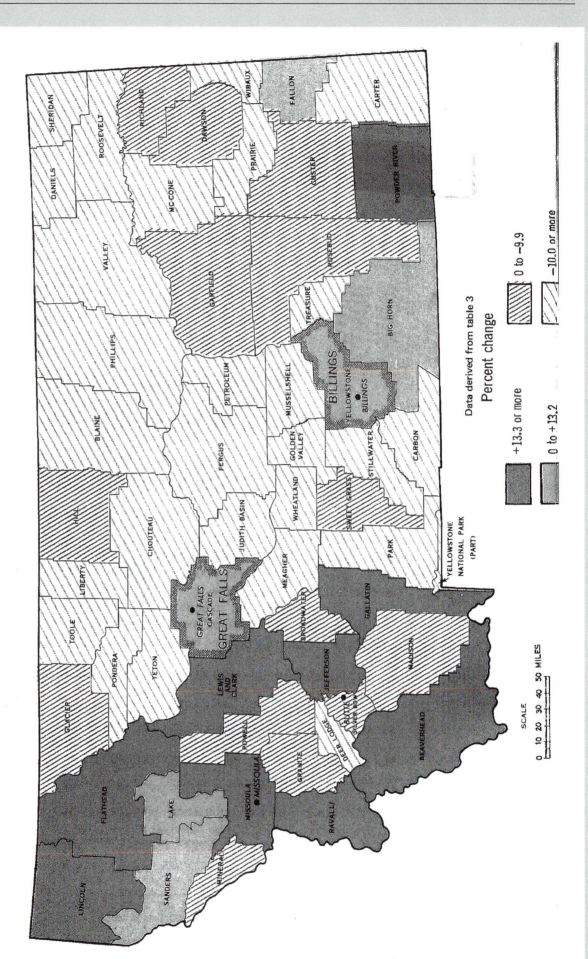

Population Change for Counties: 1960 to 1970

MONTANA

Incorporated places of 25,000-100,000
Standard Metropolitan Statistical Areas

Data derived from table 3

Percent change

+13.3 or more

0 to +13.2

0 to −9.9

−10.0 or more

SCALE

0 10 20 30 40 50 MILES

Analytical Text

POPULATION TRENDS

General

Between 1960 and 1970 the total population of Montana grew by nearly 20,000 persons, from 674,767 to 694,409, an increase of 3 percent over the population living in the State in 1960. This increase was highly concentrated in the two metropolitan areas of the State, Billings and Great Falls, which together accounted for 85 percent of the total State increase (17,000 persons). Within these metropolitan areas most of the growth occurred in the central cities of Billings and Great Falls. By contrast, the nonmetropolitan population, which is three times as great as the metropolitan population of the State, scarcely changed during this period, growing by less than 1 percent (table A).

The total number of households in the State in 1970 was 217,000 or 15,000 more than in 1960. The population living in households increased less rapidly than the rate at which new households were formed with the result that average household size decreased slightly, from 3.3 to 3.1 persons per unit.

The effect of these changes on population distribution by metropolitan-nonmetropolitan residence was very small. The proportion of the total population living in the two metropolitan areas increased by only 2 percent during the decade. About one out of every four persons in Montana now lives in metropolitan areas, compared with a national average of two out of three.

In 1960 as in 1970, 95 to 98 percent of both metropolitan and nonmetropolitan populations of Montana were white; the balance was mainly Indian (see table 1). Although numerically and proportionally very much smaller than the white population, other races increased at much faster rates. In the central cities and suburbs of both SMSA's, their numbers doubled during the decade. These changes increased the proportion of the population of races other than white which live in metropolitan areas from 10 percent in 1960 to 15 percent in 1970.

The components of population change indicate that substantial growth occurred in the State as a whole and in both metropolitan and nonmetropolitan areas as a result of natural increase (the excess of births over deaths). At the same time all areas show losses due to net outmigration, the largest being noted in nonmetropolitan areas. Although a natural increase of 78,000 was recorded for the State in this 10-year period, the population grew by only 20,000. The difference implies a net outmigration of 58,000 persons, equivalent to

Table A. Population by Race and Metropolitan and Nonmetropolitan Residence: 1970 and 1960

The State Metropolitan and Nonmetropolitan Residence	Population		Change		Percent distribution	
	1970	1960	Number	Percent	1970	1960
Total	694,409	674,767	19,642	2.9	100.0	100.0
Metropolitan residence	169,171	152,434	16,737	11.0	24.4	22.6
Inside central cities	121,672	108,208	13,464	12.4	17.5	16.0
Outside central cities	47,499	44,226	3,273	7.4	6.9	6.6
Nonmetropolitan residence ..	525,238	522,333	2,905	0.6	75.6	77.4
White	663,043	650,738	12,305	1.9	95.5	96.4
Metropolitan residence	164,543	150,086	14,457	9.6	23.7	22.2
Inside central cities	118,643	106,674	11,969	11.2	17.1	15.8
Outside central cities	45,900	43,412	2,488	5.7	6.6	6.4
Nonmetropolitan residence ..	498,500	500,652	-2,152	-0.4	71.8	74.2
Negro and other races...	31,366	24,029	7,337	30.5	4.5	3.6
Metropolitan residence	4,628	2,348	2,280	97.1	0.7	0.4
Inside central cities	3,029	1,534	1,495	97.5	0.4	0.2
Outside central cities	1,599	814	785	97.5	0.4	0.2
Nonmetropolitan residence ..	26,738	21,681	5,057	23.3	3.8	3.2

almost 9 percent of the total 1960 population of the State. Metropolitan and nonmetropolitan areas gained greatly as a result of natural increase, only to have these gains cut back by net outmigration. Nonmetropolitan areas suffered the severest migratory losses, which were almost great enough to wipe out all the growth due to natural increase.

White population growth was considerably below its natural increase, implying a substantial outmigration amounting to nearly 57,000 persons. Similarly, the growth of Negro and other races fell short of their natural increase by a figure of nearly 2,000. Net outmigration by race thus amounted to nearly 9 percent of the white population living in Montana in 1960 and nearly 7 percent of the population of other races.

All areas of the State experienced significant changes in age composition. Table 4 reveals much smaller populations under 5 years of age in 1970 than in 1960. In the State as a whole, there was a decline in the number of children in this age group from 83,000 in 1960 to 57,000 in 1970, a loss of 31 percent of the age group. There was also a drop in the number of adults 25 to 44 years of age.

Counteracting the losses to age groups under 5 and 25 to 44 are large gains in numbers of young adults 15 to 24 years of age. Statewide this group increased by 32,000 persons, a 35-percent increase over 1960. A large gain was also made by the population 45 to 64 years old, which increased Statewide by 16,000 persons.

Similar changes are found in other sections of the country and are the product in part of changing birth rates and in part are due to age selective migration: i.e., low birth rates during the Depression years and in the 1960's contribute to the diminution of age groups under 5 and 25 to 44, whereas the post-World War II "baby boom" is currently reflected in the large size of the population 15 to 24 years old.

Standard Metropolitan Statistical Areas

Considered individually, the Billings and Great Falls Standard Metropolitan Statistical Areas (SMSA's) have many features in common. They are of similar size and racial composition. They contain central cities of almost identical size, both of which acquired additional population as a result of annexation of suburban territory during the decade. Superficially, growth patterns appear to be different within the two SMSA's, but this appearance is largely caused by annexation or loss of territory. The differences which do exist between the two SMSA's are created in part by the existence of a large military installation in the suburbs of Great Falls which does not have a parallel in Billings.

Annexation of territory during the decade was responsible for addition to the cities of Billings and Great Falls of 9,000 and 7,000 persons, respectively (table B). Change from 1960 to 1970, based on the population of the city as constituted after annexation, shows a rate of population growth for Billings city twice that of Great Falls city (17 percent compared with 9 percent). While the Billings suburbs remained at a virtual standstill, thus reducing their share of total SMSA population, the Great Falls suburbs increased by 20 percent, and became a more prominent part of the SMSA. Had these annexations not taken place, the total populations of the two cities would have shown losses and the suburbs would have shown considerably greater gains.

The age distribution of the population of Billings and Great Falls shows the same tendencies noted for the State as a whole: losses for age groups under 5 and 25 to 44 years, accompanied by large gains in age groups 15 to 24 and 45 to 64 years. Changes in the city of Billings were dominated by growth of the population 15 to 24 years old, which increased by 76 percent during the decade. The same age group in Great Falls city increased by only 39 percent. In the suburbs of the two SMSA's very different age trends are evident. In the Billings suburbs, the largest proportional increases are noticed in the population 45 years of age and over; adults aged 25 to 44 years and children of all ages are down. By contrast, the Great Falls suburbs, which received additional military population between 1960 and 1970, obtained virtually all its growth from ages 5 to 44.

The net effect of all age changes within the two SMSA's is thus different: in the Billings SMSA at the end of the decade there is a greater proportion of young

Table B. Change in Population of Central Cities through Annexation: 1960 to 1970

Central Cities	1970 population			1960 population	Change 1960 to 1970 in 1960 area
	Total	In 1960 area	In annexed area		
Billings	61,581	52,546	9,035	52,851	-305
Great Falls	60,091	52,993	7,098	55,357	-2,364

people under 25 living in the central city, whereas in Great Falls in 1970 a greater proportion of young people is to be found living in the suburbs.

Counties

Between 1960 and 1970 only 15 of the 56 counties in Montana increased in population size. Nine of these counties—located chiefly in the western and north-western parts of the State—grew at a rate exceeding the 13.3-percent rate of population increase for the Nation as a whole. The two metropolitan counties of Cascade and Yellowstone, which are the most populous in the State, are not included in this list of fastest growing areas, even though their numerical increase comprised 85 percent of the total population increase in the State. Four of the fastest growing counties had populations exceeding 30,000 in 1970. The largest of these, Missoula County, the site of the University of Montana, grew by 31 percent, from 45,000 in 1960 to 58,000 in 1970. Flathead County, which was second largest in popula-tion size in 1970, increased by 20 percent from 33,000 to 39,000. Gallatin County and Lewis and Clark County, each with 33,000 population in 1970, had growth rates of 25 percent and 19 percent, respectively. Of the 42 counties which show population losses for the decade, 28 lost 10 percent or more of their 1960 population. Although these are scattered throughout the State, nine of them are contiguous to the State's two metropol-itan areas (see map). The extensive loss of population from Valley County was produced in part by the closing of a military base.

Every county had more births than deaths during the decade. In most cases, however, net outmigration was more than sufficient to wipe out the gains contributed by natural increase. Only six counties had substantial net inmigration which amounted to more than 10 percent of their 1960 populations. All six are among the eight fastest growing counties. Chief among these are Lincoln County, with an overall growth rate of 44 percent and a net inmigration rate of 26 percent; Jefferson County, with a growth rate of 22 percent and a net inmigration amounting to 18 percent; and Missoula County, with a 31-percent overall increase and a 15 percent net inmigra-tion rate.

Only six counties in the State contain a large enough population of races other than white to have this population group shown separately in the table on county components of change (see "Definitions and Explanations"). Four of these six counties grew in population size between 1960 and 1970, in spite of net outmigration. Here natural increase was clearly the dominant influence on population growth, unlike the situation described for counties with predominantly white populations.

HOUSING TRENDS

General

During the decade, the total supply of housing units in Montana increased faster than population. While housing units increased by 13,000 or 6 percent, the population grew by 20,000, or only 3 percent (table C). Similarly, the number of households increased at a greater rate than the population in housing units, resulting in lower average household size.

The metropolitan areas of the State experienced the greatest relative growth in housing, as in population. The number of housing units in metropolitan areas rose from 50,000 to 56,000 over the decade, an increase of over 6,000 units or 13 percent; this compares with an increase of 7,000 units or 4 percent in the nonmetropoli-tan areas. While only one out of four housing units is found in the Billings and Great Falls SMSA's, these areas accounted for almost half the total State increase between 1960 and 1970.

A trend toward smaller households is evident throughout the State. Households consisting of only one

Table C. **Housing Units by Metropolitan and Nonmetropolitan Residence: 1970 and 1960**

The State Metropolitan and Nonmetropolitan Residence	Housing units				Population percent change
	Total		Change		
	1970	1960	Number	Percent	
Total	246,603	233,310	13,293	5.7	2.9
Metropolitan residence	56,359	49,919	6,440	12.9	11.0
Inside central cities	41,768	36,226	5,542	15.3	12.4
Outside central cities	14,591	13,693	898	6.6	7.4
Nonmetropolitan residence	190,244	183,391	6,853	3.7	0.6

or two persons had large percentage gains, while the number of larger households grew slowly or even declined. Nonmetropolitan areas provide an example of this trend. There the number of households containing three or more persons decreased by 5,000, while households with only one or two persons increased by 13,000.

Homeownership rates in Montana are slightly higher in 1970 than in 1960, about 66 percent and 64 percent, respectively. Estimated value of housing increased during the same time from a median of $10,900 in 1960 to $14,100 in 1970. Metropolitan-nonmetroplitan differentials narrowed over the decade: The median value of metropolitan housing was 45 percent higher than the nonmetropolitan in 1960, but only 30 percent higher in 1970. Statewide, rents increased by almost one-third, with substantial increases in the number of units priced at $100 to $149. Value and rent are expressed in current dollars (the dollar value at the time of the respective censuses). Thus, any comparison must take into account the inflation which occurred over the past decade as well as changes in the characteristics of the housing inventory.

Number of persons per room is often used as a measurement of crowding. In Montana as a whole, units with 1.01 or more persons per room comprise less than 10 percent of all occupied housing units in 1970, compared with 15 percent in 1960, (table D). The number of all such units in 1970 is 21,000, a decrease of about 9,000, or 31 percent, between 1960 and 1970, with an even greater relative drop in the number having 1.51 or more persons per room. The decline occurred in metropolitan and nonmetropolitan areas alike, but in metropolitan areas the improvement was greater.

Standard Metropolitan Statistical Areas

The housing supply in each of the two SMSA's increased by over 3,000 units, or 13 percent, between 1960 and 1970. Paralleling the population changes discussed for the State, housing in Billings increased by 19 percent in the city, compared with less than 1 percent in the suburbs, whereas in the Great Falls area the rate of increase was 12 percent in the city, compared with 15 percent in the suburbs.

Average household size declined in both SMSA's during the decade. Population per occupied unit in each of the two cities is 3.0 in 1970, and reflects about the same change from 1960. The Great Falls suburbs, however, show less decennial change than the Billings suburbs; the decline for the Great Falls suburban areas is from 3.7 to 3.5 and for Billings from 3.7 to 3.3.

The two SMSA's also reveal differences in homeownership patterns. While rates of homeownership in the central cities in 1970 are nearly identical (60 percent in Billings compared with 58 percent in Great Falls), in the suburban rings, Billings shows a rate of homeownership (73 percent) considerably higher than that of Great Falls (54 percent). All the growth in housing which occurred in the Billings suburbs in this period was in owner-occupied units, while the number of rented units decreased slightly. In the Great Falls suburbs, where the rate of population growth was more than twice that of the city, the increase in renter-occupied units exceeded the increase in owner-occupied units by a ratio of 4 to 1.

The median value of owner-occupied housing in Billings and Great Falls SMSA's increased at similar rates between 1960 and 1970, from $14,700 to $17,200 in

Table D. Plumbing Facilities and Persons Per Room by Metropolitan and Nonmetropolitan Residence: 1970 and 1960

The State Metropolitan and Nonmetropolitan Residence	Percent of housing units			
	Lacking some or all plumbing facilities		With 1.01 or more persons per room[1]	
	1970[2]	1960[3]	1970	1960
Total	9.0	(4)	9.6	14.9
Metropolitan residence	5.6	13.6	7.9	13.8
Inside central cities	4.8	10.4	6.8	11.6
Outside central cities	7.8	21.9	10.9	20.3
Nonmetropolitan residence	10.1	(4)	10.1	15.2

[1] Percent of all occupied units.
[2] Percent of all year-round housing units.
[3] Percent of all housing units.
[4] Not shown because of lack of comparability with 1970.

7

Billings and from $13,500 to $16,300 in Great Falls. Both SMSA's show decreases in the number of units valued below $15,000 and large percentage increases in the number valued at $20,000 or more. However, the value distributions continue to be rather heavily weighted at the intermediate level (the suburbs at slightly lower levels than the cities) and the largest numerical increases occurred in both SMSA's in units valued at $15,000 to $24,999.

Median contract rents in the cities of Billings and Great Falls were practically identical in 1960 ($65 and $64 respectively) and relatively close in 1970 ($81 and $85).

The number of housing units in the two SMSA's with 1.01 or more persons per room and the amount of improvement which occurred during the decade are about the same. While there are many more such housing units in the central cities, units within the suburbs containing 1.01 or more persons per room comprise a higher proportion of total occupied units. In 1970, 6 percent of Billings city's housing was in that category, compared with 10 percent in the suburbs; similarly, 8 percent of Great Falls city's units had 1.01 or more persons per room, compared with 12 percent in the suburbs. Housing units having 1.01 to 1.50 persons per room declined during the decade by percentages up to 41 percent, while units having 1.51 or more persons per room decreased even more.

In both SMSA's about 19 out of 20 housing units have all plumbing facilities in 1970. The proportion represented by such units increased in the city of Billings from 92 percent in 1960 to 96 percent in 1970, and in Great Falls city from 88 percent to 95 percent.

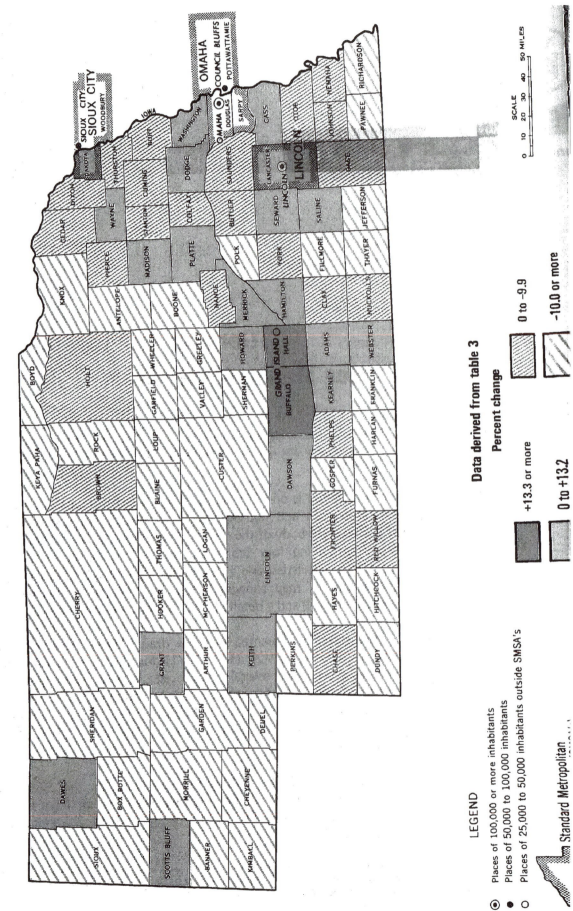

Population Change for Counties: 1960 to 1970

NEBRASKA

Data derived from table 3

Percent change

+13.3 or more

0 to +13.2

0 to -9.9

-10.0 or more

LEGEND

⊙ Places of 100,000 or more inhabitants

● Places of 50,000 to 100,000 inhabitants

○ Places of 25,000 to 50,000 inhabitants outside SMSA's

Standard Metropolitan

Analytical Text

POPULATION TRENDS

General

Between 1960 and 1970 the population of Nebraska grew from 1,411,000 to 1,483,000, resulting in an increase of 72,000, or 5.1 percent. This rate of increase is well below the rate of increase for the entire United States (13.3 percent) but is about equal to the rate for the West North Central States (6.0 percent), which in addition to Nebraska include Minnesota, Iowa, Missouri, North Dakota, South Dakota and Kansas.

The total number of households in Nebraska in 1970 was 474,000, or 41,000 more than in 1960. The population living in households increased less rapidly than the rate at which households increased with the result that average household size decreased slightly, from 3.2 to 3.0 persons.

The patterns of population change in Nebraska during the 1960 to 1970 decade varied greatly by area of residence. The metropolitan population increased by 17 percent from 542,000 to 634,000 while the nonmetropolitan population decreased by 2.3 percent from 869,000 to 849,000. As a result, the proportion of the total population living in metropolitan areas rose from 38 percent in 1960 to 43 percent in 1970 (table A). In the nation as a whole, about two-thirds of the population live in metropolitan areas.

Table A. Population by Race and Metropolitan and Nonmetropolitan Residence: 1970 and 1960

The State Metropolitan and Non-metropolitan Residence	Population		Change		Percent Distribution	
	1970	1960	Number	Percent	1970	1960
Total................	[1] 1,483,493	1,411,330	72,163	5.1	100.0	100.0
Metropolitan residence...	634,260	542,211	92,049	17.0	42.8	38.4
Inside central cities..	496,846	430,119	66,727	15.5	33.5	30.5
Outside central cities.	137,414	112,092	25,322	22.6	9.3	7.9
Nonmetropolitan residence	849,233	869,119	-19,886	-2.3	57.2	61.6
White................	1,432,867	1,374,764	58,103	4.2	96.6	97.4
Metropolitan residence...	591,110	511,569	79,541	15.5	39.8	36.2
Inside central cities..	456,630	401,451	55,179	13.7	30.8	28.4
Outside central cities.	34,480	110,118	24,362	22.1	9.1	7.8
Nonmetropolitan residence	841,757	863,195	-21,438	-2.5	56.7	61.2
Negro and other races	50,626	36,566	14,060	38.5	3.4	2.
Metropolitan residence...	43,150	30,642	12,508	40.8	2.9	2.
Inside central cities..	40,216	28,668	11,548	40.3	2.7	2.
Outside central cities.	2,934	1,974	960	48.6	0.2	0.
Nonmetropolitan residence	7,476	5,924	1,552	26.2	0.5	0.

[1]See correction note on page 9.

Nearly three-fourths of the increase in Nebraska's metropolitan population occurred in central cities. Annexation of suburban territory was an important element in this growth, however; without it the central cities would have shown a population loss for the decade (table B).

The population of Negro and other races in Nebraska increased by 38 percent during the 1960's; however, the absolute numbers are small. Negro and other races constituted only 3.4 percent of the State's population in 1970. As is typically the case in states outside the South, the population of Negro and other races in Nebraska is heavily concentrated in metropolitan areas. Eighty-five percent lived in the metropolitan areas of Nebraska in 1970. Less than 1 percent of the nonmetropolitan population was comprised of Negro and other races in 1970.

The population increase of 72,000 in Nebraska in the 1960 to 1970 decade was due to a natural increase (births minus deaths) of 145,000, and a net outmigration of 73,000. The net outmigration was equivalent to 5 percent of the 1960 population. Differences in the rates of population change by area of residence and by race were due largely to differences in rates of net migration. Net inmigration in metropolitan areas was equivalent to less than 1 percent of the 1960 population while net outmigration in nonmetropolitan areas was equivalent to 9 percent of the 1960 population. The amount of net migration among Negro and other races was small while net outmigration among whites was equivalent to 6 percent of the 1960 population.

The age composition of the Nebraska population changed significantly between 1960 and 1970. The greatest decrease occurred among the population under 5 years old and was due largely to the fall in the birth rates which occurred throughout the United States during the 1960's. The greatest increase occurred in the 15 to 24 age group and was due to the entry of the large number of persons born during the post-World War II "baby boom" into this age group. As a result of these changes, the proportion of the total population in the under 5 group declined from 11 percent to 8 percent, and the proportion in the 15 to 24 group increased from 13 percent to 17 percent. In 1970, 12 percent of the Nebraska population was in the age group 65 years and over. In the nation as a whole, 10 percent were in this age group.

The age structures of the metropolitan and nonmetropolitan segments of the Nebraska population contrast sharply. In 1970 the differential was most pronounced in the age group 65 years and over. These persons constituted 9 percent of the metropolitan population and 15 percent of the nonmetropolitan population.

Standard Metropolitan Statistical Areas

There are three Standard Metropolitan Statistical Areas (SMSA's) located wholly or partially in Nebraska: the Omaha, Nebr.-Iowa SMSA; the Lincoln (Nebr.) SMSA; and the Sioux City, Iowa-Nebr. SMSA. In 1970, 84 percent of the population in the Omaha, Nebr.-Iowa SMSA was in the Nebraska portion, and only 11 percent of the population in the Sioux City, Iowa-Nebr. SMSA was in the Nebraska portion.[1]

Between 1960 and 1970, the population of the entire Omaha SMSA, which is the largest metropolitan area in Nebraska and which is a major transportation, wholesaling, and financial center in the Midwest, increased from 458,000 to 540,000, or by 18 percent. The numerical increase was about evenly divided between the central city (Omaha) and the balance of the SMSA. However, the 1970 population of the area annexed to the city of Omaha between 1960 and 1970 was 72,000. If annexations are excluded, the city lost 26,000 population and the balance of the SMSA gained 108,000 population. Of the 82,000 increase in the population of the entire Omaha SMSA, 5,000 was due to net inmigration.

---

[1] For a discussion of the entire Sioux City SMSA, see 1970 Census Report PHC(2)-17.

Table B. Change in Population of Central Cities Through Annexation: 1960 to 1970

Central Cities	1970 population			1960 population	Change 1960 to 1970 in 1960 area
	Total	In 1960 area	In annexed area		
Omaha...................	347,328	275,460	71,868	301,598	-26,138
Lincoln..................	149,518	133,209	16,309	128,521	4,688
Sioux City...............	-	-	-	-	-

The Iowa portion of the Omaha SMSA (Pottawattamie County) grew slowly between 1960 and 1970 (from 83,000 to 87,000). The Nebraska portion of the Omaha SMSA, which grew from 375,000 to 453,000, increased by 21 percent in comparison to the 18 percent increase noted earlier for the entire SMSA.

The Lincoln SMSA grew from 155,000 in 1960 to 168,000 in 1970, yielding a growth rate of 8 percent. The city of Lincoln (the capital of Nebraska) had a population increase of 5,000 within its 1960 boundaries; however, because of annexations, Lincoln's population increase was raised to 21,000 during the decade, and the balance of the SMSA showed a loss of 8,000. The 13,000 increase in the population of the Lincoln SMSA was comprised of a natural increase of 22,000 and a net outmigration of 9,000. The net outmigration was equivalent to 6 percent of the 1960 population.

The Nebraska portion of the Sioux City SMSA (Dakota County) grew from 12,000 in 1960 to 13,000 in 1970, producing a growth rate of 8 percent. Net outmigration during the decade was 1,000.

Counties

Of the 93 counties in Nebraska, 26 gained population and 67 lost population between 1960 and 1970. (On the national level, slightly more than half of all counties gained population during the decade). Only four counties had rates of growth above the national average of 13.3 percent, and 43 counties experienced population declines exceeding ten percent.

While the nonmetropolitan population of Nebraska declined by 2.3 percent (from 869,000 to 849,000), the rate of change varied greatly with county population size. The total population of the nine nonmetropolitan counties with populations exceeding 20,000 in 1960 increased by 9 percent. Among the 26 counties with populations under 5,000 in 1960, there was a decrease of 14 percent. The explanation for this pattern apparently lies in the degree of urbanization. Each of the nine counties with a 1960 population over 20,000 contained a city with a population exceeding 10,000 (none of the other nonmetropolitan counties did), and each of these nine cities increased in population between 1960 and 1970. There was a very small net outmigration from these nine counties, suggesting an offsetting inmigration from the surrounding dominantly rural counties which had high rates of net outmigration. The population decline in rural Nebraska is dramatized by the increase between 1960 and 1970 in the number of counties with population under 1,000 from two to seven.

Only eight counties in Nebraska had a net inmigration of population during the 1960 to 1970 decade. The three counties with a net inmigration exceeding 1,000 were also the three counties with the highest growth rates. Foremost among these is Sarpy County, which is the location of Offutt Air Force Base and of much of the suburban expansion in the Omaha SMSA. The population of Sarpy County increased from 31,000 to 64,000, making it one of the less than 1 percent of all counties in the United States which more than doubled in population. Net migration into Sarpy County during the decade was 22,000.

The population of Hall County grew by 20 percent, and the population of Buffalo County grew by 19 percent as each had a net inmigration of 3,000 between 1960 and 1970. The rapidly growing city of Grand Island is located in Hall County. The growth in Buffalo County is due to the rapid expansion of Kearney State College.

There were population decreases in most of the dominantly rural counties in Nebraska from 1960 to 1970 because net outmigration exceeded natural increase. However in five counties (Franklin, Furnas, Pawnee, Thayer, and Webster), deaths exceeded births, yielding a natural decrease. Webster County was an example of a rare demographic phenomenon in the United States: net inmigration exceeded a natural decrease, resulting in population growth.

HOUSING TRENDS

General

During the decade, the total supply of housing units in Nebraska increased faster than population. While population grew by 72,000, or 5 percent, the number of housing units increased by 42,100, or 9 percent (table C).

The metropolitan areas of the State experienced the greatest relative growth in housing. The number of housing units in the metropolitan areas rose from 171,700 to 208,100 over the decade, an increase of 36,400 units, or 21 percent, compared with an increase of 5,700 units, or 2 percent, in the nonmetropolitan areas. While only 40 percent of the housing units were located in the Omaha and Lincoln SMSA's, these areas accounted for about 86 percent of the total State increase between 1960 and 1970.

Almost 80 percent of the housing in Nebraska consisted of one-unit structures in 1970. The number of units in multiunit structures, however, increased at a much faster rate than one-unit structures during the decade, 30 percent and 3 percent, respectively.

The median number of rooms in housing units (5.1) remained unchanged for the State between 1960 and 1970. However, the median rose from 4.8 to 5.0 in the SMSA's and declined from 5.3 to 5.2 in the nonmetropolitan areas.

Households were smaller in 1970 than in 1960. In metropolitan areas, the median number of persons declined from 2.9 in 1960 to 2.6 in 1970, and in the nonmetropolitan areas of the State from 2.8 persons in 1960 to 2.4 in 1970. The number of one-persons households increased by 57 percent in the SMSA's and by 44 percent in the nonmetropolitan areas.

The number of units in the State lacking some or all plumbing facilities declined from 82,700 to 31,300, a 62-percent decrease since 1960. In 1970, the proportion of such units was 6 percent of all year-round units, whereas in 1960 the proportion of all housing units was 17 percent.

Number of persons per room is often used as a measure of crowding. In Nebraska, units with 1.01 or more persons per room comprised 6 percent of

Table C. Housing Units by Metropolitan and Nonmetropolitan Residence: 1970 and 1960

The State Metropolitan and Nonmetropolitan Residence	Housing units				Population percent change
	Total		Change		
	1970	1960	Number	Percent	
Total................	515,069	472,950	42,119	8.9	5.1
Metropolitan residence.....	208,081	171,685	36,396	21.2	17.0
Inside central cities....	169,429	140,587	28,842	20.5	15.5
Outside central cities...	38,652	31,098	7,554	24.3	22.6
Nonmetropolitan residence..	306,988	301,265	5,723	1.9	-2.3

all occupied housing units in 1970, compared with 9 percent in 1960 (table D). The number of all such units in 1970 was 29,300, a decrease of about 10,600, or 27 percent, between 1960 and 1970. The decline occurred in metropolitan and nonmetropolitan areas alike for such units.

About two-thirds, 66 percent, of Nebraska's housing was owner-occupied in 1970, reflecting a slight increase from 65 percent in 1960. In the SMSA's, there was a decrease in the homeownership rate from 63 percent in 1960 to 62 percent in 1970, while in the nonmetropolitan areas homeownership rose from 66 percent to 70 percent.

Property values and rents increased over the decade. The median value of owner-occupied housing in the SMSA's increased by 32 percent from $11,800 in 1960 to $15,600 in 1970, while in the nonmetropolitan areas the median value rose from $7,300 to $9,900, or 36 percent. In the SMSA's, median contract rent was 40 percent higher than in 1960, rising from $67 to $94. In nonmetropolitan areas, rent increased 35 percent, from $46 to $62.

Value and rent are expressed in current dollars (the value at the time of the respective censuses). Thus, any comparison must take into account the general rise in the cost of living during the 10-year period as well as changes in the characteristics of the housing inventory.

Standard Metropolitan Statistical Areas

Average household size in the metropolitan area total of the State declined during the decade. Population per occupied unit was 3.1 in 1970, compared with 3.2 in 1960.

In 1970, 6,900 housing units in metropolitan areas, or 3 percent of all year-round units, lacked some or all plumbing facilities. The corresponding proportion in the central cities and the suburbs was the same, also 3 percent.

About 7 percent, 13,300 units, of all occupied units in metropolitan areas, reported more than one person per room in 1970, compared with 10 percent in 1960. In 1970, the proportion of such units was 6 percent in the central cities and 9 percent in the suburbs.

The homeowner vacancy rate for metropolitan areas increased during the decade from 1.2 to 1.3 percent reflecting an increase from 1.0 to 1.3 in the central cities and a decrease from 2.0 to 1.2 in the suburban areas. Similarly, rental vacancy rates increased from 6.7 to 8.0 percent with an increase from 6.5 to 8.4 in the central cities and a decrease from 8.1 to 6.1 outside the central cities.

Annexations

Annexations occurred in the central cities of Omaha and Lincoln during the decade (see "Population Trends" and text table B). Such annexations affect changes in the characteristics for these central cities and suburbs.

Table D. Plumbing Facilities and Persons Per Room by Metropolitan and Nonmetropolitan Residence: 1970 and 1960

The State Metropolitan and Nonmetropolitan Residence	Lacking some or all plumbing facilities		With 1.01 or more persons per room[1]	
	1970[2]	1960[3]	1970	1960
Total.....................	6.1	17.5	6.2	9.2
Metropolitan residence...........	3.3	(NA)	6.8	10.4
Inside central cities..........	3.3	8.9	6.3	9.6
Outside central cities.........	3.4	(NA)	8.9	14.0
Nonmetropolitan residence.......	8.0	(NA)	5.8	8.5

NA Not available.   [1]Percent of all occupied units.   [2]Percent of all year-round housing units.   [3]Percent of all housing units.

Population Change for Counties: 1960 to 1970

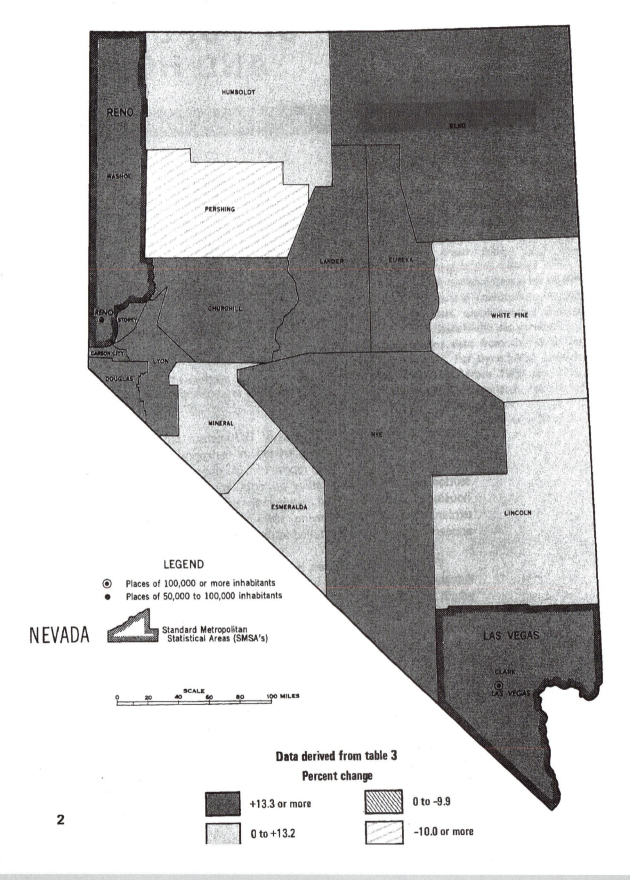

LEGEND

⊙ Places of 100,000 or more inhabitants
● Places of 50,000 to 100,000 inhabitants

NEVADA   Standard Metropolitan
              Statistical Areas (SMSA's)

SCALE
0   20   40   60   80   100 MILES

Data derived from table 3

Percent change

▧ +13.3 or more	▨ 0 to -9.9
▥ 0 to +13.2	▢ -10.0 or more

2

Analytical Text

POPULATION TRENDS

General

Between 1960 and 1970 the total population of Nevada grew faster than that of any other State. Its population increased over the decade by 203,000 persons, from 285,000 to 489,000, or by 71 percent. This rate of increase was, nonetheless, not the highest in the State's history: in the preceding decade, 1950 to 1960, the population of Nevada increased by 78 percent, but between 1900 and 1910, it grew by 93 percent.

Population growth in the State in the 1960-70 decade was highly concentrated in the two metropolitan areas of Las Vegas and Reno (table A). Together these areas accounted for 90 percent of the total State increase (183,000 persons). The effect of this growth was to raise considerably the proportion of the total population living in metropolitan areas, from 74 percent in 1960 to 81 percent in 1970. In the Nation as a whole, two persons out of three are found in metropolitan areas.

The total number of households in the State in 1970 was 160,000, or 69,000 more than in 1960. Average household size at the time of both censuses was the same, 3.0 persons per unit.

At the time of both censuses more than 90 percent of the metropolitan and nonmetropolitan populations of Nevada were white (table A). The State's population of other races is about two-thirds Negro: the balance is mainly American Indian. Practically this entire population group is found living in the two metropolitan areas. The Las Vegas SMSA alone contains 90 percent of the State's total black population (see table 1).

The components of population change indicate the overwhelming influence of migration on the growth of the State (see table 3). Two-thirds of Nevada's intercensal population increase was produced by a net inmigration of 144,000 persons, equivalent to 50 percent of the 1960 population of the State. Virtually this entire inmigration was white; only 5 percent of it was accounted for by other races.

Table A.   Population by Race and Metropolitan and Nonmetropolitan Residence: 1970 and 1960

The State Metropolitan and Non-metropolitan Residence	Population		Change		Percent Distribution	
	1970	1960	Number	Percent	1970	1960
Total.................	488,738	285,278	203,460	71.3	100.0	100.0
Metropolitan residence...	394,356	211,759	182,597	86.2	80.7	74.2
Inside central cities..	198,650	115,875	82,775	71.4	40.6	40.6
Outside central cities.	195,706	95,884	99,822	104.1	40.0	33.6
Nonmetropolitan residence	94,382	73,519	20,863	28.1	19.3	25.8
White..............	448,177	263,443	184,734	70.1	91.7	92.3
Metropolitan residence...	360,462	196,202	164,260	83.7	73.8	68.8
Inside central cities..	179,685	104,086	75,599	72.6	36.8	36.5
Outside central cities.	180,777	92,116	88,661	96.2	37.0	32.3
Nonmetropolitan residence	87,715	67,241	20,474	304.5	17.9	23.6
Negro and other races	40,561	21,835	18,726	85.8	8.3	7.7
Metropolitan residence...	33,894	15,557	18,337	117.9	6.9	5.5
Inside central cities..	18,965	11,789	7,176	60.9	3.9	4.1
Outside central cities.	14,929	3,768	11,161	296.2	3.1	1.3
Nonmetropolitan residence	6,667	6,278	389	6.2	1.4	2.2

Metropolitan areas were the chief attractors of migrants. While the two SMSA's had a natural increase of 51,000 over the decade, net inmigration added 132,000 persons, equivalent to 62 percent of their combined 1960 populations. The growth of nonmetropolitan areas likewise was due in larger part to net inmigration, which accounted for 12,000 of the nonmetropolitan population increase of 21,000.

Throughout Nevada, growth of the population of white as well as other races was dominated by increases at younger ages (see table 4). Young adults, aged 15 to 24 years, and school children, 5 to 14 years old, show highest rates of increase over the decade. In the State as a whole, the population 15 to 24 years old more than doubled, while the 5 to 14 year old group, which had a larger numerical increase, grew by 85 percent. Pre-school age children, under 5 years of age, grew most slowly of all age groups, however, by only 33 percent. By contrast, in most areas of the country, the pre-school age group declined over the decade.

Rates of increase for all age groups are considerably higher in the fast-growing metropolitan areas than in the nonmetropolitan areas. Age changes within the two areas are in proportion, however, except for the population under 5 years of age. Virtually all of the State's increase in children of this age occurred in the two SMSA's.

Standard Metropolitan Statistical Areas

Between 1960 and 1970 the population of the Las Vegas SMSA more than doubled, growing from 127,000 to 273,000. During the same period, the population of the Reno SMSA increased by 43 percent, from 85,000 to 121,000. Net migration was of primary importance to the growth of both SMSA's. Three-quarters of Las Vegas' decennial population increase and almost two-thirds of Reno's growth were produced by net inmigration. At present more than one-half (56 percent) of Nevada's total population is found in the Las Vegas SMSA; another one-fourth lives in the Reno SMSA.

During the decade the populations of both central cities and suburbs grew rapidly. Annexation of territory by the two central cities accounts to a considerable extent for their growth (table B). Between 1960 and 1970, the city of Las Vegas annexed suburban territory containing a population of 23,000, equivalent to nearly 40 percent of the city's total population gain. Without this annexation, the city would still have shown a considerable increase, but the present rapid growth of the suburbs would have been accentuated. The city of Reno, by contrast, obtained nearly all its intercensal population increase of 21,000 from the annexed territory. Without it, Reno city would appear to be at a standstill, but the suburban population would have doubled.

In the central cities and suburbs of both SMSA's, nearly all age groups show large percentage gains over the decade. The fastest-growing population in both SMSA's was 5 to 24 years of age. The proportion of the total population represented by this age group was greatly increased over the decade, particularly in the central cities. In 1970, 37 percent of Las Vegas' and 35 percent of Reno city's total populations consisted of 5 to 24 year olds, compared with 30 percent in each city in 1960.

The proportions represented by all other age groups in the two cities were diminished or remained the same, except for persons 65 and over, which comprise a slightly higher proportion of the population of each city in 1970.

Counties

Nevada's 18 counties range in population size from 600 in Esmeralda County to 273,000 in Clark County, one of the State's two metropolitan counties (Las Vegas SMSA). Washoe County, the second most populous in the State, is also metropolitan (Reno SMSA). Third in population size is Carson City, which was consolidated with Ormsby County in 1960, and is at present an

Table B. Change in Population of Central Cities Through Annexation: 1960 to 1970

| Central Cities | 1970 population | | | 1960 population | Change 1960 to 1970 in 1960 area |
	Total	In 1960 area	In annexed area		
Las Vegas...................	125,787	103,060	22,727	64,405	38,655
Reno.......................	72,863	53,035	19,828	51,470	1,565

independent city. In 1970, the population of Carson City was 15,000. The largest nonmetropolitan counties in Nevada, with 1970 populations exceeding 10,000 are Elko, Churchill, and White Pine.

Every county in Nevada gained population over the decade, except for Pershing County, which decreased by almost 17 percent, from a population of 3,200 to 2,700. Of the 17 counties which show increases, 11 grew at rates exceeding the 13.3 percent increase for the nation as a whole. With the exception of White Pine, which grew by only 3.5 percent, counties with the largest populations were among the fastest-growing.

All but two counties had more births than deaths in the 1960-70 decade. Eureka and Storey Counties each had a small natural decrease, but at the same time gained population as a result of net inmigration equivalent to more than 20 percent of their 1960 populations.

Altogether, 12 of Nevada's counties gained population through net inmigration, 10 of them at rates equivalent to 10 percent or more of their 1960 populations. The greatest attractors of migrants in the State were the two metropolitan counties and Carson City, which in combination account for 138,000 of the State's total net inmigration of 144,000. Other counties had very high inmigration rates, but numerical increases were relatively small. Chief among these is Douglas County, with a net inmigration rate of 84 percent but a numerical gain of only 3,000.

HOUSING TRENDS

General

During the decade the relative increase in the total supply of housing units in Nevada was almost the same as the increase in population. Housing units increased by 70,900, or 70 percent, while the population grew by 203,000, or 71 percent (table C).

The metropolitan areas of the State experienced the greatest relative growth in housing, as in population. The number of housing units in metropolitan areas rose from 73,000 to 137,800 over the decade, an increase of almost 64,800 units, or 89 percent; this compares with an increase of 6,100 units, or 21 percent, in the nonmetropolitan areas. While 80 percent of all housing units in the State were in the Las Vegas and Reno SMSA's in 1970, these areas accounted for 91 percent of the total State increase between 1960 and 1970.

A trend toward smaller households is evident in the State. The median number of persons per unit decreased from 2.6 to 2.5 over the decade. At the same time, there was a relatively greater increase in households with one or two persons than in households with three or more persons.

Homeownership rates in Nevada were somewhat higher in 1970 than in 1960, about 59 percent and 56 percent, respectively. Estimated value of housing increased during the same period from a median of $15,200 in 1960 to $22,400 in 1970, with large increases in homes valued at $20,000 or more. Statewide, rents increased from $77 to $123, or 60 percent, with substantial increases in the number of units renting at $150 or more.

Value and rent are expressed in current dollars (the dollar value at the time of the respective censuses). Thus, any comparison must take into account the general rise in the cost of living during the 10-year period as well as changes in the characteristics of the housing inventory.

Number of persons per room is often used as a measure of crowding. In Nevada as a whole, units with 1.01 or more persons per room comprised less than 9

Table C. Housing Units by Metropolitan and Nonmetropolitan Residence: 1970 and 1960

The State Metropolitan and Nonmetropolitan Residence	Housing units				Popula-tion percent change
	Total		Change		
	1970	1960	Number	Percent	
Total................	172,558	101,623	70,935	69.8	71.3
Metropolitan residence.....	137,769	72,977	64,792	88.8	86.2
Inside central cities....	71,147	42,456	28,691	67.6	71.4
Outside central cities...	66,622	30,521	36,101	118.3	104.1
Nonmetropolitan residence..	34,789	28,646	6,143	21.4	28.1

percent of all occupied housing units in 1970, compared with 14 percent in 1960 (table D). The decline occurred in metropolitan and nonmetropolitan areas alike, but in metropolitan areas the improvement was greater.

Standard Metropolitan Statistical Areas

In the metropolitan areas of the State (Las Vegas and Reno), the housing supply increased by 64,800 units, or 89 percent, during the past decade. A component of housing and population change in both SMSA's is annexation of territory by the central cities (see "Population Trends" and text table B). Such annexation affects to an unknown extent changes in housing characteristics for the central cities and suburbs.

Average household size in the metropolitan areas of the State remained the same during the decade. In both 1970 and 1960 the population per occupied unit in the metropolitan areas was 3.0.

In 1970, 58 percent of all metropolitan occupied units were owner-occupied, compared with 56 percent in 1960. The median value of owner-occupied housing in metropolitan areas increased by 44 percent during the past decade, from $16,100 in 1960 to $23,200 in 1970. In both SMSA's there were decreases in the number of units valued below $15,000 and large increases in those valued at $20,000 or more. Median contract rent in metropolitan areas increased by 54 percent during the decade, from $84 in 1960 to $129 in 1970.

In the central cities and suburbs of both SMSA's, one-unit structures comprised the largest proportion of all year-round housing units. Percentage increases in housing units in multiunit structures, however, greatly exceeded the growth of one-unit structures in both SMSA's.

There was a decrease in the proportion of units in metropolitan areas lacking some or all plumbing facilities, from 7 percent in 1960 to 2 percent in 1970. In addition, there was a decrease in the proportion of housing units with 1.01 or more persons per room, from 13 percent in 1960 to 8 percent in 1970.

The homeowner vacancy rate in metropolitan areas of the State increased, from 1.7 percent in 1960 to 2.0 percent in 1970, while the rental vacancy rate decreased from 6.2 to 6.1. In the Las Vegas SMSA the homeowner vacancy rate increased, from 2.1 to 2.5 percent, and the rental vacancy rate increased from 6.0 to 6.3. In the Reno SMSA, however, both rates decreased; the homeowner vacancy rate decreased from 1.0 to 0.9 percent and the rental vacancy rate decreased from 6.4 to 5.6.

Table D. Plumbing Facilities and Persons Per Room by Metropolitan and Nonmetropolitan Residence: 1970 and 1960

The State Metropolitan and Nonmetropolitan Residence	Percent of housing units			
	Lacking some or all plumbing facilities		With 1.01 or more persons per room[1]	
	1970[2]	1960[3]	1970	1960
Total.....................	3.2	9.8	8.8	13.8
Metropolitan residence...........	2.2	7.1	8.4	13.5
Inside central cities..........	2.7	7.7	7.1	10.4
Outside central cities.........	1.6	6.2	9.9	17.9
Nonmetropolitan residence........	7.3	16.7	10.6	14.7

[1]Percent of all occupied units.
[2]Percent of all year-round housing units.
[3]Percent of all housing units.

Population Change for Counties: 1960 to 1970

NEW HAMPSHIRE

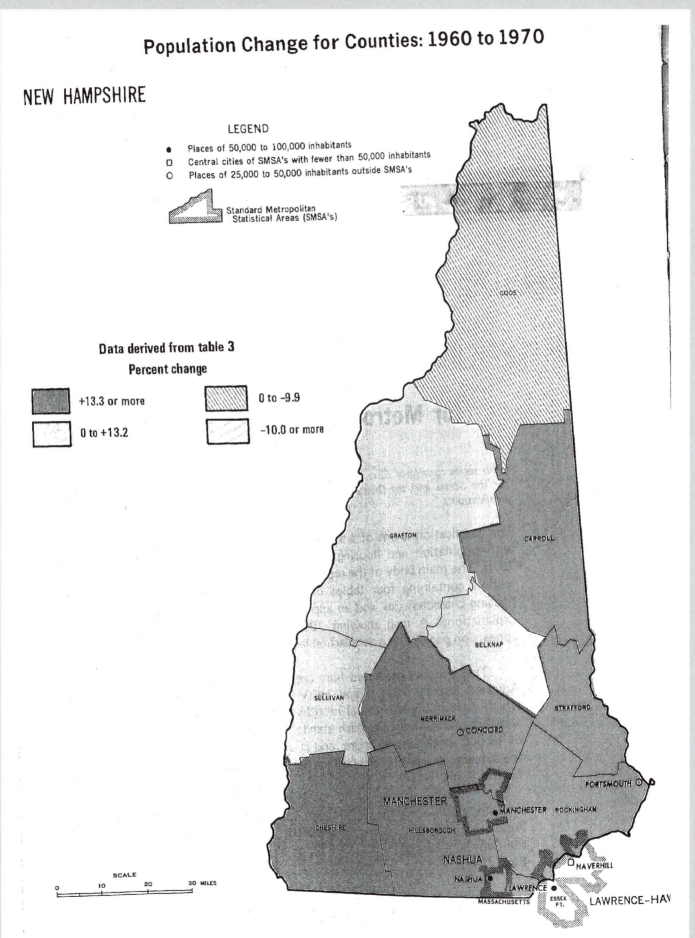

LEGEND

●   Places of 50,000 to 100,000 inhabitants

□   Central cities of SMSA's with fewer than 50,000 inhabitants

○   Places of 25,000 to 50,000 inhabitants outside SMSA's

Standard Metropolitan
Statistical Areas (SMSA's)

Data derived from table 3

Percent change

+13.3 or more

0 to +13.2

0 to -9.9

-10.0 or more

COOS

GRAFTON

CARROLL

BELKNAP

SULLIVAN

MERRIMACK

STRAFFORD

○ CONCORD

PORTSMOUTH ○

MANCHESTER

● MANCHESTER   ROCKINGHAM

CHESHIRE

HILLSBOROUGH

NASHUA

□ HAVERHILL

NASHUA ●

LAWRENCE ●

MASSACHUSETTS

ESSEX
PT.

LAWRENCE-HAV

SCALE

0   10   20   30 MILES

Analytical Text

POPULATION TRENDS

General

Between 1960 and 1970, the total population of New Hampshire increased by 131,000 or 22 percent, almost twice the national average of 13 percent, reaching a total of 738,000 persons. The 1960-70 period was the first to show New Hampshire the leader in rate of growth among the States in the Northeast region. Much of the State's spurt in growth over the last decade is attributable to its proximity to metropolitan Boston and the lower Merrimac Valley industrial centers of Lowell, Lawrence, and Haverhill. The creation of the interstate highway system which serves these areas, has encouraged considerable influx of population into New Hampshire, which could offer new residents the inducement of no State income tax or sales tax.

The total number of households in New Hampshire in 1970 was 225,000, or 45,000 more than in 1960. The population living in households increased less rapidly than the rate at which households increased with the result that average household size decreased from 3.3 to 3.1 persons.

In 1970 less than one-third of the population lived in metropolitan areas, contrasted with the national average of more than two-thirds. The metropolitan population of New Hampshire increased by 25 percent from 161,000 in 1960 to 202,000 in 1970, while the nonmetropolitan population increased 20 percent from 446,000 to 536,000 (see table A-1). Differential rates of growth in the two areas is caused not only by differential rates of migration but by higher birth rates in metropolitan areas.

Within metropolitan areas, the population of central cities grew by 13 percent from 127,000 to 144,000 and the suburban population grew by 71 percent from 34,000 to 58,000. As a result of these changes, the proportion of the metropolitan population of the State living in suburban areas increased from 21 percent in 1960 to 29 percent in 1970.

The population of New Hampshire is predominantly white. About one-half of 1 percent of the total population belongs to Negro and other races. The population of Negro and other races increased from 3,000 in 1960 to 5,000 in 1970, or 7.7 percent, the largest absolute increase since 1940. In 1960 and 1970, more than three-fourths of the population of Negro and other races lived in nonmetropolitan areas.

As with the Nation as a whole, New Hampshire's age composition changed between 1960 and 1970 (see table 4). The only decline occurred among children under 5 years old and was due largely to the decline in the birth rate which occurred throughout the United States during the 1960's. The greatest increase (53 percent) occurred in the 15 to 24 age group and was due mostly to the entry of the large number of persons born during the post-World War II "baby boom" into this age group. As a result of these changes the proportion of the total population in the under 5 group declined from 11 to 9 percent and the proportion in the 15 to 24 group increased from 13 percent in 1960 to 17 percent in 1970.

The small population of Negro and other races has a very young age structure. In 1970, 56 percent were under age 25, and only 5 percent were over age 65. Among the total population of the State 46 percent were under age 25, and 11 percent were over age 65.

Standard Metropolitan Statistical Areas

In 1970, there were three standard metropolitan statistical areas (SMSA's) in New Hampshire, including one located partly in New Hampshire and partly in Massachusetts (the Lawrence-Haverhill, Mass.-N.H. SMSA) and two located entirely in New Hampshire (the Manchester SMSA and the Nashua SMSA).[1] Each of the SMSA's gained population between 1960 and 1970 (see table A-3). The discussion of the Lawrence-Haverhill SMSA refers to the portion in New Hampshire only. The Nashua SMSA, which was designated an SMSA in 1970, includes Nashua city and Hudson town in Hillsbourgh County.

Of the 202,000 persons living in metropolitan areas in New Hampshire over one-half live in the Manchester SMSA. Between 1960 and 1970, the population of the Manchester SMSA increased from 103,000 to 108,000, by 5 percent. The population in the city of Manchester was virtually unchanged while the population in the balance of the SMSA increased by 6,000 persons or 42 percent.

---

[1] In the population tables in this report and other reports for States in New England, data are shown for two types of metropolitan areas: standard metropolitan statistical areas (SMSA's) and metropolitan State economic areas (SEA's) See "Definitions and Explanations" for a discussion of the difference between the two types of metropolitan areas. SMSA tables are shown in the Appendix to this text.

The Nashua SMSA grew from 45,000 to 66,000 or by 48 percent, between 1960 and 1970. The population in the city of Nashua increased by 43 percent while population outside central cities increased by 81 percent.

The New Hampshire portion of the Lawrence-Haverhill SMSA (Rockingham County) grew from 14,000 in 1960 to 27,000 in 1970, or by 98 percent. In 1970, 12 percent of the population of the Lawrence-Haverhill SMSA lived in New Hampshire.

Counties

New Hampshire's 10 counties range in population size from 19,000 in Carroll County to 224,000 in Hillsbourough County (see table 3). Most of the population of Hillsborough County falls within the Manchester and Nashua SMSA's. Every county in New Hampshire gained population over the decade except for Coos County, which decreased by 8 percent. Of the nine counties which show increases, six grew at rates exceeding the 13 percent for the Nation as a whole, while the remaining three grew at rates between 10 and 13 percent.

Each of the counties that gained population also gained through net inmigration, five of them at rates equivalent to 10 percent or more of their 1960 populations. The chief beneficiaries of migration in the State were metropolitan Hillsborough County and Rockingham, which in combination account for 49,000 of the State's total net inmigration of 69,000, or 72 percent.

HOUSING TRENDS

General

During the decade the total supply of housing units in New Hampshire increased more rapidly than population. While the population grew by 131,000, or 22 percent, housing units increased by 56,500, or 25 percent (table A).

The metropolitan areas of the State experienced about the same relative growth in housing as did the nonmetropolitan part. The number of housing units in metropolitan areas rose from 52,500 to 65,900 over the decade, an increase of 13,400 units, or 25 percent. There was an increase of 43,200 units, or 25 percent, in nonmetropolitan areas. The metropolitan areas contained 23 percent of the housing in New Hampshire and about the same proportion (24 percent) of the State's total housing increase between 1960 and 1970.

About 64 percent of the housing in New Hampshire consisted of one-unit structures in 1970. The corresponding proportions in the metropolitan and nonmetropolitan areas were 53 percent and 68 percent, respectively.

The median number of rooms in housing units in New Hampshire was 5.2 in 1970. In metropolitan areas the median was 5.0, compared with 5.2 in nonmetropolitan areas. While 37 percent of the metropolitan housing units had six or more rooms, 44 percent of the nonmetropolitan units were in this category.

Table A.   Housing Units by Metropolitan and Nonmetropolitan Residence: 1970 and 1960

The State Metropolitan and Nonmetropolitan Residence	Housing units				Population percent change
	Total		Change		
	1970	1960	Number	Percent	
Total..................	280,962	224,440	56,522	25.2	21.5
Metropolitan residence.....	65,903	52,543	13,360	25.4	25.7
Inside central cities....	48,220	41,139	7,081	17.2	12.7
Outside central cities...	17,683	11,404	6,279	55.1	58.3
Nonmetropolitan residence..	215,059	171,897	43,162	25.1	19.8

Households were smaller in 1970 than in 1960. Average household size in New Hampshire declined from 3.2 persons in 1960 to 3.1 in 1970. While the average household size in metropolitan areas remained at 3.2 persons, the average in nonmetropolitan areas decreased from 3.2 persons in 1960 to 3.1 in 1970. There were large percentage increases in one-person households, 55 percent in metropolitan areas and 65 percent in nonmetropolitan areas.

In 1970, 17,400 units, or 7 percent of the housing in New Hampshire, lacked some or all plumbing facilities. In metropolitan areas the proportion of housing units lacking some or all plumbing facilities was 4 percent (2,400 units), compared with 8 percent (15,000 units) in nonmetropolitan areas (table B).

Number of persons per room is often used as a measure of crowding. In New Hampshire, the proportion of housing units with 1.01 or more persons per room was 7 percent in 1970, with 14,800 such units in this category. The proportion of units with more than one person per room decreased from 8 percent in 1960 to 7 percent in 1970 in metropolitan areas, and from 7 to 6 percent in nonmetropolitan areas.

Homeownership in the State increased from 65 percent in 1960 to 68 percent in 1970. In metropolitan areas there was an increase from 57 to 61 percent, and in nonmetropolitan areas the proportion increased from 68 to 71 percent.

Property values and rents increased during the last decade. The median value of owner-occupied housing in metropolitan areas increased by 50 percent, from $12,200 in 1960 to $18,300 in 1970, while in non-metropolitan areas values increased 52 percent, from $10,200 in 1960 to $15,500 in 1970. In the State, median contract rent in 1970 was 72 percent higher than in 1960, rising from $46 to $79.

Value and rent are expressed in current dollars (the value at the time of respective censuses). Thus, any comparison must take into account the general rise in the cost of living during the 10-year period, as well as changes in the characteristics of the housing inventory.

Standard Metropolitan Statistical Areas

The suburban areas of the State experienced greater relative growth in housing than did the central cities. Housing units in the suburbs increased by 55 percent during the decade, while housing in the central cities increased by 17 percent. By 1970, there were 48,200 housing units in the central cities, and 17,700 units in the suburbs.

In 1970, 45 percent of the housing units in the central cities were in one-unit structures. In suburban areas, 77 percent of the housing units were in this category.

The median number of rooms in housing units in 1970 was 4.9 in the central cities and 5.2 in the suburban areas. While 17 percent of the housing in the central cities had three or fewer rooms, 9 percent of the suburban housing units were in this category. At the same time, 34 percent of the housing in the central cities had six or more rooms, compared with 43 percent in the suburbs.

Table B. Plumbing Facilities and Persons Per Room by Metropolitan and Nonmetropolitan Residence: 1970 and 1960

The State Metropolitan and Nonmetropolitan Residence	Percent of housing units			
	Lacking some or all plumbing facilities		With 1.01 or more persons per room[1]	
	1970[2]	1960[3]	1970	1960
Total......................	7.0	16.7	6.6	7.4
Metropolitan residence..........	3.7	10.7	7.0	7.5
Inside central cities..........	3.9	8.8	6.8	7.2
Outside central cities.........	2.9	17.7	7.7	9.0
Nonmetropolitan residence........	8.2	18.6	6.4	7.3

[1]Percent of all occupied units.
[2]Percent of all year-round housing units.
[3]Percent of all housing units.

In the central cities, 1,900 units, or 4 percent of all year-round housing units, lacked some or all plumbing facilities in 1970. In the suburban areas, about 500 units, or 3 percent, lacked plumbing. The proportion of units with more than one person per room remained at 7 percent in the central cities. Outside the central cities, there was a decrease from 9 to 8 percent.

Homeownership in the central cities increased from 51 percent in 1960 to 54 percent in 1970. In the suburbs, however, the homeownership rate declined from 84 to 81 percent. The median value of owner-occupied housing in 1970 was $18,200 in the central cities and $18,600 in the suburbs. Median contract rent was $76 in the central cities in 1970 and $128 outside the central cities.

The homeowner vacancy rate decreased from 1.1 to 0.9 percent in the central cities, and from 2.2 to 1.1 percent in the suburban areas. The rental vacancy rate increased from 4.0 to 6.7 percent in the central cities and from 3.1 to 5.5 percent in the suburbs.

Population Change for Counties: 1960 to 1970

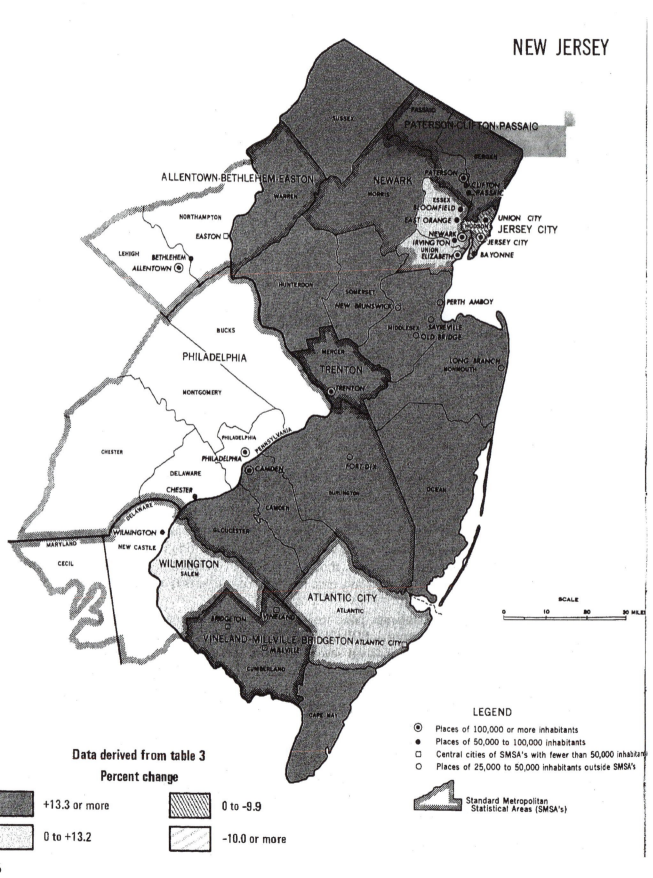

NEW JERSEY

Data derived from table 3

Percent change

+13.3 or more

0 to +13.2

0 to -9.9

-10.0 or more

LEGEND

⊙ Places of 100,000 or more inhabitants

● Places of 50,000 to 100,000 inhabitants

□ Central cities of SMSA's with fewer than 50,000 inhabitants

○ Places of 25,000 to 50,000 inhabitants outside SMSA's

Standard Metropolitan Statistical Areas (SMSA's)

Analytical Text

POPULATION TRENDS

General

The population of New Jersey was 7,168,000 on April 1, 1970, a gain of 1,101,000 or 18.2 percent over the 1960 count of 6,067,000. Only four States, California, Florida, Texas, and New York gained more population during the decade. With this population growth, New Jersey maintained its eighth ranking in population among the 50 States.

The total number of households in the State in 1970 was 2,218,000 or 412,000 more than in 1960. The population living in households increased less rapidly than the rate at which households increased, with the result that average household size declined slightly from 3.3 to 3.2 persons.

In 1970, 6,294,000 of the State's population was in metropolitan areas.[1] This amounts to 88 percent of the total population, much higher than the national average of 69 percent. Most of the State's population increase was in metropolitan areas, which grew 821,000, or 13 percent (table A). The population in nonmetropolitan areas, however, grew very rapidly during the decade, gaining 280,000 or 47 percent. Over 200,000 of this increase occurred in Monmouth and Ocean Counties, as a result of urban development in the unsettled areas between the Northeastern New Jersey metropolitan complex and Atlantic City.

---

[1] Middlesex and Somerset counties, part of the New York-Northeastern New Jersey Standard Consolidated Area, are treated as metropolitan territory although they are not included in any SMSA.

Table A. Population by Race and Metropolitan and Nonmetropolitan Residence: 1970 and 1960

The State Metropolitan and Non-metropolitan Residence	Population		Change		Percent Distribution	
	1970	1960	Number	Percent	1970	1960
Total..............	7,168,164	6,066,782	1,101,382	18.2	100.0	100.0
Metropolitan residence[1]..	6,293,515	5,472,223	821,292	13.0	87.8	90.2
Inside central cities..	1,167,044	1,212,489	-45,445	-3.7	16.3	20.0
Outside central cities.	5,126,471	4,259,734	866,737	20.3	71.5	70.2
Nonmetropolitan residence	874,649	594,559	280,090	47.1	12.2	9.8
White..............	6,349,908	5,539,003	810,905	14.6	88.6	91.3
Metropolitan residence...	5,530,141	4,985,505	544,636	10.9	77.1	82.2
Inside central cities..	771,093	955,267	-184,174	-19.3	10.8	15.7
Outside central cities.	4,759,048	4,030,238	728,810	18.1	66.4	66.4
Nonmetropolitan residence	819,767	553,498	266,269	48.1	11.4	9.1
Negro and other races	818,256	527,779	290,477	55.0	11.4	8.7
Metropolitan residence...	763,374	486,718	276,656	56.8	10.6	8.0
Inside central cities..	395,951	257,222	138,729	53.9	5.5	4.2
Outside central cities.	367,423	229,496	137,927	60.1	5.1	3.8
Nonmetropolitan residence	54,882	41,061	13,821	33.7	0.8	0.7

[1] Including the metropolitan counties of Middlesex and Somerset which are part of the New York-Northeastern New Jersey Standard Consolidated Area. See "Definitions and Explanations."

Within the metropolitan areas, there was a sharp contrast in population growth rates by race. The white population decreased 184,000 in central cities, but increased 729,000 outside of central cities. Negro and other races increased rapidly both inside and outside of central cities. The increase of 139,000 in Negro and other races in the central cities was not enough to offset the loss in white population, so total population in central cities decreased by 45,000.

At the end of this decade of sharply contrasting population change, 11.4 percent of the State's population was of Negro and other races, almost all located in metropolitan areas, and divided about equally between central cities and areas outside central cities. By contrast, only one-eighth of the white population lived in central cities in 1970, with three-fourths living in metropolitan areas outside of central cities. The remaining one-eighth of the white population lived in nonmetropolitan territory, making up 94 percent of the total nonmetropolitan population.

The growth of the Negro population was about the same inside and outside of central cities, both in amount and percent of change. This contrasts sharply with the national situation; of the 4.1 million increase in the Negro population in the Nation's metropolitan areas, only about one-fifth, or 832,000 was outside of the central cities. Of this, 117,000 occurred in New Jersey (see table 1). A substantial proportion of the 117,000 increase, however, was in areas adjacent to the central cities. For example, in Camden, which is adjacent to Philadelphia, the central city of its standard metropolitan statistical area (SMSA), the Negro population increased 13,000 from 1960 to 1970.

In the Newark SMSA, the Negro population outside of the central city increased 55,000 for the decade. Of this, 21,000 occurred in East Orange, 6,000 in Elizabeth, and 2,000 in Irvington, all incorporated cities adjacent to Newark. An increase of 9,000 occurred in Plainfield, which, though about 10 miles from Newark, is part of a continuous urban development extending from the larger city.

Thus about 38,000, or 70 percent, of the increase in the Negro population in the suburbs of the Newark SMSA occurred in four cities close to the central city. These cities are characterized by long standing urban development, with a high percentage of older housing.

In Morris County, further away from the central city in the Newark SMSA, there was rapid urban development during the decade, with a population growth of 122,000 or 47 percent. This increase was almost entirely in the white population which, at the end of the decade, constituted 97 percent of the county's population. By contrast, in the central city of Newark, the Negro population became a majority in the decade, going from

34 percent of the population in 1960 to 54 percent in 1970.

The distribution of New Jersey's population by age changed significantly between 1960 and 1970. While the total population increased 18 percent, the population under 5 years of age decreased 8 percent. This was due to the national decline in the birth rate during the past decade as compared with the higher birth rates of the fifties. The fastest growing group was that aged 15 to 24 years, which increased 56 percent. This was in line with a national trend caused by the entry into this age group of the large numbers of persons born during the "baby boom" following World War II.

The population of Negro and other races was significantly younger on the average than the white population. Only 47 percent of this group was age 25 and over, whereas 58 percent of the white population was in this category. Only 5 percent of Negro and other races was 65 years of age and over, whereas 10 percent of the white population was in this group.

Standard Metropolitan Statistical Areas

New Jersey has six standard metropolitan statistical areas (SMSA's) which are completely within the State boundaries. Portions of New Jersey are included in three metropolitan areas with central cities outside of the State: the Philadelphia, Pa.-N.J. SMSA, the Allentown-Bethlehem-Easton, Pa.-N.J. SMSA, and the Wilmington, Del.-N.J.-Md. SMSA. Of the six SMSA's completely within the State, Newark is the largest, with 1.9 million population in 1970. However, the Newark SMSA, the Jersey City SMSA, and the Paterson-Clifton-Passaic SMSA are part of a single urban complex extending through much of Northeastern New Jersey. Together with Middlesex and Somerset Counties, these three SMSA's make up the New Jersey portion of the New York-Northeastern New Jersey Standard Consolidated Area, with 4.6 million population in 1970, an increase of 13 percent over the 1960 population. This was about the same as the national average but below the average of 17 percent for all SMSA's. The Newark SMSA increased 10 percent, the Jersey City SMSA decreased slightly, while the Paterson-Clifton-Passaic SMSA increased 14.5 percent. Growth rates in all three SMSA's differ greatly by race, with the Negro population growing much more rapidly than the white population. The fastest growth in Northeastern New Jersey occurred in Middlesex and Somerset Counties, with a population increase of 204,000, or 35 percent, and a large net inmigration (120,000). Of the remaining three SMSA's, the resort center of Atlantic City had the slowest growth rate at 9 percent. The Trenton SMSA (the State capital) increased

14 percent while the Vineland-Millville-Bridgeton SMSA increased by nearly 14 percent.

Of New Jersey's 6.3 million metropolitan population, over 1 million reside in three SMSA's with central cities outside of the State. Included in the Philadelphia SMSA are three New Jersey counties, (Burlington, Camden, and Gloucester) with a combined population of 952,000 in 1970. Between 1960 and 1970, these three counties increased by 201,000, or 27 percent. One-half of this growth (100,000) was due to net inmigration.

The Wilmington SMSA includes Salem County, New Jersey. Its population of 60,000 in 1970 is only slightly larger than the 1960 population. Warren County, which is included in the Allentown-Bethlehem-Easton SMSA, experienced more rapid growth at 17 percent for the decade, with a net inmigration of 10 percent.

Counties

Of the 21 counties in New Jersey all but Hudson County (the Jersey City SMSA) gained population between 1960 and 1970. In the Nation as a whole slightly more than half of all counties gained population during the decade. Sixteen counties in New Jersey had rates of growth at least as rapid as the national average (13.3 percent) while 17 had net inmigration. This is far larger a proportion gaining inmigrants than in the Nation generally (less than one-third).

Of the metropolitan counties in New Jersey, those containing central cities grew more slowly than suburban counties, following a nationwide pattern. However, Salem County, part of the Wilmington SMSA, grew only 3 percent and Union County, adjacent to the city of Newark, grew 8 percent, slower than some central counties, but faster than Essex County, its own central county.

Just South of the Newark SMSA are two counties, Middlesex and Somerset, discussed previously as part of the New York-Northeastern New Jersey Standard Consolidated Area. Although they have a large urban population which is growing rapidly, they contain no incorporated city of 50,000 or more to qualify as SMSA's, and their work population does not commute to any nearby SMSA in sufficiently large proportions to be included in an existing SMSA.

The population in nonmetropolitan counties in New Jersey grew rapidly during the decade. East of Middlesex County lies Monmouth County, which, with 459,000 population, enjoys the distinction of having the largest population of any nonmetropolitan county in the Nation. Like Middlesex and Somerset Counties, Monmouth County is overwhelmingly urban and grew rapidly during the decade, at 37 percent. South of Monmouth County and also on the coast, Ocean County almost doubled its population during the decade. This county is still 56 percent rural, but population growth along the coastal areas is urban in character. At the southern tip of the State is Cape May County which grew 23 percent.

The remaining two nonmetropolitan counties lie in the northeast corner of the State. Hunterdon County, located about midway between the Newark, Allentown, and Philadelphia SMSA's, reached 70,000 population in 1970, growing 29 percent. Sussex County at the extreme northern tip of the State grew rapidly at 57 percent, reaching a population of 78,000 in 1970.

HOUSING TRENDS

General

Between 1960 and 1970 the total supply of housing units in New Jersey increased more rapidly than population. The population grew by 1,101,000, or 18.2 percent, while housing units increased by 389,100, or 19.5 percent (table B).

Table B. Housing Units by Metropolitan and Nonmetropolitan Residence: 1970 and 1960

The State Metropolitan and Nonmetropolitan Residence	Housing units					Population percent change
	Total		Change			
	1970	1960	Number	Percent		
Total..............	2,388,011	1,998,940	389,071	19.5		18.2
Metropolitan residence.....	2,021,143	1,721,160	299,983	17.4		13.0
Inside central cities....	405,199	404,415	784	0.2		-3.7
Outside central cities...	1,615,944	1,316,745	299,199	22.7		20.3
Nonmetropolitan residence..	366,868	277,780	89,088	32.1		47.1

The metropolitan areas of the State experienced less relative growth than did the nonmetropolitan part, in housing as well as in population. The number of housing units in metropolitan areas rose over the decade to 2,021,100, an increase of 300,000 units, or 17 percent; this compares with an increase of 89,100 units, or 32 percent, in nonmetropolitan areas. Metropolitan areas contained 85 percent of the housing in New Jersey, and additions to the housing supply in these areas accounted for 77 percent of the State's total housing increase between 1960 and 1970.

About 58 percent of the housing in New Jersey consisted of one-unit structures in 1970. The proportion of such units in metropolitan areas was 55 percent, and in nonmetropolitan areas, 78 percent.

The number of units in the State lacking some or all plumbing facilities in 1970 was 57,900 units, or 3 percent. The corresponding proportions in both metropolitan and nonmetropolitan areas were identical to that for the State as a whole, 3 percent (table C).

The proportion of Negro-occupied units lacking some or all plumbing in 1970 was the same both inside and outside metropolitan areas, 5 percent. Approximately 9,300 Negro-occupied units inside SMSA's and 700 outside SMSA's lacked the basic plumbing facilities.

Households were smaller in 1970 than in 1960. Average household size declined from 3.3 to 3.2 persons over the decade, in both metropolitan and nonmetropolitan areas. There were large percentage increases in one-person households, 70 percent in metropolitan areas and 101 percent in nonmetropolitan areas. Households with five or more persons increased 18 percent in metropolitan areas, and 52 percent in nonmetropolitan areas.

The median number of rooms in housing units in New Jersey was 5.2 in 1970. The 1970 median was 5.4 for both metropolitan and nonmetropolitan areas. One- and two-room units comprised a very small proportion of the year-round housing, 4 percent in metropolitan areas and 3 percent in nonmetropolitan areas. About 44 percent of the metropolitan housing units and 48 percent of units in nonmetropolitan areas had six or more rooms.

Number of persons per room is often used as a measure of crowding. In New Jersey, the proportion of housing units with 1.01 or more persons per room decreased during the decade. In 1960, 7 percent of all occupied housing units in both metropolitan and nonmetropolitan areas had more than one person per room. By 1970, the proportion of such units had decreased to 6 percent in metropolitan areas and 5 percent in nonmetropolitan areas (table C).

In 1970 as in 1960 the homeownership rate in New Jersey was 61 percent. In both years, homeownership was more prevalent in nonmetropolitan areas. About 74 percent owned their homes in nonmetropolitan areas, compared with 59 percent in metropolitan areas. Of the 1,349,800 owner-occupied units in the State, 1,150,900

Table C.   Plumbing Facilities and Persons Per Room by Metropolitan and Nonmetropolitan Residence: 1970 and 1960

The State Metropolitan and Nonmetropolitan Residence	Percent of housing units			
	Lacking some or all plumbing facilities		With 1.01 or more persons per room[1]	
	1970[2]	1960[3]	1970	1960
Total............................	2.5	6.5	6.2	7.3
Metropolitan residence...........	2.5	(NA)	6.3	7.3
Inside central cities..........	4.5	10.3	10.8	10.6
Outside central cities........	2.0	(NA)	5.2	6.3
Nonmetropolitan residence........	2.5	(NA)	5.4	6.9

NA Not available.
[1]Percent of all occupied units.
[2]Percent of all year-round housing units.
[3]Percent of all housing units.

were inside metropolitan areas and 198,900 were outside these areas.

About 33 percent of the Negro households in metropolitan areas owned their homes in 1970, compared with 46 percent in nonmetropolitan areas. Of the 72,400 Negro-homeowner households in the State, 66,200 lived inside SMSA's and 6,200 lived outside SMSA's.

Property values and rents increased during the last decade. The median value of owner-occupied homes in metropolitan areas rose 50 percent, from $15,900 to $23,900, while in the nonmetropolitan areas, value increased 53 percent, from $13,500 to $20,700. In metropolitan areas, median contract rent in 1970 was 63 percent higher than in 1960, rising from $68 to $111. In nonmetropolitan areas, the increase was 69 percent, from $68 in 1960 to $115 in 1970.

Value and rent are expressed in current dollars (the value at the time of the respective censuses). Thus, any comparison must take into account the general rise in the cost of living during the 10-year period, as well as changes in the characteristics of the housing inventory.

Standard Metropolitan Statistical Areas

In the metropolitan areas of the State, the housing supply increased by 300,000 units, or 17 percent. The Newark SMSA, the largest in the State, contained 30 percent of the housing units in the metropolitan areas and accounted for 22 percent of the increase. The Paterson-Clifton-Passaic SMSA, second largest, had 22 percent of the State's metropolitan housing and accounted for 22 percent of the increase.

The suburban areas of the State experienced greater growth in housing than did the central cities. Housing units in the suburbs increased by 299,200, or 22.7 percent, while housing in the combined central cities increased by 800, or 0.2 percent. By 1970, there were 405,200 housing units in the central cities and 1,615,900 units in the suburbs.

The proportion of the housing inventory in one-unit structures declined in both the central cities and their suburbs. In the central cities the proportion of such units declined from 27 percent in 1960 to 24 percent in 1970 and in the suburban areas from 70 to 63 percent.

In 1970, 50,400 housing units in metropolitan areas, or 3 percent of all year-round units, lacked some or all plumbing facilities. The corresponding proportions for the central cities were 4 percent and 2 percent, respectively (table C).

Approximately 4,900, or 4 percent, of the Negro households in central cities occupied units which lacked some or all plumbing facilities in 1970, compared with 4,300, or 5 percent of Negro households in suburban areas.

Average household size in the metropolitan area declined during the decade. In the central cities, the average decreased from 3.1 persons in 1960 to 3.0 in 1970, and in the suburbs, from 3.3 in 1960 to 3.2 in 1970. One-person households constituted 23 percent in the central cities and 14 percent in the suburbs.

The median number of rooms in the central cities declined from 4.5 in 1960 to 4.4 in 1970. In the suburban areas, the median remained at 5.4 rooms. While 26 percent of the housing in central cities had one to three rooms in 1970, 15 percent of the housing units in the suburbs were in this category. At the same time, 25 percent in the central cities had six or more rooms, compared with 49 percent in the suburbs.

Of all occupied units in the suburbs, 80,700 units, or 5 percent, reported more than one person per room, compared with 6 percent in 1960. In the central cities of the State, the proportion was 11 percent in 1970, as in 1960 (table C).

Homeownership in 1970 was greater in the suburban areas than in the central cities. About 65 percent of occupied units in the suburbs and 34 percent in the central cities were owner-occupied. The Negro-homeownership rate in the suburbs was 47 percent, compared with 21 percent in the central cities. Of the 66,200 Negro homeowners in the State's metropolitan areas, 22,700 lived in the central cities, and 43,500 in the suburbs.

In the central cities of New Jersey, the median value of owner-occupied housing rose 34 percent ($12,100 in 1960 to $16,200 in 1970) and in the suburbs, the median increased by 50 percent ($16,300 to $24,500). About 20 percent of the owner-occupied housing was valued in 1970 at $25,000 or more in the central cities, compared with 48 percent in the suburbs.

In 1970, median contract rent in the central cities was $96 and in the suburbs, $120. Approximately 8 percent of the renter-occupied units in the central cities and 25 percent of the suburban units had rents of $150 or more in 1970.

The homeowner vacancy rate increased from 0.8 percent in 1960 to 1.0 in 1970 in the central cities and decreased from 1.2 to 0.5 in the suburbs. The rental vacancy rate increased from 4.2 to 4.4 percent in the central cities, and decreased from 3.3 to 2.3 in the suburbs.

Population Change for Counties: 1960 to 1970

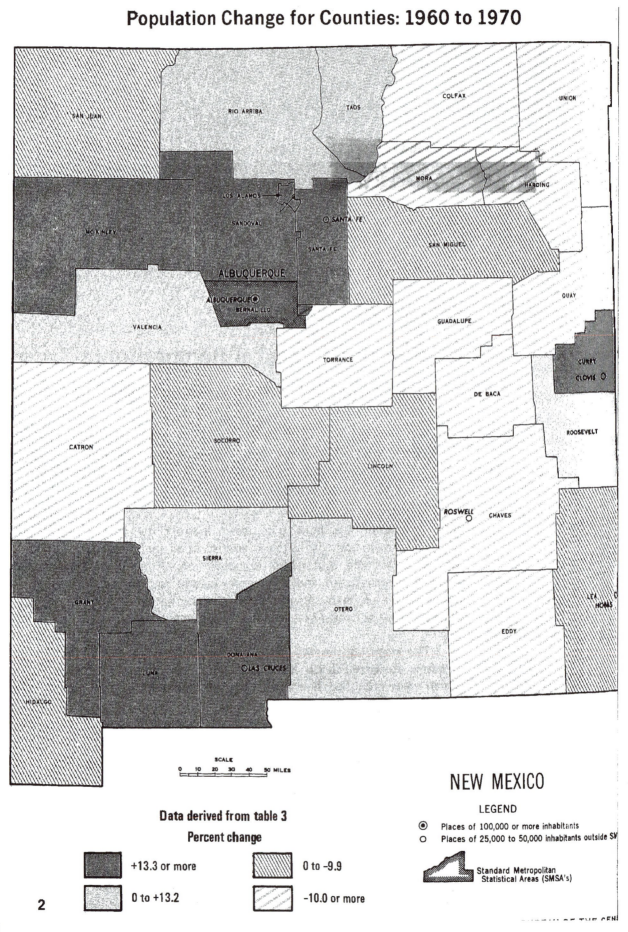

SCALE
0 10 20 30 40 50 MILES

Data derived from table 3

Percent change

NEW MEXICO

LEGEND

⊙ Places of 100,000 or more inhabitants
○ Places of 25,000 to 50,000 inhabitants outside SM

Standard Metropolitan
Statistical Areas (SMSA's)

2

■ +13.3 or more   ▨ 0 to -9.9

▨ 0 to +13.2   □ -10.0 or more

Analytical Text

POPULATION TRENDS

General

Between 1960 and 1970, the population of New Mexico grew from 951,000 to 1,016,000, resulting in an increase of 65,000, or 6.8 percent. This rate of increase is well below the rates of increase for the entire United States (13.3 percent) and for the eight states in the Mountain division (20.8 percent) in which New Mexico is located.

The total number of households in New Mexico in 1970 was 289,000, or 38,000 more than in 1960. The population living in households increased more slowly than the rate at which households increased, with the result that average household size dropped from 3.7 to 3.4 persons.

The rates of population growth in New Mexico during the 1960 to 1970 decade varied greatly by area of residence and by race. The population of the Albuquerque metropolitan area, which is the only metro-politan area in the state, increased by 20 percent from 262,000 to 316,000, while the nonmetropolitan population increased by only 2 percent from 689,000 to 700,000. As a result, the proportion of the total population living in the Albuquerque metropolitan area increased from 28 to 31 percent (table A). In the nation as a whole, about two-thirds of the population live in metropolitan areas.

The white population grew by 5 percent from 876,000 to 916,000, and the (American) Indian population, which constitutes about three-fourths of the population of races other than white, grew by 29 percent from 56,000 to 73,000. Whereas one-third of the white population lived in metropolitan areas in 1970, only about one-tenth of the Indian population lived in metropolitan areas.

The population increase of 65,000 in New Mexico in the 1960 to 1970 decade resulted from a natural increase (births minus deaths) of 195,000 and a net outmigration of 130,000 which was equivalent to 14

Table A. Population by Race and Metropolitan and Nonmetropolitan Residence: 1970 and 1960

The State Metropolitan and Non-metropolitan Residence	Population		Change		Percent Distribution	
	1970	1960	Number	Percent	1970	1960
Total...............	1,016,000	951,023	64,977	6.8	100.0	100.0
Metropolitan residence...	315,774	262,199	53,575	20.4	31.1	27.6
Inside central cities..	243,751	201,189	42,562	21.2	24.0	21.2
Outside central cities.	72,023	61,010	11,013	18.1	7.1	6.4
Nonmetropolitan residence	700,226	688,824	11,402	1.7	68.9	72.4
White...............	915,815	875,763	40,052	4.6	90.1	92.1
Metropolitan residence...	300,783	253,448	47,335	18.7	29.6	26.7
Inside central cities..	233,154	195,264	37,890	19.4	22.9	20.5
Outside central cities.	67,629	58,184	9,445	16.2	6.7	6.1
Nonmetropolitan residence	615,032	622,315	-7,283	-1.2	60.5	65.4
Negro and other races	100,185	75,260	24,925	33.1	9.9	7.9
Metropolitan residence...	14,991	8,751	6,240	71.3	1.5	0.9
Inside central cities..	10,597	5,925	4,672	78.9	1.0	0.6
Outside central cities.	4,394	2,826	1,568	55.5	0.4	0.3
Nonmetropolitan residence	85,194	66,509	18,685	28.1	8.4	7.0

percent of the 1960 population. Only three states— North Dakota, South Dakota, and West Virginia—had higher rates of net outmigration than New Mexico, and each of these states lost population between 1960 and 1970. The fact that New Mexico did not lose population, in spite of its high rate of net outmigration, is due to its high rate of natural increase which was nearly double the rate for the entire United States.

The rates of net outmigration for the white population and the population of races other than white were about equal, and thus the higher rate of population growth among races other than white was due to a higher rate of natural increase than occurred among whites. The entire net outmigration of 130,000 in New Mexico occurred in nonmetropolitan areas and was equivalent to 19 percent of the 1960 nonmetropolitan population.

The age composition of the New Mexico population changed significantly between 1960 and 1970. The largest decline occurred among the population under 5 years old and was due largely to the decline in birth rates which occurred throughout the United States during the 1960's. The greatest increase occurred in the 15 to 24 age group and was due to the entry of the large number of persons born during the post-World War II "baby boom" into this age group. As a result of these changes, the proportion of the total population in the under 5 group declined from 14 to 10 percent, and the proportion in the 15 to 24 group increased from 15 to 18 percent.

New Mexico's population has a "young" age structure. Whereas 46 percent of the United States population was under age 25 in 1970, the corresponding figure for New Mexico was 52 percent. The population of races other than white in New Mexico has a very young age structure: in 1970, 62 percent were under age 25.

Standard Metropolitan Statistical Areas

The Albuquerque Standard Metropolitan Statistical Area (SMSA), which is the only metropolitan area in New Mexico, grew from 262,000 in 1960 to 316,000 in 1970, or by 20 percent. Over four-fifths of the population growth in New Mexico during the decade occurred in the Albuquerque SMSA which in 1970 had nearly one-third of the State's population.

The city of Albuquerque, which had a population of 244,000 in 1970, and which is a major trade and financial center in the Southwest, is about six times as large as the capital city of Santa Fe, which is the second largest city in New Mexico.

The rates of population growth in the city of Albuquerque and in the balance of the Albuquerque SMSA were roughly equal during the past decade. The city of Albuquerque grew by 21 percent, and the balance of the SMSA grew by 18 percent. Nearly one-fourth of the growth in Albuquerque was due to annexation (table B).

The population of races other than white in the Albuquerque SMSA grew from 9,000 in 1960 to 15,000 in 1970, or by 71 percent. Despite this rapid rate of growth, whites constituted over 95 percent of the total population in 1970.

The population increase of 54,000 in the Albuquerque SMSA between 1960 and 1970 was due entirely to natural increase (births minus deaths).

Counties

Of the 32 counties in New Mexico, 15 gained population and 17 lost population between 1960 and 1970. (In the nation as a whole, slightly more than half of all counties gained population during the decade.) Nine counties, including Bernalillo County which is coterminous with the Albuquerque SMSA, had growth rates above the national average, and 11 counties experienced population losses exceeding 10 percent.

Only three counties in New Mexico had a net inmigration of population between 1960 and 1970. In two of these counties—Bernalillo and Grant—net inmigration was small, and the fact that the rates of growth in these counties were above the national average was due to rates of natural increase well above the rate of natural increase in the nation as a whole.

Table B.   Change in Population of Central Cities Through Annexation: 1960 to 1970

| Central Cities | 1970 population | | | 1960 population | Change 1960 to 1970 in 1960 area |
	Total	In 1960 area	In annexed area		
Albuquerque................	243,751	234,036	9,715	201,189	32,847

Sierra County experienced a natural decrease (i.e., deaths exceeded births) during the decade, and the population increased by only 12 percent. The natural decrease is due to an old age structure. In Sierra County in 1970, 25 percent of the population were age 65 and over compared to 10 percent in the nation as a whole. The old age structure in Sierra County is due to the presence of mineral springs which attract elderly inmigrants for health-related reasons.

Of the 32 counties in New Mexico, 18 had rates of net outmigration equivalent to 20 percent or more of the 1960 population. The greatest net outmigration, both numerically and proportionately, occurred in Chavez County in which the population declined from 58,000 in 1960 to 43,000 in 1970, or by 25 percent. Net outmigration during the decade was 26,000 which was equivalent to 45 percent of the 1960 population. The economy of southeastern New Mexico, and of Chavez County in particular, was set back by the closing of Walker Air Force Base and declines in oil and mineral production.

HOUSING TRENDS

General

During the decade the total supply of housing units in New Mexico increased more rapidly than population. While the population grew by 65,000, or 7 percent, housing units increased by 43,700, or 16 percent (table C).

The metropolitan area of the State (Albuquerque SMSA) experienced greater relative growth in housing, as in population, than did the nonmetropolitan part. The number of housing units in the metropolitan area rose from 76,800 to 98,600 over the decade, an increase of

21,800 units, or 28 percent; this compares with an increase of 21,900 units, or 11 percent, in the nonmetropolitan areas. While 30 percent of all housing units were in the metropolitan area, this area accounted for 50 percent of the total State increase between 1960 and 1970.

About 82 percent of the housing in New Mexico consisted of one-unit structures in 1970. The corresponding proportions in the Albuquerque SMSA and in the nonmetropolitan areas were 78 percent and 83 percent, respectively.

The median number of rooms in housing units in New Mexico was 4.7 in 1970. In the metropolitan area the median number of rooms was 5.0, compared with 4.6 in nonmetropolitan areas. While 38 percent of the housing units in the metropolitan area had six or more rooms, only 26 percent of the nonmetropolitan housing units were in this category.

Households were smaller in 1970 than in 1960. In the Albuquerque SMSA, the average household size declined from 3.6 persons in 1960 to 3.3 in 1970, and in nonmetropolitan areas, from 3.7 persons to 3.5. There were large percentage increases in one-person households, 101 percent in the metropolitan area and 46 percent in nonmetropolitan areas. Households with three or more persons showed relatively small gains in the metropolitan area and losses in nonmetropolitan areas.

In 1970, 11 percent of the housing in New Mexico lacked some or all plumbing facilities. The proportion of housing units lacking some or all plumbing facilities was greater in the nonmetropolitan part of the State than in the metropolitan area, 14 percent and 3 percent, respectively.

Number of persons per room is often used as a measure of crowding. In New Mexico, units with 1.01 or more persons per room comprised 16 percent of all

Table C. Housing Units by Metropolitan and Nonmetropolitan Residence: 1970 and 1960

The State Metropolitan and Nonmetropolitan Residence	Housing units				Population percent change
	Total		Change		
	1970	1960	Number	Percent	
Total...............	325,722	281,976	43,746	15.5	6.8
Metropolitan residence.....	98,638	76,809	21,829	28.4	20.4
Inside central cities....	78,825	60,930	17,895	29.4	21.2
Outside central cities...	19,813	15,879	3,934	24.8	18.1
Nonmetropolitan residence..	227,084	205,167	21,917	10.7	1.7

occupied housing units in 1970, compared with 24 percent in 1960 (table D). The number of all such units in 1970 was 45,200, representing a decrease of about 14,100, or 24 percent, between 1960 and 1970.

Homeownership in the State increased from 65 percent in 1960 to 66 percent in 1970. In the Albuquerque SMSA, however, there was a decrease from 68 to 65 percent; in nonmetropolitan areas the proportion increased from 64 to 67 percent.

Property values and rents increased during the last decade. The median value of owner-occupied housing in the metropolitan area increased by 17 percent ($13,300 in 1960 to $15,600 in 1970), while in nonmetropolitan areas the median increased 25 percent ($9,100 in 1960 to $11,400 in 1970). In the metropolitan area, median contract rent in 1970 was 28 percent higher than in 1960, rising from $69 to $88. In the nonmetropolitan part, rent increased during the 10-year period from $54 to $65, or 20 percent.

Value and rent are expressed in current dollars (the value at the time of the respective censuses). Thus, any comparison must take into account the general rise in the cost of living during the 10-year period, as well as changes in the characteristics of the housing inventory.

Albuquerque SMSA

The central city of the SMSA (Albuquerque) experienced greater relative growth in housing than did the suburbs. Housing units in the central city increased by 29 percent during the decade, and housing in the suburbs increased by 25 percent. In 1970, there were 78,800 units in Albuquerque city and 19,800 in the suburbs.

The proportion of the housing inventory in one-unit structures declined in both the central city and the suburbs during the decade, with a more rapid decline in the central city. The proportion of one-unit structures in the central city decreased from 85 percent in 1960 to 76 percent in 1970, and in the suburbs, from 87 to 85 percent.

Housing units increased in size in both central city and suburbs during the decade. In Albuquerque, the median number of rooms increased from 4.8 to 5.0 and in its suburbs from 4.3 to 4.8.

Average household size for the metropolitan area declined during the decade. In the central city, the average decreased from 3.5 persons to 3.2, and in the suburbs from 4.1 persons to 3.8.

The proportion of year-round housing units lacking some or all plumbing facilities declined in Albuquerque city during the decade from 5 to 2 percent. Similarly, the proportion lacking some or all plumbing facilities in the suburban areas declined from 22 to 9 percent.

There was a decrease in the proportion of units with more than one person per room in the central city from 14 to 8 percent. The proportion of suburban units in this category decreased from 31 to 19 percent.

In contrast to 1960, homeownership in 1970 was greater in the suburbs than in the central city. In

Table D.   Plumbing Facilities and Persons Per Room by Metropolitan and Nonmetropolitan Residence: 1970 and 1960

The State Metropolitan and Nonmetropolitan Residence	Percent of housing units			
	Lacking some or all plumbing facilities		With 1.01 or more persons per room[1]	
	1970[2]	1960[3]	1970	1960
Total......................	10.6	20.4	15.6	23.6
Metropolitan residence...........	3.2	8.8	10.5	17.3
Inside central cities.........	1.8	5.2	8.4	14.0
Outside central cities........	9.0	22.4	19.2	30.7
Nonmetropolitan residence........	13.9	24.8	18.1	26.1

[1]Percent of all occupied units.
[2]Percent of all year-round housing units.
[3]Percent of all housing units.

Albuquerque, homeownership decreased from 69 percent in 1960 to 65 percent in 1970, while in the suburbs, there was an increase, from 65 to 68 percent.

In the central city, the median value of owner-occupied homes increased by 17 percent ($13,800 in 1960 to $16,200 in 1970), while in the suburbs the median increased by 40 percent ($9,300 in 1960 to $13,000 in 1970). Median contract rent in the central city in 1970 was 30 percent higher than in 1960, rising from $71 to $92. Rent increased in the suburban areas from $60 to $65, or 8 percent.

The homeowner vacancy rate decreased from 1.8 to 1.1 percent in the central city, but increased from 1.1 to 1.2 percent in the suburbs. The rental vacancy rate decreased from 10.1 to 5.6 percent in the central city, and from 6.6 to 5.2 percent in the suburban areas.

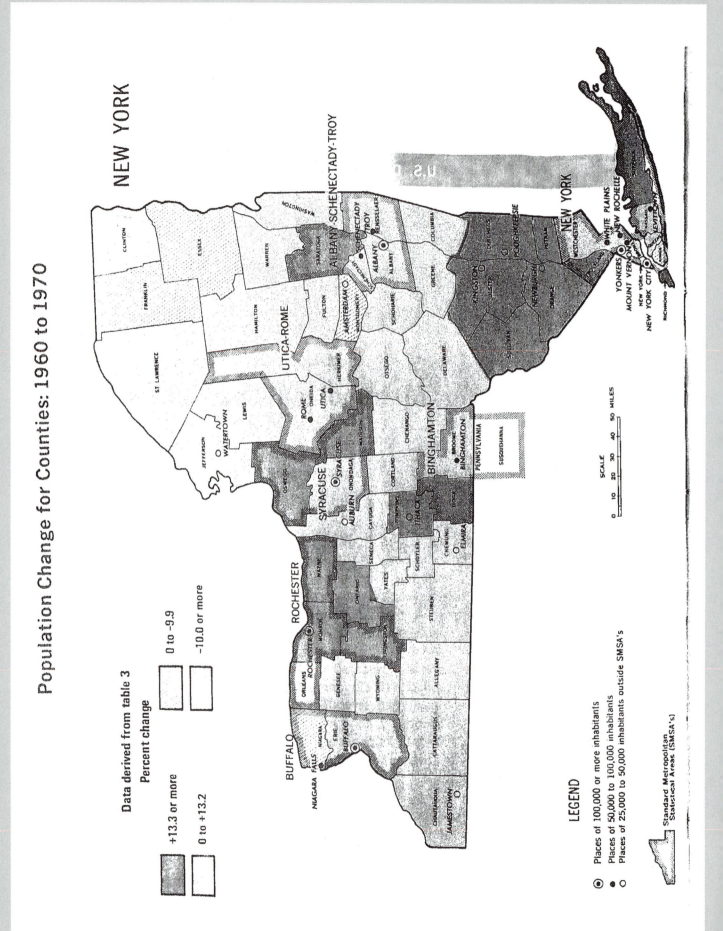

Population Change for Counties: 1960 to 1970

NEW YORK

Data derived from table 3

Percent change

+13.3 or more

0 to +13.2

0 to -9.9

-10.0 or more

LEGEND

Places of 100,000 or more inhabitants
Places of 50,000 to 100,000 inhabitants
Places of 25,000 to 50,000 inhabitants outside SMSA's

Standard Metropolitan
Statistical Areas (SMSA's)

SCALE

0 10 20 30 40 50 MILES

Analytical Text

POPULATION TRENDS

General

Between 1960 and 1970 the total population of New York increased from 16,782,000 to 18,191,000, or by 8 percent. This was the second lowest decennial rate of increase in the State's history. In the Nation as a whole, population increased by 13.3 percent over the 1960-70 decade. New York, which had been the most populous State in the Union from the time of the Census of 1800, fell to second place in 1970, behind California.

Nearly 90 percent of New York's growth occurred in metropolitan areas outside central cities. A population of 1,260,000 was added to the State's suburban areas, raising the total living there to 6,441,000 by 1970. Central cities, which in 1970 as in 1960 contained the largest population in the State, declined slightly over the decade, from 9,356,000 to 9,286,000, or by 1 percent. The proportion of New York's total population which resides in metropolitan areas was scarcely altered by these changes. In 1970 as in 1960, nearly 87 percent of the State's population was metropolitan (table A), compared to 69 percent of the national population.

The total number of households in New York in 1970 was 5,893,000 or 644,000 more than in 1960. The population living in households increased less rapidly than the rate at which households increased, with the result that average household size decreased from 3.1 to 3.0 persons.

The white population of New York State comprised 87 percent of the total population in 1970, down from 91 percent in 1960. Over 90 percent of the population of other races is Negro. Numerically the white population increase between 1960 and 1970 (503,000) comprised just over one-third of the total population growth in the State. The rate at which the white population grew (3 percent) was very much lower than that of other races which increased by nearly 61 percent, or by 905,000 persons.

Table A.   Population by Race and Metropolitan and Nonmetropolitan Residence: 1970 and 1960

The State Metropolitan and Non-metropolitan Residence	Population		Change		Percent Distribution	
	1970	1960	Number	Percent	1970	1960
Total...............	18,190,740	16,782,304	1,408,436	8.4	100.0	100.0
Metropolitan residence...	15,726,064	14,536,696	1,189,368	8.2	86.5	86.6
Inside central cities..	9,285,501	9,356,289	-70,788	-0.8	51.0	55.8
Outside central cities.	6,440,563	5,180,407	1,260,156	24.3	35.4	30.9
Nonmetropolitan residence	2,464,676	2,245,608	219,068	9.8	13.5	13.4
White...............	15,790,307	15,287,071	503,236	3.3	86.8	91.1
Metropolitan residence...	13,398,764	13,091,512	307,252	2.3	73.7	78.0
Inside central cities..	7,235,935	8,083,893	-847,958	-10.5	39.8	48.2
Outside central cities.	6,162,829	5,007,619	1,155,210	23.1	33.9	29.8
Nonmetropolitan residence	2,391,543	2,195,559	195,984	8.9	13.1	13.1
Negro and other races	2,400,433	1,495,233	905,200	60.5	13.2	8.9
Metropolitan residence...	2,327,300	1,445,184	882,116	61.0	12.8	8.6
Inside central cities..	2,049,566	1,272,396	777,170	61.1	11.3	7.6
Outside central cities.	277,734	172,788	104,946	60.7	1.5	1.0
Nonmetropolitan residence	73,133	50,049	23,084	46.1	0.4	0.3

The white population of the State grew only in nonmetropolitan areas (by 196,000, or 9 percent) and in the suburban rings of metropolitan areas (by 1,155,000, or 23 percent). Inside central cities the number of whites was reduced by 848,000, equivalent to more than 10 percent of the white population living in these cities in 1960. By contrast, a very high proportion of the growth of races other than white occurred inside the central cities of New York State (777,000 out of their total increase of 905,000). As a result, the population of Negro and other races grew significantly as a proportion of the total population of central cities, from less than 14 percent in 1960 to 22 percent in 1970, but in the suburbs and in the nonmetropolitan areas their proportion scarcely changed, growing from 3 to only 4 percent in the suburbs and from 2 to 3 percent in nonmetropolitan areas.

There was a net outmigration of 101,000 persons from New York State between 1960 and 1970, comprised of a net outmigration of 638,000 whites and a less than compensating net inmigration of 536,000 persons of other races. Within the State there was a net outmigration from the central cities of 793,000 persons, equivalent to nearly 9 percent of their total 1960 population. Other areas of the State grew in part as a result of net inmigration. More than one-half of the growth of the suburban rings between 1960 and 1970 (666,000) was produced by inmigration, but only a minor part of the growth of nonmetropolitan areas came from this source (25,000).

There were significant changes in the age composition in all areas of the State between 1960 and 1970. In both metropolitan and nonmetropolitan areas there were declines in the population under 5 years of age and declines or very little growth in the population 25-44 years old. In all areas the population 15-24 grew most rapidly. Similar changes are found in other sections of the country and are due in part to changing birth rates and in part to migration, which is highly selective by age. Low birth rates during the depression years and in the 1960's contribute to the diminution or slow growth of the population 25-44 and under 5 years, whereas the post-World War II "baby boom" is currently reflected in the large size of the population 15-24 years old.

In the central cities, where the most dramatic population changes occurred, there are great differences in the growth patterns of the white population and the population of other races. The white population, which suffered an overall loss between 1960 and 1970, had reductions in every age group except two: the 15-24 year old group, which increased by 15 percent, and the group 65 years of age and over, which increased by 8

percent. By contrast, the population of Negro and other races had very large increases at all ages, ranging from a low of 35 percent for the population under 5 years to a high of 110 percent at age 15-24. Other very rapidly growing age groups were 5-14 years (90 percent) and 65 and over (82 percent).

In 1970, less than 38 percent of the white population of New York's central cities, but one-half of the population of other races, was under 25 years of age. One of seven whites in these cities was 65 or over in 1970, contrasted with 1 of every 20 persons of other races.

Standard Metropolitan Statistical Areas

There are seven standard metropolitan statistical areas (SMSA's) in New York State. Six are located entirely within the State, and one is located partly in New York and partly in Pennsylvania (the Binghamton, N.Y.-Pa. SMSA). The SMSA's range in size from 11,529,000 population in the New York SMSA down to 268,000 in the New York portion of the Binghamton SMSA.

Each metropolitan area gained population over the decade. The highest rate of increase was attained in the Rochester SMSA (21 percent), where net inmigration was an important component of population growth. In 1970 this SMSA had a population of 883,000. The Syracuse SMSA, with a population of 636,000 in 1970, was second in rate of population increase (13 percent), and the Albany-Schenectady-Troy SMSA, whose 1970 population was 721,000 was third (10 percent). The New York SMSA grew at about the same rate as the State as a whole, 8 percent.

Only the Rochester and Albany-Schenectady-Troy SMSA's had net inmigration over the 1960-70 decade. More than 40 percent of the Rochester area's growth came from this source (64,000 of a total increase of 150,000), but less than 20 percent of the Albany-Schenectady-Troy area's growth (11,000 of a total increase of 63,000).

With the exception of Syracuse, virtually all of whose growth was produced by natural increase (the excess of births over deaths), all other SMSA's in New York State experienced net outmigration. The migratory loss from the New York SMSA was equivalent to only 1 percent of its 1960 population, but there was net outmigration amounting to 5-6 percent of the 1960 populations of the Binghamton, Buffalo, and Utica-Rome SMSA's.

All but one of the central cities in the State lost population between 1960 and 1970. New York City alone increased, at the very low rate of 1 percent. The heaviest population losses were sustained by Binghamton, which declined by 16 percent over the decade, Buffalo, which lost 13 percent of its population, and Albany, which lost 10 percent.

Every central city suffered net outmigration over the decade. The rate of loss was lowest in New York City (7 percent); in all other cities rates of net outmigration exceeded 10 percent. All central cities also had in common extensive losses of white population and substantial gains in the population of Negro and other races. Net outmigration of whites was significant in the cities of Buffalo, Rochester, Syracuse and Albany, which had rates of loss of 20 percent or more. New York City's white population was diminished by a net outmigration of 956,000, equivalent to 14 percent of the city's white population in 1960. There were significant differences in rates of natural increase by race in each city also. White rates in New York's central cities were well below the national average of 10 percent for the white population. In Albany and Buffalo, the white population had a natural increase rate of 4 percent; in New York City, 5 percent; and in Rochester and Syracuse, 6 percent and 7 percent, respectively.

By contrast, the growth of races other than white was produced by a combination of substantial natural increase (at rates ranging from 22 to 46 percent) and net inmigration (equivalent to as much as 69 percent of 1960 population). The natural increase of this racial group in New York City amounted to 267,000 for the 1960-70 decade (23 percent), while net inmigration contributed an additional 436,000 persons (38 percent of the city's 1960 total).

In consequence of these changes, in every central city there was an increase in the proportion of the total population represented by races other than white. Largest proportionate gains were realized in cities having largest numbers of Negro and other races in 1960: in New York City the percentage grew from 15 to 24; in Buffalo from 14 to 21; in Rochester from 8 to 18; and in Syracuse from 6 to 12. In the remaining central cities races other than white comprised less than 10 percent of the total population in 1970.

Both racial groups increased in the suburbs of all SMSA's during this period. In every area the suburban population of Negro and other races increased far more rapidly than the white population, but their numbers remained small and their proportion scarcely changed. In all suburbs except for New York's, this proportion in 1970 was less than 3 percent. In the New York City suburbs the population of Negro and other races grew over the decade from 147,000 to 236,000, and increased its representation there from 5.0 to 6.4 percent.

Counties

Between 1960 and 1970, 56 of the 62 counties in New York State gained population. Only 17 counties gained at rates exceeding the 13.3 percent rate of increase for the Nation as a whole. Nearly all these fast-growing counties are metropolitan, adjacent to metropolitan areas, or contain cities of substantial size (such as Poughkeepsie in Dutchess County, Newburgh in Orange County, and Kingston in Ulster County). They tend to be concentrated in two areas: eight are located in the extreme southeastern corner of the State, three of them in the New York SMSA and five just to the north of it; four others are located in the western part of the State, in and adjacent to the Rochester SMSA.

Of the six counties which lost population, three are nonmetropolitan (Essex and Franklin, located in the extreme northeastern corner of the State, and Montgomery County which connects the Albany-Schenectady-Troy and Utica-Rome SMSA's). The remaining three are the metropolitan counties of Niagara in the Buffalo SMSA and Kings County (the Borough of Brooklyn) and New York County (the Borough of Manhattan) in the city of New York. Only New York County had a population loss exceeding 10 percent.

Putnam County, which adjoins the New York SMSA on the north, had by far the fastest-growing population in the State. Between 1960 and 1970, this county increased by 79 percent. Rockland and Suffolk Counties in the suburban ring of the New York SMSA were the fastest-growing metropolitan counties: each grew over the decade by 68 percent. Net inmigration was of overwhelming importance to the growth of all three of these counties. About three-fourths of the population increase in Rockland and Suffolk Counties, but close to 85 percent of Putnam County's increase was due to net inmigration. In other fast-growing counties—Saratoga, in the Albany-Schenectady-Troy SMSA, which grew by 37 percent; Richmond, in New York City, which grew by 33 percent; and nonmetropolitan Dutchess County, which had a 26 percent increase in population—net inmigration was also of primary importance to population growth.

HOUSING TRENDS

General

Between 1960 and 1970, the total supply of housing units in New York increased more rapidly than population. The population grew by 1,408,000, or 8 percent, while housing units increased by 579,700, or 10 percent (table B).

About 86 percent of all housing units in the State were in its standard metropolitan statistical areas. The metropolitan areas experienced about the same relative growth in housing as did the nonmetropolitan areas. The number of housing units in SMSA's rose from 4,873,400 to 5,372,100 over the decade, an increase of 498,700 units, or 10 percent; the increase outside SMSA's was 80,900 units, also 10 percent.

About 40 percent of the housing in New York consisted of one-unit structures in 1970. Such units constituted 36 percent of all year-round housing units in metropolitan areas and 69 percent in nonmetropolitan areas.

The number of units in the State lacking some or all plumbing facilities in 1970 was 194,500 units, or 3 percent. The proportion of such units was 3 percent in metropolitan areas and 6 percent in nonmetropolitan areas (table C). Approximately 29,600, or 5 percent, of the Negro-occupied units in the State lacked some or all plumbing facilities in 1970. The corresponding proportions for inside and outside the metropolitan areas were 4 percent and 7 percent, respectively.

Households were smaller in 1970 than in 1960. In the metropolitan areas, the average household size declined from 3.1 persons in 1960 to 3.0 in 1970 and, in nonmetropolitan areas, from 3.3 persons to 3.2. The number of one-person households increased by 45 percent in metropolitan areas and by 52 percent in nonmetropolitan areas; in comparison, the number of households with five or more persons increased 11 percent in metropolitan areas and 8 percent in nonmetropolitan areas.

The median number of rooms in housing units was 4.7 for the State as a whole in 1970. In metropolitan areas the median was 4.6, compared with 5.6 in nonmetropolitan areas. About 27 percent of the metropolitan housing units and 11 percent of units in nonmetropolitan areas had one to three rooms. The proportion of units with six or more rooms was 34 percent inside SMSA's, compared with 53 percent outside SMSA's.

Table B.   Housing Units by Metropolitan and Nonmetropolitan Residence: 1970 and 1960

The State Metropolitan and Nonmetropolitan Residence	Housing units				Population percent change
	Total		Change		
	1970	1960	Number	Percent	
Total.................	6,275,552	5,695,880	579,672	10.2	8.4
Metropolitan residence.....	5,372,096	4,873,372	498,724	10.2	8.2
Inside central cities....	3,416,821	3,284,830	131,991	4.0	-0.8
Outside central cities...	1,955,275	1,588,542	366,733	23.1	24.3
Nonmetropolitan residence..	903,456	822,508	80,948	9.8	9.8

Number of persons per room is often used as a measure of crowding. In New York, both the number and proportion of housing units with 1.01 or more persons per room decreased during the decade. In 1960, 10 percent of all occupied housing units in metropolitan areas and 6 percent in nonmetropolitan areas had 1.01 or more persons per room. By 1970, the proportion of such units decreased to 8 percent in metropolitan areas and 5 percent in nonmetropolitan areas (table C).

The homeownership rate in New York rose from 45 percent in 1960 to 47 percent in 1970. The proportion of owner-occupied units increased from 41 to 44 percent in metropolitan areas and from 70 to 71 percent in nonmetropolitan areas. Of the 2,787,800 owner-occupied units in the State, 2,261,900 units, or 81 percent, were inside metropolitan areas and the remainder, 525,900 units, were outside these areas.

In 1970, about 19 percent of the Negro households owned their homes in metropolitan areas and 35 percent in nonmetropolitan areas. Of the 129,000 Negro-homeowner households in the State, 124,500 lived inside SMSA's and 4,500 lived outside SMSA's.

Property values and rents increased during the decade. The median value of owner-occupied units in metropolitan areas increased by 48 percent, from $16,200 in 1960 to $23,900 in 1970; in nonmetropolitan areas value increased 45 percent, from $10,600 to $15,400. In metropolitan areas, median contract rent in 1970 was 49 percent higher than in 1960, rising from $65 to $97. In nonmetropolitan areas rent increased by 48 percent, from $52 to $77.

Value and rent are expressed in current dollars (the value at the time of the respective censuses). Thus, any comparison must take into account the general rise in the cost of living during the 10-year period, as well as changes in the characteristics of the housing inventory.

Standard Metropolitan Statistical Areas

In the metroplitan areas of the State, the housing supply increased by 498,700 units, or 10 percent. Housing units in the suburbs, which comprised 36 percent of metropolitan housing in 1970, increased by 366,700 units, or 23 percent; housing in the central cities increased by 132,000, or 4 percent. The New York SMSA contained 74 percent of the State's metropolitan housing, and accounted for 72 percent of the increase.

In 1970, about 36 percent of the housing units in the State's metropolitan areas consisted of one-unit structures. The number of units in multiunit structures increased at a faster rate than one-unit structures during the decade, 10 percent and 6 percent, respectively.

In 1970, 144,600 housing units in metropolitan areas, or 3 percent of all year-round units, lacked some or all plumbing facilities. The proportion of such units in the central cities was 3 percent and in the suburbs, 2 percent. Approximately 25,300, or 4 percent, of the Negro households in central cities occupied units which lacked some or all plumbing facilities in 1970, compared with 3,400, or 5 percent, of Negro households in suburban areas.

Table C.   Plumbing Facilities and Persons Per Room by Metropolitan and Nonmetro-
           politan Residence: 1970 and 1960

The State Metropolitan and Nonmetropolitan Residence	Percent of housing units			
	Lacking some or all plumbing facilities		With 1.01 or more persons per room[1]	
	1970[2]	1960[3]	1970	1960
Total.....................	3.2	8.0	7.6	9.3
Metropolitan residence...........	2.7	(NA)	7.9	9.7
Inside central cities..........	3.0	7.2	9.5	11.2
Outside central cities........	2.2	(NA)	5.0	6.5
Nonmetropolitan residence........	6.2	(NA)	5.5	6.4

NA Not available.
[1]Percent of all occupied units.
[2]Percent of all year-round housing units.
[3]Percent of all housing units.

Average household size for metropolitan areas declined during the decade. In the central cities, the average decreased from 2.9 persons to 2.8 and in the suburbs from 3.5 persons to 3.4.

The median number of rooms for housing units in the metropolitan areas increased from 4.5 to 4.6 during the decade. In 1970, the median in the central cities was 4.0 and in the suburbs, 5.8. While 37 percent of the housing in central cities had one to three rooms, 11 percent of the suburban housing was in this category. At the same time, 21 percent of the housing in central cities had six or more rooms, compared with 57 percent in the suburbs.

Of all occupied units in the central cities 313,400, or 9 percent, reported more than one person per room, compared with 11 percent in 1960. In the suburban areas of the State, such units declined during the decade from 6 to 5 percent (table C).

Homeownership remained far greater in the suburban areas than in the central cities during the decade. In the suburbs the homeownership rate declined slightly from 75 to 74 percent. In the central cities the proportion of owner-occupied units increased from 26 to 27 percent.

About 42 percent of the Negro households in the suburbs owned their homes in 1970; the Negro-homeownership rate in 1960 was 41 percent. In the central cities, the proportion of Negro homeowners increased from 14 percent in 1960 to 17 percent in 1970. Of the 124,500 Negro-homeowner households in the State's metropolitan areas, 98,300 lived in the central cities and 26,200 in the suburbs.

In the central cities of the State, the median value of owner-occupied housing rose 42 percent ($15,700 in 1960 to $22,300 in 1970) and in the suburbs, the median increased by 48 percent ($16,500 to $24,500). About 13 percent of the owner-occupied housing in 1970 was valued at $35,000 or more in the central cities, compared with 23 percent in the suburbs.

Median contract rent in the central cities rose 45 percent during the decade, from $65 to $94. The relative rent increase in the suburbs was 72 percent, from $72 to $124. About 19 percent of the renter-occupied units in the central cities and 35 percent of the suburban units had rents of $150 or more in 1970.

The homeowner vacancy rate decreased from 1.0 percent in 1960 to 0.7 percent in 1970 in the central cities and from 1.3 to 0.5 in the suburbs. The rental vacancy rate also decreased in these areas, from 2.6 to 2.4 percent in the central cities and from 4.7 to 3.7 in the suburbs.

Population Change for Counties: 1960 to 1970

NORTH CAROLINA

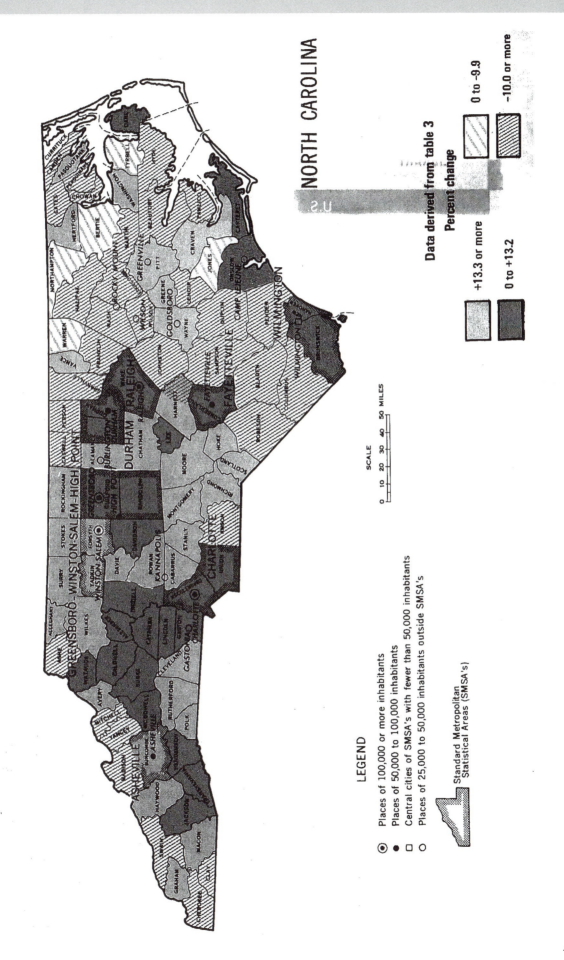

SCALE

0 10 20 30 40 50 MILES

Data derived from table 3

Percent change

+13.3 or more

0 to +13.2

0 to -9.9

-10.0 or more

LEGEND

◉ Places of 100,000 or more inhabitants

● Places of 50,000 to 100,000 inhabitants

☐ Central cities of SMSA's with fewer than 50,000 inhabitants

○ Places of 25,000 to 50,000 inhabitants outside SMSA's

Standard Metropolitan Statistical Areas (SMSA's)

PHC(2)-35
NORTH CAROLINA

General Demographic Trends
for Metropolitan Areas, 1960 to 1970

Correction Note

The key to the map showing "Population Change for Counties:
1960 to 1970" on page 2 of the North Carolina report PHC(2)-35
should be revised as follows:

Percent change

 +13.3 or more

 0 to -9.9

0 to +13.2

 -10.0 or more

Analytical Text

POPULATION TRENDS

General

Between 1960 and 1970, the population of North Carolina grew from 4,556,000 to 5,082,000, an increase of 526,000, or 11.5 percent. This rate of increase is slightly below the rate of increase for the entire United States (13.3 percent) and for the South region (14.2 percent) in which North Carolina is located.

The total number of households in North Carolina in 1970 was 1,531,000, or 326,000 more than in 1960. The population living in households increased more slowly than the rate at which households increased, with the result that average household size dropped from 3.7 to 3.2 persons per unit.

The rates of population growth in North Carolina during the 1960 to 1970 decade varied greatly by area of residence. The metropolitan population increased by 24 percent from 1,532,000 to 1,896,000 while the non-metropolitan population increased by only 5 percent from 3,025,000 to 3,186,000. As a result, the proportion of the total population living in metropolitan areas rose from 34 to 37 percent (table A). In the nation as a whole, about two-thirds of the population live in metropolitan areas.

Slightly more than one-third of the population increase in North Carolina's metropolitan population occurred in central cities. A considerable part of the growth of central cities resulted from annexation of suburban territory, however. If annexations during the decade are excluded, only about 4 percent of the

Table A. Population by Race and Metropolitan and Nonmetropolitan Residence: 1970 and 1960

The State Metropolitan and Non-metropolitan Residence	Population		Change		Percent Distribution	
	1970	1960	Number	Percent	1970	1960
Total................	5,082,059	4,556,155	525,904	11.5	100.0	100.0
Metropolitan residence...	1,896,423	1,531,589	364,834	23.8	37.3	33.6
Inside central cities..	955,746	817,880	137,866	16.9	18.8	18.0
Outside central cities.	940,677	713,709	226,968	31.8	18.5	15.7
Nonmetropolitan residence	3,185,636	3,024,566	161,070	5.3	62.7	66.4
White................	3,891,510	3,399,285	492,225	14.5	76.6	74.6
Metropolitan residence...	1,476,022	1,180,337	295,685	25.0	29.0	25.9
Inside central cities..	666,445	582,294	84,151	14.5	13.1	12.8
Outside central cities.	809,577	598,043	211,534	35.4	15.9	13.1
Nonmetropolitan residence	2,415,488	2,218,948	196,540	8.9	47.5	48.7
Negro and other races	1,190,549	1,156,870	33,679	2.9	23.4	25.4
Metropolitan residence...	420,401	351,252	69,149	19.7	8.3	7.7
Inside central cities..	289,301	235,586	53,715	22.8	5.7	5.2
Outside central cities.	131,100	115,666	15,434	13.3	2.6	2.5
Nonmetropolitan residence	770,148	805,618	-35,470	-4.4	15.2	17.7

increase in metropolitan population occurred in central cities (tables A and B).

Nearly all of the population growth in North Carolina between 1960 and 1970 occurred among the white population which increased by 492,000 or by 14 percent. The population of Negro and other races (which is largely Negro) grew by only 34,000 or by 3 percent, and as a result the proportion of Negro and other races in the State's population dropped from 25 to 23 percent. Among Negro and other races, the metropolitan population increased by 20 percent, and the nonmetropolitan population declined by 4 percent.

The population increase of 526,000 in North Carolina in the 1960 to 1970 decade resulted from a natural increase (births minus deaths) of 620,000 and a net outmigration of 94,000. The net outmigration was equivalent to about 2 percent of the 1960 population. Among whites there was a net inmigration of 81,000. Among Negro and other races, there was a net outmigration of 175,000, which was equivalent to 15 percent of the 1960 population.

The age composition of the North Carolina population changed significantly between 1960 and 1970. The only decline occurred among the population under 5 years old and was due largely to the decline in birth rates which occurred throughout the United States during the 1960's. The greatest increase occurred in the 15 to 24 age group and was due to the entry of the large number of persons born during the post-World War II "baby boom" into this age group. As a result of these changes, the proportion of the total population in the under 5 group declined from 12 to 9 percent, and the proportion in the 15 to 24 group increased from 16 to 19 percent.

The population of Negro and other races is younger than the white population in North Carolina. In 1970, 56 percent of the population of Negro and other races was under 25 years old while the corresponding figure for the white population was 45 percent.

Standard Metropolitan Statistical Areas

In 1970, there were seven Standard Metropolitan Statistical Areas (SMSA's) in North Carolina. They ranged in population from about 600,000 down to 100,000. Less than one-third of the metropolitan population in North Carolina lived in any one SMSA, and as a result the changes in metropolitan population were not dominated by changes in a single SMSA as was the case in many States. Each metropolitan area in North Carolina increased in population between 1960 and 1970 due both to natural increase (the excess of births over deaths) and to net inmigration.

The Greensboro—Winston-Salem—High Point SMSA, the largest in North Carolina now that the former Greensboro—High Point SMSA and the former Winston-Salem SMSA have been combined, grew from 520,000 in 1960 to 604,000 in 1970, or by 16 percent. About four-fifths of the growth was due to natural increase. Net inmigration during the decade was equivalent to 3 percent of the 1960 population. This rate of net inmigration was well below the rate in each of the next four largest metropolitan areas in North Carolina. The Greensboro—Winston-Salem—High Point SMSA has a diversified economy, including tobacco manufacturing (Winston-Salem leads the nation), furniture, textiles, and major commercial and financial functions.

Table B. Change in Population of Central Cities Through Annexation: 1960 to 1970

Central Cities	1970 population			1960 population	Change 1960 to 1970 in 1960 area
	Total	In 1960 area	In annexed area		
Charlotte......................	241,178	218,427	22,751	201,564	16,863
Greensboro.....................	144,076	136,421	7,655	119,574	16,847
Winston-Salem..................	132,913	98,005	34,908	111,135	-13,130
Raleigh........................	121,577	107,589	13,988	93,931	13,658
Asheville......................	57,681	55,567	2,114	60,192	-4,625
Durham.........................	95,438	76,930	18,508	78,302	-1,372
Fayetteville..................	53,510	42,020	11,490	47,106	-5,086
Wilmington.....................	46,169	35,143	11,026	44,013	-8,870
High Point....................	63,204	63,087	117	62,063	1,024

The Charlotte SMSA, one of the leading commercial and industrial hubs of the Piedmont, and the second largest metropolitan area in the State, grew from 317,000 in 1960 to 409,000 in 1970, or by 29 percent. The growth was about evenly divided between natural increase and net inmigration. Net inmigration was equivalent to about 13 percent of the 1960 population.

The Raleigh SMSA grew from 169,000 in 1960 to 228,000 in 1970, or by 35 percent. The high rate of increase was due to heavy net inmigration which was equivalent to 20 percent of the 1960 population. The Raleigh SMSA was the only metropolitan area in North Carolina in which net inmigration contributed more than natural increase to population growth during the 1960's. The rapid growth was inspired in part by the governmental functions of the city of Raleigh, the capital of North Carolina.

The University of North Carolina at Chapel Hill and Duke University at Durham, are located in the Durham SMSA which grew from 155,000 in 1960 to 190,000 in 1970, or by 23 percent. Net inmigration accounted for about two-fifths of the growth and was equivalent to 10 percent of the 1960 population.

The Fayetteville SMSA grew from 148,000 in 1960 to 212,000 in 1970, or by 43 percent, making it the most rapidly growing metropolitan area in North Carolina during the 1960 to 1970 decade. The rapid growth was due to the expansion of Ft. Bragg; however, only one-third of the growth in the Fayetteville SMSA was due to net inmigration. The Fayetteville SMSA, has an extremely "young" age structure. In 1970, 61 percent of the population was under age 25, and only 3 percent of the population was over age 65. In North Carolina as a whole, the corresponding figures were 48 percent and 8 percent. As a result, the Fayetteville SMSA had a high birth rate and a low death rate which combined to produce an extremely high rate of natural increase.

The Asheville SMSA, a major resort and the leading center of manufacturing and trade in Western North Carolina, increased in population from 130,000 in 1960 to 145,000 in 1970, or by 12 percent. One-fifth of the increase was due to net inmigration which was equivalent to only 2 percent of the 1960 population.

The Wilmington SMSA, which includes the leading port facility in North Carolina grew from 92,000 in 1960 to 107,000 in 1970. One-third of the increase was due to net inmigration, and net inmigration was equivalent to 6 percent of the 1960 population.

Counties

Of the 100 counties in North Carolina, 62 gained population and 38 lost population between 1960 and 1970. (In the nation as a whole, slightly more than half of all counties gained population during the decade.)

Twenty-seven counties had rates of growth above the national average, and six counties experienced population declines exceeding 10 percent. All 13 of the metropolitan counties increased in population, and 10 of them had growth rates above the national average.

It was noted earlier that no single metropolitan area was dominant in the total metropolitan population of North Carolina. Similarly, no single county or small number of counties dominates the total population of the State. The most populous county in North Carolina in Mecklenburg (where the city of Charlotte is located) which with a population of 355,000 in 1970, includes only 7 percent of the total for the State. None of the other 49 States has such a small percentage of its total population in its most populous county. In North Carolina, 36 percent of the population live in the nine counties with populations of 100,000 or more; 34 percent live in the 25 counties with population in the 50,000 to 100,000 range; 30 percent live in the remaining 66 counties with populations under 50,000.

Every county in North Carolina had a natural increase (i.e., births outnumbered deaths) between 1960 and 1970. In 38 counties (those losing population), net outmigration exceeded natural increase. In 30 counties, all of which gained population, there was a net inmigration; however, only three of these counties had a net inmigration exceeding 10,000: Mecklenburg County (in the Charlotte SMSA), 38,000; Wake County (coterminous with the Raleigh SMSA), 34,000; and Cumberland County (coterminous with the Fayetteville SMSA), 21,000.

The highest rate of net inmigration in a North Carolina county during the decade occurred in Watauga County. Here the net inmigration of 4,000 was equivalent to 22 percent of the 1960 population and was due largely to the rapid expansion of Appalachian State University.

Onslow County, the site of Camp Lejeune Marine Corps Base, had an unusual pattern of population change between 1960 and 1970. Despite a rate of net outmigration equivalent to 10 percent of the 1960 population, the rate of population growth in Onslow County was 20 percent, which was well above the national average. As was the case in the Fayetteville SMSA, Onslow County had a high rate of natural increase because the young age structure together with the rapid turnover of young military families was conducive to a high birth rate and a low death rate.

The six counties experiencing population declines exceeding 10 percent between 1960 and 1970 are located in the eastern half of North Carolina. The population is entirely rural and is mostly Negro. The net outmigration of Negro and other races from these counties during the decade was equivalent to 34 percent of the 1960 population.

HOUSING TRENDS

General

During the decade the total supply of housing units in North Carolina increased by 315,300, or 24 percent, while population grew by 526,000, or 12 percent (table C).

The metropolitan areas of the State experienced greater relative growth in housing, as in population, than did the nonmetropolitan part. The number of housing units in metropolitan areas rose over the decade to 608,700, an increase of 154,500 units, or 34 percent; this compares with an increase of 160,800 units, or 19 percent, in nonmetropolitan areas. While metropolitan areas contained 37 percent of the housing in North Carolina, the additions to the housing supply in these areas accounted for 49 percent of the State's total housing increase between 1960 and 1970.

About 83 percent of the housing in North Carolina consisted of one-unit structures in 1970. The number of units in multiunit structures, however, increased at a much faster rate than one-unit structures during the decade, 84 percent and 12 percent, respectively.

The size of housing units increased between 1960 and 1970. The median number of rooms rose from 4.9 to 5.0 in the State. Units with one to three rooms declined, whereas those with five or more rooms had large percentage increases over the decade.

Households were smaller in 1970 than in 1960. In metropolitan areas, population per occupied unit declined from 3.5 in 1960 to 3.2 in 1970, and in nonmetropolitan areas, from 3.8 to 3.3. There were large percentage increases in one-person households, 108 percent in metropolitan areas and 99 percent in nonmetropolitan areas. Households with five or more persons showed relatively small gains in the metropolitan areas and losses in nonmetropolitan areas.

The number of units lacking some or all plumbing facilities declined from 470,700 to 252,800, a 46-percent decrease since 1960. In 1970, the proportion of such units was 16 percent of all year-round units in the State, 7 percent in metropolitan areas, and 21 percent in nonmetropolitan areas.

Number of persons per room is often used as a measure of crowding. In North Carolina, both the number and proportion of housing units with 1.01 or more persons per room decreased during the decade. In

Table C. Housing Units by Metropolitan and Nonmetropolitan Residence: 1970 and 1960

The State Metropolitan and Nonmetropolitan Residence	Housing units				Population percent change
	Total		Change		
	1970	1960	Number	Percent	
Total................	1,638,246	1,322,957	315,289	23.8	11.5
Metropolitan residence.....	608,735	454,284	154,451	34.0	23.8
Inside central cities....	317,746	249,383	68,363	27.4	16.9
Outside central cities...	290,989	204,901	86,088	42.0	31.8
Nonmetropolitan residence..	1,029,511	868,673	160,838	18.5	5.3

1960, 14 percent of all occupied housing units in metropolitan areas and 19 percent in nonmetropolitan areas had more than one person per room. By 1970, the proportion of such units had decreased to 8 percent in metropolitan areas and 11 percent in nonmetropolitan areas (table D).

Homeownership in North Carolina increased from 60 percent in 1960 to 65 percent in 1970. In metropolitan areas there was an increase from 59 to 63 percent, while in nonmetropolitan areas the proportion rose from 61 to 67 percent.

Property values and rents increased during the last decade. The median value of owner-occupied homes in metropolitan areas increased by 58 percent, from $10,100 in 1960 to $16,000 in 1970, while in the nonmetropolitan areas, value increased 65 percent, from $6,800 to $11,200. In metropolitan areas, median contract rent in 1970 was 52 percent higher than in 1960, rising from $48 to $73. In nonmetropolitan areas, the increase was 55 percent, from $31 in 1960 to $48 in 1970.

Value and rent are expressed in current dollars (the value at the time of the respective censuses). Thus, any comparison must take into account the general rise in the cost of living during the 10-year period as well as changes in the characteristics of the housing inventory.

Standard Metropolitan Statistical Areas

The rate of homeownership was greater in the suburban areas than in the central cities of North Carolina. About 73 percent of occupied units in the suburbs in 1970 were owner-occupied, compared with 54 percent in the central cities.

In 1970, 42,200 housing units in metropolitan areas, or 7 percent of all year-round units, lacked some or all plumbing facilities. The corresponding proportion was 3 percent in the central cities, and 12 percent in the suburbs.

Of all occupied units in metropolitan areas, 47,000 units, or 8 percent, reported more than one person per room in 1970, compared with 14 percent in 1960. In 1970, the proportion of such units was 8 percent in the central cities and 9 percent in the suburban areas (table D).

The homeowner vacancy rate for metropolitan areas was recorded at 1.5 percent in 1970, as in 1960. The rental vacancy rate increased from 6.1 to 6.8.

Annexations

Annexations occurred in each of the central cities during the decade (see "Population Trends" and text table B). Such annexations affect changes in the characteristics for these central cities and their suburbs.

Table D.   Plumbing Facilities and Persons Per Room by Metropolitan and Nonmetropolitan Residence: 1970 and 1960

The State Metropolitan and Nonmetropolitan Residence	Lacking some or all plumbing facilities		With 1.01 or more persons per room[1]	
	1970[2]	1960[3]	1970	1960
Total	15.6	35.6	10.2	17.2
Metropolitan residence	7.0	(NA)	8.2	14.2
Inside central cities	2.9	13.5	8.0	12.7
Outside central cities	11.5	(NA)	8.6	16.0
Nonmetropolitan residence	20.8	(NA)	11.5	18.8

NA Not available.
[1]Percent of all occupied units.
[2]Percent of all year-round housing units.
[3]Percent of all housing units.

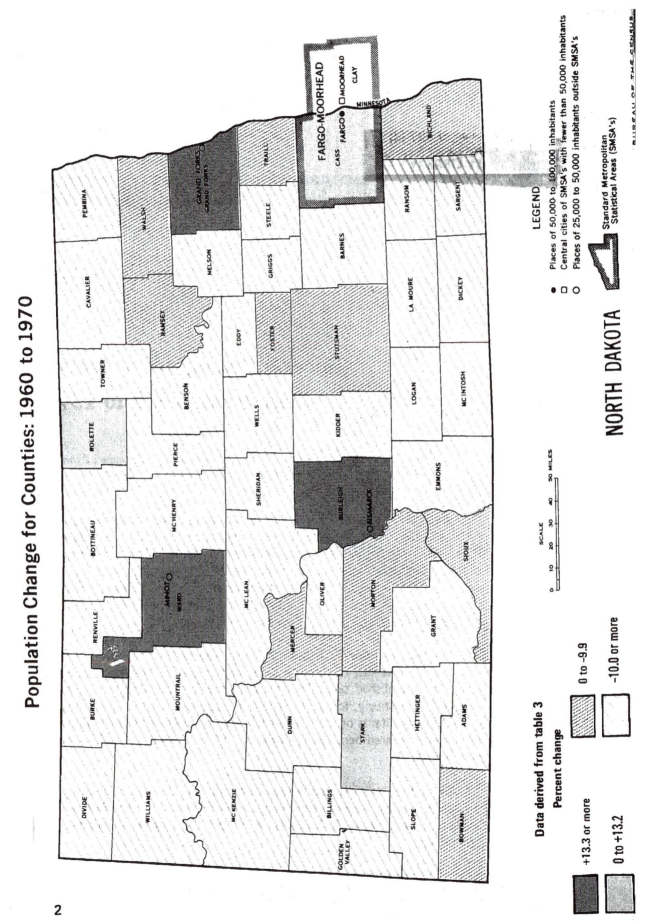

Population Change for Counties: 1960 to 1970

NORTH DAKOTA

LEGEND

• Places of 50,000 to 100,000 inhabitants
▫ Central cities of SMSA's with fewer than 50,000 inhabitants
○ Places of 25,000 to 50,000 inhabitants outside SMSA's

Standard Metropolitan
Statistical Areas (SMSA's)

BUREAU OF THE CENSUS

Data derived from table 3

Percent change

+13.3 or more

0 to +13.2

0 to -9.9

-10.0 or more

SCALE
0 10 20 30 40 50 MILES

Analytical Text

POPULATION TRENDS

General

The total population of North Dakota declined slightly between 1960 and 1970, from 632,000 to 618,000, a loss of 2 percent of the population living in the State in 1960. This decline occurred only in the nonmetropolitan areas, which show a population loss of over 21,000, or 4 percent. The State's single metropolitan area, the Fargo-Moorhead, N. Dak.-Minn. Standard Metropolitan Statistical Area (SMSA), is divided between North Dakota (Cass County) and Minnesota (Clay County). Each State contains a central city: Fargo is in North Dakota; Moorhead is in Minnesota. Somewhat more than 60 percent of the population of this SMSA is in North Dakota. Between 1960 and 1970 the population of Cass County increased by 10 percent, from 67,000 to 74,000. Neither metropolitan nor nonmetropolitan population change was great. At the time of both censuses, almost 90 percent of the population of North Dakota was nonmetropolitan (table A).

Table A. Population by Race and Metropolitan and Nonmetropolitan Residence: 1970 and 1960

The State Metropolitan and Non-metropolitan Residence	Population		Change		Percent Distribution	
	1970	1960	Number	Percent	1970	1960
Total...............	617,761	632,446	-14,685	-2.3	100.0	100.0
Metropolitan residence...	73,653	66,947	6,706	10.0	11.9	10.6
Inside central cities..	53,365	46,662	6,703	14.4	8.6	7.4
Outside central cities.	20,288	20,285	3	...	3.3	3.2
Nonmetropolitan residence	544,108	565,499	-21,391	-3.8	88.1	89.4
White...............	599,485	619,538	-20,053	-3.2	97.0	98.0
Metropolitan residence...	73,133	66,650	6,483	9.7	11.8	10.5
Inside central cities..	52,942	46,436	6,506	14.0	8.6	7.3
Outside central cities.	20,191	20,214	-23	-0.1	3.3	3.2
Nonmetropolitan residence	526,352	552,888	-26,536	-4.8	85.2	87.4
Negro and other races	18,276	12,908	5,368	41.6	3.0	2.0
Metropolitan residence...	520	297	223	75.1	0.1	...
Inside central cities..	423	226	197	87.2	0.1	...
Outside central cities.	97	71	26	36.6	...	...
Nonmetropolitan residence	17,756	12,611	5,145	40.8	2.9	2.0

The growth of Cass County between 1960 and 1970 was concentrated in the central city of Fargo, whose population increased by 6,700, or 14 percent. This increase was produced entirely by annexation of suburban territory, however. Without it, Fargo city would have shown a population loss (table B).

The total number of households in the State increased by 5 percent during the decade, from a total of 173,000 in 1960 to 182,000 in 1970. At the same time, the population living in households decreased. As a result, average household size dropped from 3.6 persons in 1960 to 3.3 in 1970.

At the time of both censuses more than 96 percent of the population of North Dakota was white. The balance, which is mainly Indian, is more highly concentrated in the nonmetropolitan areas of the State than is the white population. Less than 3 percent of races other than white were living in the SMSA in 1970, compared to 12 percent of the white population.

The growth patterns of the two racial groups are substantially different. North Dakota's overall population loss was produced by the white population, which declined over the decade by 20,000 persons, or 3 percent. The population of other races, by contrast, increased by more than 5,000 persons, or 42 percent. The white population decline was the result of an extensive net outmigration of nearly 95,000 persons, equivalent to 15 percent of the white population living in the State in 1960 (see table 3). The growth of other races, however, was due entirely to their own natural increase (the excess of births over deaths).

In both the metropolitan and the nonmetropolitan areas, there was a substantial excess of births over deaths during the decade. At the same time, both areas show net outmigration, the largest being noted in nometropolitan areas (nearly 93,000, compared to 2,000 for metropolitan areas).

There were significant changes in the age composition of North Dakota's population between 1960 and 1970 (see table 4). In the State as a whole, there were reductions in the numbers of pre-school and school age children, amounting to 36 percent and 3 percent, respectively. There was also a reduction of 11 percent in the number of adults 25 to 44 years of age. All other age groups increased, notably 15 to 24 year olds, which grew by 26 percent, and the group 65 years of age and over, which increased by 13 percent. State and nonmetropolitan rates of change are nearly identical. In the SMSA, there was a reduction only in young children under 5 years of age. All other age groups increased. In number and in rate, the greatest increases were in young adults 15 to 24 years old and in the elderly population 65 and over.

Similar changes are found in other sections of the country and are due in part to changing birth rates and in part to migration which is highly selective by age. Low birth rates during the 1960's and the depression years contribute to the diminution of the population under 5 and 25 to 44 years of a age, whereas the post-World War II "baby boom" is currently reflected in the large size of the population 15 to 24 years old.

Counties

North Dakota's 53 counties range in size from a population of 1,200 (Billings County) to 74,000 in the State's single metropolitan county (Cass). Only five nonmetropolitan counties had populations exceeding 20,000 in 1970. The largest of these, Grand Forks County, had a population 61,000 in 1970. In this county are located the city of Grand Forks, containing two-thirds of the county's population, as well as the University of North Dakota and a large military base. Other large counties are: Ward (59,000 population),

Table B.   Change in Population of Central Cities Through Annexation: 1960 to 1970

| Central Cities | 1970 population | | | 1960 population | Change 1960 to 1970 in 1960 area |
	Total	In 1960 area	In annexed area		
Fargo.........................	53,365	45,877	7,488	46,662	-785

which contains the city of Minot (32,000 population) and is the site of a college and military base; Burleigh, whose population of 41,000 is heavily concentrated in the State capital of Bismarck; Stutsman (24,000 population) and Morton (20,000 population), containing, respectively, the cities of Jamestown and Mandan.

During the decade, only six counties in North Dakota increased in population. Of these, Grand Forks, Ward, and Burleigh Counties increased at rates exceeding the 13.3 percent rate of growth for the Nation as a whole (see map). The metropolitan county of Cass, whose population increase amounted to 10 percent, ranks fourth in rate of growth. Of the 47 counties which show population losses for the decade, all but 10 lost 10 percent or more their 1960 populations.

All counties in North Dakota had more births than deaths in the intercensal period, but net outmigration played a far more important role in population change throughout the State. Fifty-one counties experienced net outmigration in this period, 49 of which had losses equivalent to 10 percent or more of their total 1960 populations. Only Grand Forks and Burleigh Counties gained population through net inmigration, but these gains were minor,   amounting to 3.2 percent and 1.5 percent of their respective 1960 populations.

HOUSING TRENDS

General

During the decade, the total supply of housing units in North Dakota increased by 9,600, or 5 percent, while the population decreased by 15,000, or 2 percent (table C).

The metropolitan area of the State (North Dakota part of the Fargo-Moorhead, N. Dak.-Minn. SMSA) experienced greater relative growth in housing than did the nonmetropolitan area. The number of housing units in the metropolitan portion rose from 20,700 to 24,300 over the decade, an increase of 3,600 units, or 17 percent; this compares with an increase of 6,000 units, or 3 percent, in the nonmetropolitan area. While the metropolitan area contained 12 percent of the housing in North Dakota, the additions to the housing supply in this area accounted for 37 percent of the State's total housing increase between 1960 and 1970.

A trend toward smaller households is evident in the State. Average household size declined from 3.6 persons in 1960 to 3.3 in 1970. Households consisting of one or two persons experienced large gains, while the number of larger households declined.

Table C. Housing Units by Metropolitan and Nonmetropolitan Residence: 1970 and 1960

The State Metropolitan and Nonmetropolitan Residence	Housing units				Population percent change
	Total		Change		
	1970	1960	Number	Percent	
Total.................	204,222	194,597	9,625	4.9	-2.3
Metropolitan residence.....	24,278	20,679	3,599	17.4	10.0
Inside central cities....	17,562	14,685	2,877	19.6	14.4
Outside central cities...	6,716	5,994	722	12.0	-
Nonmetropolitan residence..	179,944	173,918	6,026	3.5	-3.8

The proportion of units in the State lacking some or all plumbing facilities declined from 33 percent in 1960 to 14 percent in 1970.

Number of persons per room is often used as a measure of crowding. In North Dakota, both the number and proportion of housing units with 1.01 or more persons per room decreased during the decade. In 1960, 13 percent of all occupied units in metropolitan areas and 16 percent in nonmetropolitan areas had 1.01 or more persons per room. By 1970, the proportion of such units decreased to 7 percent in metropolitan areas and 9 percent in the nonmetropolitan area (table D).

Homeownership rates in North Dakota were identical in 1960 and 1970, 68 percent. Estimated value of housing increased from a median of $9,800 in 1960 to $13,200 in 1970, with decreases in homes valued at less than $15,000, and large percentage increases in those valued at $20,000 or more. In the State, rents increased from $58 to $77 with decreases in the number of units renting for less than $80 and large percentage increases in those renting at $100 or more.

Value and rent are expressed in current dollars (the value at the time of the respective censuses). Thus, any comparison must take into account the general rise in the cost of living during the 10-year period as well as changes in the characteristics of the housing inventory.

Standard Metropolitan Statistical Area
The North Dakota Part

The Fargo-Moorhead, N. Dak.-Minn. SMSA contained 38,200 housing units in 1970, a 20-percent increase over the decade. Of these, 24,300 units, or 64 percent, were located in North Dakota, i.e., Fargo central city and its suburbs, with the remainder (13,900, or 36 percent) in Minnesota, i.e., Moorhead central city and its suburbs. Of the 24,300 units in the North Dakota part of the SMSA, 17,600, or 72 percent, were located in Fargo city. The increase over the 1960 inventory in Fargo was the same as for the entire SMSA, 20 percent.

Households were smaller in 1970 than in 1960. In the North Dakota part of the SMSA, average household size declined from 3.4 persons in 1960 to 3.1 in 1970.

In 1970, as in 1960, 59 percent of the occupied units in the metropolitan area of North Dakota were owner-occupied. The median value of owner-occupied housing in the North Dakota part of the SMSA increased by 40 percent during the past decade, from $13,200 in 1960 to $18,500 in 1970. There was a decline in the number of units valued below $15,000, and relatively large increases in the number of units valued above $20,000. Median contract rent in the North Dakota part of the SMSA increased by 40 percent, from $65 in 1960 to $91 in 1970.

In both Fargo city and its North Dakota suburbs, one-unit structures comprised the largest proportion of all year-round housing units, 52 percent for the city and 70 percent for the suburban area.

There was a decrease in the proportion of units in the North Dakota part of the metropolitan area lacking some or all plumbing facilities, from 19 percent in 1960 to 9 percent in 1970. The corresponding proportion in 1970 was 7 percent in Fargo, compared with 13 percent in its suburbs. Of all occupied units in Fargo, 1,100

Table D.   Plumbing Facilities and Persons Per Room by Metropolitan and Nonmetropolitan Residence: 1970 and 1960

The State Metropolitan and Nonmetropolitan Residence	Percent of housing units			
	Lacking some or all plumbing facilities		With 1.01 or more persons per room[1]	
	1970[2]	1960[3]	1970	1960
Total.....................	13.8	33.1	9.1	15.4
Metropolitan residence...........	8.7	18.7	6.7	12.7
Inside central cities..........	7.3	13.2	6.3	12.1
Outside central cities........	12.5	32.2	7.9	14.2
Nonmetropolitan residence.......	14.5	34.8	9.5	15.7

[1]Percent of all occupied units.
[2]Percent of all year-round housing units.
[3]Percent of all housing units.

7

units, or 6 percent, reported more than one person per room in 1970, compared with 8 percent in the suburbs.

The homeowner vacancy rate in the North Dakota part of the SMSA decreased, from 1.5 percent in 1960 to 1.1 percent in 1970, while the rental vacancy rate increased, from 5.6 to 6.5.

Annexation

Annexation occurred in the central city of Fargo during the decade (see "Population Trends" and text table B). Such annexation affects changes in the characteristics for the central city and its suburbs.

Population Change for Counties: 1960 to 1970

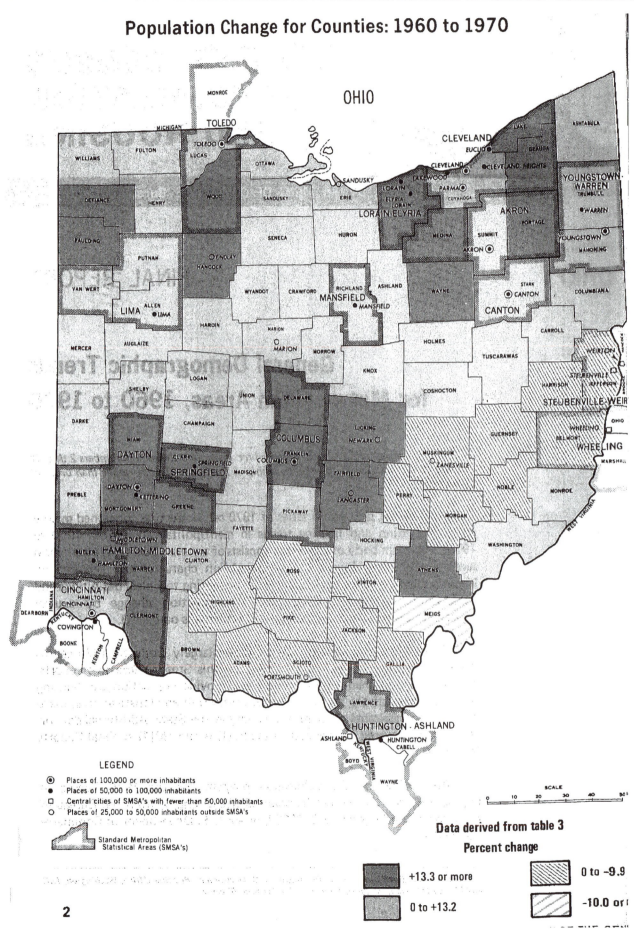

LEGEND

⊙ Places of 100,000 or more inhabitants
• Places of 50,000 to 100,000 inhabitants
□ Central cities of SMSA's with fewer than 50,000 inhabitants
○ Places of 25,000 to 50,000 inhabitants outside SMSA's

Standard Metropolitan
Statistical Areas (SMSA's)

Data derived from table 3

Percent change

▓ +13.3 or more	▨ 0 to -9.9
▒ 0 to +13.2	▨ -10.0 or l

2

Analytical Text

POPULATION TRENDS

General

Between 1960 and 1970 the population of Ohio grew from 9,706,000 to 10,652,000, or by 10 percent. This was a lower rate of increase than for the United States as a whole (13 percent) or for each of the other four States in the East Central Division (Indiana, Illinois, Michigan, and Wisconsin). Among all the States, Ohio ranked sixth in population in 1970.

The total number of households in Ohio in 1970 was 3,289,000, or 437,000 more than in 1960. The population living in households increased less rapidly than the rate at which households increased, with the result that average household size declined slightly from 3.3 to 3.2 persons.

Ohio's population increase was the result of a natural increase (the excess of births over deaths) of 1,071,000 and a net outmigration of 126,000. During the 1950-60 decade, Ohio had a net inmigration of more than 400,000 and the State's total growth exceeded 1.7 million.

More than 90 percent of the total State population was white in both 1960 and 1970. The white population grew relatively slowly, by 8 percent, to a total of 9,647,000 in 1970, while the population of Negro and other races grew by 26 percent, to a total of 1,005,000. The natural increase of the State's white population (929,000) was cut back by a net outmigration of 191,000. About one-third of the growth of Negro and other races, by contrast, was produced by a net inmigration of 66,000 persons, while natural increase added 143,000.

In 1970, 78 percent of Ohio's total population lived in metropolitan areas, compared to 69 percent in the United States as a whole. A very high proportion of Ohio's population growth during the decade occurred in the State's 16 standard metropolitan statistical areas (SMSA's). In these areas, there was an increase of 821,000 persons, but only 124,000 in nonmetropolitan areas (table A). Within the metropolitan areas, only the

Table A. Population by Race and Metropolitan and Nonmetropolitan Residence: 1970 and 1960

The State Metropolitan and Non-metropolitan Residence	Population 1970	Population 1960	Change Number	Change Percent	Percent Distribution 1970	Percent Distribution 1960
Total...............	10,652,017	9,706,397	945,620	9.7	100.0	100.0
Metropolitan residence...	8,272,512	7,451,277	821,235	11.0	77.7	76.8
Inside central cities..	3,429,005	3,501,333	-72,328	-2.1	32.2	36.1
Outside central cities.	4,843,507	3,949,944	893,563	22.6	45.5	40.7
Nonmetropolitan residence	2,379,505	2,255,120	124,385	5.5	22.3	23.2
White...............	9,646,997	8,909,698	737,299	8.3	90.6	91.8
Metropolitan residence...	7,313,606	6,695,488	618,118	9.2	68.7	69.0
Inside central cities..	2,610,973	2,831,470	-220,497	-7.8	24.5	29.2
Outside central cities.	4,702,633	3,864,018	838,615	21.7	44.1	39.8
Nonmetropolitan residence	2,333,391	2,214,210	119,181	5.4	21.9	22.8
Negro and other races	1,005,020	796,699	208,321	26.1	9.4	8.2
Metropolitan residence...	958,906	755,789	203,117	26.9	9.0	7.8
Inside central cities..	818,032	669,863	148,169	22.1	7.7	6.9
Outside central cities.	140,874	85,926	54,948	63.9	1.3	0.9
Nonmetropolitan residence	46,114	40,910	5,204	12.7	0.4	0.4

suburban population grew (by 23 percent), while central city populations declined slightly, by 72,000 (2 percent).

Ohio's net outmigration of 126,000 was the result of net outmovement from both metropolitan (40,000) and nonmetropolitan areas (86,000). The greatest net out-migration was experienced by central cities, which lost a population of 460,000 as a result. The suburban rings were the only areas to grow as a result of inmigration; between 1960 and 1970 net inmigration added a population of 419,000, equivalent to almost 11 percent of the total 1960 population in the suburbs.

The white population and other races alike increased much more rapidly in metropolitan than in nonmetro-politan areas. Eighty-four percent of the white increase and virtually all of the increase in other races occurred in metropolitan areas. While white growth was totally concentrated in the suburban rings (839,000) nearly three-fourths of the growth of other races took place in the central cities (148,000 persons). By contrast, whites in central cities declined by nearly one-quarter of a million persons, or 8 percent, between 1960 and 1970. Although races other than white living in suburban areas increased three times as rapidly as whites (by 64 percent compared to 22 percent for whites), the numerical increase of this group was small (55,000) compared to that of the white population. Consequently, the position of Negroes and other races in the suburbs scarcely changed, growing from 2 to 3 percent of total popu-lation there. In central cities, however, the proportion represented by Negro and other races grew more significantly, from 19 percent in 1960 to 24 percent in 1970.

Ohio's age distribution changed considerably over the decade. The population under 5 years declined by nearly 20 percent and 25 to 44 year olds by 3 percent. All other age groups grew, notably the 15 to 24 year old population, which increased by 48 percent. This pattern was repeated in metropolitan and nonmetropolitan areas alike.

Similar changes are found in other sections of the country and are due in part to changing birth rates and in part to migration, which is highly selective by age. Low birth rates during the depression years and in the 1960's contribute to the diminution of age groups 25-44 and under 5 years, whereas the post-World War II "baby boom" is currently reflected in the large size of the population 15-24 years old.

Standard Metropolitan Statistical Areas

There are 16 standard metropolitan statistical areas (SMSA's) in Ohio. Eleven of them lie entirely within the State. Eighty percent or more of the populations of the Cincinnati, Ohio-Ky.-Ind. SMSA and the Toledo, Ohio-Mich. SMSA are located in the State of Ohio, and nearly 60 percent of the Steubenville-Weirton, Ohio-W. Va. SMSA. Less than one-half (44 percent) of the population of the Wheeling, W. Va.-Ohio SMSA is in Ohio, and only about one-fifth (22 percent) of the population of the Huntington-Ashland, W. Va.-Ky.-Ohio SMSA.

There are two large metropolitan complexes in the State: one is in the Northeast, consisting of the five SMSA's of Cleveland, Akron, Canton, Lorain-Elyria, and Youngstown-Warren with a combined population of nearly 4 million; the other is in the Southwest corner of the State, along the Kentucky and Indiana borders, and consists of the four SMSA's of Cincinnati, Dayton, Hamilton-Middletown, and Springfield whose combined population exceeds 2.3 million. A smaller complex, consisting of the Wheeling SMSA and the Steubenville-Weirton SMSA is in the eastern part of the State, along the West Virginia border. The remaining five SMSA's are: Toledo, on Lake Erie and the Michigan border in the North; Lima in the Northwest; Mansfield and Columbus in the center of the State; and Huntington-Ashland, in the Southeastern corner of Ohio, straddling the West Virginia border.

The largest SMSA in the State of Ohio is the 4-county Cleveland SMSA, which is noted primarily as a port and center of heavy manufacturing. The area, 12th largest in the United States, contained a population of 2,064,000 in 1970. Its population increased by 155,000 between 1960 and 1970, or by 8 percent. The population of the four contiguous SMSA's adjacent to Cleveland in combination amounted to 1,844,000: Akron in 1970 had a population of 679,000; Canton, 372,000; Lorain-Elyria, 257,000; and Youngstown-Warren, 536,000. These four SMSA's grew at varying rates during the decade, from 5 percent in Youngstown-Warren to 18 percent in Lorain-Elyria, making it one of the fastest growing SMSA's in the State. Each of these SMSA's is dominated by the automotive industry.

The second metropolitan complex, located in the southwestern corner of Ohio, consists of the second largest SMSA in the State, Cincinnati (1970 population of the Ohio portion was 1,105,000), the Hamilton-Middletown SMSA (population 226,000), the Dayton SMSA (population 850,000), and the Springfield SMSA (population 157,000). With the exception of the Cincinnati area, which increased by 8 percent, these SMSA's were among the fastest growing in the State, with rates of increase ranging from 14 percent in Hamilton-Middletown to 20 percent in Springfield. Located on the Ohio River, Cincinnati has long been an important transportation center. The adjacent SMSA's have some manufacturing, and are service centers for the surrounding area.

The Columbus SMSA, the State capital, had the third largest population in 1970, and the fastest rate of growth of any of Ohio's metropolitan areas. Between 1960 and 1970, the population increased by 21 percent, from 755,000 to 916,000. Of the six SMSA's in Ohio which grew as a result of net inmigration over the decade, the Columbus SMSA had the largest net inmigration, of 50,000 persons, equivalent to almost 7 percent of its 1960 population. The Cleveland and Cincinnati SMSA's, in contrast, had net outmigration during this period.

The Dayton SMSA, with a 1970 population of 850,000, also grew at a rapid rate over the decade (by 17 percent). Net inmigration added 25,000 persons to the SMSA's population. Dayton is a manufacturing center and contains a large Air Force base (Wright-Patterson).

The Ohio portion of the Toledo, Ohio-Mich. SMSA had a 1970 population of 574,000, up 8 percent from 1960. There was a small net outmigration from the area during the decade, amounting to less than 10,000 persons. Toledo is a port and railroad center, and a glass manufacturing center.

The Lima and Mansfield SMSA's are among the smallest metropolitan areas in Ohio. Lima, with a 1970 population of 171,000, had one of the lowest rates of growth of any of the State's metropolitan areas, 7 percent. Mansfield, whose 1970 population was 130,000, grew by 10 percent. Both SMSA's experienced net outmigration.

The Ohio portions of the two contiguous SMSA's of Steubenville-Weirton and Wheeling declined slightly over the decade, by 3 and 4 percent, respectively. Both areas, which are in a bituminous coal mining district and center of the steel industry, suffered a net outmigration equivalent to over 9 percent of Steubenville-Weirton's 1960 population and 7 percent of Wheeling's 1960 population.

The small portion of the Huntington-Ashland SMSA in Ohio consists only of Lawrence County, which in 1970 had a population of 57,000. The two central cities of this SMSA are located outside the State of Ohio; Lawrence County is, therefore, one of the suburban counties of this SMSA. This county had a very low rate of growth (3 percent) produced in part by a net outmigration equivalent to nearly 8 percent of its 1960 population.

Ohio's metropolitan areas contain 17 central cities. Over the 1960-70 decade, eight of these cities grew and nine declined in population. The fastest-growing cities were Elyria (by 22 percent), Toledo (21), Middletown and Mansfield (each by 16), Columbus (by 15), and Lorain (by 13). The cities of Warren and Lima grew relatively slowly, by 6 percent and 5 percent, respectively. The rapid growth of Toledo (from 318,000 to 384,000) was produced entirely by annexation of a very large suburban population (85,000). Without this annexation, Toledo city would have shown a population loss of 19,000 and the suburbs would have shown a population gain instead of a loss (table B). Columbus city's growth (from 471,000 to 540,000) was also produced to a very large extent by annexation. During the 1960-70 decade, more than 26,000 persons were

Table B. Change in Population of Central Cities Through Annexation: 1960 to 1970

Central Cities	1970 population			1960 population	Change 1960 to 1970 in 1960 area
	Total	In 1960 area	In annexed area		
Canton....................	110,053	101,029	9,024	113,631	-12,602
Cincinnati...............	452,524	451,467	1,057	502,550	-51,083
Columbus..................	539,677	513,384	26,293	471,316	42,068
Dayton....................	243,601	240,579	3,022	262,332	-21,753
Elyria....................	53,427	52,547	880	43,782	8,765
Hamilton..................	67,865	66,708	1,157	72,354	-5,646
Lima.....................	53,734	50,225	3,509	51,037	-812
Lorain....................	78,185	75,901	2,284	68,932	6,969
Mansfield.................	55,047	47,290	7,757	47,325	-35
Middletown................	48,767	45,020	3,747	42,115	2,905
Springfield...............	81,926	78,181	3,745	82,723	-4,542
Steubenville..............	30,771	28,512	2,259	32,495	-3,983
Toledo....................	383,818	298,798	85,020	318,003	-19,205
Warren....................	63,494	61,723	1,771	59,648	2,075

transferred from the Columbus suburbs to the central city. Had this transfer not taken place, the city's population gain would have been reduced from 68,000 to 42,000, and the already considerable suburban gain (33 percent) would have been greater.

All other cities showing population gains also made annexations during the decade: Middletown's population growth (from 42,000 to 49,000), Lorain's growth (from 69,000 to 78,000), and Warren's growth (from 60,000 to 63,000) were produced to a large extent by annexation of territory; Mansfield's increase (from 47,000 to 55,000) and Lima's growth (from 51,000 to 54,000) were entirely produced by annexations, for without them the cities would have shown minor losses. Elyria's annexation, however, was very small (less than 1,000 persons were added) and population change was affected little.

Three central cities had population losses of 10 percent or more: Youngstown, which had the highest rate of loss, declined from 167,000 to 140,000, or by 16 percent; Cleveland, declined from 876,000 to 751,000 (by 14 percent); and Cincinnati dropped from 503,000 to 453,000 (by 10 percent). Cities with smaller losses were: Dayton (down 7 percent, to a population of 244,000); Akron (down 5 percent, to 275,000); and Hamilton (declined by 6 percent, to 68,000), Canton (declined 3 percent, to 110,000), and Springfield, (whose 1970 population was down only 1 percent, to 82,000), all of which lost population in spite of annexation.

Every central city, except for Toledo, Elyria, Middletown, and Mansfield, had a net outmigration during the decade. Nearly all lost 10 percent or more of their populations. Highest rates were experienced by Cleveland (24 percent), Cincinnati (22), Dayton (21), and Youngstown (21). Every city except Middletown had a net outmigration of white population. Several cities had a small net outmigration of other races (Middletown, Springfield, Cincinnati, and Cleveland), but most had an inmigration. Columbus, Dayton, Toledo, and Akron had the largest net inmigration of this population group.

The suburban populations of all SMSA's in Ohio grew over the decade, with the exception of Steubenville-Weirton and Wheeling, which had an overall population decline, and Toledo, where there was a very large annexation of suburban territory by the central city.

All central cities in Ohio had an increase in the percentage of total population of races other than white. The cities which had the largest populations of Negro and other races in 1960—Cleveland, Cincinnati, and Dayton—showed the greatest increase in the proportions represented by them. In Cleveland Negro and other races increased from 29 percent of the total population in

1960 to 39 percent in 1970; in Cincinnati, the increase was from 22 to 28 percent; and in Dayton, from 22 to 31 percent.

Suburban areas, by contrast, show little change in racial composition. The population of Negro and other races is found in significant numbers only in the suburbs of Cleveland (50,000), Cincinnati (24,000), and Dayton (21,000), but even in these SMSA's, races other than white comprise an extremely small percentage of total population (less than 4 percent in each).

The decline in the white population of Ohio's central cities affected all age groups except for the population 15 to 24 years of age, which increased 29 percent. Heaviest white losses were experienced by age groups under 5 (28 percent) and 25 to 44 years (22 percent). The growth of the population of other races was spread across all age groups except for under 5 years, which declined by 15 percent, and 25 to 44 years, which was about stationary. The most significant increases in the population of Negro and other races occurred in ages 15 to 24 (77 percent) and 65 and over (53 percent). In 1970, races other than white made up a higher proportion of the central city population at every age than they did in 1960. The proportion represented by this population group increased from 23 to almost 30 percent of children under 15; from 19 to 23 percent of the adult population 15 to 64; and from 10 to 15 percent of the elderly population 65 and over.

Counties

Of the 88 counties in Ohio, 71 gained population and 17 lost population between 1960 and 1970. Twenty-two counties had rates of growth above the national average of 13.3 percent and one county (Meigs County) had a loss of 10 percent or more. In the Nation as a whole, only slightly more than half of all counties gained population during the decade. Of the 31 metropolitan counties in Ohio, only two (Belmont County in the Wheeling SMSA and Jefferson County in the Steubenville-Weirton SMSA) lost population during the decade.

All eight counties with growth rates exceeding 20 percent are in metropolitan areas. Four counties had growth rates exceeding 30 percent: Portage County (37 percent) in the Akron SMSA, and Lake County (33), Geauga County (32), and Greene County (32) in the Cleveland SMSA. Portage County's rapid increase is in part attributable to increased enrollment at Kent State University.

Every county in Ohio had a natural increase of population (i.e., births exceeded deaths) between 1960 and 1970. During the decade, one-third (29) of the counties in Ohio experienced net inmigration. In the

Nation as a whole, 30 percent of all counties had net inmigration. In four counties in Ohio—those with growth rates exceeding 30 percent—net inmigration was equivalent to 15 percent or more of the 1960 population. The highest rate occurred in Portage County where net inmigration was equivalent to 23 percent of the 1960 population. Ten counties experienced net outmigration equivalent to 10 percent or more of their 1960 populations. The highest rate of net outmigration (16 percent) occurred in Scioto County.

In terms of absolute numbers, the largest net inmigration (47,000) occurred in Franklin County where Columbus is located, and the largest net outmigration (85,000) occurred in Cuyahoga County where Cleveland is located. In Cuyahoga County, the most populous in the State, the population grew from 1,648,000 in 1960 to 1,721,000 in 1970, or by only 4 percent.

The 17 counties in Ohio that lost population between 1960 and 1970 are all located in southern and southeastern Ohio within 75 miles of the Ohio River. Several of these counties had larger populations in 1900 than in 1970.

The only county in southeastern Ohio in which the rate of population growth between 1960 and 1970 was above the national average was Athens County. The population of Athens County changed little between 1930 and 1960, but with the rapid expansion of Ohio University, the population increased 17 percent during the past decade.

HOUSING TRENDS

General

Between 1960 and 1970 the total supply of housing units in Ohio increased more rapidly than population. The population grew by 946,000, or 10 percent, while housing units increased by 424,200, or 14 percent (table C).

The metropolitan areas of the State experienced greater relative growth in housing, as in population, than did the nonmetropolitan part. The number of housing units in metropolitan areas rose from 2,310,600 to 2,667,200 over the decade, an increase of 356,600 units, or 15 percent; the increase in nonmetropolitan areas was 67,600 units, or 9 percent. About 77 percent of all housing units were in the metropolitan areas and these areas accounted for 84 percent of the total State increase between 1960 and 1970.

About 72 percent of the housing in Ohio consisted of one-unit structures in 1970. The number of units in multiunit structures, however, increased at a faster rate than one-unit structures during the decade, 40 percent and 5 percent, respectively.

The number of units lacking some or all plumbing facilities declined from 390,400 to 178,100, a 54-percent decrease since 1960. In 1970, the proportion of such units was 3 percent in metropolitan areas and 11 percent in nonmetropolitan areas. Approximately

12,400, or 4 percent, of Negro occupied units in the State lacked some or all plumbing in 1970. The corresponding proportions for inside and outside the metropolitan areas were 4 percent and 17 percent, respectively.

Households were smaller in 1970 than in 1960. In both the metropolitan and nonmetropolitan areas, the average household size declined from 3.3 persons in 1960 to 3.2 in 1970. The number of one-person households increased by 63 percent in metropolitan areas and by 45 percent in nonmetropolitan areas. In comparison, the number of households with five or more persons increased by 7 percent in metropolitan areas and by less than 1 percent in nonmetropolitan areas.

The median number of rooms for the State was 5.3 in 1970. In metropolitan areas the median was also 5.3, compared with 5.5 in nonmetropolitan areas. About 13 percent of the metropolitan housing units and 8 percent of units in nonmetropolitan areas had one to three rooms. The proportion of units with seven or more rooms was 20 percent inside SMSA's and 25 percent outside SMSA's.

Number of persons per room is often used as a measure of crowding. In Ohio, both the number and the proportion of housing units with 1.01 or more persons per room decreased during the decade. In 1960, 10 percent of all occupied housing units in metropolitan areas and 9 percent in nonmetropolitan areas had 1.01 or more persons per room. By 1970, the proportion of such units decreased to 7 percent in both metropolitan and nonmetropolitan areas (table D).

The homeownership rate remained at 66 percent in metropolitan areas and rose from 72 to 74 percent in nonmetrpoolitan areas. Of the 2,226,000 owner-occupied units in the State, 1,685,800 were inside metropolitan areas and the remainder were outside these areas.

About 44 percent of the Negro households in metropolitan areas and 61 percent in nonmetropolitan areas owned their homes in 1970. Of the 125,900 Negro-homeowner households in the State, 119,500 lived inside SMSA's and 6,400 lived outside SMSA's.

Property values and rents increased during the last decade. The median value in metropolitan areas increased by 30 percent, from $14,400 in 1960 to $18,700 in 1970, while in nonmetropolitan areas the median increased 43 percent, from $9,400 to $13,400. In metropolitan areas, median contract rent in 1970 was 35 percent higher than in 1960, rising from $65 to $88. In nonmetropolitan areas rent increased by 40 percent, from $47 to $66.

Value and rent are expressed in current dollars (the value at the time of the respective censuses). Thus, any comparison must take into account the general rise in the cost of living during the 10-year period, as well as changes in the characteristics of the housing inventory.

Standard Metropolitan Statistical Areas

In the metropolitan areas of the State, the housing supply increased by 356,600 units, or 15 percent. The Cleveland SMSA, largest metropolitan area in the State,

Table D.   Plumbing Facilities and Persons Per Room by Metropolitan and Nonmetropolitan Residence: 1970 and 1960

The State Metropolitan and Nonmetropolitan Residence	Percent of housing units			
	Lacking some or all plumbing facilities		With 1.01 or more persons per room[1]	
	1970[2]	1960[3]	1970	1960
Total......................	5.2	12.8	6.6	9.5
Metropolitan residence...........	3.5	(NA)	6.5	9.7
Inside central cities...........	3.3	9.2	7.1	10.4
Outside central cities........	3.6	(NA)	6.1	9.1
Nonmetropolitan residence........	10.8	(NA)	6.7	8.7

NA Not available.
[1]Percent of all occupied units.
[2]Percent of all year-round housing units.
[3]Percent of all housing units.

contained 25 percent of the housing units inside SMSA's and accounted for 23 percent of the State's housing supply increase within SMSA's. The Ohio portion of the Cincinnati SMSA, the second largest area, contained 14 percent of the housing in the metropolitan areas and accounted for 12 percent of the increase. The third largest SMSA, Columbus, with 11 percent of the metropolitan housing, accounted for 17 percent of the increase.

The suburban areas of the State experienced greater growth in housing than did the central cities. Housing units in the suburbs, which comprised more than half, 55 percent, of the metropolitan housing in 1970, increased by 300,800 units, or 26 percent; in comparison, housing in the combined central cities increased by 55,800, or 5 percent. By 1970, there were 1,473,100 housing units in the suburbs and 1,194,100 units in the central cities.

In 1970, about 69 percent of the housing units in the State's metropolitan areas consisted of one-unit structures. The proportion of such units was 55 percent in the central cities and 80 percent in the suburbs.

About 93,200 housing units in metropolitan areas, or 3 percent of all year-round units, lacked some or all plumbing facilities in 1970. The proportion of such units in the central cities was 3 percent and in the suburbs, 4 percent. Approximately 8,000, or 3 percent, of the Negro households in central cities occupied units which lacked some or all plumbing facilities in 1970, compared with 2,700, or 8 percent, of Negro households in suburban areas.

Households were smaller in the central cities than in the suburbs. In the central cities, average household size was 2.9 persons compared with 3.3 persons in the suburbs. The proportion of occupied units with one-person households was 22 percent in the central cities and 12 percent in the suburban areas.

Of all occupied units in metropolitan areas, 166,800, or 7 percent, reported more than one person per room in 1970, compared with 10 percent in 1960. In 1970, the proportion of such units was 7 percent inside central cities and 6 percent outside central cities (table D).

Homeownership in 1970 was more prevalent in the suburbs than in the central cities. About 76 percent of occupied units in the suburban areas and 54 percent in the central cities were owner-occupied. The Negro homeownership rate in the suburbs was 63 percent, compared with 41 percent in the central cities.

Median value of owner-occupied housing was $16,000 in the central cities compared with $20,600 in the suburbs. About 13 percent of the owner-occupied housing in the central cities was valued at $25,000 or more, compared with 32 percent in the suburbs. Median contract rent in the central cities and the suburbs was $81 and $106, respectively. In the central cities 15 percent of renter-occupied units rented for $120 or more, compared with 41 percent in the suburbs.

The homeowner vacancy rate for metropolitan areas decreased during the decade from 1.6 to 0.8 percent, while the rental vacancy rate decreased from 6.4 to 6.1.

Annexations

Annexations occurred in each of the central cities in Ohio during the decade, except Akron, Cleveland, and Youngstown (see "Population Trends" and text table B). Such annexations affect changes in the characteristics for these central cities and their suburbs.

Population Change for Counties: 1960 to 1970

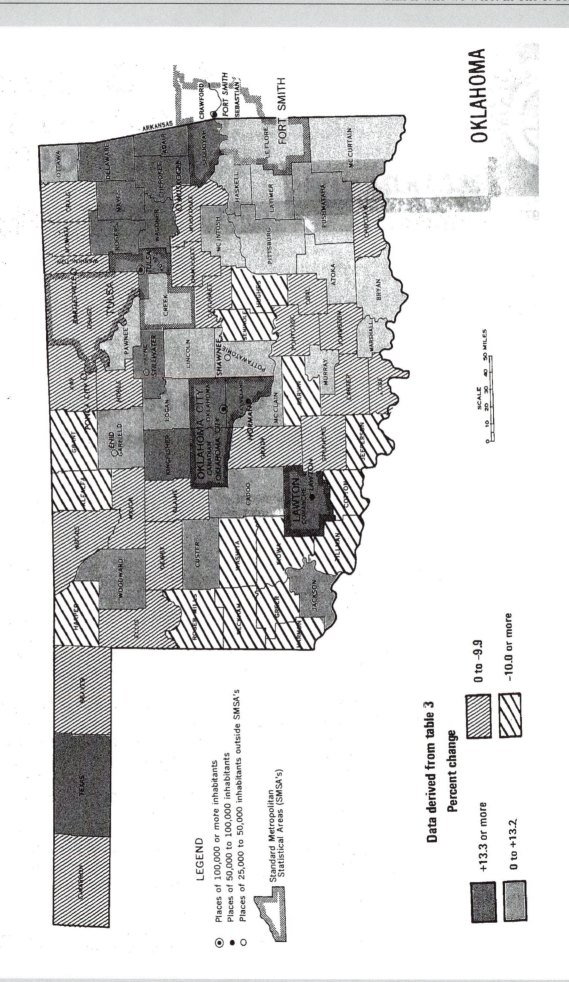

OKLAHOMA

LEGEND

Places of 100,000 or more inhabitants
Places of 50,000 to 100,000 inhabitants
Places of 25,000 to 50,000 inhabitants outside SMSA's

Standard Metropolitan
Statistical Areas (SMSA's)

Data derived from table 3

Percent change

+13.3 or more

0 to +13.2

0 to –9.9

–10.0 or more

SCALE
0 10 20 30 40 50 MILES

Analytical Text

POPULATION TRENDS

General

Between 1960 and 1970 the total population of Oklahoma grew by 231,000 persons, from 2,329,000 to 2,560,000, an increase of 9.9 percent over the population living in the State in 1960 (table A). The increase was concentrated in metropolitan areas, which accounted for 92 percent of the total increase. The nonmetropolitan population remained about the same.

The total number of households in the State in 1970 was 850,000, about 115,000 more than in 1960. The population living in households increased less rapidly · than the rate at which households increased, with the result that average household size decreased slightly, from 3.1 to 2.9 persons per unit.

The effect of these changes on population distribution by metropolitan-nonmetropolitan residence was of some significance. The proportion of the total popula-

tion living in metropolitan areas increased by slightly more than 4 percent. In 1970 one in two persons in Oklahoma lived in metropolitan areas compared to the national average of two out of three.

In 1970 as in 1960, about 90 percent of the State population of Oklahoma was white. The balance of the population was Negro and Indian, who increased at a faster rate than whites, and raised their share of the State's population from 9.5 to 11.1 percent. They increased most rapidly in the central cities of the State.

Substantial growth occurred in the State as a whole and in both metropolitan and nonmetropolitan areas as a result of natural increase. Natural increase in the State as a whole amounted to 218,000. Net inmigration was of relatively minor importance, adding only 13,000 to the State's population gain. The net inmigration was the sum of a 4,000 net outmigration for whites and a 17,000 net inmigration by Negroes and other races.

All areas of the State experienced significant changes in age composition. In the State as a whole, there was a

Table A.   Population by Race and Metropolitan and Nonmetropolitan Residence: 1970 and 1960

The State Metropolitan and Non-metropolitan Residence	Population		Change		Percent Distribution	
	1970	1960	Number	Percent	1970	1960
Total..............	[1]2,559,229	2,328,284	230,945	9.9	100.0	100.0
Metropolitan residence...	1,281,485	1,068,717	212,768	19.9	50.1	45.9
Inside central cities..	772,589	647,635	124,954	19.3	30.2	27.8
Outside central cities.	508,896	421,082	87,814	20.9	19.9	18.1
Nonmetropolitan residence	1,277,744	1,259,567	18,177	1.4	49.9	54.1
White..............	2,275,104	2,107,900	167,204	7.9	88.9	90.5
Metropolitan residence...	1,134,092	967,370	166,722	17.2	44.3	41.5
Inside central cities..	657,639	572,052	85,587	15.0	25.7	24.6
Outside central cities.	476,453	395,318	81,135	20.5	18.6	17.0
Nonmetropolitan residence	1,141,013	1,140,530	482	-	44.6	49.0
Negro and other races	284,125	220,384	63,741	28.9	11.1	9.5
Metropolitan residence...	147,393	101,347	46,046	45.4	5.8	4.4
Inside central cities..	114,950	75,583	39,367	52.1	4.5	3.2
Outside central cities.	32,443	25,764	6,679	25.9	1.3	1.1
Nonmetropolitan residence	136,732	119,037	17,695	14.9	5.3	5.1

[1]See correction note on page 8.

reduction in population under 5 years of age, from 243,000 in 1960 to 198,000 in 1970, a loss of 18 percent of the age group.

In contrast, there were substantial increases in the 15 to 24 year group. At the State level, this group increased by 36 percent, from 329,000 in 1960 to 450,000 in 1970.

Similar changes are found in other sections of the country and are the product in part of changing birth rates and in part are due to migration, which is highly selective by age. Low birth rates during the depression years and in the 1960's contribute to the diminution of age groups under 5 and 25 to 44, whereas the post-World War II "baby boom" is currently reflected in the large size of the population 15 to 24 years old.

Standard Metropolitan Statistical Areas

The populations of metropolitan areas in Oklahoma vary in size. They range from 640,000 in Oklahoma City and 475,000 in Tulsa, to 108,000 in Lawton and 55,000 in Fort Smith (Oklahoma portion). Negro and other races constitute small proportions of these populations.

Oklahoma City is the capital of the State and provides commercial and financial services for its trade area. It also carries on mining and meat production. Tulsa carries on mining and manufacturing activities; Lawton carries on financial and trade activities in its market area and is the site of a large military installation which has grown significantly over the decade. Fort Smith specializes in manufacturing, particularly furniture and fixtures, primary metals and nondurable production.

Annexation of territory during the decade was responsible for additions to the central cities of Oklahoma City,[1] Tulsa[1] and Lawton. The additions included 9,600, 93,000, and 14,300 persons, respectively (table B). Annexation by Oklahoma City pushed the growth rate for the city up somewhat, but it was

nonetheless slow (13 percent) compared to that of the suburbs (46 percent).

A very substantial annexation was made by Tulsa city which added 93,000 persons to the city's population. Without the annexation the central city would have declined in population. Similarly, Lawton city, which now shows a population increase of 21 percent, without annexation would have declined.

The age distribution of the populations of Oklahoma's metropolitan areas shows a pattern of changes similar to that described for the State as a whole. In most of the SMSA's, the population under 5 years of age declined over the decade.

In contrast, the 15 to 24 age group shows the largest increases of any age group.

Counties

Between 1960 and 1970, 38 of Oklahoma's 77 counties registered population increases and 15 of the 38 had rates of growth higher than the national average of 13.3 percent. The counties which accounted for the bulk of the State's growth are located in the eastern half of the State (see Map). The fastest growing counties were concentrated in a strip in the northeastern section of the country between the SMSA's of Tulsa and Fort Smith. These counties included Wagoner with an increase of 41.4 percent, Rogers with 37.9, Delaware with 34.6, Cherokee with 30.5 and Sequoyah with 29.8. The fastest growing county was the metropolitan county of Cleveland (Oklahoma City SMSA), which increased by 71.9 percent (from 34,000 to 82,000). Another fast growing county is Canadien, also a part of the Oklahoma City SMSA, which grew by 30.4 percent.

[1] Portions of Oklahoma City and Tulsa City are considered rural. In 1970, 9,800 residents of Oklahoma City were classified as rural, of a total population of 366,000, and 1,200 residents of Tulsa City, of a total population of 332,000. See "Extended Cities" under "Definitions and Explanations".

Table B.   Change in Population of Central Cities Through Annexation: 1960 to 1970

Central Cities	1970 population			1960 population	Change 1960 to 1970 in 1960 area
	Total	In 1960 area	In annexed area		
Oklahoma City..............	366,481	356,919	9,562	324,253	32,666
Tulsa.....	331,638	238,594	93,044	261,685	-23,091
Lawton.....	74,470	60,143	14,327	61,697	-1,554

Of the 39 counties recording population losses there were 14 which suffered declines of 10 percent or more. The largest loss, 33 percent, was experienced by Washita County in the western part of the State which had a population decline from 18,000 in 1960 to 12,000 in 1970.

There were eight small counties in which deaths exceeded births; one of these counties (Murray) had sufficient net inmigration to register a population increase over the 1960-70 period. Only eight counties had substantial net inmigration which amounted to 10 percent or more of their 1960 populations. Seven of these were the fast growing counties mentioned above. The fastest growing county, Cleveland, had the highest net inmigration rate of 53.2 percent. The eighth county was Mayes, located in the northeast, with a 10.4 percent net inmigration rate.

Twenty-three counties had sufficient numbers of Negroes and other races to have this population group shown separately in the table on county components of change (see "Definitions and Explanations"). Sixteen of these counties had population increases. Five of the sixteen had population increases despite net outmigration. The counties with large populations of Negro and other races usually recorded net inmigration. These included the metropolitan counties of Comanche with a 17.0 percent net inmigration, Oklahoma with 14.0 percent, and Tulsa with 29.3 percent.

HOUSING TRENDS

General

During the decade, the total supply of housing units in Oklahoma increased by 121,900, or 15 percent, while population grew by 231,000, or 10 percent (table C).

The metropolitan areas of the State experienced greater relative growth in housing (as in population), that did the nonmetropolitan part. The number of housing units in metropolitan areas rose from 359,600 to 450,000 over the decade, an increase of 90,400, or 25 percent; this compares with an increase of 31,500 units, or 7 percent, in nonmetropolitan areas. While almost half the housing units were in metropolitan areas, additions to the housing supply in these areas accounted for about three-fourths of Oklahoma's total housing increase between 1960 and 1970.

About 85 percent of the housing in Oklahoma consisted of one-unit structures in 1970. The number of units in multiunit structures, however, increased at a much faster rate than one-unit structures during the decade, 61 percent and 8 percent, respectively.

The size of housing units increased between 1960 and 1970. The median number of rooms rose from 4.7 to 4.9 in metropolitan areas and from 4.6 to 4.8 in nonmetropolitan areas. Units with one to four rooms declined or had only small relative gains, whereas those with five rooms or more had large percentage increases over the decade.

Households were smaller in 1970 than in 1960. In the metropolitan areas of the State, there were large percentage gains in the number of households consisting of only one or two persons and minor increases in the number of larger households. In nonmetropolitan areas, only one- and two-person households gained at all.

The proportion of housing units lacking some or all plumbing facilities decreased from 21 percent to 7 percent during the decade in Oklahoma. In metropolitan areas the proportion of units without complete plumbing facilities in 1970 was 4 percent as compared with 10 percent in nonmetropolitan areas.

Number of persons per room is often used as a measure of crowding. In Oklahoma, units with 1.01

Table C.   Housing Units by Metropolitan and Nonmetropolitan Residence: 1970 and 1960

The State Metropolitan and Nonmetropolitan Residence	Housing units				Population percent change
	Total		Change		
	1970	1960	Number	Percent	
Total...............	937,582	815,685	121,897	14.9	9.8
Metropolitan residence.....	449,991	359,573	90,418	25.1	19.9
Inside central cities....	286,305	227,784	58,521	25.7	19.8
Outside central cities...	163,686	131,789	31,897	24.2	20.9
Nonmetropolitan residence..	487,591	456,112	31,479	6.9	1.

or more persons per room comprised 7 percent of all occupied housing units in 1970, compared with 12 percent in 1960 (table D). The number of all such units in 1970 was 62,300, representing a decrease of about 25,000, or 29 percent, between 1960 and 1970.

Homeownership in the State increased from 67 percent in 1960 to 69 percent in 1970. In metropolitan areas there was an increase from 66 percent to 67 percent, while in nonmetropolitan areas the proportion increased from 68 percent to 71 percent.

Property values and rents increased during the last decade. The median estimated value of owner-occupied homes in metropolitan areas increased by 38 percent ($9,600 in 1960 to $13,200 in 1970), while in non-metropolitan areas estimated value increased 45 percent ($6,000 in 1960 to $8,700 in 1970). In metropolitan areas, median contract rent in 1970 was 48 percent higher than in 1960, rising from $52 to $77. In nonmetropolitan areas, rent increased during the 10-year period, from $38 to $51, or 34 percent.

Value and rent are expressed in current dollars (the value at the time of the respective censuses). Thus, any comparison must take into account the general rise in the cost of living during the 10-year period, as well as changes in the characteristics of the housing inventory.

Standard Metropolitan Statistical Areas

Average household size for the metropolitan area total of the State declined during the decade. Population per occupied unit was 3.0 in 1970 compared with 3.1 in 1960.

In 1970, 16,600 housing units in metropolitan areas, or 4 percent of all year-round units, lacked some or all plumbing facilities. The corresponding proportion in the central cities was 2 percent, compared with 6 percent in the suburbs.

Of all occupied units in metropolitan areas, 28,400 units, or 7 percent, reported more than one person per room in 1970, compared with 11 percent in 1960. In 1970, the proportion of such units was 6 percent in the central cities and 8 percent in the suburbs.

Homeowner vacancy rate for metropolitan area decreased during the decade from 2.1 percent to 1.5 percent. The rental vacancy rate increased from 9.4 to 11.9.

Annexations

Annexations occurred in the central cities of Oklahoma City, Tulsa, and Lawton during the decade (see "Population Trends" and text table B). Such annexations affect changes in the characteristics for these central cities and their suburbs.

Table D.   Plumbing Facilities and Persons Per Room by Metropolitan and Nonmetro-
            politan Residence: 1970 and 1960

The State Metropolitan and Nonmetropolitan Residence	Percent of housing units			
	Lacking some or all plumbing facilities		With 1.01 or more persons per room[1]	
	1970[2]	1960[3]	1970	1960
Total......................	7.2	20.8	7.3	11.9
Metropolitan residence...........	3.7	(NA)	6.8	11.3
Inside central cities..........	2.4	8.6	6.2	10.1
Outside central cities.........	6.0	(NA)	8.0	13.4
Nonmetropolitan residence........	10.4	(NA)	7.8	12.4

NA Not available.
[1]Percent of all occupied units.
[2]Percent of all year-round housing units.
[3]Percent of all housing units.

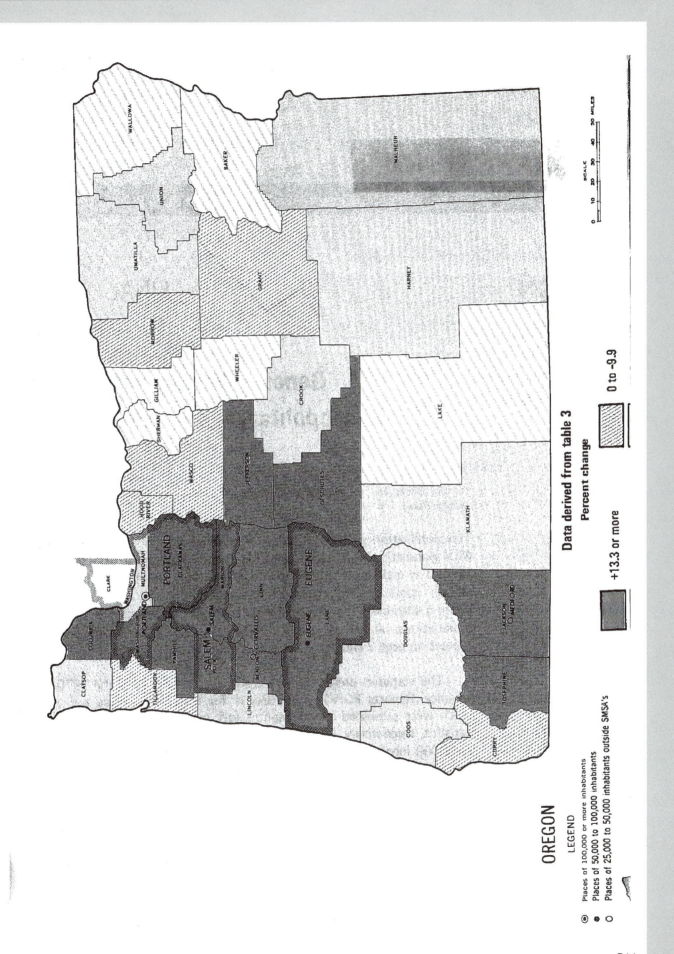

Population Change for Counties: 1960 to 1970

OREGON

LEGEND

⊛ Places of 100,000 or more inhabitants
● Places of 50,000 to 100,000 inhabitants
○ Places of 25,000 to 50,000 inhabitants outside SMSA's

Data derived from table 3

Percent change

+13.3 or more

0 to -9.9

Analytical Text

POPULATION TRENDS

General

Between 1960 and 1970, the population of Oregon grew from 1,769,000 to 2,091,000, an increase of 323,000 or 18.2 percent. This rate of increase is above the rate of increase for the entire United State (13.3 percent) but is below the rate for the Pacific States (25.1 percent), which in addition to Oregon, include Washington, California, Alaska, and Hawaii.

The total number of households in Oregon in 1970 was 692,000, or 133,000 more than in 1960. The population living in households increased more slowly than the rate at which households increased, with the result that average household size dropped from 3.1 to 2.9 persons per unit. In the nation as a whole there were 3.1 persons per unit in 1970 (table A).

During the 1960 to 1970 decade, the metropolitan population of Oregon grew twice as fast as the non-metropolitan population. The metropolitan population grew by 23 percent from 1,038,000 to 1,281,000, and the nonmetropolitan population grew by 11 percent from 730,000 to 811,000. In 1970, three-fifths of Oregon's population lived in metropolitan areas. In the nation as a whole, about two-thirds of the population live in metropolitan areas.

Within metropolitan areas, the population outside central cities grew almost three times as rapidly as the population in central cities. The central city population

Table A. Population by Race and Metropolitan and Nonmetropolitan Residence: 1970 and 1960

The State Metropolitan and Non-metropolitan Residence	Population		Change		Percent Distribution	
	1970	1960	Number	Percent	1970	1960
Total................	2,091,385	1,768,687	322,698	18.2	100.0	100.0
Metropolitan residence...	1,280,691	1,038,389	242,302	23.3	61.2	58.7
Inside central cities..	527,261	472,795	54,466	11.5	25.2	26.7
Outside central cities.	753,430	565,594	187,836	33.2	36.0	32.0
Nonmetropolitan residence	810,694	730,298	80,396	11.0	38.8	41.3
White................	2,032,079	1,732,037	300,042	17.3	97.2	97.9
Metropolitan residence...	1,237,848	1,012,243	225,605	22.3	59.2	57.2
Inside central cities..	494,091	450,727	43,364	9.6	23.6	25.5
Outside central cities.	743,757	561,516	182,241	32.5	35.6	31.7
Nonmetropolitan residence	794,231	719,794	74,437	10.3	38.0	40.7
Negro and other races	59,306	36,650	22,656	61.8	2.8	2.1
Metropolitan residence...	42,843	26,146	16,697	63.9	2.0	1.5
Inside central cities..	33,170	22,068	11,102	50.3	1.6	1.2
Outside central cities.	9,673	4,078	5,595	137.2	0.5	0.2
Nonmetropolitan residence	16,463	10,504	5,959	56.7	0.8	0.6

grew by 12 percent from 473,000 in 1960 to 527,000 in 1970. All of this growth was due to annexation (table B). The balance of the metropolitan population grew by 33 percent from 566,000 in 1960 to 753,000 in 1970.

The population of Negro and other races, slightly less than half of which is Negro, increased from 37,000 in 1960 to 59,000 in 1970, or by 62 percent. In 1970, Negro and other races constituted 3 percent of Oregon's population, and over one-half of the population of Negro and other races lived in the central cities of metropolitan areas. In contrast, less than one-quarter of the white population lived in the central cities of metropolitan areas.

The population increase of 323,000 in Oregon in the 1960 to 1970 decade resulted from a natural increase (births minus deaths) of 164,000 and a net inmigration of 159,000. The net inmigration was equivalent to 9 percent of the 1960 population. Oregon ranked eighth among the 50 States in rate of net inmigration during the 1960 to 1970 decade.

The age structure of the Oregon population changed significantly between 1960 and 1970. The only decline occurred among the population under 5 years old and was due largely to the decline in birth rates which occurred throughout the United States during the 1960's. The greatest increase (62 percent) occurred in the 15 to 24 age group and was due largely to the entry of the large number of persons born during the post-World War II "baby boom" into this age group. As a result of these changes, the proportion of the total population in the under 5 group declined from 10 to 8 percent and the proportion in the 25 to 24 group increased from 13 to 18 percent.

Standard Metropolitan Statistical Areas

In 1970, there were three Standard Metropolitan Statistical Areas (SMSA's) in Oregon including one located partly in Oregon and partly in Washington (the Portland, Ore.-Wash. SMSA) and two located entirely in Oregon (the Eugene SMSA and the Salem SMSA). Unless indicated otherwise, the discussion of the Portland SMSA refers to the entire metropolitan area rather than to the portion in Oregon.

The population of the Portland SMSA grew from 822,000 in 1960 to 1,009,000 in 1970, or by 23 percent. In 1970, the Portland SMSA was the 33rd largest metropolitan area in the United States. Nearly two-thirds of the population growth in the Portland SMSA during the decade was due to net inmigration. The net inmigration was equivalent to 14 percent of the 1960 population.

Nearly all the growth in the Portland SMSA occurred outside the central city of Portland. The population of Portland, which increased by 3 percent would have declined slightly if no annexation had occurred. The population in the remainder of the metropolitan area increased by 39 percent from 449,000 to 627,000. As a result the proportion of the population of the Portland SMSA living in the central city dropped from 45 to 38 percent.

The portion of the Portland SMSA in Oregon increased in population from 728,000 in 1960 to 881,000 in 1970, or by 21 percent. The portion in Washington (Clark County) grew from 94,000 to 128,000, or by 37 percent. In 1970, seven-eighths of the population in the Portland SMSA lived in the Oregon portion.

The Eugene SMSA grew from 163,000 in 1960 to 213,000 in 1970, or by 31 percent. One-half of the increase was due to net inmigration which was equivalent to 15 percent of the 1960 population. The rate of population growth in the city of Eugene, which increased from 51,000 to 76,000, was higher than in the remainder of the metropolitan area; however, most of the growth in Eugene was due to annexation.

The population of the Salem SMSA increased from 147,000 to 187,000, or by 27 percent. Most of the growth in the Salem SMSA was due to net inmigration, which was equivalent to 18 percent of the 1960

Table B.   Change in Population of Central Cities Through Annexation: 1960 to 1970

Central Cities	1970 population			1960 population	Change 1960 to 1970 in 1960 area
	Total	In 1960 area	In annexed area		
Eugene......................	76,346	60,202	16,144	50,977	9,225
Portland.....................	382,619	367,357	15,262	372,676	−5,319
Salem........................	68,296	45,243	23,053	49,142	−3,899

population. The city of Salem grew from 49,000 to 68,000. The growth was due entirely to annexation as the population in the 1960 boundaries declined during the decade.

Counties

Of the 36 counties in Oregon 24 gained population and 12 lost population between 1960 and 1970. Thirteen counties had rates of growth above the national average of 13.3 percent and six counties experienced population declines exceeding 10 percent. In the nation as a whole, slightly more than half of all counties gained population during the decade. All six of Oregon's metropolitan counties increased in population.

Every county in Oregon had a natural increase (i.e., births outnumbered deaths) between 1960 and 1970. In 12 counties (those losing population), net outmigration exceeded natural increase. Fifteen counties had a net inmigration during the decade. Inmigration was highest—both in numbers and in rates—in the two "suburban" counties in the Portland SMSA. Washington County had a net inmigration of 52,000, which was equivalent to 57 percent of the 1960 population, and Clackamas County had a net inmigration of 41,000, which was equivalent to 37 percent of the 1960 population. Multnomah County, which includes Portland and is the most populous county in the State (557,000 in 1970), had a net inmigration of less than 1,000.

Nearly all the population increase in Oregon between 1960 and 1970 occurred in the western third of the State. The 18 counties west of the crest of the Cascade Range (the string of counties from Multnomah County to Jackson County and all counties to the west) grew by 316,000, while the 18 counties to the east grew by only 7,000. In 1970, only about one-eighth of Oregon's population lived in the eastern two-thirds of the State.

HOUSING TRENDS

General

During the decade, the total supply of housing units in Oregon increased more rapidly than population. While housing units increased by 121,800, or 20 percent, the population grew by 323,000, or 18 percent (table C).

The metropolitan areas of the State experienced the greatest relative growth in housing, as in population. The number of housing units in metropolitan areas rose from 361,440 to 450,971 over the decade, an increase of 89,531 units, or 25 percent; this compares with an increase of 32,232 units, or 12 percent, in the nonmetropolitan areas. While 61 percent of all housing units were in the metropolitan areas, these areas accounted for 74 percent of the total State increase between 1960 and 1970.

Households were smaller in 1970 than in 1960. In the metropolitan areas, population per occupied unit declined from 3.1 in 1960 to 2.9 in 1970, and in nonmetropolitan areas, from 3.2 in 1960 to 3.0 in 1970. Households consisting of only one or two persons had large gains, while the number of larger households grew slowly and in some areas even declined.

Homeownership rates in Oregon were lower in 1970 than in 1960, about 66 percent and 69 percent, respectively. Estimated value of housing increased from a median of $10,500 in 1960 to $15,400 in 1970, with large increases in the number of homes valued at $15,000 or more. In the State, rents increased by more than one-half, with the most substantial increases in the number of units rented at $80 or more.

Value and rent are expressed in current dollars (the value at the time of the respective censuses). Thus, any comparison must take into account the general rise in the cost of living during the 10-year period as well as changes in the characteristics of the housing inventory.

Table C. Housing Units by Metropolitan and Nonmetropolitan Residence: 1970 and 1960

The State Metropolitan and Nonmetropolitan Residence	Housing units				Population percent change
	Total		Change		
	1970	1960	Number	Percent	
Total...............	744,616	622,853	121,763	19.5	18.2
Metropolitan residence.....	450,971	361,440	89,531	24.8	23.3
Inside central cities....	203,104	176,252	26,852	15.2	11.5
Outside central cities...	247,867	185,188	62,679	33.8	33.2
Nonmetropolitan residence..	293,645	261,413	32,232	12.3	11.0

The number of units lacking some or all plumbing facilities declined from 61,400 to 26,400, or a 57-percent decrease since 1960. In 1970, the proportion of such units was 4 percent of all year-round units.

Number of persons per room is often used as a measure of crowding. In Oregon, units with 1.01 or more persons per room comprised 6 percent of all occupied housing units in 1970, compared with 9 percent in 1960 (table D). The number of all such units in 1970 was 38,600, a decrease of about 9,700, or 20 percent, between 1960 and 1970. The decline occurred in metropolitan and nonmetropolitan areas alike, but in nonmetropolitan areas the improvement was greater.

Standard Metropolitan Statistical Areas

Eugene led the SMSA's in relative increase in housing units during the decade with an increase of 37 percent. The Salem SMSA followed with an increase of 28 percent, and the Portland SMSA with a 23-percent increase.

Average household size declined in all SMSA's during the decade. In Eugene, the population per occupied unit decreased from 3.3 in 1960 to 3.0 in 1970, in Portland, from 3.0 to 2.9, and in Salem, from 3.1 to 3.0.

As with the State, homeownership rates declined in each SMSA, while property values and rents increased.

In 1970, 14,100 units inside SMSA's, or 3 percent of all year-round units, lacked some or all plumbing facilities. Of all occupied units in metropolitan areas, 20,100 units, or 5 percent, reported more than one person per room in 1970, compared with 7 percent in 1960.

The homeowner vacancy rate for SMSA's decreased for the decade from 1.6 to 1.0 percent. Similarly, the rental vacancy rate decreased from 8.0 to 6.9.

Annexations

Annexations occurred in each of the central cities of the SMSA's during the decade (see "Population Trends" and text table B). Such annexations affect changes in the characteristics for these central cities and suburbs.

Table D. Plumbing Facilities and Persons Per Room by Metropolitan and Nonmetro-politan Residence: 1970 and 1960

The State Metropolitan and Nonmetropolitan Residence	Percent of housing units			
	Lacking some or all plumbing facilities		With 1.01 or more persons per room[1]	
	1970[2]	1960[3]	1970	1960
Total......................	3.6	9.9	5.6	8.7
Metropolitan residence...........	3.1	(NA)	4.7	7.1
Inside central cities..........	4.4	7.6	3.5	4.4
Outside central cities........	2.1	(NA)	5.7	9.7
Nonmetropolitan residence........	4.3	(NA)	7.0	11.0

NA Not available.
[1] Percent of all occupied units.
[2] Percent of all year-round housing units.
[3] Percent of all housing units.

Population Change for Counties: 1960 to 1970

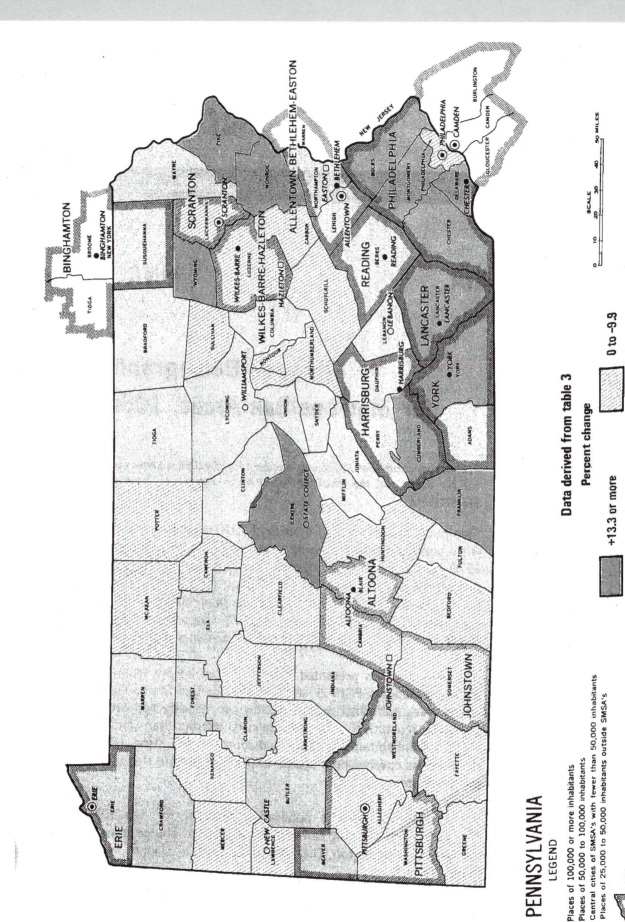

PENNSYLVANIA

LEGEND

- ◉ Places of 100,000 or more inhabitants
- ● Places of 50,000 to 100,000 inhabitants
- ☐ Central cities of SMSA's with fewer than 50,000 inhabitants
- ○ Places of 25,000 to 50,000 inhabitants outside SMSA's

Data derived from table 3

Percent change

+13.3 or more

0 to -9.9

Analytical Text

POPULATION TRENDS

General

Between 1960 and 1970, the population of Pennsylvania grew from 11,319,000 to 11,794,000, an increase of 475,000, or 4.2 percent. This rate of increase is well below the rate for the entire United States (13.3 percent) and for the Northeast Region (9.7 percent) in which Pennsylvania is located. In each decade from 1930 to 1970, the rate of population growth in Pennsylvania was less than one-half the national average. Among the 50 States, Pennsylvania ranks third in population behind California and New York.

The total number of households in Pennsylvania in 1970 was 3,705,000, or 355,000 more than in 1960.

The population living in households increased more slowly than the rate at which households increased, with the result that average household size dropped from 3.3 to 3.1 persons, just as in the Nation as a whole.

During the 1960 to 1970 decade, Pennsylvania's metropolitan population grew by 5 percent from 8,925,000 to 9,366,000 and its nonmetropolitan population grew by only 1 percent from 2,394,000 to 2,428,000 (table A). In 1970, 79 percent of the State's population lived in metropolitan areas. In the Nation as a whole, two-thirds of the population live in metropolitan areas.

Within metropolitan areas, all of the growth occurred outside central cities. The central city population declined 6 percent from 3,585,000 to 3,372,000, and the population outside central cities increased 12 per-

Table A. Population by Race and Metropolitan and Nonmetropolitan Residence: 1970 and 1960

The State Metropolitan and Non-metropolitan Residence	Population		Change		Percent Distribution	
	1970	1960	Number	Percent	1970	1960
Total...............	11,793,909	11,319,366	474,543	4.2	100.0	100.0
Metropolitan residence...	9,365,552	8,924,899	440,653	4.9	79.4	78.8
Inside central cities..	3,372,377	3,584,833	-212,456	-5.9	28.6	31.7
Outside central cities.	5,993,175	5,340,066	653,109	12.2	50.8	47.2
Nonmetropolitan residence	2,428,357	2,394,467	33,890	1.4	20.6	21.2
White...............	10,737,732	10,454,004	283,728	2.7	91.0	92.4
Metropolitan residence...	8,340,639	8,088,820	251,819	3.1	70.7	71.5
Inside central cities..	2,535,422	2,906,120	-370,698	-12.8	21.5	25.7
Outside central cities.	5,805,217	5,182,700	622,517	12.0	49.2	45.8
Nonmetropolitan residence	2,397,093	2,365,184	31,909	1.3	20.3	20.9
Negro and other races	1,056,177	865,362	190,815	22.1	9.0	7.6
Metropolitan residence...	1,024,913	836,079	188,834	22.6	8.7	7.4
Inside central cities..	836,955	678,713	158,242	23.3	7.1	6.0
Outside central cities.	187,958	157,366	30,592	19.4	1.6	1.4
Nonmetropolitan residence	31,264	29,283	1,981	6.8	0.3	0.3

cent from 5,340,000 to 5,993,000. Of the 15 central cities in Pennsylvania, five had annexations between 1960 and 1970; however, in each of these cities, the 1970 population of the annexed area was less than 1,000 (table B). With the exception of Allentown, in which the population increased 1 percent, each of Pennsylvania's central cities lost population between 1960 and 1970. The rates of decline ranged from 3 percent in Philadelphia to 21 percent in Johnstown.

The population of Negro and other races (which is almost entirely Negro) in Pennsylvania increased from 865,000 to 1,056,000, or by 22 percent. In 1970, Negro and other races constituted 9 percent of the State's population. Whereas four-fifths of the population of Negro and other races live in the central cities of metropolitan areas, less than one-fourth of the white population live in central cities. Nearly two-thirds of the population of Negro and other races in Pennsylvania live in the city of Philadelphia.

The population increase of 475,000 in the State in the 1960 to 1970 decade resulted from a natural increase (births minus deaths) of 853,000 and a net outmigration of 378,000. The natural increase was equivalent to 7.5 percent of the 1960 population, which was the lowest rate among the 50 States. In the Nation as a whole, natural increase was equivalent to 11.6 percent of the 1960 population. The net outmigration in Pennsylvania was equivalent to 3.3 percent of the 1960 population. In each decade from 1930 to 1970, the amount of net outmigration from Pennsylvania was larger than from any other State.

The age structure of Pennsylvania's population changed significantly between 1960 and 1970. The largest proportionate decline (22 percent) occurred among the population under 5 years old and was due largely to the decline in birth rates which occurred throughout the United States during the 1960's. The largest numerical decline (346,000) occurred among the population 25 to 44 years old. In the Nation as a whole, there was a small increase in the number of persons in this age group. The greatest increase in Pennsylvania (513,000, or 36 percent) occurred in the 15 to 24 age group and was due to the entry of the large number of persons born during the post-World War II "baby boom" into this age group. As a result of these changes, the proportion of the total population in the under 5 group declined from 10 to 8 percent, the proportion in the 15 to 24 group increased from 12 to 16 percent, and the proportion in the 25 to 44 group decreased from 27 to 23 percent.

Standard Metropolitan Statistical Areas

In 1970 there was 13 standard metropolitan statistical areas (SMSA's) in Pennsylvania including 10 located entirely in the State and three that cross State lines: Philadelphia, Pa.-N.J.; Allentown-Bethlehem-Easton, Pa.-N.J.; and Binghamton, N.Y.-Pa.

The Philadelphia SMSA, which is the largest in Pennsylvania and the fourth largest in the Nation, had a population of 4,343,000 in 1960 (including 751,000 in the New Jersey portion) and 4,818,000 in 1970 (including 952,000 in the New Jersey portion). The increase during the decade was 11 percent. Philadelphia is a major financial, commercial, and manufacturing center and a major port. The city is also a leading medical and educational center.

The population in the city of Philadelphia, the fourth largest city in the Nation, dropped from 2,003,000 to 1,949,000, while the population in the balance of the SMSA increased from 2,340,000 to 2,869,000, or by 23 percent. In 1970 Negro and other races constituted 34

Table B. Change in Population of Central Cities Through Annexation: 1960 to 1970

| Central Cities | 1970 population | | | 1960 population | Change 1960 to 1970 in 1960 area |
	Total	In 1960 area	In annexed area		
Allentown	109,527	108,892	635	108,347	545
York	50,335	49,473	862	54,504	-5,031
Lancaster	57,690	57,666	24	61,055	-3,389
Altoona	62,900	62,828	72	69,407	-6,579
Easton	30,256	29,371	885	31,955	-2,584

percent of the city's population (up from 27 percent in 1960) and 18 percent of the population in the entire metropolitan area. Between 1960 and 1970, net inmigration into the Philadelphia SMSA was 45,000, with a net outmigration of 207,000 from the central city and a net inmigration of 252,000 into the balance of the SMSA. The net outmigration from the central city was comprised of a net outmigration of 246,000 whites and a net inmigration of 40,000 persons of Negro and other races.

The Pittsburgh SMSA, the second largest in Pennsylvania and the ninth largest in the Nation, had a population of 2,405,000 in 1960 and 2,401,000 in 1970. None of the other 50 largest SMSA's in 1970 lost population during the decade. The population of the Pittsburgh SMSA increased at a rate less than one-half the national average in each decade from 1930 to 1960. The Pittsburgh SMSA is one of the Nation's leading centers of heavy industry with the production of steel being of primary importance. With improved technology, the employment in manufacturing has not kept pace with the volume of production during the past few decades.

The population in the city of Pittsburgh, which was 677,000 in 1950 and 604,000 in 1960, was down to 520,000 in 1970, yielding a 23 percent decline during the past two decades. In 1970, Pittsburgh was the 23rd largest city in the country. In 1910, with a population of 534,000, it ranked eighth. In 1970, Negro and other races constituted 21 percent of Pittsburgh's population compared to 17 percent a decade earlier. Between 1960 and 1970, net outmigration from the Pittsburgh SMSA was 167,000, equivalent to 7 percent of the 1960 population. In the city of Pittsburgh, there was a net outmigration among both whites (99,000) and persons of other races (6,000).

In southeastern Pennsylvania, there are five medium-sized metropolitan areas, each of which had a moderate rate of population growth between 1960 and 1970 despite a loss of population in its central city portion. The Allentown-Bethlehem-Easton, Pa.-N.J. SMSA had a 1970 population of 544,000 (including 74,000 in the New Jersey portion), up 10 percent since 1960. Net inmigration accounted for more than one-third of the growth. This SMSA, along the Lehigh River Valley, is noted for its heavy industry, especially steel production.

Reading, Lancaster, and York are all manufacturing cities surrounded by prosperous agricultural areas. In 1970, the population of the Reading SMSA was 296,000 (up 8 percent since 1960), the population of the Lancaster SMSA was 320,000 (up 15 percent since 1960), and the population of the York SMSA was 330,000 (up 14 percent since 1960). In each of these SMSA's, net inmigration accounted for about one-fourth of the growth.

The Harrisburg SMSA had a 1970 population of 411,000, up 10 percent since 1960. One-fifth of the growth was due to net inmigration. Harrisburg's economy combines the administrative functions of a State capital with heavy industry. The closing of Olmsted Air Force Base depressed the area's growth during the decade.

The Wilkes-Barre-Hazleton SMSA and the Scranton SMSA are located in the anthracite coal area of northeastern Pennsylvania. The population of these SMSA's declined slightly between 1960 and 1970 after two decades of rapid decline. The 1970 populations of 342,000 in the Wilkes-Barre-Hazleton SMSA and 234,000 in the Scranton SMSA are only three-fourths as large as in 1930. At present, manufacturing is the leading source of employment in these metropolitan areas. Net outmigration from these SMSA's was small during the past decade. Natural increase was extremely small because the heavy outmigration of previous decades has yielded a population with an old age structure. In 1970, 40 percent of the population of these two SMSA's was 45 years old and over. The corresponding figure in the Nation as a whole was only 30 percent.

The population of the Erie SMSA was 264,000 in 1970, or 5 percent more than in 1960. The net outmigration of 13,000 during the decade was equivalent to 5 percent of the 1960 population. Erie is a major port on the Great Lakes.

The Johnstown SMSA had a 1970 population of 263,000, which was 6 percent less than in 1960. The SMSA has lost population in each of the last three decades and its population in 1920 was larger than its present population. Employment in the Johnstown SMSA's coal-mining and steel industry has declined during recent years. Net outmigration of 33,000 between 1960 and 1970 was equivalent to 12 percent of the 1960 population.

The population of the Altoona SMSA was 135,000 in 1970, 1 percent less than in 1960. In 1930, the population was larger than at present. The loss in population is due to the decline in employment in the rail industry and the failure of other industries to take up the slack.

The population of the portion of the Binghamton SMSA in Pennsylvania was 34,000 in 1970, up 4 percent from 1960. Only one-ninth of the population in the Binghamton SMSA lives in Pennsylvania.

Counties

Of the 67 counties in Pennsylvania, 41 gained population and 26 lost population between 1960 and 1970. Eleven counties had rates of growth above the national average of 13.3 percent. The largest proportionate decline

(9 percent) occurred in Fayette County. In the Nation as a whole, slightly more than half of all counties gained population during the decade. Twenty of Pennsylvania's 67 counties (or 30 percent) had a net inmigration between 1960 and 1970. This is the same proportion as in the Nation as a whole. Every county in Pennsylvania had a natural increase (i.e., births exceeded deaths) during the decade; however, in most counties, especially those in the coal producing areas which have old age structures due to heavy net outmigration, the rate of natural increase was below the national average.

Six counties in Pennsylvania had rates of population growth exceeding 20 percent between 1960 and 1970. Four of these counties are in metropolitan areas: Bucks, Chester, and Montgomery Counties in the Philadelphia SMSA; and Cumberland County in the Harrisburg SMSA. Rapid growth in Centre County is attributable to the expansion of Pennsylvania State University while the growth in Pike County is attributable to its location in the Pocono Mountain resort area. Virtually all of the growth in Pike County was due to net inmigration, which was equivalent to 29 percent of the 1960 population.

The population increase of 475,000 in Pennsylvania between 1960 and 1970 was accounted for by the 16 counties located southeast of the Alleghany Mountains and the anthracite coal area. These 16 counties, which constitute one-fifth of the land area of Pennsylvania but contain one-half of the State's population, include the counties in the Philadelphia, Allentown-Bethlehem-Easton, Reading, Lancaster, York, and Harrisburg SMSA's and the nonmetropolitan counties of Franklin and Lebanon. The population of these 16 counties grew from 5,415,000 to 5,892,000, or by 9 percent, while the population in the remainder of the State remained virtually unchanged; 5,904,000 in 1960 and 5,902,000 in 1970.

HOUSING TRENDS

General

Between 1960 and 1970 the total supply of housing units in Pennsylvania increased more rapidly than population. The population grew by 475,000, or 4 percent, while housing units increased by 342,900, or 10 percent (table C).

About 78 percent of all housing units in the State were in its standard metropolitan statistical areas. The metropolitan areas of the State experienced greater relative growth in housing, as in population, than did the nonmetropolitan part. The number of housing units in metropolitan areas rose from 2,787,100 to 3,071,600 over the decade, an increase of 284,500 units, or 10 percent; the increase in nonmetropolitan areas was 58,300 units, or 7 percent.

About 73 percent of the housing in Pennsylvania consisted of one-unit structures in 1970. The proportion of such units in metropolitan areas was 71 percent, and in nonmetropolitan areas, 78 percent.

The number of units in the State lacking some or all plumbing facilities in 1970 was 198,600 units, or 5 percent. The proportions of units in this category were 4 percent in metropolitan areas and 10 percent in non-metropolitan areas (table C). Approximately 12,900, or 4 percent, of the Negro-occupied units in the State lacked some or all plumbing in 1970. The corresponding proportions for inside and outside the metropolitan areas were 4 percent and 12 percent, respectively.

Households were smaller in 1970 than in 1960. In both metropolitan and nonmetropolitan areas the average household size declined from 3.3 to 3.1 persons over the decade. There were large percentage increases in one-person households, 61 percent in metropolitan areas and 56 percent in nonmetropolitan areas. In comparison,

Table C.   Housing Units by Metropolitan and Nonmetropolitan Residence: 1970 and 1960

The State Metropolitan and Nonmetropolitan Residence	Housing units				Population percent change
	Total		Change		
	1970	1960	Number	Percent	
Total.................	3,924,757	3,581,877	342,880	9.6	4.2
Metropolitan residence.....	3,071,610	2,787,075	284,535	10.2	4.9
Inside central cities....	1,186,891	1,170,650	16,241	1.4	-5.9
Outside central cities...	1,884,719	1,616,425	268,294	16.6	12.2
Nonmetropolitan residence..	853,147	794,802	58,345	7.3	1.4

households with five or more persons increased 2 percent in metropolitan areas, and decreased 6 percent in nonmetropolitan areas.

The median number of rooms in 1970 was 5.6 in both metropolitan and nonmetropolitan areas. One- to three-room units comprised 14 percent of the year-round housing in metropolitan areas and 9 percent in nonmetropolitan areas. About 23 percent of metropolitan housing and 24 percent of nonmetropolitan housing had seven or more rooms.

Number of persons per room is often used as a measure of crowding. In Pennsylvania both the number and the proportion of housing units with 1.01 or more persons per room decreased during the decade. In 1960, 7 percent of all occupied housing units in both metropolitan and nonmetropolitan areas had 1.01 or more persons per room. By 1970, the proportion of such units had decreased to 5 percent in metropolitan areas and 6 percent in nonmetropolitan areas (table D).

Homeownership in the State increased slightly from 68 to 69 percent over the decade. In metropolitan areas the homeownership rate remained 68 percent, while in nonmetropolitan areas the proportion rose from 71 to 73 percent. Of the 2,549,300 owner-occupied units in the State, 1,996,700 were inside metropolitan areas and 552,600 were outside these areas.

About 46 percent of the Negro households in metropolitan areas owned their homes in 1970, compared with 53 percent in nonmetropolitan areas. Of the 137,300 Negro-homeowner households in the State,

133,700 lived inside SMSA's and 3,600 lived outside SMSA's.

Property values and rents increased during the last decade. The median value in metropolitan areas rose 33 percent, from $10,800 to $14,400, while in nonmetropolitan areas the median increased 43 percent, from $7,600 to $10,900. In metropolitan areas, median contract rent was 45 percent higher than in 1960, rising from $53 to $77. In nonmetropolitan areas rent increased by 49 percent, from $39 to $58.

Value and rent are expressed in current dollars (the value at the time of the respective censuses). Thus, any comparison must take into account the general rise in the cost of living during the 10-year period, as well as changes in the characteristics of the housing inventory.

Standard Metropolitan Statistical Areas

In the metropolitan areas of the State, the housing supply increased by 284,500 units, or 10 percent. The Philadelphia SMSA (Pennsylvania part), the largest in the State, contained 41 percent of the housing in the metropolitan areas, and accounted for 50 percent of the increase. Pittsburgh, second largest, had 26 percent of the State's metropolitan housing and accounted for 17 percent of the increase.

The suburban areas of the State experienced greater growth in housing than did the central cities. Housing units in the suburbs increased by 268,300 units, or 17 percent, while housing in the combined central cities

Table D.   Plumbing Facilities and Persons Per Room by Metropolitan and Nonmetropolitan Residence: 1970 and 1960

The State Metropolitan and Nonmetropolitan Residence	Percent of housing units			
	Lacking some or all plumbing facilities		With 1.01 or more persons per room[1]	
	1970[2]	1960[3]	1970	1960
Total......................	5.1	11.3	5.5	7.2
Metropolitan residence..........	4.0	(NA)	5.4	7.2
Inside central cities..........	3.7	7.1	5.8	7.2
Outside central cities.........	4.1	(NA)	5.1	7.2
Nonmetropolitan residence........	9.5	(NA)	5.9	7.4

NA Not available.
[1]Percent of all occupied units.
[2]Percent of all year-round housing units.
[3]Percent of all housing units.

increased by 16,200 units, or 1 percent. By 1970, there were 1,884,700 housing units in the suburbs and 1,186,900 units in the central cities.

The proportion of the housing inventory in one-unit structures declined in both the central cities and their suburbs. In the central cities the proportion of such units declined from 70 percent in 1960 to 62 percent in 1970 and in the suburban areas from 86 to 77 percent.

In 1970, about 121,100 housing units in metropolitan areas, or 4 percent of all year-round units, lacked some or all plumbing facilities. The corresponding proportions for the central cities and the suburbs were the same, 4 percent. Approximately 8,800, or 4 percent, of the Negro households in central cities occupied units which lacked some or all plumbing facilities in 1970, compared with 3,200, or 7 percent, of Negro households in suburban areas.

Household size in the metropolitan areas declined during the decade. In the central cities the average decreased from 3.1 to 2.9 persons and in the suburbs, from 3.4 to 3.2 persons. One-person households constituted 23 percent of the occupied units in the central cities and 14 percent in the suburbs.

The median number of rooms in the central cities declined slightly, from 5.5 in 1960 to 5.4 in 1970. In suburban areas, the median remained 5.6 rooms. While 20 percent of the housing in central cities had one to three rooms in 1970, 9 percent of the housing units in the suburbs were in this category. At the same time, 19 percent of the housing in the central cities had seven or more rooms, compared with 26 percent in the suburbs.

Of all occupied units in the central cities, 65,200, or 6 percent, reported 1.01 or more persons per room in 1970, compared with 7 percent in 1960. In the suburban areas, the proportions were 5 percent in 1970 and 7 percent in 1960.

Homeownership in 1970 was more prevalent in the suburban areas than in the central cities. About 74 percent of occupied units in the suburbs and 58 percent in the central cities were owner-occupied. The Negro-homeownership rate in the suburbs was 52 percent, compared with 45 percent in the central cities.

In the central cities of Pennsylvania, the median value of owner-occupied housing rose 22 percent, from $9,000 in 1960 to $11,000 in 1970; in the suburbs, the median increased 37 percent, from $12,100 to $16,600. In 1970, about 11 percent of the owner-occupied housing in the central cities was valued at $20,000 or more, compared with 34 percent in the suburbs. Median contract rent in the central cities and the suburbs was $74 and $81, respectively. In the central cities, 25 percent of renter-occupied units rented for $100 or more, compared with 37 percent in the suburbs.

The homeowner vacancy rate decreased in the central cities from 1.2 percent in 1960 to 1.0 percent in 1970 and in the suburbs from 1.2 to 0.6 percent. The rental vacancy rate decreased slightly from 5.8 to 5.7 percent in the central cities and from 5.0 to 4.2 percent in the suburbs.

Annexations

Annexations occurred in the central cities of Allentown, Altoona, Easton, Lancaster, and York during the decade (see "Population Trends" and text table B). Such annexations affect changes in the characteristics for these central cities and their suburbs.

Population Change for Counties: 1960 to 1970

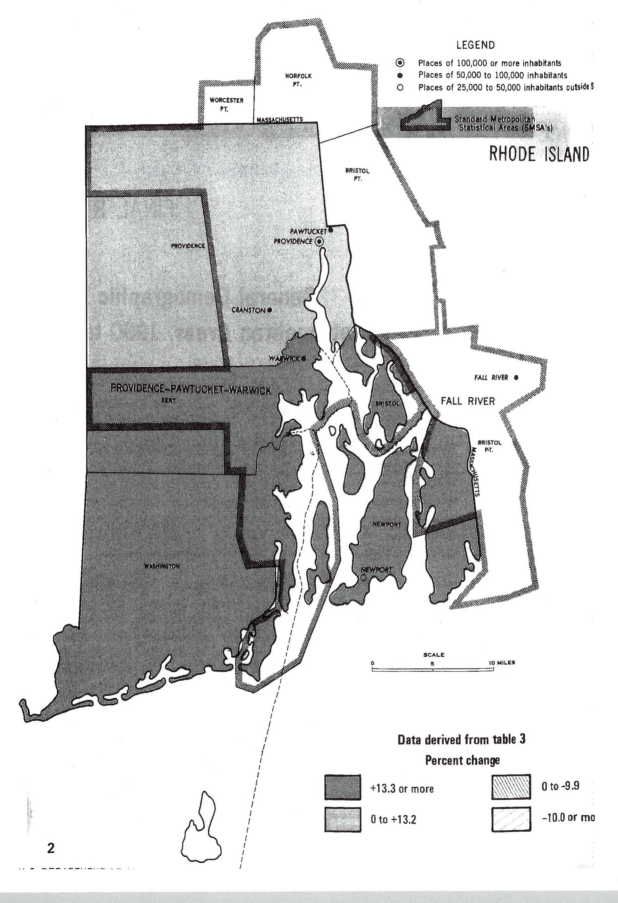

LEGEND

⊙ Places of 100,000 or more inhabitants

● Places of 50,000 to 100,000 inhabitants

○ Places of 25,000 to 50,000 inhabitants outside $

▲ Standard Metropolitan Statistical Areas (SMSA's)

RHODE ISLAND

NORFOLK PT.

WORCESTER PT.

MASSACHUSETTS

BRISTOL PT.

PROVIDENCE

PAWTUCKET
PROVIDENCE ⊙

CRANSTON ●

WARWICK ●

PROVIDENCE-PAWTUCKET-WARWICK
KENT

FALL RIVER ●

FALL RIVER

BRISTOL

BRISTOL PT.

MASSACHUSETTS

NEWPORT

WASHINGTON

NEWPORT ○

SCALE
0   5   10 MILES

Data derived from table 3

Percent change

+13.3 or more

0 to +13.2

0 to -9.9

-10.0 or mo

2

Analytical Text

POPULATION TRENDS

General

Between 1960 and 1970 the population of Rhode Island increased from 859,000 to 947,000, a growth of 87,000 or 10.1 percent. This rate of increase is below that of the United States as a whole (13.3 percent), but slightly above that of the Northeast region (9.7 percent) in which Rhode Island is located.

The total number of households in Rhode Island grew by 35,000, from 257,000 in 1960 to 292,000 in 1970. The population living in households increased less rapidly than the rate at which households increased with the result that average household size decreased slightly from 3.2 to 3.1 persons.

The metropolitan population of Rhode Island increased by 8 percent during the decade, from 741,000 in 1960 to 802,000 in 1970, while the nonmetropolitan population increased by 22 percent from 119,000 to 145,000, (see table A-1). In 1970, over four-fifths of Rhode Island's population lived in metropolitan areas, while nationwide two-thirds of the population was classified as metropolitan.

Within the metropolitan areas, the population of the central cities declined by 5 percent from 357,000 to 340,000, while the balance of the metropolitan areas increased by 20 percent, from 384,000 to 462,000.

Rhode Island's population is overwhelmingly white. In 1970, as in 1960, only about 3 percent of the total population were of races other than white.

The State's population growth resulted from a natural increase (births minus deaths) of 78,000 combined with a small net inmigration of 10,000. A high proportion of the State's net inmigration was by Negro and other races. The net inmigration of this population group (6,000), was equivalent to 28 percent of its 1960 population, and accounted for slightly more than half of its total growth (see table 3).

The age structure of the Rhode Island population was affected most significantly by the post-World War II "baby boom". The 15-24 age group in 1970 was almost 50 percent larger than the 1960 population of this age. This group grew from 117,000 to 174,000, forming 18 percent of the State's population as compared with 14 percent in 1960. The 25-44 age group, on the other hand, decreased, from 225,000 to 210,000. In 1960 this age group comprised 26 percent of the population, but in 1970 it made up only 22 percent. The major decline occurred among the population under 5 years old,

reflecting the lowering of birth rates throughout the United State during the 1960's: 76,000 children in Rhode Island were under 5 in 1970, contrasted with 90,000 10 years ago (see table 4).

As is true nationwide, the population of Negro and other races in Rhode Island has a younger age structure than the total population. On the State level, 45 percent of the total population is under 25 and 11 percent is 65 and over. Among Negro and other races, 55 percent are younger than 25, and 6 percent 65 and over.

Standard Metropolitan Statistical Areas

In 1970 there were two Standard Metropolitan Statistical Areas (SMSA's) located in Rhode Island: Providence-Pawtucket-Warwick, R.I.-Mass., and a small part of Fall River, Mass.-R.I. Both SMSA's cross the State boundaries between Rhode Island and Massachusetts; 87 percent of Providence-Pawtucket-Warwick is located in Rhode Island but only 8 percent of Fall River is in Rhode Island (see table A-2).[1]

The Providence-Pawtucket-Warwick SMSA as a whole grew by 11 percent during the decade, from 821,000 to 911,000 (see table A-3). Overall, the three central cities lost 5 percent of their population, decreasing from 357,000 to 340,000. Most of the loss, however, occurred in Providence city. Providence city decreased 14 percent during the 60's, going from 207,000 to 179,000. The change was composed of a loss of 34,000 whites and a gain of 6,000 Negro and other races. Pawtucket city's loss of 5 percent (from 81,000 to 77,000) resulted almost entirely from a decrease in the white population. Warwick city had a population increase of 22 percent (from 69,000 to 84,000), accounted for by its predominantly white population. The suburban ring of the SMSA grew by 23 percent from 464,000 to 571,000. The Rhode Island suburban portion grew at a slower rate than the Massachusetts part—20 percent compared with 36 percent. In the suburban areas in both States, the population of Negro and other races more than doubled, but their numbers remained small and their representation in the total suburban population scarcely changed.

---

[1] In the population tables in this report and other reports for the States in New England, data are shown for two types of metropolitan areas; Standard Metropolitan Statistical Areas (SMSA's) and Metropolitan State Economic Areas (SEA's). See "Definitions and Explanations" for a discussion of the differences between the two types of metropolitan areas. SMSA tables are shown in the Appendix to this text.

Counties

All five counties in Rhode Island gained population between 1960 and 1970 (see table 3). Four increased at rates above the national average of 13.3 percent. The fifth, Providence County, increased by only 2 percent, as a result of substantial white outmigration from the central cities. Net inmigration was responsible for most of the growth of three of the other counties, except for Newport, which grew mainly through natural increase (excess of births over deaths).

In the New England States, SMSA's are comprised of cities and towns (rather than of counties as in the remainder of the Nation), and thus a county may be partly metropolitan and partly nonmetropolitan (see "Definitions and Explanations"). The population of Bristol County is entirely metropolitan and Kent and Providence Counties are largely so. Almost half of the population of the Washington County is considered metropolitan but only 3 percent of Newport County falls in that category.

Washington County, with less than 9 percent of the State's population, experienced the greatest rate of growth (more than 41 percent) during the decade, increasing from 59,000 to 84,000. Over half of the growth in this suburban county was the result of net inmigration.

Kent County, containing the only central city in Rhode Island that gained population during the decade (Warwick) increased from 113,000 to 142,000, or 26 percent. The smallest county in Rhode Island, Bristol, increased by 24 percent from 37,000 in 1960 to 46,000 in 1970. Bristol, like Washington, contains no central cities.

HOUSING TRENDS

General

Between 1960 and 1970 the population and the supply of housing units in Rhode Island increased at the same rate. While the population grew by 87,000, or 10 percent, the number of housing units increased by 29,700, also 10 percent (table A).

The metropolitan areas of the State experienced less relative growth in housing, as in population, than did the nonmetropolitan part. The number of housing units in metropolitan areas rose over the decade to 270,100, an increase of 23,300 units, or 9 percent; this compares with an increase of 6,400 units, or 16 percent, in nonmetropolitan areas. Metropolitan areas contained 85 percent of the housing in Rhode Island and additions to the housing supply in these areas accounted for 78 percent of the State's total housing increase between 1960 and 1970.

About 52 percent of the housing in Rhode Island consisted of one-unit structures in 1970. The 1970 proportion of such units in metropolitan areas was 50 percent and in nonmetropolitan areas, 65 percent.

The median number of rooms in housing units in Rhode Island was 5.1 in 1970. In the metropolitan areas the median was 5.0, compared with 5.3 in nonmetropolitan areas. While 16 percent of the housing units in metropolitan areas had seven or more rooms, 24 percent of the nonmetropolitan housing units were in this category.

Households were smaller in 1970 than in 1960. In metropolitan areas average household size declined from 3.2 persons in 1960 to 3.1 in 1970, and in nonmetro-

Table A. Housing Units by Metropolitan and Nonmetropolitan Residence: 1970 and 1960

The State Metropolitan and Nonmetropolitan Residence	Housing units				Population percent change
	Total		Change		
	1970	1960	Number	Percent	
Total..................	316,477	286,757	29,720	10.4	10.1
Metropolitan residence.....	270,072	246,795	23,277	9.4	7.0
Inside central cities....	122,246	122,904	-658	-0.5	-4.8
Outside central cities...	147,826	123,891	23,935	19.3	18.6
Nonmetropolitan residence..	46,405	39,962	6,443	16.1	26.4

politan areas, from 3.3 persons in 1960 to 3.2 in 1970 During the same period in Rhode Island, there were large percentage increases in one- and two-person households, 51 percent and 19 percent, respectively. Losses occurred in the number of households with three and four persons and relatively small gains were made in households with five or more persons.

The number of units in the State lacking some or all plumbing facilities in 1970 was 9,600, or 3 percent. The proportion of such units was 3 percent in metropolitan areas and 4 percent in nonmetropolitan areas, (table B).

Number of persons per room is often used as a measure of crowding. In Rhode Island the number and proportion of housing units with 1.01 or more persons per room decreased during the decade. In 1970, 6 percent of all occupied housing units in metropolitan areas had more than one person per room, compared with 7 percent in 1960. For nonmetropolitan areas, the proportion of such units was 6 percent in 1970 and 8 percent in 1960.

Homeownership in Rhode Island increased from 55 percent in 1960 to 58 percent in 1970. In metropolitan areas there was an increase from 54 to 57 percent, while in nonmetropolitan areas the proportion rose from 57 to 61 percent.

Property values and rents increased during the last decade. The median value of owner-occupied homes in metropolitan areas rose by 47 percent, from $12,300 in 1960 to $18,100 in 1970, while in the nonmetropolitan areas, value increased 56 percent, from $12,600 to $19,700. In metropolitan areas, median contract rent in 1970 was 60 percent higher than in 1960, rising from $40 to $64. In nonmetropolitan areas, the increase was 71 percent, from $55 in 1960 to $94 in 1970.

Value and rent are expressed in current dollars (the value at the time of the respective censuses). Thus, any comparison must take into account the general rise in the cost of living during the 10-year period, as well as changes in the characteristics of the housing inventory.

Standard Metropolitan Statistical Areas

Of the 23,300 increase in housing units in the metropolitan areas of the State (Providence-Pawtucket-Warwick, R.I.-Mass. SMSA and the Rhode Island suburbs of the Fall River, Mass.-R.I. SMSA), 95 percent occurred in the Rhode Island portion of the Providence-Pawtucket-Warwick SMSA.

Average household size for the metropolitan area total declined during the decade. In the central cities, the average decreased from 3.1 persons in 1960 to 2.9 in 1970, and in the suburbs from 3.3 to 3.2.

The homeownership rate rose over the decade in both the central cities and the suburban areas. The percent of owner-occupied units increased from 47 percent in 1960 to 49 percent in 1970 in the central cities and from 62 to 65 percent in the suburbs.

In 1970, 8,000 housing units in metropolitan areas, or 3 percent of all year-round units, lacked some or all plumbing facilities. The corresponding proportion in both the central cities and the suburbs was also 3 percent.

Of all occupied units in metropolitan areas, 15,200 units, or 6 percent, reported more than one person per room in 1970, compared with 7 percent in 1960. In 1970, the proportion of such units was also 6 percent both in the central cities and the suburbs (table B).

Table B. Plumbing Facilities and Persons Per Room by Metropolitan and Nonmetropolitan Residence: 1970 and 1960

The State Metropolitan and Nonmetropolitan Residence	Percent of housing units			
	Lacking some or all plumbing facilities		With 1.01 or more persons per room [1]	
	1970 [2]	1960 [3]	1970	1960
Total.......................	3.1	13.6	6.0	6.9
Metropolitan residence..........	3.0	13.3	6.0	6.7
Inside central cities..........	2.9	13.0	5.7	6.7
Outside central cities........	3.1	13.7	6.2	6.8
Nonmetropolitan residence........	4.2	15.2	6.4	8.0

[1]Percent of all occupied units.   [2]Percent of all year-round housing units
[3]Percent of all housing units.

The median value of owner-occupied housing remained higher in the suburban areas of Rhode Island ($18,700 in 1970 and $12,500 in 1960) than in the central cities ($17,000 in 1970 and $12,000 in 1960). In 1970, the median rent in the suburbs was 72 percent higher than in 1960, rising from $39 to $67. In the central cities , the increase was 58 percent, from $40 to $63.

The homeowner vacancy rate for metropolitan areas decreased during the decade from 1.2 to 0.7 percent. The rental vacancy rate also decreased from 6.5 in 1960 to 5.8 in 1970.

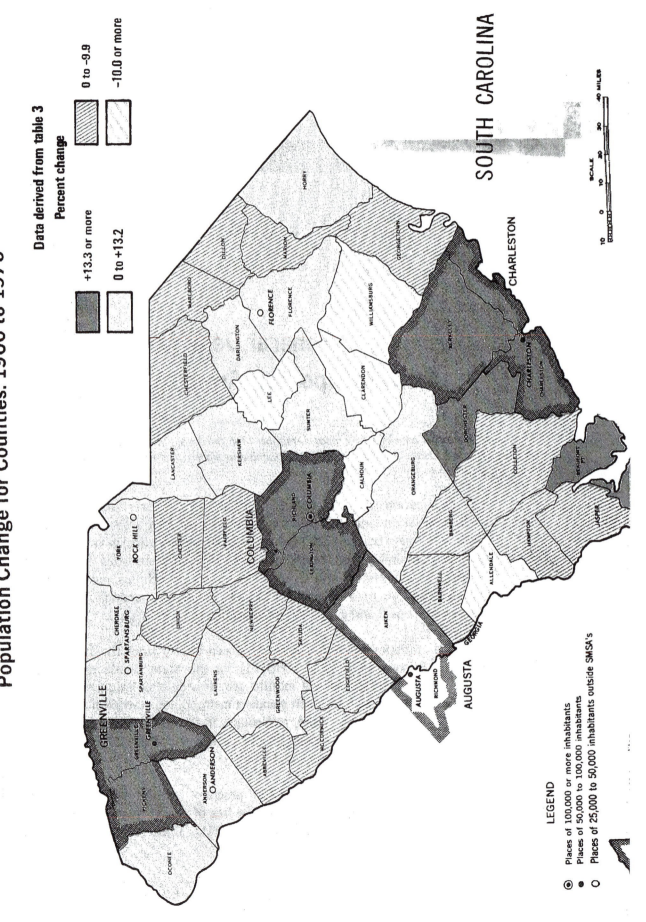

Population Change for Counties: 1960 to 1970

Data derived from table 3

Percent change

- +13.3 or more
- 0 to +13.2
- 0 to -9.9
- -10.0 or more

SOUTH CAROLINA

SCALE

LEGEND

⊙ Places of 100,000 or more inhabitants
● Places of 50,000 to 100,000 inhabitants
○ Places of 25,000 to 50,000 inhabitants outside SMSA's

Analytical Text

POPULATION TRENDS

General

Between 1960 and 1970 the total population of South Carolina grew by 208,000 persons, from 2,383,000 to 2,591,000, an increase of 8.7 percent over the population living in the State in 1960 (table A). This increase was largely concentrated in the metropolitan areas, which accounted for about 80 percent of the growth. Within the metropolitan areas, almost all growth occurred in the suburban rings. In contrast, the non-metropolitan population increased by only 3 percent over the decade. Despite the large population increase in metropolitan areas, at present only two out of five persons in the State live in metropolitan areas compared to the national average of two out of three.

The total number of households in South Carolina in 1970 was 734,000, or 131,000 more than in 1960. The population living in households increased more slowly than the rate at which new households were formed, with the result that average household size dropped, from 3.8 to 3.4 persons per unit.

The white population in South Carolina accounted for 65 percent of total State population in 1960 and 69 percent in 1970. In the metropolitan areas whites comprise a somewhat higher proportion (75 percent). The rising proportion of whites reflects the very substantial outmigration of the population of Negro and other races. Over the decade, there was a loss of 193,000 persons of races other than white, equivalent to 23 percent of their 1960 population (see table 3).

The overall population growth in South Carolina between 1960 and 1970 resulted from a substantial natural increase (births less deaths) which more than offset net outmigration. The metropolitan areas as a whole registered a significant population gain reflecting a substantial excess of natural increase over net outmigration, while growth in the nonmetropolitan area was slight because of heavy net outmigration.

In all areas of the State two age groups registered declines or had only very limited growth over the decade. These were the age groups under 5 and the 25 to 44 years of age. In the State as a whole there was a decline of 59,000 in the population under 5 years of age. This represented a loss of 20 percent from 1960 to 1970. Over the same period, 25 to 44 year olds increased by 9,000 or by only 1.6 percent.

In contrast, there were three age groups which had significant growth: 15 to 24 year olds (which increased

Table A. Population by Race and Metropolitan and Nonmetropolitan Residence: 1970 and 1960

The State Metropolitan and Non-metropolitan Residence	Population		Change		Percent Distribution	
	1970	1960	Number	Percent	1970	1960
Total................	2,590,516	2,382,594	207,922	8.7	100.0	100.0
Metropolitan residence...	1,017,254	852,250	165,004	19.4	39.3	35.8
Inside central cities..	241,695	229,546	12,149	5.3	9.3	9.6
Outside central cities.	775,559	622,704	152,855	24.5	29.9	26.1
Nonmetropolitan residence	1,573,262	1,530,344	42,918	2.8	60.7	64.2
White................	1,794,430	1,551,022	243,408	15.7	69.3	65.1
Metropolitan residence...	767,073	615,795	151,278	24.6	29.6	25.8
Inside central cities..	157,134	146,573	10,561	7.2	6.1	6.2
Outside central cities.	609,939	469,222	140,717	30.0	23.5	19.7
Nonmetropolitan residence	1,027,357	935,227	92,130	9.9	39.7	39.3
Negro and other races	796,086	831,572	−35,486	−4.3	30.7	34.9
Metropolitan residence...	250,181	236,455	13,726	5.8	9.7	9.9
Inside central cities..	84,561	82,973	1,588	1.9	3.3	3.5
Outside central cities.	165,620	153,482	12,138	7.9	6.4	6.4
Nonmetropolitan residence	545,905	595,117	−49,212	−8.3	21.1	25.0

4

by 31 percent), 45 to 64 year olds (by 25 percent), and 65 years of age and over (by 27 percent). Among Negroes, the 25 to 44 and 5 to 14 year old population declined by 11 percent, reflecting the impact of out-migration.

Changes in the overall age distribution are found in other sections of the country and are the product in part of changing birth rates and in part are due to migration, which is highly selective by age. Low birth rates during the depression years and in the 1960's contribute to the diminution of age groups 25-44, and under 5 years, whereas the post-World War II "baby boom" is currently reflected in the large size of the population 15-24 years old.

Standard Metropolitan Statistical Areas

The metropolitan areas in South Carolina are fairly close in population size (see table 1). These are the Charleston (304,000 in 1970), Columbia (323,000) and Greenville (300,000) Standard Metropolitan Statistical Areas (SMSA's). (Augusta is excepted because the central city and the largest part of the population of that area is in Georgia.) Columbia and Charleston have Negro populations of 95,000 and 84,000 respectively. Greenville, on the western border of the State, has one-half as many Negroes as the other two SMSA's.

The three areas, differ in functions. Columbia's primary function is that of the capital of South Carolina. It also has significant activity in higher education and in military operations. Both these activities were expanded substantially between 1960 and 1970. Textiles are an important product. Greenville is one of the largest textile manufacturing areas in the South. The third SMSA, Charleston, is a port and the site of significant military operations (including naval shipyards). The latter increased substantially over the 1960-70 decade. There is also private shipbuilding in Charleston.

The Columbia SMSA registered the largest relative gain in population over the decade: it grew by 24 percent. It was followed by Charleston with a 19 percent gain and Greenville with 17 percent (see table 3). The population growth of both the Columbia and Greenville SMSA's benefited by net inmigration. They both had increases in their Negro population. Charleston had a small net outmigration which was offset by the large excess of births over deaths. There was a small decline in Charleston's Negro population.

Within each metropolitan area, the largest population gains occurred outside the central city (see table 3). This was not true for the Negro segment in Columbia. These gains occurred although some suburban territory was annexed by the central cities during the decade. These annexations, which were particularly large in Columbia and Charleston, resulted in central city population gains in both SMSA's (table B). Greenville's annexation was too small to provide a population increase for the period.

The age distribution of the populations of the three South Carolina SMSA's show the same tendencies noted for the State as a whole: losses in the under 5 year group, small gains of 25 to 44 year olds, and large gains in age groups 15 to 24, 45 to 64, and 65 and over (see table 4).

Counties

Twenty-three of South Carolina's 46 counties recorded population increases over the 1960-70 period. The fastest growing counties were those associated with the three SMSA's or adjoining them (see map). The one exception is Beaufort (site of a military installation) in the Southeast. The three counties with the largest populations grew moderately over the decade: Charleston (15 percent), Greenville (15) and Richland (17). The fastest growing counties were: Berkeley (47 percent), Lexington (47), Dorchester (32) and Pickens (28). These are all "suburban" counties except for Dorchester.

There were five counties which had population losses of 10 percent or more between 1960 and 1970. These

Table B. Change in Population of Central Cities Through Annexation: 1960 to 1970

Central Cities	1970 population			1960 population	Change 1960 to 1970 in 1960 area
	Total	In 1960 area	In annexed area		
Columbia.............	113,542	84,850	28,692	97,433	-12,583
Greenville...........	61,208	59,952	1,256	66,188	-6,236
Charleston...........	66,945	48,651	18,294	65,925	-17,274

were: Allendale (15 percent), Calhoun (12), Clarendon (13), Lee (16) and Williamsburg (16).

Races other than white (mainly Negro) increased in 11 counties. These were the larger counties for the most part. Only Pickens and Richland had significant increases in Negro population, 22 percent and 15 percent respectively. The others all had gains below 10 percent, far below their rates of natural increase.

Every county had more births than deaths during the decade. Particularly large numbers of births compared to deaths were registered in several counties: Charleston, Horry, Lancaster, Lexington and Richland. As noted, however, in half of the State's 46 counties, net outmigration was more than sufficient to wipe out the gains contributed by natural increase. Only seven counties had net inmigration.

HOUSING TRENDS

General

During the decade the relative increase in the total supply of housing units in South Carolina was greater than the increase in population. Housing units increased by 136,700, or 20 percent, while the population grew by 208,000, or 9 percent (table C).

The metropolitan areas of the State experienced greater relative growth in housing, as in population, than did the nonmetropolitan part. The number of housing units in metropolitan areas rose from 243,700 to 315,800 over the decade, an increase of 72,100 units, or 30 percent; this compares with an increase of 64,600 units, or 15 percent, in nonmetropolitan areas. While 39 percent of all housing units in the State were in metropolitan areas in 1970, these areas accounted for 53 percent of the total State increase between 1960 and 1970.

About 83 percent of the housing in South Carolina consisted of one-unit structures in 1970. The number of units in multiunit structures, however, increased at a much faster rate than one-unit structures during the decade, 55 percent and 10 percent, respectively.

The size of housing units increased between 1960 and 1970. The median number of rooms rose from 4.8 to 5.1 in the State. Units with one to three rooms declined whereas those with five rooms or more had large percentage increases over the decade.

Households were smaller in 1970 than in 1960. In the metropolitan areas, population per occupied unit declined from 3.7 in 1960 to 3.3 in 1970, and in nonmetropolitan areas from 3.9 in 1960 to 3.4 in 1970. There were large percentage increases in one-person households, 85 percent in the metropolitan areas and 75 percent in nonmetropolitan areas. Households with five or more persons showed relatively small gains in metropolitan areas and losses in nonmetropolitan areas.

The proportion of housing units lacking some or all plumbing facilities in South Carolina decreased from 39 to 19 percent during the decade. For metropolitan areas the proportion of units without complete plumbing facilities in 1970 was 11 percent as compared with 24 percent for nonmetropolitan areas.

Table C. Housing Units by Metropolitan and Nonmetropolitan Residence: 1970 and 1960

The State Metropolitan and Nonmetropolitan Residence	Housing units				Population percent change
	Total		Change		
	1970	1960	Number	Percent	
Total.................	815,123	678,379	136,744	20.2	8.7
Metropolitan residence.....	315,814	243,669	72,145	29.6	19.4
Inside central cities....	74,802	69,777	5,025	7.2	5.3
Outside central cities...	241,012	173,892	67,120	38.6	24.5
Nonmetropolitan residence..	499,309	434,710	64,599	14.9	2.8

Number of persons per room is often used as a measure of crowding. In South Carolina, units with 1.01 or more persons per room comprised 12 percent of all occupied housing units in 1970, compared with 21 percent in 1960 (table D). The number of all such units in 1970 was 90,600, representing a decrease of about 34,700, or 28 percent, between 1960 and 1970.

Homeownership in the State increased from 57 percent in 1960 to 66 percent in 1970. In metropolitan areas there was an increase from 59 to 66 percent, while in nonmetropolitan areas the proportion increased from 56 to 66 percent.

Property values and rents increased during the last decade. The median value of owner-occupied homes in metropolitan areas increased by 66 percent ($9,500 in 1960 to $15,800 in 1970), while in nonmetropolitan areas estimated value increased 77 percent ($6,400 in 1960 to $11,300 in 1970). In metropolitan areas, median contract rent in 1970 was 62 percent higher than in 1960, rising from $39 to $63. In nonmetropolitan areas, rent increased during the 10-year period, from $27 to $41, or 52 percent.

Value and rent are expressed in current dollars (the value at the time of the respective censuses). Thus, any comparison must take into account the general rise in the cost of living during the 10-year period as well as changes in the characteristics of the housing inventory.

Standard Metropolitan Statistical Areas

Average household size for the metropolitan areas declined during the decade. In the central cities, population per occupied unit decreased from 3.2 to 2.9, and in the suburbs from 3.8 to 3.4.

The rate of homeownership was greater in the suburban areas than in the central cities. About 72 percent of occupied units in the suburbs were owner-occupied, compared with 47 percent in the central cities.

In 1970, 8 percent of all year-round housing units in the central cities lacked some or all plumbing facilities, compared with 12 percent in the suburbs. Of all occupied units in metropolitan areas, 28,500 units, or 10 percent, reported more than one person per room in 1970, compared with 18 percent in 1960. In 1970, the proportion of such units was 9 percent in the central cities and 10 percent in the suburbs (table D).

The homeowner vacancy rate for metropolitan areas increased during the decade from 2.0 to 2.4 percent. The rental vacancy rate increased from 9.5 to 10.1 percent.

Annexations

Annexations occurred in the central cities of Charleston, Columbia, and Greenville during the decade (see "Population Trends" and text table B). Such annexations affect changes in the characteristics for these central cities and their suburbs.

Table D. Plumbing Facilities and Persons Per Room by Metropolitan and Nonmetropolitan Residence: 1970 and 1960

The State Metropolitan and Nonmetropolitan Residence	Percent of housing units			
	Lacking some or all plumbing facilities		With 1.01 or more persons per room[1]	
	1970[2]	1960[3]	1970	1960
Total......................	18.6	38.5	12.3	20.8
Metropolitan residence...........	10.7	(NA)	9.9	17.6
Inside central cities..........	7.9	23.2	9.4	15.6
Outside central cities........	11.6	(NA)	10.1	18.4
Nonmetropolitan residence........	23.6	(NA)	13.9	22.6

(NA) Not available.
[1] Percent of all occupied units.
[2] Percent of all year-round housing units.
[3] Percent of all housing units.

Population Change for Counties: 1960 to 1970

SOUTH DAKOTA

LEGEND

● Places of 50,000 to 100,000 inhabitants

○ Places of 25,000 to 50,000 inhabitants outside SMSA's

Standard Metropolitan Statistical Areas (SMSA's)

Percent change

Data derived from table 3

+13.3 or more

0 to +13.2

0 to −9.9

−10.0 or more

SCALE

0   10   20   30   40   50 MILES

County labels (north and east portion):
GRANT, DEUEL, BROOKINGS, MOODY, MINNEHAHA, SIOUX FALLS, LINCOLN, CLAY, UNION, SIOUX FALLS

ROBERTS, CODINGTON, HAMLIN, KINGSBURY, LAKE, McCOOK, TURNER, YANKTON

MARSHALL, DAY, CLARK, MINER, HANSON, DAVISON, HUTCHINSON, BON HOMME

BROWN, ABERDEEN, SPINK, BEADLE, SANBORN, AURORA, DOUGLAS, CHARLES MIX, GREGORY

MC PHERSON, EDMUNDS, FAULK, HAND, JERAULD, BUFFALO, BRULE

CAMPBELL, WALWORTH, POTTER, SULLY, HYDE, HUGHES, LYMAN, TRIPP

CORSON, DEWEY, STANLEY, JONES, MELLETTE, TODD

PERKINS, ZIEBACH, HAAKON, JACKSON, WASHABAUGH, BENNETT, SHANNON

HARDING, BUTTE, MEADE, PENNINGTON, RAPID CITY, CUSTER, FALL RIVER, LAWRENCE

533

Analytical Text

POPULATION TRENDS

General

The total population of South Dakota declined slightly between 1960 and 1970, from 681,000 to 666,000, a loss of 2 percent of the population living in the State in 1960. This decline occurred only in the nonmetropolitan areas, which show a population loss of 24,000. The State's single standard metropolitan statistical area (SMSA), Sioux Falls, increased by 8,600 persons, or 10 percent, over the decade. These changes scarcely affected the relative positions of the metropolitan and nonmetropolitan populations (table A). At the time of both censuses, the population of South Dakota was predominantly nonmetropolitan. At present, approximately one person out of seven lives in the State's metropolitan area, compared with a national average of 2 out of 3.

The total number of households in the State increased by about 3 percent during the decade, from a total of 195,000 in 1960 to 201,000 in 1970. At the same time, the number of persons living in households declined by 36,000, or more than 5 percent—twice the rate of decrease for the population as a whole. Average household size consequently dropped, from 3.5 persons per unit in 1960 to 3.2 persons in 1970. Growth in the State's group quarters population (residents of college dormitories, military barracks, extended stay hospitals and the like) partially offsets this loss of household population. The population living in group quarters, which increased during the decade by 21,000 persons, comprised over 4 percent of the total population of the State in 1970. In the Sioux Falls SMSA, both the number of households and the population living in households increased, by 15 percent and 8 percent, respectively. However, average household size in the SMSA also declined between 1960 and 1970, from 3.4 to 3.2 persons per unit.

At the time of both censuses, the population of South Dakota was more than 94 percent white. The balance, which is mainly Indian, is highly concentrated

Table A.   Population by Race and Metropolitan and Nonmetropolitan Residence: 1970 and 1960

The State Metropolitan and Non-metropolitan Residence	Population		Change		Percent Distribution	
	1970	1960	Number	Percent	1970	1960
Total...............	665,507	680,514	-15,007	-2.2	100.0	100.0
Metropolitan residence...	95,209	86,575	8,634	10.0	14.3	12.7
Inside central cities..	72,488	65,466	7,022	10.7	10.9	9.6
Outside central cities.	22,721	21,109	1,612	7.6	3.4	3.1
Nonmetropolitan residence	570,298	593,939	-23,641	-4.0	85.7	87.3
White...............	630,333	653,098	-22,765	-3.5	94.7	96.0
Metropolitan residence...	94,320	85,961	8,359	9.7	14.2	12.6
Inside central cities..	71,732	64,882	6,850	10.6	10.8	9.5
Outside central cities.	22,588	21,079	1,509	7.2	3.4	3.1
Nonmetropolitan residence	536,013	567,137	-31,124	-5.5	80.5	83.3
Negro and other races	35,174	27,416	7,758	28.3	5.3	4.0
Metropolitan residence...	889	614	275	44.8	0.1	0.1
Inside central cities..	756	584	172	29.5	0.1	0.1
Outside central cities.	133	30	103	343.3	...	...
Nonmetropolitan residence	34,285	26,802	7,483	27.9	5.2	3.9

in the nonmetropolitan areas of the State; less than 3 percent of races other than white lived in the Sioux Falls SMSA in 1970. In contrast to the white population, which declined statewide by 3.5 percent during the decade, the population of other races increased by 28 percent, or nearly 8,000 persons.

The components of population change indicate that in the State as a whole and in both metropolitan and nonmetropolitan areas there was a substantial excess of births over deaths. At the same time both areas show losses due to net outmigration, the largest being noted in nonmetropolitan areas. Although a natural increase of 80,000 was recorded for the State in this 10-year period, the population declined by 15,000. The difference implies a net outmigration of 95,000 persons, equivalent to 14 percent of the total 1960 population of the State.

Natural increase and outmigration of the white population closely parallel State trends over the decade. The rate of natural increase for races other than white, however, was much higher (41 percent compared with 11 percent for the white population). Nevertheless, the population of other races experienced net outmigration in the intercensal period in nearly the same degree as the white population. While the white population of South Dakota had a 14 percent net outmigration rate for the decade, the rate for other races was 12.5 percent.

All areas of the State experienced significant changes in age composition, particularly the population at younger ages. One group whose position did not change over the decade is the school age population 5 to 14 years old. At the time of both censuses this was the largest 10-year age group, comprising more than 20 percent of the total population of metropolitan as well as nonmetropolitan areas. By contrast, the size of the group under five was greatly diminished between 1960 and 1970 (see table 4). In the State as a whole, there was a decline in the number of children in this age group from 83,000 in 1960 to 54,000 in 1970, representing a

loss of 35 percent of the age group. There was also a substantial decrease in the number of adults 25 to 44 years of age, amounting to 14 percent in the State as a whole.

At the same time, young adults 15 to 24 years of age showed marked increases. Statewide this group grew by 27,000 persons, or by 30 percent over 1960. The only other group to increase significantly in the intercensal period was the population 65 years of age and over, which was 13 percent larger in 1970 than in 1960.

Similar changes are found in other sections of the country and are the product in part of changing birth rates and in part are due to migration which is highly selective by age. Low birth rates during the depression years and in the 1960's contribute to the diminution of the population under 5 and 25 to 44 years of age, whereas the post-World War II "baby boom" is currently reflected in the large size of the population 15 to 24 years old.

Standard Metropolitan Statistical Areas

Between 1960 and 1970 the distribution of the population of the Sioux Falls SMSA between central city and suburb scarcely changed. At the time of both censuses, there were three persons living inside the central city for everyone in the suburban ring. Population growth during the decade was moderate throughout the SMSA, although the central city grew at a somewhat faster rate than the suburbs. Natural increase in both areas was reduced by net outmigration equivalent to 6.5 percent of the city's 1960 population and only about 1 percent of the suburban population.

Annexation of territory by the central city had an important influence on redistribution of population within the SMSA. As a result of the extension of the city's boundaries into the suburban ring, Sioux Falls city acquired and the suburbs lost a population of 4,600 (table B). Without this boundary change, population

Table B. Change in Population of Central Cities Through Annexation: 1960 to 1970

| Central Cities | 1970 population | | | 1960 population | Change 1960 to 1970 in 1960 area |
	Total	In 1960 area	In 1960 annexed area		
Sioux Falls City............	72,488	67,900	4,588	65,466	2,434

growth in the central city would have been reduced and the suburban increase would have been greater.

The Sioux Falls city and suburban populations underwent changes in age composition similar to those described for the State as a whole. In both 1970 and 1960 the largest 10-year age group was made up of school children 5 to 14 years old, which comprised one-fourth of the total suburban population and 21 percent of the central city population. Both central city and suburb experienced a sharp reduction in the number of children under five years of age, amounting to 27 percent in each area. The central city also had a small reduction in the population aged 25 to 44 years. All other groups in the SMSA gained, but young adults 15 to 24 years of age showed by far the largest increases: in the city of Sioux Falls this age group increased by 53 percent. The second fastest growing age group in the central city was the elderly population, 65 years of age and over, which increased by 25 percent. With the exception of the population 65 and over, changes in the adult population of the city were closely paralleled by changes in the suburbs.

Counties

South Dakota's 67 counties range in size from a population of 1,400 (Washabaugh County) to 95,000 in the State's single metropolitan county (Minnehaha). Only four nonmetropolitan counties had populations exceeding 20,000 in 1970. The largest of these, Pennington County, contains Rapid City, where the largest part of the county's population is concentrated (44,000 out of the county total of 59,000). Other large counties are Brown (37,000 population), Brookings (22,000 population) and Beadle (21,000 population), each of which is the site of a college or university.

During the decade, only 14 counties in South Dakota gained population. Of these, five increased at rates exceeding the 13.3 percent rate of growth for the Nation as a whole (see map). Of the 53 counties which show population losses for the decade, more than half lost 10 percent or more of their 1960 totals. The counties which show population losses for races other than white also lost 10 percent or more of their 1960 populations.

The list of fastest growing counties does not include the metropolitan county or any of the four largest nonmetropolitan counties. All the counties which grew at rates exceeding the national average had large group

quarters populations or were predominantly Indian. Meade County, whose population was 16,600 in 1970, had one of the highest rates of increase for the decade, 38 percent. This county's population growth was due principally to the addition of military personnel to the area. Clay County, with a 1970 population of nearly 13,000, is the site of the University of South Dakota. In the intercensal period Clay County increased by 2,100 persons, or 20 percent; in the same period, the group-quarters population increased by 1,200. The three remaining fastest growing counties, Todd, Shannon, and Washabaugh Counties, which are of intermediate or small size, increased by 42 percent, 37 percent, and 33 percent, respectively. The populations of all three are predominantly Indian; the white populations of these counties show minor increases or losses.

A large part of the growth in group-quarters populations is associated with increases in enrollment at the State's larger colleges and universities. Approximately one-fifth of South Dakota's counties have disproportionately large group-quarters populations. In addition to Meade and Clay Counties, mentioned above, there are 11 other counties in the State whose group-quarters populations amount to 5 percent or more of their total 1970 populations. Many of these contain one or more colleges or universities. In all but one case, the group-quarters population increased its representation in the total population between 1960 and 1970. One of the State's largest counties, Brookings, (site of South Dakota State University) has a large and rapidly growing group-quarters population. Between 1960 and 1970, the group-quarters population of this county doubled and increased its share of total population from 8 percent in 1960 to nearly 14.5 percent in 1970.

In all counties in the State there were more births than deaths in the intercensal period. Rates of natural increase for races other than white were particularly high. Net outmigration was nonetheless a prominent feature of population change in 63 of the State's 67 counties, and in 10 of the 12 counties for which data on races other than white are available. Of the counties which experienced net outmigration, 56 had losses equivalent to 10 percent or more of their total 1960 populations. Nearly all the counties with large Indian populations also had very high rates of net outmigration.

Highest rates of population loss were experienced by counties with highest rates of net outmigration; e.g. Stanley County, whose population dropped by 40 percent between 1960 and 1970, suffered a net outmigration equivalent to 55 percent of its total 1960 population.

HOUSING TRENDS

General

During the decade, the total supply of housing units in South Dakota increased by 8,800, or 4.1 percent, while population decreased by 15,000, or 2.2 percent (table C). Similarly, the number of households increased (3.1 percent) while the population living in them decreased (-5.4 percent), resulting in lower average household size in 1970.

The growth in housing was much greater (16 percent) in the Sioux Falls SMSA than in the nonmetropolitan areas of the State (2 percent). While less than 15 percent of the year-round housing units were in the Sioux Falls SMSA, the SMSA accounted for 35 percent of the total State increase in such units between 1960 and 1970, and for nearly two-thirds of the increase in number of households.

A trend toward smaller households is evident throughout South Dakota. In the SMSA, there were large percentage gains in numbers of households consisting of only one or two persons and minor increases in numbers of larger households. In nonmetropolitan areas, only one- and two-person households gained at all.

Homeownership rates were slightly higher in 1970 than in 1960 in the State and in the nonmetropolitan areas, while in the SMSA the rate remained unchanged. Throughout the State, about two out of three housing units were owner occupied in 1970.

During the decade, median estimated value of housing in South Dakota increased by about 31 percent, from $8,800 in 1960 to $11,500 in 1970. Metropolitan-nonmetropolitan differentials widened somewhat during the same period; the median value of metropolitan housing, which was 46 percent higher than the nonmetropolitan in 1960, was 50 percent higher in 1970. Statewide, rents increased by almost 35 percent, with substantial increases in the number of higher-priced units. Value and rent are expressed in current dollars (the dollar value at the time of the respective censuses). Thus, any comparison must take into account the general rise in the cost of living in the 10-year period as well as changes in the characteristics of the housing inventory.

Number of persons per room is often used as a measurement of crowding. In South Dakota as a whole, units with 1.01 or more persons per room comprised 9 percent of all occupied housing units in 1970, compared

Table C.   Housing Units by Metropolitan and Nonmetropolitan Residence: 1970 and 1960

The State Metropolitan and Nonmetropolitan Residence	Housing units				Population percent change
	Total		Change		
	1970	1960	Number	Percent	
Total................	225,253	216,449	8,804	4.1	-2.2
Metropolitan residence.....	30,386	26,094	4,292	16.4	10.0
Inside central cities....	23,544	19,979	3,565	17.8	10.7
Outside central cities...	6,842	6,115	727	11.9	7.6
Nonmetropolitan residence..	194,867	190,355	4,512	2.4	-4.0

537

with 13 percent in 1960 (table D). The number of all such units in 1970 was 18,000, a decrease of 7,400, or 29 percent, between 1960 and 1970. An even greater relative drop occurred in the number having 1.51 or more persons per room. The decline occurred in metropolitan and nonmetropolitan areas alike, but in nonmetropolitan areas the improvement was greater.

Standard Metropolitan Statistical Areas

The housing supply in the Sioux Falls SMSA increased by 4,300 units, or 16 percent, between 1960 and 1970. The metropolitan rate of increase was thus four times that in the State as a whole. Paralleling the intercensal population changes in Sioux Falls city and its suburban ring, the rate of increase in the housing supply in the city exceeded that of the suburbs (table C). A component of both housing and population change in the Sioux Falls SMSA is annexation of territory by the central city (see "Population Trends" and table B). Such annexation affects to an unknown extent these and other changes in housing characteristics described in this section for the central city and suburb.

Average household size declined in both Sioux Falls city and suburbs between 1960 and 1970. Population per household in Sioux Falls city dropped from 3.3 to 3.1, and in the suburbs, from 3.7 to 3.5.

Differences in homeownership patterns in the SMSA are apparent, and during the decade were widened. In 1970, 64 percent of the central city's housing was owner occupied, compared with nearly 77 percent in the suburbs. While renter-occupied units in the city increased more rapidly than owner-occupied units, the suburban areas reflect an increase in owner-occupied housing and a decrease in renter-occupied units.

In 1970, the value of owner-occupied units as well as the monthly contract rent was about one-fourth higher in the city of Sioux Falls than in the suburbs. While the median estimated value of housing in the city was $16,100, in the suburbs it was $13,000; contract rent in the city was $85, but only $68 in the suburbs. In 1960, however, the differences between the central city and suburbs were much greater. While the median value of housing in the city rose 33 percent in the intercensal period, there was a 53 percent increase in the value of suburban housing. Increases in median contract rent show still greater differences: an increase of 37 percent in the city (from $62 to $85) and 74 percent in the suburbs (from $39 to $68).

Between 1960 and 1970, the median size of housing units in the Sioux Falls area remained at 4.8 rooms per unit in the central city, but dropped in the suburbs from 5.6 to 5.4 rooms. In the city, there were moderate percentage increases in units consisting of three to six rooms, a minor increase in units having only one and two rooms, and a significant gain of 46 percent in units having seven or more rooms. In the suburbs, by contrast, there were increases only in the four- to six-room units; units of all other sizes recorded losses for the decade.

Table D. Plumbing Facilities and Persons Per Room by Metropolitan and Nonmetropolitan Residence: 1970 and 1960

The State Metropolitan and Nonmetropolitan Residence	Percent of housing units			
	Lacking some or all plumbing facilities		With 1.01 or more persons per room[1]	
	1970[2]	1960[3]	1970	1960
Total...................	13.6	30.3	9.0	13.0
Metropolitan residence...........	5.6	13.3	7.2	11.6
Inside central cities..........	4.3	8.6	6.4	10.9
Outside central cities........	9.8	28.7	10.0	13.8
Nonmetropolitan residence.......	14.8	32.6	9.3	13.3

[1]Percent of all occupied units.
[2]Percent of all year-round housing units.
[3]Percent of all housing units.

In both central city and suburb, one-unit structures comprise the largest proportion of all year-round housing units. In 1970, 71 percent of the housing units in the city and 87 percent of those in the suburbs were in single-unit structures. Percentage increases in housing units in 2-or-more unit structures and in mobile homes or trailers greatly exceeded the growth of single-unit structures in both central city and suburb.

Between 1960 and 1970, the number of housing units with 1.01 or more persons per room declined by 32 percent in Sioux Falls city and by 18 percent in the suburbs. While there are more than twice as many such units in the central city, within the suburbs units containing 1.01 or more persons per room comprise a higher proportion of total occupied units. In 1970, over 6 percent of Sioux Falls city's housing was in that category, compared with 10 percent in the suburbs.

In 1970 about 4 percent of the housing units in Sioux Falls city and about 10 percent of the units in the suburbs lacked some or all plumbing facilities. These proportions reflect considerable improvement in this characteristic during the decade. In 1960, 9 percent of the city's housing units were not completely equipped with plumbing facilities compared with 29 percent in the suburbs.

Homeowner vacancy rates remained relatively stable at about 1.0 percent from 1960 to 1970 for the Sioux Falls SMSA, the central city, and the suburbs. Rental vacancies, however, rose noticeably from 3.9 percent in 1960 to 7.0 percent in 1970 for the SMSA. Although the rate increased both in Sioux Falls city and in the suburbs, the rise was greater outside the city.

Population Change for Counties: 1960 to 1970

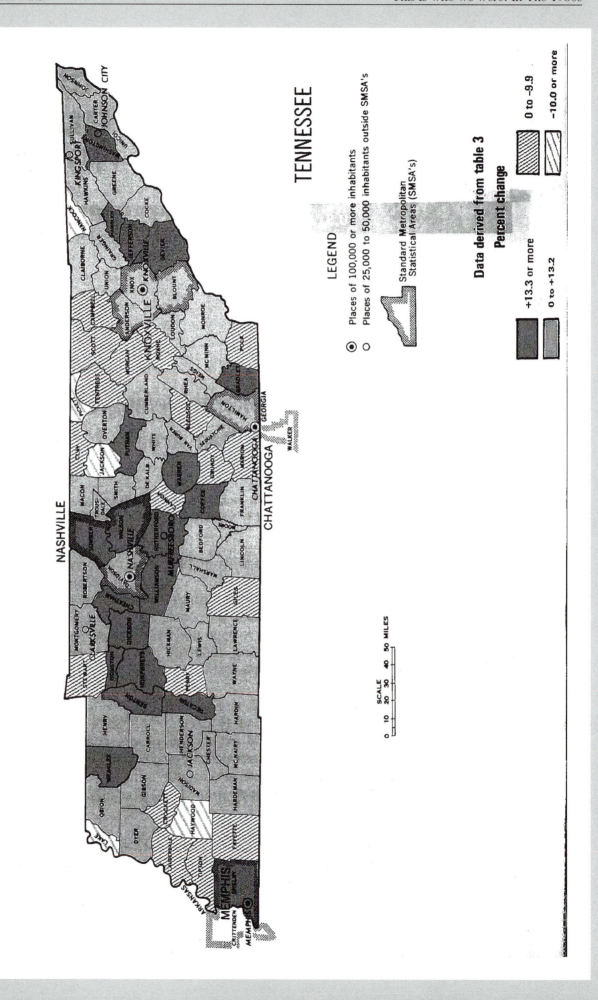

Analytical Text

POPULATION TRENDS

General

Between 1960 and 1970, the total population of Tennessee increased by 357,000, from 3,567,000 to 3,924, an increase of 10 percent over the population living in the State in 1960. This rate of increase is lower than the rates for the entire United States (13.3 percent) and for the South (14.2 percent). But among the East South Central States, which in addition to Tennessee includes Kentucky, Alabama, and Mississippi, Tennessee ranked first in rate of growth.

The total number of households in Tennessee in 1970 was 1,212,000, or 209,000 more than in 1960. The population living in households increased less rapidly than the rate at which households increased, with the result that average household size decreased from 3.5 to 3.2 persons per unit.

The rate of growth for the population living in the State's four SMSA's differed markedly from that for the nonmetropolitan population. The metropolitan areas of the State experienced greater absolute and relative population growth, increasing from 1,697,000 to 1,918,000 over the decade, or by 13 percent (table A). By comparison, nonmetropolitan areas increased at only half this rate. The effect of these changes on population distribution is very small. The proportion of the total population of the State living in the four metropolitan areas combined rose slightly from 48 percent in 1960 to 49 percent in 1970. In the United States as a whole, nearly 70 percent of the population lives in metropolitan areas.

State population growth over the decade was produced by a natural increase of 402,000 and a net outmigration of 45,000 (see table 3). Only in metropolitan areas did net inmigration contribute to population growth, although to a minor degree. Metropolitan areas

Table A. Population by Race and Metropolitan and Nonmetropolitan Residence: 1970 and 1960

The State Metropolitan and Non-metropolitan Residence	Population		Change		Percent Distribution	
	1970	1960	Number	Percent	1970	1960
Total...............	[1]3,923,687	3,567,089	356,598	10.0	100.0	100.0
Metropolitan residence...	1,917,695	1,696,632	221,063	13.0	48.9	47.6
Inside central cities..	1,365,202	1,139,103	226,099	19.8	34.8	31.9
Outside central cities.	552,493	557,529	-5,036	-0.9	14.1	15.6
Nonmetropolitan residence	2,005,992	1,870,457	135,535	7.2	51.1	52.4
White...............	3,283,432	2,977,753	305,679	10.3	83.7	83.5
Metropolitan residence...	1,473,622	1,308,305	165,317	12.6	37.6	36.7
Inside central cities..	965,537	813,434	152,103	18.7	24.6	22.8
Outside central cities.	508,085	494,871	13,214	2.7	12.9	13.9
Nonmetropolitan residence	1,809,810	1,669,448	140,362	8.4	46.1	46.8
Negro and other races	640,255	589,336	50,919	8.6	16.3	16.5
Metropolitan residence...	444,073	388,327	55,746	14.4	11.3	10.9
Inside central cities..	399,665	325,669	73,996	22.7	10.2	9.1
Outside central cities.	44,408	62,658	-18,250	-29.1	1.1	1.8
Nonmetropolitan residence	196,182	201,009	-4,827	-2.4	5.0	5.6

[1]See correction note on page 9.

gained 8,000 net inmigrants over the decade but had a natural increase of 213,000. Nonmetropolitan areas, which had a natural increase of 188,000, experienced a net outmigration of 53,000.

The white population and the population of all other races (mainly Negro) grew at very similar rates over the decade, by 10 percent and 9 percent, respectively. Growth of the white population of the State was almost entirely due to natural increase; there was a very slight change in this population group as a result of net migration. Other races, on the other hand, suffered an appreciable loss of population due to a net outmigration of 46,000 persons, equivalent to 8 percent of their total 1960 population. Tennessee has had a net outmigration of Negro and other races in each decade since at least 1940. By contrast, the white population, which had a substantital migratory loss of 97,000 during the 1940's, shows a very small net inmigration for the most recent decade.

In 1970, as in 1960, about 16 percent of the total population of Tennessee, and 23 percent of the population of metropolitan areas belonged to races other than white. Within metropolitan areas, both whites and Negroes are found in larger numbers in central cities. In 1970, 66 percent of the white metropolitan population, but 90 percent of the black metropolitan population were residents of central cities (see table 1).

The age composition of the Tennesee population changed significantly between 1960 and 1970. There was a decrease in the number of children under 5 years old, due largely to falling birth rates which occurred throughout the United States during the 1960's. The greatest increase occurred in the 15 to 24 age group and was due for the most part to the entry into this age group of the large number of persons born during the post-World War II "baby boom." As a result of these changes, the proportion of the total population under 5 years of age declined from 11 to 8 percent, and the proportion in the 15 to 24 year old group increased from 15 to 18 percent.

A comparison of changes in the age structures of the metropolitan and nonmetropolitan population shows some dissimilarities. In the metropolitan population, the age group 5 to 14 grew by 12 percent while the nonmetropolitan population in the same age group declined by about 1 percent. The metropolitan population showed appreciable gains in the 15 to 24 year old group (47 percent) and 65 years old and over (30 percent), with a 21 percent gain for both age groups in the nonmetropolitan population.

Standard Metropolitan Statistical Areas

There are four SMSA's located wholly or partly in Tennessee: Memphis, Tenn.-Ark., Nashville, Knoxville, and Chattanooga, Tenn.-Ga. Each of the SMSA's gained population during the decade. In 1970, 83 percent of the population of the Chattanooga, Tenn.-Ga. SMSA was in the State of Tennessee, and 94 percent of the population of the Memphis, Tenn.-Ark. SMSA.

Of the 1,918,000 people living in metropolitan areas in Tennessee, 40 percent, or 770,000, live in the Memphis SMSA. Memphis is the largest Mississippi port between St. Louis and New Orleans and the country's leading hardwood center. Between 1960 and 1970, the population of the entire Memphis SMSA increased from 675,000 to 770,000, or 14 percent. The central city of Memphis grew from 498,000 to 624,000, while the balance of the SMSA declined from 177,000 to 147,000. The central city growth is due to annexation (Memphis annexed a population of 137,000 population from Shelby County). Without such annexation, the city would have shown a population loss of 11,000 (table B). The Arkansas portion of the Memphis SMSA (Crittenden

Table B. Change in Population of Central Cities Through Annexation: 1960 to 1970

Central Cities	1970 population			1960 population	Change 1960 to 1970 in 1960 area
	Total	In 1960 area	In annexed area		
Memphis........................	623,530	486,986	136,562	497,524	-10,556
Nashville......................	448,003	446,470	1,533	170,874	275,596
Knoxville......................	174,587	118,449	56,138	111,827	6,622
Chattanooga....................	119,082	107,777	11,305	130,009	-22,232

County) grew between 1960 and 1970 (from 47,000 to 48,000). The Tennessee portion which grew from 627,000 to 722,000, increased by 15 percent.

The city of Nashville, the capital of Tennessee, and the site of Vanderbilt University, merged with Davidson County in 1962, becoming the first of several cities to consolidate with their county governments. The 77,000 increase in the Nashville-Davidson SMSA was comprised of a natural increase of of 55,000 and a net inmigration of 22,000—equivalent to 5 percent of its 1960 population. Most of this increase was in Nashville-Davidson County (the central city), although suburban Sumner and Wilson Counties gained substantially in population, largely through net inmigration.

The Chattanooga SMSA has less than half the population of the Memphis SMSA and grew only half as fast as Memphis between 1960 and 1970 (7 percent). The central county (Hamilton) in which the central city is located, grew by 7 percent while the suburban county (Walker, Ga.) grew more rapidly (12 percent). Population change in the entire SMSA was made up of a natural increase of 32,000 persons (59,000 births minus 28,000 deaths) and a net outmigration of 9,000. The loss of population due to net outmigration is equivalent to nearly 4 percent of the population living in the SMSA in 1960. The central city lost population between 1960 and 1970 in spite of annexation of suburban territory. The 1970 population of the area annexed to the city was 11,000. If annexation is excluded, the city lost 22,000 population.

The Knoxville SMSA had a population increase of 32,000 with a net migration loss of 7,000. Population growth is highly concentrated in the central county (Knox), which accounted for nearly 82 percent of the total SMSA's increase. Knoxville city grew from 112,000 to 175,000 while the balance of the SMSA lost 31,000.

Almost 90 percent of the growth in the city was due to annexation of surburban territory during the 1960's.

The Knoxville SMSA has a much smaller proportion of Negro and other races in its population than the other SMSA's in the State. Less than 7 percent of the total population was of Negro and other races in 1970. The proportion of the total population belonging to Negro and other races in Tennessee's three other SMSA's range from 38 percent in Memphis to 18 percent and 17 percent for Nashville and Chattanooga, respectively.

Counties

Of the 95 counties in Tennesse, 20 exceeded the U.S. average growth rate of 13.3 percent, 52 counties grew more slowly, and 23 counties lost population during the 1960-70 period.

The largest population increase in the 1960's in Tennessee was experienced by Shelby County (Memphis SMSA), a gain of 95,000. The largest relative increase occurred in Sumner (Nashville SMSA) with 55 percent; Cheatham, Williamson, Wilson, and Bradley Counties increased by 30 percent or more. Each of the seven metropolitan counties, Anderson, Blount, Davidson, Hamilton, Knox, Sumner and Shelby, experienced population growth between 1960 and 1970. Most predominantly rural counties lost population.

Sixty-six percent of Tennessee's counties gained population between 1960 and 1970, contrasting sharply with the situation in the State in 1950's, when more than 60 percent of the counties lost population.

Thirty-one of Tennessee's counties gained population through net inmigration, eight of them at rates equivalent to 10 percent or more of their 1960 populations. Twenty counties had outmigration rates of 10 percent or more. Every county in Tennessee had more births than deaths.

HOUSING TRENDS

General

During the decade the total supply of housing units in Tennessee increased more rapidly than population. While the population grew by 357,000, or 10 percent, housing units increased by 214,400, or 20 percent (table C).

The metropolitan areas of the State experienced greater relative growth in housing, as in population, than did the nonmetropolitan part. The number of housing units in metropolitan areas rose from 513,500 to 623,400 over the decade, an increase of 109,900 units, or 21 percent; this compares with an increase of 104,500 units, or 18 percent, in nonmetropolitan areas. The metropolitan areas contained 48 percent of the housing in Tennessee; the additions to the housing supply in these areas accounted for about 51 percent of the State's total housing increase between 1960 and 1970.

About 80 percent of the housing in Tennessee consisted of one-unit structures in 1970. The number of units in multiunit structures, however, increased at a faster rate than one-unit structures, 81 percent and 9 percent, respectively.

The size of housing units increased between 1960 and 1970. The median number of rooms rose from 4.8 to 5.0 in metropolitan areas and from 4.7 to 4.9 in nonmetropolitan areas. Units with one to three rooms declined in the State, whereas those with five or more rooms had relatively large percentage increases over the decade.

Households were smaller in 1970 than in 1960. In the metropolitan areas, average household size declined from 3.4 persons in 1960 to 3.1 in 1970, and in nonmetropolitan areas, from 3.6 persons in 1960 to 3.2 in 1970. There were large percentage increases in one-person households, 77 percent in the metropolitan areas and 84 percent in nonmetropolitan areas. Households with five or more persons showed relatively small gains in the metropolitan areas and losses in nonmetropolitan areas.

The proportion of housing units lacking some or all plumbing facilities decreased from 35 to 15 percent during the decade in Tennessee. For metropolitan areas

Table C. Housing Units by Metropolitan and Nonmetropolitan Residence: 1970 and 1960

The State Metropolitan and Nonmetropolitan Residence	Housing units				Population percent change
	Total		Change		
	1970	1960	Number	Percent	
Total.................	1,298,788	1,084,365	214,423	19.8	10.0
Metropolitan residence.....	623,431	513,530	109,901	21.4	13.0
Inside central cities....	449,548	351,557	97,991	27.9	19.8
Outside central cities...	173,883	161,973	11,910	7.4	-0.9
Nonmetropolitan residence..	675,357	570,835	104,522	18.3	7.2

the proportion of units without complete plumbing facilities in 1970 was 6 percent as compared with 23 percent for nonmetropolitan areas (table D).

Number of persons per room is often used as a measure of crowding. In Tennessee units with 1.01 or more persons per room comprised 10 percent of all occupied units in 1970, compared with 16 percent in 1960 (table D). The number of all such units in 1970 was 118,200, a decrease of about 44,500, or 27 percent between 1960 and 1970. The decline occurred in metropolitan and nonmetropolitan areas alike.

Homeownership in the State increased from 64 percent in 1960 to 67 percent in 1970. In metropolitan areas there was an increase from 61 to 62 percent, while in nonmetropolitan areas the proportion increased from 66 to 71 percent.

Property values and rents increased during the last decade. The median value of owner-occupied housing in metropolitan areas increased by 46 percent ($9,700 in 1960 to $14,200 in 1970), while in nonmetropolitan areas value increased 65 percent ($6,500 in 1960 to $10,700 in 1970). In metropolitan areas, median contract rent in 1970 was 54 percent higher than in 1960, rising from $46 to $71. In nonmetropolitan areas, rent

increased during the 10-year period from $28 to $48, or 71 percent.

Value and rent are expressed in current dollars (the value at the time of the respective censuses). Thus, any comparison must take into account the general rise in the cost of living during the 10-year period as well as changes in the characteristics of the housing inventory.

Standard Metropolitan Statistical Areas

Average household size for the metropolitan area total of the State declined during the decade. In the central cities, the average decreased from 3.3 persons in 1960 to 3.1 in 1970, and in the suburban areas from 3.6 to 3.3.

The rate of homeownership was greater in the suburban areas than in the central cities. In the suburbs, 75 percent of occupied units were owner-occupied, compared with 57 percent in the central cities.

In 1970, 3 percent of all year-round units lacked some or all plumbing facilities in the central cities, compared with 13 percent in the suburbs. Of all occupied units in metropolitan areas, 54,700 units, or 9 percent, reported more than one person per room in 1970, compared with 15 percent in 1960. In 1970, the

Table D. Plumbing Facilities and Persons Per Room by Metropolitan and Nonmetropolitan Residence: 1970 and 1960

The State Metropolitan and Nonmetropolitan Residence	Percent of housing units			
	Lacking some or all plumbing facilities		With 1.01 or more persons per room[1]	
	1970[2]	1960[3]	1970	1960
Total......................	14.9	34.9	9.8	16.2
Metropolitan residence...........	6.0	(NA)	9.3	14.8
Inside central cities..........	3.4	15.8	9.6	14.7
Outside central cities.........	12.7	(NA)	8.3	15.0
Nonmetropolitan residence........	23.2	(NA)	10.2	17.5

[1]Percent of all occupied units.
[2]Percent of all year-round housing units.
[3]Percent of all housing units.

proportion of such units was 10 percent in the central cities and 8 percent in the suburbs (table D).

The homeowner vacancy rate for metropolitan areas decreased during the decade, from 2.0 percent in 1960 to 1.3 percent in 1970. The rental vacancy rate increased, however, from 6.1 to 6.8 percent.

Annexations

Annexations occurred in each of the central cities during the decade (see "Population Trends" and text table B). Such annexations affect changes in the characteristics for these central cities and their suburbs.

Population Change for Counties: 1960 to 1970

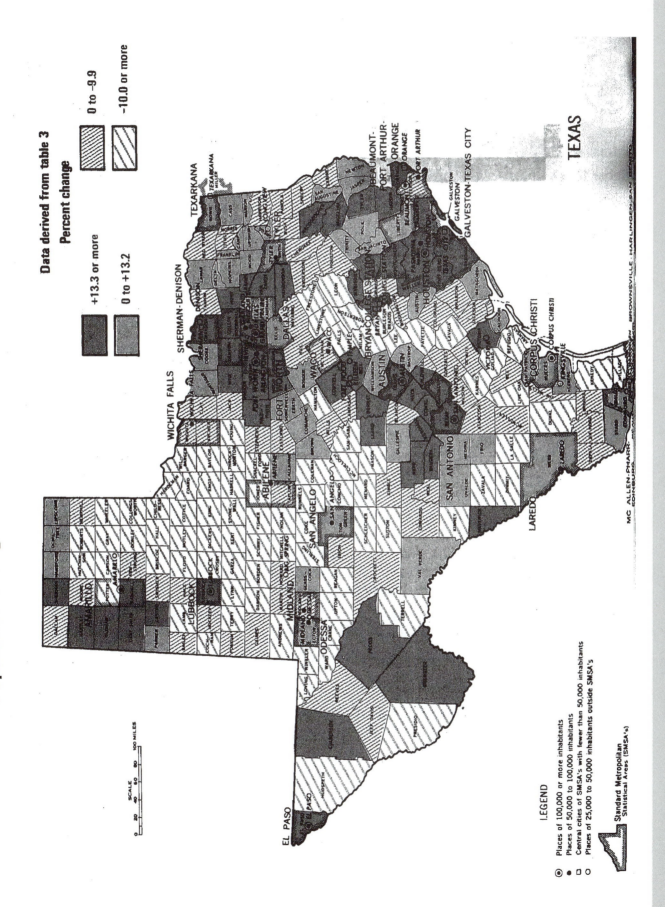

Data derived from table 3

Percent change

+13.3 or more

0 to +13.2

0 to −9.9

−10.0 or more

TEXAS

LEGEND

Places of 100,000 or more inhabitants

Central cities of SMSA's with fewer than 50,000 inhabitants

Places of 50,000 to 100,000 inhabitants

Places of 25,000 to 50,000 inhabitants outside SMSA's

Standard Metropolitan
Statistical Area (SMSA's)

SCALE

0   20   40   60   80   100 MILES

Analytical Text

POPULATION TRENDS

General

Between 1960 and 1970, the population of Texas grew from 9,580,000 to 11,197,000, an increase of 1,617,000 or 16.9 percent. This rate of increase is above the rate for the entire United States (13.3 percent). Texas ranked sixth in population in 1960 and fourth in 1970, having passed Illinois and Ohio during the decade.

The total number of households in Texas in 1970 was 3,432,000, or 654,000 more than in 1960. The population living in households increased more slowly than the rate at which households increased, with the result that average household size dropped from 3.4 to 3.2 persons.

In the Nation as a whole, there was an average of 3.1 persons per household in 1970.

Virtually all of the growth in Texas in the 1960 to 1970 decade occurred in metropolitan areas. The metropolitan population grew from 6,657,000 to 8,234,000, or by 24 percent. The nonmetropolitan population grew by only 1 percent, from 2,923,000 to 2,962,000 (table A). In 1970, three-fourths of the State's population lived in metropolitan areas compared to about two-thirds in the Nation as a whole.

Within metropolitan areas, slightly more than half of the growth occurred outside central cities. The central city population grew from 4,662,000 to 5,397,000, or by 16 percent, while the population outside central cities grew from 1,995,000 to 2,838,000, or by 42

Table A.   Population by Race and Metropolitan and Nonmetropolitan Residence: 1970 and 1960

The State Metropolitan and Non-metropolitan Residence	Population		Change		Percent Distribution	
	1970	1960	Number	Percent	1970	1960
Total...............	11,196,730	9,579,677	1,617,053	16.9	100.0	100.0
Metropolitan residence...	8,234,458	6,656,560	1,577,898	23.7	73.5	69.5
Inside central cities..	5,396,770	4,661,854	734,916	15.8	48.2	48.7
Outside central cities.	2,837,688	1,994,706	842,982	42.3	25.3	20.8
Nonmetropolitan residence	2,962,272	2,923,117	39,155	1.3	26.5	30.5
White...............	9,696,569	8,374,831	1,321,738	15.8	86.6	87.4
Metropolitan residence...	7,105,064	5,823,198	1,281,866	22.0	63.5	60.8
Inside central cities..	4,452,502	3,987,760	464,742	11.7	39.8	41.6
Outside central cities.	2,652,562	1,835,438	817,124	44.5	23.7	19.2
Nonmetropolitan residence	2,591,505	2,551,633	39,872	1.6	23.1	26.6
Negro and other races	1,500,161	1,204,846	295,315	24.5	13.4	12.6
Metropolitan residence...	1,129,394	833,362	296,032	35.5	10.1	8.7
Inside central cities..	944,268	674,094	270,174	40.1	8.4	7.0
Outside central cities.	185,126	159,268	25,858	16.2	1.7	1.7
Nonmetropolitan residence	370,767	371,484	-717	-0.2	3.3	3.9

percent. One-fourth of the growth in central cities was due to annexation (table B).

The population of Negro and other races in Texas (over nine-tenths of which is Negro) increased from 1,205,000 to 1,500,000, or by 25 percent, between 1960 and 1970. In 1970, Negro and other races constituted 13 percent of the State's population. The proportion of the population of Negro and other races living in metropolitan areas was three-fourths, the same proportion found among the white population. However, more than one-third of the white metropolitan population lived outside of the central cities, while only one-sixth of the metropolitan population of Negro and other races lived outside of the central cities. The nonmetropolitan population of Negro and other races declined slightly during the decade.

The population increase of 1,617,000 in Texas in the 1960 to 1970 decade resulted from a natural increase (births minus deaths) of 1,471,000 and a net inmigration of 146,000. Net inmigration accounted for one-eleventh of the growth and was equivalent to 1.5 percent of the 1960 population. The net inmigration of 146,000 was comprised of a net inmigration of 403,000 in metropolitan areas (equivalent to 6 percent of the 1960

Table B.   Change in Population of Central Cities Through Annexation: 1960 to 1970

Central Cities	1970 population			1960 population	Change 1960 to 1970 in 1960 area
	Total	In 1960 area	In annexed area		
Houston....................	1,232,802	1,197,278	35,524	938,219	259,059
Dallas.....................	844,401	833,065	11,336	679,684	153,381
San Antonio................	654,153	639,687	14,466	587,718	51,969
Fort Worth.................	393,476	382,431	11,045	356,268	26,163
El Paso....................	322,261	321,945	316	276,687	45,258
Orange.....................	24,457	23,325	1,132	25,605	-2,280
Corpus Christi.............	204,525	179,218	25,307	167,690	11,528
Austin.....................	251,808	207,159	44,649	186,545	20,614
Harlingen..................	33,503	33,187	316	41,207	-8,020
San Benito.................	15,176	14,567	609	16,422	-1,855
Waco.......................	95,326	92,035	3,291	97,808	-5,773
Amarillo...................	127,010	123,755	3,255	137,969	-14,214
Texas City.................	38,908	38,268	640	32,065	6,203
Wichita Falls..............	97,564	95,901	1,663	101,724	-5,823
Abilene....................	89,653	88,349	1,304	90,368	-2,019
Texarkana..................	30,497	30,399	98	30,218	181
Odessa.....................	78,380	75,155	3,225	80,338	-5,183
Tyler......................	57,770	56,193	1,577	51,230	4,963
Midland....................	59,463	57,359	2,104	62,625	-5,266
Laredo.....................	69,024	64,145	4,879	60,678	3,467
San Angelo.................	63,884	61,493	2,391	58,815	2,678
McAllen....................	37,636	35,646	1,990	32,728	2,918
Pharr......................	15,829	14,121	1,708	14,106	15
Edinburg...................	17,163	16,125	1,038	18,706	-2,581
Sherman....................	29,061	24,367	4,694	24,988	-621
Denison....................	24,923	23,901	1,022	22,748	1,153
Bryan......................	33,719	33,501	218	27,542	5,959
College Station...........	17,676	15,245	2,431	11,396	3,849

metropolitan population) and a net outmigration of 257,000 from nonmetropolitan areas (equivalent to 9 percent of the 1960 nonmetropolitan population). Among Negro and other races, net inmigration accounted for nearly one-fifth of the population growth.

The age structure of the Texas population changed significantly between 1960 and 1970. The only decline (14 percent) occurred among the population under 5 years old and was due largely to the decline in birth rates which occurred throughout the United States during the 1960's. The largest increase (50 percent) occurred in the 15 to 24 age group and was due to the entry of the large number of persons born during the post World War II "baby boom" into this age group. As a result of these changes, the proportion of the total population in the under 5 group declined from 12 to 9 percent and the proportion in the 15 to 24 group increased from 12 to 16 percent.

Standard Metropolitan Statistical Areas

In 1970, there were 24 standard metropolitan statistical areas (SMSA's) in Texas, including one that is partly in Texas (the Texarkana, Texas-Ark. SMSA).

As noted earlier, the metropolitan population of Texas grew by 24 percent. However, the patterns of population change varied greatly by size of SMSA. The demographic trends in the small SMSA's (those with populations of less than 250,000) were more similar to the demographic trends in the nonmetropolitan population than to those in the larger SMSA's.

In the two SMSA's with populations exceeding 1,000,000 (Houston, and Dallas), the population increased from 2,538,000 to 3,541,000, or by 40 percent, and net inmigration was 553,000. Close to two-thirds of the population growth in Texas between 1960 and 1970 occurred in these two SMSA's. Outside of these two SMSA's, Texas had a net outmigration of 407,000.

In the two SMSA's with populations in the 500,000 to 1,000,000 range (San Antonio and Fort Worth), there was a 26-percent increase in population and a net inmigration of 119,000.

In the four SMSA's with populations in the 250,000 to 500,000 range (El Paso, Beaumont-Port Arthur-Orange, Austin, and Corpus Christi), there was a 14-percent increase in population and a net outmigration of 52,000. In this group, only the Austin SMSA had a high rate of growth (39 percent) and net inmigration during the decade.

In the 16 SMSA's with populations under 250,000, there was only a 5-percent increase in population and a net outmigration of 218,000, or 13 percent of the 1960

population. (In the nonmetropolitan population, net outmigration was equivalent to only 9 percent of the 1960 population). Six of these SMSA's (Abilene, Amarillo, Brownsville-Harlingen-San Benito, Midland, Waco, and Wichita Falls) lost population between 1960 and 1970 and only two had rates of population growth above 15 percent (Bryan-College Station—29 percent, and Galveston-Texas City—21). Eleven of the 16 SMSA's experienced net outmigration during the decade. In the Brownsville-Harlingen-San Benito SMSA, net outmigration was equivalent to one-third of the 1960 population.

The Houston SMSA, the largest in Texas and the 13th largest in the Nation, had a population of 1,418,000 in 1960 and 1,985,000 in 1970, a 40-percent increase. Among the 33 SMSA's with 1970 populations exceeding 1,000,000, only the Anaheim-Santa Ana-Garden Grove and San Jose SMSA's had higher rates of growth. The city of Houston, which is a major port and the focal point of the huge oil and natural gas industry of the Gulf Coast, was the sixth largest city in the Nation in 1970 with a population of 1,233,000. In the decades from 1900 to 1970, the rate of population growth in the Houston SMSA ranged from two to six times the national average.

Over half of the growth in the Houston SMSA in the 1960 to 1970 decade was due to net inmigration. The net inmigration of 310,000 was equivalent to 22 percent of the 1960 population. In 1970, Negro and other races constituted one-fourth of the population in the city of Houston and less than one-tenth of the population in the remainder of the SMSA.

The Dallas SMSA, the second largest in Texas and the 16th largest in the Nation grew from 1,119,000 in 1960 to 1,556,000 in 1970, an increase of 39 percent. Dallas has a diversified economy including transportation, manufacturing, and wholesaling. In addition, the city is an important national financial center. Net inmigration into the Dallas SMSA during the decade was 243,000, equivalent to 22 percent of the 1960 population. The white population in the Dallas SMSA is evenly divided between the city of Dallas and the remainder of the SMSA. Only one-seventh of the population of Negro and other races live outside the city of Dallas.

The growth of Dallas has been only slightly less phenomenal than the growth of Houston. In 1970, the city ranked eighth in the Nation with a population of 844,000. In each of the last three decades the rate of population growth in the Dallas SMSA, as presently constituted, was between two and three times the national average.

The population of the San Antonio SMSA grew from 716,000 in 1960 to 864,000 in 1970, or by 21 percent. San Antonio is the location of several military facilities and has substantial Federal civilian employment. In addition, the city is a focal processing center for the agricultural production of southern Texas. A sizable proportion of the city's population is of Spanish-American descent. In 1970, San Antonio, with a population of 654,000, was the 15th largest city in the country. Net inmigration accounted for less than one-tenth of the growth in the San Antonio SMSA between 1960 and 1970.

The Fort Worth SMSA had a population of 573,000 in 1960 and 762,000 in 1970, resulting in an increase of 33 percent. Fort Worth has a diversified economy although aircraft production and meat packing have been of particular importance. Net inmigration accounted for more than half of the population growth in the Fort Worth SMSA during the past decade and was equivalent to 19 percent of the 1960 population. Between 1940 and 1970, the Fort Worth SMSA, as presently constituted, tripled in population.

The population of the El Paso SMSA was 359,000 in 1970, up 14 percent over 1960. This rate of growth was slightly above the national average despite a net out-migration equivalent to 11 percent of the 1960 population. The high rate of natural increase is due in part to the young population structure in the El Paso SMSA. In 1970, 55 percent of the population were under age 25 and only 6 percent were age 65 and over. El Paso, which is essentially a bilingual city, is noted for its mineral refining facilities and is also a trade and transportation center. It is the site of several military installations, including Fort Bliss. In 1970, the city had a population of 322,000.

The Beaumont-Port Arthur-Orange SMSA had a 1970 population of 316,000, just 3 percent more than in 1960. The area's economy is based largely on the oil and gas industry of the Gulf Coast. Net outmigration was equivalent to 10 percent of the 1960 population. The population growth was confined to the portion of the SMSA outside the three central cities. Each city lost population during the decade while the population in the balance of the SMSA grew by 25 percent. In 1970, Negro and other races constituted one-fifth of the population in the SMSA and one-third of the population in the central city portion.

The population of the Austin SMSA in 1970 was 296,000, or 39 percent more than in 1960. The rapid growth is due partly to the fact that the State capital and the main campus of the University of Texas are located in Austin. The population of the city of Austin grew 35 percent during the decade to 252,000 with much of the growth resulting from annexation. Net inmigration accounted for more than half of the growth in the SMSA and was equivalent to 22 percent of the 1960 population.

The Corpus Christi SMSA had a 1970 population of 285,000, up 7 percent from 1960. The petroleum industry and related manufacturing are of central importance to the area's economy. The population in the city of Corpus Christi increased 22 percent to 205,000 in 1970. Most of the growth was due to annexation, which accounts for the 19 percent decline in the population in the remainder of the SMSA.

The four SMSA's with 1970 populations in the 250,000 to 500,000 range (El Paso, Beaumont-Port Arthur-Orange, Austin, and Corpus Christi) had a combined growth rate of 14 percent during the 1960's, down sharply from the 39-percent growth during the 1950's when each of the SMSA's grew by at least 30 percent

The decline in the rate of population growth in the 16 SMSA's with 1970 populations under 250,000 was similar. Between 1960 and 1970, seven of the 16 lost population, and the combined growth rate was only 5 percent. During the 1950's, only one lost population, and the combined growth rate was 30 percent. While only four of the 16 SMSA's had higher growth rates during the 1960's than during the 1950's, most of the decline in the combined rate of growth can be traced to the cessation of growth in a few areas.

The Midland and Odessa SMSA's, which have economies based largely on the oil industry, experienced little population change during the 1960's after more than doubling in population during the 1950's. The Amarillo SMSA, which grew by 72 percent between 1950 and 1960, lost population during the following decade, due largely to the closing of Amarillo Air Force Base. In the Lubbock SMSA, which services the irrigated cotton farming area in western Texas and has shared in the prosperity generated by oil booms, the rate of population growth dropped from 55 to 15 percent during the past two decades. The Abilene SMSA, which also has benefited from oil booms and which services its agricultural hinterland, lost population during the past decade after experiencing a 41 percent growth rate between 1950 and 1960.

The Waco, Wichita Falls, and Brownsville-Harlingen-San Benito SMSA's each lost population after experiencing increases of 15 percent or more during the 1950's (Air Force bases were closed in both the Waco and Harlingen areas after 1960), while the population of the McAllen-Pharr-Edinburg SMSA remained virtually unchanged after increasing 13 percent during the 1950's.

The relatively rapid growth in the Bryan-College Station SMSA (29 percent) during the 1960's was due partly to the growth of Texas A & M University. The other six SMSA's in Texas (Galveston-Texas City, Laredo, San Angelo, Sherman-Denison, Texarkana, and Tyler) had rates of population growth ranging from 10 to 21 percent between 1960 and 1970.

Counties

Of the 254 counties in Texas, 108 gained population and 146 lost population between 1960 and 1970. Fifty-seven counties had rates of growth above the national average of 13.3 percent and 83 counties experienced losses of 10 percent or more. In the Nation as a whole, slightly more than half of all counties gained population during the decade. Of the 41 counties in Texas' metropolitan areas, 31 gained population during the decade.

Four counties had growth rates exceeding 50 percent, and all are located in metropolitan areas: Collin County (62 percent) and Denton County (59) in the Dallas SMSA; Montgomery County (84) in the Houston SMSA; and Randall County (59) in the Amarillo SMSA. At the other extreme, 25 counties had losses of 20 percent or more.

Twenty-five counties in Texas had a natural decrease (i.e., deaths exceeded births) in the 1960 to 1970 decade. Most of these counties are located within 100 miles of Dallas or Fort Worth, and all but one attained its maximum population in the 1900 to 1930 period. Several decades of net outmigration from these counties have produced old age structures; in many of these counties, the median age of the population is over 40.

Between 1960 and 1970, 68 (or 27 percent) of the Texas counties had net inmigration. In the Nation as a whole, 30 percent of all counties experienced net inmigration. Two counties in Texas had net inmigration exceeding 100,000: Harris County (including the city of Houston) had a net inmigration of 269,000, and Dallas County had a net inmigration of 201,000. The highest rate occurred in Montgomery where net inmigration was equivalent to 76 percent of the 1960 population.

The distribution of the Texas population changed considerably between 1960 and 1970. The population in the four largest SMSA's (Houston, Dallas, San Antonio, and Fort Worth) increased by 35 percent while the population in the remainder of the State increased by only 5 percent. As a result the proportion of the population living in the four largest SMSA's increased from 40 to 46 percent. In 1900, 18 percent of the State's population lived in these four SMSA's, as presently delineated.

During the 1960 to 1970 decade, there was a large area of population decline in Texas, extending from the Texas Panhandle south to Midland and Odessa and east to Wichita Falls. The 77 counties in this area, which constitute the High Plains and Rolling Plains areas of Texas, had a population of 1,423,000 in 1960 and 1,352,000 in 1970, a decline of 5 percent. Between 1950 and 1960, the population of this 77-county area increased by 26 percent, due in part to an oil boom. Of the six SMSA's in this area (Abilene, Amarillo, Lubbock, Midland, Odessa, and Wichita Falls), four lost population between 1960 and 1970.

HOUSING TRENDS

General

Between 1960 and 1970 the total supply of housing units in Texas increased more rapidly than population. The population grew by 1,617,000 or 17 percent, while housing units increased by 670,000, or 21 percent (table C).

The metropolitan areas of the State experienced greater relative growth in housing, as in population, than did the nonmetropolitan part. The number of housing units in metropolitan areas rose over the decade from

Table C.   Housing Units by Metropolitan and Nonmetropolitan Residence: 1970 and 1960

The State Metropolitan and Nonmetropolitan Residence	Housing units				Popula-tion percent change
	Total		Change		
	1970	1960	Number	Percent	
Total.................	3,823,100	3,153,127	669,973	21.2	16.9
Metropolitan residence.....	2,721,618	2,121,969	599,649	28.3	23.7
Inside central cities....	1,819,320	1,496,494	322,826	21.6	15.8
Outside central cities...	902,298	625,475	276,823	44.3	42.3
Nonmetropolitan residence..	1,101,482	1,031,158	70,324	6.8	1.3

2,122,000 to 2,721,600, an increase of 599,600 units, or 28 percent; this compares with an increase of 70,300 units, or 7 percent, in the nonmetropolitan areas. While 71 percent of all housing units were in the metropolitan areas, these areas accounted for 90 percent of the total State increase between 1960 and 1970.

About 80 percent of the housing in Texas consisted of one-unit structures in 1970. The number of units in multiunit structures, however, increased at a faster rate than one-unit structures during the decade, 91 percent and 10 percent, respectively.

The number of units in the State lacking some or all plumbing facilities declined from 626,100 to 293,300, a 53-percent decrease since 1960. In 1970, the proportion of such units was 5 percent in metropolitan areas and 15 percent in nonmetropolitan areas (table D). Approximately 74,600, or 19 percent, of the Negro-occupied units in the State lacked some or all plumbing in 1970; the corresponding proportions for inside and outside the metropolitan areas were 10 percent and 47 percent, respectively.

Households were smaller in 1970 than in 1960. In the metropolitan areas, average household size declined from 3.4 persons in 1960 to 3.2 in 1970 and in nonmetropolitan areas, from 3.3 to 3.0 persons. The number of one-person households increased by 68 percent in metropolitan areas and by 44 percent in nonmetropolitan areas. In comparison, the number of households with five or more persons increased 18

percent in metropolitan areas and decreased 9 percent in nonmetropolitan areas.

The median number of rooms rose from 4.6 rooms to 4.9 inside SMSA's and from 4.5 to 4.7 outside SMSA's. About 6 percent of the metropolitan and non-metropolitan housing units had one or two rooms in 1970, compared with 10 percent for both areas in 1960. The proportion of units with seven or more rooms rose from 9 to 13 percent in metropolitan areas and from 8 to 9 percent in nonmetropolitan areas.

Number of persons per room is often used as a measure of crowding. In Texas, both the number and the proportion of housing units with 1.01 or more persons per room decreased during the decade. In 1960, 16 percent of all occupied housing units in metropolitan areas and 17 percent in nonmetropolitan areas had 1.01 or more persons per room. By 1970, the proportion of such units had decreased to 11 percent in metropolitan areas and 12 percent in nonmetropolitan areas (table D).

The homeownership rate in Texas remained at 65 percent during the decade. As in 1960, homeownership was more prevalent in nonmetropolitan areas. In 1970, about 70 percent owned their homes in nonmetropolitan areas, compared with 63 percent in metropolitan areas. Of the 2,219,800 owner-occupied units in the State, 656,000 were outside metropolitan areas and 1,563,800 were inside these areas.

Approximately 63 percent of the Negro households in nonmetropolitan areas and 50 percent in metropolitan

Table D. Plumbing Facilities and Persons Per Room by Metropolitan and Nonmetropolitan Residence: 1970 and 1960

The State Metropolitan and Nonmetropolitan Residence	Percent of housing units			
	Lacking some or all plumbing facilities		With 1.01 or more persons per room[1]	
	1970[2]	1960[3]	1970	1960
Total....................	7.7	19.9	11.3	16.3
Metropolitan residence...........	4.9	(NA)	11.2	16.1
Inside central cities..........	3.7	11.3	11.5	15.6
Outside central cities........	7.4	(NA)	10.7	17.4
Nonmetropolitan residence........	14.8	(NA)	11.5	16.6

NA Not available.
[1]Percent of all occupied units.
[2]Percent of all year-round housing units.
[3]Percent of all housing units.

areas owned their homes in 1970. Of the 211,100 Negro-homeowner households in the State, 62,000 lived outside SMSA's and 149,100 lived inside SMSA's.

Property values and rents increased during the last decade. The median value of owner-occupied housing in metropolitan areas rose 39 percent, from $9,700 to $13,500, while in the nonmetropolitan areas value increased 41 percent, from $6,100 to $8,600. In metropolitan areas, median contract rent in 1970 was 57 percent higher than in 1960, rising from $54 to $85. In nonmetropolitan areas, the increase was 39 percent, from $38 in 1960 to $53 in 1970.

Value and rent are expressed in current dollars (the value at the time of the respective censuses). Thus, any comparison must take into account the general rise in the cost of living during the 10-year period, as well as changes in the characteristics of the housing inventory.

Standard Metropolitan Statistical Areas

In the metropolitan areas of the State, the housing supply increased by 599,600 units, or 28 percent. The Houston SMSA, the largest in the State, contained 25 percent of the housing units in the metropolitan areas and accounted for 34 percent of the increase. The second largest metropolitan area, the Dallas SMSA, contained 19 percent of the housing in the metropolitan areas and accounted for 26 percent of the increase.

The suburban areas of the State experienced greater relative growth in housing than did the central cities. Housing units in the suburbs, which comprised one-third of the metropolitan housing in 1970, increased by 44 percent, while housing in the combined central cities increased 22 percent. By 1970, there were 902,300 housing units in the suburbs and 1,819,300 units in the central cities.

About 77 percent of the housing units in the State's metropolitan areas consisted of one-unit structures in 1970. The proportion of such units was 73 percent in the central cities and 85 percent in the suburban areas.

In 1970, 132,500 housing units in metropolitan areas, or 5 percent of all year-round units, lacked some or all plumbing facilities. The corresponding proportions for the central cities and the suburbs were 4 percent and 7 percent, respectively. Approximately 14,200, or 6 percent, of the Negro households in the central cities occupied units which lacked some or all plumbing facilities in 1970; in suburban areas, 14,900 Negro

households, or 35 percent, lacked such plumbing facilities.

Households were smaller in the central cities than in the suburbs. Average household size in 1970 was 3.1 persons in the central cities and 3.4 persons in the suburbs. One-person households constituted 18 percent of all households in the central cities and 11 percent in the suburbs.

In 1970 the median number of rooms in the central cities was 4.8, and in the suburbs, 5.0. About 20 percent of the housing in the central cities had one to three rooms, and 14 percent of the housing in the suburbs was in this category. At the same time, 30 percent of the units in the central cities had six or more rooms, compared with 35 percent in the suburbs.

Of all occupied units in metropolitan areas, 279,900, or 11 percent, reported more than one person per room in 1970, compared with 16 percent in 1960. In 1970, the proportion of such units was 11 percent in both the central cities and the suburbs (table D).

Homeownership in 1970 was greater in the suburban areas than in the central cities. About 72 percent of occupied units in the suburbs and 58 percent in the central cities were owner-occupied. The Negro-homeownership rate in the suburbs was 64 percent, compared with 48 percent in the central cities.

Median value of owner-occupied housing was $13,100 in the central cities and $14,300 in the suburban areas. Approximately 15 percent of the owner-occupied housing units in the central cities and in the suburbs were valued at $25,000 or more. Median contract rent was $83 in the central cities, compared with $91 in the suburbs. In both the central cities and suburbs, about 17 percent of renter-occupied units rented for $150 or more.

The homeowner vacancy rate for metropolitan areas decreased during the decade from 2.7 to 1.9 percent. The rental vacancy rate decreased from 11.8 to 10.9 percent.

Annexations

Annexations occurred in each of the central cities in Texas except the cities of Beaumont, Brownsville, Galveston, Lubbock, and Port Arthur (see "Population Trends" and text table B). Such annexations affect changes in the characteristics for these central cities and their suburbs.

Population Change for Counties: 1960 to 1970

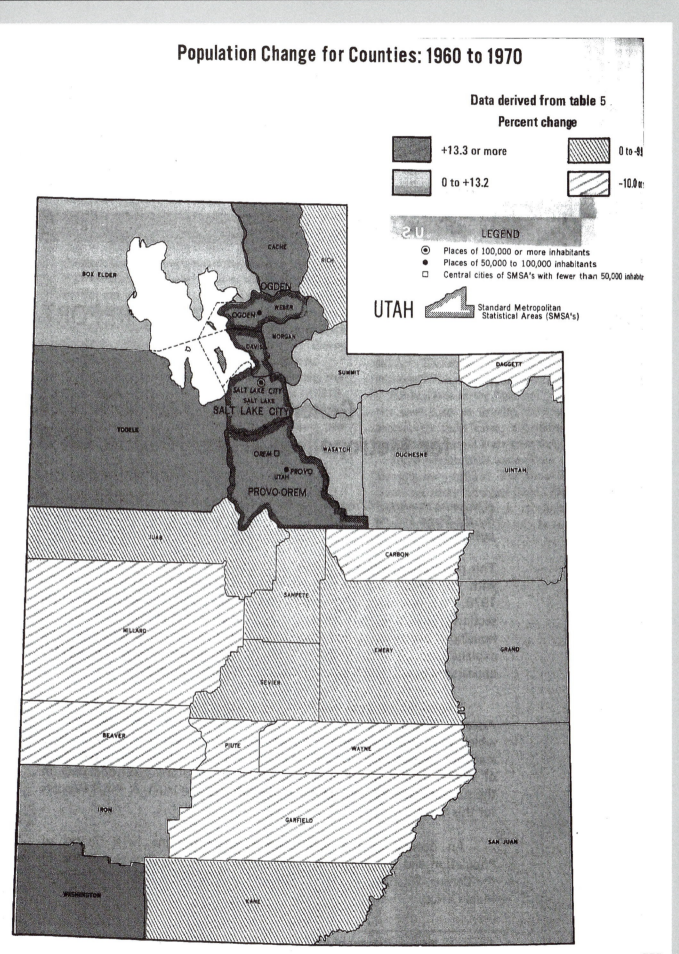

Data derived from **table** 5

Percent change

+13.3 or more

0 to -9!

0 to +13.2

-10.0 or

LEGEND

⊙ Places of 100,000 or more inhabitants
● Places of 50,000 to 100,000 inhabitants
☐ Central cities of SMSA's with fewer than 50,000 inhabit

UTAH   Standard Metropolitan
            Statistical Areas (SMSA's)

Analytical Text

POPULATION TRENDS

General

Between 1960 and 1970 the total population of Utah grew by nearly 169,000 persons, from 891,000 to 1,059,000, an increase of 19 percent over the population living in the State in 1960. This growth was highly concentrated in the three metropolitan areas of the State—Salt Lake City, Provo-Orem, and Ogden—which grew by 24 percent over the decade and together accounted for almost 93 percent of the total State increase (156,000 persons). Growth within these metropolitan areas was almost entirely suburban; the population increase of the central cities accounted for only 6.5 percent of the total metropolitan increase. By contrast, the nonmetropolitan areas acquired an additional population of only 12,000 persons, representing an increase of 5.5 percent over 1960 (table A).

The total number of households in the State in 1970 was 298,000, or 56,000 more than in 1960. The population living in households increased less rapidly than the rate at which new households were formed, with the result that average household size declined slightly from 3.6 to 3.5 persons per unit.

The effect of these changes on population distribution by metropolitan-nonmetropolitan residence was very small. The proportion of the total population living in the three metropolitan areas increased by 3 percent during the decade. Nearly four out of every five persons in Utah now live in metropolitan areas, compared with a national average of two out of three.

In 1960 as in 1970, more than 96 percent of the metropolitan and nonmetropolitan populations of Utah were white; the balance was mainly Indian (see table 1). Although numerically and proportionally very much smaller than the white population, other races increased at much faster rates (by 63 percent in the State as a whole, compared with a white rate of 18 percent). In the central cities, races other than white increased by nearly half, while in the suburban rings their numbers more than doubled during the decade. These changes increased

Table A.   Population by Race and Metropolitan and Nonmetropolitan Residence: 1970 and 1960

The State Metropolitan and Non-metropolitan Residence	Population		Change		Percent Distribution	
	1970	1960	Number	Percent	1970	1960
Total................	1,059,273	890,627	168,646	18.9	100.0	100.0
Metropolitan residence...	821,689	665,530	156,159	23.5	77.6	74.7
Inside central cities..	324,223	314,092	10,131	3.2	30.6	35.3
Outside central cities.	497,466	351,438	146,028	41.6	47.0	39.5
Nonmetropolitan residence	237,584	225,097	12,487	5.5	22.4	25.3
White................	1,031,926	873,828	158,098	18.1	97.4	98.1
Metropolitan residence...	804,419	655,710	148,709	22.7	75.9	73.6
Inside central cities..	314,383	307,325	7,058	2.3	29.7	34.5
Outside central cities.	490,036	348,385	141,651	40.7	46.3	39.1
Nonmetropolitan residence	227,507	218,118	9,389	4.3	21.5	24.5
Negro and other races	27,347	16,799	10,548	62.8	2.6	1.9
Metropolitan residence...	17,270	9,820	7,450	75.9	1.6	1.1
Inside central cities..	9,840	6,767	3,073	45.4	0.9	0.8
Outside central cities.	7,430	3,053	4,377	143.4	0.7	0.3
Nonmetropolitan residence	10,077	6,979	3,098	44.4	1.0	0.8

the proportion of the population of races other than white living in metropolitan areas from 58 percent in 1960 to 63 percent in 1970.

In the State as a whole and in both metropolitan and nonmetropolitan areas there was a substantial excess of births over deaths. At the same time losses due to net outmigration are noted for the State overall and for the nonmetropolitan areas. Although a natural increase of 180,000 was recorded for the State in this 10-year period, the population grew by only 169,000. The difference implies a net outmigration of 11,000 persons, equivalent to 1.2 percent of the total 1960 population of the State. Net outmigration from the nonmetropolitan areas was more significant, amounting to 25,000 persons, or 11 percent of their total 1960 population. The metropolitan portion of the State, on the other hand, gained population through net inmigration as well as natural increase. Migration played a relatively small part in this growth, however; while the natural increase of metropolitan areas amounted to 142,000, net inmigration contributed only an additional 14,000 persons.

Components of white population change closely parallel those for the State as a whole: a natural increase of 174,000 was cut back by a small net outmigration, amounting to 16,000 persons. The growth of Negro and other races, by contrast, was due almost equally to net inmigration (of 5,300 persons) and to natural increase (of 5,200).

Over the decade the age composition of Utah's population was altered in several important respects. A decline in the number of children under 5 years of age (of 14,000, or 11 percent) was counterbalanced by increases in the size of all other age groups. By far the greatest numerical and percentage increases were realized by the 15 to 24 year old population which grew by 78,000 persons, an increase of 57 percent over the number in the State in 1960. The elderly population, 65 years of age and over, and the population 45-64 years of age also had large increases, amounting to 29 percent

and 25 percent, respectively (see table 4). Between 1960 and 1970, the proportion of the total State population represented by children under 5 dropped from 14 percent to less than 11 percent, but the proportion represented by 15 to 24 year olds increased from 15 percent in 1960 to 20 percent in 1970.

Similar changes are found in other sections of the country and are the product in part of changing birth rates and in part are due to age selective migration. Low birth rates during the 1960's contribute to the diminution of the population under 5 years of age, whereas the post-World War II "baby boom" is currently reflected in the large size of the population 15-24 years old.

Standard Metropolitan Statistical Areas

At the time of both censuses, two-thirds of Utah's total metropolitan population lived in the Salt Lake City SMSA. In 1970, the population of this SMSA was 558,000, compared with 138,000 in Provo-Orem and 126,000 in Ogden. Each SMSA grew in population over the decade, Provo-Orem and Salt Lake City at somewhat similar rates of 29 percent and 25 percent, respectively, and the Ogden SMSA by 14 percent.

Within the SMSA's, there are marked differences between Salt Lake City and Ogden on the one hand and Provo-Orem on the other. In Salt Lake City and Ogden, only the suburban rings grew during the intercensal period, and by considerable amounts. The Salt Lake City suburbs increased by 123,000 persons, or 48 percent, and the Ogden suburbs grew by 16,000 persons, or 40 percent. Meanwhile, the central cities of the two SMSA's declined slightly, by 7 percent in Salt Lake City and 1 percent in Ogden. By contrast, the central cities of Provo and Orem grew rapidly during the decade, by 47 percent and 40 percent, respectively, and the suburban ring relatively slowly, by 12 percent.

Annexation of territory of two by the central cities—Ogden and Provo—accounts in part for the changes which occured in those SMSA's (table B).

Table B. Change in Population of Central Cities Through Annexation: 1960 to 1970

| Central Cities | 1970 population | | | 1960 population | Change 1960 to 1970 in 1960 area |
	Total	In 1960 area	In annexed area		
Salt Lake City..............	175,885	175,397	488	189,454	-14,057
Ogden......................	69,478	67,377	2,101	70,197	-2,820
Provo......................	53,131	48,170	4,961	36,047	12,123

During the decade Ogden annexed suburban territory containing a population of 2,100. Without this annexation, the direction of change already described would have been accentuated: the small decline in the population of Ogden city (700 persons) would have been greater, and the suburban population increase corresponsingly higher. Provo city's annexation of a population of 5,000 was an important component of its rapid growth. Had it not taken place, the city's increase would appear lower and the suburbs would show twice the increase they now do. Salt Lake City also annexed territory during the decade, but the population transferred from suburb to city was so small—less than 500 persons—that its effect was neglible.

As a result of the changes which actually occurred over the decade, the proportion of total SMSA populations living in central cities was reduced in the case of Salt Lake City and Ogden, and raised in Provo-Orem. In 1960, 42 percent of the Salt Lake City SMSA's population lived in the central city; by 1970, this proportion had dropped to 32 percent. Similarly, Ogden city's proportion was lowered from 63 percent in 1960 to 55 percent in 1970. Provo and Orem cities combined account for 58 percent of the SMSA's total population in 1970, compared with 51 percent in 1960. The greater advance was made by Provo city, which increased its share of the SMSA population by 5 percent over the decade.

As in the State as a whole, there were major changes in the age composition of the populations of the three SMSA's. Some changes were common to all central cities or suburban rings, but in many respects their patterns of change differ. All four central cities had gains in two age groups: 15-24 year olds and the population 65 years of age and over (see table 4). Increases in the number of persons 15-24 years of age were especially large in Provo and Orem cities, where they more than doubled. In Provo, where Brigham Young University is located, three-quarters of the total decennial population increase was accounted for by this one age group. In 1970 it comprised 45 percent of the entire population of this city compared with much lower percentages of 21-25 percent in the other central cities. The elderly population increased moderately in three of the central cities, but in Orem its rate of increase was very high, amounting to 70 percent. Changes in other age groups vary from one central city to another. In Salt Lake City and Ogden, all age groups except young adults and the elderly population were either reduced in size or show minor change. Provo city gained at all ages, but the increase in 15-24 year olds overwhelmed all other groups. Orem had significant increases, not only in the young adult and elderly population, but also in the 45-64 year old population which grew by 77 percent over the decade.

The suburban rings of Salt Lake City and Ogden show almost identical patterns of change by age. Increases in ages 15-24 (of 94 percent) and 45-64 (of approximately 80 percent) dominate all other changes. More than one-half the increase in the suburbs of Salt Lake City and Ogden in the intercensal period is accounted for by these two age groups. In the Provo-Orem suburban ring, on the other hand, there were more moderate increases at all ages except for the population under 5 years, which was reduced by 11 percent.

Counties

Utah's 29 counties range in population size from less than 1,000 (Daggett County) to 459,000 (Salt Lake County). The most populous counties are the metropolitan counties of Salt Lake, Utah (138,000 population), Weber (126,000 population), and Davis (99,000 population). The largest nonmetropolitan counties, with 1970 populations exceeding 20,000, are Cache, Box Elder, and Tooele. All seven of these counties are located in the northwestern corner of the State (see map). In combination they accounted for 86 percent of Utah's total population.

A little more than half of Utah's counties grew in population during the decade, eight of them at rates exceeding the 13.3 percent increase for the nation as a whole. Most of these fast growing counties are located in the more heavily populated northwestern corner of the State.

Counties with highest rates of population loss (exceeding 9 percent) for the decade also tend to be concentrated geographically: five of the seven counties with such losses are located in the southern and southwestern portions of the State.

Counties in Utah containing universities and colleges or military bases are among the largest and fastest-growing: e.g., Salt Lake County has the University of Utah; Utah County, Brigham Young University; Weber County, Weber State University; and Cache County has Utah State University. Each school experienced a substantial increase in enrollment over the decade. Davis County is the site of a military installation which also increased in size in this period. A considerable portion of the overall population gains of two of these counties—Utah and Cache—was due to increases in their group-quarters populations. Between 1960 and 1970, the group-quarters population of Cache County grew by nearly 1,400 persons, accounting for 25 percent of its total population increase. By 1970, residents of group quarters comprised over 6 percent of this county's total population. Utah County gained still larger numbers from this source. An increase of nearly 6,000 in the group-quarters population made up about one-fifth of the county's entire increase. In 1970, this population group comprises 9 percent of the county's total.

All counties in the State had more births than deaths over the decade. In all but four counties, however, the natural increase of the population was cut back by net outmigration. Of the 25 counties which had net migratory losses, 16 lost the equivalent of 10 percent or more of their 1960 populations. The greatest attractor of migrants in the State was Davis County (part of the Salt Lake City SMSA) which had a net inmigration of 16,000 persons, equivalent to 25 percent of its 1960 population. Other counties drew smaller numbers, even though rates were high: Utah County (Provo-Orem SMSA) had a net inmigration of 6,000 (6 percent), while Washington and Morgan Counties, with rates of 24 percent and 16 percent, respectively, gained only very small numbers.

HOUSING TRENDS

General

Between 1960 and 1970 the population and the supply of housing units in Utah increased at about the same rate. While the population grew by 169,000, or 19 percent the number of housing units increased by 53,100, or 20 percent (table C).

Housing trends in Utah, like population trends, were dominated by the metropolitan areas, which contained three-fourths of the State's housing stock. During the decade, about 88 percent (46,900) of Utah's housing increase occurred inside SMSA's.

Three-fourths of the housing in Utah consisted of one-unit structures in 1970. The number of units in multiunit structures, however, increased at a much faster rate than one-unit structures during the decade, 44 percent and 12 percent, respectively.

The size of housing units increased between 1960 and 1970. The median number of rooms rose from 4.8 to 5.0 in metropolitan areas and from 4.6 to 5.0 in nonmetropolitan areas.

Households were smaller in 1970 than in 1960. In metropolitan areas, the median number of persons per housing unit declined from 3.4 in 1960 to 3.1 in 1970, and in nonmetropolitan areas, from 3.4 persons in 1960 to 3.0 in 1970. The number of one- and two-person households in metropolitan areas increased by 51 percent and 40 percent, respectively; in nonmetropolitan areas, one- and two-person households also showed increases, 38 percent and 34 percent, respectively.

The number of units in the State lacking some or all plumbing facilties declined from 16,100 to 8,600, a 47-percent decrease since 1960. In 1970, the proportion of such units was 3 percent of all year-round units.

Number of persons per room is often used as a measure of crowding. In Utah, both the number and proportion of housing units with 1.01 or more persons per room decreased during the decade. In 1960, 16 percent of all occupied housing units in metropolitan areas and 20 percent of all occupied housing units in nonmetropolitan areas had 1.01 or more persons per

Table C. Housing Units by Metropolitan and Nonmetropolitan Residence: 1970 and 1960

The State Metropolitan and Nonmetropolitan Residence	Housing units				Population percent change
	Total		Change		
	1970	1960	Number	Percent	
Total.................	315,765	262,670	53,095	20.2	18.9
Metropolitan residence.....	238,663	191,741	46,922	24.5	23.5
Inside central cities....	108,935	100,279	8,656	8.6	3.2
Outside central cities...	129,728	91,462	38,266	41.8	41.6
Nonmetropolitan residence..	77,102	70,929	6,173	8.7	5.5

room. By 1970, the proportion of such units decreased to 10 percent in metropolitan areas and 12 percent in nonmetropolitan areas (table D).

Homeownership in the State decreased from 72 percent in 1960 to 69 percent in 1970. In metropolitan areas, there was a decrease from 71 percent to 68 percent, while in nonmetropolitan areas the proportion remained at 75 percent.

Property values and rents increased in the last decade. The median value in metropolitan areas increased by 31 percent from $13,500 in 1960 to $17,700 in 1970, while in the nonmetropolitan areas, value increased 47 percent from $9,000 to $13,200. In metropolitan areas, median contract rent in 1970 was 42 percent higher than in 1960, rising from $59 to $84. In nonmetropolitan areas, rent increased from $46 to $67, an increase of 46 percent.

Value and rent are expressed in current dollars (the value at the time of the respective censuses). Thus, any comparison must take into account the general rise in the cost of living during the 10-year period as well as changes in the characteristics of the housing inventory.

Standard Metropolitan Statistical Areas

The housing supply in metropolitan areas (Ogden, Provo-Orem, and Salt Lake City) increased by 46,922, or 24 percent, between 1960 and 1970. In 1970, there were 238,663 housing units in metropolitan areas, while in 1960, there were 191,741 units.

Average household size declined in metropolitan areas during the decade. Population per occupied units was 3.5 in 1970, compared with 3.6 in 1960.

In 1970, 3,900 housing units in metropolitan areas, or 2 percent of all year-round units, lacked some or all plumbing facilities. Of all occupied units in metropolitan areas, 23,300 units, or 10 percent, reported more than one person per room in 1970, compared with 16 percent in 1960.

The homeowner vacancy rate for metropolitan areas decreased during the decade from 1.9 to 0.6 percent. Similarly, the rental vacancy rate decreased from 7.8 to 4.8.

Annexations

Annexation occurred in the central cities of Ogden and Provo during the decade (see "Population Trends" and text table B). Such annexation affect changes in the characteristics for these central cities and their suburbs.

Table D. Plumbing Facilities and Persons Per Room by Metropolitan and Nonmetropolitan Residence: 1970 and 1960

The State Metropolitan and Nonmetropolitan Residence	Percent of housing units			
	Lacking some or all plumbing facilities		With 1.01 or more persons per room [1]	
	1970 [2]	1960 [3]	1970	1960
Total......................	2.7	6.1	10.6	16.7
Metropolitan residence..........	1.6	(NA)	10.1	15.6
Inside central cities.........	2.5	4.5	7.8	12.0
Outside central cities........	0.9	(NA)	12.0	19.6
Nonmetropolitan residence........	6.3	(NA)	12.3	19.8

NA Not available.
[1] Percent of all occupied units.
[2] Percent of all year-round housing units.
[3] Percent of all housing units.

Population Change for Counties: 1960 to 1970

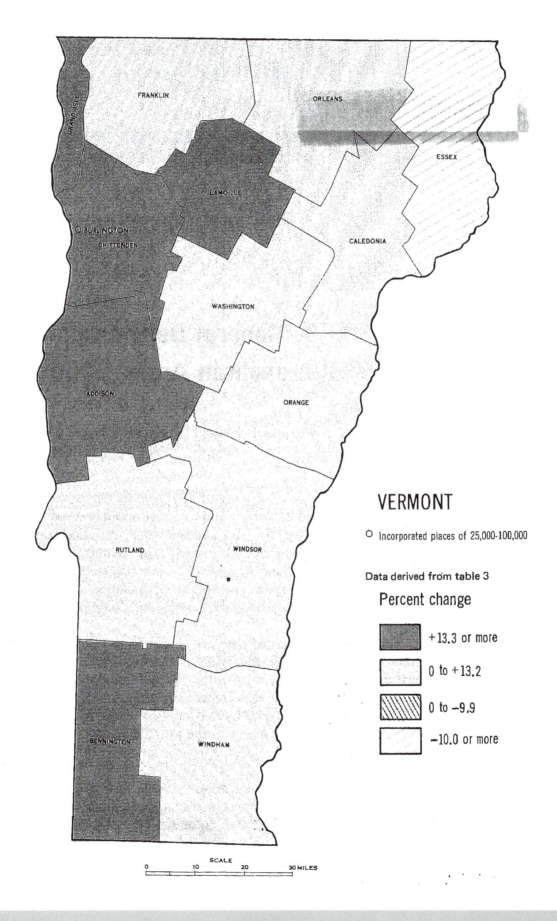

VERMONT

○ Incorporated places of 25,000-100,000

Data derived from table 3

Percent change

▓	+13.3 or more
☐	0 to +13.2
▨	0 to −9.9
☐	−10.0 or more

SCALE
0   10   20   30 MILES

Analytical Text

POPULATION TRENDS

General

Between 1960 and 1970 the population of Vermont grew by 54,000 persons, from 390,000 to 444,000. This represented an increase of 14 percent over the population living in the State in 1960, the highest decennial rate of increase in Vermont in over 100 years. The largest city in the State, Burlington, had a somewhat lower rate of growth; between 1960 and 1970 its population increased by 9 percent, from almost 36,000 in 1960 to 39,000 in 1970.

The population of Vermont is overwhelmingly white. Less than one-half of 1 percent of the total population belonged to races other than white in 1970 and in 1960.

Population change in the State was due primarily to a natural increase of 40,000 (made up of nearly 85,000 births and 45,000 deaths) and less importantly, to a net inmigration of 15,000 persons.

The total number of households in the State is 132,000, or 21,000 more than in 1960. Population increased at a slightly lower rate than number of households, resulting in a decrease in average household size from 3.4 persons in 1960 to 3.2 in 1970.

The population at every age except the youngest shows increases for the 1960-70 decade. The most significant gain was made by the population 15 to 24 years old, which increased by more than 26,000 persons, or by 49 percent during the decade. The next largest increase was in the number of school children 5 to 14 years old, which grew by 13,000. Together, these two age groups accounted for 72 percent of total population increase in the State. All age groups 25 and over grew more slowly, by about 9 percent over the decade; numerically, the population 65 and over showed least growth. The single age group to lose population between 1960 and 1970 was under 5 years, which experienced a 10-percent reduction of the number in the State in 1960.

Similar changes are found in other sections of the country and are the product in part of changing birth rates and in part of age selective migration: i.e., low birth rates during the Depression years and the 1960's contribute to the diminution of age groups 0 to 4 and 25 to 44, whereas the post-World War II "baby boom" is currently reflected in the large size of the population 15 to 24 years old.

Counties

Total population size of Vermont's 14 counties ranges from than 4,000 (Grand Isle County) to almost 100,000 (Chittenden County). All but one (Essex County) shows population increases for the decade. Counties growing at rates equivalent to or higher than the 13.3-percent rate of increase for the United States as a whole tend to be concentrated geographically in the northwestern portion of the State. These are Chittenden County—which is the site of the State's largest city, Burlington, the University of Vermont, and several colleges—and three counties which are adjacent to it: Addison, Lamoille, and Grand Isle. Chittenden County, which contains more than one-fifth of the entire population of the State, accounted for over 45 percent of total population growth in the decade.

All counties had more births than deaths, but the fastest growing counties also had very high net inmigration rates. The northwestern complex of counties was by far the greatest attractor of migrants during the decade. The opposite situation exists in the northeastern part of the State, which had lowest rates of population growth and highest rates of outmigration. Essex County, the only one which lost population during the decade, is located in this section of the State, as are Caledonia and Orleans Counties, which showed virtually no change from 1960 to 1970.

No county in Vermont had a large enough population of Negro and other races to be shown separately in the table on components of change.

HOUSING TRENDS

During the decade, the total supply of housing units in Vermont increased faster than population. While housing units increasd by 28,800, or 21 percent, the population grew by 54,000, or some 14 percent. Similarly, the number of households increased at a faster rate (19 percent) than the population in housing units (12 percent), resulting in lower average household size.

A trend toward smaller households is evident. Median population per unit dropped from 3.0 to 2.7 over the decade. Of the net increase of 21,400 households in this period, the great majority (15,900) was 1- and 2-person units. One-person households, however, experienced the greatest relative gain—61 percent.

A large increase occurred in owner-occupied housing, which had a net gain of 18,200 units during the decade.

Owner-occupied homes account for 69 percent of all occupied units, compared with 66 percent in 1960. By contrast, there was a net increase of only 3,200 renter-occupied units.

The median value of owner-occupied housing rose sharply in Vermont during the decade. In 1960, one-half of the owner-occupied households valued their housing at less than $9,700, compared with $16,500 in 1970. Median contract rent likewise increased substantially, from $43 per month in 1960 to $76 in 1970. Value and rent data are expressed in current dollars (the dollar value at the time of the respective censuses). Thus, any comparison between the two dates must take into account the inflation which occurred over the decade as well as changes in the characteristics of the housing inventory.

Number of persons per room is often used as a measurement of crowding. In Vermont, occupied housing units with 1.01 or more persons per room declined from 7.9 percent in 1960 to 6.5 percent in 1970.

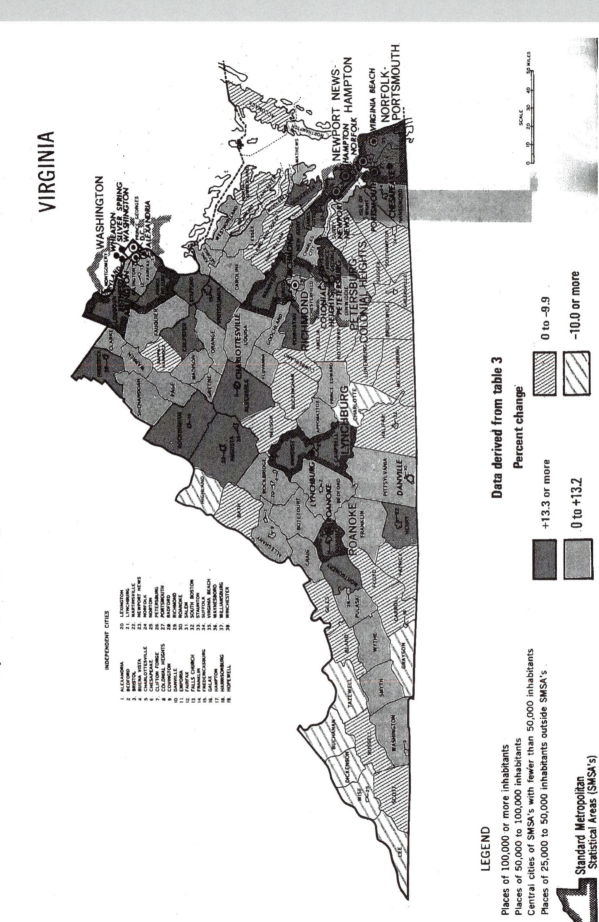

Population Change for Counties: 1960 to 1970

VIRGINIA

INDEPENDENT CITIES

1. ALEXANDRIA
2. BEDFORD
3. BRISTOL
4. BUENA VISTA
5. CHARLOTTESVILLE
6. CHESAPEAKE
7. CLIFTON FORGE
8. COLONIAL HEIGHTS
9. COVINGTON
10. DANVILLE
11. EMPORIA
12. FAIRFAX
13. FALLS CHURCH
14. FRANKLIN
15. FREDERICKSBURG
16. GALAX
17. HAMPTON
18. HARRISONBURG
19. HOPEWELL
20. LEXINGTON
21. LYNCHBURG
22. MARTINSVILLE
23. NEWPORT NEWS
24. NORFOLK
25. NORTON
26. PETERSBURG
27. PORTSMOUTH
28. RADFORD
29. RICHMOND
30. ROANOKE
31. SALEM
32. SOUTH BOSTON
33. STAUNTON
34. SUFFOLK
35. VIRGINIA BEACH
36. WAYNESBORO
37. WILLIAMSBURG
38. WINCHESTER

LEGEND

⦿ Places of 100,000 or more inhabitants
● Places of 50,000 to 100,000 inhabitants
☐ Central cities of SMSA's with fewer than 50,000 inhabitants
○ Places of 25,000 to 50,000 inhabitants outside SMSA's

Standard Metropolitan
Statistical Areas (SMSA's)

Data derived from table 3

Percent change

+13.3 or more

0 to +13.2

0 to -9.9

-10.0 or more

SCALE

0 10 20 30 40 50 MILES

Analytical Text

POPULATION TRENDS

General

Between 1960 and 1970, the population of Virginia grew from 3,967,000 to 4,648,000, an increase of 682,000, or 17.2 percent. This rate of increase is above the rate for the entire United States (13.3 percent). In both 1960 and 1970, Virginia ranked 14th in population among the 50 States.

The total number of households in Virginia in 1970 was 1,390,000, or 316,000 more than in 1960. The population living in households increased more slowly than the rate at which households increased with the result that average household size dropped from 3.5 to 3.2 persons.

Nearly all of Virginia's population growth between 1960 and 1970 occurred in metropolitan areas. The metropolitan population grew by 28 percent from 2,217,000 to 2,846,000, and the nonmetropolitan population grew by only 3 percent from 1,750,000 to 1,802,000 (table A). The proportion of the State's population living in metropolitan areas rose from 56 to 61 percent. In the Nation as a whole, almost 70 percent of the population lives in metropolitan areas.

Table A.   Population by Race and Metropolitan and Nonmetropolitan Residence: 1970 and 1960

The State Metropolitan and Non-metropolitan Residence	Population		Change		Percent Distribution	
	1970	1960	Number	Percent	1970	1960
Total...............	4,648,494	3,966,949	681,545	17.2	100.0	100.0
Metropolitan residence...	2,846,034	2,217,054	628,980	28.4	61.2	55.9
Inside central cities..	1,124,889	1,041,760	83,129	8.0	24.2	26.3
Outside central cities.	1,721,145	1,175,294	545,851	46.4	37.0	29.6
Nonmetropolitan residence	1,802,460	1,749,895	52,565	3.0	38.8	44.1
White...............	3,757,478	3,142,443	615,035	19.6	80.8	79.2
Metropolitan residence...	2,311,453	1,762,136	549,317	31.2	49.7	44.4
Inside central cities..	759,111	725,907	33,204	4.6	16.3	18.3
Outside central cities.	1,552,342	1,036,229	516,113	49.8	33.4	26.1
Nonmetropolitan residence	1,446,025	1,380,307	65,718	4.8	31.1	34.8
Negro and other races	891,016	824,506	66,510	8.1	19.2	20.8
Metropolitan residence...	534,581	454,918	79,663	17.5	11.5	11.5
Inside central cities..	365,778	315,853	49,925	15.8	7.9	8.0
Outside central cities.	168,803	139,065	29,738	21.4	3.6	3.5
Nonmetropolitan residence	356,435	369,588	-13,153	-3.6	7.7	9.3

Within metropolitan areas, most of the population growth occurred outside the central cities. The small increase in the central city population was due mostly to annexation (table B). During the decade, the metropolitan population living outside the central cities grew from 1,175,000 to 1,721,000, or by 46 percent.

During the 1960 to 1970 decade, the population of Negro and other races in Virginia increased by only 8 percent, from 825,000 to 891,000 (as opposed to a 20 percent increase in the white population), and the proportion of Negro and other races in the State's population fell from 21 to 19 percent. In 1970, two-fifths of the population of Negro and other races and only one-fifth of the white population lived in the central cities of metropolitan areas. Among Negro and other races, all of the population growth occurred in metropolitan areas, as the nonmetroplitan population dropped by 4 percent.

The population increase of 682,000 in Virginia in the 1960 to 1970 decade was due to a natural increase (births minus deaths) of 541,000 and a net inmigration of 141,000. Net inmigration was equivalent to 4 percent of the 1960 population. The difference in the rates of population growth by race was due largely to different patterns of migration. Whites experienced a net inmigration of 206,000, equivalent to 7 percent of the 1960 population. Among Negro and other races, there was a net outmigration of 65,000, equivalent to 8 percent of the 1960 population.

The age distribution of the Virginia population changed significantly between 1960 and 1970. The only decrease occurred among the population under 5 years and was due largely to the fall in the birth rate which occurred throughout the United States during the 1960's. The greatest increase (45 percent) occurred in the 15 to 24 age group and was due largely to the entry of the large number of persons born during the post-World War II "baby boom" into this age group. As a result of these changes, the proportion of the State's population in the under 5 group declined from 12 to 8 percent and the proportion in the 15 to 24 group increased from 15 to 19 percent.

Standard Metropolitan Statistical Areas

In 1970, there were seven standard metropolitan statistical areas (SMSA's) in Virginia, including six SMSA's located entirely in the State. The discussion of the Washington, D.C.-Md.-Va. SMSA is limited to the portion in Virginia.

The population in the Virginia portion of the Washington, D.C. SMSA grew from 602,000 in 1960 to 921,000 in 1970, or by 53 percent. At the latter date, nearly one-third of the 2.9 million persons in the Washington, D.C. SMSA lived in Virginia. In addition to its suburban function, the Virginia portion of the SMSA is the location of several large military installations. Net inmigration accounted for over half of the population

Table B. Change in Population of Central Cities Through Annexation: 1960 to 1970

Central Cities	1970 population			1960 population	Change 1960 to 1970 in 1960 area
	Total	In 1960 area	In annexed area		
Hampton..................	120,779	120,741	38	89,258	31,483
Lynchburg...............	54,083	53,823	260	54,790	-967
Portsmouth..............	110,963	98,602	12,361	114,773	-16,171
Richmond................	249,621	202,359	47,262	219,958	-17,599

growth in the Virginia portion of the Washington, D.C. SMSA during the 1960 to 1970 decade and was equivalent to 31 percent of the 1960 population.

The population of the Richmond SMSA grew from 436,000 in 1960 to 518,000 in 1970, or by 19 percent. In addition to being the capital of Virginia, Richmond is a financial center and a manufacturer of textiles and of tobacco and steel products. The city of Richmond grew from 220,000 to 250,000 with all of the gowth due to annexation. The 1970 population in the 1960 boundaries was 202,000. The proportion of Negro and other races in the city's population was 42 percent at both censuses. In the absence of annexation, the proportion would have increased as it did in most large central cities in the Nation. Net inmigration accounted for two-fifths of the population growth in the Richmond SMSA during the decade and was equivalent to 8 percent of the 1960 population.

In the "Tidewater" area of Virginia, two metropolitan areas, with a combined population of nearly 1,000,000, are separated only by the harbor at Hampton Roads, where the James River enters Chesapeake Bay. The Norfolk-Portsmouth SMSA, the larger of the two, is comprised of the cities of Norfolk, Portsmouth, Virginia Beach, and Chesapeake, and the Newport News-Hampton SMSA is comprised of the cities of Newport News and Hampton and of York County. The economy of the area is heavily military-oriented with the naval Atlantic Fleet headquarters, shipyards, air bases, and several forts located here. In addition, the Tidewater area is one of the principal ports and shipbuilding centers in the United States. About one-tenth of the population is in the Armed Forces, and a substantial portion of the civilian employment is directly dependent on military activities.

The population of the Norfolk-Portsmouth SMSA grew from 579,000 in 1960 to 681,000 in 1970, or by 18 percent. Virtually all of the area's growth was accounted for by the suburban ring. The city of Portsmouth lost population in spite of a substantial annexation, while the population of Norfolk increased by less than 1 percent. In the Newport News-Hampton SMSA, which grew from 225,000 to 292,000, or by 30 percent, both the central cities and the ring grew substantially. During the decade, there was a negligible net inmigration into the Norfolk-Portsmouth SMSA, while net inmigration accounted for over one-third of the growth in the Newport News-Hampton SMSA.

The Roanoke SMSA had a 1970 population of 181,000, up 14 percent from 1960. Roanoke, the largest city in western Virginia, is a rail center and textile producer. All of the growth during the past decade occurred outside the central city. More than one-third of the growth in the Roanoke SMSA was due to net inmigration.

The population of the Lynchburg SMSA in 1970 was 123,000, or 12 percent more than in 1960. All of the growth occurred outside the central city. About one-eighth of the population increase in the Lynchburg SMSA was due to net inmigration.

Between 1960 and 1970, the population of the newly created Petersburg-Colonial Heights SMSA grew by 21 percent to 129,000. About one-fifth of the growth was due to net inmigration.

Counties

In 1970, there were 96 counties and 38 independent cities in Virginia (see "Definitions and Explanations"). Between 1960 and 1970, 58 counties gained population, one county had no change, and 37 counties lost population. Twenty-three counties had growth rates above the national average of 13.3 percent, and 10 counties had population declines exceeding 10 percent. Among the independent cities, 26 gained population (including 16 with gains above the national average) and 12 lost population (including three with losses exceeding ten percent).[1] In the Nation as a whole, slightly more than half of all counties gained population during the decade.

Of the eight counties and independent cities with rates of growth exceeding 50 percent between 1960 and 1970, seven are located in metropolitan areas. Fairfax, Loudoun, and Prince William Counties and Fairfax City are in the Virginia portion of the Washington, D.C. SMSA. Virginia Beach city is in the Norfolk-Portsmouth

---

[1] In 1960, there were 98 counties and 32 independent cities in Virginia. Between 1960 and 1970, Princess Anne County was merged with the independent city of Virginia Beach; Norfolk County and the independent city of South Norfolk were merged to form the independent city of Chesapeake; and six other independent cities were established. In the groupings of counties and independent cities by rate of population change, the 1960 data were adjusted to correspond with the 96 counties and 38 independent cities existing in 1970.

In Table 3, which shows the components of population change between 1960 and 1970, only 28 independent cities are shown separately. The other 10 independent cities are included with their parent counties because the available data do not permit the compilation of births and deaths during the past decade for these independent cities as defined in 1970. These independent cities and the counties (in parentheses) in which they are included follow: Bedford (Bedford), Charlottesville (Albemarle), Emporia (Greenville), Fairfax and Falls Church (Fairfax), Franklin (Southampton), Lexington (Rockbridge), Salem (Roanoke), South Boston (Halifax), Williamsburg (James City).

SMSA; York County is in the Newport News-Hampton SMSA; Colonial Heights city is in the Petersburg-Colonial Heights SMSA. The rapid growth in James City County, which is nonmetropolitan, was due partly to increased facilities to accommodate tourists in the Williamsburg area.

The areas of most pronounced decline in Virginia between 1960 and 1970 are in the western and eastern extremities of the State. In the coal producing area of southwestern Virginia (Buchanan, Dickenson, Lee, Tazewell, and Wise Counties, and Norton city), the population declined from 176,000 to 148,000, or by 16 percent. The net outmigration of 46,000 was equivalent to 26 percent of the 1960 population.

In the two "Eastern Shore" counties on the peninsula between Chesapeake Bay and the Atlantic Ocean (Accomack and Northampton), the population declined by 9 percent. The population is entirely rural, and the economy is based on vegetable farming and fishing.

HOUSING TRENDS

General

Between 1960 and 1970, the total supply of housing units in Virginia increased more rapidly than population. The population grew by 682,000, or 17 percent, while housing units increased by 322,800, or 28 percent (table C).

About 60 percent of all housing units in the State were in its standard metropolitan statistical areas. The metropolitan areas experienced greater relative growth in housing, as in population, than did the nonmetropolitan areas. The number of housing units in metropolitan areas rose from 653,500 to 893,900 over the decade, an increase of 240,400 units, or 37 percent; this compares with an increase of 82,300 units, or 16 percent, in nonmetropolitan areas.

About 75 percent of the housing in Virginia consisted of one-unit structures in 1970. The number of units in multiunit structures, however, increased at a much faster rate during the decade than did the number of one-unit structures, 83 percent and 14 percent, respectively.

The number of units in the State lacking some or all plumbing facilities declined from 320,600 to 199,000, a 38 percent decrease over the decade. In 1970, the proportion of such units was 4 percent in metropolitan areas and 28 percent outside these areas.

Approximately 66,200, or 30 percent, of the Negro-occupied units in the State lacked some or all plumbing in 1970. The corresponding proportion for inside the metropolitan areas was 12 percent, compared with 58 percent in the nonmetropolitan areas.

Households were smaller in 1970 than in 1960. In the metropolitan areas, the average household size declined from 3.4 persons in 1960 to 3.2 in 1970 and in nonmetropolitan areas, from 3.7 to 3.3 persons. The number of one-person households in metropolitan areas increased by 105 percent; in nonmetropolitan areas one-person households increased 87 percent. In comparison, the number of households with five or more persons increased 20 percent in metropolitan areas and declined 13 percent in nonmetropolitan areas.

The median number of rooms in housing units remained unchanged at 5.1 in nonmetropolitan areas and rose from 5.0 to 5.3 in metropolitan areas. Housing units with seven or more rooms more than doubled in metropolitan areas, increasing from 115,200 in 1960 to 231,200 in 1970.

Table C.   Housing Units by Metropolitan and Nonmetropolitan Residence: 1970 and 1960

The State Metropolitan and Nonmetropolitan Residence	Housing units				Population percent change
	Total		Change		
	1970	1960	Number	Percent	
Total.................	1,491,663	1,168,913	322,750	27.6	17.2
Metropolitan residence.....	893,945	653,496	240,449	36.8	28.4
Inside central cities....	369,229	317,557	51,672	16.3	8.0
Outside central cities...	524,716	335,939	188,777	56.2	46.4
Nonmetropolitan residence..	597,718	515,417	82,301	16.0	3.0

Number of persons per room is often used as a measure of crowding. In Virginia, both the number and proportion of housing units with 1.01 or more persons per room decreased during the decade. In 1960, 11 percent of all occupied units in metropolitan areas and 17 percent in nonmetropolitan areas had 1.01 or more persons per room. By 1970, the proportion of such units decreased to 6 percent in metropolitan areas and to 11 percent in nonmetropolitan areas (table D).

Homeownership in the State increased slightly from 61 to 62 percent over the decade. In the metropolitan areas, there was a slight decrease from 58 to 57 percent, while in nonmetropolitan areas the proportion rose from 65 to 70 percent. Of the 861,900 owner-occupied units in the State, 488,100 were inside metropolitan areas and the remainder were outside these areas.

About 45 percent of the Negro households in metropolitan areas owned their homes in 1970, compared with 61 percent in nonmetropolitan areas. Of the 113,100 Negro-homeowner households in the State, 61,000 lived inside SMSA's and 52,100 lived outside SMSA's.

The median value in metropolitan areas increased by 55 percent from $13,000 in 1960 to $20,100 in 1970, while in the nonmetropolitan areas the median increased 61 percent, from $7,500 to $12,100. In metropolitan areas, median contract rent in 1970 was $109, and in nonmetropolitan areas, $54.

Value and rent are expressed in current dollars (the value at the time of the respective censuses). Thus, any comparison must take into account the general rise in the cost of living during the 10-year period, as well as changes in the characteristics of the housing inventory.

Standard Metropolitan Statistical Areas

In the metropolitan areas of the State, the housing supply increased by 240,400 units, or 37 percent. The Virginia portion of the Washington, D.C.-Md.-Va. SMSA, which contained 33 percent of the housing units in metropolitan areas, accounted for 49 percent of the increase. The Norfolk-Portsmouth SMSA, the next largest area, contained 23 percent of the housing in the metropolitan areas and accounted for only 14 percent of the increase. The Richmond SMSA, with 19 percent of the metropolitan housing, accounted for 16 percent of the increase.

The suburban areas of the State (including the Virginia portion of the Washington, D.C. metropolitan area) experienced much greater growth in housing than did the central cities. Housing units in the suburbs increased by 191,000, or 56 percent, while housing in the combined central cities increased by 49,400, or 16 percent. By 1970, there were 532,400 housing units in the suburbs and 361,600 units in the central cities.

About 68 percent of the housing units in the State's metropolitan areas consisted of one-unit structures in 1970. The proportion of such units was 65 percent in the central cities and 70 percent in the suburbs.

In 1970, about 35,900 housing units in the metropolitan areas, or 4 percent of all year-round units, lacked some or all plumbing facilities. The proportion of such units in the central cities was 3 percent and in the suburbs, 4 percent. Approximately 6,400, or 6 percent, of the Negro households in central cities occupied units which lacked some or all plumbing facilities in 1970, compared with 10,100, or 28 percent, of Negro households in the suburban areas.

Table D.   Plumbing Facilities and Persons Per Room by Metropolitan and Nonmetropolitan Residence: 1970 and 1960

The State Metropolitan and Nonmetropolitan Residence	Percent of housing units			
	Lacking some or all plumbing facilities		With 1.01 or more persons per room [1]	
	1970 [2]	1960 [3]	1970	1960
Total......................	13.4	27.4	8.0	13.8
Metropolitan residence...........	4.0	(NA)	6.3	10.9
Inside central cities..........	3.4	12.6	7.8	12.0
Outside central cities.........	4.5	(NA)	5.3	10.0
Nonmetropolitan residence........	27.6	(NA)	10.7	17.5

[1] Percent of all occupied units.
[2] Percent of all year-round housing units.
[3] Percent of all housing units.
[4] Not shown because of lack of comparability with 1970.

Average household size in 1970 was 3.1 persons in the central cities and 3.2 persons outside central cities. One-person households constituted 17 percent of occupied housing units in the central cities and 13 percent in the suburbs.

In 1970, the median number of rooms was smaller in the central cities (5.0) than in the suburbs (5.5). About 39 percent of the housing in the central cities had six or more rooms, compared with 50 percent in the suburbs.

Of all occupied units in metropolitan areas, 53,800 units, or 6 percent, reported more than one person per room in 1970, compared with 11 percent in 1960. In 1970, the proportion of such units was 8 percent in the central cities and 5 percent in the suburban areas (table D).

Homeownership in 1970 was greater in the suburban areas than in the central cities. About 60 percent of occupied units in the suburbs and 52 percent in the central cities were owner-occupied. The Negro-homeownership rate in the suburbs was 57 percent, compared with 41 percent in the central cities.

Median value of owner-occupied housing in the central cities was $15,600 and in the suburbs $24,000. About 16 percent of the owner-occupied housing units were valued at $25,000 or more, compared with 47 percent in the suburbs. Median contract rent in the central cities and in the suburbs was $78 and $135, respectively. Approximately 6 percent of the renter-occupied units in the central cities and 37 percent of the suburban units rented for $150 or more in 1970.

The homeowner vacancy rate for metropolitan areas decreased during the decade from 2.0 to 1.3 percent. The rental vacancy rate decreased from 7.0 to 5.0.

Annexations

Annexations occurred in the central cities of Portsmouth, Richmond, and Lynchburg during the decade (see "Population Trends" and text table B). Such annexations affect changes in the characteristics for these central cities and their suburbs.

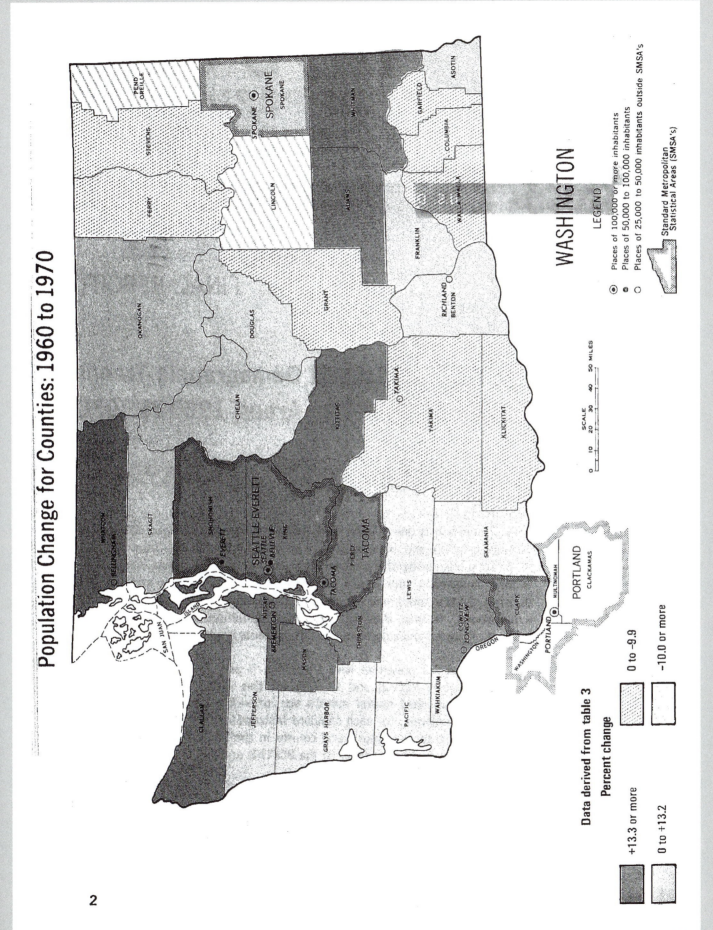

Population Change for Counties: 1960 to 1970

WASHINGTON

LEGEND

⊙ Places of 100,000 or more inhabitants
● Places of 50,000 to 100,000 inhabitants
○ Places of 25,000 to 50,000 inhabitants outside SMSA's

Standard Metropolitan
Statistical Areas (SMSA's)

Data derived from table 3

Percent change

+13.3 or more

0 to +13.2

0 to -9.9

-10.0 or more

SCALE
0   10   20   30   40   50 MILES

Analytical Text

POPULATION TRENDS

General

Between 1960 and 1970, the population of the State of Washington grew from 2,853,000 to 3,409,000, an increase of 556,000 or 19.5 percent. This rate of increase is above the rate for the entire United States (13.3 percent) but is below the rate for the Pacific States (25.1 percent), which in addition to Washington, include Oregon, California, Alaska, and Hawaii.

The total number of households in Washington in 1970 was 1,106,000 or 211,000 more than in 1960. The population living in households increased more slowly than the rate at which households increased, with the result that average household size dropped from 3.1 to 3.0 persons.

During the 1960 to 1970 decade, Washington's metropolitan population grew more than twice as fast as its nonmetropolitan population. The metropolitan population increased by 25 percent from 1,801,000 to 2,249,000, and the nonmetropolitan population increased by 10 percent from 1,052,000 to 1,160,000 (table A). In 1970, the proportion of Washington's population living in metropolitan areas was two-thirds, which was about the same as in the nation as a whole.

Within metropolitan areas, all of the growth occurred outside the central cities. The central city population dropped from 927,000 to 910,000 while the population outside central cities increased from 874,000 to

Table A. Population by Race and Metropolitan and Nonmetropolitan Residence: 1970 and 1960

The State Metropolitan and Non-metropolitan Residence	Population		Change		Percent Distribution	
	1970	1960	Number	Percent	1970	1960
Total................	3,409,169	2,853,214	555,955	19.5	100.0	100.0
Metropolitan residence...	2,248,837	1,800,945	447,892	24.9	66.0	63.1
Inside central cities..	909,550	926,978	-17,428	-1.9	26.7	32.5
Outside central cities.	1,339,287	873,967	465,320	53.2	39.3	30.6
Nonmetropolitan residence	1,160,332	1,052,269	108,063	10.3	34.0	36.9
White...............	3,251,055	2,751,675	499,380	18.1	95.4	96.4
Metropolitan residence...	2,126,547	1,725,249	401,298	23.3	62.4	60.5
Inside central cities..	821,964	867,625	-45,661	-5.3	24.1	30.4
Outside central cities.	1,304,583	857,624	446,959	52.1	38.3	30.1
Nonmetropolitan residence	1,124,508	1,026,426	98,082	9.6	33.0	36.0
Negro and other races	158,114	101,539	56,575	55.7	4.6	3.6
Metropolitan residence...	122,290	75,696	46,594	61.6	3.6	2.7
Inside central cities..	87,586	59,353	28,233	47.6	2.6	2.1
Outside central cities.	34,704	16,343	18,361	112.3	1.0	0.6
Nonmetropolitan residence	35,824	25,843	9,981	38.6	1.0	0.9

1,339,000, or by 53 percent. The loss of population in the central cities would have been nearly twice as large in the absence of annexation (table B).

The population of Negro and other races (about half of which is Negro) increased from 102,000 in 1960 to 158,000 in 1970, or by 56 percent. In 1970, Negro and other races constituted 5 percent of Washington's population, and over half of the population of Negro and other races lived in the central cities of metropolitan areas. In contrast, only one-fourth of the white population lived in central cities in 1970.

The population increase of 556,000 in Washington in the 1960 to 1970 decade resulted from a natural increase (births minus deaths) of 307,000 and a net inmigration of 249,000. Net inmigration which accounted for 45 percent of Washington's population growth during the decade, was equivalent to 9 percent of the 1960 population.

The age structure of Washington's population changed significantly between 1960 and 1970. The only decline occurred among the population under 5 years old and resulted from the decline in birth rates which occurred throughout the United States during the 1960's. The greatest increase (64 percent) occurred in the 15 to 24 age group and was due largely to the entry of the large numbers of persons born during the post-World War II "baby boom" into this age group. As a result of these changes, the proportion of the total population in the under 5 group declined from 11 to 8 percent and the proportion in the 15 to 24 group increased from 13 to 18 percent.

Standard Metropolitan Statistical Areas

In 1970 there were four Standard Metropolitan Statistical Areas (SMSA's) in Washington including three located entirely in Washington (the Seattle-Everett SMSA, the Spokane SMSA, and the Tacoma SMSA) and one located primarily in Oregon (the Portland, Oreg.-Wash. SMSA).

The population of the Seattle-Everett SMSA grew from 1,107,000 in 1960 to 1,422,000 in 1970, or by 28 percent. The Seattle-Everett SMSA was the 17th largest metropolitan area in the nation in 1970. Seattle is a major financial and trade center and port in the Northwest, and the Seattle-Everett SMSA is one of the leading centers of aircraft production in the nation. Much of the population growth is attributable to the expansion of Boeing Company during the middle to late 1960's.

All of the growth in the Seattle-Everett SMSA occurred outside the two central cities. The population of Seattle dropped from 557,000 to 531,000, and the population of Everett, whose growth was due almost entirely to annexation, increased from 40,000 to 54,000. The population outside the central cities grew from 510,000 to 837,000 or by 64 percent. In 1960, over half of the population in the Seattle-Everett SMSA lived in Seattle; in 1970, this proportion was only 37 percent. Over half of the population growth in the Seattle-Everett SMSA during the decade was due to net inmigration. The net inmigration was equivalent to 17 percent of the 1960 population.

The population of the Tacoma SMSA increased from 322,000 in 1960 to 411,000 in 1970, or by 28 percent. Nearly all of the growth occurred outside the city of Tacoma. The growth in the Tacoma SMSA was evenly divided between natural increase and net inmigration. The net inmigration was equivalent to 14 percent of the 1960 population and was due in large part to the expansion of Ft. Lewis.

The Spokane SMSA grew from 278,000 in 1960 to 287,000 in 1970, or by only 3 percent, giving the Spokane SMSA the second lowest growth rate of metropolitan areas in the 13 western States. The population in the city of Spokane declined by 6 percent and the population in the balance of the metropolitan area increased by 21 percent. Net outmigration from the Spokane SMSA was 14,000 which was equivalent to 5 percent of the 1960 population. The low rate of

Table B.   Change in Population of Central Cities Through Annexation: 1960 to 1970

Central Cities	1970 population			1960 population	Change 1960 to 1970 in 1960 area
	Total	In 1960 area	In annexed area		
Everett	53,622	40,593	13,029	40,304	289
Tacoma	154,581	154,192	389	147,979	6,213
Spokane	170,516	168,963	1,553	181,608	-12,645

population growth in the Spokane SMSA was due in part to the reduction in personnel at Fairchild Air Force Base and to a decline in the number of inmates in mental institutions.

The portion of the Portland, Oreg.-Wash. SMSA in Washington (Clark County) grew from 94,000 in 1960 to 128,000 in 1970, or by 37 percent. In 1970, one-eighth of the population in the entire Portland SMSA lived in the Washington portion.

Counties

Of the 39 counties in Washington, 29 gained population and 10 lost population between 1960 and 1970. Fifteen counties had rates of growth above the national average of 13.3 percent and two counties experienced population declines exceeding 10 percent. In the Nation as a whole, slightly more than half of all counties gained population during the decade. Four of Washington's five metropolitan counties had rates of growth above 20 percent.

With the exception of San Juan County, all of Washington's counties had a natural increase (i.e., births outnumbered deaths) between 1960 and 1970. San Juan County, which is a retirement center, has an "old" age structure. In 1970, 50 percent of San Juan County's population was age 45 and over compared to only 30 percent in this age group in the entire State.

Twenty-two of Washington's 39 counties had a net inmigration during the decade. In the Nation as a whole, less than one-third of all counties experienced net inmigration. The largest net inmigration occurred in the two counties in the Seattle-Everett SMSA. King County, which with a 1970 population of 1,157,000 is Washington's most populous county, had a net inmigration of 116,000, equivalent to 12 percent of its 1960 population. In Snohomish County, the net inmigration of 69,000 was equivalent to 40 percent of the 1960 population. This was the highest rate of net inmigration among Washington's counties.

Nearly all the population increase in Washington between 1960 and 1970 occurred in the western portion of the State. The 19 counties west of the Cascade Range (the string of counties from Whatcom County to Skamania County and all counties to the west) grew by 533,000 while the 20 counties to the east grew by only 23,000. In 1970, less than one-fourth of Washington's population lived in the eastern portion of the State.

HOUSING TRENDS

General

Between 1960 and 1970, the total supply of housing units in Washington increased at a slightly higher rate than population. The population grew by 556,000, or 19 percent, while housing units increased by 211,000, or 21 percent (table C).

The metropolitan area of the State experienced greater relative growth in housing, as in population, than did the nonmetropolitan part. The number of housing units in the metropolitan area rose from 626,600 to 789,300 over the decade, an increase of 162,700 units, or 26 percent; this compares with an increase of 48,300 units, or 13 percent, in the nonmetropolitan areas. While 65 percent of all housing units were in the metropolitan areas, these areas accounted for 77 percent of the total State increase between 1960 and 1970.

About 76 percent of the housing in Washington consisted of one-unit structures in 1970. The corresponding proportions in the metropolitan areas and in the nonmetropolitan areas were 73 percent and 81 percent, respectively.

Table C.   Housing Units by Metropolitan and Nonmetropolitan Residence: 1970 and 1960

The State Metropolitan and Nonmetropolitan Residence	Housing units				Population percent change
	Total		Change		
	1970	1960	Number	Percent	
Total...............	1,220,475	1,009,519	210,956	20.9	19.5
Metropolitan residence.....	789,283	626,633	162,650	26.0	24.9
Inside central cities....	365,485	353,817	11,668	3.3	-1.9
Outside central cities...	423,798	272,816	150,982	55.3	53.2
Nonmetropolitan residence..	431,192	382,886	48,306	12.6	10.3

The median number of rooms in housing units was 4.9 in 1970. In the metropolitan areas the median number of rooms was 5.0 compared with 4.9 in nonmetropolitan areas. While 39 percent of the housing units in the metropolitan areas had six or more rooms, 35 percent of the nonmetropolitan housing units were in this category.

Households were smaller in 1970 than in 1960. In the metropolitan areas, average household size declined from 3.1 persons in 1960 to 3.0 in 1970, and in nonmetropolitan areas, from 3.2 persons to 3.0. The number of one- and two-person households in metropolitan areas increased by 38 percent and 35 percent, respectively; in nonmetropolitan areas, one- and two-person households increased 38 percent and 28 percent, respectively. The number of households with five or more persons increased 18 percent in metropolitan areas and declined 2 percent in nonmetropolitan areas.

In 1970, 3 percent of the housing in Washington lacked some or all plumbing facilities. The proportion of such units was 3 percent in the metropolitan areas of the State and 5 percent in the nonmetropolitan areas.

Number of persons per room is often used as a measure of crowding. In Washington, both the number and proportion of housing units with 1.01 or more persons per room decreased during the decade. In 1960, 7 percent of all occupied housing units in metropolitan areas and 10 percent in nonmetropolitan areas had 1.01 or more persons per room. By 1970, the proportion of such units decreased to 5 percent in metropolitan areas and 7 percent in nonmetropolitan areas (table D).

Homeownership in the State decreased from 68 percent in 1960 to 67 percent in 1970. In metropolitan areas there was a decrease from 68 to 66 percent, while in nonmetropolitan areas the proportion declined from 70 to 69 percent.

About 50 percent of the Negro households in metropolitan areas owned their homes in 1970, compared with 44 percent in the nonmetropolitan areas. Of the 10,300 Negro-homeowner households in the State, 9,400 lived inside SMSA's and 900 lived outside SMSA's.

Property values and rents increased in the last decade. The median value in metropolitan areas increased by 57 percent from $12,500 in 1960 to $19,600 in 1970, while in the nonmetropolitan areas value increased 54 percent, from $10,000 to $15,400. In metropolitan areas, median contract rent in 1970 was 69 percent higher than in 1960, rising from $62 to $105. In nonmetropolitan areas rent increased from $51 to $76, or 49 percent.

Value and rent are expressed in current dollars (the value at the time of the respective censuses). Thus, any comparison must take into account the general rise in the cost of living during the 10-year period, as well as changes in the characteristics of the housing inventory.

Standard Metropolitan Statistical Areas

In the metropolitan areas of the State (Seattle-Everett, Spokane, Tacoma, and Portland, Oreg.-Wash.), the housing supply increased by 162,700 units, or 26 percent. The Seattle-Everett SMSA which contained 65 percent of the housing in metropolitan areas accounted for 74 percent of the increase in these areas.

In 1970, about 73 percent of the housing units in the total metropolitan areas of the State consisted of

Table D. Plumbing Facilities and Persons Per Room by Metropolitan and Nonmetropolitan Residence: 1970 and 1960

The State Metropolitan and Nonmetropolitan Residence	Percent of housing units			
	Lacking some or all plumbing facilities		With 1.01 or more persons per room[1]	
	1970[2]	1960[3]	1970	1960
Total.....................	3.4	9.8	5.5	8.3
Metropolitan residence...........	2.8	7.9	4.7	7.2
Inside central cities..........	4.0	9.1	3.9	5.2
Outside central cities.........	1.7	6.4	5.5	9.8
Nonmetropolitan residence........	4.7	12.7	6.8	10.2

[1]Percent of all occupied units.
[2]Percent of all year-round housing units.
[3]Percent of all housing units.

one-unit structures. The number of units in multiunit structures, however, increased at a much faster rate than one-unit structures during the decade, 47 percent and 18 percent, respectively.

Housing units increased in size in the metropolitan areas during the decade. The median number of rooms increased from 4.8 to 5.0. In 1970, the median number of rooms in the central cities was 4.6 and in the suburbs 5.3.

Average household size in the metropolitan areas of the State declined during the decade. In 1970, the combined central cities had an average of 2.6 persons per household and the suburbs, 3.3 persons.

Homeownership in 1970 was greater in the suburbs than in the central cities. About 72 percent of occupied units in the suburbs were owner-occupied, compared with 58 percent in the central cities. About 50 percent of the Negro households in the central cities owned their homes in 1970, compared with 44 percent in the suburbs.

In 1970, 21,700 housing units in metropolitan areas, or 3 percent of all year-round units, lacked some or all plumbing facilities. The proportion of such units was 4 percent in the central city and 2 percent in the suburbs.

Of all occupied units in metropolitan areas, 34,700 units, or 5 percent, reported more than one person per room in 1970, compared with 7 percent in 1960. In 1970, the proportion of such units was 4 percent in the central cities and 6 percent in the suburban areas (table D).

The homeowner vacancy rate for metropolitan areas decreased during the decade from 1.9 to 1.6 percent. The rental vacancy rate increased from 11.6 to 11.7 percent.

Annexations

Annexations occurred in the central cities of Everett, Tacoma, and Spokane during the decade (see "Population Trends" and text table B). Such annexations affect changes in the characteristics for these central cities and their suburbs.

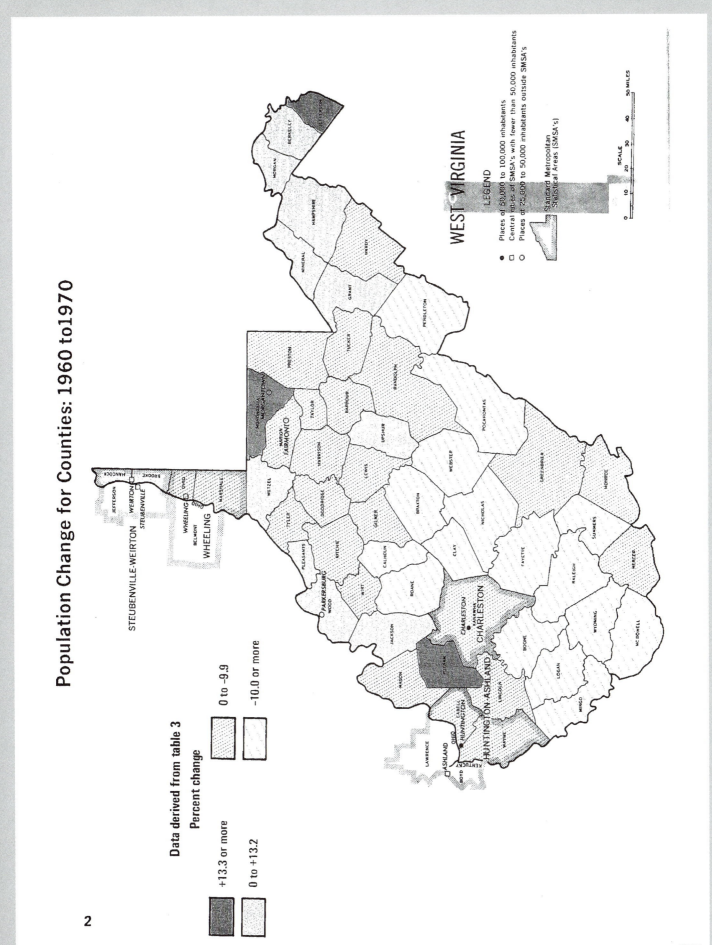

Population Change for Counties: 1960 to1970

WEST VIRGINIA

LEGEND

• Places of 50,000 to 100,000 inhabitants
□ Central cities of SMSA's with fewer than 50,000 inhabitants
○ Places of 25,000 to 50,000 inhabitants outside SMSA's

Standard Metropolitan Statistical Areas (SMSA's)

SCALE

0 10 20 30 40 50 MILES

Data derived from table 3

Percent change

+13.3 or more

0 to +13.2

0 to -9.9

-10.0 or more

Analytical Text

POPULATION TRENDS

General

Between 1960 and 1970 the population of West Virginia dropped from 1,860,000 to 1,744,000, a decrease of 116,000 or 6.2 percent. Among the three States that lost population (the other two were North Dakota and South Dakota), the numerical decline and the rate of decline were greatest in West Virginia. West Virginia, which experienced a 7.2 percent loss in population in the 1950 to 1960 decade, is the only State to lose population during each of the past two decades. Between 1940 and 1970, the population of West Virginia declined by 9 percent while the population of the nation as a whole increased by 54 percent. In 1970 West Virginia ranked 34th in population among the 50 States; in 1940, it ranked 25th. The decline in population during the past two decades was due partly to increased mechanization

in the coal industry. The reduced employment requirements in the coal industry have not been offset by increases in other sectors of the economy.

The total number of households in West Virginia in 1970 was 546,000 or 25,000 more than in 1960. The population living in households declined and average household size dropped from 3.5 to 3.1 persons per unit. In the nation as a whole the decline was from 3.3 to 3.1 persons per unit.

Between 1960 and 1970, the rates of population decline in metropolitan areas and nonmetropolitan areas were similar. The metropolitan population decreased by 5.2 percent from 575,000 to 545,000 while the nonmetropolitan population decreased by 6.7 percent from 1,285,000 to 1,199,000. The proportion of the State's population living in metropolitan areas was 31 percent in both 1960 and 1970. In the nation as a whole, about two-thirds of the population live in metropolitan areas (table A).

Table A. Population by Race and Metropolitan and Nonmetropolitan Residence: 1970 and 1960

The State Metropolitan and Non- metropolitan Residence	Population		Change		Percent Distribution	
	1970	1960	Number	Percent	1970	1960
Total...............	1,744,237	1,860,421	-116,184	-6.2	100.0	100.0
Metropolitan residence...	545,243	575,137	-29,894	-5.2	31.3	30.9
Inside central cities..	221,139	251,024	-29,885	-11.9	12.7	13.5
Outside central cities.	324,104	324,113	-9	-	18.6	17.4
Nonmetropolitan residence	1,198,994	1,285,284	-86,290	-6.7	68.7	69.1
White...............	1,666,870	1,770,133	-103,263	-5.8	95.6	95.1
Metropolitan residence...	520,885	551,034	-30,149	-5.5	29.1	29.6
Inside central cities..	205,384	234,529	-29,145	-12.4	11.8	12.6
Outside central cities.	315,501	316,505	-1,004	-0.3	18.1	17.0
Nonmetropolitan residence	1,145,985	1,219,099	-73,114	-6.0	65.7	65.5
Negro and other races	77,367	90,288	-12,921	-14.3	4.4	4.9
Metropolitan residence...	24,358	24,103	255	1.1	1.4	1.3
Inside central cities..	15,755	16,495	-740	-4.5	0.9	0.9
Outside central cities.	8,603	7,608	995	13.1	0.5	0.4
Nonmetropolitan residence	53,009	66,185	-13,176	-19.9	3.0	3.6

All of the decline in West Virginia's metropolitan population occurred in central cities which had a population of 251,000 in 1960 and a population of 1,000 in 1970. The decline would have been slightly ger in the absence of the small annexations to three of central cities (table B). The balance of the metro- litan area population was 324,000 at both dates.

In the State as a whole, the population of Negro and her races (more than 95 percent of which is Negro) pped from 90,000 in 1960 to 77,000 in 1970, a cline of 14 percent. The rate of decline for the white pulation was 6 percent. In 1970, Negro and other es constituted 4 percent of the State's population.

The population decline of 116,000 in West Virginia in e 1960 to 1970 decade resulted from a natural crease (births minus deaths) of 149,000 and a net tmigration of 265,000. Net outmigration was equiva- nt to 14 percent of the 1960 population.

The age structure of the West Virginia population anged considerably between 1960 and 1970. The mber of persons under 5 years of age and those in the to 14 and 25 to 44 age groups declined by more than 5 percent while the population 15 to 24 increased. In le nation as a whole, the population in the 5 to 14 and 5 to 44 age groups increased during the decade.

The decline in the population under 5 years old was ue partly to the decline in birth rates which occurred hroughout the United States during the 1960's. The icrease in the 15 to 24 age group was due to the entry f the large number of persons born during the ost-World War II "baby boom" into this age group.

Standard Metropolitan Statistical Areas

n 1970, there were four Standard Metropolitan Statis- ical Areas (SMSA's) in West Virginia, including one SMSA located entirely in West Virginia (the Charleston SMSA) and three SMSA's located partly in West Virginia the Huntington-Ashland, W. Va.-Ky.-Ohio SMSA, the Steubenville-Weirton, Ohio-W. Va. SMSA, and the Wheeling, W. Va.-Ohio SMSA). The following text refers to entire SMSA's rather than to just the portions in West Virginia.

Each of these four SMSA's lost population between 1960 and 1970. The rates of decline ranged from less than 1 percent in the Huntington-Ashland SMSA to 9 percent in the Charleston SMSA.

The Huntington-Ashland SMSA had a population of 255,000 in 1960 and 254,000 in 1970. Net outmigration totaled 25,000 which was equivalent to 10 percent of the 1960 population. The population in the central cities of Huntington and Ashland dropped from 115,000 to 104,000 while the population in the balance of the SMSA grew from 140,000 to 150,000.

The population in the Charleston SMSA declined by 9 percent from 253,000 in 1960 to 230,000 in 1970. The natural increase (births minus deaths) of 25,000 was more than offset by the net outmigration of 48,000 which was equivalent to 19 percent of the 1960 population. The population of the city of Charleston dropped from 86,000 to 72,000, and the population in the remainder of the SMSA dropped from 167,000 to 158,000.

The Wheeling SMSA had a population of 190,000 in 1960 and 183,000 in 1970, resulting in a decline of 4 percent. Net outmigration totaled 16,000 and was equivalent to 8 percent of the 1960 population. The population decline in the city of Wheeling was from 53,000 to 48,000, and the population decline in the balance of the SMSA was from 137,000 to 135,000.

The population of the Steubenville-Weirton SMSA declined by 1 percent from 168,000 in 1960 to 166,000 in 1970. Net outmigration during the decade was 15,000, which was equivalent to 9 percent of the 1960 population. The population in the central cities of Steubenville and Weirton dropped from 61,000 to 58,000 while the population in the remainder of the SMSA increased from 107,000 to 108,000.

Table B.   Change in Population of Central Cities Through Annexation: 1960 to 1970

Central Cities	1970 population			1960 population	Change 1960 to 1970 in 1960 area
	Total	In 1960 area	In annexed area		
Huntington..................	74,315	74,070	245	83,627	-9,557
Charleston..................	71,505	71,141	364	85,796	-14,655
Wheeling....................	48,188	46,492	1,696	53,400	-6,908

Counties

Of the 55 counties in West Virginia, 15 gained population and 40 lost population between 1960 and 1970. Only three counties had rates of growth above the national average of 13.3 percent, and 16 counties experienced population declines exceeding 10 percent. In five of these 16 counties, the rate of decline was 20 percent or more. In the nation as a whole, slightly more than half of all counties gained population during the decade.

Several States gained population between 1960 and 1970 despite the fact that the large majority of their counties lost population. Substantial gains in the populous metropolitan counties typically more than offset smaller losses in nonmetropolitan counties. In West Virginia, however, of the seven metropolitan counties five lost population and the other two had population gains of less than 1,000.

The two counties with populations exceeding 100,000 in 1960 lost population during the decade. The population of Kanawha County, which is coterminous with the Charleston SMSA dropped from 253,000 in 1960 to 230,000 in 1970. The population of Cabell County, which includes the city of Huntington, dropped from 108,000 to 107,000.

Every county in West Virginia had a natural increase of population (i.e., births exceeded deaths) between 1960 and 1970. In 40 counties (those losing population), net outmigration exceeded natural increase. Only four counties, including the three that had rates of increase above the national average, had a net inmigration of population during the decade. The largest net inmigration occurred in Monongalia County, the site of West Virginia University. Net inmigration to that county was 3,000, which was equivalent to 6 percent of the 1960 population.

The most rapid growth rate occurred in Putnam County which, with a 1960 population of 24,000 and a 1970 population of 28,000 increased by 17 percent. The population of Monongalia County grew by 15 percent from 56,000 to 64,000, and the population of Jefferson County grew by 14 percent from 19,000 to 21,000. Wood County, which had a population of 78,000 in 1960 and 87,000 in 1970 had the largest population gain of any county in West Virginia.

All five of the counties with population losses of 20 percent of more and most of the 11 counties with population losses from 10 percent to 20 percent between 1960 and 1970 have economies dominated by the coal industry and are located within 100 miles to the east or south of the city of Charleston. Three of the counties with population losses exceeding 20 percent had rates of net outmigration equivalent to more than one-third of their 1960 populations: Logan, McDowell, and Webster Counties. The highest rate of population decline occurred in McDowell County which had a 1960 population of 71,000 and a 1970 population of 51,000, a loss of 29 percent.

HOUSING TRENDS

General

During the decade, the population in West Virginia decreased by 116,200, or 6 percent, while the total supply of housing units in the State increased by 21,600, or 4 percent (table C).

The metropolitan areas of West Virginia experienced slightly less relative growth in housing, than did the nonmetropolitan part. The number of housing units in metropolitan areas rose from 179,400 to 185,500 over the decade, an increase of 6,100 units, or 3.4 percent;

Table C. Housing Units by Metropolitan and Nonmetropolitan Residence: 1970 and 1960

The State Metropolitan and Nonmetropolitan Residence	Housing units				Population percent change
	Total		Change		
	1970	1960	Number	Percent	
Total...............	595,969	574,357	21,612	3.8	-6.2
Metropolitan residence.....	185,471	179,358	6,113	3.4	-5.2
Inside central cities....	81,067	83,820	-2,753	-3.3	-11.9
Outside central cities...	104,404	95,538	8,866	9.3	-
Nonmetropolitan residence..	410,498	394,999	15,499	3.9	-6.7

this compares with an increase of 15,500 units, or 3.9 percent, in nonmetropolitan areas. The metropolitan areas contained 31 percent of the housing in West Virginia in 1970 and additions to the housing supply in these areas accounted for 28 percent of the State's total housing increase between 1960 and 1970.

About 83 percent of the housing in West Virginia consisted of one-unit structures in 1970. The number of units in multiunit structures, however, increased 51 percent while one-unit structures decreased 5 percent during the decade.

The size of housing units increased between 1960 and 1970. The median number of rooms rose from 5.0 to 5.1 in both metropolitan and nonmetropolitan areas. In the State, units with one to four rooms declined over the decade.

Households were smaller in 1970 than in 1960. In metropolitan areas, average household size declined from 3.4 persons in 1960 to 3.0 in 1970, and in nonmetropolitan areas, from 3.6 persons in 1960 to 3.2 in 1970. During the same period, in West Virginia, there were large percentage increases in one-person households and decreases in the number of households with three or more persons.

The number of units lacking some or all plumbing facilities declined from 185,700 to 108,700, a 41-percent decrease since 1960. In 1970, 8 percent of all year-round units in metropolitan areas lacked complete plumbing facilities, compared with 17 percent in 1960.

In nonmetropolitan areas such units comprised 23 percent of the housing in 1970 and 40 percent in 1960.

Number of persons per room is often used as a measure of crowding. In West Virginia, both the number and proportion of housing units with 1.01 or more persons per room decreased during the decade. In 1960, 15 percent of all occupied units had more than one person per room. By 1970, the proportion of such units had decreased to 9 percent (table D).

Homeownership in the State increased from 64 percent in 1960 to 69 percent in 1970. In metropolitan areas there was an increase from 62 to 67 percent, and in nonmetropolitan areas the proportion rose from 65 to 70 percent.

Property values and rents increased during the last decade. The median value of owner-occupied homes in metropolitan areas increased by 35 percent, from $10,900 in 1960 to $14,700 in 1970, while in nonmetropolitan areas, value increased 53 percent, from $6,200 to $9,500.

In metropolitan areas, median contract rent in 1970 was 33 percent higher than in 1960, rising from $46 to $61. In nonmetropolitan areas, the increase was 57 percent, from $30 in 1960 to $47 in 1970.

Value and rent are expressed in current dollars (the value at the time of the respective censuses). Thus, any comparison must take into account the general rise in the cost of living during the 10-year period as well as changes in the characteristics of the housing inventory.

Table D. Plumbing Facilities and Persons Per Room by Metropolitan and Nonmetropolitan Residence: 1970 and 1960

The State Metropolitan and Nonmetropolitan Residence	Percent of housing units			
	Lacking some or all plumbing facilities		With 1.01 or more persons per room[1]	
	1970[2]	1960[3]	1970	1960
Total..........................	18.4	32.3	9.2	15.1
Metropolitan residence...........	8.1	16.5	7.2	12.3
Inside central cities..........	3.7	7.5	5.4	8.9
Outside central cities.........	11.6	24.5	8.7	15.3
Nonmetropolitan residence........	23.1	39.5	10.1	16.5

[1]Percent of all occupied units.
[2]Percent of all year-round housing units.
[3]Percent of all housing units.
[4]Not shown because of lack of comparability with 1970.

Standard Metropolitan Statistical Areas

The metropolitan areas of the State also include two SMSA's which cross State lines, i.e., Huntington-Ashland, W. Va.-Ky.-Ohio, and Steubenville-Weirton, Ohio-W. Va.

Average household size for the metropolitan areas declined during the decade. For the central cities the average was 3.1 persons in 1960, compared with 2.8 in 1970. For the suburban areas, the average decreased from 3.6 persons in 1960 to 3.2 in 1970.

The rate of homeownership was greater in the suburban areas than in the central cities. The percent of owner-occupied units increased in the suburbs from 68 percent in 1960 to 73 percent in 1970, compared with 55 to 58 percent in the central cities.

One-unit structures comprised 86 percent of the housing in the suburbs in 1970 compared with 68 percent in the central cities. However, the number of units in multiunit structures showed greater increases over the decade in both central cities and suburbs, 15 percent and 99 percent, respectively.

In 1970, 15,100 housing units in metropolitan areas, or 8 percent of all year-round units, lacked some or all plumbing facilities. The proportion of units lacking complete plumbing facilities decreased from 7 percent in 1960 to 4 percent in 1970 in the central cities and from 24 percent to 12 percent in the suburban areas.

Of all occupied units in metropolitan areas, 12,700 units, or 7 percent, reported more than one person per room in 1970, compared with 13 percent in 1960. In 1970, the proportion of such units was 5 percent in the central cities and 9 percent in the suburbs.

The median value of housing remained higher in the central cities of West Virginia ($16,500 in 1970 and $12,900 in 1960) than the suburban areas ($13,600 in 1970 and $9,400 in 1960). In 1970, the median rent was $65 in the central cities and $55 in the suburbs.

The homeowner vacancy rate for metropolitan areas was 1.1 percent in 1970 as in 1960. The rental vacancy rate decreased slightly from 6.7 in 1960 to 6.6 in 1970.

Annexations

Annexations occurred in each of the central cities except the city of Weirton during the decade (see "Population Trends" and text table B). Such annexations affect changes in the characteristics for these central cities and their suburbs.

Population Change for Counties: 1960 to 1970

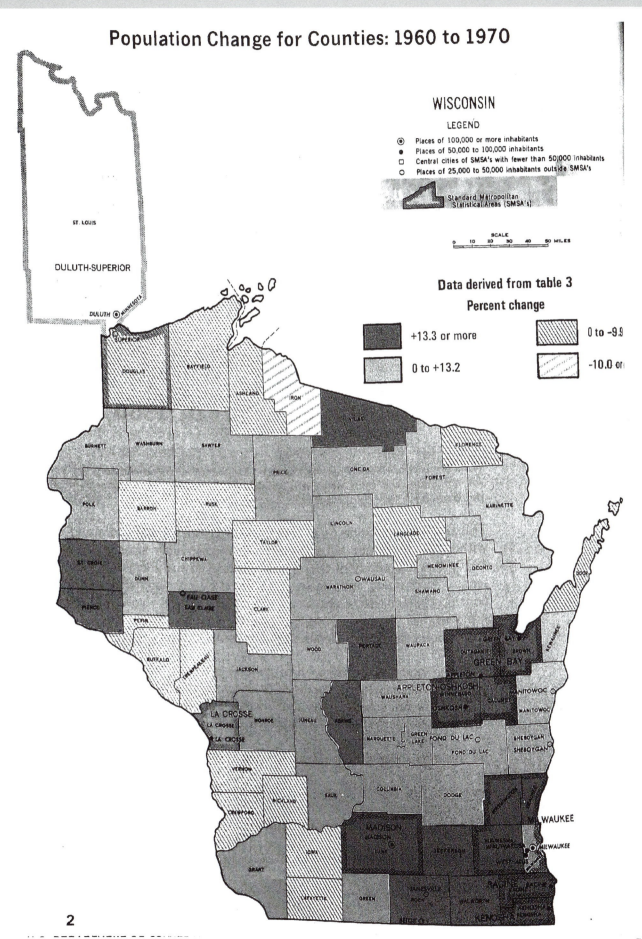

WISCONSIN

LEGEND

⊙ Places of 100,000 or more inhabitants
● Places of 50,000 to 100,000 inhabitants
☐ Central cities of SMSA's with fewer than 50,000 inhabitants
○ Places of 25,000 to 50,000 inhabitants outside SMSA's

Standard Metropolitan
Statistical Areas (SMSA's)

SCALE
0   10   20   30   40   50 MILES

Data derived from table 3

Percent change

+13.3 or more

0 to +13.2

0 to -9.9

-10.0 or

Analytical Text

POPULATION TRENDS

General

Between 1960 and 1970 the population of Wisconsin grew from 3,952,000 to 4,418,000. The rate of increase, 11.8 percent, is slightly below the national average of 13.3 percent and about the same as for the other four States in the East North Central Division. Among all the States Wisconsin ranks 16th in population size, being passed by Georgia in the past decade.

The total number of households in Wisconsin in 1970 was 1,329,000, or 182,000 more than in 1960. The population living in households increased less rapidly than the rate at which households increased, with the result that the average household size decreased slightly, from 3.4 to 3.2 persons.

The population in the State's eight metropolitan areas increased by 15 percent which is nearly double the rate of increase in nonmetropolitan areas (table A). The differential rates of growth in the two areas is caused not only by differential rates of migration but by a much higher birth rate in the metropolitan areas. (The proportion of the population in the child-bearing age is considerably higher in the metropolitan areas than in the nonmetropolitan areas.) Within the metropolitan areas,

Table A.   Population by Race and Metropolitan and Nonmetropolitan Residence:
1970 and 1960

The State Metropolitan and Non-metropolitan Residence	Population		Change		Percent Distribution	
	1970	1960	Number	Percent	1970	1960
Total..............	[1]4,417,731	3,951,777	465,954	11.8	100.0	100.0
Metropolitan residence...	2,542,975	2,217,886	325,089	14.7	57.6	56.1
Inside central cities..	1,345,887	1,262,620	83,267	6.6	30.5	32.0
Outside central cities.	1,197,088	955,266	241,822	25.3	27.1	24.2
Nonmetropolitan residence	1,874,756	1,733,891	140,865	8.1	42.4	43.9
White..............	4,258,959	3,858,903	400,056	10.4	96.4	97.6
Metropolitan residence...	2,402,888	2,138,267	264,621	12.4	54.4	54.1
Inside central cities..	1,214,464	1,187,722	26,742	2.3	27.5	30.1
Outside central cities.	1,188,424	950,545	237,879	25.0	26.9	24.1
Nonmetropolitan residence	1,856,071	1,720,636	135,435	7.9	42.0	43.5
Negro and other races	158,772	92,874	65,898	71.0	3.6	2.4
Metropolitan residence...	140,087	79,619	60,468	75.9	3.2	2.0
Inside central cities..	131,423	74,898	56,525	75.5	3.0	1.9
Outside central cities.	8,664	4,721	3,943	83.5	0.2	0.1
Nonmetropolitan residence	18,685	13,255	5,430	41.0	0.4	0.3

[1]See correction date on page 9.

the growth rate in the suburban ring was over 25 percent. In spite of substantial annexation of suburban population during the decade (table B), the rate of growth in the central cities was only about 7 percent less than that in the nonmetropolitan portions of the State. In Wisconsin about three out of five persons live in metropolitan areas, compared with two out of three in the Nation as a whole.

Although Wisconsin's population is overwhelmingly white, the increase in the population of Negro and other races is one of the highest in the Nation. Their increase in the State amounted to 66,000 or 71 percent. Most of this increase was confined to the central cities of the standard metropolitan statistical areas (SMSA's). Negro and other races comprise less than 4 percent of the State's population but nearly 10 percent of the population within central cities.

The population increase in Wisconsin was almost completely the result of natural increase (births minus deaths) which amounted to 462,000. Net inmigration added only 4,000. There was a modest outmigration of the white population during the decade (29,000), which was countered by an almost equal amount of inmigration of other races (33,000). Although the total number of inmigrants of races other than white was not large, their rate of inmigration (36 percent) was exceeded only by Nevada and Colorado.

As in the Nation generally, Wisconsin's age structure changed significantly in the decade. The population under age 5 declined almost 20 percent while every other broad age grouping showed an increase. The decline in the number of young children is caused by the greatly reduced number of births in the period 1965 to 1969 as opposed to 1955 to 1959. As a result, the population under 5 now comprises less than 9 percent of the population. Ten years ago this age group had 12 percent of the State's population.

The population of Negro and other races is considerably younger than the white. Only 40 percent of the former is over age 25 and 4 percent are over age 65. By contrast, 53 percent of the white population is over 25 and nearly 11 percent are over 65.

Standard Metropolitan Statistical Areas

With the addition of the newly created Appleton-Oshkosh and La Crosse Standard Metropolitan Statistical Areas (SMSA's) the State of Wisconsin contains eight SMSA's. Seven of them lie wholly within the State; the Duluth-Superior, Minn.-Wis. SMSA is shared with Minnesota. The major part of the SMSA is located in Minnesota.

The four county Milwaukee SMSA, with over 1.4 million residents, is five times as large as any other SMSA in the State and contains about one-third of the State's population. Over the decade the SMSA increased by 125,000, or 10 percent over the 1960 population. The SMSA had a moderate outmigration of 39,000, equivalent to 3 percent of its 1960 population. This loss was the result of very heavy outmigration from Milwaukee city. The remaining three counties of the SMSA, Waukesha, Izaukee, and Washington, rank as the three leading counties in the State in rate of inmigration. In 1970 as in 1960 the city of Milwaukee contained nearly 90 percent of the State's Negro population.

The Madison SMSA, site of the State capital and home of the University of Wisconsin, had the largest rate of increase of any metropolitan area in the State.

Table B.   Change in Population of Central Cities Through Annexation: 1960 to 1970

Central Cities	1970 population			1960 population	Change 1960 to 1970 in 1960 area
	Total	In 1960 area	In annexed area		
Milwaukee	717,099	710,176	6,923	741,324	-31,148
Madison	173,258	148,325	24,933	126,706	21,619
Racine	95,162	90,286	4,876	89,144	1,142
Green Bay	87,809	68,432	19,377	62,888	5,544
Kenosha	78,805	70,801	8,004	67,899	2,902
Appleton	57,143	55,451	1,692	48,411	7,040
Oshkosh	53,221	50,952	2,269	45,110	5,842
La Crosse	51,153	45,716	5,437	47,575	-1,859

Inmigration of 29,000 accounted for more than 40 percent of the area's growth. Because of the University, the SMSA has a very different age structure from the rest of the State. About one-fourth of the population is between 15 and 24 years of age. In comparison only a little over one-sixth of the State's and U.S. population fall into this age category.

The newly created Appleton-Oshkosh SMSA in the Fox River Valley contains a population of 277,000 and ranks 114th of all SMSA's in the United States. The rate of growth in the three county area amounted to nearly 20 percent with inmigration being responsible for one-fifth of the total growth.

The heavily industrialized SMSA's of Racine and Kenosha, lying directly to the south of Milwaukee, each had population increases of about 20 percent. In both cases natural increase accounted for the majority of the population increase, although both had some net inmigration.

The Green Bay SMSA, best known as the home of a professional football franchise (Green Bay Packers), had a population increase of twice that of the United States and currently has a population of 158,000. Its net inmigration of 10,000 was greater than for any other SMSA in the State except Madison. La Crosse, the other newly created SMSA, has a population of 80,000, an increase of 8,000 over its 1960 population. Much of the growth in the county is attributable to the increased enrollment at the branch of the State university system located in the city of La Crosse.

Douglas County, which is the Wisconsin portion of the Duluth-Superior Minn.-Wis. SMSA was the only metropolitan county in the State to lose population. The loss in this county was small, but the outmigration from the area was a substantial 6 percent.

Counties

Of the 72 counties in Wisconsin, 53 gained in population and 19 lost. The smallest county, Menominee was organized from parts of Shawano and Oconto Counties in 1961. This new county, the only county created in the United States since Los Alamos, New Mexico in the 1940's, is the Menominee Indian Reservation.

Nineteen counties in the State had population increases greater than the National average of 13.3 percent. Ten of the 13 SMSA counties fell into this category while only nine of the 59 nonmetropolitan counties could make this claim. The three suburban Milwaukee counties, Waukesha, Ozaukee, and Washington, which were the three leading counties in rate of inmigration maintained that position in terms of total growth rate. The individual rates of growth in these three counties were, respectively, 46, 42, and 38 percent. Dane County (Madison SMSA) ranked fourth with a growth rate of 31 percent.

Wisconsin's rapidly expanding State University system was in large part responsible for the growth in some nonmetropolitan counties. This was especially true at Eau Claire (Eau Claire County), Whitewater (Jefferson and Walworth counties), River Falls (Pierce County), and Stevens Point (Portage County). In these counties the increase in dormitory population alone accounts for much of the net inmigration.

The largest nonmetropolitan county in the State, Rock, with over 130,000 population, also had the largest absolute growth of any nonmetropolitan county. This county contains the city of Janesville, which is nearing the population necessary to qualify it for SMSA status, and the city of Beloit.

Not one of the 19 counties which lost population contained as many as 50,000 people in the 1970 census, and 13 had populations of less than 20,000. There is no geographic pattern to the counties losing population except that none are situated in the southeast corner of the State.

Although Milwaukee County had some population growth in the past decade, it had over 100,000 net outmigrants. This number of net outmigrants is equivalent to 10 percent of the 1960 population. The number of net outmigrants from Milwaukee County was almost twice that of the total number of net outmigrants from the 39 other counties in the State which experienced outmigration.

HOUSING TRENDS

General

During the decade the population in Wisconsin grew by 466,000, or 12 percent, while the total supply of housing units increased by 183,800, or 14 percent (table C).

The metropolitan areas of the State experienced greater relative growth in housing, as in population, than did the nonmetropolitan part. The number of housing units in metropolitan areas rose from 688,400 to 802,600 over the decade, an increase of 114,200 units, or 17 percent; this compares with an increase of 69,600 units, or 12 percent, in nonmetropolitan areas. The metropolitan areas contained 55 percent of the housing in Wisconsin and additions to the housing supply in these areas accounted for 62 percent of the State's total housing increase between 1960 and 1970.

About 71 percent of the housing in Wisconsin consisted of one-unit structures in 1970. The 1970 proportion of such units was 62 percent in metropolitan areas and 82 percent in nonmetropolitan areas.

The median number of rooms in housing units in Wisconsin was 5.2 in 1970. In metropolitan areas the median was 5.1, compared with 5.4 in nonmetropolitan areas. While 39 percent of the housing units in metropolitan areas had six or more rooms, 47 percent of the nonmetropolitan housing units were in this category.

Households were smaller in 1970 than in 1960. In both the metropolitan and nonmetropolitan areas, average household size declined from 3.4 persons in 1960 to 3.2 in 1970. There were large percentage increases in one-person households, 64 percent in metropolitan areas and 56 percent in nonmetropolitan areas. Households with three or more persons showed relatively small gains in metropolitan and nonmetropolitan areas.

The number of units in the State lacking some or all plumbing facilities in 1970 was 101,400, or 7 percent. The proportion of such units was 4 percent in metropolitan areas and 11 percent in nonmetropolitan areas.

Number of persons per room is often used as a measure of crowding. In Wisconsin, both the number and proportion of housing units with 1.01 or more persons per room decreased during the decade. In 1960, 9 percent of all occupied housing units in metropolitan

Table C. Housing Units by Metropolitan and Nonmetropolitan Residence: 1970 and 1960

The State Metropolitan and Nonmetropolitan Residence	Housing units				Population percent change
	Total		Change		
	1970	1960	Number	Percent	
Total..................	1,472,466	1,288,620	183,846	14.3	11.8
Metropolitan residence.....	802,581	688,369	114,212	16.6	14.7
Inside central cities....	447,611	404,649	42,962	10.6	6.6
Outside central cities...	354,970	283,720	71,250	25.1	25.3
Nonmetropolitan residence..	669,885	600,251	69,634	11.6	8.1

areas and 8 percent in nonmetropolitan areas had more than one person per room. By 1970, the proportion of such units had decreased to 7 percent in both metropolitan and nonmetropolitan areas (table D).

The homeownership rate in Wisconsin was 69 percent in 1970, as in 1960. The proportion of owner-occupied units remained at 63 percent in metropolitan areas and increased from 75 percent in 1960 to 77 percent in 1970 in nonmetropolitan areas.

About 34 percent of the Negro households in metropolitan areas owned their homes in 1970, compared with 52 percent in nonmetropolitan areas. Of the 11,200 Negro-homeowner housheolds in the State, 10,600 lived inside SMSA's and 600 lived outside SMSA's.

Property values and rents increased during the last decade. The median value of owner-occupied homes in metropolitan areas rose 32 percent, from $14,900 in 1960 to $19,600 in 1970, while in nonmetropolitan areas, value increased 43 percent, from $9,500 to $13,600. In metropolitan areas, median contract rent in 1970 was 43 percent higher than in 1960, rising from $70 to $100. In nonmetropolitan areas, the increase was 51 percent, from $47 in 1960 to $71 in 1970.

Value and rent are expressed in current dollars (the value at the time of the respective censuses). Thus, any comparison must take into account the general rise in the cost of living during the 10-year period, as well as changes in the characteristics of the housing inventory.

Standard Metropolitan Statistical Areas

In the metropolitan areas of the State, the housing supply increased by 114,200 units, or 17 percent. The Milwaukee SMSA, which contained 56 percent of the housing units in metropolitan areas, accounted for 42 percent of the increase.

The rate of homeownership in 1970 was greater in the suburban areas than in the central cities. About 76 percent of occupied units in the suburbs and 54 percent in the central cities were owner-occupied. About 33 percent of the Negro households in the central cities owned their homes, compared with 50 percent in the suburbs.

In 1970, 30,400 housing units in metropolitan areas, or 4 percent of all units, lacked some or all plumbing facilities. The corresponding proportion was 4 percent in the central cities and 3 percent in the suburbs.

Of all occupied units in metropolitan areas, 55,700 units, or 7 percent, reported more than one person per room in 1970, compared with 9 percent in 1960. In

Table D. Plumbing Facilities and Persons Per Room by Metropolitan and Nonmetro-
         politan Residence: 1970 and 1960

The State Metropolitan and Nonmetropolitan Residence	Percent of housing units			
	Lacking some or all plumbing facilities		With 1.01 or more persons per room[1]	
	1970[2]	1960[3]	1970	1960
Total......................	7.2	17.2	7.2	8.9
Metropolitan residence..........	3.8	(NA)	7.3	9.2
Inside central cities..........	4.2	8.5	7.1	8.7
Outside central cities........	3.4	(NA)	7.4	9.8
Nonmetropolitan residence........	11.4	(NA)	7.1	8.5

(NA) Not available.
[1]Percent of all occupied units.
[2]Percent of all year-round housing units.
[3]Percent of all housing units.

1970, the proportion of such units was 7 percent for both the central cities and suburban areas.

The homeowner vacancy rate for metropolitan areas decreased during the decade from 1.2 percent in 1960 to 0.7 percent in 1970. The rental vacancy rate decreased from 5.0 to 4.3 percent.

Annexations

Annexations occurred in each of the central cities except Superior during the decade (see "Population Trends" and text table B). Such annexations affect changes in the characteristics for the central cities and their suburbs.

Population Change for Counties: 1960 to 1970

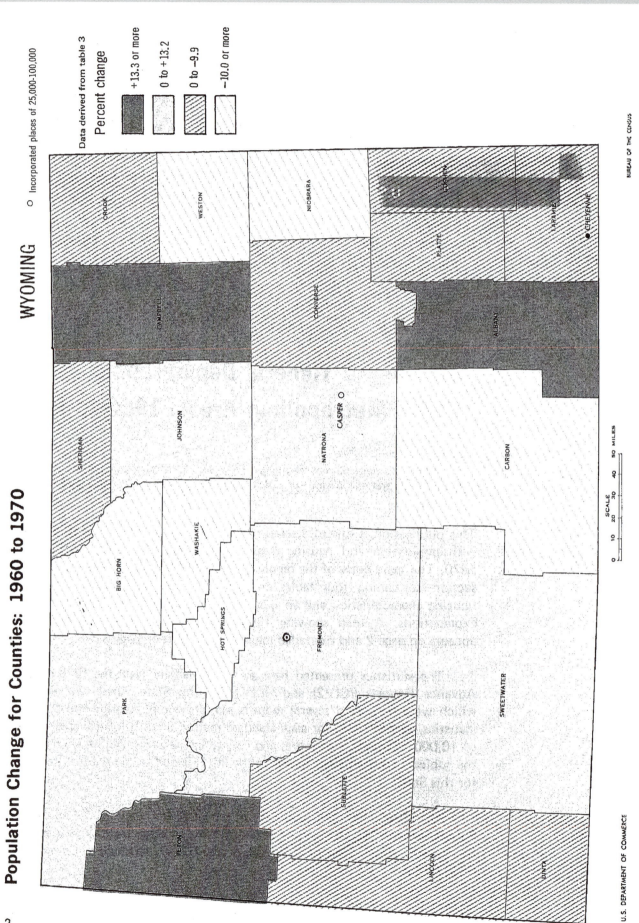

WYOMING

O Incorporated places of 25,000-100,000

Data derived from table 3

Percent change

+13.3 or more

0 to +13.2

0 to −9.9

−10.0 or more

CROOK

WESTON

NIOBRARA

GOSHEN

PLATTE

LARAMIE

CHEYENNE

CAMPBELL

CONVERSE

ALBANY

SHERIDAN

JOHNSON

NATRONA

CASPER O

CARBON

BIG HORN

WASHAKIE

HOT SPRINGS

FREMONT

PARK

SUBLETTE

SWEETWATER

TETON

LINCOLN

UINTA

SCALE
0 10 20 30 40 50 MILES

BUREAU OF THE CENSUS

U.S. DEPARTMENT OF COMMERCE

Analytical Text

POPULATION TRENDS

General

Between 1960 and 1970 the population of Wyoming scarcely changed, increasing from 330,000 in 1960 to 332,000 in 1970, or by less than 1 percent. This was the lowest decennial rate of increase in the history of the State. The largest city in the State, Cheyenne, which has a population of 41,000, also experienced a slight population loss between 1960 and 1970, amounting to 6 percent.

The population of Wyoming is predominantly white. Less than 3 percent of the total population belonged to races other than white in 1970 and in 1960.

Population change in the State was made up of a natural increase of nearly 42,000 persons (70,000 births minus 28,000 deaths) and a counterbalancing net outmigration of more than 39,000 persons. The loss of population due to net outmigration is equivalent to 12 percent of the population living in the State in 1960.

During the decade, there was an increase of more than 5 percent in the number of households in the State, from 99,000 in 1960 to 105,000 in 1970. Population living in households grew by only 1 percent, resulting in a slight decrease in average household size, from 3.3 persons in 1960 to 3.1 in 1970.

Some changes in age composition occurred during the decade which result in smaller numbers at ages under 5 and 25 to 44 years and a large increase in the population 15 to 24 years of age. The population at middle and older ages also grew during this period, but more slowly. Children of school age formed the dominant age group in 1970 as in 1960. In both years there were more than 70,000 children 5 to 14 years of age in the State, comprising over one-fifth of the population of all ages.

Similar age changes are found in other sections of the country and are the product in part of changing birth rates and in part of age selective migration: e.g., low birth rates during the Depression years and in the 1960's contribute to the diminution of age groups 0 to 4 and 25 to 44, whereas the post-World War II "baby boom" is currently reflected in the large size of the population 15 to 24 years old.

Counties

More than half of Wyoming's 23 counties lost population in the period 1960-70, and 1 out of 4 lost 10 percent or more of their 1960 populations. The most populous county, in 1960 as well as in 1970, is Laramie, which contains the State's largest city, Cheyenne. Between 1960 and 1970 the population of Laramie County declined, however, from 60,000 to 56,000, which represented a loss of 6 percent of its total 1960 population. The largest increases (at rates exceeding the 13.3-percent increase for the United States as a whole) are shown by the three widely separated counties of Campbell, Teton, and Albany. Campbell County more than doubled between 1960 and 1970, while Teton County had an increase in population of almost 60 percent. The 1960 populations of these two counties were among the smallest in the State, however, consisting of less than 6,000 persons in Campbell County and 3,000 in Teton. The population of Albany County, on the other hand, grew by 24 percent, from a total of 21,000 in 1960 to 26,000 in 1970. Some part of this increase may be attributable to a doubling of enrollment at the University of Wyoming, which is located in Albany County.

All counties in Wyoming had more births than deaths between 1960 and 1970, but only the three fastest growing counties also show net inmigration for the decade. Every other county in the State experienced net outmigration, which in many cases was sufficient to wipe out gains made as a result of natural increase. Laramie County, which had a natural increase of over 10,000, showed a counteracting net outmigration of 14,000 persons, equivalent to 24 percent of its 1960 population.

HOUSING TRENDS

During the decade, the total supply of housing units in Wyoming increased faster than population. While housing units increased by 3,200, or 3 percent, the population grew by 2,000, or less than 1 percent. Similarly, the number of households increased at a faster rate (5.5 percent) than the population in housing units (1 percent), resulting in a lower average household size.

This trend toward smaller households is evident also in the median number of persons per household, which dropped from 3.0 to 2.6 over the decade. The number of 1- and 2-person households increased by 9,500, while all larger households showed a net decrease of 4,100.

A large increase occurred in owner-occupied housing, which experienced a net gain of 7,800 units during the decade. Owner-occupied homes account for 66 percent of all occupied units, compared with 62 percent in 1960. By contrast, renter-occupied units decreased by 2,400.

The median value of owner-occupied housing in Wyoming increased by 25 percent, from $12,300 in 1960 to $15,400 in 1970. Housing units priced at $20,000 and above more than doubled during the decade. Median contract rent likewise increased by 26 percent, from $58 to $73 per month. As in the case of value of owner-occupied housing, the greatest proportional increases in rented units are at the upper end of the price scale. Households paying $100 to $149 more than doubled, and the number paying $150 or more tripled. Value and rent are expressed in current dollars (the dollar value at the time of the respective censuses). Thus, any comparison must take into account the inflation which occurred over the decade as well as changes in the characteristics of the housing inventory.

Number of persons per room is often used as a measurement of crowding. In Wyoming, occupied housing units with 1.01 or more persons per room comprise less than 9 percent of all occupied housing units, compared with 16 percent in 1960. The number of all such units in 1970 was 9,200, a decrease of about 6,300, or 41 percent, between 1960 and 1970, with an even greater drop in the percentage having 1.51 or more persons per room.

BIBLIOGRAPHY

CODE (Leave blank)	Citizenship of the foreign born	City, town, or village having 2,500 or more inhabitants. Enter "R" for all other places.	COUNTY	STATE (or Territory or foreign country)	On a farm? (Yes or No)	CODE (Leave blank)	21	22	23	24	25	E	26	27	28
		Same House			No		Yes	–	–	–	–	1	40	–	Foreman
		Same House			No		No	No	No	No	H	5	–	–	
		Same House			No		No	No	No	No	S	6	–	–	
		Same House			No		Yes	–	–	–	–	1	–	–	Laborer

General

Anderson, Terry H., *The Movement and the Sixties: Protest in America from Greensboro to Wounded Knee* (New York: Oxford University Press, 1995).

Archer, Jules, *The Incredible Sixties: The Stormy Years that Changed America* (San Diego: Harcourt Brace Jovanovich, 1986).

Baugess, James S., and Abbe Allen DeBolt, eds., *Encyclopedia of the Sixties: A Decade of Culture and Counterculture* (Santa Barbara, CA: Greenwood Press, 2012).

Berman, Ronald, *America in the Sixties; An Intellectual History* (New York: Harper and Row, 1970).

Bloom, Alexander, *Long Time Gone: Sixties America Then and Now* (New York: Oxford University Press, 2001).

Bloom, Alexander, and Wini Breines, eds., *"Takin' It to the Streets": A Sixties Reader,* 2nd ed. (New York: Oxford University Press, 2003).

Branch, Taylor. *America in the King Years, 1954–63,* 3 vols. (New York: Simon & Schuster, 1988–2006) [vol. 1: *Parting the Waters*; vol. 2: *Pillar of Fire*; vol. 3: *At Canaan's Edge*].

Braunstein, Peter, and Michael Willima Doyle, eds., *Imagine Nation: The American Counterculture of the 1960s and '70s* (New York: Routledge, 2002).

Brokaw, Tom, *Boom!: Talking about the Sixties: What Happened, How It Shaped Today, Lessons for Tomorrow* (New York: Random House, 2008).

Bromell, Nicholas Knowles, *Tomorrow Never Knows: Rock and Psychedelics in the 1960s* (Chicago: University of Chicago Press, 2000).

Burner, David, *Making Peace with the Sixties* (Princeton, NJ: Princeton University Press, 1996).

Burner, David, Robert D. Marcus, and Thomas R. West , et al. *A Giant's Strength; America in the 1960s* (New York, Holt, Rinehart and Winston, 1971).

Case, John, and Rosemary C. R. Taylor, eds., *Co-ops, Communes and Collectives: Experiments in Social Change in the 1960s and 1970s* (New York: Pantheon Books, 1979).

Chafe, William H., *The Unfinished Journey: America since World War II* (New York: Oxford University Press, 1986).

Chafe, William H., and Harvard Sitkoff, eds., *A History of Our Time: Readings on Postwar America,* 5th ed. (New York: Oxford University Press, 1999).

Chalmers, David Mark, *And the Crooked Places Made Straight: The Struggle for Social Change in the 1960s,* 2nd ed. (Baltimore: Johns Hopkins University Press, 1996).

Davidson, Eugene, *Reflections on a Disruptive Decade: Essays on the Sixties* (Columbia: University of Missouri Press, 2000).

Davies, Gareth, *From Opportunity to Entitlement: The Transformation and Decline of Great Society Liberalism* (Lawrence: University Press of Kansas, 1996).

DeGroot, Gerard J., *The Sixties Unplugged: A Kaleidoscopic History of a Disorderly Decade* (Cambridge, MA: Harvard University Press, 2008).

DeKoven, Marianne, *Utopia Limited: The Sixties and the Emergence of the Postmodern* (Durham: Duke University Press, 2004).

Delli Carpini, Michael X., *Stability and Change in American Politics: The Coming of Age of the Generation of the 1960s* (New York: New York University Press, 1986).

Dickstein, Morris, *Gates of Eden: American Culture in the Sixties* (New York: Basic Books, 1977).

Divine, Robert A., The Johnson Years, 3 vols. (Lawrence: University Press of Kansas, 1987–1994) [vol. 1: *Foreign Policy, the Great Society, and the White House*; vol.2: *Vietnam, the Environment, and Science*; vol. 3: *LBJ at Home and Abroad*].

Dudley, William G., *The 1960s* (San Diego, CA: Greenhaven Press, 2000).

Echols, Alice, *Shaky Ground: The '60s and Its Aftershocks* (New York: Columbia University Press, 2002).

Evans, Sarah, *In Personal Politics: The Roots of Women's Liberation in the Civil Rights Movement and the New Left* (New York: Knopf, 1979).

Farber, David, *The Age of Great Dreams: America in the 1960s* (New York: Hill and Wang, 1994).

Farber, David, ed., *The Sixties: From Memory to History* (Chapel Hill: University of North Carolina Press, 1994).

Farrell, James J., *The Spirit of the Sixties: Making Postwar Radicalism* (New York: Routledge, 1997).

Fischer, Klaus, *America in White, Black, and Gray: The Stormy 1960s* (New York: Continuum, 2006).

Foreman, Joel, ed., *Interrogating Midcentury American Icons* (Urbana: University of Illinois Press, 1997).

Frank, Thomas, *The Conquest of Cool: Business Culture, Counterculture, and the Rise of Hip Consumerism* (Chicago: University of Chicago Press, 1997).

Gillman, Richard, ed., *Power in Postwar America.* (Boston: Little, Brown, 1971).

Gitlin, Todd, *The Sixties: Years of Hope, Days of Rage,* rev. ed. (New York: Bantam Trade, 1993).

Goldstein, Toby, *Waking from the Dream: America in the Sixties* (New York: J. Messner, 1988).

Goodwin, Richard N., *Remembering America: A Voice from the Sixties* (Boston: Little, Brown, 1988).

Graham, Hugh Davis, *Civil Rights and the Presidency: Race and Gender in American Politics, 1960–1972* (New York: Oxford, 1992).

Graham, Hugh Davis, *The Civil Rights Era: Origins and Development of a National Policy, 1960–1972* (New York: Oxford University Press, 1990).

Greene, John Robert, *America in the Sixties* (Syracuse, NY: Syracuse University Press, 2010).

Heale, M. J., *The Sixties in America: History, Politics, and Protest* (Chicago: Fitzroy Dearborn, 2001).

Hodgson, Godfrey, *America in Our Time: From World War II to Nixon; What Happened and Why* (New York: Vintage Books, 1976).

Hurley, Jennifer A., *The 1960s* (San Diego, CA: Greenhaven Press, 2000).

Isserman, Maurice, and Michael Kazin, *America Divided: The Civil War of the 1960s* (New York: Oxford University Press, 2004).

Johnson, Lyndon B. *The Vantage Point; Perspectives of the Presidency, 1963–1969* (New York, Holt, 1971) [Johnson's official memoirs of his time as president].

Katz, Michael B., *The Undeserving Poor: From the War on Poverty to the War on Welfare* (New York: Pantheon Books, 1989).

Kennedy, Stetson, *Jim Crow Guide: The Way It Was* (Tuscaloosa, AL: University of Alabama Press, 1990) [originally published as *Jim Crow Guide to the USA: The Laws, Customs, and Etiquette Governing the Conduct of Nonwhites and Other Minorities as Second-Class Citizens*, 1959].

Keylin, Arleen, and Laurie Barnett, eds., *The Sixties: As Reported by the New York Times* (New York: Arno Press, 1980) [introduction by Tom Wicker].

Kimball, Roger, *The Long March: How the Cultural Revolution of the 1960s Changed America* (San Francisco: Encounter Books, 2000).

Klatch, Rebecca E., *A Generation Divided: The New Left, the New Right, and the 1960s* (Berkeley: University of California Press, 1999).

Koerselman, Gary H., *The Lost Decade: A Story of America in the 1960s* (New York: P. Lang, 1987).

Lemann, Nicholas, *The Promised Land: The Great Black Migration and How It Changed America* (New York: Knopf, 1991).

Leuchtenberg, William E., *A Troubled Feast: American Society since 1945* (Boston: Little, Brown, 1983).

Levy, Peter B., *America in the Sixties-Right, Left, and Center: A Documentary History* (Westport, CT: Greenwood Press, 1998).

Lytle, Mark Hamilton, *America's Uncivil Wars; The Sixties Era: From Elvis to the Fall of Richard Nixon* (New York: Oxford University Press, 2006).

Macedo, Stephen, ed., *Reassessing the Sixties: Debating the Political and Cultural Legacy* (New York: W. W. Norton, 1997).

Manchester, William Raymond, *The Death of a President, November 20–November 25, 1963* (New York, Harper and Row, 1967).

Margolis, Jon, *The Last Innocent Year: America in 1964: The Beginning of the "Sixties"* (New York: William Morrow, 1999).

Marías, Julian, *America in the Fifties and Sixties: Julian Marías on the United States*, tr. by Blanch de Puy and Harold C. Raley, ed. by Michael Aaron Rockland (University Park: Pennsylvania State University Press, 1972).

May, Ernest R., and Philip Zelikow, *The Kennedy Tapes: Inside the White House during the Cuban Missile Crisis* (Cambridge, MA: Belknap Press of Harvard University Press, 1997).

McCleary, John Bassett, *The Hippie Dictionary: A Cultural Encyclopedia (and Phraseicon) of the 1960s and 1970s*, rev. ed., ed. by Joan Jeffers McCleary (Berkeley, CA: Ten Speed Press, 2004).

McConnell, William S., ed., *The Counterculture Movement of the 1960s* (San Diego: Greenhaven Press, 2004).

McMillian, John, *Smoking Typewriters: The Sixties Underground Press and the Rise of Alternative Media in America* (New York: Oxford University Press, 2011).

McWilliams, John C., *The 1960s Cultural Revolution* (Westport, CT: Greenwood Press, 2000).

Monteith, Sharon, *American Culture in the 1960s* (Edinburgh: Edinburgh University Press, 2008).

Morgan, Edward P., *The 60s Experience: Hard Lessons about Modern America* (Philadelphia: Temple University Press, 1991).

Murray, Charles, *Losing Ground: American Social Policy, 1950–1980* (New York: Basic Books, 1984) [reprinted in 1994 with a new introduction to the tenth anniversary edition, by the author].

O'Neill, William L., *Coming Apart, An Informal History of America in the 1960's* (1971; repr., Chicago: Ivan R. Dee, 2005).

O'Neill, William, ed., *The Scribner Encyclopedia of American Lives: The 1960s*, 2 vols. (New York: C. Scribner's Sons, 2003).

Packard, Jerrold, *American Nightmare: The History of Jim Crow* (New York: St. Martin's, 2001).

Patterson, James T., *Grand Expectations: The United States, 1945–1974* (New York: Oxford University Press, 1996).

Perret, Geoffrey, *A Dream of Greatness: The American People, 1945–1963.* (New York: Coward, McCann and Geoghegan, 1979).

Rielly, Edward J., *The 1960s* (Westport, CT: Greenwood Press, 2003).

Rorabaugh, W. J., *Kennedy and the Promise of the Sixties* (New York: Cambridge University Press, 2002).

Rose, Mark H., *Interstate: Express Highway Politics, 1939–1989*, rev. ed. (Knoxville: University of Tennessee Press, 1990).

Rosenberg, Jonathan and Zachary Karabell, *Kennedy, Johnson, and the Quest for Justice; The Civil Rights Tapes* (New York: W. W. Norton, 2003).

Samuelson, Robert J., *The Good Life and Its Discontents: The American Dream in the Age of Entitlement, 1945–1990* (New York: Times Books, 1995).

Sann, Paul, ed., *The Angry Decade: The Sixties* (New York: Crown Publishers, 1979).

Schlesinger, Arthur M., Jr., *The Imperial Presidency* (1973; reprint, Mariner Books/Houghton Mifflin, 2004) [with a new epilogue, copyrighted 1989, and a new introduction].

Singleton, Carl, and Rowena Wildin, eds., *The Sixties in America*, 3 vols. (Pasadena, CA: Salem Press, 1999).

Steigerwald, David, *The Sixties and the End of Modern America* (New York: St. Martin's, 1995).

Swerdlow, Amy, *Women Strike for Peace: Traditional Motherhood and Radical Politics in the 1960s* (Chicago: University of Chicago Press, 1993).

Unger, Irwin, *The Best of Intentions: The Triumphs and Failures of the Great Society under Kennedy, Johnson, and Nixon* (New York: Doubleday, 1996).

Unger, Irwin, and Debi Unger, eds., *The Times Were A Changin': The Sixties Reader* (New York: Three Rivers Press, 1998).

Weiss, Jessica, *To Have and to Hold: Marriage, the Baby Boom, and Social Change* (Chicago: University of Chicago Press, 2000).

Westby, David L., *The Clouded Vision: The Student Movement in the United States in the 1960s* (Lewisburg, PA: Bucknell University Press, 1976).

Wofford, Harris, *Of Kennedys and Kings: Making Sense of the Sixties* (New York: Farrar, Straus, Giroux, 1980).

Wolfe, Tom, *The Right Stuff* (New York: Farrar, Straus, Giroux, 1979).

Zinn, Howard, *Postwar America: 1945–1971* (1973; repr., Cambridge, MA: South End Press, 2002).

Art and Design

Ashton, Dore, *American Art since 1945* (New York: Oxford University Press, 1982).

Belgrad, Daniel, *The Culture of Spontaneity: Improvisation and the Arts in Postwar America* (Chicago: University of Chicago Press, 1998).

Buettner, Stewart, *American Art Theory, 1945–1970* (Ann Arbor, MI: UMI Research Press, 1981).

Ettinger, Roseann, *Psychedelic Chic: Artistic Fashions of the Late 1960s and Early 1970s* (Atglen, PA: Schiffer Pub., 1999).

Garner, Philippe. Sixties Design (New York: Taschen, 1996) [in English, German, and French].

Jackson, Lesley, *The Sixties: Decade of Design Revolution* (London: Phaidon Press, 1998).

Johnson, Ellen H., ed., *American Artists on Art from 1940 to 1980* (New York: Harper & Row, 1982).

Lee, Pamela, *Chronophobia: On Time in the Art of the 1960's* (Cambridge, MA: MIT Press, 2004).

Poltorak, Joe, *Fashions in the Groove: '60s & 70s* (Atglen, PA: Schiffer Pub., 1998).

Ross, Geoffrey Aquilina, *Day of the Peacock: Style for Men, 1963–1973* (New York: Victoria & Albert Museum, 2011).

Schrijver, Lara, *Radical Games: Popping the Bubble of 1960s Architecture* (Rotterdam, Netherlands: NAi Publishers, 2009).

Whitelaw, Anne, Brian Foss and Sandra Paikowsky, eds., *The Visual Arts in Canada: The Twentieth Century* (Don Mills, Ont.: University of Oxford Press, 2010).

Wood, Paul, et al., *Modernism in Dispute: Art since the Forties* (New Haven: Yale University Press, in association with the Open University, London, 1993).

Business and Economy

Frank, Thomas, *The Conquest of Cool: Business Culture, Counterculture, and the Rise of Hip Consumerism* (Chicago: University of Chicago Press, 1997).

Squires, Gregory D., ed., *Unequal Partnerships: The Political Economy of Urban Redevelopment in Postwar America* (New Brunswick: Rutgers University Press, 1989).

United States Bureau of Labor Statistics, *Employment and Earnings, 1909–75; Bulletin No. 1312–10* (USGPO, 1976).

United States Department of Labor, *Retail Prices of Food, 1964–68; Indexes and Average Prices*, Bulletin No. 1634 (USGPO, July 1969).

United States Department of Labor, *Wholesale Prices and Price Indexes, 1963*; Bulletin No. 1513 (USGPO, June 1966).

Civil Rights Movement

Anderson, Terry H., *The Movement and the Sixties: Protest in America from Greensboro to Wounded Knee* (New York: Oxford University Press, 1995).

Bloom, Jack M., *Class, Race, and the Civil Rights Movement* (Bloomington: Indiana University Press, 1987).

Blumberg, Rhoda Lois, *Civil Rights: The 1960s Freedom Struggle* (Boston: Twayne Publishers, 1984).

Branch, Taylor. *America in the King Years, 1954–63*, 3 vols. (New York: Simon & Schuster, 1988–2006) [vol. 1: *Parting the Waters*; vol. 2: *Pillar of Fire*; vol. 3: *At Canaan's Edge*].

Brooks, Thomas R., *Walls Come Tumbling Down: A History of the Civil Rights Movement, 1940–1970* (Englewood Cliffs, NJ: Prentice-Hall, 1974).

Carson, Clayborne, *In Struggle: SNCC and the Black Awakening of the 1960s* (Cambridge, MA: Harvard University Press, 1981).

Cleaver, Eldridge, *Soul on Ice* (New York: McGraw-Hill, 1967).

Cone, James H., *Martin & Malcolm & America: A Dream or a Nightmare?* (Maryknoll, NY: Orbis Books, 1991).

Crawford, Vicki L., Jacqueline Anne Rouse, and Barbara Woods, *Women in the Civil Rights Movement: Trailblazers and Torchbearers, 1941–1965* (Brooklyn, NY: Carlson, 1990).

Dittmer, John, George C. Wright, and W. Marvin Dulaney, *Essays on the American Civil Rights Movement*, ed. by W. Marvin Dulaney and Kathleen Underwood (College Station: Texas A&M for the University of Texas at Arlington, 1993).

Dudziak, Mary L., *Cold War Civil Rights: Race and the Image of American Democracy* (Princeton, NJ: Princeton University Press, 2000).

Eagles, Charles W., ed., *The Civil Rights Movement in America: Essays*. Jackson: University of Mississippi, 1986; University Press, 1993).

Eskew, Glenn T., *But for Birmingham: The Local and National Movements in the Civil Rights Struggle* (Chapel Hill: University of North Carolina Press, 1997).

Fager, Charles E., *Selma, 1965: The March That Changed the South*, 2nd ed. (Boston: Beacon, 1985).

Fairclough, Adam, *To Redeem the Soul of America: The Southern Christian Leadership Conference and Martin Luther King, Jr.* (Athens: University of Georgia Press, 1987).

Fisher, Randall M., *Rhetoric and American Democracy: Black Protest through Vietnam Dissent* (Lanham, MD: University Press of America, 1985).

Formisano, Ronald P., *Boston against Busing: Race, Class, and Ethnicity in the 1960s and 1970s* (Chapel Hill: University of North Carolina Press, 1991).

Garrow, David J., *Bearing the Cross: Martin Luther King, Jr., and the Southern Christian Leadership Conference* (New York: William Morrow, 1986).

Garrow, David J., *Protest at Selma: Martin Luther King, Jr., and the Voting Rights Act of 1965* (New Haven, CT: Yale University Press, 1978).

Garrow, David J., *The FBI and Martin Luther King, Jr.* (New York: Penguin Books, 1981).

Graham, Hugh Davis, *The Civil Rights Era: Origins and Development of a National Policy, 1960–1972* (New York: Oxford University Press, 1990).

Greenberg, Jack, *Crusaders in the Courts: How a Dedicated Band of Lawyers Fought for the Civil Rights Revolution* (New York: Basic Books, 1994).

Hampton, Henry, and Steve Fayer, *Voices of Freedom: An Oral History of the Civil Rights Movement from the 1950s through the 1980s* (New York: Bantam Books, 1990).

Kennedy, Stetson, *Jim Crow Guide: The Way It Was* (Tuscaloosa, AL: University of Alabama Press, 1990) [originally published as *Jim Crow Guide to the USA: The Laws, Customs, and Etiquette Governing the Conduct of Nonwhites and Other Minorities as Second-Class Citizens*, 1959].

King, Martin Luther, Jr., *Stride toward Freedom: The Montgomery Story* (New York: Harper & Row, 1968).

King, Martin Luther, Jr., *Where Do We Go from Here: Chaos or Community?* (New York: Harper & Row, 1967).

King, Richard. *Race, Culture and the Intellectuals, 1940–1970* (Baltimore: Johns Hopkins University Press, 2004).

Lawson, Steven F., and Charles Payne, *Debating the Civil Rights Movement, 1945–1968* (Lanham, MD: Rowman & Littlefield, 1998).

Lemann, Nicholas, *The Promised Land: The Great Black Migration and How It Changed America* (New York: Knopf, 1991).

Lewis, George. *The White South and the Red Menace: Segregationists, Anticommunism, and Massive Resistance, 1945–1965* (Gainesville: University Press of Florida, 2004).

Malcolm X., *The Autobiography of Malcolm X* (1965; repr., New York: Penguin, 2007) ["as told to Alex Haley"].

Marable, Manning, *Race, Reform and Rebellion: The Second Reconstruction in Black America, 1945–1982* (Jackson: University Press of Mississippi, 1984).

McAdam, Doug, *Freedom Summer* (New York: Oxford University Press, 1988).

McWhorter, Diane, *Carry Me Home; Birmingham, Alabama: The Climactic Battle of the Civil Rights Revolution* (New York: Simon & Schuster, 2013) [reissue with a new Afterword by the author].

Meier, August, and Elliott Rudwick, *CORE: A Study in the Civil Rights Movement, 1942–1968* (New York: Oxford University Press, 1973).

Meier, August, and Elliott Rudwick, eds., *Black Protest in the Sixties* (Chicago: Quadrangle Books, 1970).

O'Reilly, Kenneth, *"Racial Matters": The FBI's Secret File on Black America, 1960–1972* (New York: Free Press, 1989).

Packard, Jerrold M., *American Nightmare: The History of Jim Crow* (St. Martin's, 2001).

Powledge, Fred, *Free at Last? The Civil Rights Movement and the People Who Made It* (Boston: Little Brown, 1991).

Ralph, James, *Northern protest, Martin Luther King, Jr., Chicago and the Civil Rights Movement* (Cambridge, MA: Harvard University Press, 1993).

Robinson, Jo Ann Gibson, *The Montgomery Bus Boycott and the Women Who Started It: The Memoir of Jo Ann Gibson Robinson*, ed. by David J. Garrow (Knoxville: University of Tennessee Press, 1987).

Rosenberg, Jonathan, and Zachary Karabell, *Kennedy, Johnson, and the Quest for Justice; The Civil Rights Tapes* (New York: W. W. Norton, 2003).

Van Deburg, William L., *New Day in Babylon: The Black Power Movement and American culture, 1965–1975* (Chicago: University of Chicago Press, 1992).

Weisbrot, Robert, *Freedom Bound: A History of America's Civil Rights Movement* (New York: Norton, 1990).

Westheider, James E., *Fighting on Two Fronts: African Americans and the Vietnam War* (New York: New York University Press, 1997).

Whitfield, Stephen J., *A Death in Delta: The Story of Emmett Till* (New York: Free Press, 1988).

Film, Television, and Popular Culture

Albright, Brian, *Wild beyond Belief!: Interviews with Exploitation Filmmakers of the 1960s and 1970s* (Jefferson, NC: McFarland, 2008).

Avedon, Richard, and Doon Arbus, *The Sixties* (New York: Random House, 1999).

Balio, Tino, ed., *Hollywood in the Age of Television* (Boston: Unwin Hyman, 1990).

Bapis, Elaine M., *Camera and Action: American Film as Agent of Social Change, 1965–1975* (Jefferson, NC: McFarland, 2008).

Baxter, John, *Hollywood in the Sixties* (New York: A.S. Barnes, 1972).

Bodroghkozy, Aniko, *Groove Tube; Sixties Television and the Youth Rebellion* (Durham: Duke University Press, 2001).

Braunstein, Peter, and Michael Willima Doyle, eds., *Imagine Nation: The American Counterculture of the of the 1960s and '70s* (New York: Routledge, 2002).

Brode, Douglas, *The Films of the Sixties* (Secaucus, NJ: Citadel Press, 1980).

Cohen, Lizabeth. *A Consumer's Republic: The Politics of Mass Consumption in Postwar America.* (New York: Knopf, 2003).

Corber, Robert J. *In the Name of National Security: Hitchcock, Homophobia, and the Political Construction of Gender in Postwar America* (Durham, NC: Duke University Press, 1993).

Costello, Mathew. *Secret Identity Crisis: Comic Books and the Unmasking of Cold War America* (London: Continuum, 2007).

Cowie, Peter, *Revolution!: The Explosion of World Cinema in the Sixties* (New York: Faber and Faber, 2004).

Cripps, Thomas, *Making Movies Black: The Hollywood Message Movie from World War II to the Civil Rights Era* (New York: Oxford University Press, 1993).

Dixon, Wheeler W., *The Exploding Eye: A Re-Visionary History of 1960s American Experimental Cinema* (Albany: State University of New York Press, 1997).

Finch, Christopher, *Walt Disney's America* (New York: Abbeville, 1978).

Findlay, M. John, *Magic Lands: Western Cityscapes and American Culture after 1940s* (Berkeley: University of California Press, 1997).

Gans, Herbert. *The Levittowners: Ways of Life and Politics in a New Suburban Community* (New York: Pantheon, 1967).

Gitlin, Todd, *The Whole World Is Watching; Mass Media in the Making and Unmaking of the New Left* (Berkeley: University of California Press, 2003).

Graham, Allison, *Framing the South: Hollywood, Television, and Race during the Civil Rights Struggle* (Baltimore: John Hopkins University Press, 2001).

Hayes, Harold, *Smiling through the Apocalypse: Esquire's History of the Sixties*, new ed. (New York: Crown Publishers, 1987).

Heimann, Jim, ed., *Mid-Century Ads: Advertising from the Mad Men Era*, 2 vols. (Köln: Taschen, 2012).

Hendershot, Cyndy. *AntiCommunism and Popular Culture in Midcentury America* (Jefferson, NC: McFarland, 2003).

Henriksen, Margot. *Dr. Strangelove's America: Society and Culture in the Atomic Age* (Berkeley: California University Press, 1997).

Hoberman, J., *The Dream Life: Movies, Media, and the Mythology of the Sixties* (New York: New Press, 2003).

James, David E., *Allegories of Cinema: American Film in the Sixties* (Princeton, NJ: Princeton University Press, 1989).

Lasch, Christopher, *The Culture of Narcissism: American Culture in the Age of Diminishing Expectations* (New York: Norton, 1978).

Lattin, Don, *The Harvard Psychedelic Club: How Timothy Leary, Ram Dass, Huston Smith, and Andrew Weil Killed the Fifties and Ushered in a New Age for America* (New York: HarperOne, 2010).

Lipschutz, Ronnie. *Cold War Fantasies: Film, Fiction and Foreign Policy* (Lanham, MD: Rpwman and Littlefield, 2001).

Lipsitz, George. *Class and Culture in Cold War America: A Rainbow at Midnight* (New York: Praeger 1981).

Loss, Archie K., *Pop Dreams: Music, Movies, and the Media in the 1960s* (Fort Worth, TX: Harcourt Brace College Publishers, 1999).

Marcus, Daniel, *Happy Days and Wonder Years: The Fifties and the Sixties in Contemporary Cultural Politics* (New Brunswick, NJ: Rutgers University Press, 2004).

Martinson, Tom. *America's Dreamscape: The Pursuit of Happiness in Postwar Suburbia* (New York: Carroll & Graf, 2000).

May, Lary, ed. *Recasting American Culture and Politics in the Age of the Cold War* (Chicago: University of Chicago Press, 1989).

McConnell, William S., ed., *Counterculture Movement of the 1960s* (San Diego: Greenhaven Press, 2004).

McGinnis, Joe, *The Selling of the President, 1968* (New York: Trident Press/Simon & Schuster, 1969).

McWilliams, John C., *The 1960s Cultural Revolution* (Westport, CT: Greenwood Press, 2000).

Monaco, Paul, *The Sixties: 1960–1969* (New York: Charles Scribner's Sons, 2001).

Mordden, Ethan, *Medium Cool: The Movies of the 1960s* (New York: Knopf, 1990).

Perone, James E., *Woodstock: An Encyclopedia of the Music and Art Fair* (Westport, CT: Greenwood Press, 2005).

Riley, Tim, *Tell Me Why: The Beatles: Album By Album, Song By Song, The Sixties and After* (New York: Knopf, 1988).

Schatzberg, Jerry, *Women Then: Photographs, 1954–1969*, with texts by Julia Morton and Gail Buckland (New York: Rizzoli, 2010).

Seed, David, *American Science Fiction and the Cold War* (Edinburgh: Edinburgh University Press, 1999).

Smith, Patricia Juliana, ed., *The Queer Sixties* (New York: Routledge, 1999).

Spigel, Lynn, and Michael Curtin, *The Revolution Wasn't Televised: Sixties Television and Social Conflict* (New York: Routledge, 1997).

Taylor, Ella. *Prime Time Families: Television Culture in Postwar America* (Berkeley: California University Press, 1989).

Thompson, Graham. *The Business of America: The Cultural Production of a Post War Nation* (London: Pluto, 2004).

Thompson, Hunter S. *Hell's Angels: A Strange and Terrible Saga* (New York: Ballantine/Random House, 1967).

Weiss, Jessica, *To Have and to Hold: Marriage, the Baby Boom, and Social Change* (Chicago: University of Chicago Press, 2000).

Whitfield, Stephen. *The Culture of the Cold War* (Baltimore: Johns Hopkins University Press, 1990).

Wolfe, Tom, *The Right Stuff* (New York: Farrar, Straus, Giroux, 1979).

Literature and Performing Arts

Baker, Houston, *Blues, Ideology and AfroAmerican Literature* (Chicago: Chicago University Press, 1984).

Bell, Bernard, *The AfroAmerican Novel and Its Tradition* (Amherst: Massachusetts University Press, 1987).

Booker, Keith, *Monsters, Mushroom Clouds and the Cold War: American Science Fiction and the Roots of Postmodernism, 1946–1964* (Westport, CT: Greenwood Press, 2001).

Bram, Christopher, *Eminent Outlaws: The Gay Writers Who Changed America* (New York: Twelve, 2012).

Brater, Enoch, ed., *Arthur Miller's America: Theater and Culture in a Time of Change.* (Ann Arbor: Michigan University Press, 2005).

Bromell, Nick, *Tomorrow Never Knows: Rock and Psychedelics in the 1960s* (Chicago: University of Chicago Press, 2000).

Caute, David, *The Dancer Defects: The Struggle for Cultural Supremacy during the Cold War* (New York: Continuum, 2004).

Dickstein, Morris, *Leopards in the Temple: The Transformation of American Fiction, 1945–1970* (Cambridge, Mass.: Harvard University Press, 2002).

Flowers, Sandra Hollin, *African American Nationalist Literature of the 1960s:Pens of Fire* (New York: Garland Pub., 1996).

Hendin, Josephine. *A Concise Companion to Post War American Literature and Culture.* (New York: Blackwell, 2004).

Jumonville, Neil, *Critical Crossings: The New York Intellectuals in Postwar America* (Berkeley: University of California Press, 1991).

McConachie, Bruce, *American Theatre in the Culture of the Cold War: Producing and Contesting Containment.* (Iowa City: Iowa University Press, 2003).

Nadel, Alan, *Containment Culture: American Narratives, Postmodernism and the Atomic Age* (Durham: Duke University Press, 1995).

Newhouse, Thomas, *The Beat Generation and the Popular Novel in the United States, 1945–1970.*

Phillips, Lisa, *Beat Culture and the New America, 1950–1965.* (New York: Whitney Museum, 1995).

Schaub, Thomas, *American Fiction in the Cold War* (Madison: University of Wisconsin Press, 1991).

Tanner, Tony, *City of Words: American Fiction, 1950-1970* (New York: Harper and Row, 1987).

Politics and the Presidency

Andrew, John A. *The Other Side of the Sixties: Young Americans for Freedom and the Rise of Conservative Politics.* New Brunswick, N.J.: Rutgers University Press, c1997.

Bernstein, Irving, *Guns or Butter: The Presidency of Lyndon Johnson* (New York: Oxford University Press, 1996).

Beschloss, Michael S., ed., *Taking Charge: The Johnson White House Tapes, 1963–1964* (New York: Simon & Schuster, 1997).

Brands, H. W. *The Wages of Globalism: Lyndon Johnson and the Limits of American Power.* New York: Oxford University Press, 1995.

Brennan, Mary C. *Turning Right in the Sixties: The Conservative Capture of the GOP.* Chapel Hill: University of North Carolina Press, c1995.

Caro, Robert A. *The Years of Lyndon Johnson*, 4 vols. (New York: Knopf, 1982–2009) [vol. 1: *The Path to Power*; vol. 2: *Means of Ascent*; vol. 3: *Master of the Senate*; vol. 4: *The Passage of Power*].

Carter, Dan T., *From George Wallace to Newt Gingrich: Race in the Conservative Counterrevolution, 1963–1994* (Baton Rouge: Louisiana State University Press, 1996).

Dallek, Robert, *An Unfinished Life: John F. Kennedy, 1917–1963* (Boston: Little, Brown, 2003).

Dallek, Robert, *Flawed Giant: Lyndon Johnson and His Times, 1961–1973* (New York: Oxford University Press, 1998).

Delli Carpini, Michael X., *Stability and Change in American Politics: The Coming of Age of the Generation of the 1960s* (New York: New York University Press, 1986).

Divine, Robert A., *The Johnson Years*, 3 vols. (Lawrence: University Press of Kansas, 1987–1994) [vol. 1: *Foreign Policy, the Great Society, and the White House*; vol.2: *Vietnam, the Environment, and Science*; vol. 3: *LBJ at Home and Abroad*].

Giglio, James N., *The Presidency of John F. Kennedy*, 2nd rev. ed. (Lawrence: University Press of Kansas, 2006).

Giglio, James N., and Stephen G. Rabe, *Debating the Kennedy Presidency* (Lanham, MD: Rowman and Littlefield, 2003).

Hilsman, Roger, *To Move a Nation: The Politics of Foreign Policy in the Administration of John F. Kennedy* (Garden City, NY: Doubleday, 1967).

Johnson, Lyndon B. *The Vantage Point; Perspectives of the Presidency, 1963–1969* (New York, Holt, 1971) [Johnson's official memoirs of his time as president].

Kearns, Doris, *Lyndon Johnson and the American Dream* (New York: St. Martin's, 1976) [reprinted 1991 with a new Foreword by the author].

Klatch, Rebecca E., *A Generation Divided: The New Left, the New Right, and the 1960s* (Berkeley: University of California Press, 1999).

Levy, Peter B., *America in the Sixties-Right, Left, and Center: A Documentary History* (Westport, CT: Greenwood Press, 1998).

Manchester, William Raymond, *The Death of a President, November 20–November 25, 1963* (New York, Harper and Row, 1967).

Matusow, Allen J., *The Unraveling of America: A History of Liberalism in the 1960s* (New York: Harper & Row, 1984).

May, Ernest R., and Philip Zelikow, *The Kennedy Tapes: Inside the White House during the Cuban Missile Crisis* (Cambridge, MA: Belknap Press of Harvard University Press, 1997).

McGinnis, Joe, *The Selling of the President, 1968* (New York: Trident Press/Simon & Schuster, 1969).

McGirr, Lisa, *Suburban Warriors: The Origins of the New American Right* (Princeton, NJ: Princeton University Press, 2001).

Rorabaugh, W. J., *Kennedy and the Promise of the Sixties* (New York: Cambridge University Press, 2002).

Rose, Mark H., *Interstate: Express Highway Politics, 1939–1989*, rev. ed. (Knoxville: University of Tennessee Press, 1990).

Rosenberg, Jonathan and Karabell, Zachary, *Kennedy, Johnson, and the Quest for Justice; The Civil Rights Tapes* (New York: W. W. Norton, 2003).

Schlesinger, Arthur M., Jr., *The Imperial Presidency* (1973; reprint, Mariner Books/Houghton Mifflin, 2004) [with a new epilogue, copyrighted 1989, and a new introduction].

Shesol, Jeff, Mutual *Contempt: Lyndon Johnson, Robert Kennedy, and the Feud That Defined a Decade* (New York: W. W. Norton, 1997).

Unger, Irwin, *The Best of Intentions: The Triumphs and Failures of the Great Society under Kennedy, Johnson, and Nixon* (New York: Doubleday, 1996).

Wicker, Tom, *JFK and LBJ; The Influence of Personality upon Politics* (New York, William Morrow, 1968).

Religion

Hedstrom, Matthew S., *The Rise of Liberal Religion: Book Culture and American Spirituality in the Twentieth Century* (New York: Oxford University Press, 2013).

Hudnut-Beumler, James, *Looking for God in the Suburbs: The Religion of the American Dream and Its Critics, 1945–1965* (New Brunswick, N.J.: Rutgers University Press, 1994).

Kent, Stephen A., *From Slogans to Mantras: Social Protest and Religious Conversion in the Late Vietnam War Era* (Syracuse, NY: Syracuse University Press, 2001).

Newman, William M., and Peter L. Halvorson, *Patterns in Pluralism: A Portrait of American Religion, 1952–1971* (Washington, DC: Glenmary Research Center, 1980).

Rossinow, Douglas C., *The Politics of Authenticity: Liberalism, Christianity, and the New Left in America* (New York: Columbia University Press, 1998).

Schafer, Axel R., ed., *American Evangelicals and the 1960s* (Madison: University of Wisconsin Press, 2013).

Silk, Mark. *Spiritual Politics: Religion and America since World War II.* (New York: Simon & Schuster, 1988).

Staub, Michael E., ed., *The Jewish 1960s: An American Sourcebook* (Waltham, MA: Brandeis University Press; Published by University Press of New England, 2004).

Yates, Nigel, *Love Now, Pay Later?: Sex and Religion in the Fifties and Sixties* (London: SPCK, 2010).

Vietnam War

Anderson, Terry H., *The Movement and the Sixties: Protest in America from Greensboro to Wounded Knee* (New York: Oxford University Press, 1995).

Atkinson, Rick, *The Long Gray Line: The American Journey of West Point's Class of 1966* (New York: Holt, 1989).

Davis, James Kirkpatrick, *Assault on the Left: The FBI and the Sixties Antiwar Movement* (Westport, CT: Praeger, 1997).

DeBenedetti, Charles, with Charles Chatfield, *An American Ordeal: The Antiwar Movement of the Vietnam Era* (Syracuse, NY: Syracuse University Press, 1990).

Foley, Michael S., *Confronting the War Machine: Draft Resistance during the Vietnam War* (Chapel Hill: University of North Carolina Press, 2003).

Hearden, Patrick, ed., *Vietnam: Four American Perspectives: Lectures by George S. McGovern, William C. Westmoreland, Edward N. Luttwak, and Thomas J. McCormick* (West Lafayette, IN: Purdue University Press, 1990).

Heineman, Kenneth J. *Campus Wars: The Peace Movement at American State Universities in the Vietnam Era* (New York: New York University Press, 1993).

Herr, Michael, *Dispatches* (New York: Random House, 1977).

Herring, George C. *America's Longest War: The United States and Vietnam, 1950–1975*, 3rd ed. (New York: McGraw-Hill, 1996).

Hixson, Walter L., ed., *The Vietnam Antiwar Movement* (New York: Garland, 2000).

Hunt, Andrew E., *The Turning: A History of Vietnam Veterans Against the War* (New York: New York University Press, 1999).

Kolko, Gabriel, *Anatomy of a War: Vietnam, the United States, and the Modern Historical Experience* (New York: New Press, 1985).

Logevall, Fredrik, *Choosing War: The Lost Chance for Peace and the Escalation of War in Vietnam*, new ed. (Berkeley: University of California Press, 2001)

Maraniss, David. *They Marched into Sunlight: War and Peace, Vietnam and America, October 1967* (New York: Simon & Schuster, 2003).

Oropeza, Lorena, *¡Raza Sí! ¡Guerra No!: Chicano Protest and Patriotism during the Viet Nam War Era* (Berkeley: University of California Press, 2005).

Sheehan, Neil, *A Bright Shining Lie: John Paul Vann and America in Vietnam* (New York: Random House, 1988).

Westheider, James E., *Fighting on Two Fronts: African Americans and the Vietnam War* (New York: New York University Press, 1997).

Woods, Randall B., *Vietnam and the American Political Tradition: The Politics of Dissent* (New York: Cambridge University Press, 2003).

	RESIDENCE, APRIL 1, 1935												PERSONS 14 YEARS OLD AND OW		
CODE (Leave blank)	City, town, or village having 2,500 or more inhabitants. Enter "R" for all other places.	COUNTY	STATE (or Territory or foreign country)	On a farm? (Yes or No)	CODE (Leave blank)	21	22	23	24	25	CODE	26	27	OCCUPATION
16	17	18	19	20	D	21	22	23	24	25	E	26	27	28
	Same House			No		Yes	–	–	–	–	1	40	–	Foreman
	Same House			No		No	No	No	No	H	7	–	–	
	Same House			No		No	No	No	No	S	6	–	–	
	Same House			No		Yes	–	–	–	–	1	–	–	Laborer

salmon, 142
  tribal, 142
Fisk College, 25
Fitzgerald, Ella, 97
The Flintstones (TV program), 8
Florida Education Association (FEA), 191
Florida State College for Women, 58
The Flying Nun (TV program), 189
Food and Drug Administration (FDA), 161, 177, 193
Ford Motor Company
  dealership, 14, 15
  Falcon Futura, introduction of, 16
  Mustang, introduction of, 183
"The Forgotten Prisoners" (Benenson), 180
Fortune (magazine), 65
Franklin, Aretha, 47, 190
Franklin, Mary Katherine, 171
Free DC Movement, 83
Freedom of Information Act, 188
Freedom Trash Can, 190
"free issues," 23
Friedan, Betty, 182
From Elvis in Memphis (music album), 194
The Fugitive (TV program), 182

G

Gable, Clark, 179
Gagarin, Yuri, 180
Games People Play (Berne), 187
Garroway, Dave, 11
Geary Act, 110
"Gee Whiz, (Look at His Eyes)" (song), 46, 47
Gemini 3 (spacecraft), 185
General Electric, 56, 130
General Motors, 16, 183
Geneva Basin, 123
George Peabody College, 58
"Georgy Girl" (song), 187
"Getting the Nation to Pay Attention to Farm Workers," 90
Ginsberg, Allen, 184, 190
"Give Peace a Chance" (song), 194
Gleason, Jackie, 8
Gleason, Ralph, 117
Glenn, John, 181
"Go Away, Little Girl" (song), 181
Goddard, Robert H., 194
The Godfather (Puzo), 193, 194
Goldwater, Barry, 183
golf, 119-122
"Good Lovin'" (song), 114
Goodman, Benny, 97
"Good Morning Starshine" (song), 194
"Good Vibrations" (song), 187
Gordy, Berry, Jr., 47
Gore, Lesley, 114
Goulet, Robert, 188
Graham, Katherine, 182
Grand Ole Opry House, 174-175

Grandpa Jones (performer), 174
Grant, Ted, **101-104**
Grateful Dead (music band), 189
Gray, Dan R., Sr., 57
Gray, Elizabeth Wolfenden, 57
Gray, J. J., Jr., 57
Gray, Susan Walton, *57*, **57-62**
Great Depression, 57, 66, 76, 117, 159, 163
Great Migration, 162
Green Bay Packers, 189, 191
Gregory, Dick, 143
Griffin, Merv, 183
Grissom, Gus, 185, 190
Gunsmoke (TV program), 11
Guthrie, Arlo, 113

H

Hair (musical), 190
"Hair" (song), 194
Halpern, Dina, 16
Hampton Institute, 27
Hansberry, Lorraine, 193
Happiness Is a Warm Puppy (Schulz), 181
Harper, Chandler, 120
Harris, David, 191
Harris, Ray, 49
Harrison, George, 78, 80
Harster, Wilhelm, 189
Harvard University Administration Building, 194
Harvey, Paul, 9
Hawaii, **19-23**
  after World War II, 20
  annextaion of, 20
  construction boom in, 19
  immigrants/immigration and, 20
  racial diversification and, 22
  for tourism, 21-22
  wages in, 22
Hawaii 5-0 (TV program), 192
Hawk, David, 154, 155
Hay, George D., 174
Hayes, Gabby, 175
Hayes, Isaac, 45, 48
Haywood, Carl, 60
Head Start program, 57, 60-61
"Head Start Project May Bring Changes to America's Education," 62
Hee Haw (TV program), 193
Heller, Joseph, 178
"Hemingway," 11
Henderson, Luther, *81*, **81-84**
Hendrix, Jimi, 113, 186, 193
Hermansader, John, 100
Hershey, Lewis, 191
Hewlett-Packard, 187
Highlander Folk School, 28, 29, 30, 61
Hi Records, 49
Hit Parader, 50-51
Hoffa, Jimmy, 183
Holiday, Billie, 97

Hollywood, 66
Holston Ordnance Works, 104
"Honky Tonk Women" (song), 194
Horne, Harriet Van, 164
Horton, Myles, 29, 30
Hot Wheels toy cars, 191
"Hound Dog" (song), 46
Housing and Urban Development Act, 54
Howard University, 191
Howes, Sally Ann, 188
Hudson automobile dealership, 14
Humanae Vitae (Pope Paul VI), 192
Human Sexual Response (Masters and Johnson), 188
Humphrey, Hubert, 191
Hunt Brothers Packing, 64
Hunt Foods, 64, 67-68
Huntley, Chet, 11

I

"I Fall to Pieces" (song), 173
"If I Had a Hammer" (song), 182
I Know Why the Caged Bird Sings (Angelou), 194
"I Left My Heart in San Francisco" (song), 181
ILWU. *See* International Longshore and Warehouse Union (ILWU)
immigrants/immigration
  anti-immigration, 162
  Chinese, in the U.S., 107, 108-109, 110-111
  Hawaii and, 20
  timeline, Mexican, 89-90
Immigration Act of 1924, 110
Immigration Act of 1965, 107
Immigration and Nationality Act, 89, 111
Immigration and Naturalization Act of 1965, 90, 109, 110
"The Impossible Dream"(song), 187
In Cold Blood (Capote), 187
incomes, standard jobs, 197
The Incredible Hulk #1 (comics), 181
"In Duluth, a Mother of Five Joins the Campaign against War," 155
"I Never Loved a Man" (song), 189
Intel, 191
International Days of Protest, 187
International Harvester, 130
International Longshore and Warehouse Union (ILWU), 70, 71
International Longshoremen's Association, 70
International Olympic Committee, 4
International Telephone and Telegraph, 184
Interstate Commerce Commission, 178
"In the Ghetto" (song), 194
Invading Alcatraz (excerpt), 144
Ironside (TV program), 189
"I Saw Her Standing There" (song), 73
Israel, 190
Italian Radio Company (RAI), 5
"It's My Party" (song), 114